Implementing J. D. Edwards®
OneWorld®

Check the Web for Updates:

To check for updates or corrections relevant to this book and/or CD-ROM visit our updates page on the Web at **http://www.prima-tech.com/updates**.

Send Us Your Comments:

To comment on this book or any other PRIMA TECH title, visit our reader response page on the Web at **http://www.prima-tech.com/comments**.

How to Order:

For information on quantity discounts, contact the publisher: Prima Publishing, P.O. Box 1260BK, Rocklin, CA 95677-1260; (916) 787-7000. On your letterhead, include information concerning the intended use of the books and the number of books you want to purchase.

Robert W. Starinsky

Implementing J. D. Edwards®
OneWorld®

A Division of Prima Publishing

A Division of Prima Publishing

Prima Publishing and colophon are registered trademarks of Prima Communications, Inc. PRIMA TECH is a trademark of Prima Communications, Inc., Roseville, California 95661.

OneWorld is a registered trademark of J. D. Edwards. This book is not sponsored by or affiliated with J. D. Edwards, and is used herein for referential purposes only.

Important: Prima Publishing cannot provide software support. Please contact the appropriate software manufacturer's technical support line or Web site for assistance.

Prima Publishing and the author have attempted throughout this book to distinguish proprietary trademarks from descriptive terms by following the capitalization style used by the manufacturer.

Information contained in this book has been obtained by Prima Publishing from sources believed to be reliable. However, because of the possibility of human or mechanical error by our sources, Prima Publishing, or others, the Publisher does not guarantee the accuracy, adequacy, or completeness of any information and is not responsible for any errors or omissions or the results obtained from use of such information. Readers should be particularly aware of the fact that the Internet is an ever-changing entity. Some facts may have changed since this book went to press.

ISBN: 0-7615-1956-4
Library of Congress Catalog Card Number: 0-010383
Printed in the United States of America

01 02 03 04 05 10 9 8 7 6 5 4 3 2 1

Publisher:
Stacy L. Hiquet

Marketing Manager:
Judi Taylor Wade

Associate Marketing Manager:
Heather Buzzingham

Managing Editor:
Sandy Doell

Acquisitions Editor:
Jawahara K. Saidullah

Technical Reviewer:
Michael Schultz

Book Production and Editorial:
Argosy Publishing

Cover Design:
Prima Design Team

I dedicate this book to my family—
especially to my wonderful and loving mother, Virginia, whose
tremendous work ethic is second to none and has always been an
inspiration in my work. To my loving wife, partner in life, and closest
friend, Christine, whose patience has been severely tested during this
project. Finally, to our newest family member, our daughter, who is
expected to join us shortly. She will no doubt become the center of
attention in my life for the foreseeable future.

Contents at a Glance

Contents

PART II **PREPARING FOR SUCCESS WITH ONEWORLD** **97**

Chapter 11 Tailoring OneWorld to Your Business Needs: Part II 283

Acknowledgments

There are many people that I would like to thank for their contributions and participation in the making of this book. First, hats off to Jon Reed for connecting me with Prima Publishing. Jon's knowledge of the ERP employment marketplace is second to none.

Second, to everyone at Prima Publishing, my sincere thanks for their help in preparing this book for publication and to whom I offer my unending apologies regarding my tardiness in completing this project as unfortunately my day job frequently won out. Working with a first-time author such as myself is not an easy task. As I have found out first hand, few projects require as much time, patience, or energy as does the writing of a book, *except for possibly implementing an ERP system.*

It has been my pleasure to have worked with a number of outstanding individuals over the years who served as the requisite mentors or partners in my ERP journeys, including Ms. Kay Abrams (formerly Irvine), Messrs. Don Pelka, Earl Patterson (now deceased), Jim Pope, Terry Horner, Gordon Merna, Jim Perez, Enrique Alvarez, Keith Danhoff and last, but certainly not least, Mr. William (Croft) Walker. It was this group of esteemed colleagues who challenged me on a daily basis to understand, to deliver, and most importantly to share knowledge.

Finally, special thanks is extended to the technical editor of this book, Mr. Michael Schultz, now of marchFIRST, and formerly of New Resources Corporation. Mike is an outstanding individual whose candor and experience have earned my respect; Mike has done a standout job of keeping this book on target for you, the reader.

—Robert W. Starinsky

About the Author

Robert W. Starinsky is a management consultant specializing in software-driven business process reengineering, packaged software requirements definition, packaged software selection, software package implementation, project management, and end-user training. Before he entered the consulting industry in 1998, his credentials included an impressive array of managerial and delivery leadership roles in manufacturing and financial services. He has played significant roles on numerous projects directly related to the selection and implementation of packaged software solutions for more than 20 years.

Starinsky's software experience includes knowledge of Enterprise Resource Planning software, including Financial, Distribution, and Manufacturing applications, Customer Relationship Management, Computerized Maintenance Management, Supply Chain Management, and industry-specific solutions for the financial services industry. He has worked with products from many vendors, including those offered by Best Programs, J.D. Edwards, Great Plains, P.S.D.I., Ross Systems, SAP, and Siebel Systems.

Starinsky earned an undergraduate degree in Organizational Behavior and Personnel from Northwestern University, a master's degree in accounting from DePaul University, and a master's degree in business from Dominican University. He was an adjunct faculty member at Dominican University for eight years, where he taught in the university's undergraduate business and economics department.

Starinsky has earned the professional designation of Certified Computing Professional (CCP). In addition to authoring *Implementing J. D. Edwards OneWorld*, he published and presented a paper titled "ERP Implementation Planning" at ERP World, an ERP software industry event held in Anaheim, Calif., in 2000. Starinsky can be reached at rwstarinsky@juno.com.

Introduction

Welcome to *Implementing J. D. Edwards OneWorld*. If you're reading this book, you're in good company. J. D. Edwards is one of the premier packaged software vendors in the business world today. The OneWorld client base is growing so much that across the globe, in virtually every market segment, you will likely find a J. D. Edwards' OneWorld user. J. D. Edwards has emerged as one of the "Big Five" in the ERP marketplace and is poised to become a senior member of the ERP community alongside SAP AG and Oracle as this market space is redefined.

Writing this book fulfills one of my long-standing ambitions. I first thought about writing a book on Enterprise Resource Planning (ERP) system implementation in early 1996. At that time, I was learning about one of the hottest ERP systems in the marketplace, SAP R/3. As an ERP veteran, I admittedly became impatient with the pace of these classes. At times, I pondered (actually, daydreamed about) how I could combine my earlier ERP software implementation knowledge and experience with J. D. Edwards' World software with the SAP R/3 project I found myself assigned to.

Since those moments of reflection in early 1996, I've been (informally, at least) building the knowledge and, finally, the energy to undertake the development of this book. Knowledgeable about both J. D. Edwards and SAP ERP software packages, I've seen many excellent books about SAP R/3, from both Prima Tech and other publishing houses over the last few years.

However, with respect to J. D. Edwards' OneWorld, a software product that has helped J. D. Edwards climb into the upper tier of the ERP marketplace, heretofore there has been precious little coverage by the technical press. I felt, as did Prima Tech, that, until now, a knowledge void about J. D. Edwards' OneWorld existed in the marketplace and that many people—such as you—were wanting for more information about OneWorld. This perceived void has allowed me to pen my first book and to share my knowledge and experience with you about a truly exciting product, J. D. Edwards' OneWorld.

The Purpose of This Book

As the title implies, the focus of this book is J. D. Edwards' OneWorld software. This is not a book about using OneWorld as much as it is a book about *understanding and successfully implementing* OneWorld in your organization. Of course, your first question is probably why you should read this book. Unfortunately, very little has been written about OneWorld, outside of the material published directly by J. D. Edwards. The few books about OneWorld that do exist focus on a particular aspect of the OneWorld environment, such as AS/400 implementation. Other books about ERP implementation or project management are too general to be of much value. This book has been written to fill a noticeable void in the marketplace and to provide you with the answers about OneWorld that you really need.

This book is therefore a culmination of my real-world experiences with ERP projects and my field-level observations about ERP acquired over the past decade. During this time, I have provided ERP implementation delivery and thought leadership for multiple software packages, including J. D. Edwards' World and OneWorld, to a number of manufacturing, distribution, professional service, government, and nonprofit organizations.

Why should this book appeal to you? Implementing a comprehensive business information system such as OneWorld is a significant project for just about any size of organization. It is a project that by many accounts is as much fun as having your wisdom teeth pulled. But in today's competitive, Internet-driven world, a comprehensive information system is or will shortly become an essential element in your organization's continued success.

In addition, implementing a comprehensive business information system such as OneWorld is simply not an ordinary project. It is typically not the type of project that an organization's information systems department or its other business departments likely have significant prior experience with. This is typically a one-off, long-duration project that has significant scope, risk, cost, and business impact. In short, this kind of project is best not left to chance. The information and insights provided by this book will help you achieve a successful OneWorld implementation.

You will find that the information contained in this book is quite valuable. The contents will at times be controversial or insightful. More importantly, you will find general information that is otherwise unavailable to you without significant cost.

You might choose to hire a consulting firm for guidance. As a professional in the consulting industry, I can tell you that we're always ready to help, but our services are not inexpensive. As you will come to learn, consultants are a significant part of your overall OneWorld implementation investment. Although consultants can help you get the job done, you don't want them running the show on an unchecked basis. You need to educate yourself in order to maximize the value of your consulting dollars.

You can also go it alone, learning by trial and error what it takes to make your OneWorld implementation successful. This course of action is an expensive, highly risky, and disruptive way to go about the task. If you do decide to go it alone, this book might provide a certain degree of risk mitigation for you.

Who Should Read This Book

This book is written for a multitude of audiences. If you are reading this book, I presume that your organization has either already invested in OneWorld software or is about to make the investment.

◆ If you are an information systems manager, a business or systems analyst, a department manager, or an end-user professional assigned to the OneWorld implementation team, you will find this book of interest.

◆ If you are the OneWorld implementation project manager for your organization, this book will become the driving force in your daily life, especially in the early stages of your project as you develop your going-forward plans.

◆ Finally, if you are an executive sponsor who is considering or has recently approved a OneWorld implementation, this book will provide a reality check as to what to expect and how to ensure that an adequate amount of project management and control is being exercised to promote the project's success.

I will make no excuses on this point. I wanted this book to have a wider appeal, so I purposely wrote it for a general audience. As a result, this is neither a highly technical book nor a how-to cookbook. Please understand that even after reading this book, you will still need to attend OneWorld-related classes sponsored by J. D. Edwards. Quite frankly, no amount of reading substitutes for hands-on experience when it comes to an ERP system.

Technical individuals might find that some of the material contained in this book is too simplistic. I agree. However, there is still value to the technical reader with respect to the overall dynamics of planning and organizing a OneWorld project that will no doubt be of value.

One additional note: *On the front cover of this book* is a chart indicating the appropriateness of each chapter for a specific member of the book's target audience. For obvious reasons, I prefer that you read the entire book, but there is no reason why this book can't be used as a reference tool for areas that are not germane to your particular interests.

How This Book Is Organized

This book is divided into five parts, representing what I believe are the major areas of OneWorld knowledge. Admittedly, organizing the material for this book was a difficult task. A case can be made for a number of different sequences. Therefore, I chose an organization that I felt would give the book the greatest flexibility in serving its intended audience. The five parts are described in the following sections.

Part I: General Information

The three chapters in Part I provide you with a general overview of J. D. Edwards as a company as well as the services and support you can expect from J. D. Edwards and its business partners. You also receive an introduction to OneWorld's flexible architecture.

Part II: Preparing for Success with OneWorld

In some ways, the three chapters of Part II might be the most important chapters of all. In these chapters, you gain insights into how to plan the OneWorld implementation project based on field-proven best practices and factors that are generally critical to a successful OneWorld implementation.

Part III: Understanding OneWorld

If you have not yet used OneWorld, the chapters that make up Part III introduce you to navigating in OneWorld using the Explorer and show you how to effectively use a typical OneWorld program. You are also introduced to the overall suite of OneWorld modules, or systems, that make up the complete OneWorld system.

Part IV: Making OneWorld Work for You

No doubt one of the reasons that you are either considering or have already bought OneWorld for your organization is that it can be easily configured and reconfigured. This configuration and reconfiguration can be done to meet a wide variety of business needs—all without modifying the underlying, or core, programs provided by J.D. Edwards.

The chapters that make up Part IV introduce you to the terminology and configuration steps related to OneWorld. OneWorld likely will not exist in a vacuum within your organization. You might already have J.D. Edwards' World software, or you might have other systems that will need to interface or integrate with J. D. Edwards. In addition, you might need to convert data from legacy systems into your OneWorld system. These topics are also covered in Part IV.

Finally, OneWorld is an excellent product, but it simply can't be all things to all organizations. You might be in a unique competitive situation, have a specialized industry issue, or face a regulatory issue that is not fully addressed by OneWorld. How will you address these issues? In almost all of these cases, your organization might find that its only option is to customize OneWorld to fulfill its business needs. In addition, there are numerous "extender" products available for OneWorld. Consult Appendix A for a listing of these products.

Part V: An Overview of OneWorld Functionality

The final chapters of this book provide you with a more in-depth, though still general overview of OneWorld. Each of the major business application areas within OneWorld is dealt with at a high level. In addition to the features and functions within each of these major functional areas, the data model for each of these respective areas is briefly reviewed. These chapters are an excellent way to garner a broad understanding of OneWorld's overall capabilities.

How to Use This Book

This book should be considered a part of your OneWorld toolbox. It is one of only several tools upon which you will rely while implementing OneWorld for your organization. Since I said that this book has general appeal, you might want to read it from cover to cover. If you feel more advanced in your skills, or if you already have OneWorld hands-on knowledge, you might decide to skip or merely skim through certain chapters.

Document Templates Available

For information regarding the Microsoft Office document templates that are mentioned throughout this book, please contact me at the addresses listed in the next section. You are introduced to a number of documents throughout this book, and ready-made templates are available that can be used to jump-start your OneWorld implementation. These templates include the Project Stoplight Report, a Model Project Plan, a Business Process Script Document that is useful for scripting current and future business processes, and an Issues Log. Please contact me directly, not Prima Publishing, for further information regarding these templates.

How to Contact the Author

I'm always available to discuss general management issues, packaged software implementation issues, business process transformation issues, and, last but not least, OneWorld, with other industry professionals. You can contact me through regular mail or e-mail at these addresses:

Surface mail:
Robert W. Starinsky
Tradewinds Group, Incorporated
P.O. Box 3601
Oak Brook, Illinois 60522

E-mail:
rwstarinsky@juno.com

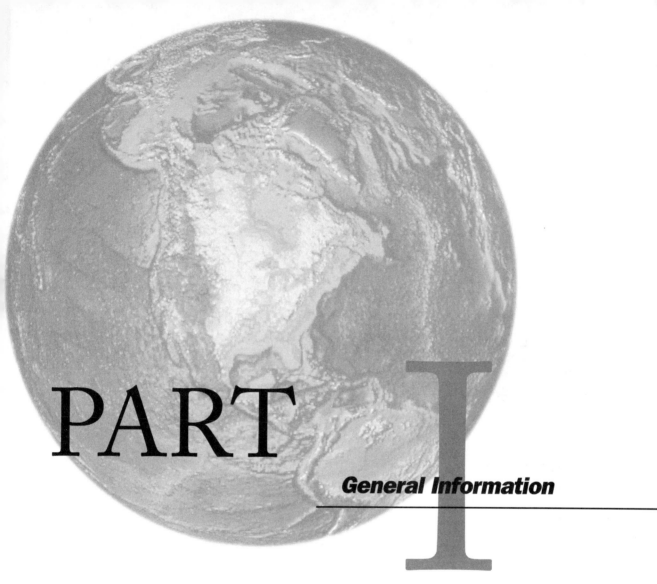

PART I

General Information

Chapter 1

Welcome to the Packaged Software Revolution

I entered the job market in the mid-1970s, about the same time that the foundational products for today's packaged software solutions for business were just beginning to take shape, including SAP and J. D. Edwards. At that time, the perception was that to get the applications you needed for your business, you had to build them. As businesses rushed to build systems during the late '70s and into the '80s, COBOL and mainframes flourished.

However, in the late '70s, the personal computer was quietly emerging from the basements and garages of a few onto the desktops of corporate America. This trend quickly became a firestorm. Personal computers brought relief from an ever-growing project backlog in the corporate information systems department. The personal computer revolution also in part spawned a software revolution. In adopting personal computer technology, the business community was increasingly relying on two emerging technologies: programmable databases and so-called shrink-wrapped software.

Early shrink-wrapped software packages included tools for creating and editing written documents and creating spreadsheets that allowed for easier calculation and presentation of financial information. Programmable databases were used to solve local or departmental computing problems.

During this era, it became commonplace for users to take on information technology roles. A new class of computer user was created—the "power user." It used to be that generating a business report was typically far down on the corporate information systems department's list of priorities and would often take months to complete. Nowadays, a business department, given a personal computer, some software and generally no more than a few weeks worth of effort by the department's "power user," can achieve real business results, quickly and cheaply.

All of these things—the power user, shrink-wrapped software, powerful programmable databases, and small, cheap computers—were changing the rules of
business computing.

Why Has Packaged Software Become So Pervasive in the Marketplace?

There are numerous reasons why packaged software—particularly ERP software—
has become so pervasive in the marketplace. This section reviews the major factors that are driving this trend toward packaged software.

It's About Constant Reinvention

Driven by competitive pressures and a desire to maximize shareholder value, most
businesses are constantly reinventing themselves. Although some accounts might
lead you to believe otherwise, businesses have always been engaged in this renewal
process.

There are a number of ways through which business change can occur. Although
this isn't an exhaustive list, some examples of significant business change that can
be drawn from a wide realm of possibilities include corporate mergers and acquisitions, corporate downsizing, business process reengineering, business expansion,
new product introductions, entry into new markets (such as going global), or entry
into a new marketing channel—the most pervasive of which includes Internet-
based marketing.

It's About Time to Market

If the revolution in business is not about reinvention, what is it all about? It is all
about time. In short, business change is occurring much more rapidly today—
more so than at any time in the past. In order to compress time, businesses are
increasingly focusing on their core competencies. Many businesses are finding the
quickest way to change is to not rely on their own capabilities and processes to
make or build things, including business processes and systems. Instead, they
build alliances with suppliers, who can fulfill their business needs on an "out-of-
the-box" basis.

Of course, time itself suggests the question of why timeliness is so important. Actually, the notion of timeliness suggests that a business can operate along two dimensions: A business can be proactive, dictating its own agenda and course of action, or it can be reactive, responding after-the-fact to business and marketplace events.

Obviously, proactive businesses stand to win all the marbles. At the end of the day, what separates a winning business from a losing business is generally how effectively it can acquire and apply business knowledge, or business intelligence. At the foundation of business intelligence is information about your past, current, and future business activities, the repository for which is generally considered to be the domain of an ERP system.

It's Not About Return on Investment

An ERP (Enterprise Resource Planning) system is not the panacea of business information and intelligence gathering. Frequently, ERP systems are cost-justified based on a series of return-on-investment criteria. Table 1-1 lists some common metrics for measuring the value of an ERP system. Vendors of ERP software will work their marketing pitches on you using metrics such as those found in this list. As your ERP journey continues, you will want to select several of these metrics as benchmarks for your OneWorld investment. As you periodically perform "health checks" on your OneWorld system (see Chapter 5), you can use these benchmarks to help you evaluate your software investment.

Table 1-1 Some Typical ERP Investment Benchmarks

Business Functional Area	Affected Business Process	Typical Benchmark or Metric	Typical ERP Benchmarks
Manufacturing	Planning and scheduling Resource management Process monitoring and control Maintenance Quality management	Predictability for on-time deliveries Reduced overhead costs Improved quality and faster throughput Increased use of subcontractors and contract manufacturing Increased equipment availability and equipment life Reduced in-field failure and rework rates Order cycle time	Availability of raw material to improve by 17 to 20 percent Reduction in the indirect costs within production by 10 percent

Table 1-1 Some Typical ERP Investment Benchmarks *(continued)*

Business Functional Area	Affected Business Process	Typical Benchmark or Metric	Typical ERP Benchmarks
Logistics and Distribution	Distribution planning Inventory management Trade management Transportation management Warehouse management	Reduced total distribution costs Improved on-time delivery Implement vendor-managed inventory Improved visibility and reduced inventory Reduced import/export time and costs Reduced delivery costs Improved space utilization and reduced picking times Order cycle time	Reduction in inventory by 30 percent On-time deliveries up 20 percent 20 percent reduction in inventory carrying costs 33 percent reduction in average delivery distance and time
Finance and Administration	General ledger Accounts payable Accounts receivable Asset management Costing Financial modeling and budgeting	Improved consolidation time and cost "Virtual" or real-time closes Minimized cash outflow Reduced credit losses/sales outstanding Increased utilization/output Implementation of activity-based costing Economically improved decision making	50 percent reduction in financial close time/cost 25 percent reallocation (reduction) in AP staff 200 percent increase in payment discounts due Reduced payment cycle time (A/R)
Sales and Marketing	Customer demand management Price and promotion management Client information systems Sales force management Configuration management Sales order entry	Improved forecast accuracy Improved price and promotion strategy Improved customer-specific expectations Improved productivity and effectiveness Improved online accuracy Improved accuracy/fill rate and on-time delivery Customer satisfaction	80 percent order cycle time reduction 65 percent reduction in pricing questions and calls 22 percent improvement in product availability
Engineering and Product Development	Production definition Product definition Product development Product rationalization and simplification	Increased product configurability Faster time to market Improved manufacturability Use of target costing/pricing Use of fewer parts Common or shared components and platforms; fewer SKUs and use of kits	Time to market cut by n months 20 percent increase in the adoption rate of incorporating changes into products Avoids unprofitable products and features Lowers cost of manufacturing and design Lowers cost of manufacturing and inventory Lowers cost of product line extensions

Let me also be the first to tell you that ERP systems typically have no cost justification. At best, an ERP system might reduce some of the overhead associated with maintaining old systems, but that's about it. If anything, generally an ERP system will increase your costs. So why are expensive ERP systems so popular?

It's All About Return on Information

Much can be said about information, or knowledge as power. Businesses that excel in their chosen markets usually do so because they have transformed information into business intelligence and can extend and leverage their business knowledge. Therefore, a far more effective measure of ERP system success is the impact an ERP system has had on an organization's return on information. In other words, how an organization has been able to leverage information is used to enhance shareholder value.

Therefore, the real return on investment for an ERP system is related to how the system is set up to gather information and, more importantly, how this information is subsequently used to alter or enhance current and future business activities. Stopping defects, speeding deliveries, and eliminating process delays are all examples of applying information as knowledge to transform a business process or activity toward shareholder maximization. Return on information can't be measured directly. Return on information must be extrapolated indirectly through traditional metrics of business performance that improve as information availability improves.

A basic tenet of a successful ERP system implementation is that it must provide sound transaction processing attributes that will let you deliver your product or service accurately and efficiently. A successful system implementation achieves high levels of integration and aggregation of information. It does so across all your business's major processing threads or cycles. At the same time, the ERP system must capture details about your business transactions, the activities and materials consumed or needed, and in what way they will enhance or detract from the value of the product or service that will or has been delivered to your customer.

Although ERP systems are good at performing transactional information, the analysis of the transactional data these systems collect is usually relegated to other data analysis tools. ERP data is typically extracted from the ERP database and stored in a data warehouse, where more sophisticated data analysis can be performed with other appropriate software tools.

It's About Core Competencies

More businesses are starting to realize that building software is not really a part of their core competencies (unless, of course, they are a software factory). At no time has this realization manifested itself more than during the recent ramp-up for year 2000 compliance. A record number of businesses adopted packaged software solutions during the late 1990s, casting aside their homegrown legacy systems in favor of packaged software solutions from vendors such as Baan, J. D. Edwards, PeopleSoft, and SAP.

Regardless of how hard most businesses try, the truth of the matter is that most businesses don't create custom applications that approach the robustness of most commercially available ERP software. When a business designs a new product, design for manufacturability should be an important consideration. However, when a firm creates software for internal use, design for manufacturability is not a common metric to apply. Usually, it's cost containment. Sadly, cost containment usually curtails the design for manufacturability attributes in an internal software product. When design for manufacturability attributes are removed, so is the robustness of the software and its ability to be easily adapted or retrofitted for business change.

Is ERP Long on Hype and Short on Results?

There are as many opponents of packaged software solutions as there are proponents. Opponents suggest that ERP packages are too complex and general for most businesses. Others suggest that they are not robust enough to support complex business processes. Still others contend that one package can't do everything well and will always require integration with other software packages and custom applications to fulfill an organization's transaction processing requirements.

Others contend that large, complex ERP packages can't be enhanced rapidly enough to keep pace with business needs. Many critics cite the industry's lack of responsiveness in Web-enabling their core software products as such an example. However, doing business in the e-business world increasingly requires the strength, integration, and flexibility offered by an ERP system.

Opponents of ERP often cite the case of FoxMeyer Drugs, the now-classic ERP train wreck. FoxMeyer was a multibillion-dollar health care products distributor that entered Chapter 11 bankruptcy as a result of massive disruptions to its ongoing business processes and supply chain caused by problems stemming from the implementation of a SAP R/3 ERP system. This is an extreme example. If business failure is so close, why do companies continue to buy and implement ERP systems? Quite frankly, when they are properly configured and installed, ERP systems can and do work.

The Next Big Thing from ERP

An ever-growing community of business pragmatists favors simplicity over complexity. With an increasing emphasis on supply-chain dynamics, the market is clearly telling businesses of all sizes to manage their operations as efficiently and effectively as possible and to strip away non-value-added activities. However, at the same time, a countervailing trend is occurring as market models increasingly move toward mass customization. In short, the time has arrived when it is necessary for your core business transaction-processing infrastructure to become a quick-change artist. It's about blowing up old business models and starting anew with relationship-driven models that require customer-by-customer adaptability.

Some contend that with Y2K now over, the market for ERP software is all but dead. However, proponents believe that the best market for ERP software is yet to come. Why would that be? As business models are reinvented around e-business, the need for ERP system backbones will increase. What's more, not every business caught "ERP fever" during the 1990s. Although the largest companies might have ERP systems in place, many smaller and middle-market businesses (those with revenues of less than $500 million) do not.

As competitive pressure mounts, information system infrastructures, including ERP systems, will move down-market. Therefore, the small- and middle-market segment represents a lucrative market for ERP software vendors going forward. In addition, the market represented by virtually all new start-up businesses in the years to come will increasingly be built around supply chain or knowledge-based competitive advantage. Again, an ERP system is a fundamental component in the e-business-centric information system infrastructure of the future.

"I Recently Read an Article That Said ERP Was Dead."

Although many will question the wisdom of writing a book about an ERP system after a truly horrible 18 months for the ERP software industry (J. D. Edwards included), understand that year 2000 compliance was not the sole reason for buying ERP software. Increasingly, ERP is about time to market. OneWorld's robust design is intended to help your business meet this time-to-market challenge.

The market for packaged ERP software exploded during the last half of the 1990s as organizations decided that ERP packages had come of age. These new-generation ERP packages represented sound alternatives to legacy systems and earlier-generation packages that faced either major rewrites or significant upgrades given that so many of these systems were not considered year 2000-compliant. Virtually all ERP software package vendors enjoyed double-digit growth rates during the industry's banner years of the late '90s. However, with the century rollover now complete, the dust is quickly settling throughout the ERP software market.

After posting outstanding results for the past several years, the growth in license fees, consulting, and training services begin to fall, on an industry-wide basis, during 1999. In addition, industry analysts and researchers have predicted significantly less growth for the ERP software industry as a whole—in the range of 3 to 5 percent for the next several years instead of rates in the 35 to 50 percent range enjoyed over the past three to five years. Certainly many of the weaker and second-tier ERP vendors have been hard hit by this downturn and will no doubt fold up shop or merge with rivals (because misery loves company).

As a matter of fact, during the last half of 1999, near-depression conditions hit the ERP software and implementation services marketplace. It was reportedly the worst year for consultants in the last 25 years. There were widespread layoffs at software companies and in consulting firms. During the first half of 2000, as this book was being written, these anemic market conditions have generally persisted.

Despite these conditions, J. D. Edwards continued to grow in a very down market during 1999. That was the year that J. D. Edwards firmly positioned itself to become the number three vendor in the ERP software marketplace. It made significant progress toward achieving the $1 billion-a-year annual sales mark and surpassing the coveted 5,000 installed customers benchmark.

More importantly, the J. D. Edwards investment in OneWorld was finally beginning to pay off. Previously, few J. D. Edwards clients demonstrated much interest in migrating from World software to OneWorld software. However, during 1999, many new clients chose to implement OneWorld instead of World software. Now, instead of dozens of customers using OneWorld, hundreds of customers were live or set to go live on OneWorld by the end of 1999. At the close of 1999, both J. D. Edwards the company and OneWorld the product emerged at the top of their class. They are clearly positioned to be in market leadership positions for many years to come.

Why Use J. D. Edwards' OneWorld?

As mentioned earlier, ERP is increasingly about time to market. OneWorld's robust design is intended to help your business meet this time-to-market challenge. The driving force behind business is and always has been change. This is not a book about business change, however. It is a book about a business transaction processing software package that represents a robust, out-of-the-box way of automating business processes that can be configured or reconfigured as business needs change. That software package is J. D. Edwards' OneWorld, one of the many sleek, configurable enterprise resource planning systems that have become increasingly popular throughout the business community.

Why should a company choose J. D. Edwards' OneWorld for its ERP system? Let me begin by offering some sage advice: Selecting and implementing any ERP system is first and foremost a business imperative, not a technology imperative.

Is J. D. Edwards' OneWorld software the right software for every business? No, it is not. I am not alone in this regard. I will tell you this, and so will Ed McVaney, chairman and cofounder of J. D. Edwards. So how can you achieve some assurance that OneWorld is the right software for your business? First, carefully analyze and determine your overall business requirements. Second, gain an overall understanding of the features and capabilities of any ERP software before you buy it. Finally, carefully consider your organization's ability to absorb and successfully implement an ERP system. There's no doubt about it—implementing any ERP system is an expensive and time-consuming process.

J. D. Edwards' OneWorld is a highly capable product that is increasingly recognized as a robust, flexible ERP package that is scalable in application from the smallest to the largest of businesses. During your ERP software selection, OneWorld deserves your fullest consideration. If you select it, OneWorld will require your undivided attention if you are to achieve a successful implementation.

I invite you to read on for a thorough introduction to J. D. Edwards' OneWorld and my model approach designed to help you achieve just such a successful OneWorld implementation. Please remember that this book alone cannot be your sole resource, nor can this author, the publisher, or J. D. Edwards guarantee your success in implementing J. D. Edwards' OneWorld in your organization. The successful implementation of any new business system must begin and end within your organization.

For my part, I will share with you my cumulative knowledge gained from over two decades of business delivery and leadership experience. For much of this past decade, I have focused on deploying and using business application software packages using both mid-range and client/server technologies. Most recently, I have been involved with numerous ERP implementations, including those specifically involving J. D. Edwards' OneWorld.

A Brief History of OneWorld

I have had the distinct pleasure of working with J. D. Edwards enterprise software since the fall of 1990. During this time, I have seen the core J. D. Edwards ERP software package, known as their World software product, evolve from a product that operated exclusively on IBM's midrange computing platform (which is more commonly known as the AS/400, which uses character-based "green screens") into a robust graphical user interface (GUI)-based multiplatform software solution.

Those who worked with J. D. Edwards software prior to its porting of World software from the AS/400 platform into the open-architecture, client/server-based system now called OneWorld knew J. D. Edwards' World software as one of the more sophisticated and robust ERP software package solutions available in the AS/400 marketplace. It was good stuff. I recall my early exposure to the J. D. Edwards future vision as moments filled with doubt about the need for and the viability of the computing model expressed in that future vision. About all I can say now is how quickly times have changed. Of course, so has my opinion of that earlier technology vision.

It is interesting to note that until SAP converted its mainframe R/2 ERP software product into the highly successful and market-leading R/3 client/server version, client/server-based ERP software packages just weren't taken seriously. However, success and market dominance have come quickly for SAP, a virtual unknown in the United States just a decade ago.

J. D. Edwards and its peers with products based on traditional mainframe or midrange platforms have had to adopt GUI-based, open system, client/server architectures to compete. J. D. Edwards has been successful in this regard, although it has been a rough road. Several of J. D. Edwards' competitors—including System Software Associates (SSA), whose BPCS software suite was at one time considered the market leader in the midrange ERP software package market—have not been as successful in the marketplace with their transition to a client/server solution.

Although SSA won many accolades for embracing object-oriented software models being used as the basis for their product rewrite, the product arrived late, it was buggy, and it was incompatible with previous versions of BPCS. As more robust products entered the market, SSA found itself less able to compete. It had some internal management turmoil, and it missed the mark on a migration path from its older-generation software. I should note that unlike SSA, J. D. Edwards has largely avoided this migration problem by allowing World and OneWorld to coexist.

As a matter of fact, while this book was being written, System Software Associates entered Chapter 11 bankruptcy reorganization. Some industry analysts fear that SSA and BPCS will not survive much longer and that BPCS users should begin considering alternatives. It would not surprise me to find over the next few years that a high percentage of these former SSA clients who used BPCS on the AS/400 will step up to J. D. Edwards' OneWorld, which can be installed in the now-tried-and-proven AS/400 environments at these organizations.

The vision that J. D. Edwards laid out in the early '90s is finally being realized through OneWorld. By no means has this evolution from the IBM AS/400 platform to an open client/server-based system been an easy one for J. D. Edwards itself or for the early adopters of OneWorld in general. Performance and data integrity problems plagued the early releases of J. D. Edwards' OneWorld software. However, I am happy to report that many of these earlier problems have been resolved in the latest release of OneWorld.

J. D. Edwards has faced a daunting task in converting millions of lines of World software code from RPG, the native procedural language of the AS/400 computer, into event-driven ANSI C-based programs, the standard for open-system GUI-based client/server software solutions. This effort has proceeded much more slowly than was initially expected, and that has meant delays in available equivalent functionality between the World and OneWorld software products. Therefore, some J. D. Edwards clients have opted to implement World software to satisfy their business requirements more completely today and will eventually migrate to the OneWorld software environment. A substantial portion of World functionality is now available in OneWorld. If you are a World client and are considering an upgrade to OneWorld, your J. D. Edwards sales representative should be able to help you determine if specific functions needed by your business are available.

In addition, some relatively recent J. D. Edwards clients who had significant year 2000 compliance issues opted for World software instead of OneWorld software in order to achieve their desired functionality levels prior to the century rollover. World software allowed these J. D. Edwards software adopters to implement year 2000-compliant business systems without incurring substantial hardware architecture or other infrastructure changeovers at this time.

Finally, many J. D. Edwards customers have opted to install J. D. Edwards' World software, a stable and reliable product that operates on an equally stable and reliable platform, instead of venturing into the unknown by implementing OneWorld at this time. I should also point out that AS/400 users have traditionally been smaller and middle-market companies that are traditionally risk-averse and cost-conscious. No doubt, if you are a World software user, eventually you will need and want to make the switch to OneWorld.

You might say that AS/400 users as a whole represent an audience that would definitely not entertain a revolutionary migration away from a proven architecture. Needless to say, many in the AS/400 community are skeptical of microcomputer-based servers supporting their businesses. However, I have seen OneWorld implementations running on AS/400 midrange platforms and others running on "Wintel"-based servers.

J. D. Edwards has had its share of the usual "new release" bugs that tend to confront most software vendors, including software powerhouses such as Microsoft and SAP. Previous users of World software have been surprised by these OneWorld problems, because they were accustomed to World software, which typically has been known for its quality, especially when compared to rival midrange products. Again, the most recent release of J. D. Edwards' OneWorld (B7.3.3) goes a long way toward correcting many of the early OneWorld release problems.

The Humbling of a Giant

In December of 1999, I attended the J. D. Edwards Mid-America User Group Conference in Chicago. The keynote speaker at this event was Ed McVaney, chairman and cofounder of J. D. Edwards. He comes across as one of the most genuine, trustworthy, and believable individuals in an industry that has not been known for these traits. Ed made two noteworthy comments in his remarks to the J. D. Edwards clients and prospects in attendance, and I would like to discuss them briefly.

The first remark I would like to share is that Ed personally apologized for the quality of the OneWorld product and committed J. D. Edwards resources to addressing current quality issues confronting OneWorld clients before moving forward with its next release of OneWorld.

Ed also indicated that J. D. Edwards has retreated from its earlier position of an announced and specific date for ending World software support. He went on to say that current J. D. Edwards' World users will play an instrumental role in establishing target dates for migrating from World to OneWorld software and therefore in ending the need to support the World software product.

These are both quite humbling statements about the software itself and about the company behind the software. I respect both Ed McVaney and J. D. Edwards as a company and fully appreciate the commitments that are being made to ensure that OneWorld is truly a world-class software product. Over the years, I have had the pleasure of working with numerous J. D. Edwards employees, and I have generally found these individuals to be knowledgeable, helpful, and genuine.

Prior to 1999, few users adopted OneWorld in large numbers. However, this has changed. This change was largely fueled by efforts to eradicate the Y2K bug that existed in so many companies. With this historical perspective in mind, it is easy to understand why J. D. Edwards faced some growing pains with respect to OneWorld support during 1999. Now that Y2K is behind us and large numbers of users are successfully using OneWorld on a daily basis, J. D. Edwards can focus on reestablishing its traditionally high levels of customer satisfaction.

At the June 2000 Focus Users Conference, sponsored by Quest, the international J. D. Edwards users group, J. D. Edwards announced that World software will be kept alive for at least a few more years, through February 2005. The J. D. Edwards Web site contains a number of press releases about the continuation of World software support and some important World software enhancements. More importantly, in October 2000, J. D. Edwards announced that an important milestone had been reached—its 1,000th client went live on OneWorld software.

J. D. Edwards as a Company

As a company, J. D. Edwards has an interesting history. This section provides a brief overview of that history.

The History of J. D. Edwards

Although I was once introduced for a meeting with a group of engineers by their secretary as Mr. Edwards from J. D. Edwards, there really isn't a person by that name at J. D. Edwards (nor have I ever worked for J. D. Edwards). J. D. Edwards was formed on March 17, 1977 by three individuals—Jack Thompson, Dan Gregory, and Ed McVaney—each of whom lent a portion of his name for the company moniker.

I've met Jack, who spoke at my technical training class in Denver in early 1991, and Ed, with whom I enjoyed a brief breakfast at the 1994 Users Conference in Denver. I would call Jack the chief technical architect behind J. D. Edwards software. I would characterize Ed as the pragmatist—the guy who gets the job done. I understand from a colleague that Ed personally called on clients and prospects in the early days.

Unlike many software start-ups, J. D. Edwards began its existence in Denver, Colorado, not Silicon Valley, and was formed by three former accountants, not college drop-outs, as was common for computer start-ups of that era.

Initially, J. D. Edwards designed software for several different computers. Eventually it focused on the IBM System/38, the predecessor to the IBM AS/400 midrange computer family. In the early 1980s, J. D. Edwards began using computer-aided software engineering (CASE) techniques. J. D. Edwards credits these CASE techniques for bringing consistency across all the programs needed to form its suite of integrated applications and paving the way to greater levels of software functionality.

In its early days, J. D. Edwards built primarily accounting software and developed a niche in the mineral extraction and construction industries, which were important markets in the Denver area. The company continued adding features and capabilities throughout the 1980s—most notably, those for distribution and manufacturing applications. During the early and mid '80s, J. D. Edwards grew its business through territory expansion, primarily in the Southwest and along the Pacific Coast. Until 1988, the company focused its growth on software sales in the United States.

In June of 1996, J. D. Edwards officially introduced OneWorld. Initially, only the financial systems were made available. When introducing OneWorld, J. D. Edwards continued its tradition of using the CASE technology it had pioneered in the 1980s by creating a robust, open system with an uncanny similarity of operation to its older-generation World software.

Until the late '90s J. D. Edwards was a privately held company. In that era of the company's history, employees with a certain tenure of company service could become an "owner" of the company by participating in the J. D. Edwards Employee Stock Ownership Plan (ESOP). As a J. D. Edwards client at the time, I always thought it was nice to see the designation of "owner" on the business cards of so many J. D. Edwards employees that I met over the years. Nowadays, J. D. Edwards is a publicly traded company on NASDAQ, its symbol being JDEC. Today, J. D. Edwards has more than 5,000 employees, almost $1 billion in annual revenue, and more than 5,000 customers that span the globe.

However, as many companies that "go public" soon find out, the financial markets can be unforgiving, unkind, and brutal at times. For instance, the recent "extended honeymoon" that so many Internet-related companies enjoyed, in which revenues and profits were largely ignored, can be viewed as an anomaly in marketplace. Generally speaking, the markets are much tougher, with the focus always being, What have you done for me lately? During the late '90s, J. D. Edwards enjoyed, just as its industry peers did, several banner years largely due to the year 2000 phenomenon. J. D. Edwards, as did many ERP vendors, found 1999 to be a rough year. I like to refer to it as the "morning after" year for ERP vendors.

Although the weaker ERP vendors have been hardest hit by this downturn, J. D. Edwards, as one of the top-tier vendors, has come through this period battered but not out of the game. J. D. Edwards shareholders, including its employee-owners, have seen the price of J. D. Edwards stock take a roller coaster ride on Wall Street over the past 12 months.

It is widely speculated that Doug Massingill, who stepped down as president of J. D. Edwards in the spring of 1999, did so in large part because of these market-place changes. Doug had replaced Ed McVaney as J. D. Edwards' CEO just a few short years ago. When Doug left, Ed returned to the helm of J. D. Edwards.

In just a few short weeks, as a second-time CEO, Ed made changes at J. D. Edwards. For instance, he announced a general restructuring of J. D. Edwards that will cause the company to reshape its organization and shrink its workforce by some 800 people. This action was reported by Ed to be a one-time alignment for J. D. Edwards that is intended to bring its cost structure in line with its revenue stream. You can conclude from these announcements that J. D. Edwards grew too fast internally and likely focused its efforts on the wrong things.

More importantly in this flurry of spring activity, Ed also shared a new market vision for J. D. Edwards. This new strategy will focus the company on collaborative commerce solutions, a business-to-business Internet strategy that has energized industry analysts and is increasingly the focus of the software industry.

How J. D. Edwards Positions Itself Within the Industry

J. D. Edwards believes that it distinguishes itself from its peers in the packaged ERP software marketplace by providing customer-centric software solutions, a strategy that the company calls Idea to Action. With Idea to Action, J. D. Edwards positions its software as being easily tailored to meet changing business needs. Currently, J. D. Edwards focuses customer attention on its ActivEra Solutions. ActivEra is best viewed as the combination of configurability, Web enablement, methodology, and flexible architecture found in its flagship OneWorld product.

J. D. Edwards does not try to do it all. For at least the past decade, the company has formed strategic alliances with hardware vendors, other software vendors whose products complement or extend J. D. Edwards software functionality, and consulting partners who can configure or customize J. D. Edwards software to meet a client's needs.

For instance, in two key areas, J. D. Edwards has formed multiple strategic and product alliances. For instance, in customer relationship management (CRM), it has chosen to partner with Siebel Sales to provide the front-office customer relationship management functions that it does not provide as a part of OneWorld functionality. In the supply-chain management (SCM) arena, it has partnered with Synquest to provide real-time supply-chain optimization on the backside of OneWorld.

In addition, it has completed the acquisition of industry-specific solutions, such as the Custom Works product configurator. Through its alliance with Ariba, the Internet-based procurement company, J. D. Edwards claims that it is one of the first software companies to deliver a business solution that is integrated within a trading community and that, as a result, it can provide true supply-chain collaboration. Obviously this is an example of the collaborative commerce model that J. D. Edwards is now promoting as a part of its future vision.

The J. D. Edwards Software Family

J. D. Edwards currently markets and supports three versions of ERP software:

◆ World software
◆ WorldVision software
◆ OneWorld software

World and WorldVision software are the most similar. Their relationship is best viewed as an evolutionary partnership, while OneWorld is considered a revolutionary architecture. The look and feel of OneWorld departs dramatically from the World software architecture in a multitude of ways. Many of these differences will be reviewed throughout this book.

World Software Architecture

J. D. Edwards claims that more than 4,000 customers now use its World software product. World software is the character- or "green-screen"-based version of J. D. Edwards enterprise software. World software operates exclusively on the IBM AS/400 midrange computer platform. J. D. Edwards cut its teeth on this product. This is also the product architecture that J. D. Edwards wisely chose to replicate in the client/server environment. World software is a robust, functionally rich product family that is fully integrated. A hallmark of World software was its use of a concept that J. D. Edwards called *soft coding*. This soft-coding architecture found in World provided the means to tailor the World software environment to a specific organization—without customizing the underlying product.

WorldVision Software

J. D. Edwards uses the software capabilities of SEAGULL Technologies to provide a graphical user interface front end for its World software product. World-Vision provides the look and feel of a Windows-based graphical user interface for this character- or green-screen-based software product. The distinguishing characteristics of World and WorldVision are largely cosmetic. WorldVision does not change the core World software product functionality and therefore can be deployed with a minimal amount of retraining. In addition, WorldVision can be used as a Windows 95/NT-style GUI for internally connected PCs. Early versions of WorldVision were slow or error-prone and required additional keypresses and mouse movements. The stability and performance issues with WorldVision have been resolved. As for the additional keypresses and mouse movements, get used to it. In general, this is a common complaint of seemingly all end-users I've encountered who must make the transition from a green screen to a GUI-based front end.

OneWorld Software Architecture

When I received word that I would soon be assigned to my first OneWorld project, I was admittedly quite nervous. I quickly hit the books and found that, much to my delight, I was not an ERP dinosaur—at least not yet.

What I quickly learned was that J. D. Edwards replicated, almost in its entirety, its World product functionality into the OneWorld product. I suspect that the J. D. Edwards product architects and product managers believed that when you have something this good, why change it? The resemblance between World and OneWorld functionality is uncanny. In addition, the concept of soft coding, along with a few new twists, also lives on in OneWorld.

Of course, that's where the similarities between World and OneWorld end. Gone are familiar report writers, the AS/400-centric security setup, and the traditional AS/400 software product installation and upgrade processes. In OneWorld, it's all done using client/server architecture, J. D. Edwards style, even on the AS/400.

OneWorld represents the future at J. D. Edwards. OneWorld was originally conceived in the early '90s as the J. D. Edwards technology vision for the future. It can be said that OneWorld represents the antithesis of World software.

World software was written in a largely platform-specific language (RPG) for a proprietary computer platform (the IBM AS/400 midrange) that used a proprietary operating system (OS/400). Was anything bad about these choices? Absolutely not! From a technology point of view, the IBM AS/400 is one of the most reliable computers available. It has a scaleable architecture based on an integrated relational database model and is widely regarded as one of the lowest cost-of-ownership computer platforms available.

OneWorld represents an "open system" architecture. No longer constrained by the AS/400 platform, OneWorld is being deployed on NT and UNIX servers as well as on the AS/400 platform. In addition, as an ODBC- (Open Database Connectivity) compliant product, OneWorld now operates on DB/2, Oracle, and Microsoft SQL Server databases, as well as on the AS/400 relational database.

What Makes OneWorld Special?

OneWorld is a robust, exciting, intelligently conceived, well-architected product. It provides a great deal of environment flexibility through its configurable network computing architecture that can be deployed on an *n*-tier basis, using either thin clients or fat clients and increasingly using browser-based delivery.

Most of what OneWorld is all about will come later, beginning in Part III of this book. For now, suffice it to say that OneWorld is a GUI-based ERP system that operates in the Microsoft Windows environment. It has an integrated report writer, called the Enterprise Report Writer. It has a number of important features that provide the ability to tailor the product's look and feel, as well as its navigation and functionality, without extensive customization requirements. As you upgrade to a later release of OneWorld, your OneWorld personalization will flow through to the next release with minimal effort on the part of your organization.

What Is Coexistence?

In an effort to protect the software investment of its current client base and to extend its reach to something beyond the IBM AS/400 midrange computing marketplace, J. D. Edwards provides a migration path for World software clients in order to move into the OneWorld environment. This migration path is called *coexistence.*

In large part, coexistence is possible due to the relational database underpinning the AS/400. J. D. Edwards did not need to rearchitect its data model around a relational database for OneWorld—it was already relational and fully normalized. However, World programs were written in RPG, the native language of the AS/400. RPG is an old-style procedural language. It is not an event-driven object-oriented language.

Therefore, J. D. Edwards faced two large tasks. First, it would need to create a middleware piece that would treat the AS/400 relational database as just another database, not as its native database. Second, it would need to rewrite or translate thousands of programs, representing many millions of lines of code (computer program instructions), into a "portable" program language that was available on multiple platforms. That choice of language was ANSI C.

Some words of caution are in order about coexistence. First, the latest version of World software (release A8.1) is not compatible with OneWorld. Therefore, World clients who are considering moving to the OneWorld environment should not upgrade from release A7.3 to release A8.1 at this time. Second, not all modules can coexist. Although I said earlier that J. D. Edwards replicated both the World functionality and the World data model into the OneWorld environment, this is not entirely true. Chapter 13 discusses coexistence in more detail.

J. D. Edwards Business Partners

J. D. Edwards has several different partnership programs. These partnership programs give OneWorld users access to independent companies who provide the following:

◆ Computer hardware products that are needed to operate OneWorld

◆ Software products that are needed to operate OneWorld, such as database and operating system software

◆ Services that are related to the support, installation, and implementation of OneWorld software

◆ Software products that provide functionality that is not now a part of OneWorld, or software that enhances or extends the basic functionality that OneWorld already has

J. D. Edwards is selective about the companies with whom it chooses to align itself. Generally speaking, the companies that are hardware or software partners of J. D. Edwards have made substantial commitments to interfacing and testing their products alongside J. D. Edwards software. In addition, J. D. Edwards is increasing its use of both hardware and software certifications to help its customers analyze their choices in the marketplace. In the case of professional service providers, these organizations typically have made substantial training, staff certification, and infrastructure investments in order to support a J. D. Edwards client base. J. D. Edwards has several categories of service providers for which different levels of qualifications apply. Details about qualification levels are available on the J. D. Edwards Web site.

Consulting Partners

J. D. Edwards partners with numerous consulting companies. It generally divides consulting alliance partners into four categories:

♦ Global strategic partners

♦ Market influence partners

♦ Select consulting partners

♦ Service partners

Each partnership category provides a unique level of client support or value to the J. D. Edwards client base. For instance, these companies might be expert in business process reengineering or might provide a unique industry perspective. These consulting alliance partners typically have service organizations that can manage every aspect of your OneWorld software implementation. Staff consultants at many of these consulting partners have completed J. D. Edwards-sanctioned certification related to one or more dimensions of OneWorld software.

Technology Partners

Technology partners can assist the OneWorld clients with their infrastructure issues. This may include hardware sizing and acquisition or providing the expertise to install your OneWorld hardware and software.

These technologists provide expertise in areas such as network configuration and management, database tuning, operating system administration, and technology deployment. Again, staff consultants at many of these consulting partners have completed J. D. Edwards-sanctioned certification related to one or more dimensions of OneWorld software.

Complementary Product Partners

J. D. Edwards has for a number of years partnered with hardware and software vendors to provide complementary products that extend or enhance the functionality of J. D. Edwards software products. Earlier, I mentioned recent strategic alliances with Siebel Systems and Synquest. These "big name" software alliances are among a litany of many alliances that J. D. Edwards has formed.

Complementary product partnerships represent a cooperative and collaborative effort between J. D. Edwards and other hardware and software manufacturers. These alliances bring together two successful products in their own right—in this case, J. D. Edwards' OneWorld and something else—things as mundane as a sales tax calculator or a wireless bar code scanner.

For instance, while Siebel Systems provides "category killer" CRM software, Vertex does the same for tax rate calculation software. In short, these are everyday products that improve your organization's productivity or efficiency. But the integration of these products can prove difficult and expensive if you attempt them on your own. Complementary product alliances mean that the up-front interfaces and integration are done for you by J. D. Edwards and its chosen business partner.

The Resource Appendix: Your Guide to J. D. Edwards Partners and Complementary Products

The appendix in this book provides a comprehensive resource guide to J. D. Edwards business partners. The appendix also includes organizations that have expertise or products that work with J. D. Edwards, although that organization might not be a J. D. Edwards business partner. The resource appendix was constructed during the summer of 2000 as this book was being prepared for publication. J. D. Edwards is constantly adding business partners. Consult the J. D. Edwards Web site at www.jdedwards.com for the latest information about business partners.

Summary

This chapter provided a historic and general introduction to the Enterprise Resource Planning (ERP) software market and in particular to J. D. Edwards as the software factory behind OneWorld the product. You were introduced to the reasons why ERP software has become such a coveted investment for many companies. In addition, you learned about the J. D. Edwards products that preceded OneWorld and the partnerships and alliances that J. D. Edwards has formed to provide a comprehensive level of business value to your organization.

Chapter 2

**What to
Expect from
J. D. Edwards**

This chapter introduces the collateral materials and services that complement your OneWorld investment. These collateral materials and services play an important role in helping you achieve a successful OneWorld implementation. The topics covered by this chapter include the following:

◆ Documentation
◆ Education
◆ Support services
◆ User groups

You will also learn about the best ways to leverage these available materials and services throughout the course of your OneWorld implementation.

Documentation

Several trends have had a profound impact on the documentation of computer software over the last decade. First, the trend has been toward the electronic publishing of documentation in a soft-copy form versus the traditional publishing of hard-copy documentation. Second, with the adoption of the Microsoft Windows graphical interface, more documentation is now being delivered through the Microsoft Windows help system. Finally, the trend is toward providing fewer examples, such as screen shots and step-by-step information on program operation.

It's easy to understand why software vendors, including J. D. Edwards, have embraced these trends. With software product life cycles shortening, and the software products themselves undergoing frequent redesign, the documentation cycle had to shrink as well. For instance, the entire library of OneWorld documentation is available at the click of a button, providing a quick drill-down into any topic of interest. This is a great time-saver and will be much easier on your back because you won't need to lug around all kinds of manuals during your implementation. CD-ROM documentation is also much more environmentally friendly.

Since J. D. Edwards users now fall into three distinct communities (World, WorldVision, and OneWorld), providing screen shots has become somewhat impractical given that a common set of core documentation works for all three environments. Therefore, in most J. D. Edwards documentation, screen shots have been replaced with menu paths. The use of menu paths over screen shots is a trend that has become increasingly popular throughout the software industry.

To its credit, J. D. Edwards continues to improve its documentation. For instance, sometimes J. D. Edwards training documentation differed in content from the documentation provided with your software. However, this is no longer the case. J. D. Edwards no longer produces separate training class documentation. Training class participant handbooks now use the standard OneWorld documentation. This documentation is supplemented by exercises based on the data in the demonstration (training) database.

Here are some documentation-related practices to help you along the way toward your successful OneWorld implementation:

- ◆ Ensure that the OneWorld help files are loaded on every client or that the path to help files at the server location are properly set up for the client.

- ◆ Ensure that each member of the OneWorld implementation has access to the OneWorld CD-ROM documentation. This is especially true for multisite organizations doing a OneWorld implementation in which the project team member must travel without a laptop computer. Moreover, it is preferable that the contents of the CD-ROM be loaded onto the member's client workstation and that they are always available for ready reference.

- ◆ The OneWorld software documentation should also be available from every client workstation in your training and conference room pilot/project team workroom environments.

- ◆ It is highly recommended that when traveling, a project team member should have available a laptop computer with the OneWorld stand-alone version installed, the OneWorld soft-copy documentation installed, and Internet dial-up capabilities in order to allow access to the J. D. Edwards Knowledge Garden.

- ◆ It pays to have an older copy of the documentation available. For instance, I work with both OneWorld and World software, so I have soft-copy documentation for each. But I also maintain an old set of documentation for each. Why? I find that sometimes features or operations change between releases, and it's nice to have these available as a basis for comparison. I've also found that sometimes documentation quality diminishes from one release to the next.

To wrap up documentation-related practices, keep in mind that OneWorld is similar to those "easy to assemble, no tools needed" toys that you buy for the kids and then spend all night trying to assemble before the birthday party. Although you receive a lot of documentation along with your OneWorld software, you won't receive anything that might resemble a "OneWorld in 10 Easy Steps" instruction guide. View documentation as a supplement to the OneWorld-related education and guidance your organization will receive through either J. D. Edwards or your implementation partner.

Education

I can't stress enough the importance of education and knowledge reinforcement to the success of your OneWorld implementation. This is also an area that is frequently under-budgeted or is taken too lightly in many ERP implementations. Thus, the challenge for the OneWorld implementation project team manager is to design a cost-effective and efficient education program that will ultimately promote your project's success.

J. D. Edwards and its implementation partners provide several education options that help you learn about your OneWorld software. There are advantages and disadvantages associated with each education option. Generally speaking, the OneWorld project team manager uses a combination of these options to provide for the education of both the project team and the organization's personnel (the end-users) who will ultimately use OneWorld on a day-to-day basis to complete transactions related to their part of the business processing cycle.

Classroom Education

Classroom-style training is the traditional form of education. In this type of education model, J. D. Edwards offers live, instructor-led, hands-on classroom training at its regional education facilities. J. D. Edwards provides these classes on a regular basis throughout the year. Training schedules are available through the

J. D. Edwards Web site or as a hard-copy catalog available from one of the regional education centers.

As a general rule, J. D. Edwards encourages attendance at its regularly scheduled classes at a regional education center location. However, J. D. Edwards as well as some of its business partners can provide on-site training as an alternative. Although it's generally a more costly option, on-site education ensures that class scheduling will fit your timetable. It also helps you avoid the cost of sending employees to a J. D. Edwards regional education center if you are not located close to one of these facilities. An added dimension of on-site education is that it can frequently be customized to meet your specific business requirements, depending on which provider you choose. This also makes sense if your organization has made software changes or significant workflow deviations from those provided in the standard J. D. Edwards documentation.

User Group Education

Traditionally, additional training opportunities have been made available during J. D. Edwards international or regional user group meetings. The courses offered in conjunction with user group meetings are typically accelerated or very focused classes on a general topic. Some recent examples include an introduction to the OneWorld Enterprise Report Writer and a class on OneWorld Security. Other types of classes include new release net change classes, upgrade planning, and classes on important new features in OneWorld, such as Business Intelligence. These classes have limited availability (such as once a year at a users conference) and therefore should not be considered a primary means of education for your project team or your end-user community.

Computer-Based Education

Self-directed or independent learning can be accommodated through a computer-based training program. The benefits of self-directed or independent learning are simply this: You are not locked into a class schedule or a particular location for training. In addition, you can proceed at a pace that's more comfortable for you.

J. D. Edwards has a multimedia computer-based training (CBT) program available for OneWorld self-education. You will pay extra for this. If you have been wondering if this is something you should invest in, my answer is yes. The following sections have some examples of how to derive value for your organization from the OneWorld CBTs. Figure 2-1 shows a typical lesson from the OneWorld CBT software.

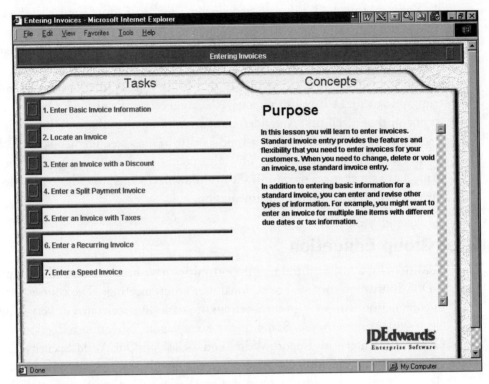

FIGURE 2-1 *A Typical OneWorld Computer-Based Training Lesson*

Making the Most of OneWorld CBTs

Now that I have told you that OneWorld CBTs can be a worthwhile investment, your next question is probably how your organization should use these training materials. There are several ways in which your organization can leverage OneWorld CBTs. Let's explore each of these.

Project Team Pre-Training Familiarization

First, the OneWorld CBT can be used to familiarize project team members with OneWorld before they ever see the actual product. This is a great way for project team members to learn something about OneWorld navigation and features before attending any formal J. D. Edwards classroom training. If you have no formal experience with OneWorld, always start with the Foundations. From there, have the project team member branch off into the business area he will attend classes in.

End-User Pre-Training Familiarization

Second, end-users can use the OneWorld CBT to familiarize themselves with OneWorld before they are exposed to any classroom or one-on-one training—but with some caveats. There is a natural tendency for project managers to assume that loading the OneWorld CBT on a laptop and sending it home for the weekend is training. In theory, this might be a way to avoid addressing issues such as "I'm too busy to attend class" or "I have no time during my busy workday for training." However, throwing a laptop at someone for the weekend is akin to saying "If you get a chance this weekend...". Most people have families, and by the time Sunday night rolls around, I'll bet that laptop has never been taken out of its carrying case.

However, some sage advice is in order. As a former educator and veteran software trainer, I must caution you that an effective education program must be planned, deliberate, and elevated to the same importance as the work itself. Any program that includes or is based solely on independent study (such as OneWorld CBTs) cannot be presumed to be any different from classroom training with respect to planning for its overall effectiveness.

Learning Differences

An important challenge facing the project manager is developing a sound educational plan that provides the right amount education to a potentially wide audience. Learning styles vary. OneWorld is not book learning—it is vocational training. In addition, computer literacy and general literacy are important considerations in the design of an effective training program. For instance, accounting clerks generally understand how to navigate a computer keyboard, but a receiving department clerk might not. Therefore, a word of caution is in order about independent study. Some individuals adapt well to independent study, and others do not. Certain people lack the motivation to study or are easily distracted when engaged in study and cannot learn without structure. Understanding learning differences is therefore an important consideration in constructing a successful training plan.

Learning differences affect all of us. I believe this is even more true for those who are pursuing independent study. For instance, does it matter if someone is well-educated or is already a frequent computer user? For instance, will this mean that he is a better candidate for CBT? Based on my experience, the answer is no. Although I have no scientific evidence to support this, I believe that a person's psychological makeup is a more important factor. For instance, did this person have attention deficit disorder as a child, or is this person left- or right-brain-dominant? This is, without a doubt, a good study area for someone completing a doctoral dissertation. For now, however, please take my advice in this regard: Independent study does not mean unstructured study. Establish goals for independent study, and provide follow-up testing to reinforce the concepts learned through independent study.

Reinforcement Training

The third use of OneWorld CBT training is for reinforcement education. If someone is unable to practice what he has learned, your training dollars will quickly become wasted. Certainly, the OneWorld CBT is one possible dimension of a training reinforcement program. Another is the availability of a practice environment where classroom or hands-on training exercises can be repeated as often as desired. You'll find that repeatable training exercises are tougher to create but pay dividends in the long run.

Web-Based Education

The newest training model emerging from J. D. Edwards is to provide Web-delivered OneWorld training workshops. These workshops leverage technology to combine location independence and live instruction. In this model, you don't need to go off-site to attend a class. Instead, you enroll for the class and then, using the Internet and a phone, attend a Web-based training workshop that typically runs for two hours.

Availability of these classes is currently limited to advanced topics for experienced OneWorld users or to World clients planning migration to or coexistence with OneWorld. Web-based education is still a relatively new and unproven medium for delivering more robust forms of training. In the future, your organization can expect J. D. Edwards to provide more Web-delivered training options to its clients. This is a rapidly emerging training delivery medium, especially in the software industry.

Custom User Education

Overall, the software documentation and training provided by J. D. Edwards is generally good. However, at times there are a small number of errors or inaccuracies present in the documentation. As for training class content, you might find that some topics are not covered in sufficient detail and others simply don't apply to your organization.

How then can you tailor J. D. Edwards-provided OneWorld documentation and training to correct for any deficiencies or to expand on these materials to satisfy your organization's specific needs? The answer is Custom User Education (CUE). Introduced several years ago, CUE is an extra-cost addition that provides a tool set designed to help your organization develop custom education specific to your OneWorld implementation.

What Do You Get If You Decide to Purchase Custom User Education?

First, you receive a Microsoft Word version of all the standard OneWorld documentation. A special document manager program and a Word document template are also included. This portion of Custom User Education is called the Custom Document Tool (see Figure 2-2).

Second, you receive administrative or content management portions of the CBT tool that allow you to create customized CBT courses. The CBT course content manager allows you to build user- or job-specific CBT programs from standard J. D. Edwards-provided CBT programs for OneWorld. Figure 2-3 shows the course-authoring portion of the CBT tool.

Train-the-Trainer Course and Documentation Writing Training

In addition to providing courses that focus on application and technical knowledge, J. D. Edwards also provides several one-day classes to help educate the OneWorld project team in two other important areas: training end-users and developing training materials.

If you have many end-users to train and you don't feel that your project team has enough knowledge or experience in classroom training techniques, consider the J. D. Edwards Train-the-Trainer class. You may choose not to have the entire project

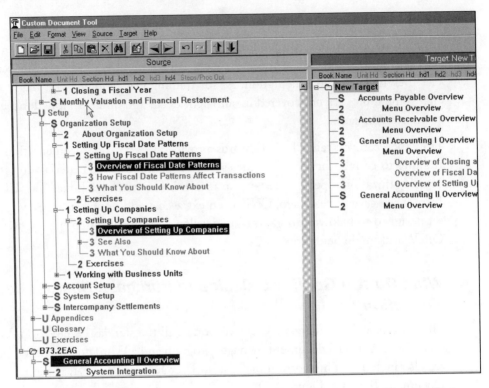

FIGURE 2-2 *Creating Custom Documentation Using the OneWorld Custom Document Tool*

team attend—only those who will be responsible for designing, developing, or delivering formal end-user education.

If your organization has purchased the Custom User Education component, some additional training classes will be of value for you to attend. First, if you will modify or rewrite any OneWorld documentation supplied by J. D. Edwards, you will want to consider taking the J. D. Edwards class on using the Custom Documentation Tool (CDT). Second, if you will use the CBT portion of CUE, consider taking the course on how to create your own individualized course tracks from the standard OneWorld CBT training modules provided by J. D. Edwards. J. D. Edwards schedules these three one-day classes on a back-to-back basis to facilitate attending all three sessions in one trip to the J. D. Edwards education center.

Technical Education

The technical personnel who provide systems support in your organization will require specific OneWorld training. Do not assume that your technical personnel

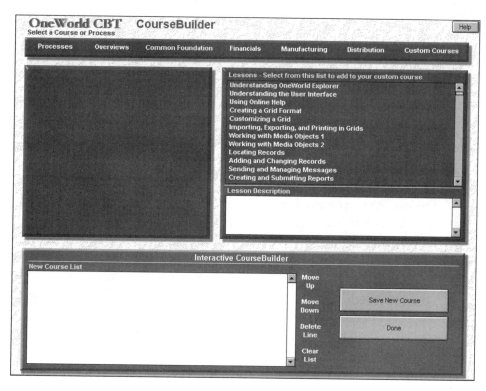

FIGURE 2-3 *Creating Custom Courses Using the OneWorld Computer-Based Training Tool*

will simply read the manual or pick up OneWorld and Configurable Network Computing as they go along.

First, *there is simply no substitute for knowledge regarding the OneWorld technical infrastructure,* referred to as Configurable Network Computing (CNC). Your organization will be well-served if one or more (preferably two or three) technically proficient individuals are trained in CNC. Not only should you possess this knowledge internally, but you'll be well-served to include CNC consulting expertise involvement in the initial rollout of OneWorld. You might also want your internal CNC experts to "shadow" consultants during the initial installation and also when the first upgrade or service pack for OneWorld is installed.

Second, if your organization expects to customize OneWorld, additional training will be needed for systems support personnel who will be responsible for completing such customizations. End-users may also require training for the Enterprise Report Writer if they will create custom reports. Although these requirements will vary by organization, I have typically found that end-users from the accounting, marketing (sales analysis), production planning, and materials planning departments are the most likely to want custom reports. However, many organizations simply do not permit end-users to create custom reports and require them to make use of their systems support department for such needs.

Keeping Up with J. D. Edwards Changes to OneWorld Education

The current mix of training class offerings and training tracks, as well as a list of the training facility locations and the contents of each class, are provided in a course catalog and class schedule. This information is available from the J. D. Edwards Web site at www.jdewards.com for download or in hard-copy form and is updated several times per year. If you need one, you can request a hard-copy catalog through a J. D. Edwards education center office. You can make arrangements to attend OneWorld classes through either the applicable J. D. Edwards education center or through the Training Central portion of the J. D. Edwards Web site.

The Best Practices in OneWorld Education

Now that I've made a case for training, the next step is to develop a training plan that promotes project success. This section provides some useful tips on how to plan and conduct end-user and project team education.

What Form of Education Is Best?

I recommend (and so does J. D. Edwards) that all your project team members receive live, instructor-led classroom training. This training is considered the basis for understanding how to use and implement OneWorld throughout your organization. Moreover, this training should be viewed as a preparatory step for the OneWorld implementation project team to provide training for non-project team OneWorld users (or end-users) in how to effectively navigate and use OneWorld.

What About End-User Education?

Although J. D. Edwards does not prevent end-users from attending their classroom training sessions, it is not something they or I particularly encourage. Why?

First, OneWorld classroom-based training, unless customized, generally provides too much information for an end-user audience. For instance, these classes tend to cover a greater amount of information that is often far too conceptual or general to be of value to an end-user. Although this information might be appropriate for your project team members, it is inappropriate for end-users.

Second, some of the information contained in these classes is directly related to configuration and setup—areas that most end-users generally won't be responsible for. You, as the project manager, probably won't want end-users to have substantial knowledge in these areas without other appropriate complementary knowledge.

Within the last few years, J. D. Edwards has begun to address OneWorld training from a new perspective. The concept of training tracks has gained favor. These audience-focused training tracks group related courses or materials into tracks that are appropriate for a given audience, including specific end-user audiences. In addition to these focused training tracks, J. D. Edwards also offers several accelerated training tracks that cover a wider scope of material.

Accelerated training tracks generally focus on an entire business process, such as distribution and logistics. Accelerated classes are aimed primarily at the OneWorld project team audience. A comprehensive accelerated class format generally does a better job of covering overall system integration, usually at the expense of subject depth or mastery. Therefore, in certain areas, you'll likely want to take specific classes that focus on details, such as advanced pricing, warehouse management, or transportation management.

Why Should Your Organization Consider Buying Custom User Education?

If your organization wants to extend or personalize the J. D. Edwards documentation, you need to purchase Custom User Education along with the OneWorld software. If your organization plans to rely extensively on OneWorld computer-based training for the purposes of educating your end-users, you'll also likely want to purchase Custom User Education.

Why Develop Custom Education Instead of Using J. D. Edwards?

Educating your user community is an expensive and time-consuming process. It is a fundamental ingredient in a successful OneWorld implementation. Too often, training gets short-changed. Your organization can't afford the time, the expense, or, in many cases, the inefficiencies of sending every affected end-user to a J. D. Edwards-provided class. Therefore, to be successful, your organization needs to formally identify and plan for the appropriate amount of education for each of your affected end-users.

It has been my experience that an education program that relies on CBT materials exclusively will not be effective. However, using CBT materials to provide introductory foundation-level knowledge will succeed. Consider training your strongest and most interested end-users via the CBT approach initially, especially if you have a number of remote locations. Allow these individuals to proceed as far as they want using the CBT approach. Bring them in from the field for a short fast-track class in the areas they have learned. You can then use these people as mentors to assist others who are less computer-literate at their remote locations to establish a level of confidence before formal training commences.

Train There or Train Here?

I've worked with both approaches. There are advantages and disadvantages to each. Consider providing OneWorld training on location in the field when you have many end-users with relatively narrow job responsibilities. You'll save travel costs by sending the instructor, not the participants. The disadvantage is that if a training area isn't already in place on a permanent basis, you'll need to worry about assembling and dismantling one in each remote facility as your training proceeds. Also, be aware that distractions can occur when training is done locally. Consider renting a conference room at a facility that is reasonably close to the remote location if you anticipate this will be a problem.

What's the good news about a road show? With OneWorld, this can be a supply of laptop computers that have the OneWorld stand-alone environment and other appropriate training materials already installed on them and an overhead LCD projector that travels with (or in advance of) the instructor to each site. The drawback of this approach is that you'll need to ensure that you leave behind, at each site, some form of OneWorld access that will let training participants perform knowledge reinforcement from their site prior to your "go-live" date.

If your training requirements aren't as grand and you have only one or a few locations to consider, training at a central location will work best. Again, plan to avoid distractions. If distractions (or space) will be an issue, consider renting a conference room at a facility that is reasonably close to your location. To save on expenses, a central location allows you to use the workstations that will be deployed as a part of your OneWorld implementation for training workstations. A good (readable from a distance) LCD projector is a small investment ($5,000 to $10,000), or one can be rented.

When Should You Train?

It has been my experience that training, like inventory, should be delivered on a just-in-time basis, or as close as possible to when the training will actually be used in some form of productive activity. For instance, there is little point in training end-users in July for the OneWorld implementation that will not happen until December.

Counter to this rule, you will want your OneWorld implementation project team trained on OneWorld at the earliest possible date. Your organization should not go too far in defining future business processes and making configuration choices prior to attending a significant portion of your OneWorld course of education. Education is your greatest ally during configuration. Engage it early and often. In addition, make sure that every team member has access to the documentation and the OneWorld stand-alone environment before, during, and after any OneWorld-related education. Please remember this important point: How will you know if your conference room pilot, training, and production environments are working correctly if your project team can't complete even the simplest of transactions within those environments?

If your OneWorld go-live date is postponed for a significant amount of time (likely more than 60 days), you will need to provide a refresher, at a minimum, for your organization's business-critical functions before the new go-live date. This will be added cost in terms of time and dollars. However, if this is not done, you are risking significant and generally unnecessary business interruption. The well-orchestrated training program should integrate CBT and some form of skill validation. This will further ensure that an organization's personnel will be ready on the go-live date, or it will at least ensure their basic navigation skills through continuous reinforcement.

Designing a Successful Training Program

First, let me say that most OneWorld implementation teams are overworked—and in some cases, they don't have to be. Why are they unnecessarily overworked? Frequently, the project team is not fully educated. When a project team's education is incomplete, the team's overall productivity and quality of work suffer. Education helps you avoid redoing work or, even worse, project failure or substantial business disruption. Training is a quest to address the proverbial paradox of "If only I knew then what I know now."

What Other Formal Project Team Training Should Occur?

In addition to the OneWorld functional or technical training that is appropriate to a given team member's involvement, some general education requirements are important skills to have.

First, the project team should receive appropriate training in any tools that you will use to facilitate your OneWorld implementation. For instance, general project management training might include training in Microsoft Project for project task planning, progress reporting, and resource planning. Microsoft Office is frequently used to prepare training documentation and presentations. You may also use Microsoft Visio or SPSS all CLEAR to create process flow diagrams. Again, some training in how to effectively use these tools might be needed. Don't assume that your team is fluent in all these tools, or that they have more than basic skills in how to use these tools.

A training requirements worksheet is a critical working paper you'll need to produce as a part of your implementation planning. The key is to analyze both project team and end-user training requirements and to obtain any additional training as needed to promote the success of your project. This is an important role, and it is one where your implementation consultant can help. The implementation consultant can assist you by recommending training, or he might even provide certain types of training for you, especially if he has developed templates for your use as a part of his implementation methodology.

For specialized OneWorld-related training, you'll need to rely on J. D. Edwards and its business partners. Besides J. D. Edwards and its business partners, there are a number of excellent training-focused consulting firms and freelance consultants that can help you.

For other types of training, such as on how to use the Microsoft Office tools, you can take a more traditional path. A good source of this type of training is generally available through a community college or through a private training-only company such as Catapult. These are good and inexpensive sources of this kind of training. However, if you want training that is customized to how you will use these tools for your specific project, consider using a training-focused consulting firm or freelance consultant.

Life in the Small Shop

In a relatively small OneWorld installation, usually one or two people serve as the OneWorld "go-to" for everything, from adding new users to creating terminals to changing user-defined codes. In some instances, these requirements can be met entirely through consultants. In a larger installation, a data administration group might be responsible for making all configuration and master data changes to OneWorld, a systems security group might add a new user, and a decision or application support group might be responsible for creating any needed custom reports for end-users. Obviously, the scale and complexity of your internal technical staff will determine to what extent OneWorld technical training is needed for individuals within your organization.

A Final Word About Training

I know that our world is increasingly an electronic one, but I find that there is still a place for live facilitator- or instructor-led classroom-style training. On the other hand, computer-based training has its place as well. Take a look at what J. D. Edwards or your implementation partner has to offer, and then sit down and work out the details of a plan that will fit your organization's OneWorld-related training needs and budget.

The Response Line

Well, the training class is over. You're now back at your office, working through the creation of a sales order. Something goes wrong. Your implementation consultant is unavailable. So what happens now? Who can you talk to? How can you determine if the problem is user- or software-inflicted? The answer is to call the J. D. Edwards response line. The response line is the customer support center for all J. D. Edwards clients, supporting both World and OneWorld software users. To access the J. D. Edwards response line, your organization must be a J. D. Edwards client that is either within its warranty period or that has subscribed to the annual J. D. Edwards software maintenance program.

The response line is available to J. D. Edwards clients during normal business hours via a toll-free number. When you call, do so from a touch-tone phone. You'll be prompted through a menu system to identify yourself and the application you need help with. You'll also need the client number that J. D. Edwards has assigned to your organization. You should sit at a workstation and generally be able to replicate or guide the customer support representative through your problem situation. Here are a few general tips to help response line calls go more smoothly or to expedite their handling:

- Validate the problem in all environments first.
- Check the Knowledge Garden for any Software Action Requests related to the program (object) that you're having a problem with.
- Check the Knowledge Garden for any white papers related to the problem you're having or that give general guidelines for troubleshooting problems.
- Place any calls to the response line from a phone at or near a development workstation.
- Know your client number before placing the call.
- Know your local fax number before calling.
- Have available copies of any screen shots, dumps, or other information related to the issue when making the call.
- Write down the call number given.
- Apply any fixes suggested by the Knowledge Garden or by response line personnel. Test them thoroughly before calling the response line about the problem again.
- Keep a record of every response line call you make and the responses you receive. Follow up with your staff regarding any J. D. Edwards-recommended actions.

If a customer support representative is not available to speak with you, after a brief wait (less than 5 minutes), your call will be answered by an attendant who will assign you a call number after asking you several identification and problem-related questions.

Generally speaking, you should receive a call back relatively quickly (usually in less than an hour). It seems that month-end and year-end are the times when the response line is the busiest. You can also initiate electronic inquiries with the response line using the J. D. Edwards Web site. I thought this would really improve my productivity. However, I don't recommend using this approach for critical issues. My experience with this method has been that the response line has not met my expectations in addressing electronic inquiries. For now, the dialog between you and the response line customer support representative simply can't be replaced efficiently.

Software Action Requests

Software Action Requests (SARs) are action items for the J. D. Edwards' OneWorld development team. The SAR is usually the last step taken toward resolving any customer issue at J. D. Edwards. This section discusses the importance of SARs.

What Is a Software Action Request?

You'll frequently hear the term Software Action Request (or SAR) when you talk to a customer support representative at J. D. Edwards. A SAR is used to track any *requested* changes to OneWorld—including those to correct any defects in OneWorld. The SAR is usually the last course of action to resolve an outstanding problem or deficiency—perceived or real—that has been identified by a J. D. Edwards client.

When Is a Software Action Request Initiated?

For instance, you might call J. D. Edwards about a particular performance or usability issue or about an error condition you've encountered. A SAR is established when the customer support representative is unable to resolve your OneWorld software issue properly and J. D. Edwards personnel have concluded that a software enhancement, modification, or repair might be warranted.

The SAR itself does not resolve a performance or usability issue or error condition— it sets the stage for resolution. SAR is only the method that J. D. Edwards uses to track such issues with OneWorld. SARs often result in *paper fixes*—a list of code changes that can be applied to the errant OneWorld program by a qualified

OneWorld developer. Also note that SARs are frequently not acted upon immediately—unless they are causing an immediate business interruption, such as the inability to print an accounts payable check.

Generally speaking, most calls that you will place to the J. D. Edwards response line will be satisfied when you call or will be satisfied with a callback from the response line within a reasonable period of time. Occasionally, you will encounter a customer support representative who hasn't dealt with your problem, so some additional research on his or her part might be necessary. When all these "quick fix" efforts fail, the issue you're experiencing is a good candidate for a SAR. As a rule, if you're unhappy with the speed of resolution or with the answer you received, consider placing another call to the response line. Be sure to let the response line operator know that the call is related to a previous issue you feel needs to be escalated. You should do this only when prior calls didn't help you resolve the problem. However, in fairness to all callers, limit these urgent messages to problems that are disrupting your business, not simply causing a nuisance.

Does a Software Action Request Guarantee Action?

It is important to note that just because a SAR has been entered does not mean that the SAR will be immediately satisfied. This is primarily true of enhancements and problems for which a workaround exists. Therefore, many of these issues are added to the list of activities that will likely be addressed in a future service pack or release of OneWorld. However, many of the software enhancements that occur are actually prioritized by the overall J. D. Edwards client community through user group voting.

Certainly, if the SAR is related to a specific performance problem or error condition, J. D. Edwards software engineers will attempt to duplicate the problem you are having. The first step at J. D. Edwards is always to determine if a similar issue has occurred previously before they act on the new request. If the new request can be satisfied through an existing SAR, the new SAR is closed, and reference is made to the existing, completed SAR.

What's a Reasonable Amount of Time to Allow?

I hope I won't be the first one to tell you that there are certain inherent disadvantages to the whole movement toward open systems. As much as you might expect to find hardware and software operating independence and no problems across platforms with the open systems model, this is simply not the case.

This lack of independence is due in part to the immaturity of the open systems movement and to the existence of competing standards in the marketplace. As a result, issues will arise that might be unique to your site and that can't be easily duplicated by the J. D. Edwards response line staff and the OneWorld product maintenance and development teams. Here are two examples to consider:

◆ One of my clients was unable to complete an accounts payable check run in OneWorld. The customer support representative on the J. D. Edwards response line was unable to duplicate the problem. It took several weeks of delay and increasing frustration, as well as a call from at least one other OneWorld client (misery loves company!) with the same problem, before J. D. Edwards was finally (after much investigation) able to reproduce the problem. In the final analysis, the resolution was simple, but pinning down the problem took much longer. The problem was caused by some inconsistencies between supposedly platform-independent software.

◆ I called the response line on a simple issue: Reversing journal entries (journal entries that reverse themselves on the first day of the next period in OneWorld) weren't being created during a general ledger batch posting run, even though the correct option on the journal entry had been set. Within a matter of hours of the SAR's being entered, J. D. Edwards made a paper fix available.

The moral of the story is that when something bad happens, you want—*and you expect*—quick attention by J. D. Edwards. If the response line is unable to respond within a period of time you deem reasonable, *which should be dictated by the severity of the problem you're experiencing,* you might need to request escalation of the problem within J. D. Edwards. Occasionally, this might require that you contact your client services manager at J. D. Edwards to help grease a few squeaky wheels and bring about the resolution of your organization's problem with OneWorld. Again, my suggestion is to work through normal channels unless that is impractical given the circumstances.

As a final note, please understand that the vast majority of calls to the J. D. Edwards response line that you will make will not result in a SAR. As a matter of fact, I've had only a few SARs entered on my behalf over the past decade.

Nonetheless, given the size of the OneWorld user base, the problem you're having has probably been identified by another client experiencing similar problems or, better yet, through J. D. Edwards' ongoing quality assurance efforts.

Electronic Support

With release B73.3.2 and above of OneWorld, instead of manually applying code change documents, which are also known as paper fixes, you may now download and apply code changes electronically. These code change downloads are known as an Electronic Software Update (ESU). An ESU can streamline the cumbersome, error-prone process of making code changes to the source code of OneWorld programs. The ESU itself is a downloadable collection of programs that address the issue or issues reported in a specific SAR. An ESU is delivered as a self-extracting executable file and must be subsequently merged into the appropriate OneWorld environment by your systems support department or a technical consultant.

The process of applying an ESU to your OneWorld environment is similar to the "update and merge" process used in the OneWorld upgrade or update process. Therefore, it is essential to track, document, and *fully* consider any customizations made in your environments prior to installing any ESU. It is essential that you load and apply the update to a test environment initially and then conduct regression (net change) testing of such changes before promoting them into your production environment if you are already "live" on OneWorld.

The Knowledge Garden

Another benefit available to a J. D. Edwards client that is within its warranty period or that has subscribed to the annual J. D. Edwards software maintenance program is access to the J. D. Edwards Knowledge Garden. Access to the Knowledge Garden is available through the J. D. Edwards Web site. Even if you are a J. D. Edwards customer, someone from your organization, who will serve as your site administrator, must initiate this service with J. D. Edwards for your organization. After the service is activated, you will receive a sign-on and password for access. The Knowledge Garden log-in page is shown in Figure 2-4.

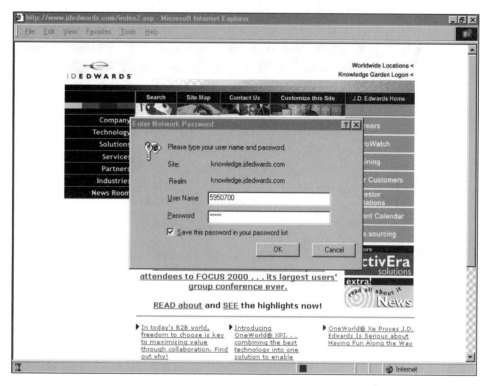

FIGURE 2-4 *The Knowledge Garden Log-In Page*

Why Use the Knowledge Garden?

The Knowledge Garden is best viewed as a self-serve customer service center. The Knowledge Garden can be used to help troubleshoot problems you might be having with OneWorld or to determine whether a particular issue has already been reported to J. D. Edwards by another customer. This is done by accessing the J. D. Edwards SAR system through the Knowledge Garden. In addition, you will also find documents that might help you understand a particular aspect of OneWorld in more detail, including downloadable, updated user reference guides when available.

The searchable SAR database through the Knowledge Garden includes all requested corrections and enhancements for both OneWorld and World Software. Although J. D. Edwards recently reduced the number of SARs available online for World Software to the current release, all SARs are still available that relate to OneWorld. J. D. Edwards updates the SAR information available through the Knowledge Garden on a daily basis, usually on a one-day delay.

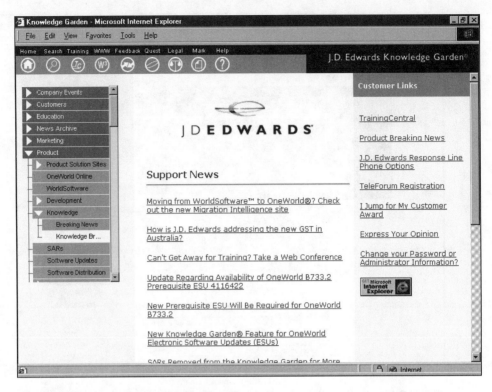

FIGURE 2-5 *The Knowledge Garden Home Page*

The Knowledge Garden home page is shown in Figure 2-5. The Knowledge Garden has replaced the response line as my primary means of accessing J. D. Edwards support services. As a consultant, I'm usually busy working with my client during business hours. I need to use the rest of my available time to prepare for the next day's activities with my client. This usually means investigating issues or resolving problems on an off-hours basis, and that, of course, means that response line support is sometimes not available to suit my schedule.

Here's a typical use of the Knowledge Garden: Using the search facilities, I can determine if a software code change (a paper fix) is available to resolve a particular problem and then immediately download it. Thereafter, it can be attached to an e-mail message and sent to a OneWorld software engineer or consultant, who will evaluate and apply the code change to the appropriate OneWorld program's source code and then compile and redeploy the changed program. All this happens without your calling the response line. The Knowledge Garden search page is shown in Figure 2-6.

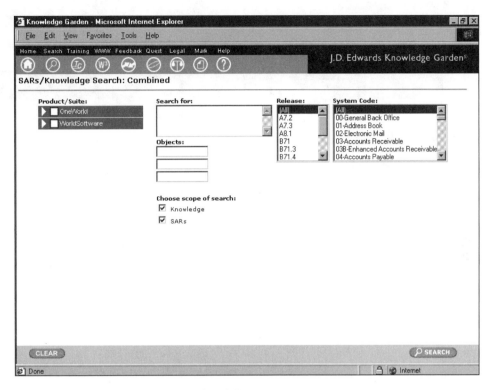

FIGURE 2-6 *The Knowledge Garden Search Page*

You can also search for white papers that have been made available on specific topics, such as financial integrity reporting or inventory valuation methods that can be useful to help configure OneWorld or that might help explain configuration options. In addition, you can download the latest versions of OneWorld reference guides or reference guides that have been published since you loaded the documentation locally, onto your workstation, from the documentation CD-ROM.

Finally, you can also find documentation related to new OneWorld features that might be included in the next release of the software. Download these manuals to preview the functionality and determine how these new features will benefit your organization or to help in planning the implementation of these new features. The Knowledge Garden documentation and white paper Web page is shown in Figure 2-7.

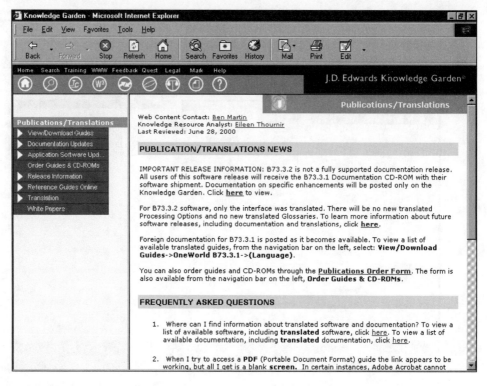

FIGURE 2-7 *Use the Knowledge Garden to Find OneWorld-Related Documentation and White Papers*

J. D. Edwards Implementation Tools and Methodologies

Over the years, J. D. Edwards has continued to enhance both the tools and methodologies that can help you implement OneWorld successfully for your organization. When I first began working with J. D. Edwards' World software in the early 1990s, its methodology was called the REP methodology (which stood for Rapidly, Economically, and Predictably). Even back then, configuration of the software was facilitated by a concept called soft coding. The business processes within J. D. Edwards' World software were just as configurable then as they are today. When you have a good thing going, you stick with it.

As J. D. Edwards began selling its World software to smaller and middle-market companies through its Genesis marketing channel in 1995, it quickly became apparent that some further help was needed to simplify the overall process for clients who generally had more limited resources.

The answer came in the form of the World tools called Composer, Teacher, and Coach. Using Composer, an organization answered a series of questions about its business practices. The answers to these questions were used to generate a pre-configured version of World software, which could then be further tweaked by the implementation consultant. Also originally intended for use in the Genesis channel were the Teacher and Coach products. These products were computer-based training tools for World software.

These early World software implementation tools for the Genesis channel are now full-fledged components of J. D. Edwards' overall methodology for implementing OneWorld, regardless of client size. The World Composer tool is the precursor to the Composer tool that is now available in OneWorld. It is an integral part of ActivEra, J. D. Edwards' latest flavor of implementation methodology. The Coach and Teacher computer-based training products are the precursors to the OneWorld CBT series.

Prior to ActivEra, there was an intermediate step. Initially, the REP methodology was combined with Composer to form a new implementation methodology, called the OnTrack methodology. The OnTrack methodology has now evolved into the ActivEra methodology based on J. D. Edwards' Idea to Action concept. The configuration tools are called activators in ActivEra. However, there are two distinct sets of activators in ActivEra. The first set is referred to as the business activators. For instance, this layer helps you configure transaction workflow and user-defined tables.

The second set of activators is called technology activators. A major difference between OneWorld and World software deployment is the Configurable Network Computing architecture, the J. D. Edwards version of client/server hardware architecture. To accommodate the rapid configuration of OneWorld, its modification, and the deployment of environmental changes as needed, J. D. Edwards has created a set of tools to facilitate this process. These tools are called technology activators in ActivEra.

The bottom line of this methodology discussion is that J. D. Edwards, or a J. D. Edwards Genesis business partner, will likely propose and use the ActivEra approach during the both the pre- and post-sale process for an implementation of OneWorld. However, most other implementation partners will have their own proprietary approach to implementing OneWorld for your organization.

Generally speaking, these alternative approaches will be experientially based and might vary substantially in content and formality from ActivEra or, for that matter, from one vendor to another. However, all these alternative approaches still rely largely on the OneWorld tools—the business and the technology activators to complete the implementation work.

Ready for more? Chapters 5 and 6 provide a more detailed discussion of implementation approach differences, including a model approach that you can adopt for your OneWorld implementation, or that can be used as a basis for comparison when evaluating potential implementation partners. In addition, beginning with Chapter 10, you will learn more about OneWorld business activators.

J. D. Edwards User Groups

Sharing your experiences with other OneWorld users can be a helpful process. User groups exist at local, regional, and national levels. In some cases, special-interest groups exist for specific industries. This section provides important information about the user groups that serve the overall J. D. Edwards software community.

Quest: The J. D. Edwards User Group

J. D. Edwards users have the opportunity to participate in a number of resource avenues besides those offered by J. D. Edwards itself. Most of these alternatives fall under the sponsorship of Quest, the international user group exclusively for J. D. Edwards clients.

Quest is a nonprofit organization dedicated to providing a forum for J. D. Edwards users to educate themselves on a continuing basis about their J. D. Edwards software investment, interact with other J. D. Edwards users, and collectively request software enhancements from J. D. Edwards.

The Quest Web Site

The Quest Web site, shown in Figure 2-8, has a variety of member-only sections. Key aspects of the Web site that are available to members include member-developed white papers, discussion groups, and chat rooms.

FIGURE 2-8 *The Quest Users Group Home Page*

Quest Publications

Quest provides its membership with a technical journal that began publication in late 1997. In addition to the technical journal, Quest also publishes a newsletter called Quest Network.

FOCUS: The Annual International Users Conference

Probably the most important aspect of Quest is its sponsorship of FOCUS, the international user group meeting that has been held annually since 1977. This conference gives the J. D. Edwards user community the opportunity to exchange information and strategies and to participate in educational and professional development programs. FOCUS is a gala event. The crowds at FOCUS have grown so large that several years back this conference had to rent a huge tent to house the keynote speeches before moving from the office and hotel campus where J. D. Edwards makes its headquarters to the Denver Convention Center.

Joining Quest

You must be a J. D. Edwards' World or OneWorld client, business partner, or complementary products and services vendor in order to join Quest. If you're not a J. D. Edwards client, the membership fees are substantially greater. Both individual and corporate memberships are available for J. D. Edwards clients.

How to Contact Quest

For further information about Quest, or for current membership pricing guidelines, contact Quest through its Web site at www.questnet.org, through the mail, or by phone:

> Quest Headquarters
> 2365 Harrodsburg Road
> Suite A325
> Lexington, Kentucky 40504
> Phone:
> (800) 225-0517
> (606) 226-4307
> Fax:
> (606) 226-4338

Regional User Groups

In addition to the Quest-organized international user group conference, in recent years regional user groups have evolved. They sponsor their own regional meetings and, in some cases, annual user conferences as well. Although they are smaller in size and scope than FOCUS, they are nonetheless quite worthwhile groups to associate yourself with.

For instance, I frequently attend the Mid-America Users Conference, which is generally held in early December in the Chicago area. The following is a list of the regional user groups that I am aware of. I have not included contact information because this information changes much too frequently. Therefore, I recommend that you obtain updated local and regional user group information from either your local J. D. Edwards office or from Quest directly.

Pacific Rim	Baton Rouge
Northern California	Mississippi

Southern California	Atlanta
Rocky Mountain	Southern Georgia/Northern Florida
Cactus League	Greensboro
Central Texas	New York
Houston	Northeast
Dallas	Mid-Atlantic
Heart of America	Nashville
Minnesota	Charlotte
Packerland	Central Florida
Chicagoland	Southern Florida
Michiana	SANLA
Southern Michigan	Hawaii
Buckeye (Cleveland)	

Special-Interest Groups

Both Quest and the regional user groups sponsor special-interest group sessions. For instance, special-interest groups might include discrete manufacturing users or government users of J. D. Edwards software. These special-interest group meetings are a good way to make contact with other J. D. Edwards users in your line of business.

Typically, organizations within the same industry (or vertical, as it's sometimes called) have common and sometimes unique business requirements. For instance, government and nonprofit corporations follow different accounting principles than do for-profit entities, while process-manufacturing requirements are generally different from discrete manufacturing requirements.

Sometimes, J. D. Edwards software might not fully meet the needs of a given vertical industry. In this case, J. D. Edwards users might employ workarounds or customized solutions to resolve some of these unique requirements. Individuals from other J. D. Edwards client sites within a given vertical who attend these special-interest groups are often more than willing to offer advice on how to solve an industry-specific problem. This can be especially helpful when you're just getting your J. D. Edwards software up and running for your business.

Since special-interest group information changes frequently, contact J. D. Edwards or Quest to determine if a special-interest group exists for your community of interest or line of business.

How to Crash the Party

If you have not yet committed to J. D. Edwards' OneWorld and you would like to attend a users conference, such as the international users conference, or possibly a regional users group conference or meeting, you can do so as an invitee of J. D. Edwards. I recommend this as a good way to speak with other users firsthand. This might help you decide about a possible J. D. Edwards' OneWorld software investment. Contact your J. D. Edwards sales representative. He or she will be able to assist you in making these arrangements.

J. D. Edwards Client Satisfaction

I have found that J. D. Edwards is genuinely interested in achieving and maintaining high levels of customer satisfaction. Prior to embarking upon my career in consulting, I was employed at a middle-market manufacturing company in the Chicago area. While in their employ, I served as the primary contact on most day-to-day matters for our J. D. Edwards software for the better part of five years.

During this time, I found the overall client experience with the J. D. Edwards pre-sales and post-sales organizations to be a very good one. In my experience, I have found that J. D. Edwards always demonstrates genuine interest in its customers. I have also heard of similar experiences from other J. D. Edwards customers over the years. In the past, J. D. Edwards regularly surveyed its customers to determine how each client viewed his or her relationship with J. D. Edwards and satisfaction with the software. As a rule, I have found that J. D. Edwards does seem to be a company that will go out of its way to ensure the satisfaction of every client.

With regard to OneWorld, the client satisfaction experience has been a mixed bag. The early versions of OneWorld were error-ridden, had performance problems, and lacked significant functionality that was available in J. D. Edwards' World software. I have heard that for a time, J. D. Edwards recommended that clients initially adopt World software and later migrate to OneWorld. However, when all is said and done, the latest version of OneWorld has largely resolved most of these earlier issues and generally works well.

One of the ways that J. D. Edwards has helped some of its earlier clients resolve at least some of their OneWorld issues is through the deployment of "SWAT" teams to help sift through customer issues during last year's Y2K surge in OneWorld implementations. J. D. Edwards experienced an unprecedented number of go-live sites in the closing months of 1999. It is well-known that OneWorld placed a strain on the support organization and software engineers at J. D. Edwards during 1999. Now that Y2K is behind us, J. D. Edwards should be able to regain some of its customer satisfaction shine in the coming year.

The J. D. Edwards Home Page

How do you keep up with J. D. Edwards and in particular with changes and enhancements planned or available for your OneWorld software? The answer is through the J. D. Edwards Web site. From the J. D. Edwards home page, you can access product information, partner information, the Knowledge Garden (for SARs, white papers, and other information), and the Quest Web site. If you have not yet decided on OneWorld, I recommend reviewing the J. D. Edwards Web site as a part of your evaluation process. Also do this for any other vendors you might be considering as an alternative to your OneWorld purchase. Understanding the depth of information on a vendor's Web site might help you arrive at a decision about a possible J. D. Edwards' OneWorld software investment. The home page of the J. D. Edwards Web site (www.jdedwards.com) is shown in Figure 2-9.

Summary

This chapter provided you with a general introduction to the collateral materials and services that complement your OneWorld investment. Special emphasis was given to planning the overall education effort related to your OneWorld implementation. Education should be an important line item in your overall OneWorld implementation budget and should be delivered on a just-in-time basis, because it will be needed to help you configure or begin using OneWorld.

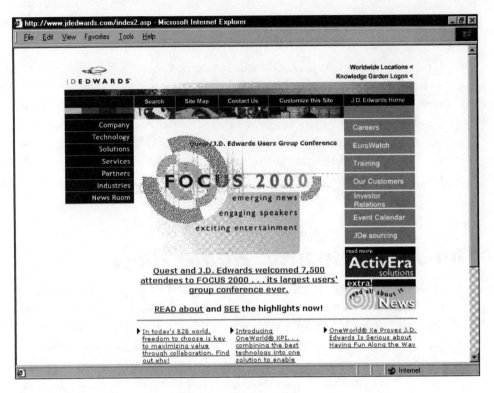

FIGURE 2-9 *The J. D. Edwards Corporate Home Page*

Other topics covered in this chapter include the following:

◆ OneWorld CBTs

◆ OneWorld Custom User Education (CUE) tools

◆ User groups

◆ The response line

◆ Software Action Requests

◆ Electronic support

◆ The Knowledge Garden

◆ The ActivEra implementation methodology

Chapter 3

This chapter gives you a fundamental understanding of the technology behind OneWorld. If you have a business background, this chapter might sound like a real sleeper to you. However, an understanding of the OneWorld technology infrastructure is important background information, even for a nontechnical person who is working on the OneWorld implementation team.

This chapter provides an overview of the OneWorld technical architecture. If you're new to both client/server and open system–based computing, you'll find lucid introductions to both of these subjects. Coverage of these two topics lays the necessary groundwork for your introduction to OneWorld's Configurable Network Computing (CNC) architecture.

From the AS/400 to the Open System Model

The evolution of OneWorld is closely associated with the history of J. D. Edwards' original ERP software product, World Software. The World Software system ran only on the IBM AS/400 midrange computer. The AS/400 has been one of IBM's most successful computers. In today's client/server-centric world, many believe the AS/400 is representative of a bygone era in computing. This section provides a brief introduction to the AS/400's impact on OneWorld.

What's the AS/400?

The Application System/400 (AS/400) is one of the most successful computers ever introduced by IBM Corporation. More than 500,000 AS/400 systems have been sold since its introduction about a decade ago. The AS/400 is considered a general-purpose computer oriented toward business applications. Being business-oriented, the AS/400 is designed primarily as a transaction processor and is not considered a "number cruncher."

The AS/400 is IBM's *midrange* computer. The AS/400 is not as powerful or as costly to own and operate as an IBM mainframe computer. It fact, its operating system, OS/400, is one of the simplest to administer—a complete departure from IBM's mainframe operating systems.

Three key aspects of the AS/400 separate it from virtually all other computers:

◆ It makes use of a proprietary processor architecture and a proprietary operating system.

◆ It includes an integrated, relational database, which is known as DB/2.

◆ About 90 percent of the business application programs that run on the AS/400 computer were written using a programming language called RPG (Report Program Generator). This represents about 90 percent of the worldwide programming that's been done in RPG. The remainder of AS/400 programs were generally written in COBOL.

By industry standards, the IBM AS/400 computer platform is likely the least open of virtually all mainstream products on the market today. However, such a lack of openness has not prevented the AS/400 from industry-wide acclaim and popularity.

The AS/400 has a proven track record as a reliable, cost-effective business computer. This has made the AS/400 extremely popular with smaller and middle-market organizations, especially in the manufacturing sector and in the "Rust Belt" region in the upper Midwest and Great Lakes areas of the United States. In addition, the IBM AS/400 computer product family has proven quite popular in Europe.

Hardware Manufacturers Embrace Open System Architectures

Traditionally, larger computer manufacturing companies such as IBM have not been known for openly sharing access to their main control program, operating system, or computer architecture. For instance, as mentioned previously, the AS/400 uses both a proprietary architecture and a proprietary operating system called OS/400. The AS/400 also features an integrated relational database architecture called DB/2.

The rules of the game for computer manufacturers have been changing over the past decade. Like its big brother, the IBM mainframe computer, the AS/400 midrange computer has been losing momentum in the marketplace. Although microprocessors spawned the PC revolution, they initially had little impact on the large-computer market. However, as microprocessors have advanced in speed and microprocessor operating systems have gained multiprocessing and multitasking capabilities, these platforms can now process vast amounts of work, especially when they are connected, either as a massively parallel processor or as a series of networked processors.

As a result of these hardware advances, organizations are increasingly adopting microprocessor-based computers and computer networks instead of selecting midrange or mainframe computers. At the same time, new computer buyers are increasingly demanding so-called "open systems."

What's in Store for the AS/400?

As this book was being completed, according to several industry analysts, IBM Corporation will shortly initiate a sweeping brand consolidation. The AS/400 will likely be included in this rebranding exercise. Speculation has it that the AS/400 will be rebranded as the "I/500." The AS/400 name change will be accompanied by name changes for the rest of the IBM product family as well, including the UNIX-based midrange RS/6000, the mainframe System/390, and the Windows NT-based NetFinity platforms.

Word also has it that the "I" in "I/500" stands for "Internet," and that the I/500 will be positioned as an electronic commerce server. At least one market analyst has cautioned that significant changes to the AS/400 architecture itself are unlikely at this time. However, others speculate that this move could be the beginning of the end for the AS/400's proprietary architecture.

Also significant are recent announcements by IBM that Linux will be available for the AS/400. Unlike Windows NT, which can run on an AS/400 using an Intel plug-in processor board, Linux will not run under the AS/400's native OS/400 operating system but instead will replace it completely. For now, however, all you can do is keep a keen eye turned toward what's happening at IBM by reading various trade journals or by checking the IBM Web site.

What Is an Open System?

An open system is a computer architecture or platform that generally permits the use of one or more commercially available operating systems such as UNIX or Microsoft Windows NT instead of proprietary operating systems such as OS/400. The fact of the matter is that open systems are *perceived* to provide choices—choices that are said to not exist when relying on the proprietary computer architecture.

Other computer manufacturers, especially those in the midrange market, have increasingly embraced the UNIX operating system. For instance, midrange computer makers NCR and Hewlett Packard are two companies that have embraced UNIX as their primary commercial operating system. IBM, however, has chosen to retain its existing mainframe and midrange architectures while adding processors that can run the UNIX operating system, and microprocessor-based servers that can run the Microsoft Windows NT-based operating system.

It is also not surprising that many previously successful computer manufacturers that hung on to proprietary architectures have gone out of business or have merged with stronger open-architecture rivals over the past decade. Two examples include Digital Equipment Corporation, which merged with Compaq, and Wang Laboratories, which left the computer manufacturing business altogether.

Software Follows Hardware Toward the Open System Model

Generally speaking, computer hardware technological change has occurred at a much faster pace than our ability to leverage these changes through improved computer software. As a result, the open system movement has been nothing less than a revolution for the software industry. As elegant and simple a concept as the open system model is, it involves adding layers of complexity behind the scenes. Therein lies a paradox of the open system model—greater complexity.

For example, J. D. Edwards used to be a "one-product" company. Its World software product would run on nothing other than an IBM AS/400 midrange system. The ERP packaged software market has existed for roughly 25 years. During this run, most ERP package vendors, including J. D. Edwards, have seen their ERP software products mature in both features and underlying complexity in order to continually meet their clients' expectations. As a result, most ERP systems are large, complex systems comprised of hundreds, if not thousands, of computer programs that represent millions of lines of computer program instructions, or *code*.

Given this underlying complexity, most ERP packaged software vendors have been slow in reengineering their systems to the open system model. In some cases, these efforts have not been marketing successes. For instance, System Software Associates, a major competitor of J. D. Edwards and the one-time ERP software market leader, created a client/server version of its popular BPCS ERP system that was largely a marketing failure. System Software Associates recently filed for bankruptcy and is currently undergoing Chapter 11 reorganization.

No doubt about it—reengineering hundreds or thousands of programs and the accompanying millions of lines of program code is a daunting task. Many credit SAP as the first company to successfully do this. SAP rearchitected its mainframe-only product, R/2, onto the client/server platform in the early 1990s. This is the enormously popular ERP package now known as R/3. However, from a purist point of view, the reengineering by J. D. Edwards of its World software into OneWorld is a much closer move toward a true open system, because SAP chose to retain its proprietary programming language, ABAP/4, for its programs. Unlike the OneWorld tool set, which can be used to create new OneWorld-like applications or modify existing OneWorld programs with few computer-programming skills, ABAP/4 requires greater programming skills. Currently, J. D. Edwards has announced plans to reengineer the OneWorld presentation layer. As soon as OneWorld Xe becomes available, it will be capable of running in thin client, HTML browser-based, or Java environments.

A good working definition of an open system is that it is largely platform- and operating system–independent. What do these industry changes mean for buyers of J. D. Edwards' OneWorld? It means that they are not limited to using an IBM AS/400 if they choose J. D. Edwards as their business application processing software. So unlike the older generations of J. D. Edwards' ERP software, which was called World and that ran only on the AS/400, OneWorld operates across a number of computer platforms. Of course, OneWorld buyers can still opt for the AS/400 as a hardware platform, or they may instead look at servers that utilize alternative operating systems such as UNIX or Microsoft Windows NT.

Why UNIX?

UNIX was an operating system first created by Bell Labs and was intended to manage the complex operations of computers that served as telephone network switches. UNIX has typically received high marks in efficiency and performance as an operating system.

Unlike proprietary operating systems, UNIX is considered an "open system," meaning that its basic command structure has been standardized and that its source code (raw computer instructions) is readily published and in theory can be modified or extended as needed. The UNIX operating system is written in the C programming language.

UNIX is generally regarded as the first open system operating system. UNIX wins this honor by being the first commercial operating system that was embraced by and incorporated into the products of multiple business computer vendors. It became a de facto industry standard, much as Digital Research's CP/M and, later, Microsoft's MS-DOS became a cross-platform, industry-standard operating system for the PC industry.

What About Linux?

It should also be noted that, increasingly, business computer users are adopting Linux, a popular UNIX operating system derivative sometimes called "poor man's UNIX." J. D. Edwards' OneWorld has not yet been certified to operate under Linux.

Why Windows NT?

Microsoft Windows NT has become a pervasive force in corporate computing environments. Although when it was first introduced, Windows NT was not considered stable or robust enough for business-critical processes, the product has matured into a full-featured, industrial-strength operating system. The hallmark of Windows NT is that it operates on virtually all Intel processor-based computers. More and more, businesses are demanding that the packaged software they buy operate under multiple operating systems, not a single one. Simply put, buyers want choices.

Although Windows NT has become a serious industrial-strength alternative to UNIX over the last few years, Windows NT is not a truly open system, because Microsoft does not make the Windows NT source code available. Therefore, a better comparison is between Microsoft Windows NT and the PICK operating system. The PICK operating system is generally considered the original multiple-platform proprietary commercial operating system. For many years, it was the operating system of choice among midrange computer makers who were competing against the IBM AS/400 and its predecessors.

Here's a final note: The use of Intel-based platforms using Windows NT has helped bring the power of feature-rich ERP systems such as OneWorld to an entirely new market segment. Previously, smaller and middle-market companies ignored higher-end software products because they generally operated on more-expensive midrange computing platforms such as the AS/400. However, the "Wintel" platform has helped change the rules.

OneWorld's Future Is in the Channel

Lower-cost hardware and operating system alternatives such as "Wintel" solutions versus midrange and mainframe platforms have brought the accessibility of high-end ERP packages to smaller scale companies—those that have less than $100 million in annual revenues.

In this regard, J. D. Edwards is likely to be far more successful in penetrating the lower end of the market using OneWorld than it was with its World software. J. D. Edwards markets its products to companies that have less than $100 million in annual revenues through a business partner program called the Genesis channel.

Given the increasing popularity of the "lower-cost" platforms I mentioned, I fully expect to see J. D. Edwards become very aggressive in the Genesis channel in the coming years. This market space is generally growing faster, and the vendor market is also highly fragmented in this market space. Many companies in this market space will eventually want to move up to the capabilities of a first-tier system such as OneWorld over second-tier products such as those marketed by Computer Associates or System Software Associates and third-tier products such as those marketed by Sage, Navison, and ROI.

The C Programming Language

Another dimension of "openness" is the programming language chosen by J. D. Edwards for OneWorld. In addition to operating system independence, programming language independence is also sought as a measure of openness. As a result, the emerging standard programming language, especially for graphical user interface and client/server computing, has until recently been the C programming language.

The C programming language was created at Bell Labs (now Lucent Technologies), along with the UNIX operating system. The combination of C and UNIX was originally used to manage the operations of computers that serve as telephone network switches.

Unlike SAP, which chose to port its proprietary programming language, ABAP/4, onto multiple platforms, J. D. Edwards rewrote OneWorld from the ground up, reengineering the functionality of its RPG programs into the C programming language. This also allowed OneWorld to be an object-oriented system from the beginning.

However, a dose of reality is needed here. OneWorld is not exclusively written in ANSI C. For instance, portions are written in C++, and for the AS/400 version, portions remain that are written in RPG. However, the portion of OneWorld that a J. D. Edwards client is most likely to change, the OneWorld business logic layer, is written in ANSI C.

OneWorld and Java

Increasingly, the world is moving toward adoption of the Java language. Java is widely considered the programming language of the Internet. Java was created by Sun Microsystems and is considered portable. As the paradigm shifts from fat clients to thin clients to browser-based presentation, Java is on the move.

Why does a browser-based model have such wide appeal for large commercial systems? In one short phrase, it's all about Total Cost of Operations (TCO). A browser-based model can operate in a thin client environment, the benefits of which will be discussed later in this chapter. Although many thought the network computer (NC) was dead, it is just now catching on in the business community.

What Makes Java Special?

Java is considered machine-independent—and the business world likes machine independence—because it's a form of openness. Java obtains machine independence through a middleware software component called the Java virtual machine. The Java virtual machine is written specifically for each computer hardware platform. However, any Java program will run, universally, on any implementation of the Java virtual machine, therefore affording maximum portability across platforms.

The Java virtual machine is by no means a new idea. A similar concept existed with the PASCAL language "P" code compilers of the early and mid-1980s. Unlike the "P" code compilers, the Java virtual machine has enjoyed much greater industry support, and it gains acceptance in the marketplace on an almost daily basis.

The move toward Java is largely fueled by the growing influence of the Internet on basic business models, including computing, where the trend is toward browser-based delivery of business software applications. In fact, at least one company, Open Software, is currently developing an ERP system that it claims will be a first because it is written completely in Java, thereby supporting true platform independence.

Events Versus Procedures

The innovators at Xerox and the Palo Alto Research Center created the forerunners of today's graphical user interfaces (GUIs), which were first popularized by the Apple Macintosh PC in the mid-'80s. In the early '90s, the Windows GUI entered corporate America. However, Windows did not gain widespread acceptance until the introduction of Microsoft Windows 95.

Behind the scenes, programs that use a GUI are much different. Prior to being GUI-based, computer programs were largely procedural or sequence-driven. As a matter of fact, all the pre-GUI programming languages are frequently called procedural languages. In a procedural language, the computer program is simply a list of computer program instructions that are executed sequentially, step by step. Hence, it can be said that activities carried out by the computer program flowed "according to procedure."

In contrast, in a GUI-based computer program, the program flow becomes *event-driven*, with those events being discretionary and much more fully under the control of the computer user. For instance, in a GUI-based program, the cursor can be at any position on the screen. From the user's perspective, the program is idling. However, when you click on a mouse button, the program comes alive. The program action is therefore completely random and must anticipate that a user can request that any of a number of tasks or events be performed. Hence, we have a definition for the event-driven program model.

Open Database Connectivity (ODBC)

The use of open database connectivity (ODBC) technology is another important aspect of OneWorld openness. ODBC is the standard application programming interface (API) that is used to allow access to data contained in a commercially available database system, such as SQL Server, DB/2, or Oracle. A special J. D. Edwards–provided software component called database *middleware* provides the services necessary to support a connection between OneWorld and one of the database systems.

Microsoft Windows was the first operating system to support ODBC. However, ODBC has steadily grown in use since its inception in the early '90s and is now used by virtually all other hardware, operating system, database management, and application software vendors.

Structured Query Language (SQL)

Working hand-in-hand with the ODBC-compliant database is OneWorld's standardized database programming language, called Structured Query Language (SQL). OneWorld constructs database queries using the industry-standard form of SQL.

In general, SQL makes programming complex transaction-based systems such as OneWorld much simpler. It allows OneWorld to use SQL requests that access the database without having to know anything about how to interface with a specific database system. This is accomplished by pushing the complexities and concerns about exchanging information with any supported database into the middleware layer. This is discussed in the next section.

The Model for OneWorld

As you will recall from Chapter 1, J. D. Edwards' AS/400-based World software is widely considered one of the more sophisticated and robust ERP software package solutions available in the marketplace. (It is also the predecessor of OneWorld.) The World software product has been steadily improved and refined by J. D. Edwards since its origin some 20 years ago. Therefore, when J. D. Edwards began establishing its future direction in the early '90s, toward an open system architecture, World software represented a strong foundation upon which J. D. Edwards could readily build.

To that end, J. D. Edwards has done an outstanding job of leveraging its prior and significant software infrastructure investment by porting much of the World software business functionality into OneWorld. As a matter of fact, current World software users will find that much of the application functionality and terminology found in OneWorld is identical in every respect to that in the World software.

When considering how much of the World software model has made its way into OneWorld, you might conclude that OneWorld is nothing more than a "pretty face" for the older World software because the user interface is different (it's a graphical user interface instead of a character-based one). However, as you have learned, OneWorld is more than just a "pretty face" for World software—there are sweeping "behind-the-scenes" technical differences between these two products.

World and OneWorld Coexistence

Much to its credit, J. D. Edwards has eased the migration from World software to OneWorld software through a strategy that permits coexistence between these two products. They share their common database elements, such as files and the fields within them. However, coexistence is not a panacea for the World software user. A later chapter provides more details about the merits and limitations of coexistence.

Comparing OneWorld Environments

To summarize much of the discussion thus far, three possible OneWorld config-uration scenarios are presented in Table 3-1. Notice in the table that there are only two elements in common across these configurations—OneWorld itself and the use of the C programming language.

Table 3-1 A Comparison of OneWorld Environments

Scenario	OneWorld Environment "A"	One World Environment "B"	One World Environment "C"
Database	DB/2	Oracle	Microsoft SQL Server
Primary programming language	ILE C	C	C
Operating system	OS/400	UNIX	Microsoft Windows NT
Computer hardware	IBM AS/400 midrange computer	Hewlett Packard server	Compaq ProLiant series server

The Evolution of OneWorld in the Marketplace

J. D. Edwards provided an open system-based architectural vision to its customers and prospects in the early and mid-'90s. The vision that J. D. Edwards laid out at that time eventually came to the marketplace as OneWorld. However, prior to 1999, OneWorld software was not widely embraced by J. D. Edwards' clients and prospects.

By no means has this evolution from the IBM AS/400 platform to an open client/server-based system been an easy one for J. D. Edwards itself or for the early adopters of OneWorld in general. Performance and data integrity problems plagued the early releases of J. D. Edwards' OneWorld software. However, the majority of these earlier problems have been resolved in the latest release of OneWorld—more specifically, release B.7.3.3.1 and later versions. In addition, release B8.1 of OneWorld is scheduled for release sometime shortly after this book is published.

As was previously mentioned, J. D. Edwards faced a daunting task in converting millions of lines of World software code from RPG, the native procedural language of the AS/400 computer, into event-driven ANSI C and C++ programs at the core of OneWorld. As you might expect, there were some bumps along the way. This effort proceeded much more slowly than was initially expected by J. D. Edwards. This resulted in delays in certain OneWorld functionality that existed in the World software product. In addition, some of the "reconstituted" OneWorld equivalents were performance- or quality-challenged. Again, most of these problems are now in the past.

The OneWorld product launch delays and the gaps in what software functions were production-ready presented problems for a number of early potential OneWorld adopters. Therefore, many J. D. Edwards prospects found that the older-generation World software was better able to satisfy their business requirements at the time of their initial software purchase. Many made the purchase with the intention of migrating to OneWorld at a future date, when OneWorld was a more "seasoned" product.

Some relatively recent J. D. Edwards clients who had significant year 2000 compliance issues opted for World software instead of OneWorld software. This was done in order to achieve their desired functionality levels prior to the century rollover. World software allowed these J. D. Edwards software adopters to implement year 2000-compliant business systems for their AS/400 environment without incurring substantial hardware architecture or other infrastructure changeovers at that time.

Finally, many J. D. Edwards customers opted to install J. D. Edwards' World software, a stable and reliable product that operates on an equally stable and reliable platform, instead of venturing into the unknown by implementing OneWorld or client/server architectures at the time of their original ERP decision. I should also point out that AS/400 users have traditionally been smaller and middle-market companies that are often risk-adverse and cost-conscious.

You might say that AS/400 users as a whole represent an audience that would definitely not entertain a "revolutionary" migration away from a proven architecture. Needless to say, many in the AS/400 community are skeptical of microcomputer-based servers supporting their businesses and view these servers as boys sent in to do a man's job.

Client/Server Computing

An important part of the appeal of OneWorld for many organizations is that it supports a variety of network architecture models, perhaps more so than do rival products found in the ERP marketplace. This section provides an overview of the client/server model and of client/server architectures.

What Is Client/Server Computing?

In its simplest form, client/server computing is a computer architecture that involves clients requesting services from a server. Unfortunately, client/server computing is not quite as simple as this definition might lead you to believe.

Although many people are quick to associate the PC and the UNIX operating system as the defining "enablers" of client/server computing, such assumptions are incorrect. Actually, several simple, though far more important, enablers or characteristics are truly the underpinnings of client/server computing:

◆ Modularity

◆ Standardization

◆ Messaging

Product designers and system designers have a lot in common. Both are concerned about similar issues, such as cost, manufacturability, and maintainability of the final product. As a matter of fact, these enablers of the client/server model are coincidentally also the fundamental tenets of product design.

Modularity

Modularity has as its fundamental assumption that the much larger or "whole" product—in this case, computer programs—can be organized into much smaller "subassemblies" of components. In the computing world, the concept of modularity is called *modular programming*.

Traditionally, computer programs were written on the premise that one program does everything. However, as both computers and the business application systems being created for them became more sophisticated, these computer programs grew larger, ran slower, and were increasingly difficult to maintain.

As computer programmers themselves became increasingly more sophisticated, they began using modular programming techniques. In the case of modular computer programs, a main or master program would call (rely on) any number of smaller single-purpose or limited-scope programs or modules that performed closely related functions.

Messaging

Once modular programming became widespread, this unitizing or separation of functionality established a new paradigm in computer programming. However, for modular programming to work, another important element was needed. These now-separated modular programs had to communicate with one another—by sending messages back and forth—about what each one had done independently of the other. Initially, this idea of computer programs passing messages back and forth was called *parameter passing*. Today, the term *messaging* is used to describe this communication process.

Standardization

It stands to reason that if messages are being sent back and forth, some form of protocol or standardization as to both the content and relative position of information within a message is necessary. Unfortunately, this is an area where the computer industry is still evolving. However, standards such as Electronic Data Interchange (EDI), Extensible Markup Language (XML), and SQL are some of the established and emerging standards in the computer industry. In fact, OneWorld relies on many of these industry standards for its internal architecture or for standard "rules of engagement" when communicating with other computer systems—such as the database management system.

How Client/Server Works: A Practical Example

How does all of this work in practice? An excellent real-life example can be found in the ERP world—the calculation of sales tax. Calculating sales tax requires knowledge of the tax rate that might apply and when it will apply. The United States has 50 states, hundreds of counties, and even more local governments that apply a sales tax in their jurisdictions—and to make matters worse, this information changes frequently.

Most ERP packages, including OneWorld, provide relatively simple "you build and maintain" tax tables for tax calculation purposes. However, many organizations prefer to use another software package—a specially designed system that calculates sales tax based on current tax rates and rules. Tax calculator vendors keep abreast of changing tax rates and rules and regularly provide table updates to their calculator software that contain this new information.

Thus, in this example, the sales order program becomes the client, and it relies on another program, the sales tax calculator or server program, to perform a sales tax calculation. For this process to work, the sales order program doesn't care about the tax applied, because its purpose is to manage order details such as the customer, products, prices, and quantities ordered. The tax calculation is the responsibility or function of the tax calculator or server program.

To service the sales order program, the tax server program needs a message from the client that requests the calculation service and provides a message containing some basic information about the order, such as what was ordered, because certain items might be exempt from sales tax. The tax server is also concerned with how much the item costs, because tax calculations are usually based on the item's price. Once the tax is calculated, this information must be provided or returned in the form of a message to the client—the sales order program—in order to complete the sales order process.

The tax calculation dilemma as described here applies to *any* ERP software package—not just OneWorld. Therefore, the tax calculator software vendor creates and maintains only one tax calculator program but establishes and publishes "interface standards" or APIs, which an ERP vendor would follow. These rules govern the entry and exit information flowing between the order entry program and the tax calculator, serving as the "rules of engagement."

Applying These Concepts to the Network

Given that program functionality could now be isolated, it also stood to reason that the programs themselves no longer needed to run on the same computer. Hence, we arrive at the birth of the client/server model.

In the client/server paradigm, it is possible to have client processes or programs and server processes. In the client/server computing model, programs run on the "most appropriate" hardware. In addition, software and hardware platforms can be related to their role or function in the overall computing process. For example, database management server software could be operated on a computer processor that is specially designed, configured, and tuned to perform database queries. A more detailed look at the roles and responsibilities for both the client and the server in the client/server architecture follows.

What the Client Does

The client represents the front end or user interface portion of the client/server application. The client has responsibility for the GUI, which has become the standard for the user interface design in modern computer software such as Windows and OneWorld. Normally a part of the client operating system, the GUI Manager detects user actions, manages the display of the form or window on the display, and the display of any data in that window or form. Application programs such as OneWorld rely on the GUI Manager.

The client validates data entered by the user and sends service requests to the server. In some instances, the client can actually execute application programs that contain "business logic" processes. The client is also responsible for some lower-level processes, including managing the local resources that the users interact with. Typically, these resources include the desktop computer and its display monitor, keyboard, and any peripherals, such as a printer.

What the Server Does

The server is best viewed as a forum or platform for the sharing of common resources and executing common processes, tasks, or procedures. The server fulfills client requests by performing the task requested. Typically, the server receives requests for its services from client programs. Server-based processing can take on many dimensions. The server process performs the back-end tasks that are common among business application systems. Examples of what server programs are responsible for include executing operations such as database retrievals and updates, managing data integrity, and dispatching responses to these client-initiated requests for services. Sometimes a server program also executes a common processing or complex business process or processes, such as financial statement preparation or manufacturing planning.

Server-based processes may run across multiple physical computers that are networked, or they might simply be a series of programs that are running on a sole physical processor. For instance, in a networked setting, one physical server computer could be dedicated to providing application-related business processing service, and another physical server computer could perform database management-related services.

Basic Characteristics of Client/Server Architectures

Client/server architectures should exhibit the following basic characteristics:

- ◆ The client/server environment should fully embrace the open system model. Therefore, a typical client/server architecture will be both diverse and multivendor. Review Table 3-1 for the various examples of three rather different OneWorld environments.
- ◆ Client and server processes should communicate through a well-defined set of standard APIs. Industry-wide standards have emerged for the messaging necessary to make client/server architectures work. For instance, ODBC is one such example of a standardized API to support messaging between a relational database and an application program, such as OneWorld.
- ◆ Another important characteristic of a client/server system is scalability. The client/server architecture can be scaled both horizontally and vertically. Horizontal scaling means adding or removing client workstations with only a slight performance impact. Vertical scaling means migrating to larger and faster server machines or sharing the computing workload among multiple server machines.

OneWorld supports these client/server architecture characteristics to varying degrees.

Client/Server Architectures

Several architectural models have emerged for client/server computing. These architectures include two-tier, three-tier, and *n*-tier models. A brief explanation of each of these client/server architectures follows.

The Two-Tier Architecture

A two-tier architecture is a very simple client/server model. In a two-tier architecture, a client communicates directly with a server. Typically, the server handles all database management, and the client provides all other processing. However, two-tier architectures have been found not to "scale" well—meaning that as transaction volume increases, the two-tier architecture is quickly saturated, and overall system performance decreases. To properly scale a client/server system to hundreds or perhaps thousands of users, a three-tier architecture is generally required.

The Three-Tier Architecture

A three-tier architecture introduces another server called an *agent* between the client and the server. The agent has several roles to fulfill in the three-tier architecture. Most importantly, the agent redistributes the workload. Typically, the client performs all presentation or end-user interaction processes, an application server handles business logic processing, and a database server handles database management services. The specific services that the agent itself typically provides in a three-tier client/server model include the following:

◆ Network traffic metering services, which monitor transactions and limit the number of simultaneous service requests made to a given server

◆ Load balancing services that can distribute server requests, such as a batch process request for a report, to another, less-utilized server for processing

◆ Intelligent mapping services that map a single service request to a number of different servers (such as to an application server and a database server), collate the results, and return a single response to the client

In OneWorld, the CNC environment provides these agent services.

The n-Tier Architecture

An *n*-tier architecture introduces another level of complexity to the three-tier architecture model. The *n*-tier architecture adds more servers, called *workgroup* servers, which are typically remotely located. This design "pushes" data and processing to the physical location where they are needed in order to improve system performance.

Therefore, in addition to the services that an agent performs in a three-tier client/server architecture, in the *n*-tier environment, the agent also provides replication and synchronization services. These agent services are necessary to ensure that programs and data that are distributed across multiple clients and servers are kept synchronized to preserve the overall integrity of the business applications using an *n*-tier client/server model. Again, the CNC in OneWorld must provide these agent services.

Fat Clients and Thin Clients

Thin clients, sometimes called network computers (NCs), are gaining in popularity among industry advocates. If you have been involved in the computer industry for some time, you have heard of network computers, but this time the thin client or network computer is *not* considered a solution without a problem.

Many organizations are beginning to grow weary of the seemingly never-ending cycle of buying or upgrading large numbers of installed desktop workstations—in some cases, as frequently as every two years. The use of a fat client actually compounds the problem. It is entirely possible that upgrades or swap-outs of the desktop workstations used as fat clients might be needed with every upgrade of the application software itself.

The attraction of the thin client or network computer is that you replace powerful desktop workstations with bare-bones stripped-down computers. These thin clients handle a relatively small number of operations. The operation of the keyboard, mouse, display, and possibly a local printer is handled by the thin client, but everything else is handled by at least one *terminal server*. On the terminal server, a client session actually communicates with the network's server resources.

A second trend is further shifting the balance of opinion toward thin clients and network computers—the Internet. In the Internet (a browser-based world), all that is really needed is a device that can run the browser software. This is indeed something that most thin clients and network computers can do. For instance, many devices now run the Microsoft Windows CE operating system, such as palm and handheld computers. These devices are therefore capable of running a version of Microsoft Internet Explorer.

What Is Thin Client Computing?

Thin client/server computing pushes *all* application processing, business logic processing, and program execution onto the server or servers. The only work remaining for the thin client is to perform GUI Manager activities and local management tasks. Thus, the thin client plays a limited role, displaying information to the computer user from a server, retrieving user input, and forwarding user input to the server. The thin client is the client/server equivalent of the "dumb terminal." A dumb terminal relies exclusively on the host computer for all processing power. All keystrokes are echoed to the main computer and are processed there, and responses are sent back to the terminal for display to the user. Client workstations generally have the ability to complete local processes without requiring total reliance on a server for its processing power.

The foundation for thin client/server computing is an enabling agent that is based on the Independent Computing Architecture (ICA) protocol. The ICA protocol is considered the de facto standard for thin client computing. This protocol provides the agent services necessary for thin clients and servers to exchange information, with a minimum amount of network traffic. Citrix Systems markets a thin client solution running under the Windows NT operating system that makes use of the ICA protocol. The Citrix thin client solution has been successfully deployed at many organizations in conjunction with OneWorld.

Why Use Thin Client Computing?

You can realize three major advantages with thin client computing: cost, administration, and flexibility. Let's take a look at these three reasons in more detail:

◆ With cost of ownership, thin clients or network computers are less costly to acquire. Thin clients or network computers average about half the cost of a typical PC workstation.

◆ Network administration and management are centralized. Individual PC workstations generally require a significant amount of administration. A thin client does not require the same degree of hands-on administration over its service life. This lowered administration requirement might also favorably affect costs in environments that have larger networks of clients.

◆ Three important trends are emerging that will have the potential to dramatically alter how software functionality will be delivered in the future. New wireless transmission capabilities, Web browser-based software front ends, and Internet-based application service provider (ASP) models are representative of a new paradigm in computing. I call this emerging trend "anywhere computing." The thin client model is clearly the superior delivery mechanism to support anywhere computing.

What's Bad About Thin Clients?

To be fair, thin client computing does have several drawbacks:

◆ The reliance on additional middleware is a consideration. This middleware adds overhead to the transaction and complexity to the network, and it complicates the overall troubleshooting of any network-related problems.

◆ Typically, one or more additional servers are needed to service thin clients. These servers are typically called *terminal servers*. These additional servers add to the network's complexity.

◆ The additional workload might saturate server capacity more quickly—something a network of fat clients might not do. Fat clients actually offload some of the processing demands from the application server to the local fat client. Therefore, a key factor when selecting a thin client solution is how well the thin client middleware performs load balancing among available terminal server resources.

Despite the challenges of a thin client architecture, momentum for its use is clearly growing.

Client/Server Communications

Connectivity is of paramount importance to both the open system model and the client/server architecture. Connectivity allows one program, process, or device to communicate with another program, process, or device. For instance, messaging and standardization, which were discussed earlier, provide for connectivity. Another important dimension of connectivity is *transparency*, or the ability to communicate with another program, process, or device, regardless of *where* it is physically located or exactly what it is, as long as it communicates using the correct protocols.

A key enabling element of connectivity for client/server communications is the computer or network operating system. The operating system provides services such as routing, distribution, messaging, file, print, and network management. UNIX, OS/400, and Windows NT are representative of the operating systems that support OneWorld.

The operating system relies on communication protocols to provide specific services related to connectivity. These communication protocols are divided into three groups: media, transport, and client/server. The operating system and other network service–related programs that run under the operating system provide both media and transport layer support needed by OneWorld.

Media protocols determine the type of physical connections used on a network. A media protocol standard determines how devices are physically or electrically connected in a computer network. Typically, a computer network consists of wires and transmission equipment, used to establish a link from the client to the server. Twisted pair is the most prevalent media protocol in the client/server world.

The transport protocol provides the mechanism for moving packets of data from the client to the server. Although multiple transport protocols are used in the industry, OneWorld relies exclusively on Transmission Control Protocol/ Internet Protocol (TCP/IP) as its transport protocol.

Other layers of protocols are also involved in a client/server architecture. These are coincidentally and collectively referred to as client/server protocols. In OneWorld, a product called JDENET facilitates client/server messaging. Another example of a client/server protocol is the ICA protocol.

Middleware

The discussion of client/server architecture mentioned clients requesting services of a given server through an agent. A special name has been given to these agents in the client/server world—they are called *middleware* components.

OneWorld Communications Middleware

After a physical connection has been established and packets of data can be moved over the physical network, a final piece is needed—the client/server protocol. The client/server protocol establishes the rule that clients will use when requesting information and services from a server and also establishes rules regarding how the server will reply to client requests. OneWorld incorporates a proprietary middleware product called JDENET for message-handling purposes between its clients and servers.

OneWorld Database Middleware

Another important piece of middleware is also needed—the database middleware layer. The OneWorld database middleware layer is the component that provides for OneWorld's database independence. An important aspect of this middleware layer, called JDEBASE, is that it provides the bridge or API to the ODBC-compliant database system. Remember my earlier comment—openness breeds complexity. The required database middleware level is an excellent example of such trade-offs.

Making multiplatform openness a reality requires some very low-level, not very open, behind-the-scenes programming in order to glue everything together. So in addition to the ODBC software that allows for SQL request processing, the middleware layer must also provide a driver for connection to the specific database that will be accessed by OneWorld. The need for such a driver is why OneWorld will not work with just any ODBC database. JDEBASE therefore provides database connectivity between OneWorld and a multitude of relational databases, such as Oracle, DB/2, and SQL Server.

This section provided a high-level introduction to client/server architecture that kept technical details to a minimum. This discussion provides an essential foundation for a discussion of OneWorld's Configurable Network Computing model.

Configurable Network Computing

This section reviews the major characteristics and requirements of Configurable Network Computing (CNC). CNC is OneWorld's flexible client/server-based architectural design. The software engineers at J. D. Edwards have made every attempt to make OneWorld flexible. Although this does make OneWorld somewhat more difficult to install and administer, these disadvantages are more than offset by OneWorld's advantages:

◆ As processing workloads or business requirements dictate, the OneWorld environment can be changed or scaled to address these external factors.

◆ You have the ability to tune the OneWorld environment in order to effect performance or productivity improvements. For example, you can add service capacity by adding terminal servers, application servers, database servers, or batch processing servers. Or you can redistribute the service workload within the OneWorld network by performing processes locally at a client workstation instead of remotely on a server.

OneWorld is flexible enough to run on a single computer, in a special "stand-alone" version of OneWorld (as discussed in the section "The Stand-Alone Version of

OneWorld"). It can also run in a multiple-server, multiple-location, fat and thin client environment—*all running simultaneously.*

For instance, here are a few examples of how OneWorld's CNC provides processing flexibility:

◆ The OneWorld database and application workload can be distributed across multiple servers and also to the clients themselves. Workgroup computers can also be employed for the further distribution of workload and data. OneWorld's CNC model is therefore based on the *n*-tier client/server model that was introduced earlier.

◆ OneWorld goes far beyond the typical *n*-tier client/server network architecture model by allowing for a mix of clients, including fat, thin, and browser-based.

◆ OneWorld achieves the characteristics of the open system model for client/server computing. One of the characteristics of this model is that computer, operating system, and database platforms can be mixed.

The OneWorld CNC model must therefore provide for a high degree of interoperability between all major network elements—clients, servers, operating systems, and databases.

A typical OneWorld network architecture consists of multiple servers and clients. At first, you might believe that only one central server is needed. Although this might be true, it is true only in a minimalist sense. Multiple servers might be needed to create optimum performance and usability in your OneWorld system. For instance, your OneWorld installation minimally includes a separate server for deployment and at least one application and database server. In addition, other servers may be added that are dedicated to database management, application processing, terminal services for thin clients, or batch processing—for instance, of reports and updates. Figure 3-1 illustrates such a network architecture.

CNC relies on several key OneWorld environmental elements and environmental processes:

Environment Elements
Environments
Path codes
Objects

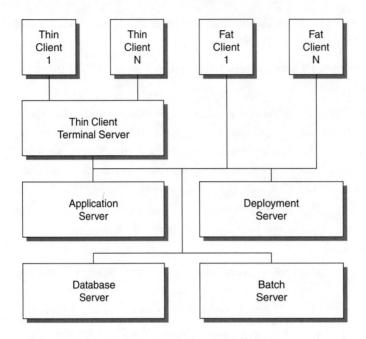

FIGURE 3-1 *The OneWorld CNC Architectural Model*

Object configuration mappings

Data sources

Environmental Processes

Replication

Deployment

Configuration management

When combined, these environmental elements—and the processes required to define and manage them—form the nucleus of the OneWorld CNC.

Environmental Elements

The environmental elements in the OneWorld CNC model can best be viewed as tables or lists of information, such as file or object names, which are used to identify and then validate network elements against. In addition, these various environmental elements are used to organize and ultimately assist in locating specific software components in the CNC network that are needed in order to make OneWorld operational. This section describes these environmental elements.

Environments

OneWorld segregates your business data and business data processing into *environments*. An environment is the result of combining path codes and Object Configuration Manager (OCM) mappings.

A typical OneWorld installation includes multiple environments. These environments minimally include a pristine environment in which unchanged common objects are stored for deployment purposes, a production environment in which "live" business data resides, and a conference room pilot or test environment.

When you sign in to OneWorld, selecting the correct environment is the important first task you must complete. Chapter 7 provides information about how to sign in to OneWorld and how to select an environment.

Another way of understanding the OneWorld environment is to view an environment as the equivalent of a directory path in either Microsoft DOS or the Windows operating system. The directory path is a sequentially arranged collection of file directories that are searched in order to find all the program and data files needed to execute a specific application program under DOS or Windows.

Path Codes

Path codes are OneWorld's way of knowing where an object is. Think of a path code as a pointer to the location of an object that is being processed. A path code exists for each set of OneWorld objects. The path code addresses the question of which processing-related objects should be used.

For instance, before introducing a new executable object—a program that will process your business data—it is generally developed in a development environment, then tested, and then ultimately promoted into your production environment.

Another way of understanding the OneWorld path code is to view a path code as a folder—such as in the Windows Explorer File Manager—which is a place where related documents or other files are stored, apart from other documents and files on your computer's disk drive.

Objects

There are many different types of objects in OneWorld. For instance, OneWorld programs are objects. Another type of object includes the tables within a database that are used to store your organization's business data. OneWorld's CNC must provide facilities for effectively managing objects—especially since they can be distributed to any number of locations across the OneWorld network.

Object Configuration Mappings

Think of OCM mappings as rules about where business data is retrieved from or sent to—the specifics as to the database and the server—and where business data processing actually occurs—at the client, on the server, or a combination of the two. Therefore, think of OCM mappings as specifically addressing these two questions:

- ◆ *Where will business data reside?* For instance, many organizations have both a production database, where live production data resides, and a training database, where sample or test data is available for startup and ongoing training purposes.
- ◆ *On what machine should a process execute?* For instance, when a button is clicked to execute a process, where does the resulting processing occur? It may be locally, on the client, a combination of client and server processing, or server-only processing.

Data Sources

A data source is the *location* for a given collection of related data, such as your business data. OneWorld has a number of different types of data sources. A data source tells OneWorld where specific types of data are stored in the OneWorld environment.

Environmental Processes

The environmental elements just described are used in the OneWorld CNC model in various ways. It is easiest to think of CNC as an orchestra conductor or an air traffic controller, but in the context of a sophisticated computer network. This section describes some of the environmental processes in which the environmental elements are used in OneWorld's CNC model.

Replication

If processing and business data is distributed from a central processor across a network of clients, replication of objects is necessary. As changes are made to any object, such as to a user-defined table of payment terms for sales orders, every distributed instance of that table must be updated with the latest version of the payment terms table.

In practice, the use of replication must be carefully planned. The extensive use of replication is generally discouraged, because coordinating replication is difficult. Also, extensive replication adversely affects network performance. For instance, you would not want to localize an object that has frequent changes to every client workstation. It is more desirable to use a departmental, workgroup, or remote site server that would be replicated from the central site database.

OneWorld has two important replication techniques that help control the impact on network performance caused by replication. The first technique is called just-in-time replication (JITR)—a process whereby data is replicated to an individual client workstation from the server only at the time the data is needed. The second technique is called *pull replication*. In this case, individual client workstations are set up as subscribers. A subscribing client workstation is notified of changes to server-managed data that it images locally, on a request basis. Usually, such requests are made of the server when an individual client workstation is logged on to OneWorld.

Deployment

Deployment is a fundamental characteristic of the CNC architecture. The first step in the OneWorld installation is to load the software onto the deployment server. Every OneWorld installation requires a deployment server. The deployment server is responsible for accepting changes in objects—including the initial load of the software—and deploying those objects throughout the OneWorld network of interconnected clients and servers.

OneWorld objects are installed, from the deployment server, to other servers and to client workstations as packages. A package is therefore considered a point-in-time snapshot of the objects available. Objects can also be installed on a just-in-time installation (JITI) basis. A core set of objects can be installed via a package installation. As other objects are needed by the client workstation, they can be replicated on a JITI basis.

Configuration Management

The Object Configuration Manager (OCM) manages all the OneWorld objects across the network of interconnected client and server computers. The OCM is the control center overseeing the OneWorld environment—where objects are, which objects are used and when, and where executable objects are actually executed. You can also think of the OCM as the tool for defining the end-user's logon environment through the use of path codes and OCM mappings.

Getting the configuration of your network right using CNC is fundamental to your organization's success in implementing OneWorld. Additional insights about the importance of CNC appear in a later chapter.

OneWorld Infrastructure Requirements

An essential and early consideration in OneWorld implementation is the selection of your computer hardware infrastructure. The driving factors to consider when making hardware choices are performance and capacity or bandwidth metrics. This section provides useful background information regarding the OneWorld hardware environment.

The Network

The first consideration is your network. As mentioned previously, OneWorld uses the widely accepted TCP/IP protocol. Therefore, the totality of your network infrastructure—including interface adapters, hubs, switches, bridges, and routers—must support this protocol. The good news is that most organizations already have installed a PC that likely supports TCP/IP and will not consider this an issue. If an organization has been exclusively using twin coaxial cabling (or "twinax" cabling) system that connects IBM 5250 or equivalent workstations to the AS/400, that organization will need to install a new network infrastructure.

The Server

OneWorld requires three technical components on the server side:

◆ A C/C++ compiler. The compiler allows the C and C++ OneWorld source code to be enabled for the specific platform on which it will run. Each supported server platform requires its own C/C++ compiler, which is generally available through the server hardware vendor. For instance, in the AS/400 environment, OneWorld requires the IBM ILE/C language environment.

◆ A relational database. As mentioned, OneWorld uses the industry-standard relational database model. Any supported relational database can be used through the open system or ODBC interfaces to OneWorld. Access to data is provided through standard SQL commands, and the relational database itself must be able to interpret SQL.

◆ TCP/IP software. Some operating system and database vendors incorporate the TCP/IP protocol as a standard features, and other vendors license their TCP/IP enabling software separately.

These required components are typically separately licensed pieces of software that are in addition to the operating system itself.

The Client

For a fat client, OneWorld requires one of the following operating systems:

◆ Microsoft Windows NT Workstation 4.0

◆ Microsoft Windows 95

◆ Microsoft Windows 98

I strongly recommend using the Windows NT Workstation 4.0 operating system on all OneWorld fat clients.

The recommended hardware requirements for a nonbrowser are as follows:

◆ An Intel-based PC, using a Pentium series processor, with a speed of 200 MHz or higher and 128 MB of RAM

◆ A 17-inch flat screen color monitor

◆ Ample storage space. A minimum of 2 gigabytes (GB) of available storage space is recommended—which likely means you need a disk with a total capacity of 4 GB or more.

Should you choose to install the computer-based training (CBT) material or the OneWorld documentation on the local fat client, even more disk storage space will be needed.

For the thin client, OneWorld requires one of the following operating systems:

◆ Microsoft Windows NT Workstation

◆ Microsoft Windows 95

◆ Microsoft Windows 98

◆ Microsoft Windows CE

The hardware requirements for a thin client workstation are significantly less demanding. This is due to the fact that all processing and storage are performed at the server level, not the client level. As is the case for the fat client, a 17-inch flat screen color monitor remains the recommendation.

Application Development Workstations: The "Bigger" Fat Client

The application development workstation can be used to modify a OneWorld application or create a new one. Even if you have not and will not customize OneWorld, you will need at least one application development workstation, if for no other reason than for the purpose of applying paper fixes. These are software action request downloads that must be made to the OneWorld source code in order to resolve an application program error or performance problem.

The application development workstation must be a nonbrowser-based fat client. Each such workstation must have a licensed copy of the Microsoft Visual C++ Compiler installed. This lets a developer recompile the application code when writing a new application using the OneWorld Tool Set or modifying an existing OneWorld application.

The Terminal Server

A thin client environment requires one or more terminal servers and additional software. In the thin client environment, a major throughput consideration—and frequently the limitation—is the terminal server configuration. This is an area where you want to work closely with vendors to ensure an adequately sized environment for the particular needs of your organization.

The Deployment Server

An important element of the OneWorld infrastructure is the deployment server. Your organization's OneWorld environment is administered from a server that is dedicated to the purposes of OneWorld software installation, deployment, and system administration or maintenance on a network-wide basis.

The deployment server must be a "Wintel" server. A Wintel server uses the Microsoft NT operating system and a high-speed Intel Pentium series processor-based server. The deployment server is used to propagate a pristine or unaltered version of OneWorld to other clients and/or servers in your CNC environment. The pristine environment in turn serves as the base environment for your custom development work as well as the base for applying software fixes or service packs and any software upgrades.

Which Vendor Platforms Does OneWorld Support?

OneWorld supports these representative platforms and databases:

- The Compaq Computer Corporation (formerly Digital Equipment Corporation) Alpha server, using Microsoft Windows NT Server and either SQL Server or Oracle Workgroup Server

- The Hewlett Packard HP 9000 using HP/UX, which is a UNIX operating system, and an Oracle Server database

- The IBM AS/400, using the OS/400 operating system and the DB2/400 database

- The IBM RS/6000 using AIX, a UNIX operating system, and an Oracle Server database

- The IBM S/390 mainframe using the OS/390 operating system and the DB2 database

- An Intel processor-based server, such as an IBM NetFinity, Compaq ProLiant, or Hewlett Packard box, running Windows NT and an Oracle Server database

- An Intel processor-based server, such as an IBM NetFinity, Compaq ProLiant, or Hewlett Packard box, running Windows NT and Microsoft SQL Server

This list of vendors that provide hardware and/or software and the specific models or versions that support OneWorld changes from time to time. Consult the J. D. Edwards Web site or your J. D. Edwards client manager for updated information prior to finalizing your OneWorld purchase or any related hardware or software purchases.

This section concludes a rather technical chapter about the OneWorld infrastructure—the hardware, software, middleware, network, and overall infrastructure configuration that is required in order to successfully implement OneWorld. A later chapter provides additional information and specific recommendations regarding OneWorld's infrastructure.

The Stand-Alone Version of OneWorld

The best way to learn about J. D. Edwards' OneWorld is through hands-on exposure. Therefore, I strongly recommend that you keep the OneWorld software handy as you continue reading this book, especially for use in conjunction with Parts III and IV. Even if your organization has not yet installed the hardware infrastructure for OneWorld, you can still enjoy access to OneWorld.

Your organization should have received a *stand-alone* version of OneWorld from J. D. Edwards when the OneWorld software was shipped to your organization. This stand-alone version is fully functional and operates with a single PC serving as both client and server. Your first task should be to install the stand-alone version of OneWorld software on a suitable PC or have someone else (such as your system administrator) do it for you.

OneWorld Stand-Alone Installation Tips

Unlike other PC software that you might be accustomed to installing, J. D. Edwards' OneWorld stand-alone software is much more particular about what versions of Microsoft software your computer is using. Therefore, please contact the J. D. Edwards response line to determine the exact Microsoft Windows– and Microsoft Office–related service packs that you will need in order to install and operate the OneWorld stand-alone version correctly.

My personal experience with the OneWorld stand-alone version suggests that the following minimum configuration is necessary. A 233 MHz or faster Pentium processor is recommended. The processor should have at least 128 MB of RAM and a 4 GB or larger hard disk. A CD-ROM drive is required for software loading. In addition, Microsoft Windows NT 4.0 Workstation is recommended as the operating system. Although I have seen OneWorld stand-alone run using a less-generous environment, you will find its performance generally unacceptable.

I feel a laptop computer is a good choice as a platform for the stand-alone version of OneWorld. For instance, as you participate in a J. D. Edwards educational class, you can practice key concepts covered in class in your hotel room in the evening. These evening practice sessions might help you identify areas that you are unsure about, and you can ask your J. D. Edwards class instructor to review that concept for you the next day. Chances are if you're having trouble, others might be too. The instructor will appreciate the effort you have gone to in attempting to understand the topic and use the class materials effectively.

Always install a printer driver, even if you won't actually have a printer attached to your workstation. Why is this necessary? If you don't install a printer or at least a printer driver, you won't be able to view any of the reports you might run when using OneWorld.

A large-screen monitor (17 inches or larger) is also recommended for best viewing OneWorld on desktop installations. This is obviously impractical for laptop installations of OneWorld. Therefore, I recommend a laptop computer that has the largest, sharpest, and brightest screen available.

Install the J. D. Edwards' OneWorld soft-copy documentation from the CD-ROM onto the OneWorld stand-alone workstation. You will want this information readily available as you learn about OneWorld.

OneWorld Stand-Alone Environment Requirements

Generally speaking, the stand-alone version of J. D. Edwards' OneWorld will run under Microsoft Windows 95 or 98 or Windows NT 4.0 Workstation. Be aware that there are some known problems when you attempt to operate OneWorld stand-alone under Windows 95 or 98. Consult the J. D. Edwards response line for specific guidance in this area.

Microsoft Office 97 Professional Edition is required. It includes Microsoft Access, which is required as the ODBC database used by the stand-alone version of J. D. Edwards' OneWorld. In addition, the Office 97 service pack SR-2 must be installed.

In order to access any of the OneWorld developer tools, including the OneWorld Enterprise Report Writer, Microsoft Visual C++ version 6.0 must be installed, and the operating system must be Microsoft Windows NT 4.0 Workstation.

At this time, J. D. Edwards' OneWorld stand-alone has not been certified for use with Office 2000 or with the Windows 2000 operating system.

How Much Time Will You Need?

If you are completing the installation of the OneWorld stand-alone version yourself, allow an adequate amount of time for this process. This could be as much as a full workday to complete all the tasks outlined here.

Summary

This chapter introduced you to a number of key technical concepts related to client/server and open system architecture. The OneWorld Configurable Network Computing (CNC) architecture was introduced, and a brief discussion of the hardware and software environments needed to support OneWorld was provided.

This chapter is not intended to answer all your questions about client/server architecture and CNC. The real of intent of this chapter is to provide a general understanding and appreciation of the hardware, software, and networking complexity that is required behind the scenes in order to implement OneWorld.

PART II

Preparing for Success with OneWorld

Chapter 4

Critical Success Factors in the OneWorld Implementation

Much has been written in the trade press lately about the failure of enterprise resource planning (ERP) systems to deliver on their promises of true business value. Cost overruns, significant gaps, missed deadlines, marginal end results, and little (if any) overall business process improvement make it clear that managing an ERP project is a complex feat.

ERP systems generally represent large-scale investments of both dollar and human capital. Because of their organization-wide scope and duration, risks in the typical ERP implementation are significant. Therefore, the defining element in the success or failure of an ERP system implementation is largely one of project management.

This chapter discusses a series of critical success factors that are instrumental to a successful OneWorld implementation.

Why ERP Projects Fail

Over the course of my 10 years of ERP software-related experience, I have seen ERP projects fail for a number of reasons. I have also observed that ERP project failures typically exhibit one or more of the following characteristics:

- The wrong ERP software package was selected.
- The ERP software package does not work as advertised.
- Too many changes or interfaces to the ERP software package were attempted.
- The overall ERP implementation project lacked the appropriate level of executive sponsorship.
- The organization has poorly organized its ERP implementation efforts and generally lacks an overall project plan.
- The ERP project team received little or no training, or the training provided was of extremely poor quality.
- The ERP system end-users received little or no training, or the training provided was of extremely poor quality.

◆ The business or technical resources committed to the project were too few.

◆ Organizational change management strategies were weak or nonexistent.

◆ Scope management strategies were weak or nonexistent.

◆ A business merger or acquisition terminated a work in process.

◆ Improperly configured networks, servers, and software environments

◆ Undersized networks, servers, and communication lines

Arguably, some of these reasons are either laughable or border on the ridiculous. However, these reasons are not made up—they represent reality.

Now that you have learned the general reasons that ERP implementations fail, let's specifically look at some strategies that offer you the best chance of achieving a successful OneWorld implementation.

What Makes the OneWorld Implementation Successful?

As a launch point for the remaining discussions in this chapter, let's review a short list of critical factors that help you achieve a successful OneWorld implementation:

◆ Properly set up and tune the Configurable Network Computing (CNC) environment

◆ Manage your overall expectations

◆ Exploit the best business practices built into the software

◆ Get the "softer" side of the OneWorld implementation (the human element) right

◆ Mitigate your project risks

◆ Take a managed approach

◆ Test and retest before going live with your OneWorld software

It is also important early on to discuss achieving a successful OneWorld implementation and some important realities about ERP implementations in general:

◆ The perfect ERP software package *does not exist*. (Not even OneWorld!)

◆ No two ERP implementations *are ever really the same.*

♦ The perfect ERP implementation *does not exist*.

♦ No ERP implementation *is ever really considered complete*.

There are no doubt other opinions on what factors should be included in this list. However, these factors should be considered the baseline for achieving a successful OneWorld implementation.

Did You Buy the Right Software?

Planning for the successful OneWorld implementation really begins before you decide to buy OneWorld. It continues during the definition of your business requirements and the evaluation of alternative software packages that meet these requirements.

If you have selected the wrong ERP software package, you will likely experience disappointment, delays, and overruns trying to make the wrong software "right" for your organization—if it can be done. However, I do have some encouragement for you: OneWorld is one of the finest ERP software products available in the marketplace today. It is a flexible and powerful package that can be configured in a seemingly endless number of ways. Your choice of OneWorld is likely a sound business decision that will be solidified as soon as your OneWorld software is operational.

I should also add that I have heard of situations in which J. D. Edwards has told a prospect that J. D. Edwards software would be not be an appropriate choice for their organization, or has allowed "test drives" of their software before a license fee changes hands.

Some Thoughts on OneWorld Implementation

Being a veteran of numerous ERP implementations and, more recently, those involving OneWorld, in this section I want to share a few of my general observations about implementations.

Every Organization Is Different

Let me begin by pointing out that no two OneWorld implementations are the same. Why is this the case? Because no two organizations are the same.

Implementation Costs: What to Expect

The implementation costs will likely exceed the cost of the software and possibly any new hardware required. You can expect implementation costs to easily exceed the cost of the software by 3 to 10 times.

For instance, a major implementation cost that you will face are consulting fees. Can you complete a J. D. Edwards' OneWorld implementation without consultants? Generally, the answer is no.

I have found that many organizations take for granted the simplicity of the hardware and software installation process. Be aware that OneWorld CNC is not simply a "load and go" proposition. Expect to spend considerable time and money getting this very important aspect of the OneWorld implementation done correctly. This usually requires expert advice from qualified CNC consultants.

Deciding how much to budget for other implementation-related consulting services is a difficult process. Generally speaking, consulting costs will be significant in the areas of process modeling, configuration, and training. They can also be significant in the areas of application integration and data conversion and migration. The general rule is that if your organization can't devote a person full time to the OneWorld project in areas suggested by J. D. Edwards or consultants, you'll likely need to fill those gaps with consultants. Even the smallest OneWorld implementation will likely involve the equivalent of three full-time people for 3 to 6 months.

How Will You Use Consultants?

At a minimum, you will need expert guidance regarding how to set up the CNC environment and the initial installation of your OneWorld software. You might also need expert assistance with the setup and installation of your database management system that OneWorld will use. Depending on your resources and abilities to undertake and manage a large-scale, organization-wide project, you also might want to use consultants to assist with project management, system configuration, and testing, or with end-user training.

In short, scores of tasks comprise the successful OneWorld implementation, and you might need the help of outsiders to get all the work done. Also, it might be more efficient to use outsiders to complete many of your one-time tasks, such as data conversions.

How Consultants Complete a OneWorld Project

I've talked quite a bit about the need for consulting help, but why is a consultant necessary, aside from possibly helping with CNC installation? One of the reasons why consultants are necessary in most ERP software implementations—regardless of the software vendor selected—is the approach to or methodology of these types of projects that a consultant will bring to the table.

Whether you use J. D. Edwards itself or another installer, such as a J. D. Edwards business partner, virtually every J. D. Edwards installer will bring an implementation methodology or approach to the table. These approaches can vary greatly.

Some of these approaches are quite exacting—almost painful at times—and others might appear fast and loose. These are two extremes, but this is also the reality of the marketplace. So what should you look for in a prospective implementation consultant's approach?

Efficiency

The first characteristic of a successful OneWorld implementation approach is that it will orchestrate activity in such a way as to maximize schedule efficiency (such as time, budget, and results) while minimizing unnecessary activity along the way. Any approach should emphasize a process orientation, should be date-driven, and should clearly identify outcomes or deliverables.

Leverage

A key question about an approach is how deliverables prepared in one task or stage will be leveraged or used in subsequent tasks or stages of the OneWorld implementation. If a clear connection is not present, be sure to question the value of such deliverables. Let the consultant defend the value or necessity of that deliverable to you.

Holistic

Another characteristic of a successful OneWorld implementation approach is that it should be holistic by definition. How does a consultant implement OneWorld holistically? By integrating people, processes, and technology.

You should look for these qualities in a holistic implementation consultant:

◆ Ask about relevant experience. The more OneWorld clients and platforms the consultant has had, the better.

◆ Ask about business experience. For a change, gray hair is good.

◆ Ask about project management experience. Has he been there and done that before? How does he control his projects and keep everyone informed and on track?

◆ Ask about change management experience. How adept is the consultant at introducing new processes, designing and conducting training programs, managing expectations and project scope, and mitigating project risks?

◆ Ask about knowledge transfer. How will the consultant document his work and ensure that your company's staff understands what work was performed? Your staff should be able to make adjustments to the configuration work performed by the consultant after he has left the project.

Adaptable

The fourth characteristic of a successful ERP implementation approach is one of adaptability. A good approach is one that can be scaled up or down as needed. Again, remember that no two organizations are the same, so no two OneWorld implementations will be the same. A cookie-cutter or purely template-driven approach is not always sufficient in all cases—it is only a starting point.

The implementation consultant must be adept at aligning his approach to his client's (your) specific needs. In short, a good consultant should be flexible in his project approach. After all, part of the reason you are paying the consultant in the first place is for his expertise and creativity in designing a "one-off" project for you (a project that is unique to you and your business).

Managed Expectations

The fifth characteristic of a successful OneWorld implementation approach is one that consistently manages your expectations. Let me begin by saying that no OneWorld implementation will be perfect. Therefore, the approach must provide for dealing with the unexpected; mitigating risks such as delays, overruns, or changes in scope; and minimizing any disruptions to your business. The elements of expectation management should include the following:

♦ Project management—how the OneWorld project is detailed and budgeted, and the mechanisms for tracking progress and keeping everyone informed and on track.

♦ Change management—how your expectations, project scope, functionality gaps, technology problems, and other project risks are identified, prioritized, tracked, and resolved.

♦ Quality assurance—how the implementation consultant provides internal quality assurance or client satisfaction. The process should provide you with reasonable assurances that a consultant's work is subject to some degree of peer review and that processes exist for measuring your ongoing satisfaction with the consultant's work.

The consulting firms that you invite to bid for your implementation work should specify what pieces of the work they will personally do versus what pieces of the work they will subcontract, or consider outside the scope of their bid. The more complicated and challenging your implementation, the more likely the consultant will use other specialists. Therefore, he will serve in the capacity of a "systems integrator" rather than as simply an implementation consultant.

Evaluate all firms equally. Remember that consultants are in the personal service business. Select an implementation consultant who has an approach you're comfortable with, who is demonstrably qualified to do the work, who is someone you are comfortable doing business with, and who prices his work fairly.

Qualify your consultants—not just the firm, but the consultants themselves. Generally speaking, most consulting firms make their pitch to you using the consultants who will actually perform the project work. If not, you should be suspect when the "A" team does the pitch but the "B" team is brought in to do the project work.

Regardless of whether the "A" team or the "B" team will do the work, make sure that your internal team members interview the consultants as prospective members of your overall OneWorld project team. Above all else, make sure you are comfortable with these individuals. Most consulting firms allow you to pick the team. After all, you are the one who is paying the bill.

Finally, be aware that consulting is a very transient business. (It is no different than the revolving-door situation that might exist in your own information technology department, and it actually might be worse.) Therefore, be prepared for the inevitable: The longer the duration of your OneWorld implementation project, the greater the possibility is that you'll lose one of your handpicked consultants along the way.

Business Process Reengineering and the OneWorld Implementation

When I hear someone suggest that "What we need is a new system," I immediately begin wondering where I have heard that before. Often, systems are both blamed for and suggested as the remedy for the ills of bad business processes.

To be fair, business process reengineering has a bad reputation. It's been viewed all too simplistically as a way to downsize the organization, an excuse for cutting jobs and management levels. However, business process reengineering is really aimed at the elimination of non-value-adding work and at leveraging the capacity or throughput of business processes and resources.

At first glance, a new system, especially one such as OneWorld, will potentially solve many of a company's issues. However, upon careful analysis, if a company has significant process issues, a new system alone might not solve any of its problems. In the words of an old and dear friend, W.C. Walker of the Viskase Corporation, "It may simply represent a new or different way to do exactly what was done before." There are two schools of thought on business process reengineering and its impact on any ERP system implementation, including OneWorld. The first approach is to engage in a more radical, or "from the ground up," reengineering effort. This approach suggests that before you can automate any process, you must seek to understand that process and then simplify it. For instance, you might ask the following of your existing processes:

◆ Should we be doing this task at all?

◆ How can we do this task better?

◆ Are there accepted best practices on how this task (or process) should be done?

◆ What are our benchmarks for the completion of this process?

Because you have (presumably) already selected a best-practice-based ERP software package called OneWorld, you might have all but eliminated the need for a radical business process reengineering project. Why? Because OneWorld is already best-practice-based, a significant reengineering of your organization's business processes should be unnecessary. In this case, business process reengineering would be evolutionary, not revolutionary. I refer to this lighter form of business process reengineering as *just-in-time* business process reengineering.

How Does Just-in-Time Business Process Reengineering Work?

During the implementation of OneWorld, your organization's business processes are modified in such a way that OneWorld can be used appropriately in your business. It's really about the alignment of your business processes with available functions and capabilities within OneWorld. You avoid the need to conduct radical business process reengineering, and you can avoid substantial OneWorld customization as well.

This "softer" form of business process reengineering therefore represents a more natural evolution or revision of your business processes toward the OneWorld-provided best business practices.

In my just-in-time business process reengineering approach, before your current business processes are automated through the use of OneWorld, you need to do the following:

◆ Understand the existing processes.

◆ Understand the best-practice-based processes available through OneWorld.

◆ Synthesize your existing processes into the best-practice-based processes that OneWorld offers.

◆ Identify any functionality gaps and assess the business impact that such gaps present.

Synthesizing your existing processes is the tough part. First, you need to reevaluate steps in your processes if they are not present in the best-practice-based process available in OneWorld. For instance, are they truly value-adding activities, or are they present in the current process to make up for shortcomings in previous information systems? Can you adjust business policies and procedures, or is that simply not possible?

In short, strive for process simplification. Having the right people in place from your organization's major business functions is a critical success factor for this synthesizing process. (Later in this chapter we'll cover the prerequisites for team member selection.)

Yes, radical business process improvements are possible simply by implementing OneWorld at your organization. However, using OneWorld is often of greatest benefit to a heavily process-challenged, manually intensive organization. In a company already well along in its business process rationalization efforts, using OneWorld's best-practice-based processes will likely yield only incremental, not radical, business process improvements.

Project Management Insights for the OneWorld Implementation

Although your boss will likely ask, "What are these line items for?" or "Is all of this necessary?" you will soon realize that these items are some of the most important line items in your project budget.

The items I speak of include project management, training, and change management. The tendency is to underestimate both the cost and value of these line items to a successful OneWorld implementation. More analysis regarding the importance of these factors to your project's success will follow a bit later in this chapter. For now, however, let's focus on what I refer to as the "soft" factors that figure heavily into the success of a successful OneWorld software implementation:

- ◆ Project sponsorship
- ◆ Project team member selection
- ◆ Project team empowerment
- ◆ Ongoing communication about the project
- ◆ Managing your consultants

Project Sponsorship

Project sponsorship does not end with an authorization for expenditure. That is only the beginning of a much longer journey. Project sponsorship should occur at the highest levels in the organization. The project steering committee should be comprised of a key executive from each major business function, the project team manager, and his consulting team counterpart.

Project Team Selection

The selection of the project team manager and the project working team itself should not rely on or tap those who are simply available. Rather, the team should be comprised of experienced, highly regarded business experts who can effectively leverage your OneWorld software investment. Also remember that OneWorld implementations are not primarily information technology initiatives; they should be viewed as first and foremost business initiatives. Be sure to select a project leader who can appreciate and share such a project vision.

Remember too that the people who staff your project team will likely devote all or most of their time to this project and likely will work above and beyond the call of duty for the duration of this project assignment. These individuals should be compensated on an ongoing basis for their dedication and effort to this project and through an end-of-project stipend.

Won't you lose your project team members to a consulting firm anyway? Not necessarily. First, let me reiterate that ERP-related hiring has slowed dramatically as the Y2K blip in ERP software sales and implementations is now all but over. Second, consulting salaries have leveled off, and overall experience requirements are up. Third, not everyone wants to be a consultant. Those who enter the ranks of consulting face frequent travel and generally long hours, and they must work without an office, cubicle, or even a desk to call their own. In short, I have found that very few people find happiness or long-term careers in consulting.

So, if you treat your project team members with respect, along with the financial rewards suggested, they will likely stay with you. After all, since these individuals represent your best and brightest, when the project is successfully concluded, that might be the time to recognize them with greater responsibilities.

Project Team Empowerment

I cannot say enough about the necessity of project team empowerment. The future of your business processes rests in the hands of your project team. If you have selected your project team wisely, their expertise and guidance in the usage of OneWorld should be definitive. As to the details of their work, the project team should be largely self-managed and empowered.

Project Communication

Periodic project communication prevents rumors and helps ensure that everyone is in tune with the expectations of your organization's executive management. Under the president's signature, an initial letter should be addressed to all employees. This letter should discuss the project's vision and lay out a rough project time line. It should also identify the project team, spell out what the project team will be doing, and encourage everyone's active cooperation and support in helping the project team complete its work.

Periodically thereafter, an executive briefing letter should be prepared and distributed as the project progresses, usually after a major phase in the project is completed. I have found that people really want to know what is happening and why, and how it will affect them and when. Such communications also enhance the accountability of the team to its deadlines. They will not want to be associated with failure and therefore will generally not provide unrealistic dates or make otherwise unrealistic projections about their work.

Managing Your Consultants

The final element is the ongoing necessity to effectively manage your consulting relationships. I have found that consultants fall into three categories:

◆ Consultants who want to leave before the job is done

◆ Consultants who don't know when it's time to leave

◆ Consultants who know when it is time to move on and who work with you to prepare an exit strategy from the project

The last type of consultant is, of course, the type you want working for you. Be assured that your consultants will offer to provide as many services as you can imagine for as long as you can tolerate them. Remember the role that you have in mind for the consultants from the start, and make sure that your expectations about their engagement scope remain in check.

Scope Creep

There is a serious disease that afflicts many OneWorld implementations. It's called *scope creep*, and it happens frequently. Scope creep is the expansion of a project beyond its original boundaries. For instance, in the case of OneWorld, if you initially elect to implement only Financials, and after a few months you decide to add noninventory purchasing to the project, you've had project expansion, or scope creep. There are times when scope creep is acceptable. Other times, it can severely cripple an in-progress OneWorld implementation.

An important role for the implementation consultant is to manage your expectations about what the software will do and to what extent you'll entertain changes to the software. However, this does not mean that your consultant will keep scope creep in check. That responsibility rests with you.

Remember that scope creep can represent additional revenue streams to the consultant and, conversely, cost overruns to you. Because of this potential conflict of interest, the consultant should present to you, for your express approval, any changes in project scope or duration and, hence, the cost of his work.

It is your responsibility to ensure that the consultant is managing your expectations effectively and is serving your best interests. By this, I mean that your consultant should prevent large-scale customization to the core functionality of the OneWorld package and should keep the project on a strict time line and budget. Also, the work that the consultants undertake should be truly value-adding.

Project Scope

What about the so-called "big bang" versus a "phased rollout" approach for OneWorld implementations? The selection of the "right" way to roll out your OneWorld software in your organization is quite circumstantial. If you have a limited number of locations, a big bang approach is very attractive. If you have numerous locations, especially across borders, phased rollouts are more appropriate.

Another common approach is to begin by rolling out three lower-risk, well-defined financial applications that are frequently single-location business functions: general ledger accounting and financial reporting, noninventory accounts payable, and fixed assets—a so-called limited scope rollout. Generally speaking, these OneWorld modules can be easily separated from other business functions and can operate on a stand-alone basis.

In addition, the underlying organizational structure and chart of accounts needed for these modules also represent the foundation for integrating the other OneWorld modules into the General Accounting system.

In general, any one of these project rollout approaches will work under the appropriate circumstances.

Project Risks

Most important when deciding how to plan your ERP software rollout is the consideration of project risks. Project risks must be mitigated. The appropriate rollout plan, even if it's more costly or time-consuming, should carefully balance the impact of any significant business interruption against the increase in implementation costs. But there are trade-offs. Long-term or multi-year ERP implementations can develop cases of significant scope creep, cost duplications, lost momentum, and disappointing returns on investment.

Summary

This chapter discussed the critical success factors that are instrumental in a successful OneWorld implementation. These critical success factors call for you to do the following:

- Properly set up and tune the CNC environment
- Manage your overall expectations
- Exploit the best business practices built into the software
- Get the "softer" side of the OneWorld implementation right
- Mitigate your project risks
- Take a managed approach
- Test and retest before going live with your OneWorld software

In the next chapter, you will gain additional insights into planning and achieving a successful OneWorld implementation through the introduction of a model implementation approach for OneWorld. The approach is specifically formulated to address the critical success factors that were introduced in this chapter.

Chapter 5

This chapter introduces you to a model approach toward achieving a successful OneWorld implementation. The approach contained in this chapter is best-practice-based, representing my cumulative knowledge and experience drawn from multiple ERP system implementations.

The OneWorld implementation approach you adopt should include stages that approximate or parallel the stages of the model presented in this chapter.

Project Planning Versus Project Execution

The model implementation approach presented in the following pages serves as a framework for the design and development of a project plan that is specifically tailored toward achieving a *successful* implementation of OneWorld.

However, before we start this discussion, I need to caution you. Any approach by itself is not a prescription for success. The approach will only provide you with a set of guidelines that promote project success. In the end, a *successful* OneWorld implementation requires not only a *successful* project plan, but *successful* project plan execution.

The Best-Practice-Based Implementation Model

The overall OneWorld implementation should be divided into stages that logically relate the complexities of the OneWorld project to plannable units of work. These stages work together to ensure that the implementation effort is planned, controlled, and monitored. Within each stage of this model approach are specific activities, or tasks, and deliverables, or outcomes, are associated with each such task or activity.

As you evaluate OneWorld project approaches or methodologies of prospective implementation consultants and solution integrators, you should encounter similarities to the model approach illustrated here. The successful OneWorld implementation approach therefore includes stages that approximate or parallel these stages:

- Chartering your project
- Selecting your project team
- Educating your project team
- Implementing the base environment
- Modeling your business
- Configuring the software for your business
- Prototyping your business processes
- Identifying functionality gaps
- Developing technical solutions
- Documenting your work
- Establishing production readiness
- Training your end-users
- Going live
- Establishing steady state
- Performing periodic health checks
- Completing periodic software updates

Figure 5-1 illustrates the sequential, or waterfall, style structure of the model implementation for OneWorld that is described in this chapter.

Chartering Your Project

During this project stage, you should develop a clear understanding of your OneWorld system implementation strategy. The project scope and objectives should be defined and communicated to all. A detailed implementation plan and project timetable should be developed. This plan should include the identification of what needs to be accomplished and who will accomplish this work. Chapter 6 provides additional tips and techniques related to project planning.

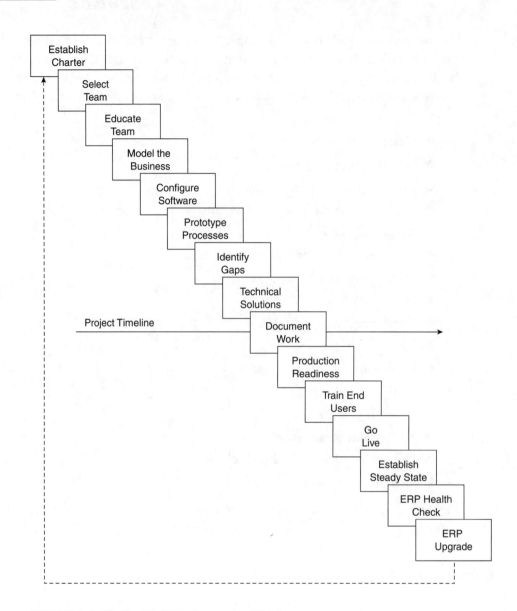

FIGURE 5-1 *The OneWorld Implementation Model*

Selecting Your Project Team

During this stage, the project working and executive teams should be defined and staffed. Formal project executive sponsorship is established. You assemble a working team of the best and brightest individuals from your representative business areas. A leader is appointed for this working project team. Consulting participants are interviewed and added to the team.

The Project Executive Team

The project executive team, or project steering committee, meets to review progress, assess project risks, and decide on project scope, budget, and schedule changes. The basic agenda for these meetings is to review the overall project status using the project plan, the project budget, and the project issues list as guiding documents.

The Project Working Team

The project working team meets to review progress, determine project status, project scope changes, and identify issues, tasks, and project risks. The basic agenda for these meetings is to review the project plan, individual action plans, task status, and project issues and to propose resolutions to issues.

Educating Your Project Team

The project team receives overview training in project and change management, business process analysis and modeling techniques, and specialized education in the base OneWorld software functionality.

Implementing the Base Environment

During this stage of the OneWorld implementation, central site preparations are completed. The central site hardware is delivered, installed, and made ready for software loading. The operating system is licensed and installed. The database and middleware software components are licensed and installed. The J. D. Edwards' OneWorld software is licensed and installed. The OneWorld baseline environments are established. Any necessary project team hardware, such as fat and thin clients, is delivered and installed, and the appropriate client software environments are deployed.

Modeling Your Business

You must analyze your current business practices within all affected functional areas. This is frequently referred to as the development of an "as-is" model for your organization. During this stage of the project, you will develop a full understanding of your current business environment, including business practices and processes, as well as an understanding of the roles and responsibilities of each member of your user community. You also identify best practices contained in the base OneWorld software product that you will use in your organization.

Using a combination of the previously developed current or "as-is" business model, an understanding of your business goals for OneWorld, and your knowledge of OneWorld best business practices, you construct a proposed or future model of the business. This is frequently referred to as the "to-be" process model for your organization.

It is during this modeling stage that an organization often relies on its implementation partner to extensively guide the process and to "fill in" the knowledge gaps about OneWorld processes and best practices that it might simply not have developed a complete competency in this early stage.

Configuring the Software for Your Business

In this stage, you configure, on a system-by-system basis, exactly how the OneWorld software will operate for your organization. The configuration of OneWorld is executed based on the input of your end-user community, the conference room pilot scripts, and the business process transaction scenarios you have previously developed.

Key deliverables from this stage include revised transaction scenarios to be used during later project stages. The business environment, workflow, and user community definitions are revised as needed during this stage.

Prototyping Your Business Processes

Proof of concept occurs in this stage. This stage is frequently called a "conference room pilot" of the software. Transaction scenarios are tested. A complete understanding of how the base OneWorld software will work is sought, and your business processes using OneWorld are documented and accepted by the appropriate business departments. Any software functionality gaps are identified for further action. The following generic business processing threads are typically exercised during this stage:

◆ Quote to cash

◆ Procure to pay

◆ Design to deploy (build)

◆ Plan to produce/plan to ship

◆ Manage the enterprise

As prototyping or "proof of concept" occurs, testing and acceptance criteria are developed. Prototyping or piloting of the software is typically an iterative process, refining the configuration based on lessons learned during this stage. The important lesson in prototyping is that it is certainly better to find out the answers to your tough questions during this stage, before these questions become an unresolved production issue.

Identifying Functionality Gaps

Further testing of any previously identified transactions containing functionality gaps occurs in this stage. A full understanding of any OneWorld gaps is sought, and workarounds are devised and modeled. Custom transactions are designed to replace or extend the functionality of the base delivered OneWorld software product.

It is important to note that tailoring, or personalizing, the base or core OneWorld software does not include the modification or customization of any of the source code of the base delivered OneWorld software product. A key tenet of any successful OneWorld implementation is to avoid customizing the core product whenever possible.

Developing Technical Solutions

Custom transactions are developed against the previous specifications to replace or extend the functionality of the base delivered OneWorld software product.

These custom transactions typically represent modifications to the source code of the base delivered software product. Custom transactions are completed and tested and then integrated into the overall workflow process of the OneWorld system.

A data migration or conversion plan is devised and executed. Master data and transaction-related data from existing legacy systems is identified and analyzed. Tools or programs are used to scrub, edit, and load this data into the appropriate OneWorld system data files or data tables.

Many ERP projects begin with lofty goals, such as rules against any customization, or they lack provisions for any data migration. However, at some point every ERP system requires data conversions—even if they are of the manual type. Customization takes many forms. A simple report can be construed as a modification. An organization that does not anticipate, at least minimally, some level of custom technical solutions is in for a surprise. In many cases, you won't know at the beginning of an ERP implementation what level of technical work is needed, but rest assured that it will be needed at some point in the project.

Documenting Your Work

Too often I have found that documentation on an ERP project becomes the "forgotten stepchild." However, it is important that documentation be completed throughout the life of the OneWorld implementation. In this stage, all the cumulative documentation efforts are cataloged, reworked, finalized, and reused. The documentation will be related to the OneWorld configuration, any customization and personalization (tailoring) of the system, and your final business processes. It is during this stage that you will develop user procedures, documentation, and training materials that are essential parts of the end-user support infrastructure that must be in place when the OneWorld system moves into production and replaces the current infrastructure and processes.

This stage commences as workflow and functionality issues are finalized. Business policies and procedures are revised and rewritten as needed to support the new OneWorld system. A training plan must be devised and executed. The design and construction of training classes and classroom collateral materials are completed.

A training schedule is devised, and participants are identified and scheduled. A training environment is defined, and training data for hands-on exercises is constructed and created in this environment. Any necessary training facilities and hardware are obtained and made operational.

You will want to provide to provide Train the Trainer education. Trainers will practice their timing and presentation skills. Trainers must ensure that they have complete competency in the software functions and business processes they will be expected to train people in.

Establishing Production Readiness

Verification of the actual stored data and the validation of business process audit trails contained in the data is an important step in ensuring the accuracy and consistency of converted data.

Testing plans should allow for individual component, module, and interface testing and, finally, end-to-end testing of the entire OneWorld system. This includes tests of converted data that your go-forward processes rely on.

All the detailed work during the prototyping and production readiness stages makes "going live" a decision point rather than an additional task to fulfill at the end of the project.

Training End-Users

In this stage, primary attention is given to the delivery of end-user training. Training should be conducted as near as possible to the go-live date. Hands-on training should be provided. Walk participants through business processes as a part of the training.

Provide participants with exercises built on sample or demonstration data drawn from data that they are accustomed to. Provide ample time to practice during formal training classes and offer a "sandbox environment" in which participants can continue to practice and improve their competency with the new OneWorld software until and after the go-live date.

Use a classroom whiteboard as a "parking lot" for unresolved questions, problems, or issues that arise. Use breaks between classes to address and resolve these issues. Review the previous days' topics and parking-lot issues before moving on. If needed, provide written follow-up for all parking-lot issues resolved after training ends.

By the way, I know the current rage is computer-based-training (CBT). As a matter of fact, J. D. Edwards has recently changed its strategy and will emphasize CBT over traditional instructor-led classroom education. I, however, remain a die-hard, favoring live instructor-led classroom education over the use of CBT.

Maybe I'll be proven wrong, but as a former college professor and software trainer, I know that most individuals prefer classroom instruction. In addition, many people do not have the self-motivation and discipline to effectively use CBT.

Going Live

A readiness assessment is completed. The management and working teams assess the overall readiness to go live with the software. A go-live decision is made, and the software launch countdown begins.

Master, configuration, historical, and transactional data is loaded into the production environment.

Your company starts conducting business through the new system. This might or might not be done in parallel with the dual entry of business transactions into both the new OneWorld system and any legacy systems.

Establishing Steady State

Support begins coincident with live production. During this stage, problem resolution and change management procedures are critical.

System performance monitoring should be conducted to ensure that both online and batch processing standards are met. The amount of tuning required depends on the initial results of production. Performance issues might also be encountered that require changing processes or OneWorld system configurations.

At this stage, a smooth and orderly transfer of knowledge to your personnel should occur, and your implementation consultants should be rolling off the project.

Performing Periodic Health Checks

Keeping your OneWorld system healthy is an ongoing process rather than a stage in the project. It begins after the first component or module of a OneWorld system enters production and extends throughout the installed life of the OneWorld system.

Periodic health checks should assess both the functional and technical results of the system. You will constantly want to address whether the OneWorld system is achieving its original objectives and whether its full benefits are being realized.

Completing Periodic Software Updates

As just mentioned, periodic health checks should assess the functional and technical performance of the OneWorld system. Active involvement in user groups and upgrade information programs or subscription services provided by the vendor will allow you to periodically assess whether an upgrade is desirable.

Upgrades generally provide cumulative fixes to known software bugs and often provide performance enhancements through design changes that leverage system performance through other middleware, operating system, and database infrastructure upgrades.

The software factory (a.k.a. J. D. Edwards guided by Quest) should also be making functionality enhancements that might further extend the value of your OneWorld system, or possibly eliminate the need for a remaining legacy system.

Upgrades can pose a significant challenge on an ongoing basis if you have made extensive customizations or have significant integration points with other legacy systems. Certainly this is the reason why J. D. Edwards and virtually every implementation partner you might consider will generally advise you to avoid or minimize customization of OneWorld (or, for that matter, any packaged software product).

In addition, remember the following additional points when considering an upgrade:

◆ Don't upgrade immediately when a new release is available. Wait about six months while you let others shake out any problems.

◆ Try to stay no more than one release level behind the current version of the software. There are several reasons for following this recommendation. Straying too far from the pack lessens the quality of vendor support you'll likely receive. Most upgrades must be sequentially applied. This might require that if you fall behind several release levels, you will need to catch up before applying the latest release.

What Can You Expect in the Way of Upgrades?

You can be bombarded with lesser releases that need to be applied against your base software. These are known as interim releases, bridge releases, quick fixes, patches, service packs, or temporary fixes. These releases are used to resolve specific problems. The problems they address will span from the mundane to the severe. Carefully weigh the merits of each such fix or patch to your system and what ramifications it might have on your system, especially if you have invested in substantial customization, integration, or personalization of the core OneWorld system.

Another release category is the year-end release or regulatory compliance release. These releases are generally available for specific regulatory changes (such as new 1099 or W2 information reporting formats). Typically, as the title implies, these releases are made to the software at year's end.

Is the OneWorld Implementation Ever Really Complete?

As an astute reader, you likely already know the answer to this question. No, because a *successful* OneWorld implementation is never really "complete." Why? Recall my comments that keeping your OneWorld system healthy is really an ongoing process rather than a stage in the project. The successful OneWorld implementation is best represented by a continuous closed-loop system. The OneWorld health check provides the impetus for the continuous improvement and tuning of OneWorld.

Periodic health checks should assess both the functional and technical results of the system. You will constantly want to assess whether the OneWorld system is achieving its original objectives and whether its full benefits are being realized. Tuning and upgrading the OneWorld system to achieve higher performance levels and greater business value is truly a journey, not a destination.

There is another way to answer this question. Your organization is not static. It is dynamic, always changing in response to its environment. Given today's e-business-centric world, nothing could be more true. Therefore, by definition, your business processes and infrastructure, which includes your OneWorld system, are constantly changing to reflect the dynamics involved in the operation of your organization.

What's Next

This section discusses the need to develop a work plan—in the form of a project plan to describe and sequence the tasks related to the OneWorld implementation. It's also vital to create frequent plan updates to reflect progress and any project issues.

The First Step: Creating a Plan

Recall from earlier discussions my point that the model implementation approach is the basis for building a project plan. Much up-front and ongoing work is required to fully define and build out lower-level work plans.

Will the initial project plan be the correct one? Generally speaking, it will not be entirely correct. Project planning is clearly an iterative process. On the other hand, the project plan should not be grossly wrong or inadequately stated. The project plan will continue to evolve and grow, generally in accuracy and to some extent in the detail it contains.

The Second Step: Working the Plan

Again recall from earlier discussions that once you have the plan, you must work the plan. There is simply no substitute available for the enormous amount of effort that is necessary to implement the OneWorld system.

Executing the project plan is not as simple as you might think. In my experience, I have found that if you dedicate personnel on a less than 100 percent basis to your OneWorld implementation, you will diminish your chances of complete success. An ERP system, regardless of how good it is or how simple and straightforward it might appear, requires tremendous effort for any organization, especially those that already have one or more legacy systems in operation.

I have frequently found that OneWorld project resources are the victims of shifting priorities. For instance, your technical personnel might spend too much time on legacy system production problems. These efforts often interfere with their expected participation in the OneWorld project at key points. If it's at all feasible, I strongly suggest that you consider making your key OneWorld technical people secondary support personnel on production systems.

Also, please understand that as a OneWorld buyer, your organization typically won't be able to efficiently implement OneWorld without an implementation partner. Even if you use consultants only sparingly, you will need them nonetheless. With that said, please understand that implementation partners can't usually complete the OneWorld implementation successfully without solid and, in many cases, full-time resource commitments made by your functional business units.

Consultants are expensive. Enormous waste occurs when consultants are not fully utilized by your project team. Ensure that your internal team members as well as your consulting team do not lose sight of the cost of being idle for any reason. The project manager has the responsibility of resourcing the OneWorld project to a "fully utilized" threshold.

Although project delays will occur, constant attention to updating and refining the project plan is absolutely essential. The project plan is not a static document. It should be as dynamic as the work on the project itself. Stay on top of things. Do not let surprises occur. Nothing should be said at a project status meeting that is not already known to the project manager. Nor should the project manager be unprepared. The project manager must regularly do impact analysis and risk assessment of project delays and unresolved issues.

OneWorld is an enormous investment for most organizations. Do not slight the after-the-fact investment in sound project management required to make OneWorld functional and successful at your organization.

Here's another key point: I find that many organizations often ignore or lose sight of the key fact that the license fee paid to J. D. Edwards for OneWorld is just a fraction of the overall OneWorld implementation costs. The project manager must create a realistic budget and find out management's expectations early on. Failure to communicate the size and scope of the effort through a budget plan early in the process can lead to enormous difficulties in the later stages of the project.

The Third Step: Repeating the First Two Steps

Although project management has been the primary focus of this discussion, please understand that on an ongoing basis, change and issue management must be integral elements in a successful OneWorld implementation experience. Therefore, you can also conclude that good planning anticipates change. You'll recall from earlier discussions that planning and implementing OneWorld is truly an iterative process.

A Change or an Issue: What's the Difference?

An issue is something that arises and must be resolved. Issues are usually unforeseen events that occur during the course of your implementation. Some issues are relatively simple to resolve, and others are not. Resolving an issue might not necessarily mean that you need to change or customize portions of your OneWorld system. However, when a configuration change or workaround can't be found, or if it proves simply unworkable, program changes are often entertained.

In this context, changes are things that affect the personalization or tailoring of OneWorld for your organization, such as its configuration, including program or report setup or the entry or conversion of master data, or customizations, which are changes that affect how OneWorld programs actually operate.

Often these changes are minor or inconsequential, and other times such changes can be significant. It is also wise to consider OneWorld or operating environment upgrades and service pack installations as changes that can and will affect your organization and potentially how or if it can conduct business through the system. One of the reasons you will need to change OneWorld programs is to resolve program operation or performance problems, commonly known as program bugs.

Change and Issue Management

Issue management should be an integral part of the overall OneWorld project management process. As soon as agreement is reached on the dimensions of the project scope, changes in scope must be carefully weighed. For instance, how will the change affect the time frame and project budget? What is the value of this change? Will a workaround suffice for start-up, or will it work on a permanent basis?

Early in the project, you need to establish acceptance criteria. Use of such acceptance criteria is intended to help you limit project scope. Acceptance criteria help you draw a line in the sand and decide when an issue can't be resolved in the working team and must be elevated to the steering committee.

For instance, here's a list of some typical scope-limiting acceptance criteria:

◆ We will implement the features and functions contained in OneWorld as delivered by J. D. Edwards.

◆ We will implement only OneWorld functions that meet our existing business needs.

◆ We will implement the following OneWorld modules: ...

◆ If a OneWorld function does not completely meet our business needs, we will attempt to find a workaround to fulfill that need. That workaround might be a combination of OneWorld and manual processes to fulfill this business need.

◆ Before we make any changes to OneWorld, we will reconsider how our business process works, and we will entertain a process change that will allow us to avoid any OneWorld customization requirements.

◆ We will not convert legacy system data into OneWorld via any automated means. All needed information for going live will be manually entered into OneWorld.

◆ We will not change any OneWorld core programs.

- ◆ We will not change any OneWorld menus.
- ◆ We will not change any OneWorld version list entries.

Again, the intent of such acceptance criteria is to limit changes to the project scope, or to OneWorld itself, and that any necessary changes are carefully thought out in terms of your overall project budget, your time line, and your OneWorld investment. Remember that when you customize OneWorld, you affect your ability to upgrade the product.

Of course, you need to be realistic. Issues representing various degrees of impact on your OneWorld implementation will invariably arise throughout the course of the project, even after the project scope has been determined and acceptance has been reached on functions, features, and processes. Therefore, I highly recommend a formal issue resolution process, which in turn authorizes and funds changes to project scope.

Many of the issues you encounter can be classified as *gaps*. A gap is an issue that represents a disconnect between business expectations, or requirements, and the intended functionality that is to be deployed. Typically, the core functionality of the software either does not support a desired business policy, procedure, or process, or does so inappropriately. For instance, functionality gaps are typically handled using one of four methods:

- ◆ A favorable change in business policy, procedure, or process is needed that will close the gap.
- ◆ A system-based workaround is found that will close the gap.
- ◆ A paper-based or manual process is used to close the gap.
- ◆ Customization of the software is used to satisfy the desired business requirement and close the gap.

A formal issue management process is therefore an important component toward ensuring that your implementation is completed within the time frame, budget, and risk level you are willing to allow.

The successful OneWorld implementation approach you adopt must provide for a sound issue-management process. Such a process provides for the orderly identification, logging, prioritization, and follow-up of functionality and technical challenges that arise during all stages of the OneWorld implementation. This process also ensures that your organization, not an implementation partner, has the final say with respect to OneWorld project issues and changes.

Certain issues or gaps are business-critical. These issues or gaps are frequently called "go-live" or "showstopper" issues. Obviously, these gaps must be resolved before you go live with OneWorld. Therefore, an important part of the overall issue-management process is determining how business-critical an issue actually is.

Unresolved issues that are considered noncritical are those that can be addressed on a post-go-live basis. For instance, if the issue represents a functionality gap, it is usually addressed (for start-up purposes) by one of the workaround techniques just discussed.

It is the responsibility of your organization, not your implementation partner, to assess whether a specific issue is considered critical or noncritical to the go-live date and to the resolution action that will be considered appropriate or acceptable.

However, a good implementation partner should stress to you that you should always be moving forward with the project, as close to the schedule as possible. It's not in the partner's best interests (as in client satisfaction) to "run up the meter." You do expect from the partner expectation management and accomplishment of as much functionality or scope as is possible within the original project budget.

A formal issue management process might work as follows:

1. As an issue is identified and logged.
2. Resolution should always begin at the lowest level possible. Often the issue can be resolved to the satisfaction of process owners through a workaround. Sometimes a promise will do.
3. For some issues, resolution is not such a simple matter. These issues are in turn prioritized and discussed in project working meetings as to their business and project impact and what the possible resolution options are.
4. If a business-critical issue is left unresolved by the working committee, it can be elevated to the steering committee.
5. The steering committee should be advised of the issue and will consider the business impact, the appropriateness of the available options, and the impact on the overall project scope, budget, and time line.

Here are a few practical tips to go along with this process: I recommend using Microsoft Excel or Access to log all issues that arise. A simple Microsoft Word document template or a Microsoft Exchange form could be designed for communicating issues to the project manager or project administrator. That person would record the issue. As issues are resolved, reviewed, deferred, or elevated to the steering committee, they can be tracked in the log. Again, my template collection might be helpful in this regard. Please consult the Introduction for information about how to obtain these templates.

In addition, every change request should be documented and tracked in much the same manner. However, with respect to making changes, they should always be done in conformance with any "site standards" you develop. Chapter 10 talks more about changes and site standards for the OneWorld environment.

Is One OneWorld Implementation Approach Better Than Another?

As I mentioned earlier, virtually every prospective implementation partner brings its own implementation approach model to the table. An obvious question is whether any of these approaches is more successful than another.

Quite frankly, it has been my experience that one approach is not really any better than—or, for that matter, much different from—another approach. When evaluating the validity of an approach model for your organization, consider an approach or methodology that complements your organization's business style.

It's All About Discipline

Are projects undertaken by your organization generally fast and loose, or are they really continuous works in process that are never quite complete? Simply put, you should leverage your successes and resource your weaknesses, such as by adding consultants to a project that complement your team's capabilities. But consider this: What really makes a project plan work is discipline. The discipline to plan and execute, above all else, will make your project a success.

Summary

This chapter focused on stepping through a model implementation approach for OneWorld. The model OneWorld approach illustrated is best-practice-based, representing my cumulative firsthand knowledge and experience drawn from multiple ERP implementations, including those involving OneWorld.

This chapter closed by discussing the need for discipline. The use of a project plan based on the model approach presented in this chapter was stressed. You also learned that your OneWorld project will be successful only when you *successfully* execute the project plan, which includes managing project scope and expectations through the use of issue and change-management procedures.

Chapter 6

The OneWorld Project—Getting It Right

This chapter provides the tips and techniques you need to implement the best practices model approach introduced in Chapter 5. In this chapter you will learn practical techniques intended to help you develop the contents of your OneWorld project plan, work packages, configuration scripts, and integration or test-case scenarios. You'll also learn a clever technique for reporting project status. Finally, you will find a discussion about business modeling techniques, including a list of key questions to ask about your business processes during the modeling stage of your OneWorld project.

The OneWorld Project Plan

I know of very few homes that have been successfully built without some form of written plan, or blueprint. In this regard, implementing OneWorld successfully also requires a written plan or blueprint. Developing and executing a successful project plan is a lot of work, but as you will discover, help is available.

In Chapter 5, you were introduced to an approach or model for the successful implementation of OneWorld. A successful OneWorld implementation project should include stages that approximate or parallel the stages of this implementation model.

How Do the Model Approach Stages Fit into the Project Plan?

The stages of the OneWorld implementation model represent the highest-level categories in your project plan. Subsequently, lower-level or detailed work breakdown structures and work packages must be developed for each stage of the OneWorld implementation project.

For instance, these work packages are sometimes called conference room pilot scripts by J. D. Edwards. Within the work package or script document, you would identify specific configuration steps and follow-up testing steps.

You should have a high-level master project plan for all the stages of your project and any subprojects. For instance, you might want to consider as subprojects the implementation of each major functional area (such as General Accounting and Procurement) or possibly use subprojects to distinguish each location being implemented. Figure 6-1 illustrates a typical work breakdown structure, or hierarchy.

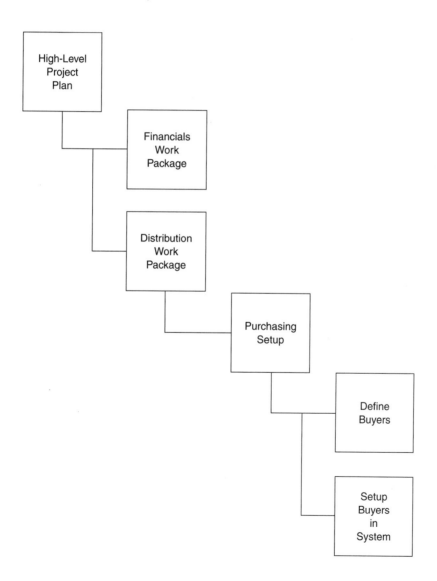

FIGURE 6-1 *A Typical Work Breakdown Structure*

How Do You Determine What Tasks to Include in the Project Plan?

There are two approaches to building work plans, and you will likely find that, to a degree, you need both types. You can build work plans that are function-oriented or process-oriented.

A function-oriented work plan starts with a list of the OneWorld modules you are implementing (for instance, Address Book, Accounts Payable, Fixed Assets, and General (Ledger) Accounting). A process- or workflow-oriented work plan builds the task list based on all the OneWorld business functions your organization uses. For instance, all the steps related to purchase order processing would be included on the "procure to pay" script, such as item and vendor setup, request quotes, compare quotes, select vendor, approve order, convert quote to order, print order, receive order, voucher order, and write payment to vendor.

Function-oriented task plans are great for controlling tasks at a micro level. These module-specific plans can ensure that a specific module is being configured and unit-tested. However, they aren't too good for planning the overall or integrated configuration planning and testing. Enter the process-oriented task plan. The process-oriented task plan is typically used to facilitate process or macro-level validation.

Function-Oriented Task Planning

The first step of function-oriented task planning is to identify the setup steps related to each module. Your starting point for this effort should be the OneWorld reference guides. These reference guides are included with your OneWorld software. You can use either the hard-copy guides or the CD-ROM version of the guides, because they are identical in content.

The table of contents in each reference guide breaks down most of the setup activities for you. These activities become a partial set of setup tasks you'll need to include in your plans. OneWorld reference guides also provide the rest of the information you will need to organize your setup and testing efforts. However, this remaining information is harder to decipher. J. D. Edwards has adopted a common structure throughout OneWorld. In general, OneWorld activities are broken into these major categories:

◆ Daily processing
◆ Periodic processing

- ◆ Setup activities
- ◆ Advanced and technical activities

You will also find that all OneWorld functional system menus are organized around these categories. In addition, the organization of every OneWorld functional system reference guide directly corresponds to these categories. Therefore, the remaining setup and related testing activities can be identified using the reference guides in much the same manner. However, the setup tasks are not as easy to identify. We'll look at why in the next section.

PLANNING TIP

Use the Reference Guide to Figure Out Your Needs

By building your task plan using the reference guide table of contents, if you're unsure whether a report or processing step applies to your project, you can quickly reference that section of the user guide and research its applicability to your project. This won't resolve all your questions, but it should help you resolve many of them.

PLANNING TIP

Preview OneWorld Reports Without Running Them

If you need to review the contents of a report in order to determine whether it will be useful or applies to your implementation, the OneWorld CD-ROM includes a report reference guide that is great for such purposes. Should a report not be in this guide, you might need to run a sample report before making your decision.

Processing Options and Versions

Virtually every program or report in OneWorld has one or more setup tasks associated with it. OneWorld is delivered with one or more preconfigured versions of each program or report. In most cases, you can define your own versions for each program or report that allow you to vary the settings for both processing options and data selection that are associated with that program or report.

Processing options are largely workflow- and navigation-related settings. They are discussed in greater detail in Chapter 11. Therefore, you will need multiple activities on your script to allow for both the setup and testing of these individual programs. We'll also discuss how to use the "versions list" in Chapter 11, but for now, each time you need a variation in workflow for a program or a variation (a different set of data) in the body of a OneWorld report, you need another version of the report or program. Although J. D. Edwards delivers OneWorld with many standard or core versions of its programs and reports, in most cases an organization needs some degree of personalization in these areas.

The Conference Room Pilot Script

The conference room pilot script document should be a comprehensive plan that will step you through the complete setup, proof of concept, and acceptance testing of all OneWorld features and functions. Figure 6-2 illustrates what a typical conference room pilot script or task list might look like. I've included this example to help you understand how you will break down the implementation, setup, and testing work that you'll need to do.

These scripts can be prepared to various levels of detail. It is my preference to support a CRP script by exercising the detailed business process itself, whether from the J. D. Edwards user reference guide, the J. D. Edwards online help text, or a procedural template prepared for you by a consultant. The CRP script is an important control document that ensures that the system's functionality has been reviewed, configured, and tested, and that any required business procedures have been prepared.

Process-Oriented Task Planning

As I mentioned earlier, process-oriented task planning is another alternative that you can employ when etching out the OneWorld task list. Although function-oriented work plans are easier to understand and construct, a process-oriented work plan stresses integration. Several core processing threads are common to all ERP systems. A processing thread is the series of activities that constitute a complete or end-to-end business process (see Figure 6-3). I recommend that you build integration scenarios around these major processing threads.

What's really the difference between a functional and a process orientation? The functional orientation considers the tasks related to a single module. This is a great way to ensure that each module is set up and tested, but it's also a silo, or one-dimensional, view of the system's functionality. A process orientation cuts across multiple modules. It is the end-to-end processing of a transaction.

To illustrate the process orientation, consider the example shown in Figure 6-4: A business regularly sells a product to its customers, but it also gives free samples

ADDRESS BOOK IMPLEMENTATION SCRIPT
SYSTEM SETUP
Address Book Setup
• Review Address Book Constants
• Review/Change Address Book Category Codes
• Review/Change Address Book Next Numbers
CRP PREPARATIONS
Gather Test Data and Information
CRP EXECUTION
Address Book Maintenance
• Add Address Book Record
• Add Supplier Information
• Add G/L Distribution
• Add Tax Information
• Add Purchasing Instructions
• Add Phones
• Add Who's Who
• Revise Supplier Master
• Revise Who's Who
• Delete Address Book Record
Address Book Inquiry
• Name Search
• Search Type Restriction
• QBE Line Search
Address Book Reporting
• Run Reports by Address
• Run Reports by Person
• Run Check for Duplicates
• Run Full Address with Codes Who's Who
CRP FOLLOW-UP TASKS
• Determine additional reporting needs
• Determine and publish standards and procedures for address maintenance

FIGURE 6-2 *Some Typical Tasks Found in a Conference Room Pilot Script*

to prospects for evaluation purposes. The difference between a regular order and a sample order is price. The regular order is priced, and the sample order is unpriced. These are two different scenarios, and both must be tested. The expectation in the priced example is that an accounts receivable entry is generated against the customer account. In the second example, an accounts receivable entry is not generated. The bottom line is that process variations represent different scenarios, and these scenarios should be sufficiently described and tested.

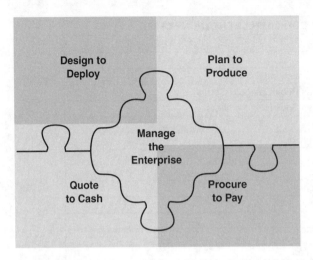

FIGURE 6-3 *Piecing Together the Puzzle: ERP Integration and Business Processes*

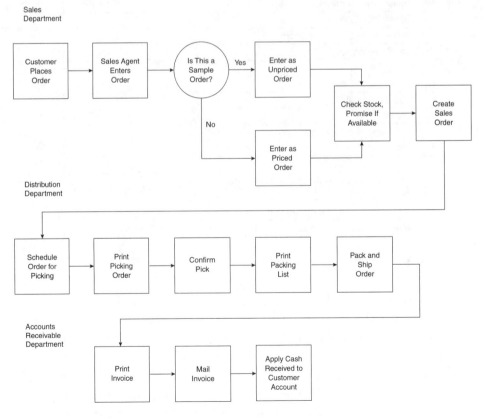

FIGURE 6-4 *Modeling the Typical Order Processing Scenario*

Finally, and most importantly, this approach focuses on the process itself, not on the individuals, systems, or departments involved. Many organizations find the process orientation in an ERP system overwhelming sometimes—realizing for the first time the degree of fragmentation, rework, and inefficiency that old, nonintegrated processes contain. The need to focus on process is paramount in an integrated systems environment like that of OneWorld. Errors made early on in the source document entry process will continue to propagate throughout the system.

Rollout Strategies and Project Planning

As you learned in the Chapter 4, there are a number of different options available regarding how you can "roll out" OneWorld to the organization at large. These approaches include the following:

- **The big bang**. In this approach, your organization goes live with the complete OneWorld system all at once for the entire organization

- **The staged approach**. In this approach, your organization initially goes live with only portions of OneWorld (such as the financial modules), followed by the startup of other modules at one or more later dates.

- **Location-by-location**. Using this approach, your organization goes live with the complete OneWorld system all at once for a single business unit within the organization. You can then use the experience and lessons learned in the initial or pilot implementation to refine your project plan into a template that can be reused in the remaining business unit OneWorld implementations. Also note that a business unit does not necessarily need to be a separate location, geographically speaking, although they often are.

Regardless of the rollout strategy you choose, it is imperative to the success of your OneWorld project that you become comfortable with and employ a robust computer-based project-planning tool such as Microsoft Project or Primavera Systems Primavera Project Planner to manage your efforts. You will want to use a project-planning software tool to construct work plans and work breakdown structures that will be used to identify your OneWorld implementation tasks and to budget project team resources for these tasks.

Iterative Project Plan Refinement

Your periodic project meetings can be used to review the progress on each task that is scheduled "for work" within a given period. Task status is then updated to reflect progress, including task completions and estimates of any delays or possible project bottlenecks. This information can then be used to determine any corrective actions needed, including changing priorities, adding resources, or adjusting deadlines and targets.

I highly recommend the use of a baseline plan. I can't emphasize enough the overall importance of instituting formal progress reporting as an integral part of your OneWorld implementation effort. This is especially true when multiple implementations will be undertaken.

Progress tracking of activities can be considered a form of continuous improvement for your baseline project plan. Actual results versus baseline plans can form the basis for the calculation of an "estimating margin of error" for each task project in your timeline and for the project on an overall, or cumulative, basis. This information can subsequently be used to refine the details in your ongoing or rolling project plan.

These plan refinements are particularly beneficial when you are doing multiple rollouts of OneWorld, such as to multiple locations within your company.

Although there will typically be variations in each of the subsequent OneWorld implementations within your organization, the knowledge gain made possible by progress tracking can be instrumental in helping you provide project budgets of increasing accuracy as you initiate each subsequent OneWorld rollout or implementation.

Does Every Detail or Task Need to Be in the Overall Project Plan?

You do not need to include every task or step in the project plan. For instance, the project plan might refer to a detailed work package (possibly a Microsoft Excel document) where all tasks are identified for a specific module, such as following the guidelines for the functional work plan described earlier. The work package would in turn represent a "block" of work or project team time.

Reporting Project Status to Management

Project management is an important and ongoing process that for all practical purposes is the daily responsibility of the project manager and will likely consume most of his or her time. However, an important role of the project manager is to keep project sponsors and stakeholders informed of project status—including the progress of any significant issues. This section discusses techniques of reporting that a project manager can employ for this purpose.

The Perils of Project Status Reporting

One day I learned, the hard way, just how far I had moved toward being a geek and away from my traditional role as a "bean counter." I remember spending countless hours perfecting my project plan for presentation to the project steering committee, a group that was largely comprised of accountants, for our new general ledger accounting system. I was rather shaken when, during our project status discussions, two of the senior accounting managers did not understand the concept of a project timeline (frequently called a Gantt chart, after its creator).

At this moment, I realized that my knowledge of accounting had extended into areas where traditional accountants typically do not venture. I often find that non-technical audiences do not have the same level of appreciation for or the same vocabulary as technical individuals.

The moral of the story is don't expect that anyone on your project working team (or anyone on your project steering committee, for that matter) understands even basic project management terminology. The challenge is how you, as the project manager, can convey the project's status in a clear, concise manner without offending anyone. About the best solution I've encountered over the years is the Stoplight Report.

Enter the Stoplight Report

One of my consulting colleagues, Gordon Merna, introduced me to a different approach toward project status reporting than I have generally been accustomed to. The concept of a traffic light to indicate project or task status has several excellent qualities of a good performance indicator:

◆ It is quite simple in concept and, more importantly, is easily and universally understood by everyone.

◆ It provides an at-a-glance status summary.

◆ It foretells of future or imminent risks.

What Does the Stoplight Tell You About the Status of a Task or Project?

- A green light means that everything is on schedule.
- A yellow light means that the task is currently on schedule, but some problems have surfaced that put the task in danger of falling behind schedule.
- A red light means that the task is behind schedule. Without resolution of the problems, the successful implementation of the process improvement is endangered.

I have found the Stoplight Report to be a clever and successful addition to my arsenal of project management tools, and it is my hope that you'll be able to use this technique as well. The Stoplight Report is not a substitute for the project plan. Consider the Stoplight Report as a summary document compiled from the detailed information in the project plan.

The Project Budget

The project budget and expenditures statement is an important document. In many cases, it might be more valuable than the project plan itself. The project budget and expenditures statement is typically an Excel or Lotus worksheet document that compares budget and actual costs of each project task in both time and dollars.

A variation of the project budget is a resource budget and effort statement. This is an especially useful report when consultants are employed. The project budget is a resource budget. The effort statement, typically an Excel or Lotus worksheet document, compares the staff allocations and actual efforts expended on each project task. An analysis of any project variances helps the project manager understand the implications of any scope changes, task delays, lack of resources, and, for multiple-phase or multiple-location implementations, whether experiences gained in an initial project will translate into future cost or time savings or increases as the project moves forward. For instance, technical infrastructure questions might delay a project's initial phase but will likely have little or no impact on future phases of the project.

Business Modeling

There are many ways to model your business. I have found that a combination of both visual and written communication techniques works best. For instance, a table-style business process script template for use with Microsoft Word can be developed and used. This can supplement the narrative script document with some form of pictorial or model of the process steps.

You might be wondering at this point why you should bother to create both a narrative and a visual model of the process. Although this might seem redundant, I find that during process reviews it is much easier to speak from the visual. On the other hand, if you can reduce a process into writing, you have also demonstrated clarity in the understanding of that process.

You can create process diagrams in a variety of ways. First, they can be created using the drawing tools available in Microsoft Word or Microsoft PowerPoint. If you already have Microsoft Office and you don't want to spend additional money or learn a new tool, consider this as an option. Additionally, there are also charting or diagramming software tools that are great for process modeling. These modeling tools vary in complexity and cost. Several of them are discussed in the next few paragraphs.

As for a visual business process-modeling tool, my preference is allCLEAR, from SPSS Incorporated. With allCLEAR, you do not need to be an artist or draftsman, nor do you need to spend countless hours aligning flowcharting elements and lines, as you would with many other similar products. This tool can create perfect charts for you if you simply type in short sentences. Some of the other products available include wizards to create a template for you, but none do the job as well as allCLEAR in my estimation.

Two additional and quite popular modeling products include Microsoft Visio 2000 and IGrafx Process (formerly called ABC Flowcharting) by Micrografx. These tools are moderately priced (less than $1,000). More-expensive business modeling tools are also available, such as Platinum BP*win* by Computer Associates and ARIS Easy Design by IDS Scheer Products.

I must point out that business process modeling is an area that has undergone tremendous maturity in recent years. New modeling techniques have been introduced, fueled in part by the business process reengineering boom and also by the move toward object-oriented analysis techniques.

For instance, Visio and ABC Flowcharting are particularly noteworthy for their abilities to create "swim-lane" diagrams. I have found that swim-lane diagrams are becoming increasingly popular with business modelers. Each swim lane represents another business unit within a business organization. Handoffs between business units within a process flow are then visualized as lines moving between swim lanes.

I prefer to limit the use of swim lane diagrams to represent business process flows at a high level only. I have found that when used at lower levels, they can become quite cluttered and therefore are not easily understood. For instance, I would represent either the overall quote to cash or procure to pay business process cycles with swim-lane diagrams.

Swim lanes do not have to be entirely "graphic" either. I have successfully used them by listing departments across the columns and then placing brief action-oriented sentences in each column. The handoff to another department shifts the flow of sentences to the next column. Finally, yet another variation on this theme is the division of processes into daily, weekly, monthly, quarterly, annual, or "as-needed" columns. I use this format to divide the daily and periodic processes found in each OneWorld system into a business process or procedure schedule that is tailored to how my client will use various OneWorld processes to satisfy their own business processes and processing schedules.

Finally, another modeling technique that is becoming increasingly popular is use case modeling. Use case modeling is frequently utilized in object-oriented software engineering methodologies. Use cases identify the actors (usually people and other systems) who interact with a system for a specific reason, or use case. In theory, the totality of actors and use cases represents the entire context of a system. Use case modeling can be done graphically, or through narration. Narrated use cases are frequently supplemented with graphical use cases. However, be forewarned that use case techniques are somewhat unseasoned. If you decide to model with use cases, adopt a consistent approach, such as using standard templates before attempting to model processes. If you don't, the results might vary so widely that they will be unusable. Although a complete introduction to use cases is beyond the scope of this book, if these techniques appeal to you, a number of books are now making their way into the marketplace on the application of use cases to business system and process design.

How Much Modeling Should You Do?

Finally, it is my recommendation that an organization limit the amount of business modeling it does, especially the as-is or current process flow portion. Quite simply, and as a practical matter, you should focus your efforts on modeling current processes for understanding and then concentrate on modeling future processes that will satisfy your business objectives through automation, elimination, simplification, or replication of an existing business process using the new system.

Is Process Understanding Through Modeling Really Necessary?

Yes, modeling is necessary, but remember, process knowledge is really what you're after. Modeling should build a path to your understanding of processes. But recall from Chapter 4 the discussion of OneWorld best business practices: They aren't free—you pay for them as a part of your software licensing fee—they are built in, and they do work. Simply put, use these best practices as much as possible.

I recommend that you focus your modeling efforts on how current processes will map, or transcend into new processes that will work within the context of your OneWorld software. In this context, you should leverage your understanding of your organization's business processes along with the formal education you have received in OneWorld software. The build-out of your new business models is an area where OneWorld functional consultants can generally provide valuable overall direction and guidance.

While you are building models of your processes, you should also be gathering current written policies and procedures used by your organization. In addition, you should be gathering samples of actual transactions and examples of any manually created or system-created documents and reports used in the current process. You should also gather examples of entry screens, inquiry screens, and forms used in completing the business process. These documents will be instrumental in mapping data and replicating current process steps using available functions within OneWorld.

Also, pay attention to the business rules used and routing workflow steps that are involved in a process. If there are standard rules or regulations that must be considered in future procedures, gather these as well. For instance, the Internal Revenue Service and the United States Postal Service have issued rules for correctly addressing documents and mailings. Use of these guidelines should be incorporated into your standard procedures for creating new address book records within your OneWorld system. (Be aware that Postal Service and Internal Revenue guidelines actually contradict each other in at least one case.)

The current or as-is process models should be confirmed with the current process enablers, subject matter experts, and participants. To help build out process models, you need to ask a number of key questions for the business process you're evaluating:

- Can you describe the event/job/process?
- What is the desired final or end result of this event/job/process?
- How does this event/job/process task start (what is the trigger)?
- When does this event/job/process start?
- What information is required to begin or execute this step or task?
- What specific steps or tasks must be completed to achieve the end result of this event/job/process?
- In what sequence must these steps or tasks occur?
- What happens?
- Who or what completes this step or task?
- Where is this step or task done?
- How much time is consumed by this step or task?
- How does this event/job/process end?
- Who receives the results of this event/job/process?
- What information (such as reports and documents) is generated about this event/job/process?
- When is this event/job/process considered complete?
- Do any quality standards apply?
- Do any time standards apply?
- What could be done differently during this step or process (along the order of improvements or streamlining)?

This is a relatively comprehensive list of questions. You might choose to alter it by adding or omitting questions as appropriate to analyze your firm's specific business processes.

Creating Business Scenarios

Now that you have constructed all of these process models, what value do they have? Although the process models themselves represent a key deliverable of the previous stage, they also factor into the creating of many other downstream deliverables, including business scenarios, the subject of this OneWorld implementation stage.

These scenarios will become the basis for configuring and prototyping OneWorld's business functionality and in identifying any potential configuration errors, omissions, or software gaps.

A business scenario should consist of two elements—a configuration plan or script and a testing plan or script. Business scenarios are created for each major business function. For instance, procuring inventory goods is a separate business scenario from that of procuring noninventory goods or from that of procuring services. Also, portions of the business scenario might be reusable. For instance, the configuration steps might be nearly identical for the two noninventory scenarios—noninventory goods and services.

Cheat to Win: Use Templates!

Wow! All this seems like a lot of work. Is there an easier way? Well, actually, there is. Your OneWorld implementation partner typically will have already developed project plan templates, system setup, and conference room pilot script templates, as well as templates covering major business processing threads, or integration testing scenarios. These templates are invaluable as launch points during project planning. They are typically tailored to the needs of your specific organization, omitting steps or modules that are inappropriate to your operations.

If your implementation partner does not have templates available, you can still get help in this area. First, you can use the guidelines in this book to create your own templates. Second, I also make available a template set that contains many templates that you can use as-is or that you can tailor for your specific OneWorld project. Instructional documents are included with these templates. See the introduction to this book for how to obtain further information about the availability of my OneWorld project-related templates.

Summary

This chapter introduced a number of tips and techniques intended to help you build a OneWorld project plan. Much of this discussion revolved around how to identify and organize the work related to setting up or configuring OneWorld, as well as the requirements for piloting and assessing OneWorld functionality and testing the configuration.

In addition, modeling techniques were discussed that can help you build narrative and visual models of your business processes, including "as-is" and "to-be" dramatizations. Also included in this chapter was a list of key questions you will need to ask about your business processes when interviewing key process enablers, subject matter experts, and participants during the modeling and visioning effort.

PART III

Understanding OneWorld

Chapter 7

Introducing the OneWorld Explorer

This chapter introduces the basics of OneWorld navigation. If you're already comfortable with Microsoft Windows 98, Microsoft Windows Explorer, or Microsoft Internet Explorer, navigating in J. D. Edwards' OneWorld won't be a difficult transition for you. However, if you're already using J. D. Edwards' World software, or if you're using any other character-based or "green screen" ERP software package or legacy system, your first challenge will be to gain confidence with navigating OneWorld through the use of a graphical user interface.

If you need further introduction to using the Windows graphical user interface, I recommend two other books from Prima Tech: *Learn Windows 98 in a Weekend* by Mike Meadhra and Faithe Wempen and *Windows 98 Fast and Easy* by Diane Koers.

Using the J. D. Edwards' OneWorld Stand-Alone Version as a Learning Environment

Quite frankly, the best way to learn about J. D. Edwards' OneWorld navigation is through hands-on experience. Therefore, I recommend that you have the OneWorld software available to you while you read this chapter (and the next chapter as well).

This chapter assumes that you or someone in your organization has already installed the stand-alone version of J. D. Edwards' OneWorld software on your PC or one that you'll use while reviewing this chapter. If that's been accomplished, you're ready to go. Otherwise, I strongly advise that you obtain access to the OneWorld stand-alone version before proceeding with this chapter. Refer to Chapter 3 for helpful information regarding the installation of the stand-alone version of your OneWorld software.

To successfully follow this chapter, you will need to have the following information available:

- ◆ Your J. D. Edwards' OneWorld user ID. This is usually "DEMO" for the stand-alone version of J. D. Edwards' OneWorld.
- ◆ Your J. D. Edwards' OneWorld password. This is usually "DEMO" for the stand-alone version of J. D. Edwards' OneWorld.
- ◆ Your J. D. Edwards' OneWorld environment name. This is usually DEMOB73 for the stand-alone version of J. D. Edwards' OneWorld.

Your organization's OneWorld system administrator should be able to assist you by giving you this information.

Accessing J. D. Edwards' OneWorld

J. D. Edwards provides a browser or Explorer-like graphical user interface in OneWorld. This browser is called the OneWorld Explorer. However, before you can access the OneWorld Explorer, you must log into the J. D. Edwards software environment that is installed on your system. This is an important step, because unless and until you log into the license manager, no other OneWorld programs can be activated.

J. D. Edwards' OneWorld Security

Your J. D. Edwards software environment is protected in several ways from unauthorized access. The first level of protection is through a password protection scheme that requires the use of a user name or ID, a password, and an environment name. The license manager within the J. D. Edwards OneWorld software environment provides a second level of protection. Without a software protection code, which is obtained from J. D. Edwards when the OneWorld software environment is installed, the OneWorld Explorer will not operate. Other levels of security are available within OneWorld. For now, we'll stop here. Other security features of OneWorld are discussed later in this chapter, as well as in later chapters of this book.

About the Software Protection Code

If your stand-alone version of OneWorld has not been completely installed (it must be activated with the assistance of J. D. Edwards before it can be used), or if the software protection code has expired (it is time-sensitive), you will receive a software lockout message. The lockout message will prevent you from using the OneWorld Explorer and therefore all other parts of the J. D. Edwards software until a new software protection code is obtained from the J. D. Edwards response line.

Also, don't worry about your data when you receive a software protection code lockout message in the future. As long as you obtain a new software protection code from J. D. Edwards, it can be applied to OneWorld in order to reactivate your software at any time without any loss of your previously entered data. Also note that approximately 10 days prior to the expiration of the software protection code, you (and anyone else who logs onto the OneWorld software) will receive a software protection code expiration warning message. When this message appears, or immediately before, the OneWorld system administrator in your organization should contact J. D. Edwards for a new software protection code.

Starting J. D. Edwards' OneWorld

To launch or start J. D. Edwards' OneWorld, locate the J. D. Edwards' OneWorld icon on your Windows Desktop, as illustrated in Figure 7-1.

Follow these steps:

1. Position the mouse cursor over the J. D. Edwards' OneWorld Explorer icon and double-click to activate the logon process.
2. After several moments, the J. D. Edwards' OneWorld Sign On screen appears, as shown in Figure 7-2.

You are now ready to enter the password protection values that allow you to access OneWorld Explorer:

1. Position the mouse cursor in the white box (input area) next to the phrase "User ID" on the screen.
2. Type DEMO.
3. Position the mouse cursor in the input area next to the word "Password."

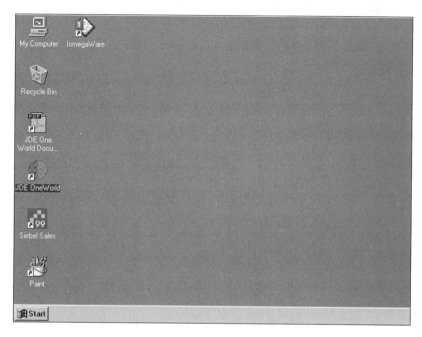

FIGURE 7-1 *The OneWorld Icon on Your Windows Desktop*

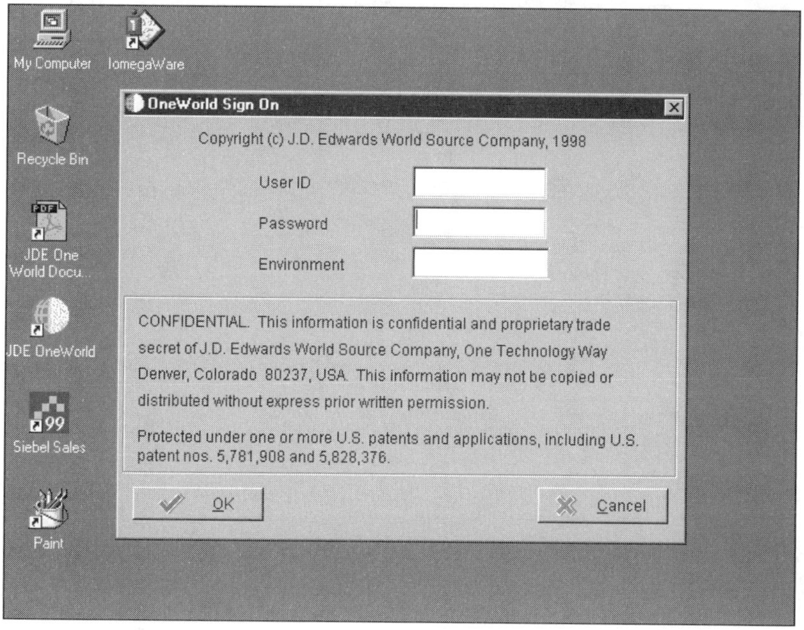

FIGURE 7-2 *The OneWorld Sign On Screen*

4. Type DEMO.

5. Position the mouse cursor in the input area next to the word "Environment."

Did you see what happened? A flashlight icon appears immediately to the right of the input box. The flashlight icon in OneWorld is called the searchlight icon. It is shown in Figure 7-3.

 NAVIGATIONAL TIP

Positioning the Cursor

You can place the screen cursor in the next field in one of two ways. The first way is to use the mouse to position the screen cursor at the beginning of the input field and click the left mouse button. The second way is to use the Tab key. When you are finished typing in the first field, press the Tab key. The cursor skips to the next input field on the screen.

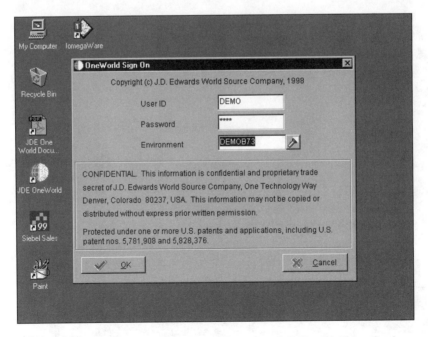

FIGURE 7-3 *The Searchlight Icon Allows You to Search for Possible Values for the Field You're Making an Entry Into*

NAVIGATIONAL TIP

Using the OneWorld Searchlight

The appearance of the searchlight icon when you position the cursor in any OneWorld input field indicates that a table of predefined values exists for the input field you are about to make an entry into. You can search the corresponding table of valid values for this field by clicking on the searchlight icon.

Let's take a look at what happens if you decide to use the searchlight search features of the OneWorld user interface:

1. Click on the searchlight.

2. After a brief pause, the Select User Environment search results window appears, as shown in Figure 7-4. Notice that a table or list of environment values is displayed in this window. This window is frequently called a "search results list." In OneWorld, a table or list of values is presented in a spreadsheet-like grid. This grid format is one of the fundamental presentation

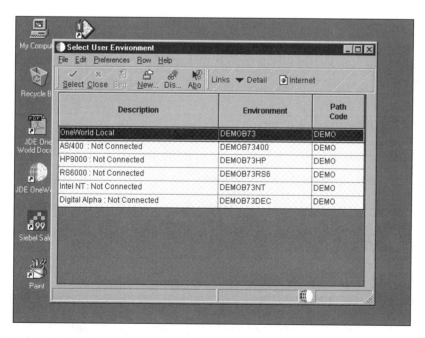

FIGURE 7-4 *The Search Results for Environment Appear as a List or Grid, Overlaying the Original Screen*

techniques used in OneWorld. Also notice that the first row of the grid is highlighted. Again, this is something that OneWorld always does.

3. Click on the grid row labeled Digital Alpha. The Digital Alpha grid row becomes highlighted.

4. Click on the grid row labeled OneWorld Local. Note that the Environment name corresponding to the One World Local is DEMOB73.

5. Click on the Select icon in the upper-left corner of the screen. The Sign On screen reappears, and the value DEMOB73 appears in the Environment entry box.

6. Click on the OK button on the bottom left of the screen.

The Sign On screen disappears. You see the OneWorld logo and copyright message on the screen for a few moments. During this brief time, password and license checking occurs, and environment variables are loaded that will be used by OneWorld Explorer. Then the moment you have been waiting for arrives! The OneWorld Explorer appears on the screen. If this doesn't happen, repeat the preceding steps. If that doesn't work, check with your OneWorld system administrator regarding your situation.

By the way, if you're wondering what an environment is in OneWorld, we'll cover that in a later chapter. For now, our mission is just to get you comfortable with navigating the OneWorld user interface, including our next topic, the OneWorld Explorer.

 NAVIGATIONAL TIP

Highlighting a Grid Row

Highlight a different grid row by clicking on that row.

 NAVIGATIONAL TIP

Selecting a Grid Row Value

Select the highlighted grid row by double-clicking on that grid row. You can also select a highlighted grid row by clicking on the Select icon in the upper-left corner of the screen. Before you perform any edit function in OneWorld, you must select a row on the grid.

A Word About Selecting Values from the Grid

OneWorld searches merely provide access to the list of entries or choices that have been preestablished for a given field in OneWorld. OneWorld validates a field against a grid table for the presence or absence of a preexisting value only.

Your OneWorld implementation team needs to define all the values for your organization that apply to this and many other grids used throughout OneWorld. Therefore, all the values they create require advanced planning and setup in your OneWorld system. This is a key part of the overall configuration or personalization of OneWorld before it can be useful to your organization. We'll discuss these configuration and personalization steps in more detail in future chapters.

Introducing the OneWorld Explorer

One of the hallmarks of OneWorld is the Explorer. The Explorer is a browser-like program that is your OneWorld command center. The Explorer controls access to all OneWorld functions, including system administration, configuring and customizing tools, development, and all application system-related menus. In addition to OneWorld system access, you can also define Internet links within the Explorer. If you're an experienced Windows user, you'll find that the OneWorld Explorer works much like the Windows 95/98 or Windows NT Explorer, which is used to find and access files and programs on the hard disk drive of your PC workstation or laptop computer. However, the Explorer has some important differences that we'll cover in this chapter and also in a future chapter.

Menus in OneWorld

OneWorld is known as a "menu-driven" system. An important aspect of OneWorld is that all system-level access is controlled through a series of menus. Presentation of menus to the OneWorld user is controlled exclusively through the OneWorld Explorer. Menus are generally set up as logical groupings of related functions within OneWorld. The highest-level menu is called the base or main system menu. In OneWorld, this base menu is called the G menu. From the G menu you can "drill down" or navigate through all of OneWorld's functions. For instance, after the stand-alone version of OneWorld has been successfully initiated, your screen should match the one shown in Figure 7-5 (which highlights the G menu).

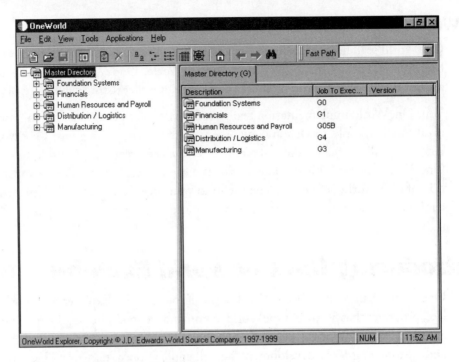

FIGURE 7-5 *The OneWorld Explorer*

Did You Get More of OneWorld Than You Paid For?

Let's say that your organization has licensed only the finance-related portions of OneWorld (Accounts Payable, Accounts Receivable, Fixed Assets, and General Ledger). As you review the G menu shown in Figure 7-5, you'll notice that you also seem to have access to both the Distribution and Manufacturing portions of OneWorld. Did J. D. Edwards err, or did you receive a windfall here? Well, maybe you did, but what you received really isn't a windfall, so some words of caution follow, especially for the adventurous.

You can activate only the portions of OneWorld that J. D. Edwards has included on the OneWorld distribution media (usually CD-ROM) in their entirety. In addition, through the technical tools within OneWorld, your system administrator can restrict access to one or more menus or to specific menu entries, which are in effect specific OneWorld programs. So although you might seemingly have access to something other than what you thought you licensed, it might not work, or, it if does work, it might work only partially.

Why Is J. D. Edwards Teasing You?

Certain OneWorld programs are shared between modules. Some examples include the Work Entry Program (Job Cost, Manufacturing, Customer Service) and the Equipment Master Screen (Equipment Billing, Fixed Assets). Therefore, a function will work properly in one portion of OneWorld, while in another portion of OneWorld, only partial functionality exists. Typically, that small shared portion of functionality is what your OneWorld license covers. For instance, sometimes enough of the functionality exists through these shared programs that you can use them to implement a specific workaround, but at other times, this will not be the case.

Menu-Level Security in OneWorld

When you first sign into OneWorld, a menu appears. The menu you see is called the initial menu. In most organizations, the initial menu that you see is determined by who you are—what your responsibilities are and what level of security or authorization you will need access in order to complete those responsibilities within OneWorld. For instance, as the credit manager in a manufacturing company, you might need access to the Sales Order Processing and to the Accounts Receivable portions of OneWorld, but you would not need access to the Inventory, Purchasing, or Manufacturing portions of OneWorld.

The OneWorld system administrator in your organization is typically responsible for identifying OneWorld access requirements and for establishing access to the portions of OneWorld needed by a given OneWorld user. Inadvertent access to portions of OneWorld by an untrained individual or unauthorized user is typically a dangerous and irresponsible business practice. Your organization will want to establish and maintain an appropriate level of access control for your OneWorld "production" system.

In addition to specifying which menus OneWorld users can access, the OneWorld system administrator also can establish the "initial" menu that any given user will encounter at the time of OneWorld sign-on. The initial menu value is maintained as part of the definition of a user to the OneWorld system. For instance, the initial menu can point to an entirely custom menu structure that is used to restrict access at the highest level possible within OneWorld.

Recall the DEMO logon that you used to access OneWorld on a stand-alone basis. It has access to almost all the functions and activities in OneWorld. This is not the typical or recommended level of security for your users.

Biology 101: Dissecting the OneWorld Explorer

As mentioned earlier, the OneWorld Explorer is the launch point for all the features of OneWorld. You'll also find that Explorer is somewhat customizable to your particular tastes. Figure 7-5 illustrates the OneWorld Explorer. If your screen does not look like Figure 7-5, you might want to check on the issue with your OneWorld system administrator. For now, however, let's start your introduction to the OneWorld Explorer by defining the various elements that appear on the Explorer screen. As you continue reading this introduction on the OneWorld Explorer, you will want to refer to Figure 7-5 as needed.

The Title Bar

We'll start at the top of the screen with the title bar. It has two sections. The left section of the title bar shows the name of the running program. For instance, when you're in Explorer, the title bar reads "OneWorld." The right section of the title bar includes buttons you can use to minimize, maximize, or close the window you're viewing. (In the case of the OneWorld Explorer window, the close button also closes your OneWorld session.)

The Menu Bar

Underneath the title bar is the menu bar. Additional Explorer program functions are performed from here. For instance, to change the appearance of the Explorer screen or to close Explorer (and your OneWorld session), you select from the entries on these menus. You can also access OneWorld help from the menu bar.

The Tool Bar

The third bar atop the OneWorld screen is the tool bar. It has two sections. On the left side are buttons or icons that represent one-click shortcuts to Explorer program functions. Many of the Explorer program functions can be performed by clicking on one of the tool bar buttons instead of selecting an entry from one of the menus on the menu bar. For instance, you can use these buttons to change the appearance of the lower-right portion of the screen, where details about OneWorld menu entries appear. If a button or icon is grayed out, that program function is disabled and is therefore unavailable for use.

The Fast Path Entry Window

To the right of the tool bar you see the Fast Path area. If you are familiar with J. D. Edwards' World software, this area represents the former command line, where menu entries were entered. If you know a particular menu number, you can enter it here. By doing so, you can bypass navigating OneWorld menus using the Explorer menu tree, which we'll review next. Later in this chapter you will learn more about how to effectively use Fast Path commands. Note that a drop-down list is available. The most recent Fast Path commands you have used are listed. This speeds access and might help you remember an obscure menu you stumbled onto.

The Menu Tree and the Menu Entry Windows

Your OneWorld screen has two major windows. These windows appear below the title, menu, and button bars we just reviewed. The left window is called the OneWorld menu tree window. The right window is called the menu entry window. You can resize these two windows by repositioning the center or dividing line between them. For instance, you might need to resize the windows to allow a greater portion of the menu titles to appear.

To resize these windows, do the following:

1. Position the cursor on the line separating the two windows.

   When correctly positioned, the arrow representing the cursor should change to the vertical resizing icon. The vertical resizing icon is two parallel vertical bars with two arrows pointing toward opposite sides of the screen.

2. Press and hold down the left mouse button. You can drag the line separating the windows to the left or right as desired. When you let up on the mouse button, the separating line locks the windows to that position.

 NAVIGATIONAL TIP

Resizing Windows in OneWorld

OneWorld windows can be resized by repositioning the line that separates windows.

Understanding the Menu Tree Window

The left window of the OneWorld Explorer screen represents a tree structure. Again, if you're familiar with Microsoft Explorer, it is akin to how your directory structure appears. Each item in the OneWorld Explorer tree structure represents OneWorld menus.

When a plus sign (+) appears next to a tree structure entry, additional branches or menus are available. To view the contents of a branch in the OneWorld menu tree structure, place the cursor on the plus sign next to the branch you're interested in exploring, and click.

 NAVIGATIONAL TIP

Go Forward Using the Plus Sign

Click on any plus sign in the OneWorld Explorer menu tree to see additional branches or menus.

When a minus sign (−) appears next to a tree structure entry, you have opened that particular branch. To close that branch, place the cursor on the minus sign and click. This closes or hides the contents of that branch from view.

 NAVIGATIONAL TIP

Go Backward Using the Minus Sign

Click on any minus sign in the OneWorld Explorer menu tree to hide lower-level branches or menus.

The menu tree allows you to surf through OneWorld. Using the menu tree, you can access all OneWorld business processes and all the tools used to configure, personalize, or customize OneWorld. Explorer is always active while you are logged into OneWorld. This means that you can switch back to Explorer as you would with any other Windows program, using the Alt and Tab keys to navigate to another menu and initiate another OneWorld process or session.

Understanding the Menu Entry Window

The right portion of the OneWorld Explorer screen shows the contents of the highlighted menu entry from the left or menu tree portion of the screen. The appearance of this portion of your Explorer screen can vary. Five formats are available to depict menu entries:

- ◆ Large Icons view
- ◆ Small Icons view
- ◆ List view
- ◆ Details view
- ◆ Web view

These views can be activated in two ways:

- ◆ By using the buttons on the Explorer button bar.
- ◆ By selecting an option from the View menu on the menu bar.

What's the Best Way to View OneWorld Menus?

During all the discussions in this book, I'll use the Details view. Why? This OneWorld view option provides the greatest amount of information about the OneWorld menu entries. For instance, if you use one of the icon views of the menu structure column, you lose important information, such as the menu number. Besides, you'll find that the icons are not really that easy to read and are not always representative of the underlying function. I've found that I'm occasionally baffled by the software engineer's choice of icon to represent a particular function. Therefore, you might want to heed this suggestion: Forget the graphics and go for the words.

 NAVIGATIONAL TIP

Use the Details View

Use the Details view for the menu entry window in OneWorld Explorer.

Let's now turn our attention to deciphering OneWorld menu entries on the Explorer screen. Notice that the first row in the menu entry window appears as a file folder tab. On this tab is the title of the menu you're currently viewing

(Master Directory (G) in Figure 7-5). When you look at the menu structure using Detail view, a second row of information appears. This information represents column labels or legends for the menu entries below.

When you see the contents of the current or selected menu on the right side of the Explorer screen, navigating OneWorld is unlike navigating in other Windows-based application software systems that rely primarily on drop-down menus (such as SAP R/3) to ultimately navigate to their underlying programs. In the OneWorld Explorer, drop-down menus are used to operate the Explorer program itself, not to navigate throughout OneWorld. It has been my experience that end-users are sometimes perplexed by the stare of a blank screen. However, sometimes a "busy-looking" screen can also be frightening to some end-users. Therefore, a happy medium is sometimes difficult to find.

The choice of OneWorld's menu structure is due in part to OneWorld's heritage. OneWorld is based on J. D. Edwards' World software. World Software was also a menu-driven system that operated exclusively on IBM AS/400 computers. Each menu in World software allowed up to 24 entries. These entries could be entry points to other menus or to actual World software application programs. As a matter of fact, OneWorld can coexist with World software. Coexistence allows a J. D. Edwards' World client to transition from the World to the OneWorld environment. With such a coexistence philosophy, it stands to reason that each system would need to share some principles of operation—and they do. The OneWorld Explorer menu navigation structure is one such example. If you happen to be a curious World software user, a more detailed discussion of coexistence appears in a later chapter.

The third row in the menu entry portion of the Explorer screen (and all subsequent rows) represents the details of each particular menu entry. Some of these menu items represent entries on other menus (as indicated by the plus signs in the menu tree), and other menu items are entries to specific OneWorld programs or *executable objects*. We'll take a detailed look at deciphering a menu entry a bit later in this chapter. For now, let's complete the discussion of the OneWorld Explorer screen.

The Status Bar

With the introduction of the status bar, we're done with our introduction to the OneWorld Explorer screen. The status bar appears at the very bottom of the OneWorld Explorer screen. The status bar has two sections. The left section contains the standard J. D. Edwards copyright notice. The right section of the status bar has three keyboard status indicators (Caps Lock, Numeric Keypad Lock, and Scroll Lock) followed by the current time (if it's set right for your computer). Note that the three keyboard status indicators are a carryover from the AS/400 environment. Virtually all modern PC keyboards have keyboard status LED indicators that render this information obsolete.

Deciphering the OneWorld Menu View

Let's take a detailed look at menu entries now, starting by attempting to decipher the quirky little icons that appear along the left side of the menu entry column. Generally speaking, the three icons shown in Figures 7-6, 7-7, and 7-8 collectively represent the three major varieties of menu entries that you will encounter in OneWorld.

FIGURE 7-6 *The Icon for Other OneWorld Menu Entries*

FIGURE 7-7 *The Icon That Invokes a OneWorld Interactive Process*

FIGURE 7-8 *The Icon That Invokes a OneWorld Background Process*

You are no doubt wondering what these odd-looking icons are supposed to represent.

The icon in Figure 7-6 represents other OneWorld menu entries. This icon looks like a small screen of icons overlaying a file folder. The icon in Figure 7-7 represents the OneWorld menu entry that invokes a OneWorld interactive process. This icon is a small OneWorld logo. The icon in Figure 7-8 represents a OneWorld menu entry that invokes a OneWorld background process. This icon is a flowcharting symbol for a report.

I guess you need to stretch your imagination a little to understand the subject of any of these icons, except possibly the last one. A colleague of mine, Charles Ban, suggests that user interfaces should be "self-navigating" and that user choices should be "self-evident." I find that OneWorld, as do so many application programs and other systems nowadays, violates the latter criteria for user-centered system interface and screen design. By the way, don't worry if you don't know what an "interactive" or "batch or background" process or program is. We'll get to that shortly. That discussion might help you understand (just a little) why these icons look like they do.

In the case of the menu we have been looking at thus far, it is called the G or home menu in OneWorld. Notice that all the other icons appearing on the G menu represent additional menus. In Figure 7-9, which illustrates menu G43A11, the mix of icons includes a shape we haven't discussed yet.

Although we reviewed only three icon shapes, there are many other icon shapes within OneWorld—but they all generally fall into one of the three definitions just provided. But don't try to make too much of OneWorld icons. Although it is true that icons in a Windows-based system are supposed to depict the action available through a pictorial representation, OneWorld program icons really aren't too useful in this regard.

If an Icon Won't Necessarily Tell You What You're About to Do, What Will?

Because icons don't tell the story, I recommend identifying OneWorld menu entries through their "Job to Execute" value. This value appears as the second column in the Details view of the Explorer screen. Again, I've described only three

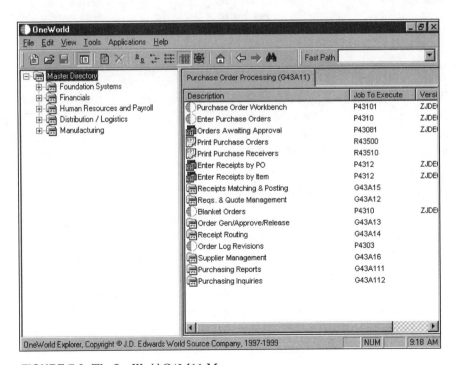

FIGURE 7-9 *The OneWorld G43A11 Menu*

icons thus far because ultimately all OneWorld menu entries fall into one of the three broad categories associated with these icons. Thus, you can conclude that all menu entries in OneWorld will perform one of the following functions:

- Execute another menu
- Execute an interactive process or program
- Execute a batch process or program

Values in the Job to Execute column in Figure 7-9 provide some further guidance.

The "Value to Execute" Column

The first letter in a Job to Execute value represents the highest level of naming conventions used throughout OneWorld. The following list describes the first character of the Job to Execute value:

G This menu entry refers to another menu.

P This menu entry refers to an interactive program.

R This menu entry refers to a batch process program.

There is some additional significance to these menu entry names. It is identified in the object-naming conventions used by J. D. Edwards for OneWorld. A naming convention is a common format for or method of naming related groups of executable objects, such as interactive processes or batch processes. Files or tables containing master and transaction data also follow a standard naming convention. For instance, all elements related to Procurement (Purchasing) in OneWorld begin with 43. A future chapter clarifies naming conventions for the major OneWorld objects you'll encounter.

 NAVIGATIONAL TIP

Know Your Menu Entry Conventions

Names of OneWorld interactive processes begin with P.

Names of OneWorld batch processes begin with R.

Names of OneWorld menus begin with G.

Navigating Using OneWorld Menus

The navigation of OneWorld relies heavily on the use of menu numbers. Therefore, menu numbers can be considered a fundamental OneWorld building block. This section discusses OneWorld navigation using menus. It also covers the consequences of selecting a menu option.

Selecting and Executing Menu Entries

It has been a long time coming, but now we are ready to talk about understanding and using the OneWorld menu entries. First, let's look at how to select menu entries. To highlight a menu entry, position the cursor on the entry and click. To select the highlighted menu entry, click on it again. A menu entry can also be highlighted and selected in a single action or step. This dual-action step is done by positioning the cursor over the menu entry and double-clicking.

What Happens When a Menu Entry Is Selected?

You know that OneWorld is a menu-driven system that relies on a series of executable programs or objects that are selected from menus. These menu entries invoke or call upon another executable object or program to perform a function. In OneWorld, a menu entry represents a call to one of three types of executables:

◆ Menus
◆ Interactive executable objects
◆ Background executable objects

What Is a OneWorld Interactive Process?

An interactive process is one that you work with using the screen. For instance, an interactive process might be the program that allows you to enter customer information into the OneWorld database. Another might be the OneWorld program that allows you to inquire about the status of a previously entered order for a customer. Virtually all OneWorld processes begin from a "Work With" program. More information is provided about Work With programs in the next chapter.

What Is a OneWorld Batch Process?

OneWorld also has functions that are executed or performed as batch processes that you initiate through an interactive screen, but the actual processing occurs in the background on your server while you attend to other matters. Examples of batch processes might include the printing of purchase orders that have been created in OneWorld today or the creating of billings in OneWorld Accounts Receivable for customer orders that shipping confirmation occurred on today. (Generally speaking, the term *batch process* is used throughout this book instead of *background process*.)

The OneWorld Universal Batch Engine

The OneWorld batch or background process is sometimes called a Universal Batch Engine (UBE). The easiest way that I can describe what the universal batch engine does is that conceptually it allows OneWorld to run programs in a sequential order. For example, this helps ensure that invoices are printed before orders are closed. The sequence of background processing is very important in an integrated package such as OneWorld.

Menu Numbers

Menu numbers are important for a number of reasons. First of all, your J. D. Edwards' OneWorld documentation and likely most of the internal procedures you write will favor providing menu paths rather than menu names.

Second, having a menu number handy means you don't have to fumble through the menu structure to find a menu. As you might recall from our earlier discussions, if you know a menu number, you can save time by typing that menu number as a Fast Path command. This can save you several steps, especially if you are on the telephone trying to resolve a customer inquiry expeditiously. Also, fewer clicks can be important, especially for remote users connected over phone lines.

Third, if you are having difficulties using OneWorld, your internal help desk as well as the J. D. Edwards response line personnel will want to know specifically what version of a menu you're using.

Menu Naming Conventions

In OneWorld, virtually all menus provided by J. D. Edwards begin with the letter G and are generally followed by a series of numbers and letters. These trailing numbers and letters have significance within J. D. Edwards. For instance, menu G4 provides access to Distribution and Logistics system functions. Within Distribution and Logistics, menu G43 accesses OneWorld Procurement, menu G42 represents Sales Order Management, and G41 represents Inventory Management. Table 7-1 lists the high-level menus available within OneWorld.

Table 7-1 OneWorld System-Level Menu Numbers

Software Function	Menu Number
Main Menu	G
Financials	G1
Address Book	G010
Accounts Receivable	03B
Accounts Payable	G04
Fixed Assets	G12
General Accounting	G09
Profit Management	G16
Job Cost	G51
Human Resources/Payroll	G05B
Human Resources	G05B1
Payroll Processing	G07BUSP
Distribution/Logistics	G4
Inventory Management	G41
Sales Order Management	G42
Procurement	G43
Warehouse Management	G46
Material Planning	G34
Electronic Commerce	G47
Transportation Management	G49
Agreement Management	G38
Manufacturing	G3
Product Data Management	G30

Table 7-1 OneWorld System-Level Menu Numbers *(continued)*

Software Function	Menu Number
Shop Floor Management	G31
Configurator	G320
Resource and Capacity Planning	G33
Material Planning	G34
Forecasting	G36
Plant and Equipment Management	G13
Work Order/Service Billing	G48
Quality Management	G370
Customer Service Management	G17

There is some additional significance to these menu entry names. When you are in a given part of the system through the use of one of these menus, such as Accounts Payable, you'll notice that the next menu levels are labeled as shown in Table 7-2.

Table 7-2 OneWorld Accounts Payable Menus

Software Function	Menu Number
Daily Processing	G0410
Periodic Processing	G0420
Advanced and Technical Operations	G0430
System Setup	G0441

This format is carried throughout most of the other business functions within OneWorld. There are some exceptions. For instance, Procurement (G43) and Customer Service Management (G17) add additional levels of menus that are related to specific types of business events or processes, as shown in Table 7-3.

Table 7-3 Contract Management Menus

Software Function	Menu Number
Installed Base Management	G1701
Service Contract Management	G1702
Call Management	G1703
Service Order Management	G1704
Customer Service Setup	G1740
Stock-Based	G43A
Non-Stock-Based	G43B
Services/Expenditure-Based	G43C
Subcontract-Based	G43D

As you can sense from these discussions, menu-naming conventions can vary within OneWorld. Sometimes menus are grouped logically and you can guess which menu number you need for a specific function after you become comfortable with OneWorld. Other times, it's a bit more complicated than that. In a future chapter, I'll cover how related groups of executable objects such as interactive processes, batch processes, and files or tables containing transaction data are similarly identified.

Menu Names and Fast Paths

Perhaps the most important reason for discussing how to identify a menu number or why you would want to use the Details view of Explorer is the important navigational role that a menu number plays in OneWorld. Simply put, the OneWorld menu number is the meat of the Fast Path command.

What Is a Fast Path?

The Fast Path command line allows you to circumvent the normal menu path to any OneWorld menu. The Fast Path technique is also called *menu traveling*.

How to Fast Path

1. In order to Fast Path, you first need the OneWorld menu number. If you don't know the menu number you need to use, some of the OneWorld documentation includes quick reference charts that include menu num-

bers. You'll also find quick reference charts in the later chapters of this book that provide overviews of each OneWorld application suite. Also, you'll likely want to create quick reference charts of your commonly used OneWorld menus and functions. We'll discuss this topic later in this chapter. For now, let's look at an example of how to Fast Path. Refer to Figure 7-10 for guidance with this example.

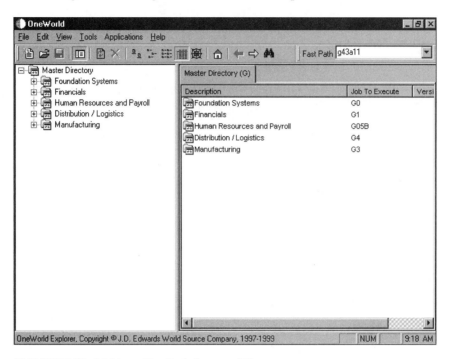

FIGURE 7-10 *Making a Fast Path Command Entry*

2. Locate the Fast Path command box on the OneWorld screen.

3. Enter the menu number you want to go to. For this example, use g43a11.

NOTE

Note that the Fast Path command entry box is not case-sensitive. Therefore, you don't need to enter the Fast Path command value as all capital letters.

4. Click, or press the Enter key.

The menu G43A11 should now appear on the screen.

NAVIGATIONAL TIP

Use Fast Path Commands

Enter any OneWorld menu number in the Fast Path command entry box on the Explorer screen to quickly access any OneWorld menu without following the standard menu path.

How to Go Back

If you get "lost" in OneWorld, it's easy to return "home." In OneWorld, your home is the base or initial menu you saw when you logged into OneWorld. Refer to Figure 7-10. On the toolbar is a button with a house. In OneWorld, this is called the Home button. See Figure 7-11.

FIGURE 7-11
*The OneWorld
Home Button*

For the DEMO user ID that is used with the OneWorld stand-alone version, this will be the G menu (refer to Figure 7-5). However, do not forget that this value might be set differently by your organization's OneWorld system administrator.

 NAVIGATIONAL TIP

Use the Home Button

Return to the initial OneWorld menu that appears when you log onto OneWorld by clicking on the Home button on the OneWorld Explorer toolbar.

Training Best Practices and Menu Paths

Here are two final comments on menu numbers. First, it is recommended that your organization make use of menu paths, using menu numbers, for training materials and all other internal documentation. The following format is typically used to represent a menu path:

> Base (home) menu > menu number > **submenu number** > menu option (entry) name to be executed

Note that the submenu number representing the Fast Path menu number is typically bold for emphasis and quick reference in any given menu path. Second, prepare and provide quick reference cards or "cheat sheets" with menu paths to your end-users during training. These can be laminated one- or two-sided cards. Some other ideas are to print frequently used menu paths on a mouse pad (a better idea). Or (the best idea), if you use a mouse pad that has a lift-up clear plastic surface, the card containing this information can be inserted under the lift-up surface.

 NAVIGATIONAL TIP

Prepare Menu Quick References

Provide quick references (by business function or focus) to end-users, indicating menu paths with the Fast Path menu number highlighted.

Helping End-Users Learn Through the Use of Humor

I have effectively used two parodies during my end-user training classes. The first is "Show me the menu path," which is based on the 1996 movie *Jerry Maguire* and its famous line "Show me the money." The other line I have used effectively (also unoriginal) came from a SAP (those "other" guys) training class I attended several years ago. SAP instructor Jeff Dahl introduced me to the phrase "Cheat to win," and it has been a staple in my vocabulary ever since. I use "cheat to win" as a way of introducing quick-reference materials and the Fast Path commands in OneWorld.

Also, while we're on this subject, it's always a good idea to make use of humor, but don't overdo it. Training is not a laughing matter, so be careful in your use of classroom humor. Its sole purpose is to regenerate the audience's interest level (or to "wake up" the class every so often). Training is not as simple as it seems; not everyone can pull it off. Choose your trainers wisely. If you don't have the right people, or if they're uncomfortable with training, call on professionals for assistance.

Creating Your Own Menus

J. D. Edwards provides tools in OneWorld that you can use to create your own menus or change standard OneWorld menus. Such changes can be made to OneWorld without any programming. When created correctly, your custom menus will be preserved when you upgrade to a later version of OneWorld. However, changes you make to the standard OneWorld menus will not necessarily be preserved. As a matter of practice, you should always copy standard OneWorld menus and create new menus with similar names. In a later chapter, I will cover how your custom menus should be named, as well as the processes for creating custom menus and changing existing menus.

OneWorld Versus World Menus

If you use J. D. Edwards' World software in your organization, I have some good news. You are already familiar with OneWorld menus! J. D. Edwards has used common menu-naming conventions so that functions are identical between OneWorld software and World software. But there is one point you should be aware of, especially if you have written documentation that refers to option numbers on specific World software menus. In World software, menu options or entries are numbered. However, in OneWorld, menu entries are *not numbered; only the menu option's one-line description appears.*

Closing OneWorld

You can close your OneWorld session in one of two ways. The first technique is to click the cancel/close button in the upper-right corner of the title bar. The second technique is to use a menu. From the menu bar, choose File, Exit.

When you are done using OneWorld, it is important to correctly close or log off the software. This includes closing any and all windows that you opened or launched while using OneWorld. OneWorld will not shut down until all open windows are closed. For instance, if you are attempting to exit OneWorld and you see the error message shown in Figure 7-12, you have open windows that must be closed before you can exit the OneWorld application.

You can check for open OneWorld windows by pressing the Alt and Tab keys simultaneously. Select each open OneWorld window, close any open processes, and ultimately close OneWorld.

 NAVIGATIONAL TIP

Close All Open Windows to Exit OneWorld

You might have created multiple OneWorld windows during your current session. All windows must be closed before you can close OneWorld.

Advanced Topics

Several Explorer-related topics have been omitted from the discussion. Some other OneWorld Explorer features allow you to do the following:

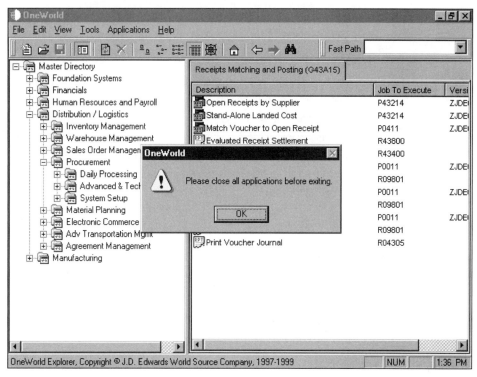

FIGURE 7-12 *A Reminder to Close All Open Windows Before Exiting OneWorld*

◆ Search for menus, by words and phrases or portions of words

◆ Create tabs and then put content references on them

◆ Create shortcuts for OneWorld menus and programs and then add them to your Windows desktop

I have not seen frequent use of these features at my OneWorld clients. Most folks seem to stick with the basics. When you're first learning OneWorld, that is sage advice. Focus on expanding your knowledge of using the software the long way, and then work your way up to these shortcuts to use OneWorld smartly and efficiently.

Should Your Organization Use Fast Paths and Menu Searches?

Every organization must decide whether using the Fast Path menu entry is valuable and does not pose any unnecessary security risks. Understand that although you can control the user's use of Fast Paths, you can't control which Fast Path menu numbers are entered. Therefore, Fast Path has some risks, but none that can't be effectively reduced through the use of menu-level security.

As for menu word searches, they're great for the project team members. You can use them to "explore" or "mine" sections of OneWorld functionality that you're unfamiliar with. However, these searches do not replace proper training and documentation of end user-performed tasks in OneWorld. Simply put, I have found that menu searches often lead to end-user confusion rather than end-user navigational help. Therefore, my recommendation is simple: Don't go there for end-users, just for the project team!

Summary

Although this was a relatively short chapter, we covered an important topic—getting some hands-on experience accessing and navigating within OneWorld. As was stressed in this chapter, from this point forward, get as much hands-on exposure to OneWorld as you can to really learn the material. The availability of the OneWorld stand-alone version as you're reading is helpful in providing a true hands-on learning experience for you.

Here are the major topics that were covered in this chapter:

- How to log on to J. D. Edwards' OneWorld
- How to navigate in OneWorld using the OneWorld Explorer and OneWorld menus
- The three types of OneWorld menu entries
- How menu numbers can be used as Fast Path commands to "menu travel" within OneWorld
- How to log out of J. D. Edwards' OneWorld

The next chapter covers OneWorld program functionality in depth. You'll find a thorough introduction to several types of OneWorld interactive programs, including Work With, Header, Detail, and Tab Entry panels. You'll also learn about the fantastic OneWorld data grid.

Chapter 8

Getting Comfortable with OneWorld

This chapter provides further information about the look and feel of OneWorld. As you will recall from the preceding chapter, the OneWorld Explorer is used to navigate menus from which any of the various OneWorld programs are activated. Also note that OneWorld programs are frequently called *executable objects* or simply *executables*.

The specific types of OneWorld programs covered in this chapter and the next are called *interactive* programs. The OneWorld documentation provided by J. D. Edwards calls interactive programs *forms*. You will find that these terms are used interchangeably. A key aspect of OneWorld interactive programs or forms is the *user interface*. Therefore, much of this chapter focuses on introducing the OneWorld user interface.

OneWorld Software Architecture

Perhaps, one day after using the OneWorld sales order entry program for awhile, you find yourself "lost" in another portion of OneWorld. The accidental path you have taken leads you to an interesting discovery. You have accidentally stumbled into the purchase order entry program. You notice that the purchase order entry program looks remarkably like the sales order entry program you use daily. However, this fact about OneWorld isn't accidental—it's deliberate. It is an important characteristic of the OneWorld software architecture.

A key component that contributes to OneWorld's overall usability is its software architecture. The software engineers at J. D. Edwards have "architected" a common look and feel for the various OneWorld interactive programs you will use. In fact, these same software engineers started creating OneWorld by first creating a "toolbox" or "tool set" containing programs that could in turn be used to create other programs based on predefined *model programs* or *templates*. In the industry, this technique is called computer-aided software engineering (CASE). The OneWorld CASE tool is the subject of a later chapter.

For now, however, much of the discussion in both this chapter and the next will focus on explaining what functions these various types of OneWorld model programs perform and how they actually work. Understanding the look and feel as well as the user interface aspects of these model programs will in turn lead to a general understanding of how virtually all other OneWorld programs work. Therefore, much of the discussion in this chapter sets the stage for you to be able to navigate within almost any form you will encounter in OneWorld.

OneWorld Program Models

This chapter introduces the Work With program. This program is also called the Find and Browse Form in the OneWorld documentation. Ever practical, I prefer to use the term Work With to describe these programs because that's what they are called on the form when in use. The next chapter introduces the other members of the family of interactive programs that are common throughout OneWorld.

However, before beginning your introduction to any specific OneWorld program, you should note that OneWorld programs include some basic features that are common to most Windows GUI-style programs, such as drop-down menus and program functions that are activated when you click on a related button. So if you are used to working with a Microsoft Windows-based program such as Word or Excel, you should find the transition to OneWorld easy.

The Work With Program

One of the most prevalent interactive program types that you will encounter in OneWorld is the Work With program. It is the standard *front-end* or *gateway* form for virtually all OneWorld transaction processing and master file maintenance functions. It is from this program that existing transaction or master file records, such as those in the Address Book, can be searched. It is also from this program that a new transaction or record can be created or that an existing transaction or record can be updated.

The Address Book

The Address Book is the collective set of master data files where the names and addresses of your organization's customers, suppliers, employees, and physical locations are stored in OneWorld. Creation of Address Book records is therefore one of the most basic tasks you will perform during the startup and ongoing use of OneWorld within your organization. It is for this reason that Address Book-related programs and forms are used for many of the examples in this chapter.

Following Along in OneWorld

If you want to test the contents of this chapter, as with the previous chapter, you need hands-on access to the OneWorld stand-alone version. Therefore, if you will follow along online, first make sure you're signed onto the OneWorld stand-alone version. If you have forgotten any of the details of signing onto OneWorld, refer to the previous chapter.

Reviewing the Address Book Work With Form

To activate the Address Book Work With form, you need use the OneWorld Explorer to navigate to the proper menu. Here is the menu path you should follow:

> Master Directory (G), Foundation Systems (G0), Address Book (G010), Daily Processing (**G01**), Address Book Revisions (P01012)

If you follow this menu path correctly, your form should look like the one shown in Figure 8-1.

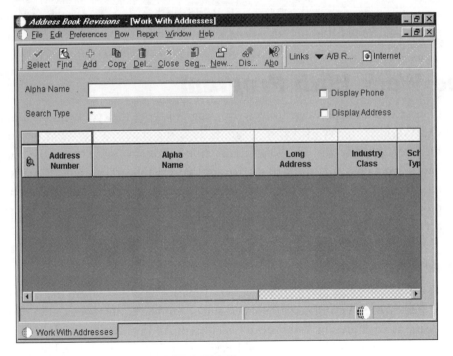

FIGURE 8-1 *The Address Book Work With Form*

NAVIGATIONAL TIP

Describing OneWorld Menu Paths

Menu paths in this book follow these conventions:

- Menu paths appear on a separate line. The menu name is first, followed by the menu number, which appears in parentheses.

- The Fast Path menu number is bold.

- The name of the menu option to be selected is the last entry in the menu path description. A program number appears in parentheses immediately following the menu option name.

Using the Work With Program

As mentioned earlier, OneWorld programs include some basic features that are common to most Windows GUI-style programs, such as drop-down menus and program functions that are activated when you click on an icon. For instance, much like any other Windows-like drop-down menu, when an option is "grayed out" or "ghosted" on a OneWorld program drop-down menu, it can't be selected. Therefore, if you are used to the look and feel of most Windows-based programs, you will find that OneWorld does not differ dramatically from what you might be accustomed to.

Like the OneWorld Explorer form, the Work With form is partitioned into common areas that always appear on every Work With form in OneWorld. The following sections describe how the OneWorld Work With form is partitioned. Refer to Figure 8-1 while reviewing the following information.

The Title Bar

The top line of the Work With form is called the title bar. It always contains two pieces of information. The first is the menu option title or description, which is italic, and the second is the program title, which appears in brackets.

The Menu Bar

The second line on the form is the drop-down menu bar. Actually, most of the frequently used OneWorld Work With functions are represented by buttons, which appear on the third line of the Work With form. Therefore, on a daily basis, the drop-down menus will not be used as frequently as they are in other types of OneWorld programs. In other OneWorld program forms, you will see that drop-down menus are extremely important, because they are used to initiate many follow-up functions and activities within a transaction. Like any other event-driven Windows-style program, the menu bar options can be used at any time to activate a program function.

The Button Bar

The third line of the Work With form is the button bar. This line contains a row of buttons that are used to activate a Work With program function. These program functions are associated with selected items from the Data Grid or Search Information form areas. For instance, to add an Address Book record, you would click on the + (plus sign) or Add button. To find a name that contains "ALLEN," you would type ALLEN into the Alpha Name field on the form and then click on the Find button. The following sections discuss the Search Information and Data Grid areas of the form in more detail.

The Search Information Area

The next common area found in all Work With forms is the Search Information area, which is the gray area immediately below the row of buttons. Although all Work With forms have a Search Information portion, the contents of this form vary from program to program. In OneWorld documentation, these fields are called *filter* fields. This book uses the term Search Information.

In Figure 8-1, the Address Book Work With form contains two entry fields, Alpha Name and Search Type, and two check boxes, Display Phone and Display Address. However, the Journal Entry Work With form, shown in Figure 8-2, shows a completely different set of fields in the Search Information area, including entry fields for Batch Number and Batch Type and check boxes for Models and Summarize.

How Searches Work

Typically, a meaningful field related to the underlying data is raised to (appears in) the Search Information portion of the form. These meaningful fields are frequently called *key* or *index* fields in database terms. Simply put, these meaningful

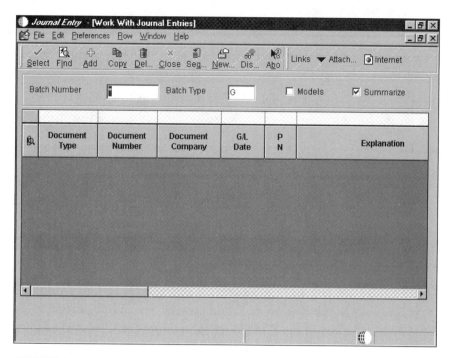

FIGURE 8-2 *The Journal Entry Work With Form*

fields are used to catalog, index, or organize information for you within OneWorld data files. Without indices, finding information (or data, as it is more frequently called in computing circles) is difficult and time-consuming, both for you and for your computer system. Imagine finding someone's address or phone number in a telephone directory that is not alphabetized by name.

Generally speaking, here are the most common ways to find transaction or master data in OneWorld:

◆ Using a document or batch number, such as a sales order or purchase order number

◆ Using an Address Book number, such as a customer or supplier (vendor) number

◆ Using an alpha name or description, using names or portions of names, such as "ALLEN" or "BIKE"

Table 8-1 lists some examples of the key fields that are used by various Work With forms to search against OneWorld data files.

Table 8-1 Work With Forms and Key Search Fields

Work With Form	Key Fields
Addresses	Alpha Name, Search Type
Items	Item Number, Description
Sales Orders	Sales Order Number, Customer (Sold To) Number
Purchase Orders	Purchase Order Number, Supplier Number
Work Orders	Work Order Number
Journal Entries	Batch Number, Batch Type
Voucher Entries	Supplier Number, Document Status
Cash Receipt Entries	Payor Number, Document Status

Actually, there are two ways to search for information in OneWorld. Thus far, you've only learned about how OneWorld uses the Search Information fields found in the middle portion of the Work With form. However, OneWorld also provides extended search capabilities using the Data Grid's Query by Example (QBE) feature. The Data Grid and its QBE feature are discussed in the next sections.

The Data Grid

If you are familiar with Microsoft Excel, you are well along in understanding how the OneWorld Data Grid functions. The Data Grid is perhaps the defining feature of OneWorld graphical user interface capabilities. The Data Grid occupies the lower portion of the Work With form. Also note that several other OneWorld interactive program models make use of a Data Grid. Therefore, all of the following information regarding how the Data Grid works also applies to the Data Grids found in the other program models.

The OneWorld Data Grid consists of these key elements:

◆ The Query By Example row. This is the first row of the Data Grid.

◆ The column name row. Column names are frequently also called field names. This is the second row of the Data Grid.

◆ The data row area. Initially, this area is blank.

◆ The horizontal (left to right) slider bar.

◆ The vertical (up and down) slider bar. The vertical slider bar does not appear on the grid initially. It shows up as soon as the Find button is clicked and data is loaded into the form. The appearance of the vertical slider indicates that the number of data rows exceeds the number of rows that can appear on the Data Grid form at one time.

How the Data Grid Works

As just mentioned, when the Work With form is initially displayed, the data row area of the Data Grid is always blank. The Data Grid is populated only after you initiate a search for records. When the grid remains blank after a search is completed, it is for one of two reasons:

◆ The search criterion was incorrect.

◆ The transaction or data file is empty.

Recall that the Work With form provides two ways to initiate searches. We've discussed how Search Information and key fields are used. The Data Grid also provides additional search capabilities. The first row of the Data Grid, which initially appears as the empty yellow row above the column name row, is called the Query by Example (QBE) line.

Also note that on some Work With forms, one or more entry fields in the QBE row might be gray. When any entry field is grayed out, it is considered a *protected* or *display-only* field for which data entry is not possible. These fields are usually values that are brought into the form through a reference to another file. For instance, on the Order Header Inquiry form, the underlying sales order header file contains only an Address Book number, not the actual name of the customer or supplier. By not copying the alpha name to every order header, table size is reduced, and searches against the database can be performed more effectively. However, before a name can be displayed, it must be retrieved from another table—the Address Book. Therefore, a *join* operation is performed between the order header and Address Book tables on the Address Book number in order to determine the customer or supplier alpha name appearing on the form. As you can tell from this example, OneWorld must perform many "behind-the-scenes" activities to populate a form with data from many different tables.

 NAVIGATIONAL TIP

Identifying Protected Fields in OneWorld

When any OneWorld entry field is grayed out, it is considered a protected or display-only field for which data entry is not possible.

Data Grid Columns

Much like Microsoft Excel, the Data Grid displays all the fields contained in a selected OneWorld data file as *columns,* from left to right, along the Data Grid. When a row of data is displayed, some of the data columns for a given row of data might be blank. This is a typical and perfectly normal situation. Depending on how OneWorld has been configured, each OneWorld data or transaction entry program performs a check or validation of required fields. When a field is not required, an entry into a field is optional. Note that since many of the fields in OneWorld are driven by validation tables called user-defined codes, this usually means that a blank code exists within the user-defined code table used to populate a given field. Therefore, "blanks" will serve as the default value.

Why Are Some Fields Optional in OneWorld?   OneWorld data files typically have dozens of fields. Every OneWorld client uses the OneWorld data model to a varying degree, either by the number of OneWorld functions used or by the sophistication of a given organization's needs. This is one of the more pervasive features available in OneWorld and is frequently mentioned by J. D. Edwards in its sales presentations.

For instance, certain fields might pertain only to manufacturing-related information on a sales order line. However, suppose your organization is a distribution company that doesn't use the OneWorld manufacturing functionality. Manufacturing-related fields are therefore typically left blank in any given sales order line in your organization's OneWorld order detail file.

On the other hand, some organizations have specialized reporting requirements and might require entries into user-defined fields that are generally available in every major OneWorld transaction or master data file. In these cases, your transactions or data rows will have information in them that might be left blank by another organization that uses OneWorld.

Data Grid Rows

Individual data records from any given OneWorld file appear as rows in the Data Grid of the Work With form. For other OneWorld forms, such as an Order Detail form, each row on the form typically represents one line associated with a given order.

Data Grid rows are typically sorted or sequenced in some kind of order, such as item number, address number, document number, or order line number. The sequence of data rows can be rearranged as well. Details regarding the rearranging or sorting of rows appearing in a Data Grid are provided later.

Personalizing the Data Grid

Of particular note is the ability to "personalize" the appearance of the OneWorld Data Grid. Much like Microsoft Excel, the OneWorld user can control both the sizing and location of Data Grid columns. These personalized grid columns can then be saved. This is a great feature for transaction entry purposes. Frequently used fields can be shifted left on the grid, in view of the data entry operator, and lesser-used fields can be shifted right. Such personalization can increase the usability of OneWorld and promotes the productivity and efficiency of an organization's data entry operators.

Recall from an earlier discussion that there are dozens of fields in a typical OneWorld data file. It is not uncommon for many of these fields to be either optional or unused in your organization. Therefore, these fields are excellent candidates to be shifted "out of sight and out of mind" of the data entry operator. This is another pervasive feature of OneWorld and is frequently highlighted by J. D. Edwards in its sales presentations.

Working with the Data Grid

By now you've read enough about the Data Grid and are likely ready for some examples of how it works. Again, the Address Book "Work With" program is used in this example.

Populating the Grid with Data

Recall that your first step will generally be to search the data file, which is attached to the Work With form. In this case, it is the Address Book search file.

1. Click on the white box next to Alpha Name. This step properly positions the cursor on the form for data entry purposes.

2. Type in the name ALLEN, allen, or Allen in the Alpha Name field. Note that any combination of uppercase and lowercase characters can be used.

3. Click on the Find button.

Figure 8-3 shows the results of this search.

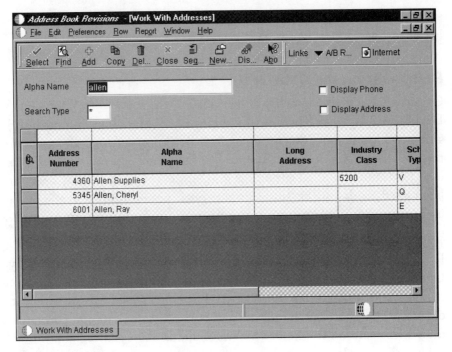

FIGURE 8-3 *The Successful Address Book Search*

Error Messages in OneWorld

If your search is unsuccessful (for instance, if you pressed the Enter key instead of clicking on the Find button), you see an error message in the lower-left portion of the screen, as shown in Figure 8-4.

Sometimes more than one error occurs when you're working with OneWorld programs. How would you know that? Notice in the bottom-right portion of the screen that a message appears, indicating the number of errors and other warnings that occurred.

So now that you know how many errors occurred, how do you find out why they occurred? In the button bar, notice the button that has eyeglasses overlaying a stop sign. This is the Display Errors button. When you click on it, the additional error messages appear in a list box that replaces the bottom portion of the Data Grid, as shown in Figure 8-5. In many cases there are multiple entry points, or ways to activate OneWorld program actions. For instance, another way to review error messages is by double-clicking on the stop sign in the right corner of the status

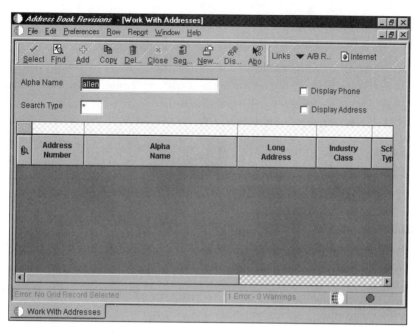

FIGURE 8-4 *An Unsuccessful Address Book Search*

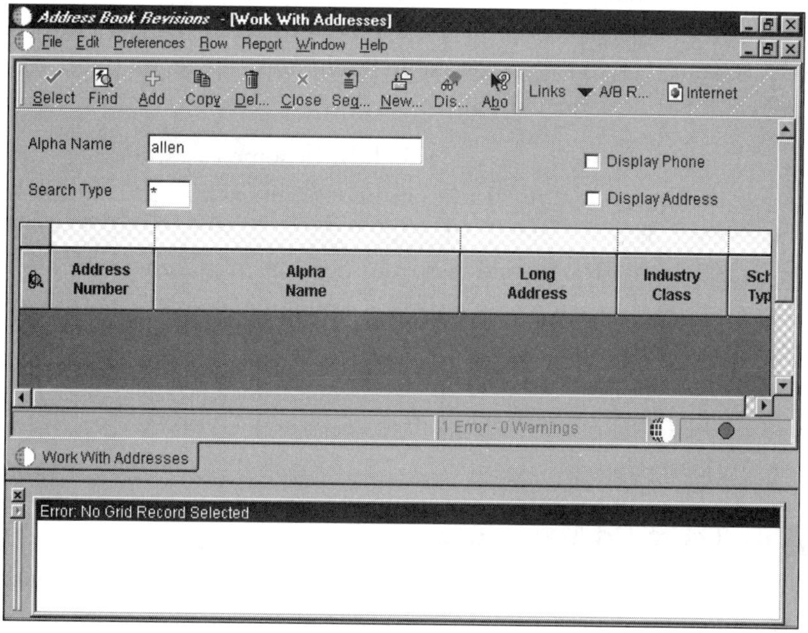

FIGURE 8-5 *The Display Errors List Box*

row along the bottom of the window. Also, the menu bar has a Help, Display Errors option that will access and display any program-related error messages.

You can get additional information about an error message by double-clicking on the error message line. This opens a second window containing additional error-related information or possible corrective actions.

After you have reviewed the errors, you can close or minimize the Display Errors List Box by clicking on the cancel button (the button with an X in the upper-left corner of the Display Errors list box. The next section provides further information about errors in OneWorld.

Errors Versus Warnings

OneWorld programs can issue both warning messages and error messages. What's the difference? Warnings are less severe than errors.

A warning is also called a *soft* error. Warnings are yellow and are further identified by the yield sign. You can generally clear or bypass a warning by pressing the Enter key or by clicking on the transaction-related button you previously clicked on (such as the check mark, Select button, or OK button).

Error messages are red and are further identified by a stop sign. When a transaction or form contains an error, it is usually a field-related error. An error is considered *hard* and stops you from completing a specific transaction (until, of course, the error condition is corrected).

You should not take warning messages lightly. In some cases, these messages are intended to prevent you from taking an undesirable action in connection with your OneWorld data without further thoughtful consideration. For example, posting an accounting transaction to a prior period is something you might need to do from time to time but would not do as a matter of course. Arguably, the case can be made for making hard errors instead of soft errors in these cases. OneWorld System constants and processing options, which you'll learn more about in a future chapter, are used to control certain conditions as soft errors or warnings versus a hard error.

Why Are There So Many Errors?

No doubt as a new OneWorld user, you will grow accustomed to seeing and responding to error messages. However, do not be frustrated by them. Sometimes trial and error is the best way to learn a new system and to ensure its proper configuration. As long as this is done in a nonproduction environment, such as in the stand-alone version, there is minimal risk.

OneWorld Errors can be cryptic in that they frequently provide little information or information that is (in my opinion) meaningful only to an experienced systems person. Over time, you will become familiar with the common error messages and the corrective actions to clear them. As you prepare to train others in how to use OneWorld, prepare a list of common error messages and their corrective actions.

Correcting Errors

Here's a practical strategy for dealing with OneWorld errors. First, when an error occurs, always check the data. Often the error is in the data entry, such as a typo or a missing entry field. Second, check your understanding of how a program should work. Use the OneWorld reference guides or online help (discussed later in this chapter) for such purposes. Finally, if neither of these steps corrects the situation, review the system configuration.

When errors are repeated or always present, system configuration is usually the problem. If the system configuration is not at fault, it is possible that your OneWorld environment has an error or that the OneWorld program has a bug in it. (A *bug* is programming lingo for an error in the program itself.) These kinds of problems typically require a call to the J. D. Edwards response line and the involvement of your OneWorld system administrator for assistance in resolving them.

Using the Query by Example Row on the Data Grid

As mentioned, an alternative way to populate the Data Grid is to use the Query by Example (QBE) row. Any field that is "unprotected" (not grayed out) in the QBE row can be used as the basis for selecting data and populating the Work With form. For instance, to perform an Alpha Name search using the QBE line, do the following:

1. Position the cursor in the Alpha Name entry field in the QBE row.
2. Type Allen*.
3. Click on the Find button.

The results of the QBE search are shown in Figure 8-6. The asterisk (*) you entered as a part of the Alpha Name is called a *wildcard* character. A *wildcard* character replaces one or more characters in a string of text when a search is performed.

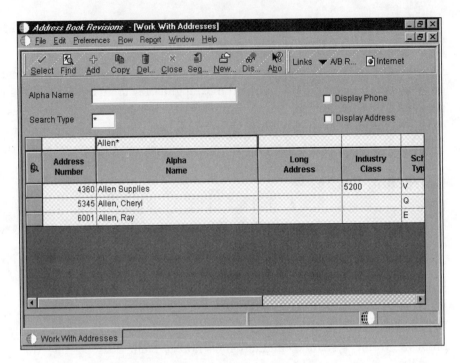

FIGURE 8-6 *The Results of the QBE Address Book Search*

Equality Operators

You can "condition" a QBE search by using the less than (<), greater than (>), and not equal to (<>) operators. The equality (=) operator is always implied for a QBE line entry. For instance, a typical customer service query might be "Show all sales orders to be delivered after 7/1/05." In this case, you would type >07/01/05 in the Request Date field on the QBE line and then click on Find. If you wanted to review all orders for Capital System (customer 4242), you would simply enter 4242 in the Sold To field on the QBE line and then click on Find. The equality operator is implied. If you wanted to review all orders to be shipped on or before 06/30/05, you would enter <=06/30/05 in the Request Date field on the QBE line and then click on Find.

Compound Searches

A QBE search can also have compound search criteria. This means that you can enter search values for more than one field. For instance, a typical customer service query might look like this:

Show all sales orders against any branch/plant location, for customer 4242, (Capital System), to be delivered after 7/1/05.

For each additional field that you specify when entering compound search criteria, the "and" relationship is implied between the conditions. An illustration should help here. Although you might not be familiar with the Customer Service Inquiry in OneWorld, Figure 8-7 illustrates how the preceding "search script" would be set up on that particular form.

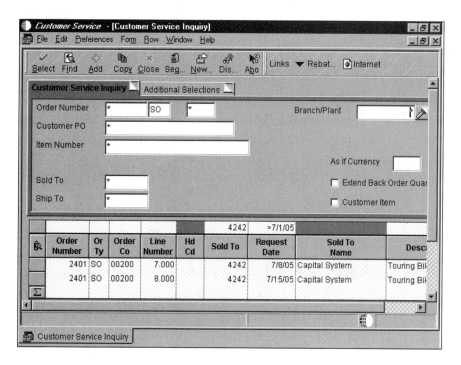

FIGURE 8-7 *The Results of the QBE Customer Service Inquiry Using a Compound Search*

 NAVIGATIONAL TIP

Using the Wildcard Character in Searches

Use an asterisk to replace one or more letters in a string of text. For example, to retrieve values containing AL, enter *AL*. To retrieve values beginning with AL, enter AL*.

How a QBE Search Differs from a Filtered Search

So what's different about a QBE search? QBE searches are much more flexible. The Search Information fields are limited to those that J. D. Edwards has chosen for you. With a QBE search, virtually all fields are fair game. Recall that if a Search Information field in the QBE line is grayed out, the field can't be used in a QBE search—and that's really the only exception.

More importantly, the QBE line offers both _conditioned_ searches, which use equality operators, and _compound_ searches, which allow the use of multiple filters or search fields. You might wonder why you should use a filtered search at all, given the QBE line. Simply put, because of system performance. Standard searches are generally faster than if the QBE line is used.

Case Sensitivity

A search is _not_ case-sensitive. However, our eyes _are_ case-sensitive. Therefore, here are a few words to the wise: When creating data in OneWorld, especially master data such as addresses and items, adopt standards for the formatting of data. OneWorld does not do this for you. Adopting and following naming conventions will dramatically improve the readability of your data.

 ONEWORLD IMPLEMENTATION TIP

Adopting Standards for the Formatting of Data

When creating data in OneWorld, especially master data such as addresses and items, adopt standards for the formatting of data. OneWorld does not do this for you. You will dramatically improve your ability to find data efficiently by doing so.

Position Sensitivity

The QBE search is column position-independent. Names entered as "Allen, Edward" or "Edward Allen" are in different formats. Retrieving values such as these requires an alternative strategy. The Search Information fields are typically "position-dependent." Therefore, QBE has the flexibility to find values that are not position-dependent within the data field itself. In our Address Book example, the Alpha Name Search can read data from only the leftmost position first. Therefore, the "key" or significant portion of the Alpha Name must begin in the first position. Again the case is made for standardizing the data formats related to information that will be entered into OneWorld.

ONEWORLD IMPLEMENTATION TIP

Performing "Test" Searches

It is a good practice to build a representative sample of different products (item master records) and names (address book records) and perform "test searches" *before* you commit a vast amount of effort toward the conversion or rekeying of your organization's data into OneWorld. Understanding how data is stored and retrieved will provide long-term productivity benefits to your organization.

Personalizing the Data Grid

Earlier, the ability to personalize the OneWorld Data Grid was briefly introduced. The Data Grid's appearance is personalized much like it would be in a spreadsheet program such as Microsoft Excel. The OneWorld user controls both the sizing and location of Data Grid columns. These personalized grid column settings can then be saved as a view of the Data Grid that is called a *tab* or, more correctly, a *format* for the Data Grid. Grids are saved based on the user ID used when you initially log on. Therefore, the use of "generic" User IDs is generally not a good idea. (However, I have seen my share of J. D. Edwards installations where no one took the time to create individual user IDs.)

ONEWORLD IMPLEMENTATION TIP

Personalizing the Data Grid

The Data Grid can be personalized. Personalization can be used to raise, or shift, important entry fields to a more prominent column position in the grid.

What can be personalized on the Data Grid? OneWorld allows several appearance-related changes to the Data Grid:

◆ Changing the font

◆ Changing the colors

◆ Freezing rows or columns

◆ Changing the format of rows or columns

◆ Changing the position of a column

◆ Changing the sort sequence of the data in the Data Grid

◆ Establishing an "auto return" field

Some of these features work quite similarly to how they might in any other Windows program, although the results might not be what you expect. In other cases, some of these features are unique to OneWorld. In addition, certain functions affect the entire grid, and other functions affect only the cell, column, or row where the cursor is positioned. Table 8-2 lists some ideas on how to make effective use of some Data Grid features that are discussed here.

Table 8-2 Ideas for Personalizing the Data Grid

Action	Result
Change the font or font size used on the Data Grid	Improved screen readability
Change the background color used on the Data Grid	Improved screen readability
Change a column's background color	Indicates a special or mandatory column (field)
Move a column (field) to the left	When a column (field) is required or mandatory
Move a column (field) to the right	When a column (field) is not used or is optional
Change the Data Grid's sort sequence	Displays data in a more logical or user-friendly manner
Establish a column as the auto return column	Speeds up data entry for multiple-line transactions

Effecting Grid Changes

Now that you have a good idea as to what "personalization" features are available for the Data Grid, this section introduces, by example, how some of these features can be used.

But first, here are a few words of advice: Not every person or organization will want or need to make use of all of the Data Grid's features. I recommend caution when you're considering to what extent your organization's staff will be introduced to many of these features. If an organization's staff is unfamiliar with Windows-based programs, initially you likely won't want to go beyond search and navigation skills as part of your training curriculum. Consider in such cases introducing these "personalization" features to your organization's staff on an as-needed basis.

Whether they are used or not, all of these features will always be there, because they are an integral part of OneWorld. When a future need arises in your organization for a practical use for one or more of these features, you'll look like the OneWorld hero that you are when you pull up one of these features on a menu. As the OneWorld trainer or implementation specialist for your organization, you must be comfortable with using these features before you introduce them to the OneWorld user community at large. With that said, we'll move on to a discussion of Data Grid-related personalization features.

Changes to the Data Grid are relatively easy to perform. Most changes are accomplished simply by positioning the mouse cursor somewhere on the Data Grid, right-clicking, and choosing a menu option from the drop-down menu. For certain functions, you make personalization-related changes by positioning the cursor over a specific cell, column, or row within the Data Grid. The next section contains the specific steps to follow regarding personalizing the Data Grid.

Data Grid Formats

The first step to perform when personalizing the appearance of the Data Grid is to always save the current format. When a new format is created, it appears as a tab along the top or bottom edge of the Data Grid. For instance, I generally save the original Data Grid format as the *base* format. Only after saving the original Data Grid do I create a new tab or format. You might wonder why. By saving the original format, you can always revert to the look and feel of the original or base format for any given Data Grid with a simple mouse click.

Creating a Personalized Data Grid Format

OneWorld includes a number of Excel-like capabilities that are useful in changing the Data Grid's appearance. This section discusses a necessary first to personalization—the creation of a base grid—and also what can be personalized on the Data Grid.

Understanding Grid Personalization

Table 8-3, shown in a moment, summarizes the Data Grid personalization actions in OneWorld. In order to perform the personalization actions outlined in Table 8-3, you must first access the drop-down menu related to the Data Grid:

1. Position the cursor anywhere on the Data Grid. Recall that the Data Grid is always the lower portion of the screen, beginning with the QBE line.

2. Right-click. A drop-down menu appears.

3. Slide the cursor from top to bottom along the drop-down menu. Notice as you pass over each item on the menu that it expands to another menu whenever an arrowhead appears at the end of the line. Also notice that some of the entries are grayed out and can't be selected.

The Base Format

In this section, you will save the current Data Grid format as the base format:

1. Position the cursor anywhere in the Data Grid portion of the form, and right-click. A drop-down menu appears.

2. Position the cursor over Format. A second drop-down menu appears.

3. Choose New Format. A pop-up entry window appears called New Format.

4. Type BASE as the name of the new format.

5. Click on the OK button. The Data Grid is redisplayed without the pop-up entry box or menus.

The Data Grid should now display a tab identifying it as the BASE format. It appears along the tab edge of the displayed Data Grid, as shown in Figure 8-8.

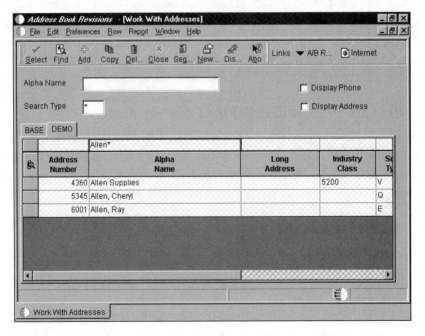

FIGURE 8-8 *Tabs Appear When Multiple Data Grid Formats Exist*

ONE WORLD IMPLEMENTATION TIP

Creating Base Data Grid Formats

For quick reference, create a base Data Grid format when personalized Data Grid formats will be used.

The Personalized Format

Once the original grid format has been saved as the base grid format, the same steps can be followed to create a personalized grid, by naming it differently:

1. Position the cursor anywhere in the Data Grid portion of the form, and right-click. A drop-down menu appears.

2. Position the cursor over Format. A second drop-down menu appears.

3. Choose New Format. A pop-up entry window appears called New Format.

4. Type DEMO as the name of the new format. Note that typically you might use your initials or first name to identify a personalized new format—it's your choice!

5. Click on the OK button. The Data Grid is redisplayed without the pop-up entry box or menus.

Note that a new tab has been added along the tab edge of the Data Grid called the DEMO format. Figure 8-8 illustrates the tabbed Data Grid with the DEMO format in the foreground.

Notice in Figure 8-8 that the DEMO tab is slightly raised or dominant on the form. This indicates which Data Grid Format is active and on the form at this time. To switch to a different Data Grid format, simply click on the desired tab.

When the new Data Grid format is initially created, it does not contain any personalization. Now that the DEMO Data Grid format has been established, the next step is to "personalize" it. Table 8-3 summarizes all the available personalization options that are associated with the Work With program's Data Grid. They are available when you right-click anywhere on the Data Grid.

Table 8-3 OneWorld Data Grid Personalization Features

Menu Item	Description
View System Log	Displays the "jdedebug" log file. The response line might ask you to view this file when they help you troubleshoot OneWorld problems.
Contents	An entry point into OneWorld online help (discussed later in this chapter).
How To	Another entry point into OneWorld online help.
What's This?	Provides access to field-level help for any OneWorld field. This is discussed later in this chapter.
Grid, Print	Selects and prints all or a portion of the Data Grid's contents.
Grid, Sequence	Sequences or sorts the Data Grid's contents.
Grid, Check for Attachments	Lets you access and view an attachment file for a given row. A paper clip symbol appears in the leftmost column of the Data Grid associated with a given row or line item to indicate that an attachment file exists for that given row or line item.
Grid, Font	Selects and changes to an alternative font style and size for the overall grid.
Grid, Color	Selects and changes to an alternative background color for the overall grid.
Maximize/Restore	Hides the Search Information or the top portion of the form to provide additional room for the Data Grid. Also restores the Search Information.
Zoom	Reduces or enlarges the Data Grid portion of the screen.
Cell, Visual Assist	This is simply another name, or entry point, to the search features behind the searchlight icon for a given field. Choose the Visual Assist option to exit to another program that can search for a valid value for this field. The Visual Assist option is not available for every field.
Cell, Undo	Undoes the last cell action, such as a cell entry.
Column, Font	Changes the font style and size for this column only.

Table 8-3 OneWorld Data Grid Personalization Features *(continued)*

Menu Item	Description
Column, Color	Changes the background color for this column only.
Column, Freeze/Unfreeze	Freezes or unfreezes a specific portion of the Data Grid when you scroll a large file.
Column, Auto Return	Designates the column as the last column in a row for data entry purposes. When this tab is chosen, the cursor is positioned at the first entry column in the next row on the form. This option functions only on an input-capable form.
Row	Allows exits to other OneWorld programs based on the contents of a given row on an input-capable grid. For example, more than a dozen exits are available from a sales order transaction row in the Customer Service Inquiry form. Because the Work With form is not input-capable, row options are not available on it.
Export, Microsoft Excel	Exports selected contents of the grid from OneWorld to Microsoft Excel.
Export, Microsoft Word	Exports selected contents of the grid from OneWorld to Microsoft Word.
Export, Lotus 1-2-3	Exports selected contents of the grid from OneWorld to Lotus 1-2-3.
Export, Lotus WordPro	Exports selected contents of the grid from OneWorld to Lotus WordPro.
Export, Corel QuattroPro	Exports selected contents of the grid from OneWorld to Corel QuattroPro.
Export, Corel WordPerfect	Exports selected contents of the grid from OneWorld to Corel WordPerfect.
Import, Microsoft Excel	Imports selected contents of the grid from OneWorld to Microsoft Excel. This feature does not apply to every grid form.
Import, Lotus 1-2-3	Imports selected contents of the grid from OneWorld to Lotus 1-2-3. This feature does not apply to every grid form.

Table 8-3 OneWorld Data Grid Personalization Features (continued)

Menu Item	Description
Import, Corel QuattroPro	Imports selected contents of the grid from OneWorld to Corel QuattroPro. This feature does not apply to every grid form.
Import, Remove Link	Removes an import link. Works only in conjunction with other import-related features. An import can be linked to another application when the import is initially established.
Format, New, Grid	Creates a new Data Grid format or tab.
Format, New, Chart/Graph	Creates a new Data Grid chart or graph.
Format, Rename	Renames an existing Data Grid format or tab.
Format, Remove	Removes an existing Data Grid format or tab.

Figure 8-9 illustrates the Data Grid-related drop-down menu with the Grid option and its related drop-down menu.

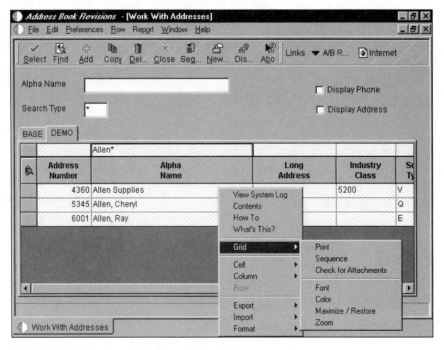

FIGURE 8-9 *The Data Grid Drop-Down Menu*

The creation of a Data Grid format was previously covered for the purposes of completing this example. Although it isn't possible to illustrate by example all the Data Grid personalization features listed in Table 8-3 in this chapter, we will look at several of the most important:

◆ Sequencing the data that appears in the Data Grid

◆ Reducing or enlarging the overall size of the Data Grid (which is called zooming)

◆ Relocating a column on the Data Grid

◆ Changing the size of a column on the Data Grid

Examples are also provided for the following:

◆ Renaming a Data Grid format

◆ Removing a Data Grid format

I will conclude this chapter by covering how to access the online help functions in OneWorld, represented by the What's This? and How To selections appearing in the Data Grid drop-down menu.

Sequencing the Data Grid Contents

OneWorld does not always list data or information in the Data Grid in a manner that might be appropriate for your use or needs. In the old days of computing, this was usually a problem—but not with OneWorld! Without any reprogramming or other technical requirements, the sequence of rows appearing in the Data Grid can be reordered, resequenced, or sorted in a different way.

For instance, to sequence the data in the DEMO format for the Address Book Work With form, follow these steps:

1. Position the cursor anywhere on the Data Grid and right-click. A drop-down menu appears.

2. Position the cursor on Grid. A second drop-down menu appears.

3. Choose Sequence. A pop-up window appears called Select Grid Row Sort Order.

4. Click on the field labeled Address Number in the right column labeled Columns Sorted.

5. Click on the left-arrow button along the bottom of the window.

6. The Address Number field no longer appears in the right column.

7. Click on the Sch Typ field in the left column, labeled Columns Available.

8. Click on the right-arrow button along the bottom of the window.

9. The Sch Typ field should be listed in the right column.

10. Click on the OK button to accept this new Data Grid sequence.

The Data Grid is redisplayed without the pop-up entry box or menus. Notice that the order of the data or information appearing in the Data Grid has been rearranged according to this new sequence. It might be necessary to move the horizontal slider along the bottom of the Data Grid to the right in order to view the effects of this example.

Here's a final note about the Grid Sequence feature: Any of the fields listed under Columns Available can be used to sequence information that will appear on the Data Grid.

Reducing or Enlarging the Data Grid View

Sometimes the important columns in a Data Grid might "overrun" the viewable width of the Data Grid, or perhaps your eyesight is failing but you refuse to admit your need for bifocals. The Zoom feature can help in either case. For instance, the Address Book Work With form's Data Grid can be shrunk to fit within the viewable area of a monitor as follows:

1. Right-click anywhere on the Data Grid. A drop-down menu appears.

2. Position the cursor on Grid. A second drop-down menu appears.

3. Position the cursor on Zoom.

4. A pop-up selection window appears called Zoom.

5. Click on the button next to 75%.

6. Click on the OK button.

The Data Grid is redisplayed without the pop-up entry box or menus. Notice that in this exercise, the Data Grid portion of the screen has decreased. Do the following to compare the appearance of the base format to the DEMO format:

1. Click on the format tab labeled BASE.

2. Review that Data Grid size.

3. Click on the format tab labeled DEMO.

To change the format to a larger (or still smaller) magnification, use the Zoom feature accordingly.

Relocating a Column

To relocate a column along the Data Grid, do the following:

1. Position the cursor on the column label or field name for the column. For the purposes of this example, position the cursor on the Industry Class column.
2. Press and hold down the left mouse button. A column icon with a left and right arrow appears.
3. Move the column icon left or right to the desired location for this column on the grid. For this example, position the Industry Class column immediately after the Alpha Name column.
4. Release the mouse button. The column "snaps" into its new position along the Data Grid.

Any number of columns on any given form can be reorganized in this manner.

Changing a Column's Size

Changing the size of a Data Grid column works much as it does in any Microsoft Windows program. To resize a column along the Data Grid, do the following:

1. Position the cursor on the column label or field name row.
2. Position the cursor on the vertical bar that separates one column from another on the Data Grid. For this example, position the cursor along the right side of the Alpha Name column. A vertical bar with a left and right arrow appears. This is the standard icon for column resizing in any Microsoft Windows-based program.
3. Press and hold down the left mouse button.
4. Drag the cursor left or right to the desired width for the column. For this example, drag the cursor left about an inch for the Alpha Name column.
5. Release the mouse button. The column is resized.

Any number of columns on any given form can be resized in this manner. When a column is resized, none of the data or information appearing in that column is lost. It is only hidden from view until the column is resized again as needed.

The preceding examples illustrate only a few of the features available to create a personalized OneWorld Data Grid format. So what does the masterpiece DEMO Data Grid look like now? Figure 8-10 shows you. (The "before" version of the DEMO Data Grid Format appeared in Figure 8-8.)

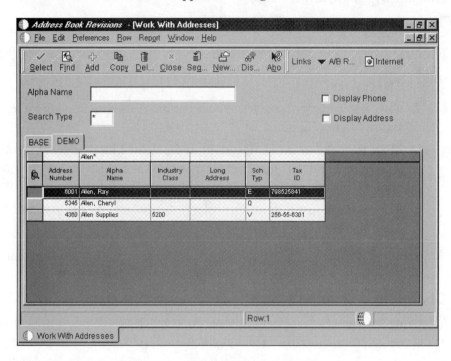

FIGURE 8-10 *The "After" Version of the DEMO Data Grid*

Renaming and Removing Data Grid Formats

The steps to rename or remove a Data Grid format are essentially the same as they were for creating a new Data Grid format.

Renaming a Data Grid Format

To rename a Data Grid format, do the following:

1. Right-click on the tab corresponding to the Data Grid format that is to be renamed. A drop-down menu appears.

2. Position the cursor on Format. A second drop-down menu appears.

3. Choose Rename Format. A pop-up entry window appears called Rename Format.

4. Type RENAMED as the replacement name for the format.

5. Click on the OK button.

The Data Grid is redisplayed without the pop-up entry box or menus. The tab should now be named RENAMED.

Removing a Data Grid Format

To delete or remove a Data Grid format, do the following:

1. Right-click on the tab corresponding to the Data Grid format that is to be removed. A drop-down menu appears.

2. Position the cursor on Format. A second drop-down menu appears.

3. Click on Remove Format. The Data Grid is redisplayed.

The tab corresponding to the removed format no longer appears.

This section showed you how to create, personalize, rename, and remove a Data Grid format. The steps that were covered here apply for any given version of a Data Grid in any OneWorld program.

Getting Help in OneWorld

The last topic in this chapter is perhaps the most important one—how to obtain help online while working in OneWorld. OneWorld has a rich set of online help that in many cases will help you avoid cracking open the reference guides.

Actually, one of the forms of online help in OneWorld was discussed earlier—the display of error messages. Field- and program-specific help are also available in OneWorld. These two types of help are discussed in this section.

Field- or Cell-Level Help in OneWorld

In OneWorld, field-level help is also called What's This? help. Field-level help provides a general description and purpose for any given field on the OneWorld form. Do the following to access field-level help:

1. Position the cursor on a field that you need assistance with, and right-click. A drop-down menu appears.

2. Choose What's This?. A pop-up window containing descriptive information about this field is displayed.

3. To remove this pop-up window, click anywhere on the form, outside the pop-up window.

Here's another way to obtain field-level help in OneWorld:

1. Position the cursor on a field that you need assistance with.

2. Press the F1 key on the keyboard. A pop-up window containing descriptive information about this field is displayed.

3. To remove this pop-up window, press the F1 key again, or click anywhere on the form outside the pop-up window.

Program- or Form-Level Help in OneWorld

In OneWorld, each form provides help information that is specific to the form itself. Program-level help in OneWorld is called How To help. This level of help information is intended to guide you through the use of the form itself.

There are two ways to access form- or program-level help. Here's the first method:

1. From the menu bar of any OneWorld form, select Help, How To. A standard Microsoft Windows Help System window appears, titled Help topics for this form.

2. Use the mouse to drill down through Help categories and topics.

3. To remove the Windows Help window, click on the cancel or X button in the upper-right corner of the OneWorld Help form.

Note that OneWorld form-level help relies on the Microsoft Windows Help System. Windows Help has various other menu options that you can use, including printing specific topics and copying text from the Help System into a word processor, such as Microsoft Word. These two features of the Help System might be particularly valuable to you when you're creating custom documentation. I have found the OneWorld How To or form-level help to be particularly well-written. A more detailed discussion of the Microsoft Windows Help System is beyond the scope of this book.

There is another way to obtain How To or form-level help. You can obtain help on any form by following these steps:

1. From any position on a form, right-click. A drop-down menu appears.

2. Position the cursor on the How To menu item and click.

3. The standard Microsoft Windows Help System window appears, titled Help topics for this form.

4. Use the mouse to drill down through Help categories and topics.

5. To remove the Windows Help window, click on the cancel or X button in the upper-right corner of the OneWorld Help form.

General Online Help

If you need assistance on another aspect of OneWorld, you have two choices. One is the OneWorld documentation, either in hard-copy or soft-copy (online) format. The second is the "totality" of OneWorld online help. I refer to this form of help as "general online help." However, don't be scared away by this type of help, because you will not need to go form by form to review all of the OneWorld help. In this case, the "help" that appears in the Windows Help system is really the table of contents for the entire collection of OneWorld Help. What a system! There are two ways to access general or system-level help. Here's the first way:

1. From the menu bar of any OneWorld form, select Help, How To. A standard Microsoft Windows Help System window appears, titled Help topics for this form.

2. Use the mouse to drill down through the help categories and topics.

3. To remove the Windows Help window, click on the cancel or X button in the upper-right corner of the OneWorld Help form.

The second way to obtain general help is by following these steps:

1. From any position on a form, right-click. A drop-down menu appears.

2. Select the Contents menu item. The standard Microsoft Windows Help System window appears, titled OneWorld Help.

3. Use the mouse button to drill down through help categories and topics.

4. To remove the Windows Help window, click on the cancel or X button in the upper-right corner of the OneWorld Help form.

Custom Help

It is also possible for the astute OneWorld shop to incorporate its custom documentation into the Microsoft Windows Help System, much as J. D. Edwards has done with OneWorld. Developing help files that are compatible with the Microsoft Windows Help System is beyond the scope of this book. On the surface, there is nothing wrong with an online solution or custom documentation. However, when possible, I highly recommend using the standard OneWorld user reference guides and the online help documentation as delivered. Writing and maintaining custom documentation is a big job and frequently does not get done. Of course, there will always be a need for a certain amount of custom user documentation, but it is best to keep this effort to a minimum.

Summary

This has been perhaps the most engaging chapter thus far in terms of topics covered. A hands-on introduction to navigating and using OneWorld interactive programs or "forms" was presented using an important OneWorld program model called the Work With form. The Work With program "front ends" most OneWorld master data maintenance and transaction processing business functions.

Most of the examples provided in this chapter were based on the Address Book, a key set of master data files related to the names and addresses of customers, suppliers, employees, and facilities. Additional information about the Address Book will appear in a later chapter.

Also introduced was an important user interface element in many OneWorld programs—the Data Grid. The Address Book was used to introduce the concept of searching using the Data Grid's Query by Example (QBE) feature. The Data Grid can be customized to improve both readability and ease of data entry. Techniques for personalizing the Data Grid were illustrated through examples.

This chapter also included important information about how to understand and respond to OneWorld error messages. It provided examples of how to receive help at the field and program levels while using OneWorld.

Chapter 9

Much of the discussion in this chapter focuses on explaining, mainly through examples, the remaining OneWorld model programs. Recall from the introductory sections in the preceding chapter that a key contributor to the overall usability of OneWorld is its architecture. J. D. Edwards software engineers have architected a common look and feel for OneWorld that is propagated throughout these model interactive programs—or *forms,* as they are also frequently called.

The examples in this chapter represent the look and feel as well as the user interface aspects of OneWorld programs in general. Therefore, the examples serve as your guide to how virtually all other OneWorld programs and applications behave in daily operation.

In addition to OneWorld's model programs or forms, it should be noted that OneWorld programs include certain basic features that are common to virtually any Windows GUI-style program, including drop-down menus and click- or icon-activated program functions. Therefore, if you or your OneWorld end-users are accustomed to working with a Microsoft Windows-based program such as Word or Excel, the transition to OneWorld should be an easy one.

The OneWorld Program Models

When any menu option is selected in OneWorld Explorer, that option generally performs one of the following three activities:

- ◆ The menu selection activates another menu.
- ◆ The menu selection activates a report or batch-style program.
- ◆ The menu selection activates an interactive program or form.

Recall that Chapter 7 discussed how menus work and explained the differences between OneWorld interactive and batch programs. Chapter 8 introduced OneWorld interactive programs using the Work With model program as an example. This chapter introduces the remaining interactive model programs using examples. The OneWorld model interactive programs or forms include the following:

◆ The Work With program
◆ The Search and Select program
◆ The Fix and Inspect program
◆ The Parent/Child Browse program
◆ The Header Detail program
◆ The Header-Less Detail program

After the introductions to these interactive programs, the report or batch-style program will be introduced through an example. Your overall use of OneWorld will be based on the working examples introduced in this chapter.

Using OneWorld Interactive Programs

The most prevalent type of program in OneWorld is the interactive program. Interactive programs provide for master data entry, transaction entry, and all related inquiries into the OneWorld database.

The Work With Program

The Work With program was introduced in the preceding chapter. This program is also called the Find and Browse form in OneWorld. The Work With program is one of the most prevalent interactive program types you will encounter in OneWorld.

Recall Chapter 8's characterization of the Work With program as the standard front-end or gateway form for virtually all OneWorld transaction processing and master file maintenance functions. It is from the Work With program that any existing transaction or master file, such as the Address Book, can be searched for a specific record—such as a customer or supplier record. It is also from the Work With program that a new transaction or record can be created or that an existing transaction or record can be updated.

For further information about the OneWorld Work With program, refer to Chapter 8. Figure 8-1 shows the OneWorld Work With program.

The Search and Select Program

The Search and Select program is usually associated with or *called* by another program. The Search and Select program is typically used to give the OneWorld user a way to search a master data table—such as a user-defined code (UDC) table—for a specific value and to then select or return that value for use within the original or *calling* program. This kind of system feature is sometimes called *table lookup*.

The Data Grid of the Search and Select program represents the contents of the underlying OneWorld data file or table from which a value can be selected. A separate interactive program is used to maintain the underlying OneWorld data file or table that is being used for reference or lookup purposes. Therefore, as a general rule, the Search and Select program is not used to access and maintain values in the underlying data file or table.

Actually, you have already seen several examples of the Search and Select program in previous chapters. Recall the examples in Chapters 7 and 8 in which a pop-up window appeared when the searchlight button was clicked. Those pop-up windows were actually working examples of the Search and Select program in action.

The following example uses the OneWorld Address Book Work With form as the calling program that calls the Search and Select program. To begin this example, initiate the Address Book Work With form. Recall the menu path from Chapter 8:

> Master Directory (G) > Foundation Systems (G0) > Address Book
> (G010) > Daily Processing (**G01**)> Address Book Revisions (P01012)

Follow these steps to see how the Search and Select program is called from within the Work With form:

1. Click on the entry box for Search Type. The searchlight button appears to the right of the Search Type entry box.
2. Click on the searchlight button. The Select User Defined Code form appears. One or more possible Search Type values appear on the Data Grid.
3. Use the mouse to move the cursor down the Data Grid until you see the Suppliers entry.
4. Click on Suppliers to highlight it.
5. Click on the Select button. The value V is returned to the Search Type entry box on the Work With form.

Figure 9-1 shows the Select User Defined Code for Search Type, and Figure 9-2 shows the Address Book Work With form.

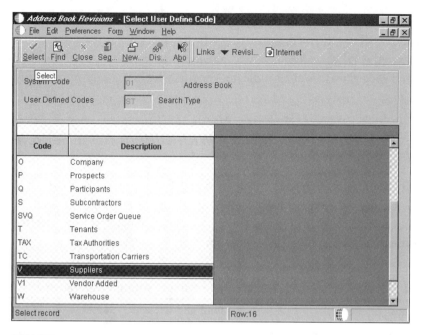

FIGURE 9-1 *The Select User Defined Code Form Using Search Type as an Example*

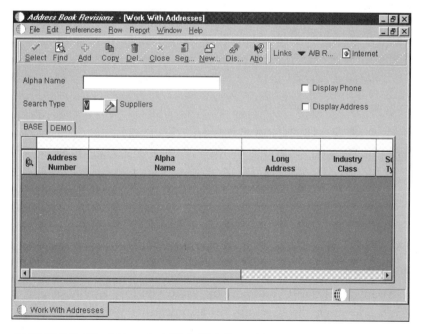

FIGURE 9-2 *The Address Book Work With Form After a Selection Is Made*

Note that, in the preceding steps, the UDC value of V corresponds to the Suppliers Search Type. If you're wondering why the letter S was not used for this code, note that the UDC value of S was already used to indicate a Sub Contractor Search Type. V was used to indicate Vendor, which is a common synonym for Supplier.

How Find and Browse/Work With Differs from Search and Select

Initially, you might believe that the Find and Browse or Work With and Search and Select are two ways of saying the same thing. However, there are subtle differences between these two program models. These small but nonetheless important differences are summarized in Table 9-1.

Table 9-1 Work With Versus Search and Select Program Differences

Feature	Find and Browse/ Work With	Search and Replace
Search using key field entry	Yes	Yes
Search using QBE row entries	Yes	Yes
Typically a stand-alone program	Yes	Limited use in OneWorld
Select record(s) for further processing	Yes	No
Typically called by another program	No	Yes
Select one record as a reference value	No	Yes
Action bar buttons for table maintenance	Yes	No
Menu bar options for table maintenance	Yes	Limited application; typically through the menu selection Form, Revisions

Must You Use the Search and Select Program to Select Valid Entry Choices?

The short answer is no. If you know the value, you may simply type it into the entry field. However, the short answer assumes that you already know a valid choice or value for an entry field. Suppose you have relatively few codes that are used often in a short amount of time. I have found that frequent OneWorld users often memorize these values. For the occasional OneWorld user, the Search and Select program provides access to a "cheat sheet" of possible values.

 TRAINING TIP

Selecting Versus Keying Field Values

Show end-users how to select valid values for fields, as well as how they can simply enter a valid value into a field.

The Fix and Inspect Program

The Fix and Inspect program is used for the maintenance of both master data and transaction-related data into OneWorld. When the Fix and Inspect program is used for entry into a transaction record, it can also be considered a Header record maintenance program. An excellent example of the Fix and Inspect program is the Address Book Revisions form.

The following example uses the OneWorld Address Book Revisions form to illustrate how the Fix and Inspect program actually works. To begin the example, initiate the Address Book Revisions program from within the Work With program. The menu path is

> Master Directory (G) > Foundation Systems (G0) > Address Book
> (G010) > Daily Processing (**G01**) > Address Book Revisions (P01012)

To see how the Fix and Inspect program is initiated from within the Work With form, click on the Add button. The Address Book Revisions form should appear.

Generally speaking, when a Fix and Inspect program is initiated in Add mode, it appears as a form with one or more blank entry fields. Figure 9-3 shows the Address Book Revisions Fix and Inspect program.

Entering Values in a OneWorld Entry Field

You can enter information into a field on the OneWorld program form several different ways. Information can be entered manually or systemically. This section discusses data entry into OneWorld forms.

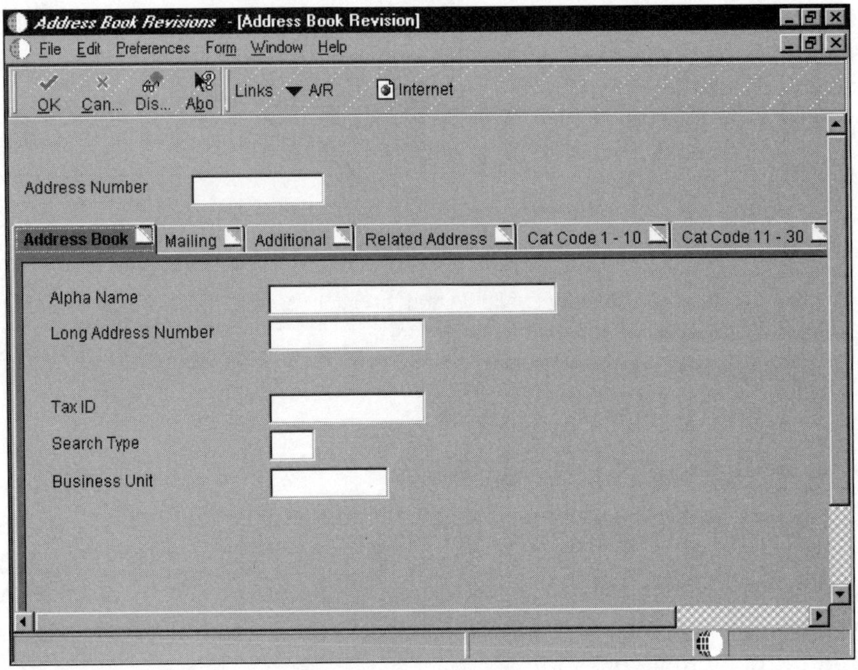

FIGURE 9-3 *The Address Book Revisions Fix and Inspect Program*

Types of Fields

A typical OneWorld form includes a variety of entry fields. In some cases, these fields are structured or formatted, as is the case for the Search Type field, which is considered a table-validated or table-driven field. In other cases, form entry fields are unstructured, such as in the case of the Alpha Name field on the Address Book Revisions form.

Although they do not appear on the Address Book Revisions form, date entry fields, dollar and numeric entry fields, and quantity entry fields are all examples of data entry field types that are considered structured entry fields. They appear throughout OneWorld in various data entry forms.

Leaving the Field Blank or Accepting Default Values

One of the hallmarks of OneWorld is that through configuration, many entry fields can be preselected, thereby minimizing repetitiveness in the data entry process. In these cases, entry fields can be left blank, and default values, when defined, default into the entry form as the record is being added to the OneWorld data file or table. Values for these fields default into the form when they have been predefined.

 IMPLEMENTATION TIP

Establishing a Default Entry Field Value

Consider using blanks as a valid code value to correlate to the usual value for an entry field.

Introducing the OneWorld Data Dictionary

These predefinitions for entry fields are determined by the Data Dictionary definition for a given OneWorld field. For instance, the Data Dictionary is where a link is made between the Search Type field and the UDC Table for Search Types, which is referenced by System Code 01, and User-Defined Code ST. Note these references, as protected fields, in the top portion of the Search and Select form shown in Figure 9-1.

There are other cases where field values are automatically determined when left blank. In such cases, a default value has been defined for a field. Again, the default value for a specific field is also established in the Data Dictionary.

Next Numbers

A special type of automatically determined field value in OneWorld is a next number field entry. Most master data record numbers, such as the Address Book record number, as in the case of our example here, and most transaction document numbers, such as Purchase Order numbers, are based on a unique table of next numbers for that entry field.

The OneWorld user can enter a specific value for a next number value or can let OneWorld find the next available number using the Next Number table for the specific entry field. When the user lets OneWorld determine the next number, it assigns that number to the master data record or transaction document as it is being added to the OneWorld data table.

Making Entries into a Field Mandatory

In other cases, you might determine that, for various reasons, your organization wants an entry for a given field to be mandatory or required. Therefore, the user must either know a valid value for the field or look it up through the use of a Search and Select form of values associated with a given entry field. By eliminating "blank" as an acceptable or valid value for a given entry field, by definition, an entry other than blank is now mandatory.

On the other hand, the blank value entry for other OneWorld tables is often defined as the most frequently used, typical, usual, or, more precisely, the *default* for the entry field. Again, it is your choice.

 IMPLEMENTATION TIP

Establishing a Required Field

To establish a field as a mandatory entry field, remove "blank" as a valid code value in a table. In some cases, the Data Dictionary default value might need to be changed to blanks as well.

Processing Option Override Values

In certain cases, default values are provided through a processing option override. The Data Dictionary, Next Numbers, Processing Options, and User-Defined Code tables are important components in the overall configuration of OneWorld for use in your organization. All of these topics will be discussed at length in future chapters.

Determining Required Fields

The mandatory or required entry fields for any given OneWorld data entry form can be easily determined. For instance, this can be done for the Address Book Revisions form, shown in Figure 9-3. If you have been following this chapter's examples you will already be at this form. To access this form again, choose

> Master Directory (G) > Foundation Systems (G0) > Address Book
> (G010) > Daily Processing (**G01**)> Address Book Revisions (P01012)

Then click on the Add button.

To see how a blank entry form can be used to determine the required values on a form, do not make any entries in the Address Book Revisions form, and then click on the OK button.

The underlying OneWorld program validates the contents in the entry fields on the form. Any mandatory or nonblank fields will trigger an error. To view the error messages generated by the blank Address Book Revisions entry form, from the program's menu bar, select Help, Display Errors. The error messages should be displayed as another window, replacing the bottom portion of the Address Book Revisions Fix and Inspect form.

Figure 9-4 shows the Address Book Revisions Fix and Inspect program with blank form-related errors displayed.

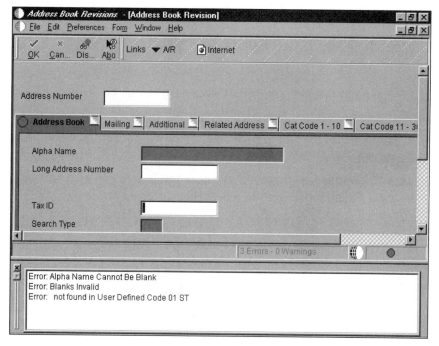

FIGURE 9-4 *Address Book Revisions Fix and Inspect Program Illustrating Blank Form Errors*

The first error message relates to a single field being blank—the Alpha Name field. The third error message indicates that in this case "Blank" or "Blanks" is not defined as a value in the UDC table for the Search Type field. However, the second error message listed—Blanks Invalid—applies equally to both of the Address Book Revisions form fields that contain errors.

As illustrated by this Address Book Revisions form example, OneWorld does not always provide clear error messages. Sometimes you will find that corrective actions are not straightforward in OneWorld. Successive or iterative correction of entry errors on any entry form will help you better understand and clear each OneWorld error message or error condition.

TRAINING TIP

Finding the Required Fields on Any Entry Form

For any given OneWorld entry form, to determine the entry fields that are considered mandatory or required entries, first click on the Add button from within a Work With form, and then click on the OK button. The program processes the blank form and highlights any required fields as errors.

Correcting Field Entry Errors

To clear entry form errors, do the following:

1. Click on the entry field.

2. Enter (or search and select) a valid value for the field. In our Address Book Revisions example, enter My First Address Book Entry as the Alpha Name value.

3. Click on the OK button. If any errors still exist, the error message window should be updated to reflect the correction just made.

4. Make additional corrections to the entry form as needed.

A valuable technique for correcting errors is to make corrections, one entry field at a time, clicking on the OK button after each entry field correction is made to determine if any additional errors exist on the entry form.

For example, do the following to continue the Address Book Revisions example:

1. Select a value from the UDC table for Search Type by positioning the cursor in the Search Type field.

2. Click on the searchlight button.

3. Find and select V (for Supplier) from the UDC table for Search Type.

4. Click on the OK button.

The Supplier Master Revisions form now replaces the Address Book Revisions form.

Determining If OneWorld Saved Your Form Entries

The appearance of the next form in a sequence of related forms or programs is your indication that the first or preceding step completed successfully. Also note that sometimes a record number or document number is assigned when this happens. In the case of the preceding example, a Supplier Number was assigned from the Address Book Next Numbers table. It appears in the top portion of the Supplier Master Revisions form. Figure 9-5 shows the subsequent Supplier Master Revision form and the default Supplier Number.

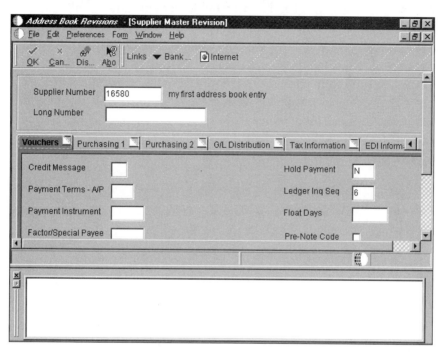

FIGURE 9-5 *The Supplier Master Revisions Form*

What If a Blank Form Appears Instead?

Sometimes all the field entries disappear from the form, as well as any remaining error messages in the Display Errors window. So why does the form simply "go blank"? After all erroneous field entries—such as blanks in this case—are corrected, the appearance of a blank entry form generally indicates that the previous record was successfully added or saved and that the running OneWorld program is ready to receive and process the next record entry. Although I'm not sure I like the way OneWorld indicates that all errors were corrected—by showing a blank form—this is one of the *few* idiosyncrasies you'll encounter in OneWorld.

What If You No Longer Need to Review Error Messages?

Notice something about Figure 9-5: Although there are no form-related errors, the Display Errors window is still open or maximized on the viewable portion of the screen. This is what I consider another idiosyncrasy of OneWorld: When all form errors are corrected, the Display Errors window does not automatically close or minimize itself. Therefore, if the error message window still appears on successive entry forms, it can be closed or hidden at any time—and then recalled if needed. To close the error message window, click on the cancel or X button in the upper-left corner of the Display Errors window. The Display Errors window subsequently closes, minimizes, or, in reality, disappears from view, while the program's data entry form consumes the entire viewable area of the screen. Figure 9-6 shows the subsequent Supplier Master Revision form *after* the Display Errors window has been closed.

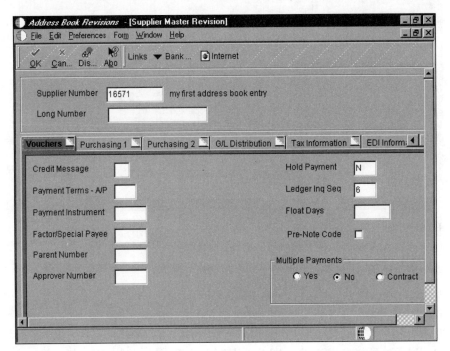

FIGURE 9-6 *The Supplier Master Revision Form Without the Display Errors Window*

 TRAINING TIP

Successively Correct Entry Form Errors

Successively correct entry form errors by correcting entry errors one entry field at a time, clicking on OK after each correction to determine if additional errors exist.

Saving Entered Data

After entering values for all required and optional data fields in the OneWorld Fix and Inspect program entry form, you must add or save the contents of this entry form to the appropriate OneWorld tables.

The OneWorld Fix and Inspect program associated with the entry form determines through its internal business logic which tables the form contents will be appended to. To save the current contents for any OneWorld Fix and Inspect program entry form, click on the OK button. If all fields were successfully validated, the entry form contents are added to the appropriate OneWorld tables. Either a blank entry form or a follow-on data entry form appears. In some cases, OneWorld displays the document number of the previous document at the top of the blank form as another indicator that the previous entry was accepted.

Note, however, that if any errors exist, the form will not be saved or appended to any OneWorld tables until any required corrections are made on the entry form and its contents are subsequently revalidated by again clicking on the OK button to attempt the save again. As soon as all remaining corrections are considered valid, the record is appended or, in the case of changes to an existing record, the existing records are updated in the appropriate tables.

To discontinue additional record entry, click on the Cancel button. The Fix and Inspect program operation will be terminated.

When any Fix and Inspect program is terminated, the program or menu that initiated the Fix and Inspect program appears. Typically, this will be the related Work With form. In this case, the Work With Address Book form will appear.

Canceling Data Entry

If data has already been entered on a form, but you *do not* want to save this information, click on the Cancel button. The record will not be saved, and the Fix and Inspect program operation will be terminated.

Canceling a Form Entry in World Versus OneWorld

If you were a World software user, OneWorld does not have the Clear Form function that was provided by a function key command in World software. You must cancel the form operation and reinitiate the form operation to achieve the same result.

Business Logic Errors

In some cases, "business logic" rules define relationships between required values. For instance, if the Search Type of an Address Book record is E—for employee—an entry in the Tax ID field is required as well. Generally speaking, these business logic rules are "embedded" within a given OneWorld program. Business logic errors are different and distinct from field entry validation errors. Business logic validation typically occurs during program execution, whereas field validation generally occurs during data entry. Generally speaking, it is easier to understand and resolve field validation logic errors than it is to identify and resolve business logic errors.

How Can OneWorld's Business Logic Be Determined?

Understanding OneWorld's business logic is really the essential reason for spending what might seem like an enormous amount of time and effort prototyping your processes according to OneWorld's business rules. The modeling, configuring, and testing of your business processes using OneWorld and the iteration of these steps until a configuration or workaround is reached are essential to the successful implementation of OneWorld in your organization.

During the business modeling, configuration, and testing stages of your OneWorld implementation, the field validation and business logic of OneWorld should be identified, defined, and, when applicable, configured. OneWorld should be thoroughly tested to determine how the chosen configuration affects—or is affected by—OneWorld's business logic. Certainly the outcome or impact on your business transactions to be processed through OneWorld should be identified, tested, and measured for accuracy and completeness. This is frequently called *integrated* or *end-to-end* testing. Observing test transactions as they flow through every part of the system is the best way to validate the system configuration and overall operation of OneWorld programs. For example, consider the impact of a purchase order on inventory, accounts payable, and the general accounting systems within OneWorld—not just from within the context of the purchasing system alone.

You should also consider the impact of OneWorld's business logic on your organization's nonsystemic processes and activities. For example, consider the impact that OneWorld's field validation and business logic validation will have on your organization's standing policies, procedures, and training materials. Such an impact is not always obvious.

How to Correct Business Logic Errors

Resolving a business rule violation generally requires one of the following actions:

◆ Correcting the business rule violation by canceling the incorrectly structured transaction and reentering it correctly. In some cases, this might mean reversing the effects of transactions that have already occurred.

◆ Expanding the business rules, through OneWorld configuration, to allow for processing of the incorrectly structured transaction and then reprocessing this transaction through the step or steps that were previously prevented.

In summary, it is always advisable to thoroughly consider the implications of selecting one table value over another with respect to how the underlying OneWorld program will behave. This is especially true when table values are either copied or deleted so that undesirable program actions do not occur or so that additional configuration testing and rework are unnecessary. Understanding OneWorld's business logic can be challenging. However, one of the tasks of an implementation consultant is to help you understand OneWorld's business logic and correctly apply it to your business transactions. Rely on your consultant to assist you in this important area.

 IMPLEMENTATION TIP

Understand Entry Field Validations

Before deleting, copying, or documenting how an entry field value works, understand how the entry field is validated within each specific OneWorld program that your organization will use.

Tabbed Entry Forms in OneWorld

A number of OneWorld programs have file folder-style tabs at either the top or the bottom of the entry form. Tabs are used in the OneWorld program to logically group related fields. Do not confuse these entry-related tabs with the Data Grid formats (discussed in the preceding chapter), which are user-defined. These data entry-related tabs are not user-defined.

The Address Book Revisions form provides an excellent example of how tabs are used to organize related data entry fields. For instance, one tab can be used to represent fields related to supplier or vendor type Address Book records, and another tab can be used to represent fields related to a customer Address Book record type.

You will notice examples of tabs in the Address Book Revision form in Figure 9-3 and in Figure 9-6, the Supplier Revision form.

Business-Required Versus Systemically-Required Fields

Recall from Chapter 8 how the Address Book is used—to store all name and address information, regardless of the type of address. Different types of addresses are known by their search type value in OneWorld. From the earlier example in this chapter, you might recall that an address was never really entered prior to the address record being saved. Why did the address get omitted from the entry? As you might recall, the address entry fields were blank. The OK button was then used to generate errors that determined the required fields for entry purposes on the form. Therefore, no address-related fields were actually considered required fields.

Several points need to be made here. First, some fields are said to be "required by business or company policies and procedures or by statute." These fields are said to be "business- or company-required" fields. A business-required field differs dramatically from a "systemically-required" field. Second, in day-to-day practice, the *last* step of data entry is clicking the OK button. This should happen only after you follow your business procedures regarding data entry standards for the field-by-field contents of any given OneWorld form.

On this final point, I can't emphasize enough that during your CRP testing, it is important to exercise the software and come to an understanding of how each field on every form will be used—or not used—in your day-to-day business operations. OneWorld requires that certain fields be entered—even when they are user-defined. In other cases, user-defined fields are strictly informational but can be used to influence data selection.

There is simply no substitute for common sense. Flagging every appropriate data entry field as "systemically required" might be either impractical or, in some cases, impossible—such as in the case of the Address Book, where different types of address records are maintained. Therefore, end-users and the implementation team should work together closely to document field usage within OneWorld that is specific to your business processes.

A Cautionary Note on OneWorld Programs with Tabs and Windows

Unfortunately, unless your client or terminal server workstation is equipped with Windows NT, I have found that tabs don't always work correctly. In such cases, the related field groupings normally associated with a tab are still available, but they must be accessed through the menu bar's Row option. This option lists all the tab views that are available for the Address Book record. To correct any problems related to the display of form tabs, check with the J. D. Edwards response line to determine the proper Microsoft Windows-related Service Packs and OneWorld Service Packs that are necessary for tabs to work correctly at your site.

Tabs have a strong advantage during data entry. If an error is contained on any tab—such as a blank field that requires a mandatory, nonblank value—when such a form-related error is detected, not only will the field be highlighted (in red), but so will the entry form tab.

Where Have All the Function Keys Gone?

In J. D. Edwards' World software, the equivalents of many of these tabbed entry forms, such as those appearing for the Address Book Revisions program, were previously accessed through the 12 or 24 function keys along the top of most keyboards. As a general rule, the World software function keys have been replaced by menu options under Row on the menu bar for any given OneWorld program.

In the case of J. D. Edwards' WorldVision users, this Windows-based front end for World software retained function key capabilities and also provided them as drop-down menu options—but OneWorld does not do so. It is also interesting to note that J. D. Edwards' arch-rival, SAP AG, chose to provide in its GUI-based R/3 software the function key equivalents from its R/2 character-based software as drop-down menu options. This is another example of what I consider an idiosyncrasy of OneWorld. But I will quickly add that if you're unfamiliar with either J. D. Edwards' World or WorldVision software or SAP software products, this is likely a moot point.

The Parent/Child Browse Program

The Parent/Child Browse program has a similar look, feel, and functionality as several programs already known to you—Microsoft Windows Explorer and OneWorld Explorer. Currently, there are relatively few examples of this program in OneWorld. One such example is the Parent/Child Balance Inquiry in the OneWorld Accounts Receivable system. Figure 9-7 shows the Accounts Receivable Balance Inquiry program using the Parent/Child Browse program model.

The left portion of the Parent and Child form provides a list of data records—in this case, customers. On the right side of the screen is detail information about

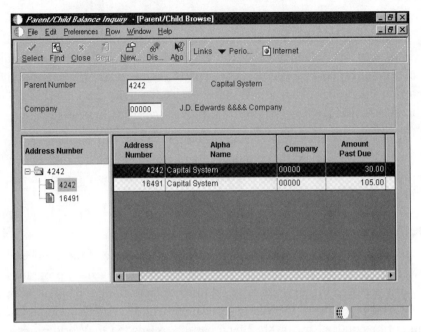

FIGURE 9-7 *Accounts Receivable Balance Inquiry Using the Parent/Child Browse Program*

the selected entry in the left portion of the screen—account balance information in this example.

Unfortunately, unlike previous examples, demonstrating how this form works is not quite as simple as navigating the form. The population of this form typically requires that a substantial amount of business processing activity precede its use. For instance, creating Figure 9-7 required an extensive amount of "behind the scenes" activities—several steps involving multiple OneWorld applications were used to create this example. Creating this example required the following steps:

◆ Several Address Book records were created as "customers."

◆ One of these Address Book records was designated as the *parent* Address Book record.

◆ Customer 4242 was designated as the parent Address Book record.

◆ Two *children,* or related Address Book records, for this customer were also created—records 16491and 16539.

◆ On each of these two child records, the Parent Number entry field under the Address Book entry form tab Related Addresses was updated to reflect the parent record number of 4242.

◆ Stand-alone invoices were entered against two of these customer accounts into the OneWorld Accounts Receivable system and posted.

◆ The Credit Analysis Refresh was run.

Only after all of these tasks were completed was the example in Figure 9-7 possible.

To understand the power and utility of this relatively straightforward form type, consider for a moment why the Accounts Receivable application provides for such Parent/Child relationship views of account activity. It is all about credit exposure or risk associated with a given customer relationship.

For instance, if one of your customers buys for multiple locations, the Sold To address typically does not change, but the Ship To address on each order might be different. It is easy to find the totality of open invoices due or past due for this customer—simply find this information using the Sold To address value. Now suppose each location this customer has actually represents a stand-alone company. Without a parent/child account balance inquiry, it would be necessary to inquire on each account individually and manually calculate the total or aggregate exposure using balance information from each such individual inquiry. The Parent/Child Browse form, as illustrated here, solves these kinds of business data aggregation dilemmas quite easily.

The Transaction Model and OneWorld Forms

Most business transaction-style forms—whether paper-based or systemically based, generally contain two major data entry areas. The top half of the form is usually called the transaction header. It contains general information that is typically transaction-specific and that applies to the specific articles or contents of the business transaction in a general way. Consider a sales order. Generally speaking, the transaction header for a sales order contains information such as the customer name and address, billing or shipping information, an order date, an assigned order or reference number, and the method of payment.

The detail portion of a transaction contains information that is typically specific to each component in a business transaction. For instance, in the case of a customer order, it identifies each item or service ordered, usually as a separate order line on the transaction document. The specific information provided generally includes a part number or description, a quantity, and a price or cost per item.

The standard business transaction model just described is also how OneWorld organizes and works with information about your business transactions. To that end, OneWorld has several program models that are specifically designed for entering and processing transaction-related information. Although a fill-in-the-blank form is convenient for the end user, these types of transaction processing programs are some of the most sophisticated in all of OneWorld.

OneWorld Business Views

Before we enter a detailed discussion of OneWorld transaction processing forms, it might be helpful to define the concept of a business view. Although a discussion of relational database theory is beyond the scope of this book, in order to understand how the next several types of OneWorld interactive programs or forms actually work, an understanding of the concept of business views in OneWorld is appropriate, if not required. OneWorld relies extensively on the use of the relational data model or a relational database, such as Oracle, Microsoft SQL Server, or DB/2.

In OneWorld, a business view is really a way of referencing the OneWorld data file or table. For World software and AS/400 technical individuals, a business view is conceptually similar to a logical file. A single data file or table typically contains multiple records or rows of business-specific information that is organized in a similar format—with each file containing multiple data entry fields or columns of information. A database is a collection of related data files or tables. *The data model is the equivalent of an organization chart for business data, as it is organized within OneWorld.*

For instance, one example of such a database is the Address Book. The Address Book data model in OneWorld is actually comprised of multiple files—with each file having a singular use in the data model. The records between these files together constitute the "whole" of the OneWorld Address Book record.

When information in one file relates to information in another file—or business view—at least one field or column-level entry in each data record or table row must be common between them in order for a relationship to exist. These related—but different—records are connected through at least one common data column or field in each individual file or table.

In the case of the Address Book, every table that is part of the Address Book data model is related by way of one common field—the Address Book Number.

So how does OneWorld find information within a database? Through the use of business views. A business view represents the logical organizing or indexing of similar or related records or rows of information that are typically stored in a single data file or table. In most cases, OneWorld program execution is based on a single business view of the data. However, in some cases, such as with the Header Detail program, two business views are used. Generally speaking, OneWorld logically organizes header-related information into a single business view, and the transaction details are organized into another business view. For instance, the common fields between the transaction detail and the header business views are typically the transaction document number and transaction type fields.

In addition, it is also possible to have additional views of data that span multiple files or tables. These are called *joins*. For instance, OneWorld does not need to copy every column of information about an Address Book record for a supplier into the Header table for every purchase order transaction created for any given supplier. However, if a vendor purchases report based on an Address Book reporting code is needed, a join can be created between the Address Book reporting codes table and the Purchase Order detail table. Thus, in this case, a special business view might be needed. This business view would be used in the OneWorld Enterprise Report Writer to create a report to fulfill your business needs. This report is possible using the business view created by joining two files or tables—in this case, using the supplier number value—in order to fill in the missing pieces of Address Book-related information needed during report creation.

OneWorld Header Programs

A transaction header-style data entry program can typically be used to maintain both master data and transaction-related data. For instance, in OneWorld, a header-style form is really nothing more than a variation of the Fix and Inspect program model (discussed earlier).

An option for some OneWorld transaction cycles, such as Sales Order entry, is the ability to perform transaction entry in one or two steps. If transaction entry is performed in one step, it typically means that the use of the Fix and Inspect program related to the transaction header is bypassed. Instead, the required header fields are combined in the Header Detail program. The Header Detail program used for Sales Order Header entry is shown in Figure 9-8. Ignore for a moment the open drop-down menu. Note the use of tabs on the Sales Order Header entry. Not all Fix and Inspect programs used as transaction header forms use tabs.

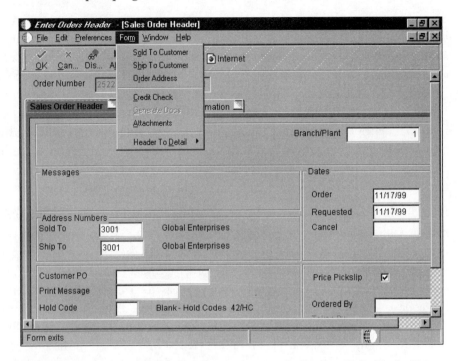

FIGURE 9-8 *The OneWorld Fix and Inspect Program for Purchase Order Header Entry*

The Header Detail Program

The Header Detail program is an all-in-one transaction entry form. The Header Detail program combines the data fields contained in a transaction header form, along with the contents of a transaction detail form, into a single on-screen entry form. Typically, the Detail section of the on-screen Header Detail form contains an abbreviated or abridged version of the Header form for a transaction.

The Header Detail program typically provides the quickest way to record a product or service sale or establish a purchase order in OneWorld. The Header Detail program is designed for speed. It works best in a repetitive order environment where the customer or supplier is already known to your organization. The reason for this is that the Header portion of the form window includes or raises only the fields that would vary by order.

For instance, each purchase order entered is typically for a different supplier number. However, payment terms and shipping instructions are typically the same for every order to a given supplier and need not be reviewed or entered. This information can be established for the order from previously entered information about the supplier that resides in the Address Book. Figure 9-9 shows the OneWorld Header Detail form for Purchase Order entry.

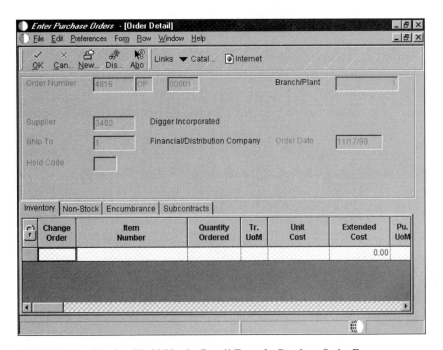

FIGURE 9-9 *The OneWorld Header Detail Form for Purchase Order Entry*

Thus far, the discussion of the Header Detail program has been focused on the header. However, an important aspect of the Header Detail program is the transaction detail or row entry portion of the form window. In OneWorld, the Data Grid (introduced in Chapter 8) is used as the lower portion of the transaction data entry form in a Header Detail program. The Data Grid represents the Detail portion of the Header Detail program. The good news is that the navigation and formatting rules you have already learned—including the use of a custom or user-specific format for the grid, represented as tabs—still apply here.

Maintaining Header Data for OneWorld Transactions Created Through a Header Detail Program

It is important to understand that information not contained in the Header portion of the Header Detail or on the Header form itself in some cases should not be considered as simply unavailable or irrelevant to the underlying business transaction. For example, a customer might request that this order be shipped or diverted to a different location than he normally receives goods at. It's possible to effect such a change in the Ship To information for the order. You do this through the OneWorld program menu bar by selecting Form, Ship To Customer.

Other options or "exits" under Form allow similar header-level changes to OneWorld transaction-related data fields. The open drop-down menu in Figure 9-8 illustrates the form or header-level changes that are possible for an *existing* Sales Order Header. In OneWorld, these form-level program exits are sometimes unavailable until *after* a header record has been created and saved. For instance, this is true for the Sales Order Header example shown in Figure 9-8.

The Header-Less Detail Program

The Header-Less Detail program is another type of OneWorld interactive data entry program. As suggested by its name, this program does not permit entry or modification of any header-level data associated through the form itself. The form generally relies on only one business view of the data, unlike the Header Detail program, which typically relies on two business views of data. A typical use of the Header-Less Detail program is to maintain lower-level master data records related to a single master data record. A good example is the existence of multiple phone numbers for a single contact person at a customer or supplier record maintained in the Address Book through Who's Who. Figure 9-10 shows a Header-Less Detail program example.

Most likely, you're wondering how the Header-Less Detail and the Header Detail programs really vary, since they look nearly identical. Generally speaking, the easiest way to distinguish between them is simple: Do any editable fields appear in the header portion of the screen? If not, you're typically dealing with a Header-Less Detail program. If so, you're typically dealing with a Header Detail program. The bottom line is really to what extent related pieces of data can be maintained from a single OneWorld program. As a final note about the OneWorld Header-Less Detail form, the Data Grid portion of the screen functions the same way it would on the Header Detail program. The OneWorld Data Grid was discussed at length in Chapter 8.

Where Do Entry Form Details Originate?

It is also of particular importance to understand how an actual transaction or *data row*—such as a purchase order detail line—is built or constructed in OneWorld.

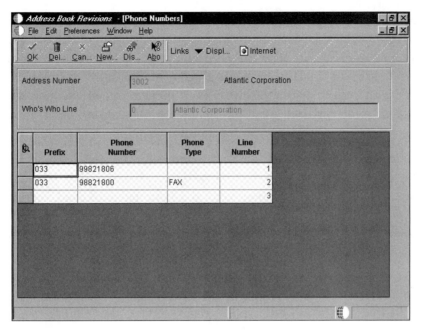

FIGURE 9-10 *The OneWorld Header-Less Detail Form for Phone Numbers of an Address Book Who's Who Entry*

Every OneWorld transaction is built or constructed from a complex series of business rules that determine default values as well as any override values. In effect, a "data source hierarchy" determines the default and override values that build or construct the OneWorld transaction details. In some cases, a data source hierarchy also exists for master data records—such as item master records and item branch/plant records.

OneWorld Data Hierarchies, Data Integrity, and Data Administration

Data hierarchies also have important ramifications for changes to or the deletion of any existing OneWorld transaction or master data record.

For instance, for any given item in a master data record (such as the item master record) to be deleted, the item must have been reduced to zero quantities on hand or must be on order for all locations. All master data references to that item must first be deleted. For instance, a cross-reference table entry that allows substitution of another item by the deleted item should be deleted. As soon as all references are eliminated, the item can be deleted in the branch/plant table and finally in the item master table.

Changes can have equally serious ramifications. Configuration changes, such as removing a UDC table value used by an existing purchase order awaiting goods receipt, might in fact not allow goods receipt to occur because of a transaction error indicating an invalid value for a given field. The incorrect value must be replaced with a valid value on the order document before goods receipt is allowed. I have even encountered situations in which master data records had to be re-created in order to complete an in-process transaction.

I can't stress enough the need for your organization's implementation team to develop a keen appreciation of the OneWorld data model and, in particular, the data hierarchy for each application. With this information in hand, your organization will need to determine the appropriate measures for master data and configuration security, as well as data administration procedures that are appropriate for your organization.

Documenting OneWorld Data Entry as a Part of Your Business Procedures

In an earlier chapter I mentioned that J. D. Edwards and its competitors are moving away from system documentation that contains screen examples. There are numerous reasons why software vendors are doing this. There are both pragmatic and economic reasons for eliminating screen shots in documentation.

For instance, in the case of J. D. Edwards, it does simplify the process of maintaining documentation for roughly identical application functionality that can appear in as many as five different formats. These include OneWorld Windows, Java, or HTML GUI interfaces; the World Vision Windows front end for World software; and the World software interface itself. In addition, as software becomes more configurable—as in the case of OneWorld—the relevance of vendor-provided screen shots within the vendor-delivered documentation becomes even more suspect.

However, there are some compelling reasons to provide your end-users with screen shots within your OneWorld training and procedural documentation. For instance, the use of "before" and "after" screen shots is a particularly helpful practice for both master data entry and transaction entry screens. Sometimes a picture is worth a thousand words. I generally use the "before" screen shot to illustrate user-entered fields and the "after" screen shot to represent the combination of user-entered and "system-defaulted" or "system-completed" values—the end result.

If your organization sees value in such documentation practices, you should consider the Custom User Education product, discussed in Chapter 2. Custom User

Education allows you to combine your company's procedural and training materials, such as "before" and "after" screen shots, along with other custom annotations, with the contents of the standard OneWorld Reference Guides.

 DOCUMENTATION TIP

Use Screen Shots in Your Documentation

Using "before" and "after" screen shots is a particularly helpful practice for both master data entry and transaction entry screens. "Before" snapshots can illustrate user-entered fields, and "after" screen shots can illustrate both user-entered and system-entered values.

The OneWorld Batch or Report Model Program

The final program model that must be discussed is the OneWorld Batch or Report Model program. Recall from previous discussions that OneWorld has two general types of programs that are activated through OneWorld Explorer menu entries. The first type is interactive programs, which were introduced in this chapter and the last. The second type of OneWorld program is the batch or report program. These types of programs are typically submitted on an interactive basis for processing in the background or as a batch process.

Report programs, such as a report containing all customer records, and update programs, such as a program that posts all general ledger transactions associated with the Accounts Payable system to the general ledger, are two examples. Much like OneWorld provides a common way to access all programs (through a menu), OneWorld also provides a common way to activate all OneWorld batch or report processes.

Version Prompting

In the World software, J. D. Edwards called this batch process activation method DREAM Writer, which stood for Data Record Extraction And Management system. In OneWorld, J. D. Edwards employs a similar method for batch process activation. However, it is no longer called DREAM Writer. It is now called the Version Prompting form.

The OneWorld Version Prompting form is really a Work With program that lists the available versions of any given OneWorld program. Generally speaking, all OneWorld batch programs typically have one or more versions. In later chapters, you'll learn other important uses for the Versions List, in addition to its role as the entry point for initiating batch processes, such as reports.

How Version Prompting Works

Most batch processes are performed periodically rather than daily. When batch processes are performed on a daily basis, they are generally referred to as "end of day processing." Therefore, it stands to reason that batch processes typically reside on OneWorld menus with names like "End of Day Processing," "Periodic Processing," and "Reports and Inquiries." As an example, consider Address Book reports. For instance, if you want a report of all Address Book entries, follow this menu path:

> Master Directory (G) > Foundation Systems (G0) > Address Book (G010) > Periodic Processing (**G0121**)

As you can see in Figure 9-11, the Address Book Periodic Processing menu (G0121) has numerous Address Book-related reports.

For the purposes of this example, do the following:

1. Highlight the first menu entry, Reports by Address (R014021).

2. Click on this entry to select it.

The Work With Batch Versions form, shown in Figure 9-12, appears for Batch Application R014021: One Line Per Address.

The next step is to select and submit, or *execute,* a batch version. There are two ways to submit a report for processing:

◆ Without specifying any overrides on the Version Prompting form

◆ With overrides specified on the Version Prompting form

Overrides allow for the modification of data selection, sequencing, and other advanced version functions. For the purposes of this example, overrides will not be specified. Follow these steps:

1. Highlight the first entry, Version XJDE0001, One Line Per Address.

2. Click on the Select button.

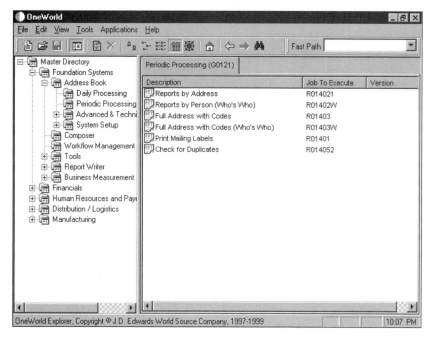

FIGURE 9-11 *The Address Book Periodic Processing Menu*

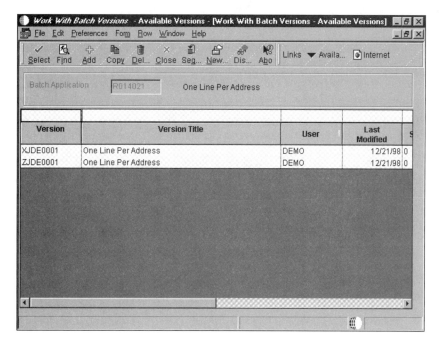

FIGURE 9-12 *The Work With Batch Versions Form*

The Work With Batch Versions - Available Versions - [Version Prompting] form appears, as shown in Figure 9-13. It is from this form that a version is actually submitted for processing.

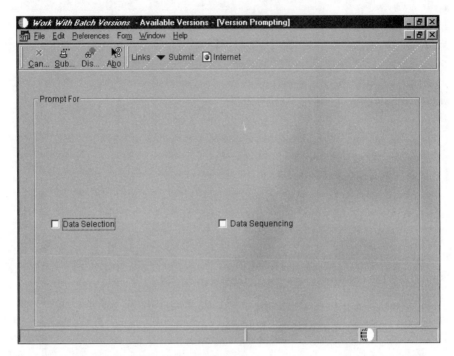

FIGURE 9-13 *The Version Prompting Form*

At this point, there are always two options. The first option is to submit the report for processing. The second option is to cancel further processing of the report.

Notice the placement of the Cancel and Submit buttons on the Version Prompting screen. This placement is intentional and differs from the Cancel or close button used in OneWorld interactive programs. The placement is meant to encourage thoughtful review of your intentions here. Due diligence is stressed here for two reasons. First, reports and batch processes often update your organization's business data. Second, batch processes are generally time-consuming and might place an unusual amount of workload on your server. Therefore, before executing these processes, you must always exercise caution. The placement is meant to check that you understand how any given batch process will affect your system before you make such submissions.

The next and subsequent chapters provide further information about batch and report processing using Version Prompting. In particular, the use version overrides—particularly the Data Selection, Data Sequencing, and Processing Options—will be discussed. For now, to complete this exercise, click on the Submit button. The Report Output Destination form appears, as shown in Figure 9-14.

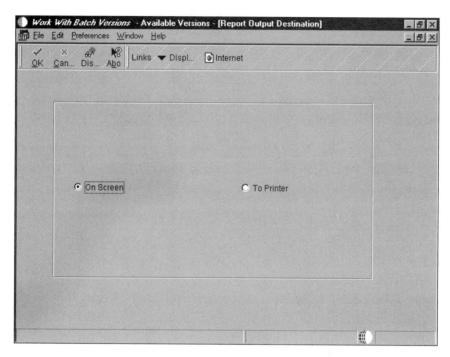

FIGURE 9-14 *The Report Output Destination Form*

Using this form, you can preview the contents of a report before sending it to a printer. For the purposes of this exercise, click on the On Screen button. The screen reverts to the Versions List for this report. Your workstation's disk drive should be busy. After a few moments, a report should appear on your screen in the Adobe Acrobat reader. All OneWorld reports are spooled in the Adobe Acrobat reader format.

When you're done viewing any report appearing in Adobe Acrobat, from the Acrobat menu bar, select File, Exit. The Adobe Acrobat reader program closes. As you will notice, Adobe Acrobat does not immediately display the report in a highly readable manner. There are Adobe Acrobat features that allow for increasing the magnification and thereby increasing the readability of the on-screen version of a

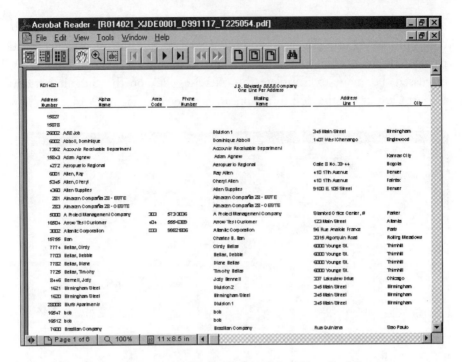

FIGURE 9-15 *The Adobe Acrobat Reader Version of the Address Book Report*

report. Adobe Acrobat also allows the report to be saved. A complete discussion of Adobe Acrobat is beyond the scope of this book. However, more information is available in the Acrobat Help file. To view Adobe Acrobat Help, from the Adobe Acrobat menu bar, select Help, Reader Online Guide. If this file is missing, it can found on the OneWorld Documentation CD-ROM.

If, on the Report Output Destination form, To Printer is selected instead of To Screen, a Printer Selection form appears on the screen instead. The appearance of this form varies by system. For example, the form that appears when you run the stand-alone version of OneWorld is shown in Figure 9-16.

The Address Book report example is the typical manner in which all OneWorld reports and batch processes are submitted with version prompting. However, it is also possible to submit the OneWorld report or batch processing without ever prompting the user for any information. In addition, a report or batch process version can be scheduled for processing at a predetermined time on a regular or one-time basis. Future chapters provide more information about these version submission alternatives.

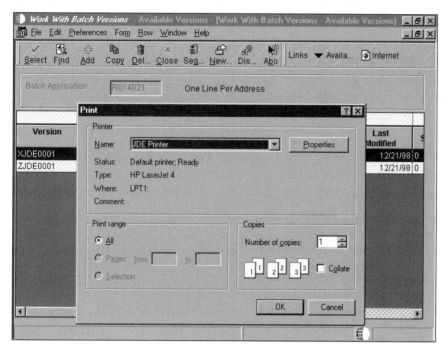

FIGURE 9-16 *Printer Selection Form for OneWorld Stand-Alone*

Summary

This was a lengthy chapter that provided a number of important explanations and that featured numerous examples. The various OneWorld interactive model programs were introduced:

- ◆ The Work With program
- ◆ The Search and Select program
- ◆ The Fix and Inspect program
- ◆ The Parent/Child Browse program
- ◆ The Header Detail program
- ◆ The Header-Less Detail program

In addition to these examples and explanations, numerous other concepts were introduced, including

- ◆ Business views
- ◆ Business logic versus field validation logic

You also saw an explanation and an example of how the OneWorld batch or report-style program works, particularly using the concept of version prompting. The examples provided in this chapter represent the look and feel as well as the user interface aspects of all OneWorld programs in general. Therefore, this chapter's examples are representative of how virtually all other OneWorld programs and applications operate.

PART IV

Making OneWorld Work for You

Chapter 10

**Tailoring
OneWorld to Your
Business Needs:
Part I**

Often the reason why an organization chooses to replace its existing business application software with a system such as OneWorld is the important benefits provided by the tools included with the system that will allow your organization to personalize or configure the software to your organization's specific needs.

It is frequently said that in business, the one thing you can count on is change. In OneWorld, you will find a rich set of personalization tools that will help you meet the challenges of business change. The tools that you will learn about in this chapter will allow your organization to respond quickly to its ever-changing business requirements.

What Benefits Are Provided by Personalization?

Certainly from a business case point of view, responsiveness to change is the primary benefit your organization will derive through personalization. Although OneWorld business applications provide the potential to improve end-user productivity and streamline processes, the OneWorld personalization tools will improve the productivity of your systems support department.

For instance, if your company uses the term "catalog number" instead of "part number," through the personalization functions within OneWorld, you can make such a substitution with relative ease—all without reprogramming any portion of OneWorld. Need an address book report that contains only customers for a certain city? That's easy. Just create another version of the report that contains the zip codes for that city—again, without any reprogramming of OneWorld.

The Soft-Coding Concept

It also stands to reason that your OneWorld system will be easier to maintain given the ability to personalize the software to your organization. When I was first introduced to J. D. Edwards' World software back in 1990, its term for this personalization capability was *soft coding*. Although this term is not a major part of the J. D. Edwards vocabulary today, it remains a fundamental concept underlying OneWorld, so I'll use it here to help you gain the right perspective on personalization.

Traditionally, much of a computer program's data and logic was *hard coded*, or built into the computer program itself. When program requirements were simpler and computer storage costs high, hard-coding had its merits. As computer hardware and software have matured, the wisdom of hard coding just about anything in a computer program has been severely challenged. Today, hard coding is considered among the worst of computer software design practices. So if hard coding is not an option, it stands to reason that soft coding is the way to go.

When soft coding is used, much more of the logic and conditional values related to the system become stored *and changeable* values. These stored values exist in a file or table. Such files or tables can be altered when needed through a set of additional programs that are written specifically for such table maintenance. So when soft coding is used, the program does not change, but the table does.

Table Configuration Replaces Programming

For many, the tough part of understanding the implementation of an ERP system such as OneWorld is the amount of effort required to successfully implement or set up such a system.

Previously, if an organization wanted to solve a business information problem through automation, a specialized computer program was usually prepared. Such efforts typically required the skills of a business systems analyst to translate a business problem, articulated by a business domain or subject matter expert into a system requirement. The business systems analyst would then provide the system requirements to a skilled computer programmer, who would create the system necessary to solve the business problem. Under the package software model, *configuration replaces programming*—and a substantial amount of configuration is necessary to make the typical ERP system, such as OneWorld, work for the typical organization.

Although many business processes are considered as highly standardized, they can and do vary. For instance, inventory accounting practices differ between manufacturing and distribution companies. Therefore, to be successful, software vendors such as J. D. Edwards must make their software configurable by the customer to suit their individual business practices. Failing to do this would limit the market for the software product and the software maker's long-term prospects as well.

How Much Customization Should You Do?

My former colleague and manager, William Yost, said it best: "When you buy a software package, also in the box is a way of doing business. You therefore have but two choices: Change the way you do business, or change the package." I have searched but have not found a more realistic perspective about both the challenges (adapting your organization to the package, or changing the software) and the limitations (every software package has them) that accompany a packaged software implementation.

Over time, I have found that many organizations engage in unnecessary and costly modifications to their packaged software. You might believe that as a consultant in this industry, I might advocate more change, not less, to the core package. However, I do not adhere to such a self-serving perspective. Rather, I believe that only necessary changes should be made to a software package, even to OneWorld, which has a robust tool set for creating and maintaining custom enhancements to the core product. Therefore, my recommended best practices are that OneWorld customization should be limited to just three areas:

◆ Make necessary customizations to comply with the applicable regulations that affect your operation within a certain industry or jurisdiction where OneWorld clearly does not provide built-in functionality or a suitable workaround cannot be determined to fill this gap in functionality.

◆ Make only essential customizations that will truly provide a competitive advantage or that are deemed necessary to meet a competitive threat. Competition-matching customizations only allow your organization to sustain market share and generally don't provide any competitive advantage. In this latter instance, your organization might be better served if a short-term workaround is identified and if your full attention is devoted to challenging the competitive threat through market enhancements that will provide a competitive advantage. I recommend this latter course as taking a market-matching instead of a market-enhancement course of action. It might require additional or different custom enhancements to OneWorld.

◆ Make only essential customizations that will prevent cost escalation. This typically is caused when implementing OneWorld cripples a lean or best-of-breed business process you already have in place. An example might be the need to replicate, in OneWorld, the tight integration of a process control-based data collection system with an existing business information or *legacy* system.

I evaluate OneWorld customization decisions almost exclusively on return on investment criteria. Therefore, any customization made to the OneWorld core software should be influenced by the identified customization's ability to do the following:

◆ Generate revenue in excess of its cost

◆ Reduce costs that exceed its own costs

◆ Contain or prevent cost escalation by an amount that is less than its own cost

You might say that my position on software package modification is nothing less than controversial. However, I believe it is the right way to make a sound business decision about how much customization should actually occur to your organization's OneWorld system.

Here's a final note, especially if you are still evaluating OneWorld and other software packages for your organization: It is my contention that if you have done your homework on the front end, during the software selection process, you will likely pick a package that represents the best fit for your organization's business requirements and should therefore require the least amount of customization.

Will a Smaller Organization Have Less Configuration Work?

It has been my experience that smaller companies can and do have business processing requirements that are as complicated as the largest multinational corporation. Of course, the simpler your business processes are, or the more adaptable and amicable your organization is toward accepting and embracing change, the less likely it will be that you will need to make substantial changes to OneWorld. To be sure, there are differences.

One of the hallmarks of OneWorld is scalability, both functional and technical. For instance, a smaller organization generally has a shorter workflow, or thoughtful review process, for the approval of a purchase order or a purchase order requisition. For instance, with OneWorld you can create as simple or as complicated an order processing flow as you want. Of course, as you complicate the flow, you also complicate the configuration steps.

What likely has a more dramatic impact on the amount of configuration that will be needed to successfully use OneWorld is your organization's line of business. For instance, a manufacturer of standard cataloged parts (typically called a "make to stock" manufacturer) requires greater configuration than will a distributor of preassembled cataloged parts (such as a catalog house, wholesaler, or manufacturer's representative). However, a manufacturer of semicustom- or custom-engineered products (typically called a "make to order" manufacturer) will likely have more configuration work to do than the "make to stock" manufacturing company.

Also, expect more configuration work if any of the following situations apply to you:

◆ Your organization is a nonprofit or governmental body

◆ Your organization has multiple companies (subsidiaries) and divisions or operates from multiple physical locations

◆ Your organization sells consumer products in several states

◆ Your organization operates internationally, dealing with multiple currencies

The moral of the story is simple. Regardless of your "vertical," or industry, if your business model is simple, OneWorld configuration is straightforward. If your business model is complex, OneWorld configuration will be more complex as well.

Your organization might find that your implementation consultant prefers to work from a template for the OneWorld implementation that is industry-specific to your "vertical." Note that not all consultants have these templates, and note further that sometimes these templates won't fit your business model. As a matter of fact, sometimes these "implementation templates" can be more trouble than they are worth. They are sometimes long on process and short on results.

Therefore, a cautionary note about configuration templates is in order. If your organization has processes that closely resemble those that are within the template, some efficiency might be gained in the overall configuration process. Although these templates might jump-start your implementation, they will not eliminate the need to review your processes and ensure that OneWorld has been properly configured to suit your business requirements. If the template can't be easily retrofitted for your organization's business model, question the value of using it. A consultant who can work only from a template is likely an inexperienced consultant who might be a bit naive.

Can a Large Organization Get by with Less Configuration Work?

Despite some of the horror stories you might have heard or read, large organizations can and do implement ERP systems successfully. Many do so without extensive customization of the core package. However, larger organizations usually couple an ERP implementation with process change—also known as business process reengineering or business transformation.

Despite the ugliness and job insecurity that are sometimes associated (often incorrectly) with business change, especially in the case of an ERP system, organizations are more successful when processes are changed as opposed to making the software fit the business.

On the same note, most ERP implementations create new and enriched jobs for business analysts and certain other professionals within the organization while reducing the number of application developers needed. However, the application developer can also benefit by learning new skills—in this case, the OneWorld tools. As for end-user personnel, when all is said and done, OneWorld alone generally does not reduce head count. However, if other productivity-enhancing programs are instituted, such as evaluated receipt settlements or automated shop floor data capture, some labor savings might be possible.

For instance, I have worked with a $50 million company and a $500 million company that needed to change their standard voucher check layout. Configurability differences cause havoc, so it makes sense to buy a computer program off the shelf that could be used immediately or with little modification to fit your industry.

ActivEra

Over the past several years, ERP vendors such as J. D. Edwards and SAP have strived to simplify the configuration of ERP implementation. SAP introduced ASAP (Accelerated SAP), and J. D. Edwards introduced ActivEra (discussed briefly in Chapter 2), as its answer to simplifying OneWorld configuration and change.

Wouldn't it be wonderful if OneWorld could tell you exactly what to configure? Actually, it can. With the introduction of ActivEra, J. D. Edwards lets its customers script themselves through a particular aspect of OneWorld configuration, thereby ensuring that each configuration element is reviewed and that any necessary additions or adjustments are made.

ActivEra was introduced in December of 1998. It is a part of the J. D. Edwards Idea to Action initiative. I consider the concept of Idea to Action more a clever marketing program than an approach toward the implementation of OneWorld. What Idea to Action does is play off the amount of change an organization faces, as well as the need for fast response. The story is simply that as an organization needs to quickly reconfigure itself and its business processes, OneWorld can quickly adapt to these changes as well.

I have found the explanations that J. D. Edwards provides about ActivEra and Idea to Action on its Web site and in its marketing literature lacking in substance. Previously, I have found that J. D. Edwards did a better of job of explaining itself with regard to explaining its approaches or methodologies, such as R.E.P. and OnTrack. So with all of that said, here is a brief introduction as to ActivEra.

ActivEra is a multifaceted solution or approach that lets the organization easily adapt its OneWorld software before or after its implementation. The ActivEra solution consists of three components:

◆ The ActivEra Console

◆ ActivEra Activators

◆ The ActivEra Extension Architecture

More accurately stated, ActivEra is a tool that both simplifies and accelerates configuration or change in OneWorld. The next section further explains how ActivEra works.

How ActivEra Works

This section introduces several ActivEra concepts. A grasp of these basic concepts will give you an overall understanding of ActivEra.

The ActivEra Console

The ActivEra Console can be thought of as an adaptation or change workbench. The ActivEra Console guides a person who is responsible for a particular OneWorld functional or technical configuration activity through the necessary steps to configure OneWorld to the business or technology requirement.

ActivEra Activators

The necessary configuration activities or steps are defined in scripts called ActivEra Activators. You can view these Activators as wizards, much like those that guide you through completing the installation of a Windows-based program. Another way to think of the ActivEra Console is as an Explorer-like front end for accessing the ActivEra Activators. The ActivEra Activators are further identified as Business Activators or Technology Activators. The current release of OneWorld includes more than 100 individual Activators. J. D. Edwards has indicated that future releases of OneWorld will offer more than 200 Activators and will provide more extensive ActivEra Console capabilities.

Business Activators

A Business Activator is intended to simplify the configuration process. Business Activators streamline the complexity of the configuration. A *knowledgeable* business professional—not necessarily a systems professional—can make needed changes to the OneWorld configuration. Business Activators let you make OneWorld functional configuration changes—such as adding a warehouse facility or creating a new sales order processing procedure.

Arguably, many of these Business Activators are in my estimation too advanced in scope for the business professional who has only moderate or average skills and knowledge of OneWorld. Unfortunately, I cannot provide hard and fast guidelines as to which Activators are clearly within the domain of the business professional and which should rest with the systems professional.

It is my opinion that you will need a OneWorld power user or business systems analyst who owns the OneWorld configuration. This person should assume responsibility for all OneWorld nondevelopment activities. At larger organizations, several people might divide these responsibilities, such as by line of business, by business processing thread, or by groupings of related OneWorld systems.

Figure 10-1 is one of the screen panels from the OneWorld Add a New User Business Activator.

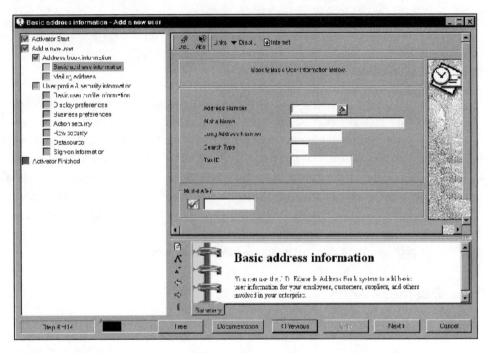

FIGURE 10-1 *A Representative Panel from the OneWorld Add a New User Business Activator*

Technology Activators

A Technology Activator is intended to simplify the tasks associated with OneWorld system management and maintenance. As such, Technology Activators are generally used by systems professionals. For instance, your organization has or likely will designate someone as the OneWorld system administrator. Technology Activators let you make OneWorld technical configuration changes—such as adding a new user to the system, designing a new business report, or administering the server.

Arguably, many of these Technology Activators can be used by a *knowledgeable* business professional just as easily as by a systems professional, such as in the case of adding a new user or designing a new business report. However, I must stress that a *knowledgeable* business professional in this case is one who is knowledgeable about OneWorld as well as his or her particular business process or requirement.

The demarcation between a Technology Activator (which a *knowledgeable* business professional would work with) and a systems administrator task is a simpler choice. If the configuration task concerns object management or Configurable Network Computing (CNC), it is clearly a task for the OneWorld systems administrator, not the power user.

The ActivEra Extension Architecture

The ActivEra Extension Architecture lets the organization that uses OneWorld create its own or custom Activators. For example, a company might need to develop a repeatable process to add a new branch office.

Relying on the ActivEra Console, Activators, and the ActivEra Extension Architecture, the criteria to add a new branch office can be built into ActivEra, enabling the use of this custom process each time a branch office is added.

ActivEra and Soft Coding

Two topics introduced in this chapter might now sound similar to you—soft coding and ActivEra. These topics were discussed in the context of being tools for the configuration of OneWorld. In case you are wondering whether these two topics are related, the answer is yes.

Behind those ActivEra Activators are individual programs that carry out the actual OneWorld configuration action or step. In many cases, these are the programs that carry out a particular soft-coding step, such as adding a user-defined code value. In other cases, ActivEra relies on some of these actual OneWorld application programs, such as the Address Book.

Recall that the Address Book contains the names of your organization's employees, who are OneWorld users as well. So, when you are setting up a new user, it stands to reason that employee users must either already exist in the Address Book or must be set up in the Address Book as they are defined as OneWorld users.

In conclusion, another way to look at ActivEra Activator is as a way of grouping multiple steps that really fill out a complete configuration process—such as adding a new user. Thus, you might say that ActivEra Console, along with the ActivEra Activators, puts a pretty face on the configuration of OneWorld. It's a shortcut approach to the configuration process that requires a minimum amount of OneWorld configuration-related knowledge. The long way home in OneWorld configuration is understanding what all the steps are and accessing individual OneWorld programs to complete those steps. Recall that in Chapter 6, I outlined a process whereby configuration tasks can be identified and a configuration script can be written for each particular system that is a part of your organization's OneWorld implementation. In this case, J. D. Edwards has already done this for you through the standard ActivEra Activators.

Some Final Thoughts on ActivEra

In Chapter 2, I said that ActivEra is the current J. D. Edwards methodology or approach for implementing OneWorld, and that it has evolved from some previous generations of approaches or methodologies, such as R.E.P. and OnTrack. The earlier explanation of ActivEra was an oversimplification, because it was not entirely correct in indicating that ActivEra alone will get the job done for you. As a software company, J. D. Edwards' emphasis or focus is on the tools necessary to get the job done—not necessarily on the process. Chapters 4 through 6 addressed many of the process-related initiatives needed to successfully implement OneWorld.

Should You Use ActivEra?

For a new OneWorld client, the ActivEra "scripted" approach is perhaps easier to follow. However, in some other cases, this might not be true. A good example comes from my world. A fellow consultant who was an expert in warehousing but who possessed no knowledge of OneWorld attended a 10-day immersion class on OneWorld. In this class, his only observation or knowledge of how OneWorld is configured was based on the activators he saw in class. Using activators as the configuration script, he found the process easy. However, with this road map, a deeper understanding and hands-on knowledge of the software is needed. For instance, a business or systems professional with extensive OneWorld or World software experience might perceive ActivEra as more of a novelty—and therefore might find that it is faster to rely on his previous experience and knowledge of OneWorld configuration steps than to use ActivEra. I suppose that I, along with many of my consulting colleagues, fall into this group—or maybe it is a case of not being able to teach an old dog a new trick.

System Setup Without ActivEra

The most confusing part of OneWorld configuration is probably locating where all the configuration components actually are. As a matter of fact, one of the major reasons motivating J. D. Edwards to create the ActivEra configuration front end—or organizer, as I like to view it—was to address this concern.

The good news is that even without ActivEra, understanding OneWorld configuration is still within the reach of most business and systems professionals. It is my belief that a good level of business process understanding, some commonsense knowledge of the configuration process, and a general knowledge of the OneWorld master data requirements are a sufficient knowledge base for understanding how the OneWorld application is configured and maintained. With that said, we'll begin a general introduction to the various OneWorld configuration tasks.

The OneWorld Back Office

The soft-coding tools and the ActivEra tools, along with developer and CNC tools, constitute the OneWorld "back office" system. The back office system is therefore considered one of the foundation, core, or cornerstone systems in OneWorld. A future chapter will introduce the remaining back office systems.

The OneWorld soft-coding tools and ActivEra both allow for the configuration and personalization of OneWorld. On the other hand, the OneWorld Developer tools allow an organization to complete OneWorld customizations. For example, the Enterprise Report Writer is an important back office system that allows your organization to create "custom" reports in OneWorld. The CNC tools are used to define, configure, and administer the OneWorld operating environment.

These "technical" or "back office" systems, along with certain "functional" systems— the OneWorld Address Book, General Accounting, and Inventory Management systems—constitute the set of "core" or "foundation" systems within OneWorld. All other OneWorld modules minimally rely on the back office systems as well as one or more of the functional foundation systems.

At the core of ActivEra is a set of configuration components that can actually be used on a stand-alone basis, without ActivEra as your guide. These components represent the key business-related configuration elements of OneWorld. The soft-coding components that I refer to include

- ◆ Constants
- ◆ User-defined codes

◆ Vocabulary overrides

◆ The use of versions of programs, each with potentially different processing options, data selection, and data sequencing options

◆ Menus

An understanding of what these components are and how they are typically used to configure OneWorld provides essential background for the business or technical professional, regardless of the approach toward OneWorld configuration that your organization will take—using ActivEra or using a self-scripted process.

From the standpoint of OneWorld setup, two specific menus are primarily used on a system-by-system (or application module-by-application module) basis:

◆ System Administration Tools menu

◆ Application-specific setup menus

System Administration Tools

Many of the configuration steps discussed in this chapter and the next rely on the System Administration Tools menu.

To access the System Administration Tools, select

G > Foundation Systems (G0) > Tools (GH90) > System Administration Tools (**GH9011**)

The System Administration Tools menu is shown in Figure 10-2.

The soft-coding components found on the System Administration Tools menu are discussed in this and subsequent chapters of this book.

Application-Specific System Setup Menus

The remaining application-related configuration steps or tasks are available from application-specific setup menus. Table 10-1 (shown in a moment) provides a comprehensive listing of the OneWorld configuration or setup modules by application. The Procurement System Setup menu for stock-based procurement (G43A41) is shown in Figure 10-3.

The intent of these application-specific setup menus is to organize the setup steps or tasks for you. Generally speaking, the contents of these menus approximate the topics covered in the Setup portion of each OneWorld Application Reference Guide.

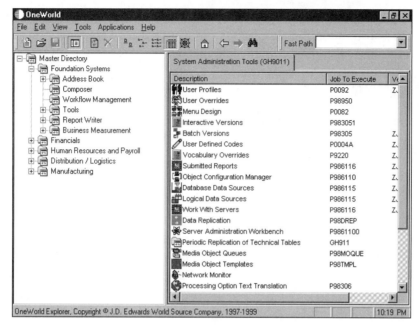

FIGURE 10-2 *The System Administration Tools Menu (GH9011)*

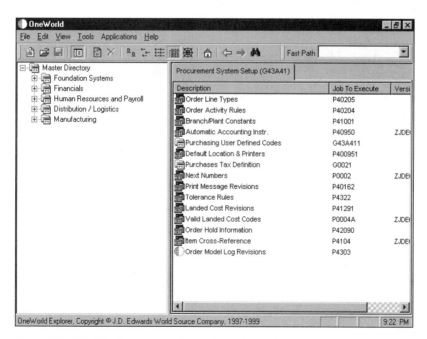

FIGURE 10-3 *The Procurement System Setup Menu for Stock–Based Procurement (G43A41)*

These application-specific setup menus are discussed in this and subsequent chapters. For instance, the next section discusses a typical configuration component on many application-specific setup menus.

Constants

A constant is simply a value that does not change over time. An example of a constant would be the company or plant numbering scheme your organization decides to use in OneWorld, or the number of periods in your organization's fiscal year. Constants are typically established at one or more levels within OneWorld. For instance, a constant could be a system-level constant, a company-specific constant, or a branch/plant constant.

Constants are generally the first configuration components that are defined and established for each OneWorld module or system that is being implemented, such as Accounts Payable or Sales Order Processing. Generally speaking, each specific OneWorld system has its own unique set of constants that must be reviewed and appropriately configured to the specific requirements of your organization.

Constants are perhaps the most important configuration values in any OneWorld module or system. Figure 10-4 illustrates OneWorld's General Accounting Con-

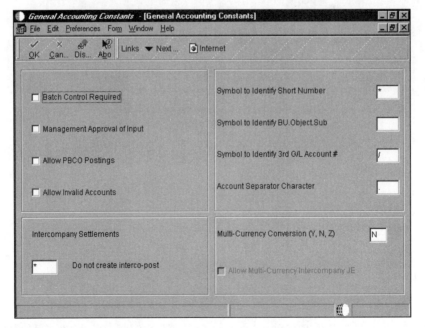

FIGURE 10-4 *The OneWorld General Accounting Constants*

stants. The reference guide for a given OneWorld system identifies the constants that must be correspondingly maintained for that system.

Table 10-1 summarizes the system-level constants that must be reviewed. In addition to these constants, many other user-defined code tables and special-purpose tables are typically associated with each specific module or system within OneWorld. There are cascading interdependencies between OneWorld tables that must be understood and dealt with during the configuration of OneWorld. Table 10-1 has a second purpose in that it also serves as an overall guide to the OneWorld systems and the menu on which configuration for a given module or system is completed.

Table 10-1 OneWorld Application System Setup Menus and Systems with System-Level Constants

OneWorld System	Configuration Menu (Fast Path)	System-Level Constants
Address Book	G0141	Yes
Accounts Receivable	G03B41	Yes
Accounts Payable	G0441	Yes
General Accounting	G094	Yes
Fixed Assets	G1241	Yes
Profit Management	G1641	No
Job Cost	G5141	Yes
Human Resources	G054	Yes (System options)
U. S. Payroll	G07BUSP4	No
Inventory Management	G4141	Yes (Branch/plant constants)
Warehouse Management	G4641	Yes (Branch/plant constants)
Sales Order Management	G4241	No
Pricing Management	G4222	No
Advanced Pricing	G434A41	No
Procurement/Stock Items	G434B41	No
Procurement/Non Stock	G434C41	No
Procurement/Services	G434D41	No

Table 10-1 OneWorld Application System Setup Menus and Systems with System-Level Constants *(continued)*

OneWorld System	Configuration Menu (Fast Path)	System-Level Constants
Procurement/Sub Contracting	G3441	No
Materials Planning/Forecasting	G3442	No
Materials Requirement Planning	G3443	No
Advanced Transportation Management	G4941	No
Product Data Management	G3041	No
Shop Floor Management	G3141	No
Product Configurator	G3241	No
Capacity Requirements Planning	G3341	No
Plant/Equipment Maintenance	G1341	No
Work Order/Service Billing	G4841	No
Quality Management	G3741	No
Customer Service Management	G1740	No

User-Defined Codes

Before we discuss user-defined codes, perhaps some background on exactly what *codification* is would be a more appropriate starting point. Codification is the process of preidentifying values that are commonly used so that they may be consistently applied or used in the future. Codification has several advantages, including consistency, accuracy, and efficiency.

Consistency occurs because the same code is always used to describe the same characteristic, such as the colors. The codes themselves do not change over time. Accuracy occurs because in terms of a computer system, the codes can be stored in a table, and new entries for a code can be validated against the code table, thereby preventing data entry errors. Efficiency occurs because, again in terms of a computer system, the user can call for a list of valid values.

In OneWorld, a significant number of the data entry fields have been codified in one of several ways. For instance, all date fields are codified against a calendar table. Many of the other codified fields use a predefined table or list of acceptable values or codes. The usual way these predefined tables or lists are accessed is by clicking on the searchlight button in OneWorld. A code can be looked up or found in the table or list, and the selected value can be returned to the data entry field as the input value. When a code is established in OneWorld, a definition or description is usually provided for each code as it is defined.

The OneWorld Data Dictionary maintains a list of all OneWorld field names, as well as other important information about each field. One such piece of information maintained by the Data Dictionary is the type of field. The Data Dictionary also maintains information about whether a field is table-driven. When a field is table-driven, the data dictionary also maintains information about which user-defined code table is used to provide an "edit list" of available values for that field. As a result, many tables in OneWorld codify the entries that are valid for a given OneWorld data field.

The majority of these lists or tables are defined as a user-defined code (UDC) in OneWorld. This also suggests that the vast majority of these codified fields in OneWorld are user-maintained. That is largely true, but there are some caveats. Many UDCs have special meanings or formats. For instance, in the case of document types in OneWorld, a specific naming convention applies. In other cases, values are predetermined and can't be changed, such as in the case of General Accounting Batch Types.

One example of a UDC in OneWorld is the Address Book Search Type. Figure 10-5 illustrates the UDC table for the Address Book Search Type.

Given that all name and address information (such as customers, employees, and suppliers) appears in the OneWorld Address Book, wouldn't it be helpful if Address Book records could be classified by type of record—or name and address—they represent? Not a problem! J. D. Edwards created the Search Type field for just this purpose. Notice that OneWorld provides for one type of Customer in the Search Type field.

However, what if you have several types of customers—not just one as OneWorld provides for in the Search Type UDC table? Again, this is not a problem. In this case, the UDC table can be modified to include one or more additional customer types that are specifically needed by your organization. How are entries added to a user-defined table? It is a relatively simple operation, such as in the case of the Search Type field:

1. From any form containing the Search Type field, tab to or click on the entry portion of the field. The searchlight button appears next to the Search Type field.

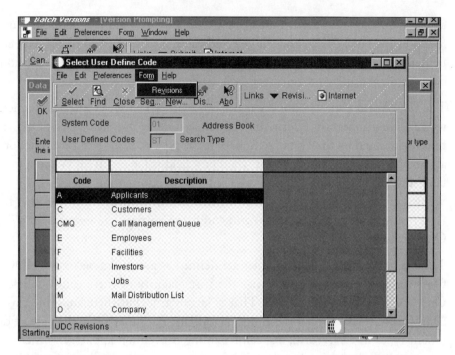

FIGURE 10-5 *User-Defined Code Form for the Address Book Search Type Field*

2. Click on the searchlight button. The Select User Defined Code form appears.

3. Select Form, Revisions. You can now maintain the UDC table you are viewing. In this case, it is the UDC table for the Address Book Search Type field.

4. The Work With User Defined Codes form appears, as shown in Figure 10-6.

You now know the quickest route for maintaining a UDC table in OneWorld. But that's not the entire story on configuring OneWorld's UDC tables!

Another way to maintain UDCs is through System Administration Tools menu. Refer again to Figure 10-6. Notice the fields at the top of the screen—System Code and User Defined Codes. If you know these two values, you can maintain the UDC table through the System Administration Tools menu. To access the System Administration Tools, select

> G > Foundation Systems (G0) > Tools (GH90) > System Administration Tools (**GH9011**)

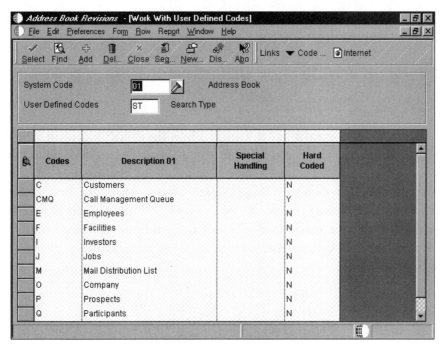

FIGURE 10-6 *The Work With User-Defined Codes Form for the Address Book Search Type Field*

(The System Administration Tools menu is shown in Figure 10-2.) To modify *any* UDC table, do the following:

1. Select User Defined Codes (P0004A) on the System Administration Tools menu.
2. Enter the System Code value.
3. Enter the User Defined Codes value.
4. Click on the Find button. The current values for the selected UDC table appear.

Now you have just two paths that effectively arrive at the same place in OneWorld. With that said, add an additional value to the UDC table:

1. Click on the Add button.
2. Type a unique code value, such as C1, as a Search Term value. Note that the code value cannot be a duplicate of any value that exists in the table.
3. Type a description for the code value, such as Class 1 Customers.
4. Click on the OK button.

The UDC table reappears, and the new value appears in the table. (You might need to scroll through the UDC table to find it.)

Changing and Deleting UDC Values

Deleting UDC values isn't quite as simple. The problem arises from any transactions that relied on these previous values. The reason for this is that you might have already used an existing UDC that is now the subject of a change or that is being deleted. All previous transactions entered into your database relied on these "obsolete" values. If they were never used, or if any records have already been purged from the system with these values in them, you're safe. But actually, you are always safe, because there really isn't a major problem with obsolete data until the record must be maintained. For instance, an error will now occur, forcing changes to the UDC to another value in the UDC table before any changes to the record can be saved.

Changes are usually to a description of the UDC code itself. Therefore, they are inconsequential, because OneWorld relies on the code—not on the descriptions of the code.

Securing Access to the UDC Tables

The title of this section says it all—you should secure access to the UDC tables. Changes to these tables should be routed through a knowledgeable business or technical person. These changes should not be made by end-users. In a later chapter, you will learn about some OneWorld security features that can help secure UDC tables against unauthorized changes.

Other Tables and Fields in OneWorld

Numeric fields, such as dollar amount entries and quantities, and text entry fields, such as a name or description, are examples of the types of fields that OneWorld does not codify. However, in some cases you will want to self-impose guidelines on how the contents of certain fields—such as Alpha Name or Item Descriptions—should be entered in order to make searches against your master data tables more efficient.

OneWorld has many special types of tables. Although the searchlight button can retrieve values for these fields during transaction data entry or inquiry, these special types of tables cannot be maintained in the same way that UDC tables are maintained. These special types of tables implement complex business rules, such as sales tax calculations and payment terms. A special OneWorld program is required to maintain each of these special tables. The reference guide for a given OneWorld system identifies the special types of tables that must be correspondingly maintained for that system.

Configuration Sharing

Each individual OneWorld system, such as Accounts Payable or Sales Order Management, generally requires the configuration of multiple elements. This is especially true of UDC set values—but in reality, there are many additional shared configuration tables.

When a configuration is shared by multiple OneWorld systems, it is important to consider the sum of the configuration required, not simply the configuration that is applicable to a single system or, for that manner, a single user or process. Therefore, many configuration elements are shared by multiple OneWorld systems and therefore need to be configured only once in a manner that represents the overall needs of your organization.

If you're wondering what Accounts Payable and Sales Order Processing have in common, the answer is sales taxes. Sales taxes represent only one example from a series of tables shared between OneWorld applications.

This "configure once, use many" scenario is possible even when your organization phases or stages the rollout of OneWorld systems. For instance, your organization might elect not to install OneWorld all at once—sometimes called a "big bang" or "full" implementation. Instead, your organization might opt for a "partial" or "phased" implementation of OneWorld, starting with implementing only the Financial systems, followed by the Distribution systems at a later date, and implementing the Manufacturing systems at an even later date. Both of these scenarios are quite typical.

Putting It All Together: Some Tips on OneWorld Configuration

Configuring a system like OneWorld requires a significant time commitment. This is certainly one of the major reasons why consultants like me are frequently engaged to help organizations. Most organizations have employees who, given the right amount of time, can figure out how to make OneWorld work for their organization. Unfortunately, many organizations can't afford to commit staff members to do nothing else except configure OneWorld. This is one reason that consultants are frequently called in to help.

An experienced consultant can be used to reduce the learning curve regarding OneWorld configuration for your staff. This consultant can also be called on to configure OneWorld for you, with minimal input from your staff. However, the more "face time" your staff has with the configuration aspects of OneWorld, the better off your organization will be over time. If you rely too much on consultants, you might not be able to maintain your configuration without their assistance in the future. If your staff can't spend much time with the consultant, insist on adequate documentation for your configuration. Many of the configuration steps mentioned next will be discussed in upcoming chapters. My recommended steps toward achieving a successful OneWorld configuration are as follows:

◆ Develop a general understanding of how each business process will be affected by OneWorld. This is the As Is model.

◆ Develop a general understanding of each OneWorld system or module being implemented.

◆ Create a configuration inventory or checklist for each OneWorld system being implemented. Use the reference guide(s) and OneWorld itself for this purpose.

◆ Develop a general understanding of how your business will look in OneWorld. This is the To Be model.

◆ Understand and establish system-level constants.

◆ Understand user-defined codes, and establish code values.

◆ Understand tables other than UDCs, and establish code values. These include Sales Tax tables, Payment Term tables, the Chart of Accounts, and Automatic Accounting Instructions.

◆ Understand the workflow or process of the OneWorld module. This includes Sales Order, Purchase Order, and Work Order document processing steps.

◆ Configure the workflow or process for the OneWorld module.

◆ Understand the processing options used by each OneWorld program.

◆ Establish any organization-specific versions for each OneWorld program as needed.

◆ Establish the processing options in each organization-specific version of a program.

◆ Create custom menus as needed to access organization-specific versions of programs.

◆ "Unit test" or test on a program-by-program basis your configuration settings. Tune them as needed.

◆ Develop business-specific test cases, and pilot the system on an integrated or end-to-end or process-level basis. For example, consider the entire procure-to-pay or order-to-cash process.

◆ Implement any needed security locks on menus, options, approval paths, and routings.

◆ Retest to ensure that your security measures are working.

These steps are not comprehensive, but they provide a good framework for the early stages of OneWorld implementation—including process understanding, software configuration, and testing.

How OneWorld Configuration Compares to "Brand X"

It has been my experience that OneWorld is relatively easy to configure. You might be wondering, "Relatively easy compared to what—other ERP systems?" This is a fair question. One of those "brand X" systems happens to be SAP. Having completed configuration work in both of these products, I have always felt that J. D. Edwards' World and OneWorld software provide a more straightforward, logical, and consistent approach to overall system configuration than is provided by SAP.

There is one aspect of SAP configuration that I do prefer over J. D. Edwards. That is SAP's Implementation Guide (IMG). The IMG is a Windows Explorer-like listing of R/3 configuration steps. I find that the IMG does a much better job of organizing all the configuration steps for you in one place. Unfortunately, OneWorld does not have an equivalent. Although ActivEra configuration scripts look like the IMG, they are not quite the same.

Although it is easier to find the totality of configuration steps (and there are many) in SAP, I much prefer the consistency that J. D. Edwards provides in its configuration steps. You could say this is a preference for the approach and architecture that J. D. Edwards has chosen to employ over that of SAP. For example, SAP has many one-up tables that are the equivalent of OneWorld's user-defined tables. In SAP, however, each configuration screen varies in format to conform to the configuration of the table. In OneWorld, all user-defined tables reside in one physical file and are configured with one consistent method—using system codes and UDC identifiers.

Although it's a subtle difference, this example does illustrate the difference in approach that these two major vendors have taken. From what I have seen of Oracle Applications Software, its configuration look and feel follows the SAP table-by-table approach. This is an admittedly small problem and might be a bit too mundane or petty to really be of concern, but it could also explain why it seemingly takes a small army to configure and implement SAP versus a small team to configure and implement OneWorld.

Summary

This chapter introduced the major configuration steps in OneWorld. The concept of soft coding was discussed. Soft coding is J. D. Edwards' method for allowing personalization or configuration of OneWorld without requiring custom programming.

The various tools for personalizing OneWorld were introduced, as well as some of the major configuration elements in OneWorld. J. D. Edwards' ActivEra OneWorld configuration product was also introduced. ActivEra can automate or simplify configuration by scripting a specific configuration scenario, such as the creation of a new branch/plant location within the system.

Soft coding relies extensively on the use of tables. These tables are externalized from OneWorld programs and are maintained independently. In addition, many of these configuration tables are shared throughout OneWorld, thereby requiring the configuration of a common or shared table only once. Examples were provided as to what makes OneWorld's system-wide configuration relatively consistent. Additional configuration topics will be introduced in future chapters.

Chapter 11

**Tailoring
OneWorld to Your
Business Needs:
Part II**

This chapter continues with the introduction of the major soft-coding components that was begun in the preceding chapter. Recall that these components represent the key business-related configuration elements of OneWorld. The soft-coding components that are specifically introduced in this chapter include the following:

◆ The Versions List

◆ Data Selection and Sequencing

◆ Processing Options

◆ Menus

In each case, these components are introduced through an example. The soft-coding components that were covered in the preceding chapter were

◆ Constants

◆ User-Defined Codes (UDCs)

An understanding of these five core OneWorld soft-coding components and how they are typically used to configure OneWorld during its implementation provides essential background for any business or technical professional in your organization who will play an active role in configuring and implementing OneWorld—if for no other reason than to understand the capabilities and limitations of OneWorld soft coding.

The Versions List

In OneWorld, a version is a set of predefined specifications that control how each batch or interactive program runs. Therefore, each OneWorld program has a list of versions (a "Versions List") that apply to it.

The utility or value of the version is simple. The behavior or operation of a program can be specifically altered or controlled without requiring an additional, modified copy of the program to be maintained. Instead, the single program contains the logic to read the specifications and alter its behavior accordingly. The ability to define versions is therefore one of the fundamental building blocks of OneWorld configuration.

Base Versions

J. D. Edwards provides one or more "base" versions for each OneWorld program. The naming convention that is generally used by J. D. Edwards is to refer to its specific or "delivered" versions with either XJDE or ZJDE followed by a version number, such as 0001 or 0002.

It is my recommendation that you not delete or modify the base versions that J. D. Edwards provides. If you need to make version changes, create a new version by copying one of the existing "delivered" versions provided by J. D. Edwards, make your changes to the "new" or "copied" version, and save it. OneWorld programs do not operate properly without a version specification.

DREAM Writer Versus the Versions List

If you're moving from the World to the OneWorld software environment, the Versions List concept is not new to you. Actually, it is a new name for an old friend—DREAM Writer (Data Record Extraction and Management). However, World users should not assume that the OneWorld version and a World DREAM Writer version are identical. OneWorld has a few new twists—and very important ones at that—that World users need to understand. These are described in the following discussion.

Batch Versus Interactive Versions

There are two types of programs in OneWorld: batch programs, such as reports, and mass updates and interactive programs, such as data entry or inquiry programs. It also stands to reason that there are separate and distinct types of versions that are unique to each of these OneWorld program types.

Version Maintenance

OneWorld uses two different version maintenance programs. One is for interactive versions, and the other is for batch versions. Note that this is a departure from World software, in which a single DREAM Writer version maintenance program existed and took care of both interactive and batch version specifications.

To create, delete, or modify a OneWorld specification version, follow this menu path:

G > Foundation Systems (G0) > Tools (GH90) > System Administration Tools (**GH9011**)

To create, delete, or modify an *interactive* program specification version, select Interactive Versions (P9803051). To create, delete, or modify a *batch* program specification version, select Batch Versions (P98305).

How do you know if the program you need a version for is a batch or interactive program? Recall from discussions in previous chapters that the letter P as the first character in the program name identifies interactive programs, and the letter R as the first character in the program name identifies batch programs. Figure 11-1 shows a Versions List for the One Line Per Address Report (R014021).

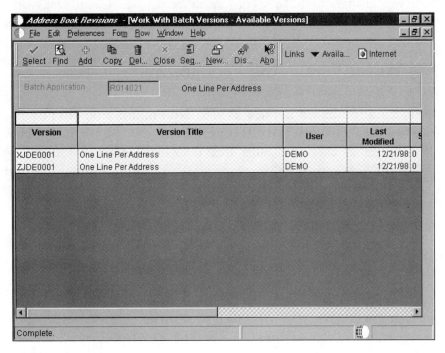

FIGURE 11-1 *The Versions List for the One Line Per Address Report (R014021)*

There is another way to access the Versions List related to a specific OneWorld program—through the OneWorld Explorer menu:

1. Position the cursor on the desired OneWorld program menu entry.
2. Right-click on the desired menu entry. A pop-up window appears.

3. Click on the Prompt for Version menu entry. The processing options for the selected OneWorld program version called by the Explorer menu option are displayed.

The Versions List for the selected OneWorld program can now be maintained. One advantage of using this approach is that you do not need to concern yourself with the type of program (interactive versus batch) you're dealing with. However, accessing and changing the Versions List for a OneWorld program in this manner can be dangerous in the wrong hands. Therefore, this capability should be kept from most of your OneWorld users.

Interactive Versions

The key reason for maintaining multiple specifications or versions for OneWorld interactive programs is the need to maintain more than one set of processing options for each OneWorld program. An example should help illustrate why.

OneWorld has only one program for Purchase Order Entry. However, you can define more than one type of Purchase Order document in OneWorld, and, as you will learn in a later chapter, each order type can have a unique set of order processing rules or workflow steps. For example, OneWorld comes with both a Purchase Order and a Purchase Requisition document type. Both document types use the same Purchase Order Entry program. Therefore, OneWorld needs to know which type of Purchase Order document you want to work with because each document works differently—just like they would in your organization.

These document processing differences are identified to OneWorld through a set of processing options that are unique to the Purchase Order entry program. Although processing options have not been fully introduced here, for now it is sufficient for you to understand that they are maintained by version for each OneWorld program.

Batch Versions

Batch program specifications differ from interactive specification versions in that additional specifications are typically included that allow for the selection and sequencing of data.

An important use of batch versions is to create location-specific versions of reports, such as preparing a sales order backlog report for a given warehouse or branch office. A batch report version would typically be created using location-specific selection criteria for each location in this case.

Data Selection

At the version level, data selection is probably the most important and useful function outside of processing options. For instance, a version of the Purchase Order Print program (R43500) might select and batch all print purchase order documents for a given branch or plant location. Another example might be the creation of an Address Book single-line listing (R014021) that includes only Customers (where Search Type equals C). The data selection criteria statement found on each Batch Program Version Data Selection form or data selection row requires the specification of four elements, or form columns:

◆ Operator

◆ Left operand

◆ Comparison

◆ Right operand

The purpose of each data selection column is described in the following sections. For reference purposes, see Figure 11-2 (shown in a moment), which illustrates the Batch Program Version Data Selection form.

The Operator

The Operator column specifies how multiple criteria are joined (*concatenated*). The first row is always the Where operator. If additional data selection rows or conditions are needed to further qualify or limit data selection (such as when a range of data must be selected), they are appended to the Where row by use of the And operator. When specific additional values are needed, additional data selection rows are typically appended to the Where row by use of the Or operator.

If multiple sets of criteria must be used, such as when selecting data that is in non-contiguous ranges, they are generally arranged in a row sequence such as Where-And-And-Or-And-And-Or-And-And.

The Left Operand

The Left operand column is the field your selection is based on. Every OneWorld batch program has a "based on" file or table associated with it. The fields that are available for use as data selection criteria are drawn from that "based on" file or table.

The Comparison

The Comparison column uses standard equality and inequality operators to specify how OneWorld will compare a record that is read into the OneWorld program. Here are the allowed comparisons:

- ◆ Is equal to (=)
- ◆ Is not equal to (<>)
- ◆ Is greater than (>)
- ◆ Is greater than or equal to (>=)
- ◆ Is less than (<)
- ◆ Is less than or equal to (<=)

The comparison is always carried out against the value appearing in the Right operand column of the data selection.

The Right Operand

The Right operand is the "test" value or condition. Typically, a test is made against a known or specific value that is valid for a given data field. For instance, from the earlier Address Book report example, the test was for records where the Search Type value is equal to C. In other cases, it might be necessary to test for blanks in a given field. OneWorld allows several data selection tests, including a single or specific value, a range of values, or a list of values. When you choose values for a given data field, select "literal." Another form with tabs appears, allowing you to enter the data selection.

Why Versions Frequently Don't Produce Reports

Whether one or multiple data selection rows are defined, as long as data exists within the parameters provided to OneWorld, the batch program should run correctly based on the data selected. However, in my experience with J. D. Edwards software, the number one reason why something usually doesn't work is faulty data selection.

As noted earlier, multiple data selection criteria or rows can be used. The overall selection of data depends on the "correctness" of the logic or criteria used to select data. If the data selection criteria can't be satisfied by OneWorld, the infamous

"No records selected" message appears. Here are few tips to help you avoid some problems:

◆ Use the equality and inequality operators with specific values and ranges of values.

◆ Use the greater-than and less-than operators with single or specific values.

◆ Do not use the greater-than or less-than operators with lists or ranges of values.

Another error that frequently happens in data selection is that sometimes processing options for a given batch program also contain data selection criteria. In these cases, the criteria on the Data Selection form should be thought of as a *subset* of any processing option-related data selection criteria. Observing this rule should help you avoid the infamous "No records selected" message.

Figure 11-2 illustrates the completed Data Selection form of the Address Book single-line listing (R014021) sample report cited earlier.

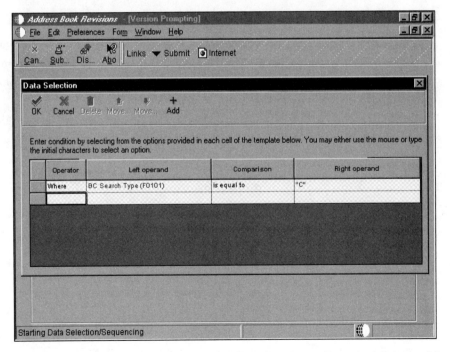

FIGURE 11-2 *Data Selection Form for the Address Book Report (R014021) Customer List Example*

Data Sequencing

Data sequencing applies primarily to reports. However, not all OneWorld reports provide for data sequencing. For instance, the previous Address Book report example does not include data sequencing.

Field selection and ordering in the Section Data Sequencing form for a version work in a nearly identical fashion to the methods covered in Chapter 8 (sorting data rows that appear in a Data Grid). For instance, a given data field can be sorted in ascending or descending order. However, there are a few differences. First is the addition of a "page break" column in the Columns Sorted portion of the screen. Second, in some cases a report has predefined report totals that might be affected if the sequencing is changed. Finally, in order to toggle between page break (P/B) or ascending or descending order (A/D), point the cursor to the appropriate field and click to toggle the value in that field.

Manipulating the data sequencing for a given OneWorld report might or might not work. Test any changes made to a report's data sequencing with a small quantity of transaction data that will sequence in the desired manner. Often data sequencing changes fall into the category of OneWorld customization rather than simply a configuration task. The reason for this problem is that report totaling and subtotaling are frequently directly related to data sequencing. At times, the sequencing of the report is more complex than the data sequencing function can handle. In these scenarios, the sequencing is done through hard-coding and therefore requires program modifications to make changes.

A Best-Practice Tip: Test Your Versions

One way to avoid problems with a version is to make a test or trial run of any new version you create or make changes to. For instance, preliminary testing will help you avoid situations in which you get the "no records selected" error or a report is improperly sequenced.

Many batch update processes provide for a "proof" or no-update run as well as "final" or "update" run. It goes without saying that a proof version should be run first. To ensure that test runs produce predictable results and do not adversely affect your system, consider using fewer records that are known to you.

Testing will go a long way toward saving trees and avoiding unsanctioned updates to your data that might in turn result in data integrity issues.

Batch Versions and Menus

Typically, there are two ways to execute a batch version of a report or update. One method is by the overt user action of selecting and executing the batch version from a menu. Another way is the "blind" or "background" execution of a batch version. This occurs when another program triggers the selection and execution of the program version. Several examples are provided next.

Example 1: Many OneWorld batch programs can provide for the automatic execution of another OneWorld batch program, as a "follow-on" activity to the first batch program. The Sales Order Update program (R42800) is one such example. For instance, the first batch program, Sales Order Update, triggers execution of the second batch program, the Sales Price/Cost Update program (R42950), when certain Sales Order Update program processing options are established correctly.

Example 2: Several OneWorld interactive programs can provide for the automatic execution of a "print document" batch program. For instance, the Purchase Order program (P4310) and the Purchase Order Receipt (P4312) program can trigger batch programs to print documents related to the *specific* purchase order being processed, such as the "print on demand" Purchase Order document (R43500) or the Receipt Traveler (R43512). In such cases, the processing options in the interactive program version must be established correctly for the interactive execution of a batch print program.

Example 3: In addition to triggering execution of a batch version from a menu or from within another OneWorld program, you can take another approach. A batch program can be scheduled by version for *automatic* after-hours execution. Recall the earlier example of creating location-specific versions of reports. Using this technique, these batch reports can be run automatically after the close of business. Within the version for each location, the remote location's printer can be specifically identified, and presto: Reports are produced and sent to the branch for use the next day. Automatic after-hours execution is accomplished through the OneWorld Scheduler, which is discussed in the next chapter.

These examples should provide not only some useful insights into how batch versions can be executed, but also as to the power, flexibility, and extent of the OneWorld configuration and implementation process. Although OneWorld includes "out of the box" predefined versions, most organizations must personalize OneWorld to a certain degree.

Differences Between Batch and Interactive Versions

This section discusses the differences between OneWorld batch and interactive versions. Also, it should be noted that for previous users of J. D. Edwards' World software, this is an area where OneWorld is much different from World in that each type of version is maintained independently.

Processing Options

Processing options typically exist for both interactive and batch programs. However, not all OneWorld applications include processing options. This rule applies equally to batch and interactive program versions. When processing options do not apply to a given OneWorld program, the option of modifying processing options on the Versions List (Work With Versions, Row, Processing Options) is grayed out.

Selection and Sequencing

Generally speaking, the data selection and sequencing options are predetermined for OneWorld interactive programs and are not changed. For instance, the specific OneWorld tables that an interactive Work With program uses are generally *keyed* or *indexed* on specific fields, such as Address Number or Search Type. Therefore, which fields appear in the search information section of the Work With form are determined by the "based on" file or table used by the Work With program and the specific key or index fields for that given "based on" file or table. It is for this reason that the Selection and Sequence options do not appear on the Versions List menu (Work With Versions, Row) for interactive program versions.

Advanced Topics: Versions

For previous users of J. D. Edwards' World software, OneWorld batch versions are machine-dependent. For example, clients can maintain and run versions locally, and interactive versions are machine-independent—all clients run the same version. Version check in and check out manages machine dependencies.

Version Check In/Check Out

An important distinction between interactive and batch versions is that a batch version can exist at the client workstation as well as at the central server level.

Interactive versions are maintained centrally, at the server level, but are executed locally, at the client. Batch versions can be executed locally at the client workstation as well on the central server. Batch versions are therefore created and maintained locally. For a batch version to be available centrally, it must first be "checked in" to the central server's version list. Likewise, if changes need to be made to a centrally stored version, it must be "checked out" to the local client workstation first. The bottom line is that versions that are not checked in to the central server are not universally available to the client workstations.

For organizations that come from the World environment, this is another important difference between World and OneWorld. Here's a simple step-by-step approach to batch version creation and maintenance in OneWorld:

1. Copy an existing version.
2. Provide a version name and version description.
3. A new version is created.
4. The new version is checked out to the local client workstation.
5. You can modify the new version. For example, you can change processing options and data selection and sequencing criteria to meet your organization's business requirements.
6. The new version is tested.
7. As soon as the new version is working, it must be checked in.

There is no limit to the number of times a version can be checked in or checked out. However, only one client workstation can check out a version at any given time.

Version Security

Several levels of version security can be applied to a batch version. The general recommendation I offer here is that batch report versions should be only *minimally* secured. Batch update programs can be more highly secured. Table 11-1 lists and describes the batch version security levels.

J. D. Edwards uses the term "Last Modified By" instead of "Original Author." Generally speaking, the creator of the version determines the level of security needed. Hence, the Created By and Last Modified By values are typically the same in OneWorld.

Table 11-1 Batch Version Security

Security Level	Level of Security Provided
0	No security is provided. This is the typical default for a new version. Anyone can copy, run, modify, or delete the version.
1	Minimal security is provided. Anyone can copy or run the version, but only the original author can modify or delete the version. All J. D. Edwards-provided versions are delivered with this level of security.
2	Medium security is provided. Only the original author can run, modify, or delete the version. However, anyone can copy the version.
3	Complete security is provided. Only the original author can do anything with the version.

World Versus OneWorld Version Security

In World software, it was my preference as the system administrator to limit access to the DREAM Writer Versions List program altogether and to create menus containing versions that were specific to an individual or a given department or plant location. However, in OneWorld this technique is inadvisable. Unfortunately, an important "prompting" option is missing that was available in the World software. The option to preface the running of a version by entering data selection criteria is missing from OneWorld. The only options now are to either prompt for processing option values or "blindly execute" the version.

Previously, I used the "missing" option I just mentioned to prompt a user to enter a known, specific document number into the version at runtime. For instance, this was a quick way for a business department user to reprint a processed document, such as a purchase order. My alternative now would be to create a custom program to allow this using the OneWorld development tools. (Perhaps this would be a good future project.)

"Copied Version" Problems

Sometimes a copied version, for reasons not always known, does not work correctly. In such cases it might be advisable to create a new version from scratch using the Add button on the Work With Versions form. If you are having trouble getting a copied version to work, try adding a version before calling the J. D. Edwards response line, because this might provide a quick resolution to your problem. When all else fails, contact the J. D. Edwards response line about a failing version.

Version Names

A version name in OneWorld may contain any alphanumeric character (A to Z or 0 to 9). The version name must not exceed 10 characters in length. A version name must be unique. A version name can be deleted and then reused. It is generally recommended that your organization adopt a standard naming convention for the versions you create.

For instance, here is a standard I frequently use:

◆ For an organization-wide standard version, I typically use A*NNN0000*. *NNN* represents the organization's initials, and *0000* represents a sequentially assigned version number.

◆ For versions that are specific to an individual, I typically use B*CCC0000*. *CCC* represents the person's initials, and *0000* represents a sequentially assigned version number.

I refer to the first letters in the version name as a version class identifier. The A represents an organization-wide version, and the B represents an individual's version. Both A and B distinguish your organization's versions from those delivered by J. D. Edwards with OneWorld, which typically begin with J or X.

An organization that requires versions by location or branch/plant might have an additional letter. For instance, B might represent branch/plant versions, and C might represent individual versions.

As a final cautionary note, do not use XJDE or ZJDE in your version names. These values are always reserved for use by J. D. Edwards.

Do You Need Your Own Versions?

Strictly speaking, as long as your organization can accept the version's configuration "as built" or "as delivered," the answer is no. However, this is usually not the case. When that happens, you will want to create versions that are specific to your organization, and perhaps to your individual users or departments. It is wrong to assume that merely changing the standard or delivered OneWorld version is sufficient.

It is strongly recommended that all version-level changes, such as data selection and processing option changes, be done in your own versions—not the standard delivered versions from J. D. Edwards (those that have names beginning with XJDE or ZJDE). The simple fact of the matter is that when J. D. Edwards provides a new release level of OneWorld, it will likely contain replacement XJDE and ZJDE versions that will overwrite their old equivalents. Hence, your system configuration will be overwritten as well.

Processing Options

Processing options represent another important dimension of OneWorld configurability. As a matter of fact, much of the time required to configure OneWorld is spent reviewing, setting, testing, and adjusting to processing options to arrive at the OneWorld configuration settings that are appropriate for your organization. Processing options generally perform one of the following tasks:

◆ Serve as a switch to enable a feature in the OneWorld program.

◆ Establish a basic value, such as a document type value, needed by the OneWorld program.

◆ In some cases, processing options are used to provide comparison values for data selection purposes. These are usually based on a from/to date range. In some cases, they represent date buckets (30/60/90 days). However, for most batch processes and reports, comparison values are a part of the data selection and sequencing in the version.

Although most OneWorld programs have processing options, it should be emphasized that not every OneWorld program does.

Some programs have only a few processing options, such as the Address Book Revisions program (P01012), shown in Figure 11-3. In OneWorld Release B.7.3.3.1, this program had only six processing options. Other OneWorld programs have dozens of processing options. For instance, the Sales Order Entry program (P4210), shown in Figure 11-4, had 92 processing options in Release B.7.3.3.1. Figure 11-3 shows some of the processing options for Address Book Revisions program P01012. Figure 11-4 shows some of the processing options for the Sales Order Entry program P4210.

Both of these programs use tabs to organize related processing options. Also note that in the Sales Order Entry Processing Options window, left and right arrow buttons appear at the top-right of the window. These buttons indicate that more

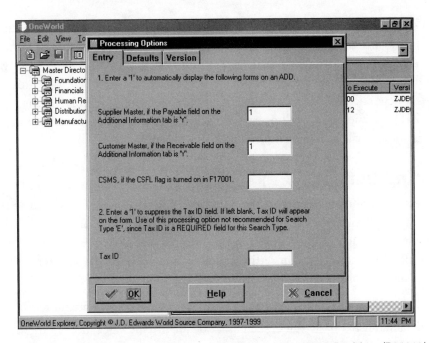

FIGURE 11-3 *The Processing Options Form for the Address Book Revisions (P01012) Program*

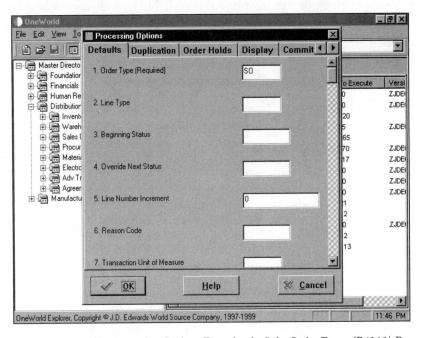

FIGURE 11-4 *The Processing Options Form for the Sales Order Entry (P4210) Program, Illustrating the Defaults Tab*

tabs of processing options exist beyond what is shown. After clicking on a given tab, you might see a vertical slider bar along the right side of the window, as shown in Figure 11-4. This vertical slider indicates that more processing options exist than can be shown in the window.

Every OneWorld program that has processing options has at least one version. One of the key tasks your organization will engage in during the initial implementation of OneWorld is determining how to set up *each* OneWorld program to reflect how you want to conduct business using OneWorld. As stated earlier, a major part of the overall setup process is determining how all the various processing options should be configured for each of the many OneWorld programs your organization will use.

When your organization determines that the standard processing option values that were established by J. D. Edwards are not properly configured for your organization, you have several options. The first is to simply change the processing options in the version supplied by J. D. Edwards. Recall that I strongly recommend against making any changes to the standard XJDE or ZJDE versions that are supplied by J. D. Edwards for each OneWorld program.

The second and highly recommended option is to create your own versions for each OneWorld program when the standard XJDE or ZJDE versions are not appropriately configured for your organization as delivered. You would then subsequently change processing options in the new version to the settings needed by your organization.

However, there is one additional consideration when creating your own versions—how they will be accessed. Again, you have two options. The first is to change the version reference on the menu to the new version. The second option is to reference your versions through a custom menu. The next section has more information about custom menus.

How to Access and Maintain Processing Options

There are two ways to access processing options for any given OneWorld program. The first technique is to use the Versions List for the program. It is accessible through System Administration Tools:

> G > Foundation Systems (G0) > Tools (GH90) > System Administration Tools (**GH9011**)

(The System Administration Tools menu is shown in Chapter 10 in Figure 10-2.)

Recall that there are two Versions List manager programs. One is for interactive programs and has a P as the first character of the program name. The other is for batch programs and has an R as the first character of the program name.

The second technique for accessing processing options related to a specific version of a OneWorld program is through the OneWorld Explorer menu:

1. Position the cursor on the desired OneWorld program's menu option and right-click. A pop-up window appears.

2. Choose the Prompt for Values menu entry. The processing options for the selected OneWorld program version called by the Explorer menu option are displayed.

The processing options for the selected OneWorld program can now be maintained. One advantage of using this approach is that you do not need to concern yourself with the type of program (interactive or batch) that you're dealing with. Accessing and changing processing options for a version in this manner can be dangerous in the wrong hands. Therefore, this capability should be kept from most of your OneWorld users.

Document Processing Option Settings

An important and often overlooked part of configuring OneWorld is documenting the configuration settings and the reasons why certain settings have been made. Perhaps the "why" represents the more important component of any OneWorld configuration documentation effort.

Generally speaking, the "why" of configuration is determined only after research and often through trial-and-error iterations of testing to make a given program work correctly for your organization. Imagine your project team spending hours configuring a OneWorld program in a certain way, only to lose that version. What is even worse is trying to understand the thought process that went into configuring this OneWorld program, especially if any time has elapsed.

Therefore, one of the best practices I have adopted and that I use when implementing OneWorld is to document my configuration settings. I have created a Microsoft Word template for this purpose. If you would like a copy of this template, refer to the Introduction section of this book for information on how to obtain this template, along with the other templates I have referenced throughout this book.

Menus

After you have created versions that are specific to your organization, you need a way to access them. Although batch versions can always be accessed, maintained, or executed from a Versions List, this is not the case for an interactive version. Interactive versions must be initiated from a menu. Therefore, establishing organization-specific or *custom* menus is an integral part of the OneWorld configuration process.

Recall from previous discussions in this chapter that you do have an option other than creating custom menus. That option is to substitute the version number of your organization-specific version for the standard XJDE or ZJDE version provided by J. D. Edwards. Again, this version substitution is also done at the Explorer menu level. If you have a minimal number of versions or user groups or minimal custom workflow requirements, custom menus might be overkill for your organization. However, I do not want to minimize the value or versatility that custom menus can provide to an organization.

There are some valid reasons for minimizing the use of custom menus. For instance, the OneWorld reference documentation provided by J. D. Edwards—as well as this book and others like it—typically references the OneWorld menu numbers that are supplied by J. D. Edwards. If your organization has opted to purchase the Custom User Education product from J. D. Edwards, you can make the necessary documentation adjustments related to your custom menus.

There are also valid arguments for creating custom menus. Custom menus can be used to build logical step-by-step workflow paths in the business language your organization is more comfortable with—not the words chosen by J. D. Edwards. Custom menus can also be used to build a more secure system by groups of end-users. For instance, in one case, I used custom menus to *completely* control access to specific functions and provide overall navigation in J. D. Edwards software. The major drawback of custom menus occurs when an upgrade is applied to your OneWorld software. You must review and update your custom menus for any differences against standard OneWorld programs, such determining if any new programs exist or if any old programs are now obsolete.

In some cases I have found that J. D. Edwards has not created menus that logically bring together all the important components to master or unlock the power of a given portion of the system. An excellent example is in the area of Non Stock Items. Although J. D. Edwards has done a good job of grouping programs on menus related to stock item maintenance, transaction processing, and inquiry, it has not done so for nonstock items. Organizations that do not engage in the selling of products—such as government entities, nonprofit groups, trade associations, and professional service firms such as engineering and consulting firms—typically use nonstock items rather than stock items.

Menu Naming Conventions

Menu names may contain up to 10 alphanumeric characters (0 to 9 and A to Z). Menu names generally start with a letter. For instance, over the 10 years that I have worked with J. D. Edwards software products, I have seen three generations of application menu naming conventions, including the M, the A, and currently the G menus.

Suffice it to say that a common menu naming hierarchy does exist in OneWorld. Here are the common tenets behind J. D. Edwards' menu design:

◆ Group related system activities by frequency of use, such as daily versus periodic processes.

◆ Provide access to as many processes as possible from each menu in order to reduce the number of menus overall. Such a design tenet helps eliminate multiple lower-level menus, thereby eliminating layers of menus. (This is often called *menu nesting*.) Fewer menus means faster system navigation.

◆ Group related system activities by task and level of difficulty. For instance, Technical and Advanced Operations are isolated on separate menus. Another example is from Procurement, where an entire series of tasks for a given type of material is organized together.

The last example also provides an excellent illustration of how a common menu structure can be adopted, making only version number changes for the unique menu options in similar process-oriented menus.

System codes 55 through 59 have a special meaning or purpose in OneWorld. These system codes are reserved for the client's use in customizing OneWorld. It is generally recommended that custom menus follow the standard J. D. Edwards menu-naming hierarchy. For instance, as a general rule, when I replace an existing OneWorld menu for the purposes of creating my own version of a menu, I generally use the existing menu name, preceding it with a 55 or 56 after the letter G.

Creating and Maintaining Menus

OneWorld menus can be maintained through the System Administration Tools menu. To access the System Administration Tools, select the following:

> G > Foundation Systems (G0) > Tools (GH90) > System Administration Tools (**GH9011**)

(The System Administration Tools menu is shown in Figure 10-2 in the preceding chapter.)

To modify *any* OneWorld menu, from menu GH9011, select the Menu Design option.

Menus are organized by system code. The two or three characters that follow the G in the OneWorld menu name generally represent a system code. For instance, Accounts Payable is system code 04, and Enhanced Accounts Receivable is system code 03B. Table 11-2 lists common OneWorld system codes.

Table 11-2 Common OneWorld System Codes

System Code	System Name
00	Foundation Environment
01	Address Book
03B	Enhanced Accounts Receivable
04	Accounts Payable
05A/05U/08U	Human Resource Management/U. S. Payroll
09	General Accounting
10	Financial Reporting
12	Fixed Assets
13	Plant/Equipment Maintenance
17	Customer Service Management
30	Product Data Management
31	Shop Floor Control
32	Configuration Management
33	Capacity Planning

Table 11-2 Common OneWorld System Codes (continued)

System Code	System Name
34	Requirements Planning
36	Forecasting
37	Quality Management
40/41	Inventory Management
42	Sales Management
43	Procurement (Purchasing)
45	Advanced Pricing
46	Warehouse Management
47	Electronic Commerce (EDI)
48	Work Order Processing
49	Transportation Management
50/51	Job Cost
55 through 59	Reserved for Client Use

Usually the easiest way to create a new menu is to copy an existing menu that is similar to the one you need to create. For instance, if it is your organization's practice to make a copy of an existing menu and change the version references to your own, the first step is to make a copy of the menu, such as the Daily Menu for Stock Based Procurement (G43A11). To complete the copy, do the following:

1. Enter 43 in the System Code field.

2. Click on the Find button.

3. Select the entry labeled G43A11—Purchase Order Processing.

4. Click on the Copy button.

5. Enter a name for the menu in the Menu Identification box. For this example, enter G5643A11.

6. Replace the System Code value of 43 with 56.

7. Click on the OK button. The Work With menu screen reappears.

8. Type 56 in the System Code field.

9. Click on the Find button.

The custom menu G5643A11 that you just created should be listed.

Making changes to a menu is a relatively simple two-step process. For instance, let's say you need an entry to access a Special Procurement Reports menu option on the menu you just created. First, you add an entry to the menu by doing the following:

1. Select the entry labeled G5643A11—Purchase Order Processing.
2. Click on the Select button. The Work With Menu Selections form appears. You see the menu entries for the selected menu.
3. Click on the Add button. The Menu Selection Revisions form appears.
4. Enter any unused sequence number.
5. Enter a desired form name or menu title for the Selection Description value.
6. Enter a 2 for the selection consequences.
7. Indicate a Selection Type by clicking on the appropriate type. For this example, click on Menu.
8. Click on the OK button.

This completes the first step in the process of adding an entry to an existing menu. Another common need you might have in menu design is changing a menu sequence so that your addition appears where you want it to. If a desired sequence number is already in use, it might be necessary to renumber one or more menu entries. To renumber a menu entry, from the menu bar on the Work With Menu Selections form, select Form, Renumber.

Menus are just one of the menu option selection types that are a part of overall menu design in OneWorld. The typical menu selection options that you will likely use include the following:

◆ Selecting the OneWorld application (interactive program)
◆ Selecting the OneWorld report (batch or background application)
◆ Selecting another OneWorld menu
◆ Creating a nonfunctioning or title-only menu line entry. These are typically used to group related menu entries.

The completion of the second step—activating the menu option—varies based on the menu option selection type. Figures 11-5, 11-6, and 11-7 show the three forms and the requisite information that defines each selection type for a menu entry.

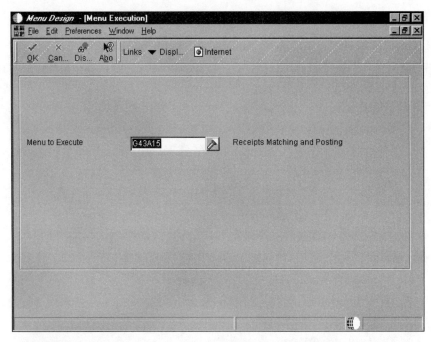

FIGURE 11-5 *A Typical Define Form for the Menu Selection Type*

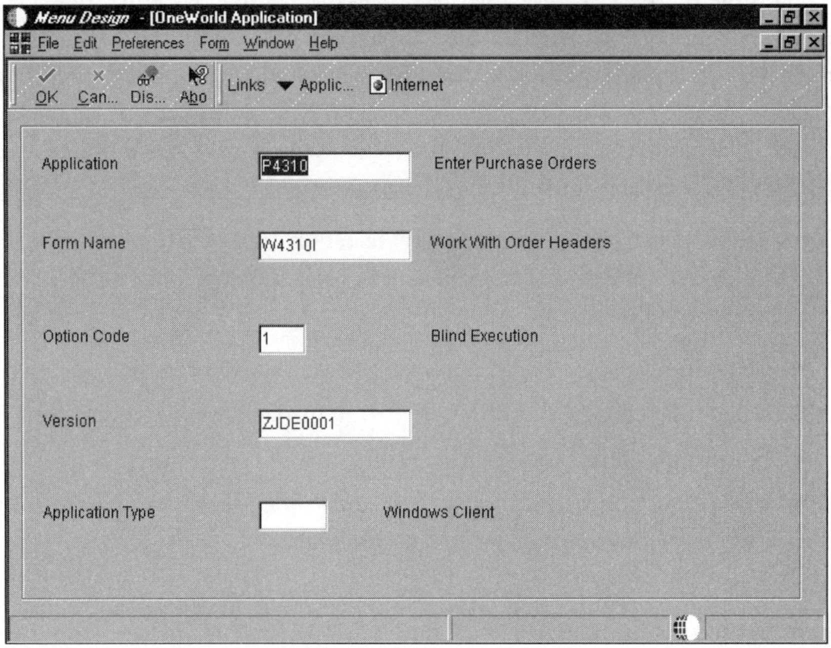

FIGURE 11-6 *A Typical Define Form for the Interactive Program Selection Type*

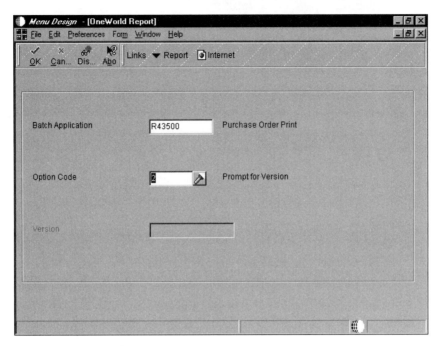

FIGURE 11-7 *A Typical Define Form for the Batch or Report Program Selection Type*

In the first step of menu entry creation, you did nothing to really activate the option. In the second step, the information required to activate the added menu option is provided to OneWorld. This second step must be performed for every OneWorld menu, application, and report selection type. If the selection type is a subheading, no further configuration of the menu option is necessary.

To complete the second step of OneWorld's menu entry creation process for menu, application, and report selection types, do the following:

1. Click on the Cancel button to exit from the Menu Selections Revisions form. The Work With Menu Selections form reappears.

2. Click on the Find button to refresh the Data Grid.

3. Scroll through the Data Grid until the menu entry that was just added appears.

4. Click on the Select button. The Menu Selection Revisions form appears.

5. From the menu bar on the Menu Selection Revisions form, select Form, Define. A single entry field labeled Menu to Execute appears, as shown in Figure 11-5.

6. Enter a menu number. For this example, enter G5643A11.

7. Click on the OK button.

8. Click on the Cancel button. The Menu Selection Revisions form appears.

This example applies only when you're adding a menu type selection. An obvious next question is what happens when a program is added as a menu selection entry? You can explore this option by changing the selection type:

1. Click on OneWorld Application under Selection Type.

2. From the menu bar on the Menu Selection Revisions form, select Form, Define.

3. You must enter values for the following fields (this form is shown in Figure 11-6):

   Application—The program name. It usually begins with the letter P.

   Form Name—The form name. It usually begins with the letter W.

   Option Code—For interactive programs, this is generally a value of 1 if versions exist for the program. When versions do not exist, 0 is used. Version—The version number, such as XJDE0001.

   Application Type—Currently left blank. J. D. Edwards intends to make use of this field in the future.

4. Click on the Cancel button.

This example applies only when you're adding an interactive menu type selection. Now we'll look at how the screen varies for the OneWorld report or batch-type menu selection. Again, you can explore this option by changing the selection type:

1. Click on OneWorld Report under Selection Type.

2. From the menu bar on the Menu Selection Revisions form, select Form, Define.

3. You must enter values for the following fields (this form is shown in Figure 11-7):

   Batch Application—The program name. It usually begins with the letter R.

   Option Code—For batch programs, this value is generally set to 2. The 2 triggers the appearance of a Versions List for the program. If 0, 1, or 3 is used, a version number must be provided.

Version—When a specific version is to be executed by this menu option, you enter the version number, such as XJDE0001.

4. Click on the Cancel button.

Although you know how to find program numbers and version numbers, the use of a form number value is a new concept here. Do the following to determine a form number for any OneWorld *interactive* program:

1. Select Help, About OneWorld from the menu bar of any OneWorld form. The following information is displayed:

   The OneWorld application program number

   The corresponding OneWorld form name

2. Click on OK to exit this display.

This concludes our discussion of OneWorld menu design and maintenance activities, as well as this chapter. Although there are additional soft-coding components, such as security, these are generally technical topics and will be discussed in a future chapter.

Summary

This chapter concluded the introduction to OneWorld's major soft-coding configuration components. These components are J. D. Edwards' way to allow the personalization or configuration of OneWorld without requiring custom programming. Many how-to examples were provided regarding the following:

◆ The Versions List

◆ Processing options

◆ Menus

In addition to these soft-coding components, other discussion topics included security concerns and naming conventions for versions and menus. Configuration best practices were discussed and comparisons were made to J. D. Edwards' World software where appropriate. Additional configuration topics will be introduced in future chapters.

Chapter 12

When Tailoring Doesn't Work: Customizing OneWorld

J. D. Edwards has a rich history of providing customizing tools as a part of its overall suite of applications. As a matter of fact, this history is shared throughout the AS/400 application software community. Much of the customization provided through the AS/400 computer platform relies on the concept of shared, reusable objects, especially those related to the user interface, as well as on the relational database model. So in many ways, the AS/400 application software community had a head start on much of the client/server world.

Although J. D. Edwards has attempted to provide the widest array of choice and flexibility within OneWorld as it is delivered, there are times when your organization's requirements will exceed the software's capabilities. Assuming that your configuration options have been exhausted and that any available workarounds have been explored and deemed unacceptable, your organization's final answer will be to customize OneWorld. When the answer is customization, J. D. Edwards has built into OneWorld a wide array of customizing tools that will make the job easier.

Perhaps you're wondering if customizing OneWorld is really necessary. My short and preferred answer is generally no. However, the practicality of the matter is that this is rarely true. Don't feel that your organization is alone in needing to customize OneWorld in some way in order to meet its business requirements. As good as OneWorld is, a client will always need to do some degree of customization. For instance, the change could be as mundane as changing the placement of the address information on the OneWorld invoice document in order to use an existing stock of window envelopes.

I don't advocate OneWorld customization, and neither does this chapter. In addition, this chapter should not be considered a how-to guide for customizing OneWorld. Instead, the intent of this chapter is to provide an appreciation of what is possible in terms of OneWorld customization and how this is accomplished in the OneWorld environment. *My experience tells me that I must strongly advise against packaged software customization.* After all, by selecting packaged software, you have outsourced the software development process to the package vendor. When customization is necessary, a strong business case, rooted in your organization's overall strategy or due to regulatory necessity, should factor strongly into making any OneWorld customizations.

Of course, the good news is that given all the flexibility provided by OneWorld configuration over business functions, workflow, and the graphical user interface, the need to customize OneWorld to the needs of your organization's business processes or user preferences should be substantially diminished.

Additional Back Office Tools

In addition to the back office tools discussed in the previous two chapters, OneWorld provides several additional tools that can in effect prevent customizing OneWorld. Although end-users can make changes to OneWorld using these back office tools, it has been my experience that traditionally these tools are generally within the domain of technical individuals, such as database or system administrators and developers. I have therefore chosen to speak about these additional back office tools outside the context of the OneWorld configuration. These tools include the following:

- The OneWorld active Data Dictionary
- The OneWorld Workflow Manager
- The OneWorld Security Workbench

This chapter introduces the OneWorld active Data Dictionary. The active Data Dictionary is a cornerstone of OneWorld application. The Workflow Manager and Security Workbench tools are introduced in the next chapter.

The Active Data Dictionary

The OneWorld Data Dictionary is the central repository containing both the definition and technical attributes for all OneWorld data items. The OneWorld Data Dictionary is called an active Data Dictionary because any changes made to a data item are automatically reflected throughout OneWorld applications without any further software-related actions, such as the recompilation of a program using a changed data item.

I prefer to include a discussion of the active Data Dictionary in this chapter because one of the first steps that any OneWorld customization effort requires is an identification of the data model needed to support the required customization. Not only does this require working with existing OneWorld data fields, but it also likely means that new fields will be necessary. Therefore, an initial development step is for the developer to properly create and annotate these new fields in the OneWorld active Data Dictionary.

Before going into a more detailed discussion about the Data Dictionary, a cautionary note is in order. I do not recommend, nor do I endorse, changing the specifications of existing fields. This is a very intrusive practice that can affect scores of existing OneWorld tables and any underlying data.

Instead, the typical practice employed by programmers working with complex ERP systems requiring custom modifications and additional fields is to create new tables for the storage of such data fields. These new tables, called *tag files,* in effect "tag along with" the transaction and master files in the ERP database. This approach and recommendation do not differ for OneWorld.

Changing a table to add a new field requires the recompilation of all affected programs. Considering the complexity of OneWorld, this is simply not recommended. In fact, it's discouraged. Data item changes are best utilized to change field descriptions, default values, and acceptable values, and vocabulary overrides are used to provide alternative field names on forms and reports.

In general, modifying a field in the Data Dictionary or modifying any underlying OneWorld database table is discouraged and should be avoided. In some cases, J. D. Edwards has predefined user-definable fields within a table structure. Consider using these fields for your custom applications instead of tag files whenever possible.

Using the Data Dictionary, your organization determines how data items will be

◆ Formatted on OneWorld reports and forms
◆ Validated during data entry within an application

In addition, data field-related textual descriptions are defined in the Data Dictionary. Field-related text descriptions include the following:

◆ Column and row descriptions used for Data Grid column headings and report headings
◆ Field-sensitive help information when using the right-click drop-down menu "What's This" feature or the F1 key

The OneWorld active Data Dictionary itself is another series of tables residing in the OneWorld relational database on the enterprise server.

The enterprise server version of the OneWorld active Data Dictionary is also called the "publisher" Data Dictionary. All Data Dictionary changes must be replicated—or published across the network—to other servers and workstations throughout the OneWorld Configurable Network Computing environment. Therefore, when configuring the OneWorld environment, the OneWorld system administrator uses Configurable Network Computing tools to establish "pull replication" for the Data Dictionary.

When OneWorld is initially installed or deployed onto a client workstation, the active Data Dictionary is not installed as a part of that process. When a user accesses an application for the first time, OneWorld installs or pulls down the Data Dictionary information needed on a *just-in-time basis*. At that time, OneWorld replicates Data Dictionary information from the relational Data Dictionary to tables residing on the workstation.

The workstation's Data Dictionary is kept *active* by using pull replication. Using pull replication, each time a user logs into OneWorld, all changed Data Dictionary specifications are removed from the workstation tables. Then, the next time the user accesses an application that requires that deleted Data Dictionary information, OneWorld retrieves this information on a just-in-time basis from the publisher Data Dictionary.

Generally speaking, the typical OneWorld configuration has all OneWorld environments (such as production, development, and CRP) map the Data Dictionary to the publisher tables. Therefore, the Data Dictionary can be changed at any workstation in any environment.

Creating and Maintaining Data Dictionary Entries

To work with the OneWorld active Data Dictionary, do the following:

1. Access the System Administration Tools menu by selecting G > Foundation Systems (G0) > Tools (GH90) > System Administration Tools (**GH9011**).

2. Select Data Dictionary Design. The Data Dictionary Design menu (GH951) appears.

3. Choose Work With Data Items (P92001).

Figure 12-1 illustrates the Work With Data Items (P92001) form.

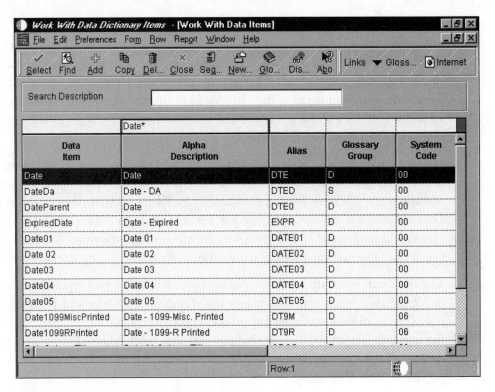

FIGURE 12-1 *The Work With Data Items Form*

Understanding the Data Dictionary

This section defines some of the important informational fields contained in the OneWorld active Data Dictionary.

The Data Item Value

The Data Item field is a 32-position "character-only" field that is used to identify OneWorld data items that are used as the basis for field names in OneWorld data tables and applications. Note that blanks, special symbols, and punctuation marks cannot be used in this character-only field. This field is the basis for all C programming language data names used in OneWorld business functions, data structures, and event rules.

It is essential when customizing OneWorld to have this value available. The Data Item value appears in the lower-left corner of the field-level help window. For instance, end-users and business analysts can identify data fields for technical designers using this value.

The Alpha Description

The alpha description is used to further identify and classify OneWorld data items. Using OneWorld's search capabilities, related fields are found using this value. Although this is a free-form or unstructured entry field, the entries made in the field are generally structured to begin with one of the following values:

- ◆ Date
- ◆ Amount
- ◆ Unit
- ◆ Name
- ◆ Prompt
- ◆ Address Number

The Alpha Description appears in the upper-left corner of the field-level help window. This information is not considered as valuable to technical designers as the Data Item value is.

The Alias Value

The OneWorld Alias value is recognized by World software as the four-character AS/400 data item name. Within any given data file or table, this four-character field name is preceded by a unique two-character prefix that is related to the table's purpose or use. For instance, "PH" stands for Purchase Order Header, and "PD" stands for Purchase Order Detail.

OneWorld data tables created in any database (such as DB/400, Oracle, or SQL Server) use the Alias value as the field name within the context of the database table. This is an important consideration should you attempt to query the OneWorld file or table using any other ODBC-compliant reporting, data extraction, or manipulation tool.

When you create a new Data Dictionary item, the Alias is an eight-character alphabetical code that should not contain blanks, special characters, or punctuation symbols. A new data item should be given an alias that includes a dollar sign ($) as a prefix. For example, a new field might have an alias name of $DAT. Note that an Alias value cannot be changed. However, a practical size limitation does exist for AS/400 users. The alias value is used to create the field name on the AS/400. For this reason, the size of the alias should be kept to four characters, including the $—for example, $DAT, not $DATA. The $ is used to differentiate JDE data items from client data items.

The Glossary Group

Glossary Group is a table-validated field that designates the type of data item. Items in glossary group D or S can be included in database tables. Data items in other glossary groups cannot be added to a table. In World software, this field was used to designate and select types of Data Dictionary items for printing purposes.

Working with Data Items

There are some important rules regarding defining and maintaining data items in the OneWorld Data Dictionary. First, when creating new data items, use a system code value of 55 through 59. These system code values are reserved by J. D. Edwards for client use and are considered "user-defined" system codes. These code values should be used in conjunction with all custom development efforts. Second, after a data item is created, you can change only the Alpha Description value; the data item name and alias cannot be changed. Finally, when a data item is added, the Data Dictionary edits the Data Item and Alias fields to ensure that they are unique values.

To add a new data item to the Data Dictionary, from the Work With Data Items form, click on the Add button. The Data Item Specifications form appears. Figure 12-2 illustrates the Work With Data Item Specifications form from the B.7.3.3.1 version of OneWorld. In OneWorld Xe (B.7.3.3.3), the appearance of this screen has changed. The buttons for High Level Default Triggers are tabs instead. While we're on this subject, it is interesting to note that OneWorld forms do change in appearance from release to release. These "form" changes are likely more pronounced within the context of OneWorld Development tools than perhaps in the OneWorld applications themselves. In short, the OneWorld Development tools are undergoing constant revision by J. D. Edwards' software engineers.

To maintain an existing Data Dictionary data item, do the following:

1. Find and select the desired data item using the Work With Data Items form.
2. Click on the Select button to access the selected data item for maintenance purposes.

The Data Item Specifications form appears (see Figure 12-2).

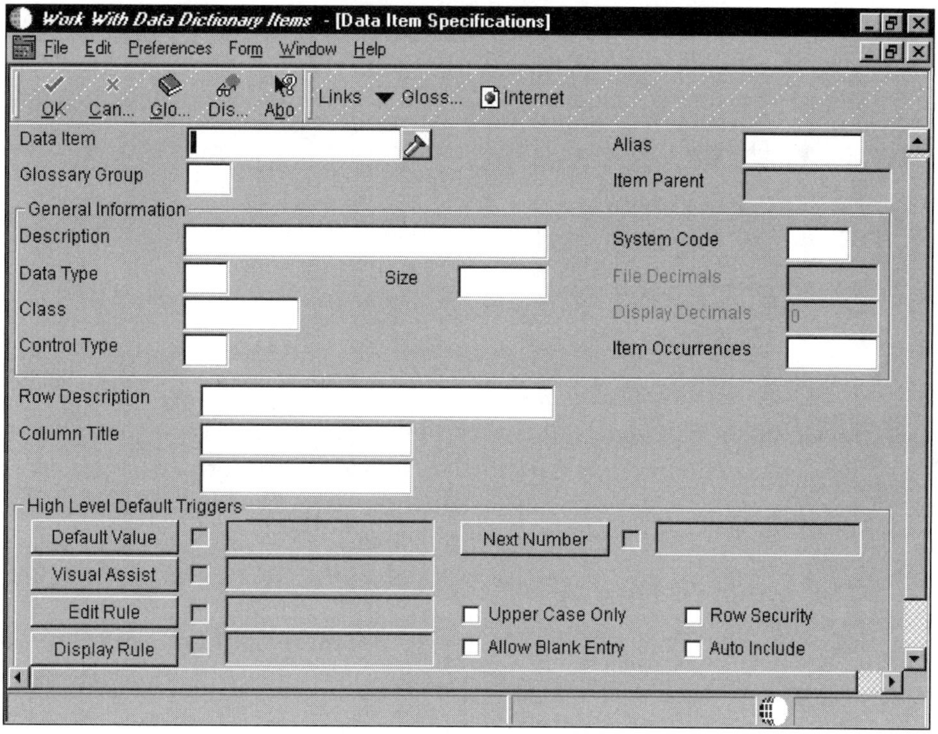

FIGURE 12-2 *The Work With Data Item Specifications Form*

Using the Data Item Specifications Form

You must enter a number of required or mandatory fields when defining a new data item. The required fields on the Data Item Specifications Form include

- ◆ Alias
- ◆ Description
- ◆ System Code
- ◆ Data Type
- ◆ Control Type
- ◆ Row Description
- ◆ Column Title

Although they aren't required fields when describing a data item, some of the most important fields in the Data Dictionary are found on the other tabs (or, in the case of earlier versions of OneWorld, buttons) for High Level Default Triggers. In addition to the main form or first tab for Item Specifications, the remaining tabs or buttons include provisions for defining and maintaining the following:

- The Item Glossary
- A default value
- Defining a visual assist
- Defining an edit rule
- Defining a display rule
- Establishing Next Numbering for a field

However, the developer will find that merely changing a value for a given field in the Data Dictionary item is insufficient by itself. Frequently, other actions are necessary to activate processing using either the Form Design or Report Design tool.

Decimals in OneWorld

OneWorld employs a floating or implied decimal point feature called the Display Decimals value. This feature is necessary to accommodate both differences in currencies and in business models and practices. You should decide how many decimal positions are needed for both currency-related and quantity fields *before* you begin entering data in OneWorld. Although J. D. Edwards provides a method for changing the position of the decimal for specific field classes, it does not provide any way to convert the underlying data. If you change the decimal position *after* you enter data, the data you entered before changing the display decimal value will be wrong.

Using the Display Decimals feature, you can change the position of the display decimal for specific classes of fields, such as currency or quantity fields. For example, data items that belong to the currency class are initially delivered with the display decimal set at 2, but this value can be changed to another value, such as 4. Therefore, instead of a currency value's being displayed as 100.00, it would be displayed as 100.0000 throughout all OneWorld applications. In addition, fields in the quantity class are delivered with a display decimal value of 0.

As a final note, you should disable OneWorld replication when you update Display Decimals. Depending on how replication has been set up in your OneWorld environment, failure to do so might create hundreds of replication messages.

World Versus OneWorld Dictionary Differences

If you are using OneWorld and World coexistence, you must maintain two Data Dictionaries. You cannot share one dictionary, because the dollar sign ($) has a different use in World software. You will note that the procedure for maintaining text in the Data Dictionary differs slightly between OneWorld and World. In addition, a number of the file formats in World are different from those in OneWorld.

Maintaining Error and Workflow Messages

Error messages and workflow messages are defined and maintained through processes similar to those for defining and maintaining data items in the Data Dictionary. To maintain OneWorld message text, the Data Dictionary Design menu (GH951) is used. Individual options appear on this menu for maintaining both error messages and workflow messages. These message type fields require minimal definition because they are primarily text. OneWorld workflow management has not been discussed thus far, but an overview is provided in the next chapter.

Vocabulary and Text Overrides

One of the benefits that the OneWorld active Data Dictionary provides is the ability to change the vocabulary used throughout OneWorld to that which is common to your organization or industry. For instance, a distributor might want to rename several item master-related fields. It may be desirable to rename the second item number field Catalog Number and the third item number field UPC code. With OneWorld, this type of change is generally made through the Data Dictionary. It is also possible to access and change the field-level help information for a specific field through the active Data Dictionary.

An important cautionary note about such changes is in order. Although these changes affect the report or form, they do not have any impact on either the OneWorld online documentation or the contents of the OneWorld reference guides provided by J. D. Edwards. Your organization must carefully weigh the merits of making vocabulary and text changes using the active Data Dictionary against the impact on OneWorld documentation used for training and future reference purposes. My general advice is to avoid or minimize making vocabulary and text changes using the active Data Dictionary. In this case, the easy part is making the system change; the hard part is following through on documenting and communicating such changes.

The OneWorld Developer Tools

This section discusses the overall process of developing new applications that maintain the same look, feel, and processing properties of OneWorld. In addition, when an existing OneWorld application must be customized to meet specific requirements that are unique to your organization, the OneWorld application is modified using the same process. However, before we discuss the OneWorld tools, some introduction to object-oriented software development and to some of the vocabulary specific to OneWorld development is in order.

OneWorld Is Object-Based

The current approach in the system development community is the use of objects. Object orientation represents a paradigm shift for the software industry. Objects offer many advantages to software designers. Object-oriented programming is the prevalent development technique in the Internet age, especially with the emergence of Java, a machine-independent object-oriented language that is browser-based. If you use AS/400, do not confuse AS/400 objects with the concepts of object-oriented software development. AS/400 developers will find that many parallels do exist, but there are some important differences.

Object orientation is rooted in the concepts of modularity and messaging—concepts that most software developers are already comfortable with. It is not surprising that *n*-tier client/server computing solutions, such as OneWorld, rely on object orientation. An object is considered a stand-alone or self-sufficient entity that contains or encapsulates both data and the functions used to manipulate that data. Traditionally, data and the functions used to manipulate it were separated. Objects are by design highly reusable entities—and are highly "distributable" as a result.

OneWorld Is Event-Driven

OneWorld is considered an event-driven system. Events are an important concept in the overall OneWorld development framework. Events are perhaps the greatest difference between a procedural programming language such as Report Program Generator (RPG), the native programming language of the AS/400 environment, and the base development language for most of J. D. Edwards' World software, an event-driven language such as Visual C++.

In the event-driven world, the developer must build programs that respond to an array of activities or events that are not necessarily sequential or procedural in nature. The event-driven program therefore is a program that can respond to any of a series of randomly selected events by the application program's user. Such events include the movement between tabs on a form or the use of a drop-down window to dynamically resize a column or move a column to another position in a grid.

As complex as event-driven programming is, the good news for the developer is that much of the complexity in building event-driven programs is simplified through the use of reusable components or objects. In addition, OneWorld further simplifies the process of software development to the point that it is more of an assembly process, bolting reusable components together to form a new OneWorld application.

Creating Objects and Applications in OneWorld

In OneWorld, developers create both objects and applications. Objects are considered the building blocks for all applications. The suite of OneWorld development tools is used to create these objects. Although new objects can be built, OneWorld is delivered with scores of prebuilt objects. Here are some of the major OneWorld object types that are used as application building blocks:

- Business functions
- Business views
- Data Dictionary items
- Data structures
- Event rules
- Processing options
- Tables

The OneWorld application is considered a collection of objects that perform a specific task. The OneWorld developer uses the OneWorld development tools to build both batch and interactive applications—from objects—that satisfy a given business process requirement.

In many instances, the creation of a new OneWorld batch or interactive application is done without the need for any new program code generation. Instead, the new application is "assembled" from the existing collection of OneWorld objects. Of course, this is very idealistic. Therefore, it is often necessary for a programmer to write lines of code to completely satisfy an application requirement.

A Primer on OneWorld Objects

Earlier we discussed the OneWorld active Data Dictionary. However, before we proceed, I will define the other major OneWorld object types that are used as the building blocks for creating OneWorld applications.

The OneWorld Business Function Object

The OneWorld business function groups related business logic. A business function is used to perform a specific task. A business function generally enhances the value of a given OneWorld application. For instance, calculating depreciation is an example of a business function that has application-enhancing value. Business functions are created by one of several methods, including

◆ Use of the OneWorld event rules scripting language.

◆ Use of C language programming code

These business functions are generally designed in such a way as to promote their reusability throughout a number of OneWorld applications.

The Event Rules Scripting Language

Business functions in OneWorld are generally created using the event rules scripting language. These scripts are generally called business function event rules. When it is not possible to create a business function using the OneWorld event rules scripting language, a C language-based business function is necessary to complete your organization's specific business requirements.

Also note that larger business functions can be broken into smaller, individual functions. These smaller blocks of code or event rules can then be called from a larger or "umbrella" business function. After you create business functions, they are incorporated into OneWorld applications, thereby providing additional processing capabilities.

The OneWorld Business View Object

Although the concept of the business view was introduced in the preceding chapter, its role and importance to the OneWorld application is a central concept. This is further reinforced here from the developer's perspective.

A business view is essential to OneWorld application processing. Both interactive and batch applications rely on business views. The business view restricts data access to what is "necessary" based on the data selection made in the application. In addition, a business view can contain data items from more than one table. The business view "links" the OneWorld application to the data tables in the OneWorld database. For instance, without a business view, the developer would be unable to create an interactive form application or generate a report.

The OneWorld Business View Design Tool

A business view is a selection of data items from one or more tables. After a table is created, the OneWorld Business View Design tool is used to select only the data items that are required by the application. This step is called defining business view specifications.

After business view specifications have been defined, they must be saved. The developer uses the OneWorld Business View Design tool to generate the new business view. The generation process uses the business view specifications to generate the appropriate SQL statements needed to retrieve data from the OneWorld database.

Before a business view definition can be used by the developer, the business view must be generated. A business view can be generated at any time. For instance, if one or more data items are added to the business view, a new business view must be created. Tables and business views are closely related. For instance, the OneWorld application will fail when there is an inconsistency between the tables and business views, such as a missing data item, a missing business view, or a missing data table.

Another way to think of business view is that it represents the "rules" for the selection of data items from one or more tables. For instance, a developer uses the Business View Designer tool after creating a new table to select between data items from old tables and any added OneWorld tables within the context of the new application. OneWorld subsequently uses a business view to generate the appropriate SQL statement or statements needed to retrieve data from the OneWorld database. Perhaps the most important use of business views is not for custom development work in OneWorld, but to simplify report generation when using the Enterprise Report Writer. Therefore, in many cases, adding a business view might actually eliminate the need to further customize OneWorld.

Finally, coupling data selection criteria with the OneWorld application minimizes the movement of data over an organization's network and thus improves OneWorld's overall processing performance.

The OneWorld Data Structure Object

Data structures are an essential element in any computer programming language. A data structure represents a list or grouping of data items that are used to pass data between the application itself and a database table. OneWorld uses several important types of data structures:

- ◆ Business Function data structures
- ◆ Form data structures
- ◆ Report data structures

In addition to these more common data structures, OneWorld has other types of data structures. The OneWorld Development Tools Guide provides further details about these additional data structure types.

Business Function Data Structures

Any OneWorld business function relying on OneWorld Business Function Event Rules or on C programming language code must have a defined data structure to send or receive information to or from applications. Although the OneWorld Business Function includes a predefined data structure, the developer is responsible for defining data structures related to any C programming code.

Form Data Structures

Each form that includes a business view has, by default, a data structure. The default data structure contains all fields associated with a given business view. This data structure is used to receive or send information between forms. The default data structure for a form is maintained using the Form/Data Structure menu option in Forms Design.

Report Data Structures

A batch application that includes a business view receives and sends information to a data structure. Unlike a form data structure, the report data structure is not automatically populated with any data item references. The Report/Data Structure menu option in Report Design is used to create and maintain a batch application data structure.

The OneWorld Event Rule Object

Event rules are an important building block of the OneWorld application development process. Event rules are best thought of as a way to "assemble" existing OneWorld business logic into an application program. Event rules provide the "programmed response" to a user-driven event in the world of object-oriented or event-driven programming as embraced by OneWorld. This section introduces the event rules that are a fundamental part of OneWorld's underlying program architecture.

Business Function Event Rules

Although it's possible to customize OneWorld without writing code, this is somewhat of a misnomer. What the developer really does is write business function event rules. These rules represent an encapsulated, reusable business logic component that relies on event rules rather than on C language program statements. Like a C language program, the business function event rule is stored as an object and is compiled. There are different types of event rules.

OneWorld developers frequently spend much of their effort defining event rules that represent application or business processing logic. A good way of understanding the purpose of an event rule object is to think of it as a container for the logic statements that are attached to or associated with a given OneWorld event.

Consider for a moment OneWorld interactive form processing. Each type of OneWorld form includes a basic level of processing or logic to handle various events. For instance, saving the contents of the form or canceling the form are two events that an application user can initiate. In addition, each form has a certain degree of business logic associated with it. Given that OneWorld automatically defines a basic level of forms processing logic for a new application program, the developer is free to concentrate on defining event rules related to business processing.

Controls Versus Events

A *control* is a reusable object that appears on the OneWorld form. Controls are part of the forms processing logic defined for a new application program. Examples of controls include buttons, edit fields, and data grids. *Events* are activities that occur on a form, such as entering a form or exiting a field using the Tab key. Controls are user interface components that initiate or trigger one or more events.

Events are typically initiated by user actions—using controls. However, the running OneWorld application itself can also initiate additional events that a user might not know have occurred. For instance, for any given OneWorld application that is active and where OK is clicked, the form is then processed. Processing usually implies a validation of the contents of each data item. If validations are successful, the transaction record is saved to the database. This forms processing example represents an entire assembly of individual events. There are also events that are system-initiated when certain actions occur. For instance, if the forms processing encounters data item validation errors, the system highlights field errors and presents one or more error messages to the user.

Other Event Rules

In addition to business function event rules, there are other types of event rules. They include:

- ◆ Embedded event rules
- ◆ Application event rules
- ◆ Table event rules

These event rules are briefly described in the following sections. More information about event rules can be found in OneWorld's Online Help. Refer to the Published Application Program Interface (API) section for information about an individual event.

Embedded Event Rules

Embedded event rules are specific to a particular table, interactive application, or batch application. When an event rule is embedded, it is by definition not reusable. Examples include a form-to-form call, or the hiding of a field based on a processing options value. An embedded event rule can also be an application event rule (interactive or batch) or a table event rule.

Application Event Rules

Application event rules are the addition of business logic that is specific to a particular application. Event rules are connected or assembled for interactive applications using Form Design, and batch event rules are connected or assembled using Report Design.

Table Event Rules

Table Design is used to define table-related event rules. A table event rule is a rule associated with a given table—a database trigger. The logic attached to a table is executed whenever any application initiates that database event. A developer might want to maintain referential integrity for a master data table by having a rule associated with it that all child records must be deleted when a parent record is deleted, which maintains referential integrity. For instance, the OneWorld item master table requires that all branch/plant records for a given item be deleted before the item master record itself is deleted. If this parent/child relationship logic is attached to or embedded in the table definition, this parent/child deletion rule definition is also embedded in the application itself, because its definition resides at the table level.

Processing Option Template Objects

An integral part of most OneWorld applications is processing options. Processing options control how an interactive or batch application processes data. Processing options work closely in conjunction with versions. Processing option settings are maintained through a version. Processing option settings may vary from version to version. A version provides a wide degree of user control over data processing. Versions reduce the need for continual customization of OneWorld applications. Here are some examples of what processing options can provide:

- Controls the path a user follows in an application
- Provides a container for default or override values
- Allows an application to be customized for different companies, business units, or even different users

◆ Provides control over the format of forms and reports

◆ In certain instances, processing options provide overrides for data selection

◆ Controls page breaks and totaling on reports

Processing options can be defined for custom applications. Or, if needed, processing options of existing applications can be modified. Processing options are made possible through the use of a processing options template. The processing options template is another type of OneWorld data structure. A processing options template in turn contains one or more processing options.

When the OneWorld batch or interactive process is initiated, the processing option template displays a set of tabs within an area called a *page*. Each tab represents a category of processing options. When you click the tab, the page changes to show the set of processing options for that category. Each processing option appears on a row within the template and is defined by three components:

◆ Tab title

◆ Comment

◆ Data item

The tab title categorizes processing options by page within the processing options template. This text appears on the tab for a given processing option. J. D. Edwards has standardized these tab entries. Consult the OneWorld Application Design Standards Guide for specific directions regarding processing option tab titles to help ensure that any custom applications mimic J. D. Edwards applications.

Comments represent additional or optional text that appears on the form along with the processing option itself. Each comment takes the place of a processing option on the page, so adding comment lines eliminates space for processing option entries.

Every processing option must be associated with a data item in the Data Dictionary. When the processing options template is defined, the developer selects data items for inclusion in the processing options template.

Here are the general steps for creating and implementing processing options for a given application:

1. Create processing options by building a list of parameters called a template.

2. Attach this template to an application, and create event rules for the application to make use of these values.

3. Create versions of the application. Specify how the processing options will be handled at runtime.

When an application program is initiated, depending on how configuration options have been set at the version level, the user will be allowed to review and modify processing options. However, these configuration options also allow for the protection or masking of the processing options from review or modification by the user.

Tables

One or more relational database tables or files stores the data that any given OneWorld application will use. In a relational database, data is stored in two dimensions—as a spreadsheet or as a table consisting of columns and rows. Each column represents a data field or data item, and each data row is considered a record.

Relational database tables needed to complete all OneWorld batch and interactive application processes already exist when J. D. Edwards ships OneWorld to a client. However, if your organization will develop custom applications to complement or extend OneWorld's delivered functionality, new database tables will likely be needed. When building a new OneWorld application, the developer may also use existing OneWorld tables. The OneWorld table Design tool is used to

◆ Define a table to the OneWorld database

◆ Identify the Data Dictionary fields or data items that comprise a table definition

◆ Define the table index by defining the key fields for a given table

The developer uses OneWorld Table Design to define and generate a new table. This is an important step that must be done through the Table Design tool in order for OneWorld to recognize that the table exists. Before you create the physical table, it must be generated. Data cannot be added or updated in the table until it is physically generated. The table generation process also creates special files that are needed when compiling business functions and table event rules. A table must be regenerated when

◆ A data field or item is added to or deleted from a table definition

◆ A table index is added or modified

A table must be regenerated *after* you modify the table definition to accommodate any of these changes.

The Data Dictionary's Role in Table Design

Before a table can be created, data fields or data items must be defined. Recall from earlier discussions that data items are defined in OneWorld's active Data Dictionary.

Indices and Tables

As a part of the table definition process, the index for the table must be defined. An index identifies records in a table. Every table definition includes at least one index, although additional indices are frequently used. Identifying certain data fields as *key fields* creates the database table index. An index is composed of one or more data fields or data items, referred to as *keys* within the table.

A table can have multiple indices; however, every table must have only one primary index. The primary index is the one identifier that is unique for each record in the table. However, as a practical matter, the application should use an index that returns the most detail from the database. This does not mean that the primary index is always useful and is why additional indices are often needed. A good example to consider is the Address Book. Although the Address Book is unique to each record in the Address Book Table, a combination key of Address Book number and Search Type might be a more appropriate key to locate customer records specifically.

Indices are used by the database for the purposes of retrieving and updating data in the database. Indices allow the database to locate, retrieve, or sort records as efficiently and quickly as possible. The goal of an index is to prevent having to read through the data sequentially, which can be time-consuming. Indices are created for the database based on when the OneWorld middleware generates a SQL statement that is in turn translated by the underlying database. For instance, the Oracle, IBM DB/2, or Microsoft SQL Server database creates an index for the file or table based on OneWorld's middleware instructions.

Flat Files Versus Relational Database Files

You will frequently hear the term *flat file*. There are several major differences between a flat file and a relational database file. Although a flat file also stores data in two dimensions—as a spreadsheet or as a table consisting of columns and rows—a flat file has no index. Therefore, an application using flat files has no index to rely on when processing the data. A second major difference is that flat files are typically not normalized, meaning that all the data needed by an application is contained within a single file. The data is therefore not broken out into a series of smaller, logically organized and related fields.

The typical use of a flat file in a relational database environment is generally restricted to data conversion and application integration or interface files and tables. For instance, your organization might build flat files containing legacy system data that will be converted into OneWorld. For instance, flat files containing annualized budget data, as well as the legacy system trial balance information (as of the conversion date), can be used as input data sources for the OneWorld batch interface processors. More information about the OneWorld batch interface processors can be found in the next chapter.

OneWorld Application Development Steps

Here are the initial steps that a developer would typically follow in creating a new OneWorld application. They are common to both interactive and batch processes:

1. Determine the features needed in a new application. Use cases are an excellent tool to use when designing an object-oriented application, such as a new OneWorld application.
2. Sketch out the forms, or user interface design, for the new application.
3. Design the data model for the new application. Identify existing tables and data items, as well as new tables and data items that are needed.
4. Create data items in the Data Dictionary.
5. Create tables using the Table Design tool.
6. Create business views using the Business View Designer tool.

Previous sections have discussed the Data Dictionary, the Table Design tool, and the Business View Design tool.

The remaining steps vary, depending on whether an application is considered an interactive or batch application. If the application is interactive, do the following:

7. Create and attach a Processing Options template to the application.
8. Create the required forms using the OneWorld Form Design tool.

If the application is a batch update or report application, do the following:

9. Create and attach a Processing Options template to the application.

10. Create the required forms using the OneWorld Report Design tool.

After the application is completed, tested, and accepted by users, the developer promotes or moves the objects that comprise the OneWorld application into production.

11. Use the Object Librarian and Promotion Manager to stage the new application for distribution to clients.

12. Perform a package build to assemble and distribute new objects to the client workstations.

Although these steps are an oversimplification of the exact steps in the typical OneWorld application development process, they do serve to highlight the steps a developer can expect and that will be minimally necessary when designing the OneWorld application. These steps will vary with the complexity of the application, or if an existing application is being modified or copied and modified.

Customization Without Programming

OneWorld development tools are intended to keep changes at a high-enough level so as to prevent the need for program development at the source code level. As a result, much of OneWorld customization is accomplished through the assembly of prebuilt components—called business functions—using a point-and-click or drag-and-drop style of development environment.

The developer who is familiar with a visual tool such as Visual Basic or Visual C++ should be comfortable in the OneWorld application development environment. RPG programmers coming from the AS/400 environment will experience a longer ramp-up period before they are comfortable with OneWorld development tools.

Plan for Upgrades Before Beginning Customization

This is an area where J. D. Edwards offers some sage advice for organizations that are about to embark on efforts to customize OneWorld. Quite simply, before beginning any OneWorld customization effort, consider how the customization will be impacted by any future upgrade to OneWorld. While we're on this subject, the same holds true for configuration actions—they too can be adversely affected by an upgrade if certain rules are not followed. The next chapter includes a section that summarizes important information about how any configuration changes, including customization, are affected by an upgrade of your OneWorld software.

Batch Versus Interactive Applications

A batch process is an application that completes all processing automatically without the need for any user intervention. More specifically, there is typically no user interaction with batch processes. Once a batch process is initiated, the user has no control over the logic flow within the batch process. If a change in the logic flow is needed within the batch process or report, the logic flow within the batch application must be modified by a developer using the OneWorld Report Design tool.

Examples of OneWorld batch processes include:

◆ Reports

◆ Update processes

◆ Batch input processing

◆ Table conversion

◆ Subsystem processing

In OneWorld, a subsystem process is a batch process that runs constantly in the background. A subsystem process is typically used to monitor and route applications or for "on-demand" document printing applications.

Although you observed in previous chapters that the Versions List initiates a batch process, along with the ability to define data selection, sequencing, and processing values at runtime, it is absolutely unnecessary to complete these steps in OneWorld in order to initiate and execute a batch process. In fact, OneWorld menu options can be defined so as to allow nothing but job initiation by the user. Throughout OneWorld there are numerous examples where another batch or interactive process calls another OneWorld batch application and executes that application unbeknownst to the user. In addition, a batch application can be scheduled to execute automatically on a one-time or recurring basis using OneWorld Scheduler. The OneWorld Scheduler is discussed in the next chapter.

An interactive process is *functionally opposite* of a batch process. The interactive process relies on the user for one or more interactions with the application to complete processing. The interactive process pauses at certain points and waits for user interaction with the application before the application continues processing.

The interactive application decides what to do next based on the context or content of the user's response.

Accessing the OneWorld Development Tools

To work with the OneWorld development tools, access the Development Tools menu by selecting

> G > Foundation Systems (G0) > Tools (GH90) > Application Development Tools (GH901) > Cross Application Development Tools (**GH902**)

Figure 12-3 shows the Cross Application Development Tools (GH902) menu.

FIGURE 12-3 *The Cross Application Development Tools Menu*

Interactive Applications

In OneWorld, interactive application development revolves around the creation of forms. A form is the interface between a user and the OneWorld data table. A form presents the data from the table in an organized manner and contains the functionality necessary for the user to enter and manipulate data.

A typical OneWorld application contains more than one form. For instance, a Work With or Find and Browse form is the first form displayed for the typical OneWorld application. This form provides a way for the user to locate a specific record that is to be updated. After you select a specific record that appears on the Work With form, a subsequent form, such as the Fix and Inspect form, is displayed; it is populated with the contents of the specified record. The user can subsequently review and update the data for that record.

Interactive Application Development

The One World Form Design tool is used to construct interactive applications and forms. Interactive application design is a relatively complex assembly task. Not only does it involve laying out the controls and fields on a given form, but it also requires the definition of all the behind-the-scenes processing that is required for the processing of the data that is entered into a form by the user. OneWorld forms are comprised of multiple elements:

◆ Form types

◆ Business views

◆ Controls

◆ Properties

◆ Data structures

◆ Event rules

As in all software development efforts, design of the application should proceed its actual coding or development. Although OneWorld has specific tools and rules for creating an application, the need to think through and define what is to be accomplished within an application remains the starting point. For the OneWorld developer, one of the most important initial choices is the selection of a form type. The form type establishes the basic functionality of a form. Each form type has a set of basic or default controls and processes. The OneWorld Forms Design tool supports creation of these form types:

◆ Find/Browse

◆ Parent/Child

◆ Fix/Inspect

◆ Header Detail

◆ Header-Less Detail

◆ Search and Select

◆ Message

The application developer must understand the available form types, because each form has characteristics to accommodate different tasks. You must use this understanding to select the correct form type when developing the new OneWorld application.

The business view plays an important role in the creation of a form. Business views link forms and tables. Generally speaking, all forms except the Message form type must be associated with a business view.

In the context of form design, all objects on a form are considered controls. For instance, controls include the Data Grid, a check box, or a button. In addition to form controls, properties must be defined. Properties define appearance and functionality characteristics for the application itself as well for the form, controls, and the Data Grid.

Data structures define the data that will be passed between forms within an application or between several applications. Form interconnections are then used to specify how data flows from one form or application to another form or application.

Event rules contain the application or business logic that brings the form alive. Event rules provide instructions on how specific events are handled by the application. An event is typically a user action that occurs on a form, such as clicking a button or tabbing to the next field. Use event rules to attach business logic to any event. Events can also be the result of a system-initiated process, such as loading a grid with contents from the OneWorld table.

This is an admittedly brief and overly simplistic introduction to OneWorld interactive application development. A more complete discussion of the process of developing OneWorld interactive applications is beyond the scope of this book.

For additional information about developing OneWorld interactive applications, consult the OneWorld documentation CD-ROM. The soft-copy documentation contains a Development Tools guide that provides further information. However, in addition to this documentation, it is highly recommended that developers from your organization attend a formal J. D. Edwards training class regarding how to create both batch applications and interactive applications.

The Use of Caching in OneWorld

One final note about OneWorld interactive applications: For performance reasons, OneWorld interactive applications are typically cached. A cached OneWorld application does not read all the contents of a database into the form at once. Instead, only the visible rows of data in the Data Grid are loaded. As the user pages or scrolls down through the Data Grid, additional table records are loaded while the already loaded grid data is saved into cache memory. If the user then pages or scrolls back to a previous record, the interactive application retrieves the records from cache memory, not from the database again.

The Enterprise Report Writer

The OneWorld Report Design tool and the OneWorld Enterprise Report Writer are synonyms for the process of creating reports as well as batch update applications in OneWorld. The Report Design Tool will likely be the OneWorld customization tool that your organization will ultimately use the most.

Although it's billed as a user-oriented report writer, in practice I have found that few organizations provide end users with training or, in some cases, even allow access to this tool by their end-users. Since the tool can actually allow for data manipulation, its use cannot be taken lightly. I have not found the OneWorld Report Design tool to be a "point and click" report writer. As a matter of fact, OneWorld Report Design has some annoying traits. With each new OneWorld release, the OneWorld Report Writer seems to undergo some degree of revision, although it is not yet at the level of maturity where I believe it is ready for end-users to handle. Therefore, I continue to recommend that its use generally be restricted to developers.

Batch Application Development

In OneWorld, both batch processes and report applications are created using the Report Design tool. Completed batch and report applications are then added to OneWorld menus. A key difference between a batch process and a report is that a batch process usually performs table update processing, while a report does not perform table update processing.

Although batch update processes are frequently designed in such a way as to not print a report, this is a practice I strongly advise against. I frequently recommend several batch update process printing alternatives:

◆ Use of a *before-and-after* snapshot report.

◆ Use of a *proof* or *final* update mode.

If neither of these alternatives is considered, another alternative is a *follow-up* application that prints a report showing the results of a batch update process.

The Before-and-After Snapshot

The first reporting alternative is to create a report during a batch update process that indicates both the "before" and "after" values of a data item being changed or updated by the batch update.

Proof Versus Final Mode Processing

The well-designed batch update process should be capable of running in a "proof" or "preliminary" mode. In this mode, the batch process sends the database update to a report for thoughtful review or "proofing" before committing to the database update. The database update occurs when the batch update process is run in "final" mode. The "switch" for preliminary and final processing is generally provided through a processing option.

Report Design Versus Report Design Directors

OneWorld Report Design also uses configurable *Directors*. A Director works much like a help wizard in Microsoft Office applications. OneWorld comes with several preconfigured Directors. For example, a Director exists that guides you through the steps of creating a financial report.

Level-Break Processing

For AS/400 developers, the concept of a level break is not new. However, for developers in other environments, this concept may be an unfamiliar one. A level break is used to identify a change in the data that is being processed. The level break compares the current data record being processed to the previous record. If there is a change between records, a level break occurs. When a level break occurs, other processing typically occurs. For instance, level breaks are often used to initiate page breaks or print subtotals, totals, headers, or footers.

Level-break processing is based on fields or data items that are associated with a business view being used in a batch process.

The Anatomy of a OneWorld Report

The OneWorld report contains all the specifications for the report, including layouts for sections and fields, business views, event rules, data selection, sequencing, and specifications for any database output. Every report is named with a unique identifier.

Each report contains one or more *sections*. Sections are self-contained elements that are used as building blocks to construct a report. OneWorld sections include headers, footers, and body sections. There are three body sections:

◆ Group sections

◆ Columnar sections

◆ Tabular sections

A *group section* is used to print data in either a vertical or horizontal format. Group sections display row headings each time a new record is read. A free-form group is displayed based on the process performed. The printing of transaction documents such as sales orders, invoices, purchase orders, mailing labels, and checks relies heavily on group sections.

A *columnar section* prints data in a columnar fashion, with column headings at the top of each report page and rows of data beneath each heading. A columnar section presents data in a manner similar to the Data Grid. Therefore, column headings are not repeated when a new record is read from the table. Most business reports that present information one row or line per record fit this model. The One Line Address Book Report, described in previous chapters, relies on a columnar section.

A *tabular section* prints data in columns, rows, and *cells*. Tabular sections are used when there is a need to control the information on an item-by-item basis. This is a common requirement when producing financial reports, especially consolidated information. A tabular section prints data *only* when a level break occurs. A tabular section automatically sums and totals at *each* break level.

Group, columnar, and tabular sections are considered independent sections, and header and footer sections are considered dependent sections. Because each kind of body section in a report has certain properties and characteristics that are specific to it, a key aspect of custom report development is determining the report body section that best satisfies your specific business requirements.

World Versus OneWorld Report Writers

If you're a former World software user, be aware that everything you learned about previous report writers provided by J. D. Edwards or IBM no longer applies in the OneWorld environment. The OneWorld Report Design tool combines and replaces all the functionality previously provided through World Writer, the general-purpose report writer; STAR, the fixed-asset report writer; FASTR, the financial report writer; and World CASE Report Design Aid (RDA) into a single report development tool. This also means that any custom report applications making use of these former tools need to be redesigned using the OneWorld Report Design tool.

Third-Party Report Writers

If your platform is AS/400, you might wonder why AS/400 Query can't be used to design custom reports for OneWorld. Actually, it can be. However, two potential issues must be considered. First, J. D. Edwards uses a standard Julian date format across all its applications that is not a standard IBM-defined Julian date format. Second, the decimal point is missing from any OneWorld numeric data field. Recall from earlier discussions in this chapter how OneWorld uses the Display Data Decimals feature of the active Data Dictionary when displaying or printing a decimal data field.

If you are compelled to use a report writer other than OneWorld's Report Design tool, J. D. Edwards' complementary products such as those from Showcase and Business Objects should provide accommodations for these two OneWorld data anomalies.

Application Design Standards

Frequently throughout this and previous chapters, mention has been made of standards that J. D. Edwards adheres to in its OneWorld product development. These standards also provide guidelines that any developer or consultant that is customizing for your organization should adhere to. J. D. Edwards periodically publishes and updates its Application Design Standards guide for OneWorld. A copy of this guide is included on the OneWorld documentation CD-ROM. An updated version of this guide can be downloaded from the J. D. Edwards Web site to ensure that any custom applications are in compliance with the latest standards.

The Application Design Standards guide includes valuable information for developers:

- Application development checklists
- OneWorld naming conventions
- Performance considerations
- Acronyms and abbreviations
- Standard verbs

For instance, a major standard is the use of system code values 55 through 59 throughout OneWorld. These code values are reserved for client and business partner use when developing custom applications. The reserved values also apply to other objects, including data tables and user-defined codes.

Following application design standards prescribed by J. D. Edwards is the best way to ensure that your applications are "future-proofed" from conflicts with OneWorld updates provided by J. D. Edwards.

OneWorld Object Management

The OneWorld development tool set provides for the management of OneWorld-related objects—including control over both the creation and changing of objects. Managing software modifications can be more difficult than making the actual application changes, especially if a team of developers is necessary. Therefore, it is important to establish and communicate to all developers a plan for controlling and tracking software changes—by object. Although OneWorld includes systemic tools that aid in object or change management, these tools alone are likely insufficient.

OneWorld Object Librarian

The OneWorld Object Librarian manages the creation and maintenance of OneWorld objects. The main functions of the Object Librarian include the following:

- Serving as the entry point into the OneWorld development tool set
- Managing the creation and modification of OneWorld objects

◆ Tracking the location of OneWorld objects

◆ Identifying which developers are using specific objects through a check in/check out process

The OneWorld developer uses the OneWorld Object Librarian in conjunction with the OneWorld Development Tools to control the movement of objects between the client and the server. When an object is initially created, it exists only on the local client workstation. For the object to be available to other users, it must be "checked in" to the server. The process of checking in an object copies the object to the server.

When the OneWorld developer needs to modify any object, the OneWorld Object Librarian is used to "check out" an object. When an object is checked out, it is copied from the server to the local client workstation using the OneWorld Object Librarian. Other developers are then prevented from modifying this object. This restriction is made using processing options related to the OneWorld Object Librarian itself, so making this restriction is therefore highly recommended.

Object Management Workbench

In the latest version of OneWorld, referred to as B.7.3.3.3 or OneWorld Xe, the Object Librarian of old has been replaced by a new object manager, the Object Management Workbench. OneWorld's object manager sports more than just a new name. It has a new look along with an improved user interface that makes development somewhat more intuitive. Most of a developer's application development activities are initiated through the Object Management Workbench. The Object Management Workbench provides significant advantages over its predecessor, the Object Librarian, for OneWorld Xe technical personnel in administering and deploying objects.

Accessing the Object Management Workbench

To work with the OneWorld development tools, access the Development Tools menu by selecting the following:

G > Foundation Systems (G0) > Tools (GH90) > Application Development Tools (GH901) > Cross Application Development Tools (**GH902**)

If you're using an older version of OneWorld, select

Object Librarian (P9860)

If you're using the latest version of OneWorld, select

> Object Management Workbench (P98220)

Figure 12-4 shows the Object Management Workbench (P98220) form, and Figure 12-5 shows its predecessor, the Object Librarian (P9860).

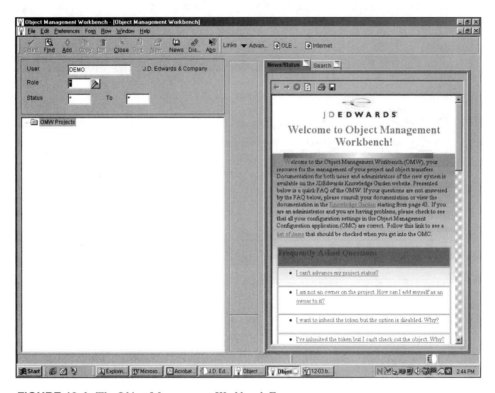

FIGURE 12-4 *The Object Management Workbench Form*

Regardless of what version of OneWorld your organization has installed, object management is the fundamental starting point for creating OneWorld interactive applications as well as for most other OneWorld development tasks. For instance, several entry points exist for entry into the OneWorld Report Designer, which is used to create batch update and report applications. However, batch application development can also be initiated through the Object Management Workbench or the Object Librarian.

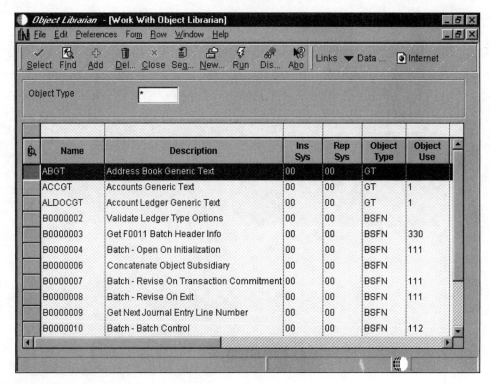

FIGURE 12-5 *The Object Librarian Form*

OneWorld Promotion Manager

The OneWorld Promotion Manager is used to determine which objects have been checked out to a local client workstation—typically a developer's workstation. For instance, developers who will be away from the work site for several days can use this tool to determine what objects they have checked out. In addition, the OneWorld Promotion Manager lets the developer check in a series of related objects at the same time or move objects from a development environment to a testing environment.

The Path Code

When object check-out, check-in, or promotion occurs in OneWorld, the movement of the object is based on the *path code*. The path code is used to keep track of where objects are located in OneWorld. The path code serves as a pointer to an object's location. Related sets of objects are typically maintained in a specific OneWorld environment, such as a development environment versus a test environment.

Environments as well as object configuration mappings and path codes are considered fundamental building blocks of OneWorld's Configurable Network Computing environment. They are established using OneWorld's Configurable Network Computing tools. The Promotion Manager and the Package Assembly, Package Build, and Package Deployment functions rely heavily on OneWorld's Configurable Network Computing building blocks.

Building and Deploying Packages

Before the new OneWorld application or changes to an existing OneWorld application appear at the end-user client workstation, certain steps must occur. It should be clearly understood that merely checking in the changed objects does not distribute them to client workstations.

For new or changed application objects to reach client workstations, deliberate system administration actions must be taken. This process is called package creation and deployment. A package is used to administer the objects resident at the client workstation. In general, the three steps of the package creation and deployment process are

- ◆ Package assembly
- ◆ Package build
- ◆ Package deployment

Objects that constitute an application or changes to an application are assembled or collected into a package. The first step in building and deploying a package is to assemble the package. In this step, the type of package to be built is identified, and the objects are selected or assembled for inclusion in the package. In general, there are three types of OneWorld packages:

- ◆ The full package
- ◆ The partial package
- ◆ The update package

The full package includes all OneWorld applications. If you need access to the full suite of OneWorld applications, this type of package should be deployed to your client workstation.

The partial package is a minimum configuration version of OneWorld. The main advantage of a partial package is a significant savings in client workstation disk space. For the user who receives this package, OneWorld subsequently loads, at runtime, only the applications needed, rather than deploying all and possibly many unused OneWorld applications during the initial installation of OneWorld to the client workstation.

Generally speaking, a full package installation occurs only once. Unless the workstation configuration is corrupted for some reason, a full package installation should not be required again. Instead, update packages are applied thereafter.

The update package is used to update or overlay an existing OneWorld installation on the client workstation. Any new objects from the package are added to the existing OneWorld installation by replacing any existing objects that have changed with new versions from the update package. All other OneWorld objects on the workstation are left untouched. This type of package can be used to efficiently deploy OneWorld software fixes and application enhancements. The Package Director can be used to search for changed objects and then build a list of changed objects that can be included in an update package.

The second step is the package build. Its purpose is to group OneWorld software modifications so that they can be deployed to workstations. A package describes where to find all the components that are to be deployed to the client workstations. A package can contain everything needed to run OneWorld, as in an initial installation for a new workstation, or only updates and changes to an existing OneWorld client workstation configuration.

The third step is package deployment. After a package is built, it must be deployed. OneWorld provides several package deployment methods. Each of these methods has specific advantages. In general, the deployment method selected depends mainly on the type of package to be deployed. The three types of package deployment are

♦ The workstation installation
♦ The full or partial package deployment
♦ The multitier deployment

The Workstation Installation program is used to deploy full and partial packages. Update packages cannot be deployed using the Workstation Installation program.

Update packages are always deployed using the Package Deployment program. Although full and partial packages are normally deployed using the Workstation Installation program, package deployment of a full or partial package is possible in cases where OneWorld is already on a machine and redeployment is desired.

Multitier deployment lets the OneWorld client workstation install software objects from more than one deployment location and from more than one deployment machine. Although this is more complex, if your organization has a large number of client workstations or uses a wide area network for deployment purposes, multitier deployment might prove beneficial.

Server Packages

OneWorld application development takes place on a local client workstation, typically called a developer workstation. After it's promoted, the OneWorld object is stored in a central location. The OneWorld Configurable Network Computing environment allows business applications to be partitioned or split between enterprise servers.

Therefore, application objects must be distributed to these multiple enterprise servers in addition to the client workstations. This is done through the use of a server package. Although server packages are not the same as workstation packages, they are built and deployed using the same OneWorld processes: package assembly, package build, and package deployment. It is important to understand that when an update package is created for workstations, a corresponding server package must deploy the same objects to your enterprise servers.

Package Deployment Administration

Package deployment can have an adverse impact on network resources and on your organization's personnel. Therefore, packages should be built and deployed only on an "as necessary" basis. An excessive number of package builds can place a strain on developers, end-users, and system administrators who are responsible for building and deploying packages. It is generally advisable to build and deploy packages on a set schedule. A schedule ensures that everyone involved knows when objects are due, when packages will be built and deployed, and, more importantly, when system resources might be adversely affected.

Evaluating Software Change Requests

Your organization will derive maximum benefit from its investment in OneWorld software—or, for that matter, any packaged software—if you can utilize the software as delivered and adjust or change your internal processes, policies, practices, and procedures to meet the software rather than change the software. Once any packaged software changes are made, these changes must be constantly administered, and they might complicate your ability to follow the software vendor's usual upgrade process.

As a general rule, evaluate packaged software changes by deciding whether the change is of regulatory or competitive necessity. If the change will create a competitive advantage or will sustain or increase your competitive position, its value can typically be dollarized, and a return on investment can be calculated. For statutory or regulatory compliance, most organizations will have few options but to comply with making customization or workarounds a necessity.

When changes to a software package are necessary, such as to OneWorld, it is best to develop customizations as follow-on or stand-alone processes rather than making an inline customization of a vendor-delivered application.

Finally, a OneWorld owner leverages its software investment by involving itself in Quest, the International Users Group for J. D. Edwards software, and by participating in vertical industry and other special-interest groups sponsored by Quest. These affiliations can be used to spirit forward OneWorld best-practice adaptations and change initiatives with J. D. Edwards, to further protect your investment in OneWorld, and to influence its future direction.

Summary

This rather lengthy chapter provided an overview of the OneWorld application development process. In OneWorld, application development is facilitated through a series of individual tools. These OneWorld tools give the technical individual, referred to as the OneWorld developer, the ability to create new OneWorld applications or to modify OneWorld applications provided by J. D. Edwards.

This chapter is perhaps the most technical chapter presented in this book. This chapter is not intended as a how-to for developing OneWorld applications. Instead, its purpose is to provide an overall appreciation of the OneWorld development tools and the possibilities that exist. Given a talented and experienced developer, new OneWorld applications that maintain the same look, feel, and processing capabilities of any delivered J. D. Edwards' OneWorld application are possible using the development tools provided with OneWorld.

Chapter 13

This chapter provides a brief introduction to a number of advanced OneWorld technical topics. Although coverage of any one of these topics is not exhaustive, this chapter nonetheless provides a basic understanding of these important OneWorld-related subjects. Here are the topics that are covered in this chapter:

◆ Workflow management

◆ System security

◆ Batch process scheduling

◆ Software installation and upgrades

◆ System and data integrity

◆ OneWorld coexistence with World software

◆ Data migration using OneWorld table conversions and batch interface processor tools

◆ System integration tools

Although your organization might not have concerns about or an interest in all of these topics, you will at the very least have an interest in at least several of these topics.

Enterprise Workflow Management

Workflow management is an integral part of OneWorld software. Workflow management is all about document routing and processing. Workflow management is an important element in an organization's administrative control processes to fulfill its everyday business obligations, as well as managing business risk, detecting fraud, and managing compliance with internal and external policies. Most organizations have both formal and informal procedures or rules regarding workflow.

Many organizations have not yet taken advantage of integrated back office systems such as OneWorld that can serve as the basis for reducing document preparation and management requirements, not to mention the possibilities of further automating the workflow. In his latest book, *Business at the Speed of Thought,* Bill Gates, the founder of Microsoft, provides many examples of how e-mail can be used to further reduce administration and paperwork and to automate workflow. He makes a strong case for doing so. In short, workflow automation increases process efficiency.

Closely associated with workflow management is document management. Previously, paper documents were a part of almost every business process in virtually every organization. However, with the electronic signature act that was recently signed into law, the predisposition toward and general dependency on paper in business transactions is expected to begin a rapid decline. Electronic documents are now poised to replace paper within the next decade for the majority of business-to-business transactions. Currently, paper documents are digitized through imaging equipment and then stored electronically. These electronic or digital documents are then indexed by their document number reference to a back office system such as OneWorld.

OneWorld Enterprise workflow management provides a means for automating high-volume paper-based processes by using e-mail flow across an organization's network. The e-mail system thereby replaces the routing of paper documents throughout your organization. Using workflow management, documents, information, and tasks pass from one individual to another for subsequent review and action based on a set of preestablished procedures or rules.

Most organizations will find that workflow automation does the following:

◆ Reduces paper consumption and the clutter and storage problems created by paper.

◆ Reduces errors and delays by reducing or eliminating paper movement. Prevents the loss of important work-in-process paperwork by automating its representation and movement electronically.

◆ Focuses knowledge worker attention on exception management, thereby improving knowledge worker productivity.

Workflow automation can be used to streamline existing business processes, thereby increasing efficiency and reducing overall processing or order turnaround times.

Workflow management relies on and leverages tools that are already in place within OneWorld. For instance, among the workflow management features that are an integral part of OneWorld are facilities that provide important document and workflow controls such as these:

◆ Accounting transactions can be held for review and subsequent posting to the general ledger.

◆ Budget checking can be instituted for procurement documents.

◆ Credit checking can be instituted for sales documents.

◆ Documents can be held for dollar or general acceptance or approval in order processing paths.

◆ Approval path routings can be created for held documents in order processing paths.

◆ An inspection step in the goods receipt process is provided.

Some of these workflow management capabilities rely on e-mail. For instance, e-mail is used to inform an approver that held documents await his or her approval.

In addition to OneWorld's built-in workflow management capabilities, the OneWorld Workflow Management tools let your organization "workflow-enable" virtually any OneWorld application. This capability allows your organization to facilitate workflows that might be unique to your business or industry.

Finally, OneWorld itself uses workflow management. For instance, when a batch process is initiated, a job status message is typically generated when the batch process terminates either normally or abnormally. When a batch processing job fails, the error messages associated with the batch process are associated with the e-mail that provides job status information. The OneWorld user reviews these error messages in order to determine what went wrong and to decide on a course of action to correct the processing errors that were encountered.

Scripted Versus Ad Hoc Workflows

OneWorld supports two types of workflow models. Your organization should review its processes to determine which of the two models is appropriate for its workflow processes.

The first type of workflow process is a scripted workflow. A scripted workflow is used to automate a business process that is repetitive in nature and that can be predefined. Approving a purchasing requisition as part of a predefined approval process is an example of a scripted workflow process.

The second type of workflow is an ad hoc workflow. An ad hoc workflow has less structure. In these scenarios, the workflow is generally fluid and cannot be predefined. Often, an individual's business or product expertise or knowledge factors heavily into the workflow. A sample ad hoc workflow process might begin by sending an electronic message to a supervisor, requesting review and approval of supplier payments in Accounts Payable. If an organization closely monitors its cash flow, the controller would typically generate a cash requirements forecast and then manually approve each payment item based on its business criticality or similar criteria. In this case, the controller's approval of certain supplier payments completes the ad hoc workflow.

As previously mentioned, OneWorld is delivered with certain workflow management facilities already built in and operational. These workflows are typically activated or deactivated through the normal course of configuration. They represent both scripted and ad hoc workflows. However, it is also possible to design custom workflows that are specific to your organization using OneWorld.

Much like the Enterprise Report Writer, discussed in the preceding chapter, the OneWorld Enterprise Workflow Management tools require an advanced technical acumen that the typical OneWorld user doesn't have. Therefore, it is recommended that the OneWorld developer be responsible for workflow design and definition within OneWorld.

The Workflow Director

The OneWorld Workflow Director is used to set up automated business information processing flows using e-mail. The Workflow Director guides the workflow administrator or developer through the step-by-step process of setting up a workflow process.

The workflow process in OneWorld employs a workflow engine. The OneWorld workflow engine relies on user-defined workflow-related routes and rules. A route defines the path along which an object will move. In OneWorld, the object can be a message, a document, or a form. A route can be a simple, sequential process, or it can be a complex process involving branching and iteration. Rules define what object is routed and to whom it is routed. A rule also defines the conditions that must be met at one step in the workflow route before the object can progress to the next step in the workflow route.

The Workflow Director therefore establishes the overall workflow process, which includes workflow routes and their associated rules. Workflow processes as well as workflow routes and rules can also be established and maintained independently of the Workflow Director.

Planning for Workflow Automation

Before considering workflow management, it is a good idea to clearly understand the process that will be automated. Perhaps by taking a fresh look at a process, you can visualize improvements. If an existing process is poorly designed, automating it typically won't improve the process—it will only automate the process. As a matter of fact, throughout the course of any OneWorld implementation, the standard approach should be to determine to what degree some business process improvement through reengineering using OneWorld best practices is possible. However, as a general rule, keep in mind that simple processes still work best.

When planning for workflow automation using OneWorld, complete the following steps:

1. Name each process.

2. Describe the process in detail from beginning to end, listing the activities as they occur in the process. If desired, complete a graphical representation of the process if that will help you understand and describe the process.

3. Define any activity conditions. Activity conditions are rules that determine when an activity is performed, as well as what happens after an activity has been completed.

4. Identify the data upon which the process relies. Determine all the relevant data that will be needed throughout the entire process. This information constitutes the data model for the process.

5. Define the messages that the process generates.

6. Define the recipients of messages generated by the process. Group similar recipients into distribution lists.

7. Define recipient rules that can affect the process. Recipient rules determine to whom or to which distribution list a message is sent.

The workflow administrator or developer uses this information as the basis for completing a low-level design of the workflow process that can in turn be used as input to the OneWorld Workflow Director.

Workflow Process Design

The workflow administrator or developer must further identify the individual activities in the process, such as whether a business function will be called, at what point a message will be sent, or if another application will be launched. Using the data model for the process, the developer must determine which data items to include in the data structures for the process and which tables will be updated at the outcome of the process. Data structures are used to pass information back and forth between different objects, such as forms, business functions, and reports that constitute a workflow. With this level of understanding in hand, the developer can begin creating and testing custom workflow processes in OneWorld.

Workflow Management Features

This section provides a brief introduction to the Workflow Management features available in OneWorld. A number of important OneWorld workflow concepts and features are explained here.

Workflow Messages

As was mentioned at the beginning of this chapter, not every organization will have the same degree of interest in or concern about the topics covered here. However, workflow messaging is a topic that affects every OneWorld implementation, regardless of whether your organization even uses OneWorld's workflow facilities.

In OneWorld, workflow management-related e-mail messages and tasks are accessed from one of several places:

- From the Work Center Manager
- From the Employee Queue Manager
- From a third-party e-mail system such as Microsoft Exchange or Microsoft Outlook

Even if your organization does not design any custom workflow objects minimally, the Work Center Manager and, depending on your configuration, the Employee Queue Manager will be used by the OneWorld applications that your organization has implemented.

The OneWorld Employee Work Center

An important and integral part of your organization's OneWorld training program should be to provide instructions for end-users on how to access and use the Employee Work Center. For instance, every batch process that an end-user runs creates a message in one or more of the queues found on this form. These messages should be regularly reviewed for possible job errors and discarded from these queues.

The OneWorld Employee Queue Manager form is divided into two sections. The left portion of the form contains a directory of queues for messages sent by OneWorld applications. If a specific message is opened from within an individual queue, the contents of that message appear in the right portion of the form. The menu path to access the Employee Work Center form is as follows:

> G > Foundation Systems (G0) > Workflow Management (**G02**) > Employee Work Center (P012501)

Figure 13-1 shows the Employee Work Center.

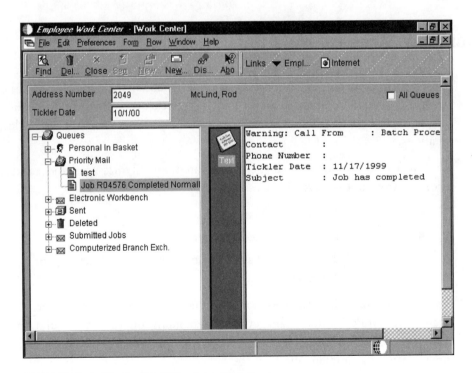

FIGURE 13-1 *The OneWorld Employee Work Center*

Using OneWorld's E-Mail Capability

If your organization did not have an e-mail system before acquiring OneWorld, your wait is over. Not only will OneWorld applications initiate e-mail messages, but any OneWorld user can also initiate a personal e-mail message through the OneWorld Employee Work Center. To send a personal message to another individual within your organization, do the following:

1. On the Employee Work Center form, click on the New button. The Send Internal Mail form appears, as shown in Figure 13-2.

2. Enter the recipient's Employee Number (Address Book Number) in the Send To box.

3. Enter a subject for the message. This is a required field.

4. Enter any message text in the bottom portion of the form. Message text is not required. The Subject field can serve as a one-line message to the recipient if you want.

5. Click on OK to send the electronic message to the recipient.

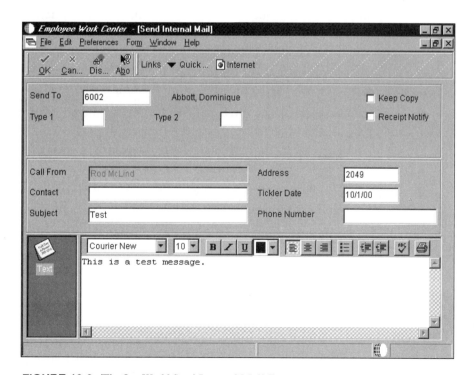

FIGURE 13-2 *The OneWorld Send Internal Mail Form*

The OneWorld Employee Queue Manager

The Employee Queue Manager is a Workbench-like tool designed to manage your electronic message queues. From this form, the user may review queues and messages, initiate messages, or check in or out. In a call center environment or professional services environment, check in/check out is particularly valuable to determine who is in the office today or if a particular call center operator is currently online to accept a callback. However, the important aspects of queue management and message handling can be performed exclusively from the Employee Work Center form.

Message Queues

As has been discussed, both the Work Center Manager and the Employee Queue Manager can be used to access workflow and personal electronic messages. Typically, the following queues are predefined in OneWorld:

- ◆ The Sent Messages queue. This queue stores a copy of each personal message a user initiates.

- ◆ The Deleted Messages queue. Messages must be specifically deleted from a queue. After a message is deleted, it can still be viewed until it is purged from the OneWorld database. A special purge program, generally run on a periodic basis at the direction of the OneWorld system administrator, removes all deleted messages from the OneWorld database.

- ◆ The Submitted Jobs queue. System-generated messages generated by batch processes are directed to this queue. Review the contents of this queue regularly and carefully. When a batch process fails, error details are contained in messages in this queue.

- ◆ Action queues. These are queues where system-generated messages from OneWorld-delivered workflow facilities, such as purchase order approval requests, are directed. Each specific OneWorld workflow facility generally has a unique action queue.

It is possible for your organization to define and use additional OneWorld-related message queues as necessary for your organization and its workflow processes.

OneWorld and Third-Party Mail Systems

Depending on how OneWorld is configured and how an individual user's electronic message preference is defined using the Employee Queue Manager, electronic messages can be routed to third-party-provided e-mail software, such as Microsoft Exchange or Microsoft Outlook. OneWorld's e-mail middleware product, JDE-MAIL, is used to interface with third-party-provided e-mail software using the extended MAPI-compliant message format.

Workflow Process Monitoring

An integral part of OneWorld workflow management is the ability for workflow process monitoring to occur. Workflow activities and processes can be monitored in the following ways:

♦ The OneWorld end-user monitors workflow through the Employee Work Center. The Employee Work Center displays messages that require user action.

♦ The workflow administrator monitors workflow through the Process Activity Monitor. The Process Activity Monitor gives the workflow administrator the override authority required to process certain activities and to monitor the activity flow to workflow queues.

Generally speaking, most process monitoring occurs through the Employee Work Center. The Process Activity Monitor is, strictly speaking, an administrative tool.

Workflow Processing Features

When defining workflow processes that are specific to your organization, here are some of the key features that are provided by OneWorld Enterprise Workflow Management:

♦ The ability to attach a workflow process to any event in an application or batch process.

♦ The ability to perform conditional processing.

♦ The ability to create messages specific to a process using message templates that are defined in the active Data Dictionary.

♦ The ability to include both interactive and batch applications in a workflow process.

♦ The ability to support multiple-level approvals.

♦ The ability to manually escalate activities. The workflow administrator can override or bypass certain activities or users in a predefined workflow process.

◆ All workflow activities within a process are automatically time-stamped.

◆ Once a workflow process is initiated, the process and activity definitions are protected. This prevents changes to process definitions and activities while a process is running and preserves the integrity and accuracy of the audit trail generated by the process.

This introduction to the Enterprise Workflow Management facilities within OneWorld is not meant to be exhaustive. Consult the OneWorld Documentation CD-ROM to review the Enter Workflow Management reference guide or the OneWorld online help for additional information about OneWorld workflow.

OneWorld Security

OneWorld includes extensive application security capabilities. In general, OneWorld security is at the object level. A specific object can be secured within OneWorld. Object-level security provides a high degree of control over user interaction with a given OneWorld application. For example, a given user can be restricted from a specific form, and no matter how he tries to access this form, OneWorld will prevent him from doing so.

Establishing a sound degree of security for the OneWorld environment is an important challenge that your organization will face during OneWorld implementation. In all likelihood, the greatest amount of effort will be spent in determining the appropriate level at which to secure objects from certain users within your organization. For example, if a given menu were secured, this would not necessarily prevent users from accessing the specific applications found on that menu. The users might be able to access these applications from other menus on which they appear, or through an application that accesses the applications that are to be secured.

It is for this reason that OneWorld does not directly support menu or system code-level security. If you are familiar with World Software, you will likely identify this as a departure. Using object-level security, OneWorld can provide a much higher degree of security over menu or system code-based security.

Given the voluminous number of objects within OneWorld, establishing object-level security could therefore be time-consuming without the right tools. The OneWorld Security Workbench simplifies and accelerates the process of securing objects by establishing security for hundreds of objects at a time. For instance, all objects on a specific menu, or all objects under a specific system code, can be secured en masse.

Establishing Security in OneWorld

There are two dimensions of security to be defined in OneWorld. The first dimension is the population of users. The second is defining what objects must be secured.

Users

In OneWorld, user security is established

◆ By a specific user

◆ For a group of users

◆ For all users

From a maintainability standpoint, it is generally best to maintain security at the group level. Therefore, in most security scenarios, users of a system are segregated into user group classes. In OneWorld Xe, a user group is called a user role. In previous versions of OneWorld, the term user group prevailed. Suffice it to say that all members of a given user group class typically have common system requirements. If group-level security is defined, a group ID, not the individual user ID, controls object access.

In addition to a user group class, subclasses and superclasses might exist for a given user group class. For example, a superclass might include purchasing managers in order to allow access to document-approval features, while the purchasing user group class does not. A subclass of a user group might exclude certain functions. For instance, receiving-dock personnel might be restricted from purchase order entry and change functions of the purchasing user group class. Strictly speaking, each user group class, subclass, or superclass is simply another user group.

When security must be applied to all users, a special system-level group ID value is used. The designation *PUBLIC is a special group-level ID within OneWorld that automatically includes all system users.

Objects

The second dimension of OneWorld security is defining objects. At specific object levels, the following levels of security, alone or in combination, can be established for both users and user groups:

◆ Action security

◆ Application security

◆ Column security

◆ Exclusive application security

◆ Exit security

◆ External calls security

◆ Menu filtering

◆ Processing option security

◆ Prompting

◆ Row security

◆ Tab security

◆ Version security

Table 13-1 defines each of these types or levels of OneWorld object security.

Table 13-1 OneWorld Object-Level Security Definitions

Type or Level of Security	Description
Action	Prevents a user from executing a particular action, such as adding, deleting, revising, inquiring, or copying a record.
Application	Prevents a user from running or installing a particular application or form within an application.
Column	Prevents a user from viewing a particular field or changing a value for a particular field.
Exclusive application	Permits access to a specific application, regardless of any other security that might be set. When exclusive application security is used for a user, that user gains access to just that specific application. All other security still applies.
Exit	Prevents a user from using a menu option to exit the OneWorld form.
External calls	Prevents a user from accessing external stand-alone executables from within OneWorld.
Menu filtering	Secures an unauthorized menu option from a user's view.
Processing option	Prevents a user from changing the values of processing options.
Prompting	Can be used to prevent or force processing options to appear when initiating a specific version. Prompting security is established within a given application version on the Version Detail form and is independently maintained from the Security Workbench.

Table 13-1 OneWorld Object-Level Security Definitions *(continued)*

Type or Level of Security	Description
Row	Prevents a user from accessing a particular range or list of records in any table.
Tab	Prevents a user from seeing a tab or tabs on a given form.
Version	Determines if a user can copy, run, modify, or delete a given version. Version security is established within a given application version on the Version Detail form and is independently maintained from the Security Workbench.

Implementing Security

Implementing security in OneWorld is a multistep process that requires careful planning, execution, and testing. As mentioned previously, both users and objects form the basis of OneWorld security. Follow these steps when establishing the OneWorld security scheme for your organization:

1. Identify each user group.
2. Identify each user.
3. Classify each user into the appropriate user group.
4. Identify each application to be secured by user group.
5. Identify the objects to be unsecured within each application (by user group).

Identifying the objects to secure includes identifying which application, form, report, or table (in the case of row and column security) must be secured. This includes the object name, such as F0101 for the Address Book Master file, P0101 for the Address Book interactive application, or *ALL for all objects. Generally speaking, I recommend using application-level security (security by product code) and then selecting which object within a given application is to be unsecured and to which level for the user group. For the majority of OneWorld installations, simple application and object-level security as I just described are sufficient. However, for some installations, row- and column-level security might be appropriate.

An additional step is necessary when establishing row and column security. This step requires the identification of specific columns by their Data Dictionary item name as well as the specific values that represent the basis of the security. For instance, it might be desirable to limit access to employees' Address Book records (Search Type = E) to all but a few people in the Payroll or Human Resources departments.

SECURITY TIP

Prevent Identity Theft

Row- and column-level security can be used to help prevent identity theft and the commission of fraud using such information.

A common requirement is to secure access to employee data within the Address Book. In this case, row-level security is used for the search type data item where the value equals "E." Other examples of security to prevent identity theft include using column-level security on fields such as date of birth, credit card number, social security number, or taxpayer identification number.

Also note that an important difference exists between World and OneWorld security. OneWorld does support Cost Center security in the same manner as World Software. To duplicate Cost Center security in OneWorld, use row-level security.

The available template diskette that I mentioned in the Introduction includes a security planning worksheet to help your organization construct an effective OneWorld security scheme.

IMPLEMENTATION TIP

Duplicating World Cost Center Security in OneWorld

OneWorld does not support Cost Center security in the same manner as World Software. To duplicate Cost Center security in OneWorld, use row-level security.

After this information has been prepared, the next step is to implement the security scheme that has been devised for OneWorld. OneWorld security setup consists of a number of steps:

1. Create any user group IDs.
2. Attach application-level security to these user group IDs.
3. Create individual Address Book records for each employee.

4. Create the user ID.

5. Add the appropriate environments to the user ID.

6. Create security for the user ID by copying security from one or more user groups.

7. Establish passwords for the user IDs.

8. Create any user-specific object-level security records.

The Address Book Revisions form is used to establish all name and address information, including employee records. As noted previously, employee records are required even if your organization does not process its payroll through OneWorld. Here is the menu path to reach the Address Book Revisions form:

> G > Foundation Systems (G0) > Address Book (G010) > Daily Processing (**G01**) > Address Book Revisions (P01012)

In most environments, it is necessary to define a user ID within the context of your technical environment. For instance, a network or system-level user ID is typically needed. The system administrator or system security officer for your organization typically has this responsibility and knows what is needed for your organization's technical environment.

Within the context of OneWorld, setting up a user ID is the next step in the process. User IDs are also called user profiles in OneWorld. The menu path to set up user profiles is as follows:

> G > Foundation Systems (G0) > Tools (GH90) > System Administration Tools (**GH9011**) > User Profiles P0092

A group profile is created using this same form. Special conventions apply when you create a group profile. You create a new group profile by entering the group name in the User ID field and by entering a value of *GROUP in the User Class/Group or Role field.

Creating object-level security records is the next step. Object-level security is established from the Security menu under System Administration. The menu path is as follows:

> G > Foundation Systems (G0) > Tools (GH90) > System Administration Tools (**GH9011**) > Security (**GH9052**) > Security Workbench (P00950)

Figure 13-3 illustrates the OneWorld Security Workbench (P00950). The Form menu has been selected to illustrate how to add an object-level security record for a given object.

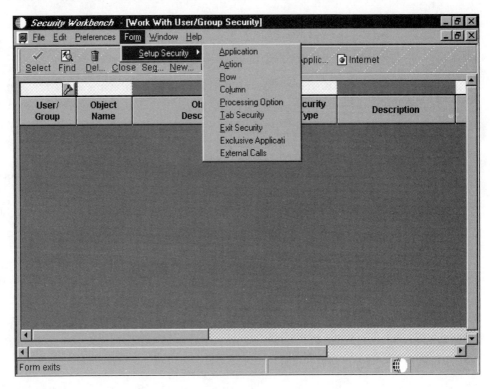

FIGURE 13-3 *The OneWorld Security Workbench*

The final step in establishing OneWorld security is typically the activation of user IDs. This is done through the User Passwords function. It's on the Security menu under System Administration. The menu path is as follows:

> G > Foundation Systems (G0) > Tools (GH90) > System Administration Tools (**GH9011**) > Security (**GH9052**) > User Passwords (P98OWSEC)

This form is used to enable, disable, or reset a user's password. It is not necessary to establish passwords for user group IDs, because they typically are not used for entry to the system—only as a template or grouping for the purposes of storing object-level security records that are then copied to an individual user ID.

Creating User IDs En Masse

If Address Book records already exist for employees, a batch process can be run that will automatically create user IDs (user profiles) based on existing Address Book records. User IDs are created through the Create User Profile from A/B records batch process (R0092), which is found on the System Administration Advanced Operations menu (GH9012). Processing options for R0092 are used to assign environments, user preferences, and a user group for the purposes of attaching object-level security. This process creates any number of new user IDs at a time.

How OneWorld User ID Security Works

OneWorld initially checks for any security associated with the user ID. If no security is found for the user ID, OneWorld checks the group- or role-level security if the user ID indicates that it belongs to a specific user group. Finally, *PUBLIC is checked for security. If security exists at any point, OneWorld displays a message informing the user that he cannot proceed. On the other hand, if security is not established at any of these levels, OneWorld allows the user to continue.

 SECURITY TIP

Affecting Security

As a general rule, if security is changed while the user is logged into OneWorld, the user must log out of OneWorld and then log back into OneWorld before any security changes that were made are applied.

Menu Filtering

OneWorld filters menus based on a user ID. Menus are filtered so that only menu options that are available to a certain person appear on the menu when it is displayed to the user. The content of the menu is predicated on the menus and options that apply to a given user's role or responsibilities as defined through the security setup. Again, because OneWorld does not directly support menu- or system code-level security, it uses object-level information to determine the menu options that apply to a given user.

Fast Paths

Fast Path commands are used to access frequently used applications. Although I mentioned in a previous chapter that OneWorld doesn't ship with program-level Fast Paths for all applications, unlike its counterpart, SAP, this precludes your organization from creating Fast Paths to individual application programs on a case-by-case basis. J. D. Edwards provides only a small number of such Fast Paths in OneWorld. They generally access technical and configuration-level applications. For instance, to access the Universal Table Browser, a quick and dirty way to browse any OneWorld table, the Fast Path of UTB is used. A Fast Path command can be defined as follows:

- ◆ A user-defined abbreviation
- ◆ The combination of a menu option and menu number referencing the menu location where the application is usually accessed

The quickest way to create a new Fast Path command is by using a Fast Path command. In the Fast Path command window, do the following:

1. Enter UDC (for User-Defined Codes). The UDC form appears.
2. Enter 00 as the System Code value.
3. Enter FP as the User-Defined Codes value.
4. Click on Find. The existing Fast Path commands are displayed.
5. Review the existing Fast Path commands to determine the availability of the desired mnemonic.
6. Click on Add.
7. Enter the letters for the mnemonic to be used in the Codes field.
8. Enter a description for the Fast Path command in the Description 1 field.
9. To fast-path to a menu, enter the menu number as the Description 2 field value.
10. Click on OK to save.

To fast-path to a given OneWorld program instead of to a menu, you also need the menu option number. This is found on the Menu Design form. If the menu option number is unknown, you might want to use the system administration method to create a Fast Path. To create a Fast Path using the system administration method, follow these steps:

1. Access system design. The menu path is G > Foundation Systems (G0) > Tools (GH90) > System Administration Tools (**GH9011**) > Menu Design (P0082).
2. Use the Work With Menus form to select the menu containing the selection for which you want a Fast Path command.

3. On the Work With Menu Selections form, determine the menu option number corresponding to the program for which you want a Fast Path command.

4. Make a note of both the menu number and the menu option number.

5. Select Form, Fast Path Revs from the Work With Menu Selections form.

6. Click on Add. The UDC form appears.

7. Click on Find. The existing Fast Path commands are displayed.

8. Review the existing Fast Path commands to determine the availability of the desired mnemonic.

9. Click on Add.

10. Although the first line is not blank, it is still OK to type over the information appearing on that line.

11. Enter the letters for the mnemonic to be used in the Codes field.

12. Enter a description for the Fast Path command in the Description 1 field.

13. To fast-path to a specific menu option, enter the menu option number, followed by a slash, followed by the menu number, as the Description 2 field value.

14. Click on OK to save.

Using a given Fast Path command does not bypass any object-level security that might apply. Use of Fast Path commands can be restricted by user. When a user profile (user ID) is established, an option exists in the User Profile/User ID record to disable or enable the use of Fast Path commands.

This concludes the introduction to OneWorld's security management facilities. It was not meant to be exhaustive. Consult the OneWorld Documentation CD-ROM to review the System Administration reference guide or the OneWorld online help for additional information about OneWorld security.

Batch Process Scheduling

OneWorld provides a job-scheduling tool that allows your organization to create and maintain a schedule of jobs or batch processes that are performed on a regular basis. Although other system management tools have overlapping capabilities, they are also available as a part of the OneWorld back office environment. For users of J. D. Edwards' World software, the OneWorld Job Scheduler replaces the Unattended Operations or "Sleeper" function.

Many jobs can or must be processed after-hours, when online users place fewer demands on OneWorld server resources. For instance, the sales order update, the credit refresh, an MRP plan regeneration or plan net change update, statement cycling, G/L batch postings, and the printing of informational and financial reports can be scheduled. In addition, scheduling certain update processes to occur without human intervention is a good way to ensure that they are consistently performed so as to prevent other operational glitches or data integrity issues from arising.

When a batch process is scheduled to run through the Scheduler, a *recurrence pattern* can be established for the job. When a recurrence pattern is established, the job is started at a predefined interval. There are a wide array of recurrence patterns to select from:

- Every *n* minutes
- Every *n* hours
- Every *n* days
- Every weekday
- Every week on *x* day
- Every *n* weeks on *x* day
- Day *n* of every *x* month
- Day *n* of every fiscal period
- The first or last day of every fiscal period

Quarterly and annually recurring jobs can be established. For financial reporting-related jobs, specific companies can be designated in order to use the fiscal calendar that is associated with that company for job-scheduling purposes. In addition, an ending date can be established for a recurring job pattern. Jobs are scheduled based on the local time of the server on which the job will run. The OneWorld system administrator typically establishes and maintains the job schedule.

OneWorld Installation, Upgrades, and Service Packs

This section provides an overview of the process by which OneWorld software is installed and upgraded across your client workstation and server environments.

The Initial OneWorld Installation

The installation of your OneWorld software and the configuration of the OneWorld Configurable Network Computing architectural components are, quite frankly, tasks that can't be left to chance. Consider this as perhaps my most important advice to you—advice that may well be worth many times what you paid for this book:

> If you use external consulting assistance for only one task in your entire OneWorld implementation, this should be where those dollars are spent.

Although you might think I'm simply trying to sell consulting services by giving this advice, I'm not. Actually, I'm trying to save your organization money in the long run. As for myself, although I am a management consultant, my focus is on the functional side of OneWorld, so this is not even an area where I do consulting work. But what I do know, based on my experiences with multiple OneWorld clients where I have helped implement OneWorld, you will want help in this area if in no other.

A "Best of Breed" Hardware Architecture for OneWorld

I am frequently asked what is the best approach for implementing OneWorld. This section provides my recommendations regarding a "best of breed" approach for implementing OneWorld.

Should You Go with Fat or Thin Clients?

I am frequently asked what is a good OneWorld hardware foundation. I am inclined to recommend a predominantly thin client-based or network computer architecture. Your organization really cannot get by completely by using thin clients, but for the vast majority of everyday business-related users, thin clients work just fine. Those who complete OneWorld program modifications or develop new OneWorld business functions and reports will still need to use fat clients.

So why do I like thin clients? Quite simply, thin clients are much easier to administer. Although thin client technology has not yet proven popular, its usage is steadily increasing. There will always be a need for fat clients, but not on every corporate desktop. Cost will also be another consideration. I believe that within a short period of time, a thin client, or network computer, will approach the $100 price point.

Should You Use Big Iron or Little Boxes for OneWorld?

I still like the AS/400 midrange platform as an enterprise-level server. In my estimation, microprocessor-based servers remain akin to sending in a boy to do a man's job. In addition, the AS/400 midrange computer family is a scalable, highly reliable platform. However, if you insist on a microprocessor-based platform, IBM Netfinity servers seem to perform adequately. No matter what you buy, always buy more than you need. I say this because as your application usage and database requirements increase, you'll save time and money in the long run. It is my experience that your system requirements will grow at least as fast your business grows, if not faster.

If your organization is not experienced with packaged software or relational database systems, there are a few more things to keep in mind. Bigger and faster processors and more core (main) memory are always desirable when you're using a relational database or any packaged software.

These types of systems place a high degree of overhead on your system. For instance, an executable program for a packaged software solution typically has dozens of files open at any one time. Most homegrown business software does not reach the same level of sophistication as does the typical program found in a packaged software product. Although this might be considered less efficient, it does provide a highly configurable software product that can be used by a wide cross section of users—such as across different computing platforms and in different industries, countries, currencies, and languages.

OneWorld Upgrades

Each new release of OneWorld typically brings changes to the installation and upgrade process. Therefore, careful research and planning prior to undertaking an upgrade are essential to your success and, possibly, to your continued employment. Your measure of success for any OneWorld upgrade is actually a simple one: Integrity, integrity, integrity. The areas of your concern should include the following:

◆ Data integrity

◆ Configuration integrity

◆ Environment integrity

Planning for an upgrade is a big deal. Upgrades generally go more smoothly when they are planned and deliberate.

Have a Plan

The first step in any OneWorld upgrade should be to have a plan. A software upgrade is significantly more complex than simply loading a CD-ROM and clicking on Go. You need to understand what will change, how it will impact your existing business processes and your environment, and exactly how the upgrade process itself works.

If you have completed any OneWorld customizations, be aware that they might be adversely affected by the upgrade. J. D. Edwards occasionally refines OneWorld through greater normalization of the database or by adding fields to implement new functionality into the OneWorld product.

When planning the OneWorld upgrade, if something is unclear to you, do not leave it to chance. For instance, when you review the technical information for the upgrade, it should be your practice to contact the J. D. Edwards response line and request assistance from a technical support representative to clear up any ambiguity, confusion, or questions.

Choreograph the Upgrade

An upgrade is serious business in the systems business. Upgrades can be tricky for any software package that is already in production. I like to compare a software upgrade to a rocket launch. Rocket launches require extensive planning and advance preparation. They also rely on several key elements that any upgrade plan should include:

- The upgrade launch plan
- The upgrade launch checklist
- The upgrade diary
- The upgrade clock
- The backup and recovery plan

I like using the rocket launch analogy—not because an upgrade is rocket science, but because a rocket launch is a "choreographed" event. Therefore, technical activity choreography is the best practice gained from using the rocket launch analogy. For instance, many organizations used such an analogy as an integral part of their year 2000 readiness and rollover process.

Conduct a Dress Rehearsal

For most businesses, OneWorld is the backbone of their business processes. When your business depends on the system's being available and accurate, you can't leave anything to chance. Therefore, I recommend that you always conduct a dress rehearsal of the upgrade process.

The most effective method I know of is for you to do this by maintaining a separate test environment. For instance, the test environment can be a snapshot of your product environment as of a certain date. Apply the upgrade to the second test environment first. When the upgrade is completed in that environment, you'll want to thoroughly test your business functions before going forward.

A dress rehearsal should be just that. The intent is to conduct a simulated upgrade. I like to call this a dress rehearsal of the upgrade. The purpose of an upgrade dress rehearsal is to minimize your chances of a possible business disruption. The dress rehearsal helps you get your timing issues down and your questions out of the way.

I like an upgrade dress rehearsal to take on the form of the now-familiar rocket launch countdown. For my upgrade clock, I use a stopwatch and a clock to track the process. Start and stop the clock for every question or issue that arises along the way. Also, take notes on everything that happens along the way. I do this in my upgrade diary.

Afterward, take on the role of launch director, and ask the hard questions. Review your upgrade diary, and ask why the clock stopped during the upgrade. For how long did the upgrade stop? Was the stop preventable (for instance, were you unprepared for this step), and can the issue causing the clock to stop be resolved now in such a way that during the real upgrade it will not stop the upgrade countdown? An upgrade is not rocket science, but that doesn't mean you can't learn how to choreograph your OneWorld upgrade using rocket science best practices.

Backup and Recovery

Generally speaking, you can avoid a complete business disaster in the upgrade process. Ensuring that you have a full system save before starting does that. It's your fallback position. By the way, ensure that your upgrade plan includes a time provision for recovery from a backup and an alternative upgrade date.

Again, just like a rocket launch, the OneWorld upgrade must occur when conditions are right. However, unlike with the rocket launch, you aren't considering weather conditions. Instead, you're considering business conditions. The rule here is simple: Avoid upgrades during peak business periods, such as during December if you are a retailer or during the first week of the fiscal period when you're trying to close the books. The simple fact is that you must allow adequate time to complete the process.

Finally, if you're doing the installation after regular business hours, you might need to ensure the availability of a J. D. Edwards technical support service representative on an after-hours basis.

Upgrades, Configuration Settings, and Custom Applications

With every OneWorld upgrade, careful and deliberate consideration must be given to its impact on the soft coding or configuration settings, such as processing options, versions, and menus, as well as what the impact will be on any custom applications your organization has required throughout its course of being a OneWorld license holder.

Lessening the Pain

Following a few simple rules will help ensure that minimal damage or disruption is caused to your OneWorld environment by an upgrade:

- The starting point in any upgrade is always a full system backup.
- When creating data items, fields, user-defined codes, menus, tables, interactive applications, or batch applications—in short, any OneWorld object—use a *system code value* of 55 through 59 to identify the object to OneWorld. J. D. Edwards has reserved these specific system code values for use by customers and third-party application software providers for all software customizations. When an upgrade or service pack is installed properly, OneWorld doesn't overlay or replace your custom programs and applications using these system code values.
- When adding a new OneWorld object or copying a J. D. Edwards-provided object for modification, always identify the object to OneWorld using your naming conventions that include reference to a system code value of 55 through 59. For instance, a revised or modified version of the Open Order Report R43525 might be named R5543525. This identifies the object as a custom report that is based on the standard R43525

report. This simplifies troubleshooting and, for menus, it correlates with the standard J. D. Edwards documentation and online help text. However, note that renaming certain OneWorld objects might not be quite so easy. For instance, reports and batch jobs are usually easier to rename than business functions or interactive applications. The reasons are quite simply the number of programs that rely on or call the business function or interactive application. These other applications would also require changes that reflect your references to a new object.

◆ Do not use a version name that begins with ZJDE or XJDE. These version name prefixes are reserved for the standard version templates that J. D. Edwards provides for each version-driven batch or interactive application. In addition, these specific version templates should not be deleted or changed unless this is by specific directive of J. D. Edwards (such as when you're advised to do so by the J. D. Edwards response line).

◆ Follow the application development standards published by J. D. Edwards.

◆ Do not delete objects that are supplied by J. D. Edwards unless this is by specific directive of J. D. Edwards (such as when you're advised to do so by the J. D. Edwards response line).

Although this is not an exhaustive list, it does provide a minimal amount of guidance that will prevent data, configuration, or object loss in the OneWorld environment.

System and Data Integrity

There are several dimensions of integrity in OneWorld. The first dimension of system integrity is what I call environment integrity. In the World software and AS/400 environment, much of the environment integrity was controlled through library lists. In OneWorld, environment integrity is more complicated.

The second dimension of system integrity is data integrity. In general, users and applications control data integrity. Provided that the OneWorld program is working correctly—and most do—data integrity is, generally speaking, a user or organizational issue. OneWorld provides numerous integrity reports to ensure that the financial and inventory information that your organization must rely on is complete. These data integrity-related reports are discussed in later chapters.

When data is converted or is integrated with OneWorld from a legacy system, special care must be taken to ensure the quality of the inbound data. Batch interface processors for financial data have built-in edits to ensure incoming data quality and should be used for both data conversion and system integration purposes.

In general, when you convert other data into OneWorld from a legacy system, data integrity rests solely with your organization and how the data is mapped into OneWorld through the use of OneWorld table conversion processes. OneWorld table conversion processes do not have the built-in data quality checks that OneWorld batch interface processors include.

Environment Integrity: Do Not Proceed Without It!

It is quite important that the integrity of your environments be confirmed. Unfortunately, many organizations that implement OneWorld simply do not realize the technical complexities of the Configurable Network Computing environment. Until you get the base configuration right, you should not proceed with your OneWorld implementation. Consider this sage advice.

An improperly configured environment will result in a continuous series of problems during your OneWorld implementation. These problems can cause project delays and substantial rework. In addition, if left unresolved, these problems can result in production environment inconsistencies and will present difficulties when you attempt to make any upgrades to the OneWorld software.

Here are the areas that I recommend you thoroughly understand and validate:

- ◆ What object configuration mappings are and how they have been defined for your OneWorld installation
- ◆ What environments are, how they are created and used, and what interrelationships exist between them in your OneWorld installation
- ◆ What packages are and how they are deployed to an environment
- ◆ What replication is and how it is used in your OneWorld installation

Integrity is not a matter of concern only at startup. Recall from the discussion on OneWorld Installation and Upgrades that your measure of success for any OneWorld upgrade is actually a simple one—integrity, integrity, integrity—and that the areas of concern in an upgrade include data integrity, configuration integrity, and environment integrity.

If you don't recall some of the specifics about these concepts, consult Chapter 3, which provided an overview of OneWorld's Configurable Network Computing environment.

Conversion and Integration

Unless your organization happens to be the newest dot-com startup, no doubt you already have a combination of manual and system-based back office systems in place that will be supplanted by OneWorld. In some cases, OneWorld might need to operate alongside a legacy system for an indefinite period, or your organization might choose to phase or migrate applications over a longer period of time rather than "flipping the switch" and going live all at once on OneWorld.

Although manually reentering information into OneWorld at or near startup is an option, if your organization has significant volumes of data to transport into OneWorld on a one-time or recurring basis, manual efforts might not be practical. However, there is always a cost/time trade-off when you load data electronically instead of manually.

Converting either several hundred or thousands of Address Book records requires about the same amount of technical design and development time. However, manual entry for thousands of records varies greatly from the scenario of entering only several hundred records. In addition, when multiple sources of legacy data exist, or when they are in different formats or at different quality levels, significant preprocessing of the data might also be required before it can actually be loaded into OneWorld. Every organization needs to carefully assess the quality and quantity of its legacy data in determining to what extent the data conversion should be automated.

Similar cost/time trade-offs exist when standing interfaces with legacy systems are necessary. However, the business case evaluation should be on the basis of periodicity, volume, and duration of redundancy in determining if feeds or interfaces from or to legacy systems make business sense.

As a general rule, I recommend manual entry of data when there are fewer than 500 records or rows in a table. The technical costs related to conversion usually exceed the cost of labor in these instances. As the number of records or the complexity of data increases, manual entry of data decreases in attractiveness from both a cost and data quality point of view.

Assuming your organization has made a business case for electronic data conversion or interfacing with OneWorld, J. D. Edwards provides tools within OneWorld that can ease the transition from your organization's legacy systems into OneWorld. These tools fall into two categories: table conversion processes and batch interface processors.

Table Conversions

Table conversions are a type of OneWorld batch process that provides a facility for performing high-volume manipulation of data contained in files and tables. Table conversions can be used for both data conversion and legacy system integration.

The table conversion tool provides support for four different table conversion scenarios, each of which allows for a different degree of data manipulation:

◆ Data conversion
◆ Data copy
◆ Data copy with table input
◆ Batch delete

It is important to understand that table conversion does not perform any data validation as such. However, business logic can be added to a conversion definition to facilitate data validation.

The data conversion scenario allows the transfer or copying of data from an input table or business view into one or more output tables. Data conversion is also used to update records in a table or business view. The data copy scenario allows for the copying of one or more tables from one environment, which is also called a data source, to another environment or data source. The data copy with table input scenario provides a method for scripting a conversion scenario using directives about what to copy and to where from an input table. The batch delete scenario provides a method for deleting records from a table or business view.

The OneWorld Table Conversion tool can be used with any OneWorld table or business view. In addition, a text or flat file, as well as any table that resides in a database supported by OneWorld, such as IBM's DB/400, Microsoft SQL Server, or Oracle, can be used with the OneWorld Table Conversion tool. These "non-OneWorld" tables are generally called *foreign tables*. When a foreign table is used, an ODBC data source must be established for each such table before it can be used with the Table Conversion tool. After this step is completed, a data source, environment, and OCM mapping must be established in OneWorld for the table. User-defined formats can be defined for flat or text files used as input or output tables.

The developer uses a Director to set up a table conversion definition or scenario. Table conversions can be saved and run multiple times. A table conversion can be run in proof mode to review the conversion results before any actual table updates are performed. The table conversion tool can access any available environment, for both data input and output.

Here are a few of the important preliminary steps a developer would follow before setting up a table conversion:

♦ Typically, conversions involve the use of non-OneWorld tables. For non-OneWorld tables, remember to set up the data source and environment information for these tables.

♦ If data is being mapped or input from multiple tables, a *joined* business view must be created over the tables. In addition, business views are used as inputs only.

♦ If any data validation is necessary as part of the conversion process, business functions must be created by the developer to perform any such validations.

♦ Authority to foreign tables is a frequent issue in data conversion. The developer must have authority for read/write access to all environments and tables that will be used in a table conversion definition.

Additional information regarding table conversion can be found both in the OneWorld online help and in the Table Conversion Reference Guide under the Technical tab of the OneWorld soft-copy documentation that is available on CD-ROM from J. D. Edwards.

Batch Interface Processors

The batch interface processors provide a means of introducing data from the outside world into OneWorld. Batch interface processors are akin to an internal and proprietary electronic data interchange (EDI) transaction set. Batch interface processors allow other systems to provide data to OneWorld financial systems. To ensure the integrity of your financial systems, as a general rule, all interfaces to your financial systems should be handled through these predefined batch interface processors, not by table conversions or other custom programs that you might otherwise consider developing.

For nonfinancial transactions, OneWorld table conversions or EDI transaction input batch processes must be used for these other interfacing and data conversion requirements. Unlike the OneWorld table conversion application, the financial batch interface processors perform the requisite business logic processing and data cleansing and validation associated with these transactions. Note that the OneWorld EDI transaction processor programs work in much the same way as the financial batch interface processors and perform both validation and update processes.

Batch interface processors are supplied by J. D. Edwards for

 ◆ General accounting journal entries
 ◆ Accounts receivable invoices
 ◆ Accounts receivable cash receipts
 ◆ Accounts payable vouchers

Additional input processors are predefined for these additional external data inputs:

 ◆ Address Book records
 ◆ Bank statement debit and credit records
 ◆ Spreadsheet budget input

The processing flow for these input processes varies somewhat from that of the previously discussed financial batch interface processors. Also, please be aware that OneWorld batch processing programs have gained a dubious reputation; they are generally considered to be slow-running and resource-intensive.

How the Batch Interface Processors Work

In general, the batch interface processors work in a similar manner. The batch interface processors can be run in proof or final mode. A processing option makes this determination. In proof mode, the batch interface processor produces an error report, and no file updates are made.

Errors can be corrected directly in the input file produced during the conversion process. These files are known as Z1 files. An important ability is the ability to edit the Z1 file without needing to rerun the input process. This can save a considerable amount of processing time if only a few errors exist in the inbound data. In general, if any errors occur during processing, they are noted on an edit report with additional details as to what caused the error, available in the form of a work center message. These errors can then be corrected, and the batch can subsequently be reprocessed. Note that if one transaction in the batch is in error, the entire batch does not process.

When a batch-input processor is run in final mode, each input record is marked as processed. Optionally, based on a processing option setting, these records can be deleted as they are processed. If the record is not deleted from the Z1 file as it is processed, it needs to purge processed records from the Z1 file using OneWorld's general-purpose R00PURGE program.

All journal entries created out of a batch input process job are created as unposted transactions. A processing option allows for the submission of a general accounting post program to post any journal entries that were created. Each batch-input processor also creates the other application-related documents in their respective transaction files. Figure 13-4 illustrates how the overall batch input process works.

Errors in Processing

Although these interfaces can be run in proof mode, this is not absolutely necessary. It is possible to review the batch and its transactions before posting. Provided that posting has not occurred, the batch and its contents may simply be deleted, without affecting financial balances. As stated previously, the only thing that prevents a batch from processing is an error. Warning messages alert you to nonstandard conditions or events but do not prevent processing.

Unless there is wide variation in the inbound data, the results from these interfaces are fairly predictable: They will typically process every transaction correctly or incorrectly, so most errors that occur in one record occur in all records. Thus, it is always best to isolate and process related records in smaller batches, not as one large batch. This reduces investigative and troubleshooting efforts needed to correct any errors. It follows that this same sequence of steps applies when you process a larger number of records in a batch. When thousands of records are involved, and the same error is present in every record, it might be more practical to apply an "electronic fix" rather than the alternative of manually correcting every transaction. A SQL script or a third-party database utility such as TOAD in the

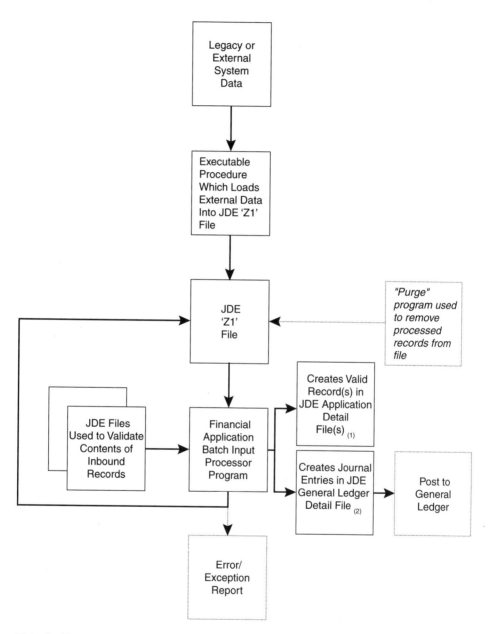

Notes for Figure 13-4:

[1] Write of this record does not apply for journal entry batch interface processors.

[2] Write of this record does not apply for Address Book batch interface processors.

FIGURE 13-4 *Financial Batch Input Processing*

Oracle environment or DBU in the AS/400 environment might be appropriate for making such mass corrections to the inbound data.

Although batch posting and the concept of automatic accounting instructions to facilitate system integration surfaced in this discussion, these topics will be formally introduced in Chapters 14 and 15.

Journal Entries

The General Accounting Journal Entry batch interface processor allows the creation of journal entries outside of J. D. Edwards and introduces them into J. D. Edwards through the batch processing facility. Regardless of the originating operating environment—personal computer, midrange computer, or mainframe computer—the data presented to the batch interface processor process must be in a specific file format used by J. D. Edwards. Journal entries must be introduced as balanced journals unless they are budget entries.

A popular use of this application is to aid in the startup of OneWorld. In these cases, the final trial balance figures or "as of" date account balances are extracted from the legacy system and are used as the input to OneWorld. Several other popular applications for this type of interface include interfaces with external or outsourced payroll processing systems and maintenance management software, usually for the distribution of work order-related charges to consuming business units and work centers. Note that a payroll outsourcing provider usually assesses a setup charge and a per-transmission charge for this type of service.

When OneWorld is implemented in a phased approach, it is not uncommon for financial applications to be the first phase. In addition, many organizations, especially in the nonprofit, government, and financial services arena, use only the OneWorld financial and purchasing systems, based on the strength of these applications when compared to competitive products. However, these organizations typically find other industry-specific software solutions to provide the functionality they need that are often outside the domain of an ERP software package. Therefore, it is not uncommon to strip the general ledger transactions from a legacy system, use an intermediate or preprocess program that performs account number conversion and validation when needed, and finally reformat this information in the format required by OneWorld.

Of course, there are numerous other applications. For instance, process manufacturers in the oil and gas, mining, chemical, and pharmaceutical industries, as well as water treatment facilities, could use SCADA devices to gather production volumes and periodically send this information to statistical accounts defined in the general ledger chart of accounts that can in turn be used for daily flash reports and other financial analysis purposes. In short, the existence of these interfaces supports any number of unique, innovative, or transitional requirements your organization might have.

Accounts Payable Vouchers

The Accounts Payable Voucher batch interface processor allows the creation of accounts payable vouchers that originate outside OneWorld and introduces them to OneWorld through the batch processing facility. A voucher is a representation of an invoice, presented by a supplier or vendor, that your organization must make payment for, typically for a good or service that was previously purchased. Voucher transactions differ from general ledger transactions in that they are presented without complete general ledger information. The offsetting payables account is determined automatically by OneWorld using automatic accounting instructions.

Accounts Receivable Invoices

The Accounts Receivable Invoice batch interface processor allows the creation of accounts receivable invoices that originate outside OneWorld and introduces them to OneWorld through the batch processing facility. An invoice is your bill, to your customer or client, for a good or service that was previously ordered and shipped or provided to that customer or client. It too differs from general ledger transactions in that it too is presented without complete general ledger information. The offsetting receivables account is determined automatically by OneWorld using automatic accounting instructions.

Cash Receipts

The Accounts Receivable Cash Receipts batch interface processor is used to load cash receipts information into OneWorld that is typically received from your bank or a customer-supplied EDI remittance advice. If this information is provided by your financial institution, a setup charge and a per-transmission charge are usually associated with this type of service.

This information is then used for automatic application of cash receipt processing against invoices. Separate post input processing steps use predefined algorithms to apply received cash based on invoice number and amount parameters. Any received cash processing exceptions must be manually matched against invoice documents for a given customer or client account. No general ledger account information is presented with a cash receipts transaction. The accounting information is derived from the matched invoice document. For unmatched cash receipts, accounts are determined automatically by OneWorld using automatic accounting instructions.

Names and Addresses

The Address Book batch interface processor loads Address Book information from other systems, such as the loading of new employees from an outsourced payroll system or the loading of new customers or vendors that were recently created in a legacy system. Note that a payroll outsourcing provider usually assesses a setup charge and a per-transmission charge for this type of service.

The primary difference between this input processor and those for accounting-related transactions is that no financial entries or transactions are created in any financial system. Note that updates to existing Address Book records are not possible with this interface; only the addition or deletion of Address Book records is possible using this batch interface processor.

If Address Book updates must be passed to OneWorld, you must use the OneWorld Address Book Revisions application program, or a custom interface is required. Although it is possible to delete an Address Book record using this interface, this is not a recommended practice. An inactive address record is frequently needed well into a new calendar year in order to comply with the information reporting requirements for annual 1099 statements for nonwage income for the Internal Revenue Service.

Other Financial File Input Processors

There are several other finance-related file input processors. They are discussed in this section.

Bank Statements

The Bank Statement Input Processor is used to load checking account statement items for account reconciliation purposes. Your financial institution can generally provide this information to your organization as an electronic file transmission. A setup charge and a per-transmission charge are usually associated with this type of service. A transaction code is assigned to each statement entry or type of record in the file supplied by your financial institution. The transaction code determines how the statement item is processed for reconciliation purposes. This information is subsequently used with the account reconciliation features found in the General Accounting system.

Budget Information

It is not uncommon for an organization to develop annual and future-year detailed financial information, by business unit or account, outside of its OneWorld software. For instance, a financial modeling and budgeting tool might be used at a large multinational organization, and a smaller organization might develop budgets using Excel or Lotus spreadsheets. As previously mentioned, budget information can be loaded as "one-sided" journal entries. Alternatively, OneWorld has a facility that uploads budget information directly into the account balance file, eliminating the need to create a journal entry transaction that must subsequently be posted in order for the account balance file to be updated.

General Batch Input Processing Requirements

Implementing any of these batch interface processors requires a substantial degree of effort. Not only are there technical issues to be addressed, but typically external parties apart from your organization are involved in the overall design and development of these interfaces. End-user training issues are involved as well. Process results must be reviewed, errors corrected, and batches posted. Finally, for recurring interfaces, job scheduling and coordination are significant operational issues. Your organization must develop the appropriate procedural and thoughtful review procedures necessary to ensure that completeness and accuracy of data prevail, as well as to ensure that measures are taken to prevent any inbound transaction duplications—a frequent problem that I have seen when external interfaces between systems are needed.

Each batch interface processor provided in OneWorld has its own set of required fields and other idiosyncrasies regarding both content and format for the incoming information into a specific batch interface processor. Unfortunately, J. D. Edwards does not provide a single, comprehensive guide on how to implement batch input processing for your organization. Instead, it is necessary to consult the individual One World application system reference guides found in the

OneWorld Softcopy Documentation Library, available on CD-ROM from J. D. Edwards.

World and OneWorld Coexistence

There are two dimensions of coexistence. The first type is called application or functional coexistence. This form of coexistence provides for application coexistence—essentially, database sharing between systems. The programs that use the data do not need to be technically compatible—only the database must be common. This means that the data structure, format, and access technique must be compatible.

The second dimension of coexistence is technical or multiplatform coexistence. It allows the same set of application programs to run on many hardware platforms—for instance, on personal or microcomputer equipment, on servers and midrange systems, and on large-scale multiprocessor and mainframe systems.

For many years, both J. D. Edwards and its clients relied on the IBM AS/400 midrange platform as a preferred platform. The AS/400 is a business-oriented computer that has a well-established reputation for low total cost of ownership as well as for its overall performance and reliability, especially for transaction processing. In short, the AS/400 has become one of the leading midrange computing platforms used by many small and midsize organizations around the world. As the AS/400 has matured, J. D. Edwards has continually refined its World software, a character-based ERP system that runs exclusively on the AS/400, with business functionality very similar to that of OneWorld, since it was first introduced to the market in the late 1970s.

Foreseeing fundamental changes in the marketplace that required systems that were graphical instead of character-based and that used open multiplatform environments, not just an AS/400 environment, brought about the creation of OneWorld. However, J. D. Edwards faced a huge dilemma—how to help its customers cope with this transition. In short, the answer was coexistence. Another way to view coexistence is as a salesperson's dream and a technician's worst nightmare. Coexistence, like an electric car, is something we all want, but that is not, practically speaking, technically feasible. J. D. Edwards is not the only ERP vendor to embrace coexistence. For instance, PeopleSoft, a leading J. D. Edwards competitor, attempted to port its system to the AS/400 environment but recently stopped supporting the AS/400 version of its product for basically these reasons.

The good news is that J. D. Edwards does provide coexistence—but not complete coexistence—at the application level between its World and OneWorld software products. For J. D. Edwards, making the transition from the character-based to the GUI or now browser-based world, this is a potentially important consideration. The news is even better if your organization is running OneWorld exclusively, because both application and technical coexistence are possible.

Back Office Tools

World and OneWorld software require separate Data Dictionaries. However, J. D. Edwards has stated that with release B8.1 of OneWorld, a single Data Dictionary is planned. The User-Defined Codes are between OneWorld and World software. Security has been enhanced in OneWorld. Therefore, separate OneWorld and World software security must be maintained. For the first time, J. D. Edwards now provides field-level security. It dropped menu-level security, but its functionality can be replicated. Although the application menu structures are virtually identical between World and OneWorld software, the menu definition process is not. Therefore, it is necessary to maintain separate menu definitions for both systems.

Applications

For the most part, World software and OneWorld applications work or share data interchangeably. However, there are specific instances in which coexistence does not work, primarily due to enhancements made to the OneWorld application but not to a World application. Two such examples of systems that do not coexist include Accounts Receivable and Payroll. Your organization must decide which environment to use. If it's OneWorld, it's a reimplementation decision. This also involves data conversion between World and OneWorld software.

Development Tools

J. D. Edwards provided multiple Report Writer tools for World software. These tools included FASTR for financial reporting, STAR for fixed-asset reporting, and World Writer for all other custom reporting requirements. These reporting tools operated without issues in a coexistence environment. However, OneWorld consolidates all reporting functions into a single tool, the Enterprise Report Writer. OneWorld has no automatic conversion tool that converts a World software-based custom report into OneWorld Enterprise Report Writer specifications. In effect, you must redesign all existing reports that you need on a go-forward basis using OneWorld's Enterprise Report Writer. World's DREAM Writer data selection and sequencing front end is replaced by the Versions List, and there is some variation between how these two front ends work.

As for any custom applications, batch or interactive, the development environment is nothing less than a paradigm shift. OneWorld is an object-oriented event-driven system. Although its underlying database is still relational and although the application functionality is generally preserved between World and OneWorld software, little else is. Some of the development tools might have the same or a similar name, but they are indeed different and incompatible, as are any of the World software programs. The preceding chapter provided a more complete discussion of OneWorld application development and this new approach.

All Good Things Must Come to an End

J. D. Edwards currently supports two distinctly different software products— OneWorld along with World and World Vision. As ever-increasing numbers of J. D. Edwards clients find value in moving to its GUI- or browser-based product, OneWorld, how long can J. D. Edwards be expected to endure the costs of supporting these two products? Obviously this has been a frequent and heated question posed to J. D. Edwards by World software customers over the past several years.

World software customers have already made a significant investment, and many are not quite ready to make such a transition, especially after expending considerable effort updating to the year 2000-compliant version of World software. Therefore, after consulting with its customers, J. D. Edwards announced at its annual user group meeting, FOCUS 2000, held in Denver last summer, that it will extend support for World software through what is now considered to be both a final and realistic date of February 2005.

At that time, it also created a new division devoted specifically to World software support. Thereafter, J. D. Edwards will support only the OneWorld software product.

Why Bother with Coexistence?

This is obviously a question that many organizations will struggle with over the next few years. In many ways, OneWorld represents an opportunity for many organizations to reconsider their current implementation and any previous customizations of World software. In many cases, the preference might be a reimplementation rather than coexistence. Again, every organization needs to weigh the benefits of each strategy. If a total change in platform will occur, obviously it will be a reimplementation project. On the other hand, implementing OneWorld now for no other reason than to use the Enterprise Report Writer to develop and deliver new custom reports to end-users might be an excellent way to get started.

Summary

This chapter introduced a number of advanced OneWorld technical topics. Although the coverage of these topics was not exhaustive, this chapter nonetheless provided a basic understanding of OneWorld, including the following:

◆ Workflow management

◆ System security

◆ Batch process scheduling

◆ Software installation and upgrades

◆ System and data integrity

◆ Data migration tools, including OneWorld table conversion and batch input processing applications

◆ System integration tools

◆ Coexistence with World software

This chapter was not intended to answer all the questions you might have about any of these important topics. However, it does provide a general overview of the subject so that you can appreciate its value to your organization as you proceed with your OneWorld implementation.

PART V

An Overview of OneWorld Functionality

Chapter 14

This chapter introduces the OneWorld *foundation* application systems. They are called foundation systems because all the other OneWorld application systems rely on one or more of these systems. These systems are also frequently called the "cornerstone" or "core" OneWorld systems. The OneWorld foundation systems include the following:

◆ Back office
◆ Address Book
◆ General Accounting
◆ Inventory Management
◆ Product Data Management

In general, these foundation systems fulfill an important objective. They serve as a repository for data that can be shared across multiple applications in OneWorld. This type of shared data is frequently called *master data*. Note that master data files and tables that are shared across application modules or systems are a common characteristic and key benefit of an ERP system. Most ERP systems will not function correctly without at least some amount of master data being present. In this regard, OneWorld is no different from other integrated ERP systems. Therefore, this data sharing is essential to the successful operation of OneWorld.

On a final note, few other implementation areas require as much planning and advance preparation than does the task of master data setup in OneWorld. Most organizations underestimate the amount of effort this will require. It is a part of the "production readiness" phase of the implementation plan.

Master data setup is not simply a matter of rekeying or converting legacy data. Instead, a significant amount of cleansing and reformatting of data is typically necessary. For an organization that has used manual processes or rudimentary legacy systems, the amount of work frequently elicits responses such as "Is all this information necessary?" The short answer is no. The long answer is, of course, yes. For OneWorld to process transactions as efficiently as possible, all of this advance work is necessary.

The Foundation Systems

This section introduces the OneWorld foundation systems. These systems are at the core of OneWorld. Virtually all other applications rely on these systems to some degree.

Back Office

Prior chapters have introduced many of the general "back office" functions that exist in OneWorld. In OneWorld, the back office is comprised of the configuration and personalization tools that allow your organization to personalize the software to fulfill your business requirements. Examples of these back office functions include Security Management, User-Defined Code Maintenance, and Workflow Management.

These configuration tools go a long way in helping an organization completely avoid (or at least significantly reduce) the degree of custom programming necessary in order to achieve a successful OneWorld implementation. If custom programming is still needed, OneWorld developer tools such as the Enterprise Report Writer are also available. The OneWorld developer tools were introduced in Chapter 12.

Application-Specific Back Office Activities

In addition to the general back office functions, each module or set of modules has a related setup menu. These menus typically include references to a back office system for setup tasks that are related to a given application. At times, these references will seem and actually are redundant with tasks found on other setup menus. This does not mean that you need to once again set up new values in the table. The tables are changed only if the values in the table already do not completely include the full range of possible values used by your organization. Two excellent examples of shared tables are the payment terms table and the freight terms table. The values from these two tables are shared minimally, between OneWorld accounts payable, accounts receivable, procurement, and sales order management.

With respect to OneWorld configuration, the general rule is "set up once and reuse often." Again, the single payment terms table is a good example of this approach. An important role played by an implementation consultant is to provide intervention throughout the OneWorld setup process to your organization. Depending on the service level your organization has negotiated with its implementation consultant, the intervention level can range from substantial and complete to serving in a very limited role.

The consultant might be engaged to provide overall guidance to the process, placing the burden of configuration on your organization. On the other hand, the consultant might be engaged to perform the actual configuration of OneWorld for your organization, with minimal involvement by your organization's staff. If your organization chooses the latter approach, insist that your consultant provide a minimal level of knowledge transfer upon conclusion and acceptance of the configuration. Also insist that complete documentation of the configuration actions be provided. This documentation will serve as a ready reference should questions arise about your configuration. Also, it is a reference if any configuration changes are needed or for some reason, the documentation must be replicated.

There are numerous back office references in OneWorld. For instance, sometimes you hear the terms "general back office" or "distribution back office" used. Generally speaking, these references are to the setup menus or processes needed in each of these areas. Back office functions are not discussed as a separate topic here. Instead, the back office or setup functions for each application system are discussed as they are introduced throughout the remaining chapters. For a more complete discussion of OneWorld's general back office capabilities and features, refer to Chapters 10 and 11.

Address Book

Previously, the Address Book was introduced for purposes of the examples presented in Chapters 8 and 9. As you will recall from some of that earlier discussion, the Address Book is the central repository of name and address information for your organization in OneWorld. The Address Book is the application system where all customers, employees, suppliers, taxing authorities, other stakeholders, and even your own facilities are also defined for use by all other OneWorld applications.

General Accounting

At the heart of OneWorld is the General Accounting system. In many other systems, this application system is simply called the General Ledger system. All applications that interface to—or, more specifically, that create General Ledger transactions—rely on the General Accounting system. It is within the General Accounting system that the chart of accounts, fiscal periods, and companies is defined.

Although these master data-related functions are an important aspect of the General Accounting system, this system, unlike the Address Book, is not solely a master data repository. The General Accounting system also provides a number of important transaction-processing capabilities. This secondary role of the General Accounting system is discussed in Chapter 15.

Automatic Accounting Instructions

Although technically they aren't part of the General Accounting system, the automatic accounting instruction tables play an important role in OneWorld. Automatic accounting instructions are frequently called AAIs. All general ledger transactions that are created by any OneWorld application system (other than those that are manually entered as journal entries in the General Accounting system) rely on these tables.

Instead of entering or looking up accounting code values for every transaction, based on some facts about the transaction itself, OneWorld can use these tables to fill in the missing pieces of a journal entry that can subsequently be posted to the general ledger through OneWorld's General Accounting system. The validation of account numbers remains the task for the chart of accounts, not the automatic accounting instructions. Automatic accounting instructions are discussed in future chapters about OneWorld application systems in the context of General Accounting system integration.

Inventory Management

Much like the General Accounting system, the Inventory Management system serves two roles. The first role is serving as the central repository for information about stock items or products, nonstock items, and services that your organization will consume, produce, or sell, generally speaking, on a repetitive basis. To the other OneWorld distribution and manufacturing systems, Inventory Management represents the essential starting point in that these other systems rely on Inventory Management for item-related information.

The second role that the Inventory Management system fulfills is as a *perpetual inventory system*, providing the necessary transaction processing functionality for controlling stock item balances and locations and facilitating stock valuation, disposition, and movement. This secondary role of the Inventory Management system is discussed in Chapter 16.

Product Data Management

The Product Data Management module is required when you implement OneWorld manufacturing-related application systems. Product Data Management essentially provides a series of enhancements above and beyond the basic item master information found in the Inventory Management system that relate specifically to manufacturing.

In addition, Product Data Management serves as the repository for other essential data, such as work centers, routings, bills of materials, and manufacturing standards information, that is subsequently used in OneWorld manufacturing applications. A complete discussion of OneWorld's Product Data Management capabilities and features can be found in Chapter 17. However, this chapter's discussions and recommendations about master data planning and setup practices for the OneWorld implementation apply equally to Product Data Management.

An In-Depth Look at the Address Book

Much has already been said about the Address Book in earlier chapters. Therefore, some of the following material might repeat certain elements from those earlier discussions. However, to be fair, those previous discussions barely touched the surface of the content and relevance of the Address Book to OneWorld. Consider the following questions I generally encounter during any serious Address Book-related discussion or training session that I have with a client:

◆ "Why is so much data necessary?"

◆ "Why does this overall process seem so overwhelming or even clumsy to me?"

Of course, these questions come up repeatedly, and they generally do not stop with the Address Book; they also resurface with Item Master and Product Data Management discussions. With that as a preface, the Address Book will be further introduced.

What Is the Address Book?

The Address Book is not one file, but a set of files or tables where the names and addresses of your organization's customers, suppliers, employees, and physical locations are stored in OneWorld. Another way to look at the Address Book is that anytime a street address might be involved, an Address Book record is required. The creation of Address Book records is one of the most basic tasks that your organization performs during the startup and ongoing use of OneWorld.

The Address Book Data Model

A number of primary data files or tables are maintained through the Address Book system. Table 14-1 identifies each table and defines the table's primary purpose in the Address Book data model.

Table 14-1 Address Book Data Model

Data File Number	Data File Name	Data File Contents
F0101	Address Book Master	Stores the name, address number, search type, and category code (reporting) information.
F0111	Who's Who	Stores information about individual contacts or people, including given names, nicknames, and salutations for each Address Book entry. A single Address Book entry can include any number of related individual contacts.
F0115	Phone Numbers	Stores the area code and phone number by type of phone number, such as home, office, fax, or cellular. E-mail addresses can also be identified and stored. A single individual in an Address Book entry can have any number of related phone numbers.
F0116	Address Organization	This is an "as of" file for street address information. The Address Book maintains street address lines, state or region, country, and postal code information, along with an "effective date" for each such entry.
F0150	Address by Date	Parent and child record structures are maintained in this file. For instance, relationships such as internal organizational structures and employee/supervisor relationships are defined in this manner.

Table 14-1 Address Book Data Model *(continued)*

Data File Number	Data File Name	Data File Contents
F01815	Word Search	Stores words that are referenced during a "search by name" operation. Once established, the Address Book Word Search master table facilitates Address Book-related queries using text strings. For example, name, city, postal code, phone number, or portions thereof can be used. To reduce extraneous search hits, common words should be bypassed. These common words are maintained in the User-Defined Code table 01/SW. OneWorld does not add any words from this table to the Address Book Word Search Master table.
F0301	Customer Master	The customer master stores accounts receivable, billing, and pricing-related information about the customer.
F03012	Customer Master by Line of Business (LOB)	Stores the customer by company information.
F0401	Supplier (Vendor) Master	Stores accounts payable information and other related information about a supplier.

Category and Reporting Codes in OneWorld

The Address Book has a number of fields called category or reporting codes. The concept of category or reporting codes is found throughout OneWorld, not just in the Address Book. Therefore, the general information about category or reporting codes that is provided in this section applies to OneWorld in general.

A simple though powerful concept, category or reporting codes provide a *completely user-defined method* for classifying or categorizing information. In addition, as a general rule, the use of category or reporting codes throughout OneWorld is completely optional, although in actual practice, your organization will likely find numerous applications for category or reporting codes throughout your business processes. For instance, the Address Book defines 30 separate user-defined codes, although in practice, I rarely find that more than just a few are actually used.

Although at first it might seem logical that search types should be defined for each type of customer, such as retail, wholesale, and large accounts, this information is typically unnecessary for order-taking purposes, because in the end, customers are, simply stated, just that—customers. However, such classifications are usually necessary for analysis and compensation purposes, but these classifications are arbitrary, discretionary, and change frequently. Therefore, a category or reporting code is the more appropriate method for classifying or categorizing information.

Of course, any such classifications using a category or reporting code are meaningless unless there is "downstream value" to be derived from them. In OneWorld, this occurs in a number of ways, including the following:

◆ Default values. In some cases, one or more category or reporting codes can be extracted from the Address Book and used to subsequently classify a transaction that occurs in another system, such as in another OneWorld financial or distribution system. Reports and searches in these other systems may then rely on such values.

◆ Search values. Using the OneWorld's Query by Example feature in conjunction with category or reporting codes, specific Address Book records can be located and viewed.

◆ Report selection or sequencing criteria. Category or reporting codes can be used to control data record selection or sequencing for Address Book-related reports. For instance, you can use category or reporting code values to print mailing labels for the president or CEO at each of your large accounts for your organization's annual golf or polo match outing.

As mentioned earlier, your classification schemes are subject to change as your business model or business processes change. When large numbers of master data records exist, making changes to category and reporting codes can be a significant and important task, because they serve as default values for transactions and as the basis for other analyses performed.

To ease such changes, in some cases OneWorld has predefined batch processes available to perform mass changes of category or reporting code information—from one value to another value. For instance, account assignments by regions, branches, or offices change frequently, and realignments become necessary. As new regions, branches, or offices open, or as markets are abandoned, existing accounts might be reassigned.

To complete this discussion of category and reporting codes, Figure 14-1 illustrates the Address Book Reporting Code form for Codes 1 through 10. A separate form is used to maintain codes 11 through 30.

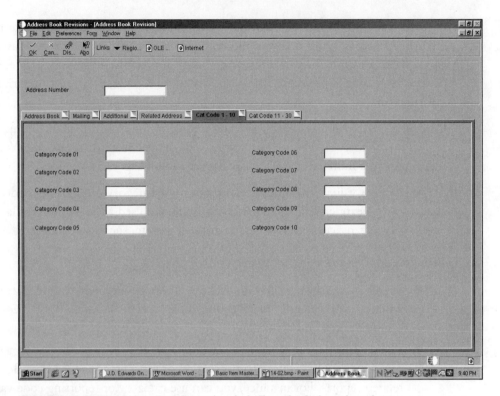

FIGURE 14-1 *The Address Book Reporting Code Form for Codes 1 through 10*

Maintaining Address Book Information

This section discusses maintaining Address Book information by covering some of the more frequently asked questions I encounter, as a consultant, during Address Book setup.

Where Do You Send the Bill?

With so many organizations being acquired by others, it's sometimes hard to know who the real customer is or how many customers are really the same customer. In addition, the general trend is toward a shared services model, especially for financial operations. As a result, the "invoice to" address is frequently different from the "ship to" address on the sales order document. Knowing and storing addresses and information about address relationships is facilitated through the parent/child relationship feature of OneWorld's Address Book. The parent/child relationships are established as follows:

1. Define a parent record for the primary role.
2. Define a child record for the secondary role.
3. Use OneWorld's parent/child relationship capabilities within the Address Book to link or relate these two records. This is done using the Related Addresses form in Address Book Revisions.

For example, the parent record might be the corporate headquarters where invoices are sent, and subsidiary companies, branch offices, and plant locations would be considered child records. Figure 14-2 illustrates the Address Book Related Addresses form.

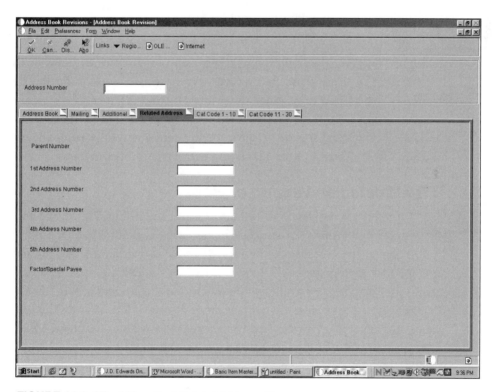

FIGURE 14-2 *The Address Book Related Addresses Form*

OneWorld also includes more sophisticated techniques for managing parent/child relationships of customer- and billing-related records. In certain businesses, the availability of additional levels of customer addressing is critical to the sales order management and billing processes. Although Figure 14-2 shows both parent/child and related addresses, OneWorld also includes a form that shows only parent/child relationships and allows for more sophisticated maintenance of these relationships.

Whom Do You Pay?

It is common practice for suppliers to request payments to a third party—usually to their bank in order to expedite the collection process. For big-ticket items, payment is made to a factor, who finances the inventory prior to its sale. In cases where a bankruptcy filing has occurred, payments are made to a third party, to a debtor in possession account, or to a court-appointed trustee. How does OneWorld handle payment diversions?

The first step is to define a *supplier* record. Second, define a *special payee* record. Third, use OneWorld's parent/child relationship capabilities within the Address Book to link or relate these two records. Again, this is done using the Related Addresses form in Address Book Revisions. In this instance, the special payee address is noted in the reserved field Factor/Special Payee. The OneWorld accounts payable system must be subsequently configured to override the supplier address with the special payee address on the payment instrument.

Is It a Customer, Vendor, or Both?

Can customers also be vendors? In both real life and in OneWorld, the answer is yes. For the vast majority of situations, one Address Book record should suffice. In other instances, however, it might be desirable to maintain separate Customer and Supplier master records. In such situations, where multiple Address Book records are used, be sure to follow the parent/child relationship setup procedures previously noted. Also note that an advanced feature in OneWorld's financial systems is the ability to perform receivables/payables netting for these "dual" relationships that you might have with customers and suppliers.

Legacy System Relationships

If address information was previously maintained in a legacy system, that system likely assigned its own identifier, much like the Address Book number that is assigned in OneWorld to every customer, supplier, or employee. A legacy system Address Book-like number can be entered into OneWorld's Long Address Number field.

For instance, if your conversion is a phased implementation, this number serves as a cross-reference to customers from your legacy sales order processing system who are now being entered into OneWorld accounts receivable. What's more, OneWorld financials allow the use of the legacy system number during transaction entry and make the account number conversion automatically.

There are other possible uses for the Long Address Number field than simply the legacy system illustration. Because it is a free-form field, the actual use of this field is left to the discretion of your organization.

Other Uses for the Address Book

Long before customer or supplier relationship management systems existed, J. D. Edwards designed the Address Book functionality available in OneWorld for use in its World software product. It seems that no matter how many fields J. D. Edwards has added to the Address Book, over the years more always seem to be needed.

Generally speaking, these additional field requirements support other uses that a J. D. Edwards customer invents for the Address Book, such as maintaining unique customer or supplier relationship management information. For these purposes, J. D. Edwards provides facilities that provide for extending the Address Book database. This is done through the use of OneWorld's supplemental database feature, described later in this chapter.

Contact Management

I previously suggested that I have seen the OneWorld Address Book used as a customer or supplier relationship manager. An important aspect of relationship management is contact management. Contact management usually involves recording a summary of any conversation held with the customer or supplier in a journal or log. OneWorld also supports this requirement through the supplemental database.

I don't want to oversell the supplemental database or its ease of use. If you really need a customer relationship management system, Chapter 18 discusses J. D. Edwards' alliance with Siebel. Siebel products provide a much more robust customer relationship and contact management tool, especially for high-volume usage. For instance, I have used the supplemental database to maintain supplier-related information and notes—a much less demanding application for the supplemental database.

Periodic OneWorld Address Book Tasks

For the most part, unlike other OneWorld transaction processing systems, the Address Book is free of a litany of periodic processes that must be performed. However, your organization should perform several periodic processes:

◆ Running the Build Word Search batch process. This process is found on the Address Book Advanced and Technical Operations menu (G0131) as the Word Search Build option. Note that to reduce extraneous search hits, common words such as "company," "and," "the," and "corporation" should be bypassed. These common words are maintained in User Defined Code table 01/SW. The list of common words should be reviewed prior to executing the Build Word Search batch process.

◆ Running the Check for Duplicates batch process. This process is found on the Address Book Advanced and Technical Operations menu (G0131) as the Check for Duplicates option.

These two tasks can be added to the OneWorld Scheduler for automatic and periodic execution on a frequency that is determined by the frequency and volume of Address Book changes and that is balanced with other processes that must be regularly scheduled. The OneWorld Scheduler was discussed in Chapter 13.

Maintaining Address Book Information

To create and maintain Address Book information in OneWorld, use the Address Book Revisions program (P01012), found on the Address Book Daily Processing menu (G01). Here is the overall menu path:

> Master Directory (G) > Foundation Systems (G0) > Address Book (G010) > Daily Processing (G01) > Address Book Revisions (**P01012**)

Note that customer master information is maintained through the Address Book revisions menu option Form, Accounts Receivable (A/R), while vendor master information is maintained through the menu option Accounts Payable (A/P).

An In-Depth Look at General Accounting Master Data

As previously stated, all applications that interface to—or, more specifically, that create General Ledger transactions—rely on the General Accounting system.

More specifically, they rely on the master data that is maintained in the General Accounting system. This master data includes the definition of

- ◆ Companies
- ◆ Fiscal years and periods for companies
- ◆ Business units and model business units
- ◆ Object accounts
- ◆ Reporting codes related to business units or object accounts
- ◆ Legacy system account numbers

Collectively, this master data is called the chart of accounts for the General Accounting system.

The Chart of Accounts Data Model

Three primary data files or tables are maintained through the General Accounting system. Table 14-2 identifies each table and defines the table's primary purpose in the chart of accounts data model.

Table 14-2 Chart of Accounts Data Model

Data File Number	Data File Name	Data File Contents
F0006	Business Unit Master	Stores the business unit definition, including name and number, company, and category codes.
F0008	Fiscal Date Patterns	Stores the fiscal date patterns.
F0010	Company Constants	Stores company definitions, including number and name and fiscal date pattern.
F0901	Account Master	Stores the object account definition, including account number and description on a one-record-per-account basis.

Account Code Structure

The OneWorld account code structure consists of three fixed segments:

- ◆ A Business Unit value of up to 12 characters
- ◆ An Object Account value of up to six characters
- ◆ A Subsidiary value of up to eight characters

The business unit, object account, and subsidiary portions of the account number are generally separated or segmented by a period. However, this separation character is user-defined and can be changed to another character in the system constants for General Accounting. For example, dashes are frequently used as an account code separation character.

A Business Unit value and an Object Account value are *mandatory* entries in every OneWorld journal entry. The Subsidiary value is considered an optional part of the account number.

It should be noted that the company number is an integral part of every accounting transaction. However, unless specifically stated, the Business Unit value determines the Company Number value. The determination of company number from business unit is possible because every business unit value is both unique and company-specific.

Companies

The definition of "company" is that it is typically a separate legal entity that requires a balance sheet. From a legal and tax perspective, the affairs of separate, legally chartered organizations should always keep separate books of records.

As noted previously, the company value is not an explicit part of the OneWorld account structure. However, company is an implicit part of the OneWorld account structure, because every business unit must be assigned to, or defined within, the context of a company.

If your organization operates multiple companies for legal or tax purposes, each company should be set up in OneWorld as a separate company. If your organization operates joint ventures that maintain common assets that are shared among your "companies," a company is also needed for these structures. In addition, OneWorld requires a default company, referred to as company 00000.

Before you set up companies in the General Accounting system, you should establish an Address Book record for each company that will be defined in OneWorld for accounting purposes. Generally speaking, the same number is used for both the company and its Address Book. If necessary, however, the company number can be cross-referenced to a different Address Book number. An Address Book record is not established for the default company, 00000.

Business Units

A business unit is considered an organizational demarcation. J. D. Edwards calls this the "Who" portion of the account number. The term Cost Center is an obsolete term that is synonymous with business unit and is still used in a few isolated cases within OneWorld. Business unit reporting can be further controlled through the use of user-defined reporting codes.

In addition, you should be aware that often, if a new business unit is added to the chart of accounts, such an action might mean that additional automatic accounting instructions are also needed.

Every company minimally has two business units defined. These are typically a balance sheet business unit, which is typically the company number, and at least one income statement business unit. OneWorld further requires that every business unit name must be unique across companies.

Object Accounts

The object account is the main classification scheme for assets, liabilities, capital, income, and expenses in OneWorld. J. D. Edwards calls this the "What" portion of the overall account number. An object account may contain up to six characters. Here are some characteristics of the object account:

◆ Every account is assigned to a specific level of detail for rollup purposes.

◆ An account can be defined as a summary account (not eligible for journal entry postings) or as a detail account (eligible for journal entry posting).

◆ Postings can be further restricted to manual or automatic entries.

◆ Reporting by account

With respect to reporting by object account, the following points are true:

◆ Object accounts can be grouped by level of detail.

◆ Object accounts can also be grouped through the use of user-defined reporting or category codes.

Do not underestimate the importance of level of detail. I was once called into a situation where all of a client's accounts were established at the same level of detail. Unfortunately, the client had been ill-advised by their implementation consultant.

Hence, this arrangement completely negated what they thought was their chart of accounts hierarchy, rendering the standard level-of-detail-driven inquiries and reports useless. The client's intent was to develop custom reports. This made for a lot of follow-on consulting work but made little sense otherwise. Fortunately, this was discovered and corrected before the client went live on OneWorld. They in turn were able to use all the standard general accounting reports and inquiries. Although some custom reports were still needed, they were needed for very different reasons than to replace the standard chart of accounts hierarchy that is integral to OneWorld.

Also note that when new object accounts are defined, additional automatic accounting instructions will be needed.

Subsidiaries

The subsidiary provides for greater detail in your organization's accounting records. Quite frankly, I have used Subsidiary values sparingly. For some accounts, they make sense, but in other cases, they do not. Another option for detailed level accounting is the use of sub-ledger accounting.

Note, however, that these are two different methods of performing detail-level accounting—they are not identical. Sub-ledger accounting does not require defining any additional accounts within the chart of accounts. Instead, sub-ledger accounting relies on an existing value to demarcate the detail, such as an Address Book number or a work order number.

Sub-Ledger Accounting

Optionally, accounting journal entries can be carried to a lower level of detail through the use of the Sub-Ledger field. Valid sub-ledger references can include the following:

◆ Address Book numbers

◆ Business units

◆ Equipment item numbers

◆ Work order numbers

◆ User-defined numbers

Sub-ledger accounting is activated at the account level. A typical use of a sub-ledger value is for special projects. Although the Job Cost system within

OneWorld is specifically intended to serve as a project accounting system, many organizations cannot justify the Job Cost system for this purpose given their limited project accounting requirements.

With some discipline, sub-ledger accounting can be used to fulfill this requirement. All that is really needed, systemically, in order to establish a special project, is a work order number. However, use of a Sub-Ledger value on an optional instead of a required basis requires a tremendous amount of discipline. If your usual account number values are used, they are typically not set up to require sub-ledger accounting. Therefore, proper codification of source document transaction rests with the end user, because no validation or check to force entry of a sub-ledger-related account is made.

If you're wondering how work orders are created, refer to Chapter 17. Please be aware that the work order header function is distributed to every J. D. Edwards customer as a part of OneWorld, even if your organization has not purchased the application systems that genuinely rely on a work order, such as shop floor control.

General Ledger Reporting Codes

User-defined category or reporting codes are also prevalent throughout the OneWorld chart of accounts structure. These user-defined category or reporting codes can in turn be used as the basis for selecting and analyzing accounting information and creating financial reports. As with the case of the Address Book, each business unit and each account number has 30 category or reporting codes available.

For instance, departments can be grouped into divisions. A divisional income statement is then possible by using the division reporting code for purposes of selecting all business units within that division for inclusion on the requested income statement.

Maintaining General Accounting Information

The chart of accounts information is maintained through the General Accounting system. To create and maintain the OneWorld chart of accounts, use the General Accounting Organization and Account Setup menu (G09411). Here is the overall menu path:

> Master Directory (G) > Financials (G1) > General Accounting (G09) >
> System Setup (G0941) > General Accounting Organization and
> Account Setup (**G09411**)

This menu includes numerous options. Table 14-3 summarizes the more important menu options and which chart of accounts setup functions are performed through those options.

Table 14-3 Chart of Accounts Setup

G09411 Menu Option	Functions Performed Using This Option
Company Names and Numbers	Create or maintain company information. Establish date patterns through Form, Date Patterns.
Business Units by Company	Create or maintain a business unit. Copy accounts from the selected business unit to the desired business unit using Row, Accounts, Copy Accounts.
Accounts By Business Unit	Create or maintain an object account for the selected business unit (such as a model business unit).

Legacy Account Numbers

OneWorld provides a 25-position free-form or unstructured field that can be used for the entry of an account number value that was assigned by a legacy system. This field is called the "third account number" in the OneWorld account master record. This field is often used if you want to continue using the same account number from a prior system. It is also possible to use the third account number value as an alternative way of entering an account number when you're creating the journal entry.

Restructuring the Chart of Accounts

As with most documents and master data records, OneWorld creates a "short account number" for every account defined in the chart of accounts. This value is assigned on a "behind-the-scenes" basis for account numbers. The value of this additional number is quite simple. The transactions and the balance file records are associated with this short number, not the long account number consisting of the cost center, object account, and subsidiary values. What this really means is that the cost center, object account, and subsidiary can be changed independent of the underlying data, thus giving your organization enormous flexibility to restructure your chart of accounts should that become necessary.

Designing the Chart of Accounts

In general, the steps required to establish a chart of accounts within OneWorld are as follows:

1. Determine your organizational structure and reporting needs.
2. Set up companies.
3. Define your fiscal year by setting up fiscal date patterns.
4. Set up business units.
5. Set up model (nonposting) business units (this is optional but recommended).
6. Determine category codes for business units (this is optional).
7. Assign category codes to business units (this is optional if category codes are not used).
8. Design the overall chart of accounts (object account) structure.
9. Copy the appropriate accounts into one or more model business units (this is optional if model business units are not used).
10. Copy the accounts from model business units into operating business units.

Although it isn't comprehensive, this list represents the steps that I typically employ as a consultant when configuring OneWorld software.

Creating a Model Chart of Accounts

The easiest way to establish a multiple business unit chart of accounts is through the use of one or more *model business units*. A model business unit-based chart of accounts is a template for creating other business units. The model business units themselves are therefore established as nonposting business units, thus preventing any journal entries from being made to the accounts defined in them. Model business units are used as chart of accounts templates when you create other business units.

When model business units are used, typically multiple business units are created to represent different types of business units that exist throughout your business. Examples include business units to represent expense, overhead, or administrative departments versus production departments. Other uses might include separate business units by salesperson or product line. A model business unit is defined in

OneWorld as any other business unit would be, with two exceptions. The business unit should be designated as a *model* business unit and should also be designated as a *nonposting* business unit. As discussed previously, this latter practice denies postings to accounts of the model business unit.

Alternatively, a model chart of accounts can be maintained through the use of a single master model business unit that includes the entire chart of accounts. For the simplest of organizational structures, this is an acceptable solution. In larger organizations, the use of model business units is generally a more efficient practice. Some tips regarding the use of a model business unit-based chart of accounts appear in the next few paragraphs.

As a general rule, maintain a chart of accounts model to reflect your organizational structure. Use a model business unit for every different type of business unit found in your organizational structure. Assign only the object accounts that are relevant to that type of business unit to the model business unit. These business units form your overall model chart of accounts that are used as a basis for creating your actual chart of accounts.

A "lean" chart of accounts for each business unit is possible with model business units. This serves multiple purposes. First, it facilitates copying object accounts across all business units and eliminating portions or ranges of numbers when inappropriate. Second, financial reporting rollups are easier when you use account ranges as the selection criteria if account ranges are consistent between business units. Third, the account balance file will be smaller in size, because a balance record is maintained for every defined account, thereby streamlining inquiry and report generation. Fourth is the "out of sight, out of mind" principle: If an account is defined for a business unit, it will not be used inappropriately or mistakenly.

Use a consistent numbering scheme for all object accounts; accounts should be standardized across business units and companies. Carefully proofread your model chart of accounts to ensure that the descriptions, including their spellings, are appropriate and that the level of detail assignments and posting edit codes for each specific account are accurate. Revise accounts as needed to correct errors *before* copying the model accounts to your actual business units. Remember that the chart of accounts model is the basis for your entire chart of accounts. If it's left unchecked and the models are copied as is, they will potentially reproduce any undetected errors into one or more destination business units, which must then be corrected manually.

Chart of Accounts Design Considerations

After the necessary companies are designed to reflect your organizational structure, the next task is to create business units for each company. Typically, this is done when your organization implements OneWorld, but it might be necessary to set up new business units due to changes in your organizational structure. Each business unit must be uniquely named and assigned to a specific company.

Generally speaking, every company defined in your OneWorld implementation requires at least two business units. These two mandatory business units relate to the balance sheet and the income statement, the two fundamental accounting statements of any business entity. Additional business unit values are optional, but in practice, additional organizational demarcations are quite typical for all but the smallest and simplest of organizations.

Balance sheet accounts—asset, liability, and equity accounts—are usually associated with a single balance sheet business unit. A balance sheet business unit is therefore required for every company that is defined. Note that J. D. Edwards recommends that the business unit number for your balance sheet business unit be the same value as the one used to define your company. In other words, the balance sheet business unit is also the company number.

If you require balance sheets for "nonlegal" entities within your organization, such as balance sheets at a division, district, regional, or other level, these entities can be defined as separate companies. Such a balance sheet structure in turn provides for reporting and accounting at a lower level. However, such arrangements usually require the use of OneWorld's intercompany accounting transactions and procedures.

Here are some of my additional best-practice recommendations:

◆ Account numbers should be assigned in increments of 5 or 10, thus permitting growth in the chart of accounts numbering scheme. For example, use patterns for account numbers such as 1100, 1110, 1120, and so on or 1100, 1105, 1110, 1115, and so on.

◆ Although OneWorld permits the use of letters, do not use them. Use only numbers for the naming of your business units, account numbers, and subsidiary values. This will simplify report data selection and sequencing. One final note on this subject: I typically violate my own rule and use character-based business unit names for model business units exclusively.

◆ Account numbers should generally be four positions in length.

◆ My preference is for company number values to be two or three digits in length.

◆ Consider designing business unit suffix values as base numbers for business unit numbers. A division, location, or company number can be used as a unique prefix value, and the common business unit type suffix designation follows. For example, suppose your organization is comprised of three companies, designated as company numbers 95, 96, and 97. In addition, there are four types of business units in each company: Sales and Marketing (100), Administration (120), Purchasing (140), and Distribution (160). Therefore, company 95 has four business units defined as 95100, 95120, 95140, and 95160, and company 96 likewise has four business units defined as 96100, 96120, 96140, and 96160.

◆ The base or suffix portion of a business unit number value should generally be three or four digits in length, depending on the number of business units, such as your organization's multiple physical locations.

◆ Although a company number is entered as 00010, I generally omit the 000 when using it as a business unit prefix value.

◆ Although OneWorld provides nine levels of detail, practically speaking, only levels 3 through 9 are available. Level 1 is reserved for company processing. Level 2 is reserved for business unit processing. If your organization will implement the OneWorld Job Cost application system now or in the future, please be aware that levels 8 and 9 are reserved for use specifically with job cost. However, when job cost is not a consideration, I have successfully used levels 8 and 9 for other purposes.

Although it isn't comprehensive, the preceding list is experientially based, representing my collective experience with OneWorld software. The overall account number scheme that I usually employ appears in Table 14-4.

Table 14-4 A Typical OneWorld Account Numbering Scheme

Account Classification	Account Number Range
Assets	1000 to 1999
Liabilities	2000 to 2999
Capital/Equity	3000 to 3998
Income Summary/Year to Date Net Income/Loss	3999

Table 14-4 A Typical OneWorld Account Numbering Scheme *(continued)*

Account Classification	Account Number Range
Income	4000 to 4999
Cost of Goods Sold/Manufactured (Direct Costs)	5000 to 5999
General and Administrative Expenses (Indirect Costs)	6000 to 6999
Other Income	7000 to 7999
Other Expense	8000 to 8999
Statistical Accounts	9000 to 9999

OneWorld uses a special income summary or year-to-date net/income loss account. This account is used to update the balance sheet to reflect the aggregation of profit and loss information from income statement accounts into the balance sheet. This account is always the last balance sheet account. The automatic accounting instructions must be adjusted to accommodate your organization's account number range structure.

If you do not know where to start with the design of your chart of accounts, consider reviewing the OneWorld demo database, which includes a complete model chart of accounts. Carefully reviewing this model merits your consideration, especially if your organization is on a very short implementation timeline. This model is implementation-ready, and I have found that it works well for most nonmanufacturing businesses. In addition, the table of automatic accounting instructions delivered to you by J. D. Edwards generally reflects account number values from this model chart of accounts. However, if I had to design a chart of accounts from scratch, I would likely devise a slightly different structure, more along the lines of what was shown in Table 14-2.

To review the model chart of accounts described here, refer to the Appendixes of the OneWorld General Accounting Reference Guide, where this model is called the "training" chart of accounts.

Finally, do not take the design of your organization's chart of accounts lightly. This is an important first step in configuring OneWorld to work correctly for your organization's business model. You must do some "tuning" to properly reflect your organization's organizational structure and business model in order to get the chart of accounts correct.

An In-Depth Look at Inventory Management Master Data

In its role as a repository, Inventory Management is the application where any product- or item-related information—whether it is a product that is purchased, sold, or manufactured—is defined and stored by OneWorld. In its other equally important role, the Inventory Management system is responsible for the movement and location of items within OneWorld—which, generally speaking, should mirror where items are physically stored or warehoused throughout your organization.

The Inventory Management system relies on the existence of an item master and one or more branch/plant master records for each stock item. A branch/plant location is typically defined as a physical location, such as a plant, distribution center, public warehouse, sales office, or other type of facility.

These branch/plant records identify where stock is as well as attach a value to the stock, or quantity on hand. Nonstock items are, by definition, items that are defined in the item master but are not carried in the inventory balance or as an asset on an organization's balance sheet.

Nonstock items are typically expensed when purchased. Alternatively, nonstock item costs are accumulated as a prepaid expense and are allocated on a periodic basis. Nonstock items consumed or sold in the ordinary course of business are typically described in the item master as a matter of convenience and for efficiency during order entry processing. For instance, nonstock item descriptions don't need to be re-entered on each order document.

The Inventory Management Data Model

The item master and item branch/plant or master data portions of the OneWorld Inventory Management system include a number of primary and secondary files in the overall data model. Note that the Inventory Management system data model is significantly more complex than the two other cornerstone systems of OneWorld that were introduced earlier in this chapter.

The major reason for this complexity is that significantly more transaction processing is item-driven in OneWorld. For instance, every distribution system—including sales order processing, procurement, transportation, warehouse management, distribution requirements planning, and stock valuation—relies on the item master and item branch/plant information. The same case can be made when considering OneWorld's manufacturing-related systems.

The OneWorld Item Information Hierarchy

Fully understanding the OneWorld Inventory Management data model first requires that in terms of items, OneWorld expects and requires that item-related information be built in a strict, hierarchical manner. This item-related information hierarchy looks much like the organizational structure for a typical enterprise or organization. Figure 14-3 summarizes the OneWorld item-related information hierarchy introduced in this section.

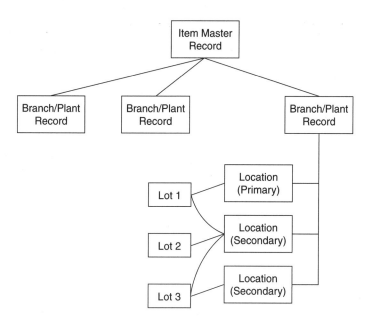

FIGURE 14-3 *The OneWorld Item Information Hierarchy*

Item Master Information

At the highest level is the item master record itself. There is one and only one item master record for every unique item that is purchased, sold, or manufactured. Item master records are always predefined in OneWorld.

Item Branch/Plant Information

At the next level, one or more item branch/plant records are maintained. An item branch/plant record is maintained for every physical plant or warehouse facility your organization might operate. Any inventory transaction processing requires the existence of the item branch/plant record. The branch/plant records define important information, such as costs and prices used by OneWorld inventory-related transactions. However, there is much information redundancy between the item master and the item branch/plant record. For many installations, the item master information defines the information and therefore becomes default values for use on branch/plant records. This is often a confusing and misunderstood area of OneWorld.

Like the item master record, each item branch/plant record must also be predefined in OneWorld. For example, an item cannot be processed by another OneWorld system from one branch/plant facility to another branch/plant facility without both the sending and receiving branch/plant facilities being predefined.

Item/Location Information

At the next level of the item information hierarchy, an item's location is taken into consideration. It is at this level that perpetual inventory information is maintained. Every item in OneWorld has, at a minimum, at least one item/location record for each branch/plant in which an inventory balance is maintained. At a minimum, all stock items are maintained in at least one unrestricted or primary stocking location within a given physical plant or warehouse facility. An item can also be maintained at multiple secondary locations. Generally speaking, a location is often defined as the physical storage space or location where an item is located within a branch/plant location.

These locations within a branch/plant facility are usually predefined. For instance, many branch/plant facilities maintain storerooms and warehouses with strict rack-, shelf-, and bin-level segmentation for ease of material stocking. However, this is not an absolute requirement. In addition, an item may be location-controlled at one physical plant or warehouse facility but not at another. It is also possible to accommodate satellite storage locations within the same facility through the use of location levels in OneWorld.

Lot/Location Information

Optionally, information can be maintained at a lower level of detail in OneWorld. This next lower level of detail is called the *lot* information for a stock item within a given stocking location. One or more lots can be stored within a single storage location in OneWorld. For instance, some organizations, such as those that manufacture food products, drugs, or other regulated items, such as automobiles and appliances, are typically *lot-controlled*. Product source location and date of manufacture are typically captured on a transaction-by-transaction basis. This information is in turn available for use in conjunction with product recalls or service and repair campaigns that are mandated for public health and safety purposes, or to preserve customer goodwill or honor product warranties.

In general, lot level information gathering and tracking are typically called *lot tracing*. Lot level information is not predefined in OneWorld. Instead, lot level information is usually created dynamically as transaction processing occurs, such as with the recording of a serial number as a product is assembled and shipped to the customer or selling agent.

It should be noted that lot tracking requires very deliberate procedures. Many organizations want the benefits of lot tracking but are unwilling or unable to instill the discipline necessary to properly identify a lot every time an inventory transaction is made.

Nonstock Items and the Item Hierarchy

Although nonstock items do not require the existence of an item branch/plant record, certain information for nonstock items is typically maintained at the plant level, such as supplier-related information. Branch/plant, location, and lot information is not captured or tracked by OneWorld. Although a goods receipt or shipment confirmation transaction can occur for a nonstock item, no inventory quantity information is captured as an Inventory Management system transaction, nor is any update ever made to an item balance record for a nonstock item.

The Item and the Bill of Materials

Note that in the case of a manufactured item, each component that makes up the manufactured item requires a complete item definition in OneWorld. These individual items are combined into a recipe or formula for building a product that is generally called a *bill of materials*. This term is frequently abbreviated as BOM and is pronounced "bomb." A bill of materials, when "exploded," identifies all the components and the quantities needed in the manufacture of an item.

A bill of materials for a manufactured item might consist of a combination of internally manufactured components, which might each have an associated bill of materials and purchased components. These manufactured components or *sub-assemblies* must be further exploded to arrive at a complete or overall bill of materials for the manufactured item. For these types of manufactured items, it is said that a multilevel bill of materials is necessary to fully describe or identify the component items.

Note that what is meant by a complete item definition in OneWorld is the complete build-out of the item information in the context of the item information hierarchy that has been introduced in this section.

Given the preceding introduction to the OneWorld item information hierarchy, you should now better understand the primary data model for the item-related information portion of the OneWorld Inventory Management system. Note that the item-related data model is comprised of more than two dozen primary and secondary files in the overall data model. Only the primary item-related data files from the Inventory Management system are listed in Table 14-5.

Table 14-5 Primary Item-Related Files in the Inventory Management System

Data File Number	Data File Name	Data File Contents
F4100	Location Master	Contains basic information about each storeroom or warehouse location within a plant or warehouse.
F4101	Item Master	Contains basic information about each item, including item number, description, category code, item class, and unit of measure values.
F4102	Item Branch	Contains essential information related to transaction processing and storage for a given item within the context of a defined facility, such as a plant or warehouse.
F4104	Item Cross Reference	Contains item descriptions used by the general-purpose OneWorld Item Search program. (The item word search table is built through a special batch process that must be run on a daily or periodic basis.)
F4105	Cost Ledger	Contains inventory cost records.
F4106	Base Price	Contains inventory price records.

Table 14-5 Primary Item-Related Files in the Inventory Management System (continued)

Data File Number	Data File Name	Data File Contents
F4108	Lot Master	Contains lot processing information.
F41002	Item Specific Unit of Measure Conversion	Contains the unit of measure conversion equations that are unique to a given item.
F41021	Item Location	Contains each item's quantity, general ledger classification, and lot status for each location within the context of a defined facility, plant, or warehouse.
F41023	Item Location Definition	Contains item location definitions.

What Information Does the Item Master Record Contain?

Virtually all of the information contained in the item master record must be defined and entered by your organization. The information in the item master record can be divided into two major categories: information that is used to describe or classify items, and information that is used to control OneWorld program functions.

What Additional Information Does the Item Branch/Plant Record Contain?

Much like the item master, virtually all of the information contained in the item master record must be defined and entered by your organization. However, at the item branch/plant level, information in this record defaults from the item master record and can be changed to reflect a branch- or plant-specific value. The item/branch plant record contains additional user-maintained information, such as price, cost, supplier, and buyer information, that is often branch- or plant-specific.

What Information Does the Item/Location Record Contain?

Virtually all the information contained in both the item master and the item branch/plant record must be defined and entered by your organization. The information in the item/location file is system-maintained. This record contains valuation and stock control information that can be updated only through

OneWorld application programs. For example, OneWorld updates the stock balance, which resides in the item branch/plant record, for an item when an inventory receipt or issue transaction is posted.

Control Information

This section describes some of the more important control information that can be found in both item master and item branch/plant records for an item defined in OneWorld.

G/L Category Codes

In order to properly value inventory, a general ledger (G/L) category code value is assigned to every item. The G/L category code is a user-defined code value. The G/L category code itself does not define the general ledger account number. Rather, this value serves as a pointer to the correct inventory account that is contained in the distribution/manufacturing-related automatic accounting instructions.

Line Type

The line type controls how OneWorld programs process this item when it is encountered on a transaction document, such as a sales order or purchase order. Specifically, the line type controls how a transaction interface will work, or whether the item is included in a calculation. Table 14-6 lists OneWorld's hard-coded line types. Line types are largely user-configurable. Only the W line type cannot be changed. It is also possible to define multiple line types that have identical setups.

Table 14-6 OneWorld Line Types

Code Value	What It Indicates
S	Stock Item
J	Job Cost
N	Nonstock Item
F	Freight
T	Text Information
M	Miscellaneous Charges and Credits
W	Work Order

Reorder Point Information

The minimum, maximum, and normal reorder quantities for an item are specified at the item branch/plant record level. Various OneWorld programs use these branch/plant quantities as control information that in turn provides recommended reorder alerts or messages in order to prevent stock-outs of items.

Stocking Types

The stocking type is a user-defined code that indicates how you stock an item—for example, as finished goods or as raw material. Certain stocking types are hard-coded within OneWorld. Your organization should not change these hard-coded values. Within the user-defined code definition itself, the second description column (Description 2) is used to indicate if the item is purchased (P) or manufactured (M). Table 14-7 lists the hard-coded stocking types in OneWorld.

Table 14-7 OneWorld Stocking Types

Code Value	What It Indicates
0	Phantom Item
B	Bulk Floor Stock
C	Configured Item
E	Emergency/Corrective Maintenance
F	Feature
K	Kit Parent Item
N	Nonstock

Valuation Information

This section describes some of the more important valuation-related information found in the context of the item branch/plant for an item defined in OneWorld.

Costs

OneWorld provides for up to eight cost definitions per item within any given branch/plant record. These definitions include both average cost and last-in-cost buckets. It is also possible to do lot-level or lot by lot costing in OneWorld.

The branch/plant constants establish definitions as to which cost-related field should be used during inventory valuation and in conjunction with inventory transaction processing. These branch/plant constants are used to specify the cost method that OneWorld uses to determine the cost of an item when it is necessary to calculate costs of goods sold or to calculate a purchase order document. For example, weighted average cost might be used to determine both transfer costs between locations as well as an item's cost of goods sold, and the last-in-cost method might be used to cost out purchase orders. Your organization can define additional cost methods using user-defined codes. Note that your organization defines its own cost methods, and that codes 01 through 19 are reserved by J. D. Edwards. In the absence of a cost method, OneWorld assigns a 0 cost method and a 0 cost for the item.

Prices

OneWorld allows the maintenance of multiple base or list prices for any given item within the context of any given branch or plant. In addition, item, item group, and customer-level prices can be established in OneWorld. Note that some item pricing features fall within the domain of OneWorld's Advanced Pricing capabilities, described in Chapter 16. However, these advanced pricing features rely on the maintenance of a base price using the maintenance functions found in the item branch/plant.

Descriptive and Classifying Information

This section describes three methods of defining and classifying item information within OneWorld. These methods include item or part numbers, item or part descriptions, and item classification or grouping using category codes. As a general rule, descriptive text and classifying information is generally defined at the item level within an ERP system.

Item Numbers

OneWorld provides for three item or identifying numbers in the item master. The first item number is typically a sequential next number value assigned by OneWorld. This value is called the *short item number*.

The second item number is a 25-character position alphanumeric value that your organization typically assigns to an item. Generally speaking, this value is an existing item or part number that your organization is already using to describe its items in legacy systems. This value is frequently called a long item number. This is an optional entry. If the second item number is left blank during item setup, OneWorld automatically assigns the short item number as the second item number.

The third item number, labeled Catalog Number on the OneWorld item master form, is also a 25-character alphanumeric value. Again, your organization typically assigns this number to an item. This is also an optional entry. If the third item number is left blank during item setup, OneWorld automatically assigns the short item number as the third item number. Frequent uses of the third item number field include Universal Product Code (UPC) numbers and military specification (MIL-SPEC) part numbers.

The important consideration in part numbering is that although the short, second, or third item number fields might be one and the same for any given item, each item master record in the OneWorld database must have a unique value for each of these three-part number fields. In other words, a part number value across the short, second, or third item number fields cannot be duplicated in OneWorld.

During data entry, OneWorld allows any one of these three numbers to be used when retrieving item-related information when using an identifier character in front of the value entered. These identifying characters are identified to OneWorld during inventory management setup.

Any number of additional or alternative part numbers by item can be established as needed in the item number cross-reference file. Cross-reference types must be predefined and are used to identify different types of item numbers, such as vendor or customer part numbers. These numbers can be used to determine or cross-reference to your organization's assigned OneWorld part number through the use of OneWorld's item cross-reference search program.

Item Descriptions

The OneWorld item master provides for a common, reusable, standard description for every item. Two 30-position item description fields are provided. An entry in the first 30-position item description field is mandatory for every item established in OneWorld. The second 30-position item description field is optional.

Longer descriptions are also possible by creating a user-defined print message field for selected items. The print message associated with a given item can in turn be used on order processing documents, such as sales orders and purchase orders.

Item Search Key Words and Phrases

Optionally, a single 30-position field can be maintained with key values or search words related to any given item. This search word string value can then be used in conjunction with both item and word search capabilities.

Finding Items in OneWorld Using Text

As previously mentioned, OneWorld provides several facilities to assist users in determining or identifying parts by descriptive information instead of by part number. First, using OneWorld's word search capabilities, items can be identified based on text that appears in any of more than 30 item master information fields. Second, the OneWorld item word search capability lets you identify items by the value in the predefined search text in the item master discussed previously.

When using item word search, the system accesses the Item Word Search table (F41829) as the basis for performing a search request. However, the OneWorld search table is not built and maintained on a real-time "as-you-go" basis. The Item Word Build batch program is used to create and update the Item Word Search table. Therefore, it is important to note that when any of the descriptive information is changed in the item master, OneWorld does not automatically update the Item Word Search table. However, the Item Word Build program can be run as often as necessary. For example, your organization might choose to run the program weekly or monthly, depending on the number of changes to descriptions. I recommend that you add this program to the OneWorld Scheduler as a process performed on a daily basis.

Item Classification

There are additional ways to group or identify related items in OneWorld. For instance, it might be desirable to group items by common or shared characteristics. By grouping items in such a manner, it becomes possible to identify, select, and work with an entire group of items at the same time. For example, grouping items for purposes of creating a sales analysis report, such as by product line, is a common practice.

Grouping items in OneWorld requires defining and assigning one or more category code values to each item. This step typically is done when a new item master record is created. The category or classification codes are created on the Item Category Codes tab for either the item master or the branch/plant record. Generally speaking, these values are assigned at the item master level and default to the branch/plant record.

Five types of category codes are available in OneWorld. They can be used as classification codes. The item-related category codes include the following:

◆ Sales category codes

◆ Purchasing category codes

◆ Inventory category codes

◆ Transportation category codes

◆ Warehouse category codes

Figure 14-4 shows the OneWorld tab form used to maintain many of the item-related classification codes.

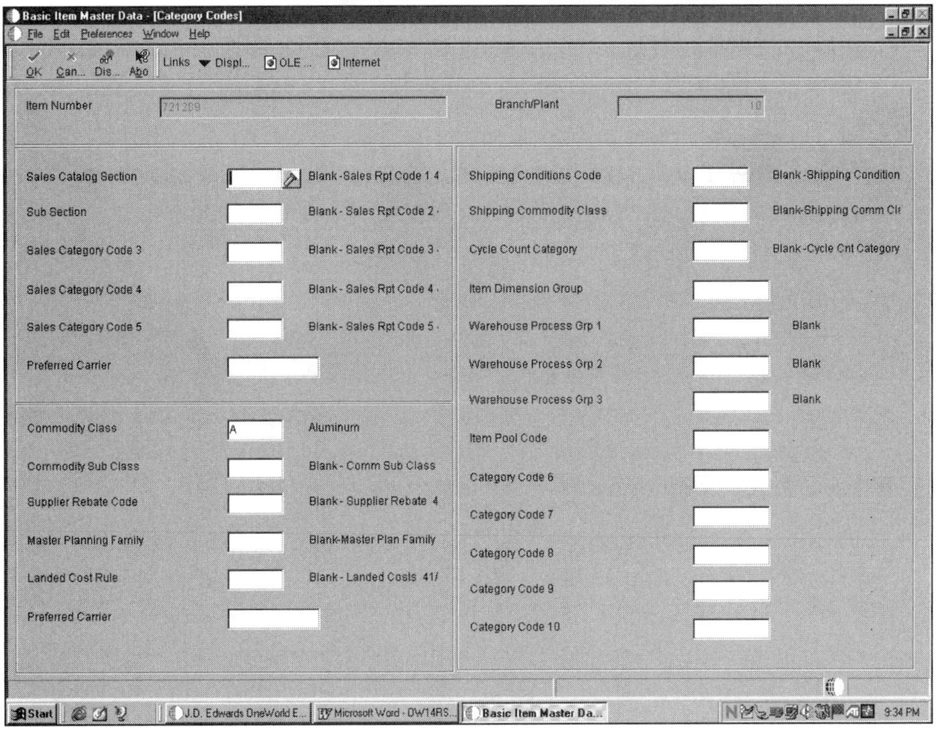

FIGURE 14-4 *Item-Related Category Codes*

Careful and deliberate definition of item-related category codes is needed during your OneWorld implementation. The steps include defining the number of categories or classifications needed (fewer categories are always better) and then establishing the actual values to distinguish each category definition. In addition, it is necessary to understand how these category codes default to transaction documents and on through the system into any related transaction documents. These codes are frequently used as the basis for selecting data during OneWorld program processes.

Item Master Design Strategies

One of the most important tasks you will have in setting up any new ERP system, including OneWorld, is the task of master data design. The best time to tackle data cleansing and standardization is *before* old data corrupts the new system. An old system often becomes unusable because of the database contents, not the system itself. Therefore, item master design is an important consideration in the new ERP system implementation process. This section presents some various strategies for achieving a successful item master design.

Intelligent Versus Nonintelligent Part Numbering Conventions

Arguments abound about the use of intelligent or significant part numbering conventions versus the use of nonintelligent or randomly assigned part numbering conventions. Because many legacy systems lacked the ability to classify items based on shared item properties, such as OneWorld's category codes, structured or intelligent part numbers became commonplace. However, in the current era, intelligent or structured part numbers are largely unnecessary, but old habits die hard, so this form of part numbering remains prevalent.

For instance, the majority of ERP implementations that I have been personally involved with rely on a client's existing part number scheme, which is generally a structured part number. In OneWorld, the legacy part number typically becomes the long or second item number value in the item master. This is, of course, a perfectly reasonable and understandable action and does mitigate some of your implementation risk.

A wholesale renumbering of your existing part numbers might be a business risk that your organization is unwilling to accept. This is a frequent issue, especially when engineering specifications and drawings exist that make use of your existing part numbering scheme.

Although I do not strongly advocate the use of structured part numbers, it is my preference to use separate numbering schemes or number assignment groups for major classes of materials. For example, I prefer separate number ranges for each major material group, such as raw materials versus finished goods, work in process, or consumables, and spare parts when starting anew with part numbers. However, unlike SAP, OneWorld does not systemically support my preference. Therefore, in OneWorld, I generally let sequential next number assignment perform as intended.

Item Naming Conventions

Item naming conventions are almost as controversial as item numbering conventions. Because descriptions are not as significant as item numbers in an automated world, their importance has diminished. Most systems, including OneWorld, force reliance on part numbers over descriptions.

In addition, it is not uncommon to find that an organization maintains two item descriptions. A short description is frequently used for computer-generated screens and reports, while a long description is also maintained. For instance, longer descriptions are frequently used in conjunction with vendor item conformance and certification programs as part of an organization's ISO 9000 quality-management initiative. In OneWorld, the short description is the first description line, and longer descriptions are maintained as item print messages.

Note that I do not advocate the use of longer descriptions, except in cases when a customer might require them. Instead, you should find ways to abbreviate or shorten descriptions when possible. Otherwise, you have signed up for the ongoing and onerous task of maintaining multiple descriptions.

Although I do not strongly advocate the use of structured part numbers, I do strongly advocate the use of an item classification scheme as well as standardized, structured descriptions.

I frequently see examples of bad item descriptions. Misspellings, varying or cryptic abbreviations, formats, and key word placements are commonplace. I have a strong preference for the use of hierarchical, structured descriptions, sometimes called a military-style part description. For instance, a part described as a "25-watt yellow bug light bulb" might be better described as a "Light Bulb—25W—Yellow—Insect Repelling."

I find that OneWorld category codes remain largely reporting codes in my view of things. Characteristic groups for your items can quickly build, especially when tens of thousands of items are involved. In general, I find that SAP has a stronger item classification scheme. However, this scheme can largely be replicated in OneWorld by using the item master supplemental database.

Item numbering, naming, and categorizing design are important steps in any ERP system implementation. Their design must be finalized before master data input is gathered and entered into the new system. Do not take this portion of your OneWorld implementation planning lightly.

Maintaining Item Information

The item master and item branch/plant information are maintained through the Inventory Management system. To create and maintain items in OneWorld, use the Item Revisions menu (G4112). Here is the overall menu path:

> Master Directory (G) > Distribution (G4) > Inventory Management (G41) > Daily Processing (G4110) > Item Revisions (**G4112**)

To create and maintain item cross-references in OneWorld, use the Item Inquiries menu (G41112). Here is the overall menu path:

> Master Directory (G) > Distribution (G4) > Inventory Management (G41) > Daily Processing (G4110) > Inventory Inquiries (**G41112**) > Item Cross Reference

To create and maintain item-related pricing information in OneWorld, use the Price Management menu (G4222). Here is the overall menu path:

> Master Directory (G) > Distribution (G4) > Sales Order Management (G42) > Periodic Processing (G4220) > Price Management (**G4222**)

Although this menu includes the obvious option, Base Price Revisions (P4106), the maintenance of pricing is typically a complex process within most organizations. OneWorld supports numerous pricing options beyond mere maintenance of a base or list price per item through its advanced pricing capabilities. However, the base price record itself is a required record for use by these advanced pricing functions. For instance, items can be priced by customer or item group. Chapter 16 provides additional information regarding item pricing options within OneWorld.

Effective Dating of Item Information Changes

Engineering change notice (ECN) processing capabilities within OneWorld have the ability to control and affect future dated changes to item-related information in both the item master record and the branch/plant record. Chapter 17 provides additional information regarding effective date item updating options through the use of engineering change notices within OneWorld.

Other Important Master Data Files

In addition to the master data files or tables discussed earlier, there are other shared master data tables in OneWorld. This section introduces the fixed asset/equipment master table and the OneWorld supplemental database tables.

Fixed Asset/Equipment Master Records

The OneWorld Fixed Asset accounting system has its own unique item master, called the equipment master. Instead of defining products that are bought, sold, or consumed, this database is used to describe your organization's long-lasting assets that will be capitalized or depreciated over a longer period of time, usually anywhere from 3 to 40 years, depending on generally accepted accounting principles or tax guidelines. As such, its information content varies dramatically from the standard item master data model.

Fixed asset- and equipment-related information is stored in one primary table, the F1201 table. This table stores basic information about each asset, such as

- ◆ Asset number
- ◆ Asset description
- ◆ Account coding
- ◆ Asset-related category codes

In addition to the fixed asset system, other OneWorld applications use the equipment master data model. The other OneWorld systems that rely on the Fixed Asset Item/Equipment Master file include Equipment Billing and Equipment/Plant Maintenance.

OneWorld Supplemental Databases

In addition to the general and required data fields and user-defined category and reporting codes that are maintained in the standard master data tables, it is also possible to define and maintain your organization's other unique data as "supplemental data" in specific OneWorld application systems.

This is made possible through OneWorld's generic supplemental database feature. This generic database provides a standard approach for defining, maintaining, and editing supplemental data for selected OneWorld application systems. These application systems include

- Accounts Payable
- Accounts Receivable
- Address Book
- Equipment and Plant Management
- Fixed Assets
- General Accounting
- Human Resources
- Inventory Management
- Payroll
- Work Order Management

OneWorld includes predefined supplemental databases for each of these systems.

Data types are user-defined codes that are used to organize supplemental data. Data types are determined by the specifics of the information your organization must track. For each user-defined type, OneWorld provides a number of predefined fields that can be used to capture and track information that is unique to your organization and that otherwise would not be included in the OneWorld application database. When working with supplemental data, OneWorld allows for several different display modes, including a narrative format that allows entry of notes.

For additional information about how the supplemental database is used within each of the specific OneWorld application systems, consult the appropriate OneWorld application system reference guides.

Master Data Transformation Planning

Moving master data into OneWorld from legacy systems and even your manual systems—such as travel cards and Rolodexes and business cards—requires considerable planning and considerable attention to detail.

Generally speaking, organizational and chart of accounts information is not a significant conversion issue given OneWorld's account coding structure and the availability of a cross-reference to and the ability to use a legacy system account number within a OneWorld transaction. However, name and address information, as well as item-related information, are quite another issue. Frequently, such master data is scattered, out of date, unstructured, or maintained in multiple systems with little relationship between systems. Sometimes it is simply unavailable due to a lack of sophistication in prior processes.

Overall Category or Reporting Code and User Defined Code design is another significant, high-impact area that requires careful analysis of how and when OneWorld master data records default this information into the transactions created by other OneWorld programs. Many legacy processes likely include both hard-coded and soft-coded tables that must be reviewed and migrated into the appropriate equivalents. This step should be completed *before* commencing with the entry of master data into your OneWorld production environment.

Migrating from one or more legacy systems to OneWorld is an excellent time to complete a data quality audit in order to identify, cleanse, and purge obsolete master data information. In order to cleanse data properly, your organization should engage in a complementary data standardization effort. This effort should develop standards for part numbering, naming, and classification schemes. In addition, name and address standards should be developed and implemented.

The OneWorld development tool supports your organization's data migration efforts through the use of table conversions used for organizational, account number, and item information conversions and the batch input processor for Address Book information conversion.

Summary

This chapter introduced the OneWorld foundation systems. These foundation systems are the repository for essential master data records that are used by other OneWorld application systems. The OneWorld foundation systems discussed in this chapter included

- ◆ The Address Book system
- ◆ The chart of accounts portion of the General Accounting system
- ◆ The item master portion of the Inventory Management system

Additional common or shared master data elements are defined in

- The OneWorld back office
- The Product Data Management system

The back office portions of OneWorld represent the many configuration-related tables in OneWorld, while the Product Data Management system provides a repository for manufacturing-related information. In turn, other OneWorld application systems also rely on these two additional OneWorld foundation systems.

OneWorld makes extensive use of master data for default values, thereby minimizing data entry on transactions. In addition, OneWorld provides for numerous user-defined category or reporting codes. When properly configured, many of OneWorld's individual application systems use these user-defined category or reporting codes to classify, sort, and report on OneWorld transactions.

By using OneWorld's predefined supplemental databases for certain applications, you can store other information that is unique to your organization, thereby filling in any master data gaps.

Finally, master data design and standardization and migration into OneWorld is a significant task that can't be underestimated. It requires careful planning and attention to detail.

Chapter 15

This chapter introduces the OneWorld Financial systems. The OneWorld Financial systems require the least amount of effort from the standpoint of software configuration and implementation planning. The OneWorld Financial modules include

◆ Address Book
◆ Accounts Receivable
◆ Accounts Payable
◆ General Accounting

The additional OneWorld Financial applications that are frequently implemented include

◆ Fixed Assets
◆ Job Cost Accounting

Financial reporting and financial modeling functionality, including facilities for budgeting and allocations, is considered a part of the General Accounting module. These latter functions are implemented to varying degrees by any given organization based on its overall business needs and business model complexity.

I find that many organizations, especially multinationals and holding companies, use other tools for consolidations and financial statement preparation as well as for short- and long-range budget and forecast preparation. Therefore, although I find the financial reporting capabilities in OneWorld somewhat unimpressive, they are often good enough given that the financial reporting focus is limited to the trial balance with respect to an ERP system.

Less frequently implemented is the OneWorld multicurrency accounting module. It has been my experience that many companies with ERP systems that are capable of multicurrency operation typically operate their ERP system in "single currency" mode. I have found that many multinational organizations maintain separate sales and distribution facilities for each country. Each such operation represents a "wholly owned" or "joint venture" subsidiary and generally maintains its own set of books and in turn reports its results to the parent for consolidation and translation.

Finally, it has been my experience that financial-related applications are typically implemented first in the schema for most ERP implementations. In addition, most organizations do not implement the full complement of remaining ERP system application modules, except for those within the Financial suite of applications. These observations apply equally to both J. D. Edwards-based and non-J. D. Edwards-based ERP implementations. For instance, as a consultant, I have been frequently engaged to help organizations "fast track" the implementation of their new ERP system, including World and OneWorld software.

I should also point out that the core Financial systems—Address Book, General Accounting, and Accounts Payable—were among the first systems to be ported from the J. D. Edwards' World software environment and made available in the OneWorld software environment. However, the OneWorld Accounts Receivable system represents a design departure from World software and therefore cannot coexist with OneWorld.

General Accounting

In addition to managing the chart of accounts and organizational structure that defines your organization to OneWorld, the General Accounting system performs basic double-entry bookkeeping tasks. For most organizations that adopt OneWorld, its complete integration of the general ledger with all other business processes can eliminate virtually all error-prone, highly repetitive hand postings to the general ledger. This section discusses the significant accounting features of the OneWorld General Accounting system. For a discussion of the OneWorld chart of accounts and organizational structure, refer to the preceding chapter.

The Data Model

The data model of the General Accounting system is rather simple. OneWorld maintains three essential files in the General Accounting system:

- The Account Balance file (F0902)
- The Transaction Detail file (F0911)
- The Batch Header file (F0011)

In addition to these files, the General Accounting system is used to maintain the chart of account-related files that were discussed in the preceding chapter.

The Account Balance File

OneWorld maintains multiple account balance records, by account ID, fiscal year, and ledger type. Maintaining account balances by fiscal year greatly simplifies both the period and year-end close process in OneWorld. Given that transaction detail is posted into the account balance file, the transaction detail of previous fiscal years can be removed. However, account balances of prior years can be retained for comparative reporting purposes.

The Transaction Detail File

In OneWorld, journal entries are written to the Transaction Detail file. Initially, all transactions that are entered into the transaction detail file are written in an "unposted" state. This means that the individual account balance records contained in the account balance file do not reflect the account-by-account debit/credit activity for the transaction.

The Batch Header File

A batch consists of one or more related journal entries in OneWorld. Given that transaction detail records are initially written in an unposted state, a special batch process is initiated on demand to post the account-by-account debit/credit activity represented by the transaction against the individual account balance records contained in the account balance file. The batch header file controls the posting state of a batch. Also note that as each record is posted to the account balance file, the posting status is updated on each transaction record.

Important General Accounting Features

The OneWorld General Accounting system has numerous features. This section introduces the most significant ones.

General Accounting Setup

In addition to the organizational and chart of account setup, a series of general ledger constants must be established. Most of these constants relate to using one or more of the many features discussed in the following sections.

Fiscal Date Patterns

In OneWorld, the company definition is also the location where a company's fiscal year is defined in the system. OneWorld supports 12-, 13-, and 14-period fiscal years. It is also possible to use a 52-week fiscal year, but it has been my experience that use of this feature is not extensive. The fiscal year pattern is user-defined insofar as the starting date of the fiscal year and the fiscal period ending dates. Note that fiscal years can be established in advance, in order to support future dated transactions, such as fixed asset accounting entries. The fiscal date pattern also establishes the date-checking parameters for any transaction that has general ledger impact.

Ledger Types

Multiple ledger types are maintained in OneWorld. For instance, one ledger type—the AA ledger type—is used to represent actual financial results. Budget information is maintained in a separate ledger type, the BA ledger type. Other ledger types are also possible. For instance, if encumbrance accounting is used, the PA ledger is used to record purchasing commitments.

Levels of Detail

In OneWorld, financial reporting rollups are facilitated through the Level of Detail (LOD) setting related to each account number. The Level of Detail is maintained in the account definition within the chart of accounts. If an account is created at a higher level and does not allow transaction posting, it is said to be a rollup or summary-level account. The use of the Level of Detail setting on an account is an important consideration when designing the basic financial reports that will be produced from OneWorld. The following hierarchy should be followed with respect to the Level of Detail settings for your accounts:

- ◆ Level 1 represents the Company level.
- ◆ Level 2 represents the Business Unit level.
- ◆ Levels 3 through 7 represent the Object Account level.
- ◆ Levels 8 and 9 are reserved for use with the Job Cost (Project Accounting) system.

If your organization will not use the Job Cost system, levels 8 and 9 can be used to extend the Object Account level of detail range.

Multi-Company Accounting

If your organizational structure is complex, involving multiple companies or balance sheets, any transactions between companies or balance sheets will be out of balance unless an intercompany balancing, or settlement, entry is created. An intercompany settlement or balancing entry can be created automatically by OneWorld when a transaction occurs between two or more OneWorld companies. This settlement entry ensures that each company's net balance is 0. OneWorld supports two methods of multi-company accounting: the *hub* method and the *detail* method.

The hub method is more frequently used and results in a summary-level transaction at the batch level for the intercompany settlement. As the name implies, one company is designated as the hub company, through which transactions between the subsidiary companies must flow.

The detail method creates, as its name implies, detailed journal entries between companies. No summarization to a hub or clearing company occurs—all transactions are between companies. The detail method requires more transactions to achieve the same result. The detail method produces a clearly stated audit trial in that intercompany settlements appear as stand-alone balanced journal entries in the transaction ledger. This technique is commonly used by government entities, which typically maintain and operate separate, legally chartered entities such as water districts, sewer treatment districts, school districts, and park districts. In these cases, funds cannot be comingled between entities. Also note that OneWorld requires use of the detail method for intercompany settlements if transactions between companies are denominated in different currencies.

Both the hub and detailed methods rely on automatic accounting instructions to create the journal entries necessary for the intercompany settlement. Regardless of accounting method, each company involved in the intercompany settlement has an automatic offset to the appropriate intercompany account. The intercompany accounting process in OneWorld relies on subledger accounting. The system uses the subledger field to indicate the Address Book number of the other company involved in the intercompany transaction. Therefore, all companies must be set up in the Address Book system. The company number is used as the Address Book number for the company.

Multi-Currency Accounting

If your organization has business operations in more than one country, your organization currently works with multiple currencies. Therefore, you might elect to set up and use the multi-currency accounting features provided in OneWorld. Use of multi-currency accounting has significant ramifications.

Each company must have a designated operating currency, called the *domestic* currency. In addition, a single currency is designated as the *common* or *reporting* currency. The base currency is generally the domestic or operating currency of the parent company. When working with multiple currencies, it is necessary for financial reporting purposes to "restate" foreign currencies in terms of the base currency.

There are two kinds of transaction-level accounts in multi-currency accounting: monetary and nonmonetary. Generally speaking, your organization will want to record transactions in any currency for any given account. However, certain accounts, such as those representing bank accounts denominated in specific currencies, are designated as monetary accounts. An account is designated as a monetary account by assigning a currency code in the account's definition.

Financial account balances are typically restated on a period-end basis into the parent company operating currency. In OneWorld, currency restatement is based on exchange rates maintained by effective dates. Currency restatements are subsequently made against a restatement ledger type.

Euro Support

The *Euro* is the new single currency for Europe. The majority of the European Union (EU) countries have begun adopting this new currency over the past two years. The intent of the Euro is to achieve a single market and provide for an economic basin that is on a more even keel with the United States. In theory, this interlocking of economies should help promote political and economic stability and tariff-free trading and allow the whole of Europe to compete in the global economy.

Currently, the Euro exists on a noncash basis. However, beginning in 2002, Euro coins and currency will appear. The Euro itself is divided into 100 cents, much like the U.S. dollar. At the present time, the central banks of Europe are using the Euro. Although the Euro has gotten off to a rocky start in currency markets, the longer-term objectives behind the economic and monetary union of European nations remain fundamentally sound.

The impact of the Euro on most organizations and their transaction processing systems—such as OneWorld—is twofold. First, organizations operating in Europe must begin adopting the Euro, in "book form" as a reporting currency. This is called the Euro transition period. Therefore, during this transition period, a typical multinational company located in the United States might need to convert or restate its account balances from the operating currency of a specific country where it operates subsidiaries, such as Spain or France, into the Euro and ultimately into the U.S. dollar.

Second and ultimately, organizations operating in Europe will negotiate all business transactions in the Euro as the currency itself becomes available. Thereafter, the same multinational company will only need to restate its balances from the Euro into the U.S. dollar. The Euro phase-in will be complete on July 1, 2002, when the Euro will represent the sole legal tender of the participating European countries.

J. D. Edwards has provided for both transition and post-transition support of the Euro. For further information, consult the OneWorld documentation CD-ROM, which includes a special Euro implementation guide.

Journal Entries

The journal entry is the fundamental transaction in the now centuries-old and universally adopted double-entry accounting system. A journal entry consists of at least two entries to specific general ledger accounts: at least one debit entry and at least one credit, or offsetting, entry. In other words, the total of the debit entries within any given journal entry must total the sum of the credit entries, resulting in a net balance of 0 for the transaction. This is called a *balanced* journal entry.

OneWorld provides two formats for the creation of journal entries. The first format is a single-column entry method. When this format is employed, all credits are entered with a minus sign. The second format is a double-column format in the familiar T account. Debit amounts are entered in the first column, and credit amounts are entered in the second column. The minus sign is not used with the double-column format. The single-column format is more suitable in a high-volume data entry environment. Hopefully, given OneWorld's integration with its other modules, manual journal entries will not be significant in your general ledger environment.

Reversing Journal Entries

OneWorld provides a *reversing entry* transaction. When a journal entry is flagged as a reversing entry, a second journal entry occurs. This second journal entry is set up with a general ledger date as the first day in the next fiscal period, meaning that the original transaction is automatically reversed on the first day of the next period. Note that the second transaction does not automatically post. It must be posted just like any other journal entry.

Model Journal Entries

Model journal entries can be created, stored, and reused within OneWorld. Model journal entries have many applications. The allocation of occupancy costs based on the square footage consumed by each department is such an example. In addition, model journal entries can be applied either to the accounts receivable invoice distribution for revenue booking or to an accounts payable voucher for an expense-related distribution. For instance, a model journal entry could be established and used to distribute the contents of an expense report to accelerate expense reimbursement payments.

Journal Entry Revisions

In OneWorld, any unposted journal entry can be revised or even deleted. However, once a journal entry is posted, it cannot be deleted. Deleting a previously posted journal entry would violate the integrity of the audit trail. Therefore, a posted journal entry must be *voided.* When a journal entry is voided, an identical transaction is created, with signs reversed. Note that a "reversing journal entry" and "voiding or reversing" a journal entry are two fundamentally different transactions for an accountant and should not be confused.

The Batch Post Process

OneWorld provides an enterprise-wide platform to efficiently manage, on an up-to-the-minute basis and in real time, the information necessary to conduct your business operations. This includes managing information related to a diverse number of activities, including the processes of buying materials from suppliers, paying for them, manufacturing products, selling products, and receiving payments from customers.

However, one aspect of OneWorld is not necessarily real-time—and this is by design. Although OneWorld is considered an online, integrated, enterprise-wide system, it is not real-time with respect to the General Accounting system or financial reporting purposes. For instance, subsystem activities are not immediately reflected in an account balance. For purposes of this discussion, any system that affects a general ledger account is called a *subsystem.* For example, the Accounts Receivable and Accounts Payable systems are considered subsystems.

The OneWorld general ledger is not immediately updated by subsystem journal entry transactions or upon completion of a manual journal entry. Instead,

OneWorld employs a *batch post* process to update the account balance file. Therefore, these journal entries are read on an after-the-fact basis and are posted to the account balance file through a special update program.

Batch posting allows the accountant to control and review the flow of transactions from subsystems into the general ledger and ultimately onto financial reports. Transaction-related errors can be detected and corrected before they have a financial impact under a batch post arrangement. This time-proven technique of providing systems auditability and control has been employed by J. D. Edwards for many years throughout its World and OneWorld software product lines.

Increasingly, a "real-time" post is becoming desirable to meet the ever-increasing interest in the "virtual" close instead of simply a monthly close of the books. OneWorld software addresses this need through the use of either automatically triggered general ledger batch posts (such as a result of a successful sales update or check run batch process) or through daily or scheduled batch postings of all unposted batches in the general system. However, this is an overly simplistic approach to the virtual close concept. Numerous other "matching" issues likely must be addressed using allocations based on business flow assumptions that likely are also necessary.

In OneWorld, general ledger journal entries are created by batch. A batch is typically made of up related journal entries, such as all the transactions entered or created at the same time, or all the transactions of a given type that were entered or created within a subsystem at the same time. When a batch is created or saved, it is saved in an unposted state.

Note that for each OneWorld journal entry line, a posting status is maintained. When posting occurs, the account balance is updated from an unposted to a posted state. The posting status at the journal entry line level is intended to prevent duplicate postings, should a batch require reposting. Reposting batches is discussed later in this section. Figure 15-1 illustrates the OneWorld batch post process.

After posting journal entry batches, it is a recommended best practice to ensure that the batch post process completed successfully. The post program creates an audit trail within OneWorld as to the batch's posting status. This audit trail includes

◆ One or more workflow messages

◆ The General Ledger Posting report

◆ The General Ledger Posting error report. Note that this report is produced on an as-needed basis.

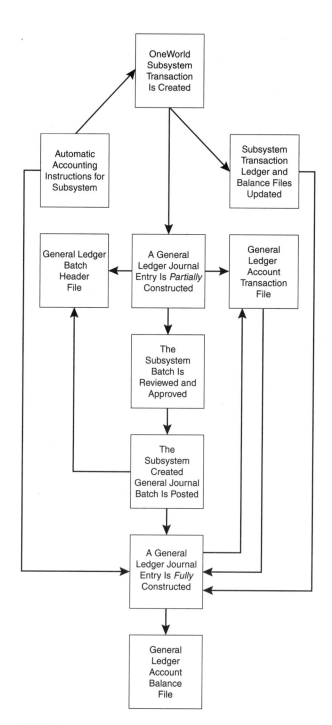

FIGURE 15-1 *The OneWorld Batch Post Process*

As a general rule, the batch status is usually determined from a review of the General Ledger Posting report. If the batch posted successfully, this report provides details about the posted batch, such as the journal entry number, accounts affected, and the debit and credit entries made to each account. This report is typically retained as a record of the entries posted to the general ledger.

Although the post program might have completed successfully, the batch itself still might not be posted. Typically, if the batch does not post, an error message appears on the General Ledger Posting report instead of the usual details about the posted batch. In addition to this message, in most cases a General Ledger Posting error report is also generated. A General Ledger Posting error report provides more detailed information regarding why the batch failed to post. When a batch does not post, the errors must be found and corrected, the batch status must be changed to approved, and the batch must be reposted.

If the General Ledger Posting Report or the General Ledger Posting Error Report was not produced for a batch (or cannot be found), this typically indicates that something went wrong with the post program—the equivalent of a plane crash. The aircraft flight data recorder equivalent in OneWorld's batch posting process is called *workflow messaging*. After a batch post job completes processing, the post program sends one or more workflow messages to the Employee Work Center for every batch post performed. If the Post program completes all processing steps normally, a "batch processing completed normally" notification message is provided.

If the post program does not complete normally, one or more error messages are generated. Typically, one error-related message provides notification that a job failed, and additional messages typically provide more detailed information about the errors encountered during the posting process.

Batch Control

An optional feature is the use of batch control. Batch control is activated from the General Accounting Constants Setup form, found on menu G0941. If batch control is used, a batch control dollar amount is entered before a manual journal entry session commences. When journal entries are completed—that is, upon exit from the Journal Entry form—the journal entries that were entered in the batch must total the previously entered batch control amount. Also note that each journal entry within a batch must be balanced in that debit entries must equal credit entries in the batch.

Note that batch control can also be activated separately for the Accounts Payable and Accounts Receivable systems. Generally speaking, batch control over Accounts Payable and Accounts Receivable is desirable, but not necessarily over general ledger transactions.

Batch Approval

Batch approval is another option that can be activated. Batch approval is activated from the General Accounting Constants Setup form. Batches can be saved in an "unapproved" state. Each batch must then be specifically reviewed and approved before it can be posted to the general ledger. Generally speaking, batch approval is a desirable control mechanism. Batch contents can be verified for "reasonability" before they are posted to the general ledger. However, note that in high-volume environments, use of batch review and approval may prove unwieldy.

Batch Types

OneWorld has numerous journal entry batch types. A batch represents a group of related journal entries that must be posted to the general ledger. Batch types differ by OneWorld system. Certain subsystems in OneWorld produce more than one type of batch. Therefore, the batch type identifies both the subsystem that created the journal entries and the type of batch. Table 15-1 identifies many of the important batch types in OneWorld. For each type of journal entry batch, a batch-specific batch posting program version and a special review/approval interactive form must be used. In other words, batches are posted from within the subsystem that created them.

Table 15-1 OneWorld Batch Types

Batch Type	Batch Origination/Content
0	Manufacturing
E	Fixed Assets/Asset Transfer
G	General Accounting
I	Invoice Entry
K	Accounts Payable/Checks
M	Accounts Payable/Manual and Void Checks
N	Inventory

Table 15-1 OneWorld Batch Types *(continued)*

Batch Type	Batch Origination/Content
O	Purchasing/Receipts
R	Cash Receipts and Adjustments
S	Stock Transfers
W	Manual Checks without Match
X	Fixed Assets/Depreciation
Z	Fixed Assets/Disposals

Achieving the Virtual Close

Organizations are increasingly interested in shortening (in some cases, dramatically) the monthly accounting close. In the last few years, the accounting and finance professions have frequently discussed the term "virtual close." ERP systems, such as OneWorld, bring the concept of a virtual close into a much more realistic perspective. Their tight integration between business processing systems and the general ledger makes the concept of a virtual close much more feasible.

For OneWorld users, achieving a virtual close really means circumventing much of the traditional batch review and post process. In OneWorld, much of the batch review and post process can be circumvented. This is made possible through processing options related to individual programs, such as the Payment Status Update program in Accounts Payable or the Sales Order Update program found in Sales Order Management. These batch processes can initiate a general ledger batch post program to execute following completion of the subsystem update process. In addition, the OneWorld scheduler can be used to "post" all other unposted general ledger batches on an overnight basis. For instance, inventory-related transactions can be posted to the general ledger prior to the beginning of each business day, or possibly several times throughout the course of a business day. Therefore, it is certainly possible to "automate" virtually all of the necessary general ledger postings within OneWorld.

Posting Out of Balance

OneWorld allows a batch to be posted "out of balance." For instance, budget journal entries are typically entered as "one-sided" entries. In addition, system integrity might identify a partially unposted batch. The batch posting can be completed if the remaining contents are printed using the post out of balance flag. A cautionary note applies here. Although you have the ability to post batches out of balance, in practice this feature is rarely used. Its typical use is strictly for posting budgets or to correct an integrity error caused by a partially unposted batch.

Posting to Another Financial Period

OneWorld allows journal entries to be posted to both past and future periods, including to a prior year. For good reason, some extra effort is required in order to post a batch to a prior period or prior year. In addition, if posting to a prior year, the year-end close must usually be rerun in order to correct the prior year-ending balance-forward amount in the account balance file.

Although in theory OneWorld allows postings to previous periods, as a standard business procedure, this might not be desirable. In practice, you likely won't have many instances where you will want to allow this after your period is considered closed. For instance, if the change will not impact profit and loss at the external reporting level, such as the usage of a wrong expense account or cost center within the context of the same rollup, the change may be easily made. However, correction of an error through a subsequent period journal entry is the more conservative approach—and the one that my accounting training would suggest that I would typically employ.

In short, *carefully* control your postings to previous periods. Also note that unresolved integrity errors can cause cross-period errors. Integrity reports ensure (among other things) that OneWorld itself is in balance. The potential for this type of problem makes a persuasive case for running integrity reports as an essential step in your organization's routine month-end closing process. Integrity reports are discussed in a moment, in the section "System Integrity."

Prior Period Entries

To post a transaction in a prior period, you must change the General Ledger date to the desired period and then post the transaction to that period. Note that the date should be changed back to the current period immediately after you post the batch to a prior period. Creating a transaction for a prior period requires opening the prior period first. Then the entry is made into the prior period. Thereafter, the batch can be posted.

Understanding Date Posting Errors

Most general ledger date-related errors are detected and corrected during normal transaction entry. OneWorld has eight major calendars, or processing period settings:

- ◆ The General Accounting date
- ◆ The Accounts Payable date
- ◆ The Accounts Receivable date
- ◆ The Financial Reporting date
- ◆ The Inventory Management System date
- ◆ The Shop Floor or Factory Calendar
- ◆ Payroll pay period definitions
- ◆ Payroll holidays

Of these, the first five dates have an impact on the general ledger. The general ledger or G/L date is the date that identifies to which period a transaction should be posted. Generally speaking, the G/L date is the current period or month. OneWorld uses the G/L date value in determining if a transaction can be posted. Transactions can be posted to the current period or to the next period in OneWorld.

PACO, WACO, PBCO, and PYEB

When a transaction has a future date beyond this two-month horizon, a PACO (Posting After Cut-Off) error occurs. When a transaction has a future date that falls in the next or a subsequent fiscal year, a WACO (posting Way After Cut-Off) error occurs. These two errors create "soft" errors or warnings. In general, for any OneWorld warning message, you should click on OK (or press Enter) a second time on the transaction entry form; transaction processing should then proceed.

When a transaction has a prior period date, no grace period is allowed for posting purposes. Therefore, the error message received will be a "hard" error. The transaction can't be completed or saved until the period is changed. A PBCO (Posting Before Cut-Off) error occurs when you attempt to post a transaction to a closed period within the current fiscal year. A PYEB (Prior Year Ending Balance) error occurs when you attempt to post a transaction to a closed fiscal year.

Batch Revisions

Many of the same rules apply to batches that apply to journal entries. For instance, an unposted batch can be revised or voided. Also note that a posted batch can be reversed. Batch revisions are also made to repair a damaged batch. A batch is damaged when the posting process is not completed. Posting errors are discussed in the next section.

System Integrity

The batch posting process introduced in the previous section helps ensure the accuracy of your database in another way—through the verification of the subsystem detail against general ledger system balances. This verification process is called *system integrity* in OneWorld. This section introduces the concept of system integrity in OneWorld.

How Subsystems Interact with General Accounting

Recall that although OneWorld is considered an online, real-time, integrated system, the "integration" to the general ledger does not occur in real time. Although a subsystem to the General Accounting system, such as the Accounts Payable or Inventory Management system, creates its own transactions in real time and updates its own subsystem balances in real time, the associated journal entries are not fully created, nor are they posted in real time.

As subsystem-created batches of journal entries are posted to the general ledger, the "missing pieces" required to form a balanced journal entry must be constructed. These journal entries are constructed through the use of the automatic accounting instructions that are specific to a given subsystem.

In the normal course of business, general journal batches are approved and posted on a daily basis. For example, here are several key subsystem general ledger postings that must be completed, usually as a part of your organization's daily processing:

◆ The posting of purchase order receipts

◆ The posting of invoices matched to purchase order receipts

◆ The posting of cash receipts posted against customer balances

In a number of cases, OneWorld program processing options can be used to initiate these batch post processes automatically, as a follow-on process to another OneWorld batch or interactive process.

Batch Posting Errors

When a batch is submitted for posting to the General Accounting system, a series of preposting edit checks are made to ensure the following:

- Each journal entry line references valid accounting codes, such as a valid business unit and a valid object account number. In addition, both the business unit and object account must allow journal entry postings.

- Each journal entry line references a general ledger date that is currently valid for posting purposes.

- Each journal entry line references a valid general ledger category code or automatic instruction code in order for the post program to determine an offset account when completing the "missing" or automatic balancing portion of a journal entry.

Batches found to have errors are not posted. When a batch error is noted, it should be corrected. When a batch has an error, the batch posting status is noted as "in process" or "error."

The first step in correcting any batch-level error is to review the batch for any obvious errors. When a batch fails to post, an error report is usually produced. If the posting report (R09801) for the batch is blank, it will usually state that "one or more batches had errors." This error message on the first report generally means that a *second* report exists. The second error report is the batch out of balance and posting error report (R09801E). Generally speaking, this second report will contain sufficient information for you to diagnose and correct the error. Note that when a batch error report is generated, the posting process has usually completed in its entirety. However, in a batch that has errors, no part of the transaction is posted. I have seen instances where this second error report is not generated. In such cases, a careful review of the system constants, the chart of accounts, and the detailed contents of a batch usually reveals the nature of the problem. Also, refer to the Employee Work Center to determine whether any error messages related to the batch post job were sent to this queue.

The second step in resolving a batch error is to correct the problem. The third step is to change the batch status to approved for posting. Finally, post the errant batch again. If you have resolved all the errors successfully, the batch should post.

A final note: A batch that has encountered errors during the posting process is not itself a violation of OneWorld system integrity, because many user errors can result in a batch's not posting. Integrity errors are usually caused by batch posting job failures or cancellations.

Damaged Batches

A batch is referred to as *damaged* when the posting process is not completed for the batch. The posting process usually *does not* complete when one of the following situations occurs:

- A hardware failure or software error occurred.
- Someone terminated the batch process before it completely posted the batch.
- An attempt was made to run more than one batch posting process simultaneously.

It is entirely possible that a portion of the transactions in a batch posted and the remaining portion of transactions remains in the general ledger transaction file as an unposted transaction. Correcting a batch posting error when some of the transactions are found "unposted" requires reposting the batch out of balance.

When a batch contains errors, a batch error report is generally produced. If it's available, review the associated batch posting report, discussed earlier. Correct any obvious errors and repost the batch. Obvious errors include an incorrect G/L date, use of a nonposting account, or an out of balance entry. Note that it is possible to exit from a batch entry form on an out-of-balance basis.

Generally speaking, when a job fails, an error message is generated and sent to the job-related messages queue. These messages are reviewed through the Employee Work Center form. Here is the menu path to access this form:

> Master Directory (G) > Foundation Systems (G0) > Workflow Management (**G02**) > Employee Work Center > *Submitted Jobs*

However, when a hardware failure occurs, no such message is generally created. Hardware failures are usually obvious, unless your system operates unattended for part of the business day, such as in the evening and overnight for batch processing.

As a general business practice, your system administrator should review system logs on a daily basis to determine if any anomaly, such as a power-down and restart, occurred. The system administrator should then run (or alert others to run) the various OneWorld integrity reports discussed later in this chapter. In addition, he should be sure to review the status of any Scheduler jobs to determine if they completed or failed and whether they must be rerun.

Batch Header Revisions

As previously mentioned, once a batch is posted and an error is detected, the batch status is changed to "error." To repost a batch after errors are corrected or to repost a damaged batch, batch header revisions are necessary. The batch status must be revised to approved/ready-to-post status through use of the Batch Header Revisions form. Here is the menu path to access this form:

> Master Directory (G) > Financials (G1) > General Accounting (G09) > Advanced and Technical Operations (**G0931**) > *Batch Header Revisions* > Row > Revise (Change Batch Status here) > *Overrides* (Allow Out of Balance Post here)

In general, carefully control when, why, and who may change batches or post batches out of balance by carefully controlling access to the Batch Header Revisions form.

Where There's Smoke, There's Fire!

As previously mentioned, a batch posting error alone usually does not imply that an integrity problem exists within your OneWorld system. However, the batch post process also performs a series of batch-level checks. These checks are intended to ensure the following:

◆ The batch itself is in balance. This is true when the debit and credit journal entries within the batch total 0.

◆ The batch is complete. Completeness implies that all transaction-produced journal entries are present within a given batch. This process is known as batch control. Batch control must be activated in setup for this test to work successfully. However, it has been my experience that many organizations do not use batch control.

As a general rule, if a batch fails a batch-level edit check, this usually foretells of an integrity error. When a batch-level error is detected, it is a good practice to consider running integrity reports as soon as practical thereafter.

When a batch integrity error occurs, this is usually a telltale sign that one or more other integrity issues might exist in OneWorld. Also note that a batch error might mean that other errors exist. OneWorld provides a series of integrity reports to help ensure that the general ledger account balances are correct. Integrity reports are also available to help ensure that subsystems are in balance with the general ledger.

Why Integrity Checking Is Necessary

There are a number of reasons why integrity checks are necessary. The most important reason is to ensure that debit and credit entries are in balance between the subsystem ledger and the transactions presented to the general ledger. This process is known as transaction matching and balancing.

Resolving integrity errors is essential to the overall integrity of your OneWorld system and ultimately to the reliability of your organization's financial reports that are produced by OneWorld. Failure to catch integrity errors can result in cross-period errors. Research all integrity errors by first running the reports, in the order given, and then analyzing the batch and transaction contents. Typically, integrity errors occur when parts of the transaction are missing. As previously discussed, part of the transaction is posted, but another part might not be.

Integrity tests are typically done at the end of an accounting period for the simple reason that you want everything in balance before you close the books. As previously mentioned, it is always desirable to perform integrity tests after any system failure.

Before executing any integrity-related batch processes, approve and post all journal entry batches in the normal course of business. Note that batch integrity reports are typically long-running processes and should be done during nonbusiness hours. It is not necessary to run all subsystem integrity reports at the same time, and it is only necessary that integrity reports be executed for the subsystems that are actually in use at your organization. For example, if your organization does not perform intercompany accounting, those reports would not apply.

Table 15-2 lists the integrity reports found in OneWorld, by subsystem. Generally speaking, these reports should be run in the sequence noted. Report sequence is critical for integrity reports because some of the reports *resolve* errors, shortening the remaining reports, and other reports *mask* errors from a series of remaining reports if they are run out of sequence.

Integrity reports are found on the respective Advanced and Technical Operations menu for each subsystem noted. The reports might not appear in the order in which they should be run on these menus. As errors are found and corrected, the reports need to be rerun to verify that errors have been resolved.

Table 15-2 OneWorld General Accounting-Related Integrity Reports

Report Number	Report Title	Menu Number
R007011	Unposted Batches	G0922
R007031	Batches Out of Balance	G0922
R007021	Transactions to Batches	G0922
R09706	Company with Batch Out of Balance	G0922
R097001	Companies in Balance	G0922
R097011	Inter-Company Accounts in Balance	G0922
R097041	Account w/o Business Unit	G0922
R097031	Account Balance w/o Account Master	G0922
R097021	Transactions w/o Account Master	G0922
R09705	Account Balance to Transactions	G09322
R099102	Repost Account Ledger	G09316
R04701	A/P Original Document to G/L	G0421
R04702A	A/P Payments to G/L	G0421
R047001A	A/P to G/L by Offset	G0421
R03B701	A/R Original Document to G/L	G03B21
R03B702	A/R Receipts to G/L	G03B21
R03B7001A/R03B707	A/R to G/L by Offset	G03B21
R127011	Fixed Assets to G/L	G1224
R12301	Unposted Fixed Assets	G1224
R127012	Fixed Assets Transaction Integrity	G1224
R127013	G/L to Fixed Assets Integrity	G1224
R41543	Item Ledger to Account Integrity	G41111
R41544	Item Balance to Ledger Integrity	G41111

As previously noted, unresolved integrity errors can cause cross-period errors. This is why running integrity reports on a period-end basis should be an essential step in the accounting close—to ensure that OneWorld itself is in balance.

J. D. Edwards has published a series of white papers regarding system integrity. These white papers can be found in the Knowledge Garden on the J. D. Edwards Web site.

Online Account Reconciliation

OneWorld includes an online account reconciliation feature. This feature is frequently used for the purpose of reconciling monthly bank statements with the accounts payable check register and accounts receivable cash receipts ledger. Another application of this OneWorld feature is the reconciliation of any suspense accounts and cash advance accounts that your organization may use.

A one-time setup process is required *for each account* to be reconciled through this process. The online account reconciliation setup includes the following:

◆ Creation of an automatic accounting instruction. This instruction tells OneWorld to copy journal entries for the subject account into a work file for reconciliation purposes.

◆ Creation of a version to mark all previous transactions as reconciled; otherwise, this step must be done manually.

◆ Menu changes must be made. It is necessary to create a menu entry for *each* specific account reconcilement.

Once set up, the online account reconciliation process requires that

◆ All batches to be considered are posted.

◆ The reconciliation work file is then refreshed.

◆ The reconciliation interactive form is then used to review and, where appropriate, "check off" all entries as reconciled.

Optionally, OneWorld can receive reconciling items through an interface. The batch process interfaces were discussed in Chapter 13.

Financial Reporting

OneWorld includes a number of standard financial reports and online inquiries. The standard inquiries include an online trial balance, an account ledger inquiry, and a consolidations inquiry form. OneWorld provides a number of standard reports, including a comparative balance sheet, a comparative income statement format, a trial balance, and an account journal or ledger detail report. In addition, OneWorld also includes excellent capabilities to perform online consolidated financial reporting.

Although OneWorld financial reports are generally adequate, it is not uncommon to find that complex financial reporting requirements require more than is available or possible within the scope of the standard delivered reports. For instance, OneWorld *does not* provide a predefined Statement of Cash Flows statement format.

Several options are available to organizations requiring more complex or flexible financial reporting capabilities than are included within OneWorld. Several tools can be used to analyze and report on financial information contained within the OneWorld database, including the following:

◆ The OneWorld Enterprise Report Writer. The Enterprise Report Writer is an included component of the OneWorld system and is considered a part of the OneWorld foundation systems. The Enterprise Report Writer includes built-in access to OneWorld business data tables using business views related to financial information tables. It also includes a template for creating financial-style reports. Although it's billed as an end-user reporting tool, many organizations find that report writers—including the OneWorld Enterprise Report Writer—are not necessarily user-friendly and in some cases are not friendly themselves, requiring an excessive amount of system time and/or tuning.

◆ The FRx Visual Financial Reporting tool. This report writer is not a J. D. Edwards-produced product, but it is a very popular financial report writer add-on, especially for second- and third-tier ERP packages. Within the last 24 months, FRx and J. D. Edwards have formed a business alliance that has extended the capabilities of FRx into the OneWorld environment. Accounting departments that already use FRx might want to inquire about its availability for OneWorld as well. However, although FRx might be familiar to your organization, it will still be necessary to remap existing report specifications into OneWorld.

◆ The Hyperion Financial Consolidation Reporting and Analysis tool. This report writer is not a J. D. Edwards-produced product, but Hyperion is a highly regarded financial reporting tool. It is especially popular with multidivision and multinational corporations and is used by a significant number of Fortune 1000 companies. For instance, trial balance data can be extracted from OneWorld and loaded into Hyperion using OneWorld's standard export capabilities.

Every organization will have a litany of reasons for favoring one choice over another with regards to a financial reporting tool. For instance, many organizations will not want to incur the added cost and support required by multiple report writers, so they will choose to use the Enterprise Report Writer. On the other hand, some organizations might want to retain the familiar look and feel of current reporting tools in the OneWorld environment, yet incorporate OneWorld-produced transactional data.

Important Information for World Software Users

World software users will find that the Enterprise Report Writer combines or replaces three of their familiar report writers into a single tool. Gone is FASTR for financial reporting, STAR for fixed-asset reporting, and World Writer for all other custom reporting requirements. One tool now suffices for creating reports against all types of files. Note that STAR, FASTR, and World Writer report specifications are not compatible with, nor is a conversion available to recast these specifications into, an Enterprise Report Writer specification.

Note that it is possible to coexist using World software report writers against OneWorld-produced transactions in data files contained on an AS/400 computer serving as the file server. The library list or path code must point to the correct environment to retrieve and report on the desired financial or other information. In addition, if the file server remains an AS/400 system, the AS/400 query tool and, for that matter, other query and data extraction tools can still be used against OneWorld-produced data files. In a non-AS/400 environment, ODBC tools for SQL databases can be used in a similar manner. However, there are some nuances in J. D. Edwards data formats that must be understood and appropriately translated.

Ultimately, both end-users and technical personnel using report writers will be required to transition to the Enterprise Report Writer.

Budgeting

An important tool used by organizations of all sizes is the budget. The budget is an integral part of the short- and long-range planning process. A budget plan helps your organization coordinate its activities toward achieving strategic plan goals by predicting future revenues, expenses, and capital outlays.

Business Unit Planning

Business Units are an essential part of the overall planning process. The overall budget plan is typically the consolidation of individual Business Unit plans, which include forecasts at the account level of revenues, direct costs, and overhead. Typically, the Business Unit manager is accountable for the revenue contribution or expense control as it relates to the individual Business Unit. Business Unit managers must have influence on and responsibility for the costs and revenue produced at the Business Unit level.

Business Unit managers must set realistic target values so that the activities in the individual Business Units within your organization can be controlled effectively. To carry out comprehensive Business Unit planning, it is necessary to take both internal or business conditions and external or market conditions into account during the planning process.

Planning is typically an iterative process. Any number of preliminary budgets are prepared until an acceptable or final budget is approved for your organization. For instance, OneWorld supports up to three budget plan entries, typically viewed as requested, revised, and final budgets for each account within the domain of a Business Unit.

OneWorld supports the Business Unit manager's role in the planning and controlling process in a number of ways:

◆ Several methods for entering your budget information into the system, including direct entry or journalized entry against the account balance.

◆ Facilities that can recast current operating results or budgets as future or revised results. If these values are realistic, these forecasted figures likely require only limited revision.

◆ Reports and inquiries built from account balance information contained in the General Accounting system. These facilities help the Business Unit manager control performance and make "mid-course adjustments" by providing for the comparison between planned values and actual results at the Business Unit level.

When budgeting at the Business Unit level, the direct entry method is typically employed.

Direct Entry Budgeting

Using the direct entry method of budgeting, the budget can be entered in one of two ways:

◆ By cost center, where all appropriate accounts that are associated with a given cost center are displayed for budget entry or revision on the direct entry budget form

◆ By account

Using the direct entry method, a budget can be entered on either an annual or period-by-period basis. When budgets are entered on an annualized basis, they must be "spread out" to the monthly buckets on a prorated basis.

Spreading the Annual Budgets

After a budget is entered, based on a "spread pattern," the annual budget entry can be spread into month-by-month entries for comparative reporting purposes. These spread patterns are established by your organization. They allow the budget to be seasonally adjusted by allocating a higher or lower percentage to the account balance for a given month. Note that the total allocation cannot exceed 100 percent of the account balance.

Journalized Budgeting

Since budget information in OneWorld is maintained in a separate budget ledger type, it is also possible to make journal entries containing budget information in the general ledger. Admittedly, this is a less than desirable technique for budget input. Generally speaking, the budget entry will use a one-sided journal entry.

Spreadsheet Budgeting

Many organizations use spreadsheet programs, such as Lotus 1-2-3 or Microsoft Excel, in order to prepare budget forecasts. Instead of manually re-entering a spreadsheet-prepared budget into OneWorld, it might be possible to upload the spreadsheet into OneWorld using the OneWorld spreadsheet upload program. Carefully review the information in the General Accounting reference guide to determine if the spreadsheet upload program will work for your organization. In general, the spreadsheet program must present the account number and budget amount in a predetermined columnar format.

Allocations

Allocations are defined for many purposes. They are used to redistribute amounts from one or more business units to accounts in other business units. Allocations can be made for a variety of reasons. Examples include allocation of occupancy costs, such as lease payments and electric service.

OneWorld provides two techniques for performing allocations: the indexed allocation technique and the variable-numerator technique. Regardless of the technique employed, the result is the same—the allocation program creates a journal entry. This journal entry must subsequently be posted to the general ledger, like any other journal entry.

Indexed Allocations

The indexed allocation is the more flexible of the two techniques. This technique can be used to recast or restate a balance through use of the copy feature found in this technique. Here are some of the possibilities using an indexed allocation:

- ◆ Set up annual or monthly budgets by copying current-year information, and use this information as the basis for a future year's budget projection.
- ◆ Allocate dollars from one company to another company.
- ◆ Multiply the amount subject to allocation by a positive or negative factor before carrying out the allocation.

Variable-Numerator Allocations

The variable-numerator allocation is considered the less flexible of the two techniques. However, it is also the more dynamic. The variable numerator usually represents a static or variable statistic. For instance, a statistic might change annually, such as budgeted headcount or square feet, while other statistics might change monthly, such as sales order counts. Some of these statistics will change infrequently.

Statistics used in allocations can be maintained in the general ledger. A special ledger type can be established for statistical accounts. Note that units instead of dollars can be maintained. Nonbalancing journal entries can be posted to statistical accounts. For instance, if statistics change monthly, create a new journal entry to update statistical account information each month. For statistics that change infrequently, create a model journal entry. Update it monthly if needed, and then use this model for the current month's allocation.

Complex Allocation Schemes

Chains, or tiers of allocations, can be defined. Up to nine allocations can be chained sequentially. When a chained allocation scheme is used, subsequent allocation calculations use the results or allocation amounts from the previous tier.

Allocation Setup

Significant preparatory work is required in developing appropriate allocations. In general, here are the steps required to establish an allocation:

1. Identify and define the account(s) to be allocated
2. Identify and define the business unit(s) to be allocated
3. Identify and define the basis for allocation
4. Identify and define the business unit(s) to receive the allocation

Once allocations are defined, procedures and/or processes must be defined for the capture of the appropriate statistics that any allocations are based on. These business procedures and/or processes must cover the following:

◆ What manually and systemically gathered statistics will be needed

◆ How the manual and systemic statistics will be gathered

◆ How the manually and systemically gathered statistics will be summarized

◆ Identify the frequency of the update. For instance, will this statistic be updated monthly, periodically as needed, or only annually?

Note that if category codes are used within an allocation, as new business units (including projects) are added to the chart of accounts, they must be properly coded with the appropriate category code or codes in order for these new entities to be included in any allocations.

Performing Periodic Allocations

After allocations are established, significant periodic (usually monthly) maintenance and processing work are required. Here are the preliminary steps in performing monthly allocations:

1. Review individual business unit category code definitions.
2. Update any individual business unit category code definition(s) as necessary.

3. Review allocation definitions.

4. Update any allocation definition(s) as necessary.

The actual monthly allocation processing steps include the following:

1. Compile current-month statistics for specific allocation statistics.

2. Journalize and post current-month statistics to the general ledger.

3. Run allocations in the proper sequence in proof mode.

4. Review allocation results.

5. Run allocations in the proper sequence in final mode.

If multiple allocations are required, these steps should be repeated. This section on the account balance allocation facilities available in OneWorld concludes the introduction to the OneWorld General Accounting system.

Accounts Payable

The OneWorld Accounts Payable system administers accounting information related to your organization's suppliers. The Accounts Payable system provides facilities for entering invoices received from suppliers for amounts owed them for goods or services. The invoice entry process is generally called *vouchering* an invoice for payment. When an invoice or voucher is "paid," it is also said to be "settled."

The Accounts Payable system includes features to voucher and pay supplier invoices. In addition, the Accounts Payable system has other capabilities and uses:

◆ Tracking expenditures for goods and services provided by the supplier, including summarization of dollars spent by the supplier (supplier ranking)

◆ Tracking expenditures for goods and services provided by purpose, including drill down to source documents

◆ Managing and analyzing cash (liquidity) requirements

The OneWorld Accounts Payable provides numerous features to ensure accurate and timely payments in accordance with your business procedures and to better manage supplier relationships. These features include payment and vendor "holds" to prevent payments, and invoicing error tolerance ranges to settle invoices where differences are considered immaterial.

Data Model

Here are the major data tables in the Accounts Payable system data model:

- The Supplier Master (F0401)
- The Accounts Payable Ledger (F0411)
- The Accounts Payable Matching Document (F0413)
- The Accounts Payable Matching Document Detail (F0414)
- The Procurement System Goods Receipts Transaction Table (F43121)

In addition to these tables, the General Accounting system transaction and chart of account-related files play a major role in the Accounts Payable data model.

Supplier Master

The Supplier Master table contains voucher-related information for suppliers, including payment terms, method of payment preference (check versus electronic payment), tax information, and vouchered amounts for the year.

Accounts Payable Ledger

The Accounts Payable Ledger table contains information about the invoice entered in the form of a voucher. Transaction-related information includes the invoice date and amount, the due date, and the purpose of or explanation for the expenditure. Note that reporting codes from the Address Book can be used to further classify supplier payments contained in this table.

Matching Summary Document

The Accounts Payable Matching Document table contains the payment summary information. The payment or check number, amount and date paid, and bank account used are a part of this summary-level information. For each summary payment record, one or more payment detail records exist.

Matching Document Detail

The Accounts Payable Matching Document Detail table contains payment transaction details. For every paid item reflected in a given payment or summary record, one line of information exists in this table. Think of the matching document detail as the "check stub" contents. This information includes the payment gross amount, any discounts taken, and the accounting information to use during general ledger posting.

Goods Receipts

The Procurement System Goods Receipts Transaction Table (F43121) includes purchase order receipt information created through formal receipt of goods or services against a purchase order. Initiating a voucher requires a three-way match between a purchase order, a receipt, and a supplier invoice. OneWorld provides for both a three-way matching process and an informal payment vouchering process that uses a two-way matching process that bypasses the formal receiving process. It essentially is used to receive and voucher the invoice in a single step. Purchases for inventory must use the formal receiving process, while purchases to a general ledger account number can rely on either receiving process.

Although it's technically a part of the Procurement system, the matching of invoices against purchase orders and goods receipts is typically an Accounts Payable department function in most organizations. Therefore, although technically speaking J. D. Edwards classifies the matching process as a Procurement system function, practically speaking this is usually a topic more appropriately discussed under the Accounts Payable banner.

Workflow

This section provides an overview of the OneWorld Accounts Payable system's workflow and highlights many of the important features available within the system.

Procurement System Document Matching and Invoice Vouchering

The vouchering process is best described as both a verification and scheduling process. The invoice is for goods or services that were legitimately procured for the use in the normal course of business. The invoice is considered for payment only after receipt of the goods can be confirmed through a process known as matching. After the invoice is verified or matched, it is then scheduled for payment. Payment terms vary significantly by industry. Payment terms can range from Net Invoice (Due on Receipt) to Net 60 Days or more.

Invoice vouchering may include a two-way match process, where the invoice is validated against a purchase order document, or a three-way match, where the invoice is validated against a purchase order and a purchase order receipt. It is also possible to perform automatic vouchering based on the existence of a purchase order receipt. This is called Evaluated Receipt Settlement (ERS). When used together, the OneWorld Procurement and Accounts Payable systems support two-way matching, three-way matching, and ERS business processes.

Non-Procurement System Invoice Vouchering

In many other instances, invoices may be received for payment without reference to a specific purchase order document. Utility bills and property tax bills are examples of such types of amounts. Also, lease payments represent a fixed, monthly amount that must be paid to the lessor. These types of payments are generally called *recurring payments*. Other types of expenses also require vouchering. These are generally regarded as nonrecurring payments—including, for example, the reimbursement of employee-related business travel and living expenses. The OneWorld Accounts Payable system provides support for manually entered one-time or nonrecurring payment vouchers and recurring payment vouchers. Debit memorandums can be entered to account for credits that a supplier has or can be expected to issue against an open account balance.

Cash Requirements Forecasting

An important function of the OneWorld Accounts Payable system is its role in cash requirements forecasting. Cash requirements are determined from the backlog of vouchered invoices and scheduled recurring payments for purposes of optimizing the liquidity of your organization. For instance, the OneWorld cash requirements planning and payment system allows you to consider many variables before submitting a payment to the supplier, such as the due date of the invoice, whether a discount can be taken, and the amount of cash on hand versus the amount due the supplier. Individual supplier obligations can be accelerated or decelerated based on cash availability or delivery or performance-related disputes.

The Accounts Payable system provides for the total review of commitments and obligations to suppliers. On a supplier-by-supplier basis, you can review information such as the account balance, or the payment status of any given voucher, using the OneWorld Supplier Ledger Inquiry form. A number of reports are included in the OneWorld Accounts Payable system. The open Accounts Payable vouchers can be "aged" using the Open Accounts Payment Detail report with Aging. The Cash Requirements report allows establishing payment windows and showing cash requirements within each of these windows. In addition, a Payment Register report and a Voucher Detail report can be generated.

Duplicate Payment Detection

OneWorld includes several features to help eliminate or reduce the number of duplicate supplier payments. These features include duplicate invoice number checking at the time of voucher entry and a batch report that analyzes payment information and determines if any payments have been duplicated based on invoice number, date, or amount paid.

Payment Processing

Vouchers that are outstanding and payable to your suppliers are "settled" through the OneWorld payment processing process. The OneWorld Accounts Payable system supports standard payment methods, including support for both check payments (in printed form) and electronic payments such as a data transmission or sending information to a diskette. OneWorld's payment process can be set up to take advantage of trade or cash discounts offered by early or timely payment.

Manual Payment Processing

One World includes features to support two types of payment processing. These include processes to support manual payment processing. The manual payment typically produces a single printed check or can be used to record a hand-drawn check. In addition, both vouchering and manual check payment processing can occur as an integrated or single event. It has been my experience that manual payments, if used at all, are used for transactions to replenish petty cash, postage meters, to pay truck drivers for cash-on-delivery orders, or to provide a cash advance to a traveling employee. In general, given the wide acceptance of corporate charge or debit cards, the use of manual checks continues to decline.

Automatic Payment Processing

Most organizations choose to use automatic payment processing for their routine payments to suppliers. It has been my experience that most organizations process supplier payments on a weekly basis, producing checks to be mailed or due through the date of the next scheduled payment or check run. In OneWorld, a payment group is used to select and lock down vouchers as payments to be written. The payment group is then used to select and write payments en masse.

In addition, the use of payment groups allows maximum flexibility in canceling and rerunning a payment run, such as when check stock is damaged during printing or when checks are printed incorrectly due to incorrect forms loading. The

Work With Payment Group feature allows a payment run to be deleted and re-created as necessary to exclude or include payments. After payments are successfully written, the payment group is used again, this time to select and update payment information into the Accounts Payable system tables. Thereafter, payments are posted to the general ledger using the General Accounting system batch post and review process.

Here are some additional features of Automatic Payment processing:

♦ You can make payments from one or more bank accounts.

♦ Payments can also be made from the same bank account for a number of companies when necessary.

♦ You can prepay for goods or services in advance of constructive receipt. Examples of prepayments include travel advances to employees.

♦ It provides for payment retainage. A retainage is a hold-back of a certain percentage of an invoiced amount. For instance, this is a common occurrence in construction-related transactions.

Figure 15-2 provides an overview of the basic Accounts Payable process workflow found in OneWorld. This process is highly configurable and is largely user-driven based on data selection criteria, particularly at the time of report or payment generation.

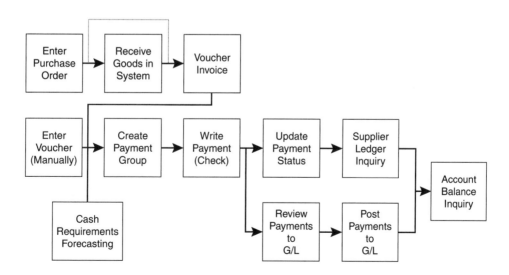

FIGURE 15-2 *The OneWorld Accounts Payable Process*

Accounts Receivable

The OneWorld Accounts Receivable system administers accounting information related to your organization's customers. The Accounts Receivable system provides facilities for entering customer-related invoices and applying cash receipts, as payments are received, against specific open invoices on a customer's account. In addition, OneWorld cash receipts processing provides facilities for processing a cash receipt payment in a number of ways, including as payment in full or as unapplied cash against the customer's account. At a later time, unapplied cash can be applied against specific open invoices.

Data Model

The OneWorld Accounts Receivable system includes the following major data tables:

- ◆ The Customer Master (F0301)
- ◆ The Accounts Receivable Ledger (F03B11)
- ◆ The Receipts Ledger (F03B13)
- ◆ The Receipts Detail Register (F03B14)
- ◆ The Credit and Collection Workfiles (F03B15, F03B16, and F03B16S)

In addition to these tables, the General Accounting system transaction and chart of account-related files play a major role in the Accounts Receivable data model.

Customer Master

The customer master record is created in the Address Book system and contains customer billing and credit-related information.

Accounts Receivable Ledger

The Accounts Receivable Ledger contains a record to represent each entry on an invoice as a record in this file. Invoice lines are created in OneWorld using one of two methods. When the sales order management system is used, invoices are created through a sales order processing invoice/billing process. When the sales order management system is not used, invoices can be entered directly (manually) through the Accounts Receivable system. A batch interface process program (discussed in Chapter 13) can also introduce a properly formatted invoice *electronically* into OneWorld.

Cash Receipts Ledger

The Receipts Ledger table is used to store the payment record header. This header stores the receipt amount, any unapplied balance remaining, and the customer's payment reference number.

Cash Receipts Detail

The Receipts Detail Register table contains records of information about how the cash receipt is applied to an invoice, including the amount applied in addition to any discount, write-off, or chargeback amount associated with the invoice.

Credit-Related Files

The Credit and Collection-related workfiles or tables store statistical information used for credit and collection purposes. The information stored in these files includes aging information, balance information, days outstanding (DSO), average days late, last invoice date, and the amounts invoiced in the current and previous year.

Workflow

The OneWorld Accounts Receivable system is used to support the order to cash business processing cycle. The process begins when a customer sale is completed. A sales transaction is completed when a product is shipped or delivered to the customer, or when the performance of a service has been completed for the customer. Typically, the customer is billed or invoiced for the sale amount when the sale is completed. This billing is usually in the form of a printed invoice document mailed to the customer. A record is also made of the amount owed by the customer and when it is due. It is a common practice to provide a discount if the amount is paid in full by a certain date. The discount serves as an incentive to the customer to settle his account quickly.

In a perfect world, the customer remits a payment by the date it is due. When the customer remits a payment for the amount due, the cash receipt must be acknowledged or recorded, and the amount must be deducted from the amount owed by the customer. This is called cash application or cash receipts processing. Typically, cash is applied on an invoice-by-invoice basis. Account-related records are also adjusted as cash received is applied against the customer account.

In the imperfect world in which we live, frequently the amount paid by the customer is different from the amount that is actually due per the invoice that was sent to the customer. Differences arise for any number of reasons, including disputes, errors, the customer's inability to pay the full amount due, or taking a discount based on the invoice terms. The goal is that on an invoice-by-invoice basis, no balance remains open or uncollected. To achieve this goal, any differences between the invoiced amount and the amount paid must be resolved. Differences can be resolved in a number of ways. These ways include making a charge back to the customer account, writing off a minor difference in the interest of customer goodwill, reducing and matching the amount due (as in the case of allowing a discount), or as the basis of a credit memo issued to the customer's account.

A customer is usually given a certain number of days in which to pay the amount due before the amount due is considered past due. An organization may choose to apply delinquency fees, often in the form of a late payment charge or interest on the past-due balance. The typical practice for an organization is to produce an aging report of customer accounts on a daily or periodic basis. This report is used to determine what customer accounts are considered past due. This report is typically used as the basis for making reminder calls to customers that their payments are past due and that the payments are expected immediately.

Periodically, usually monthly, a statement listing the unsettled or unpaid invoices is produced and sent to the customer. This statement serves as a summary and a reminder to the customer about the amount that is owed and due now or by a future date.

The Accounts Receivable process just discussed is fully supported by OneWorld. Figure 15-3 illustrates a typical Accounts Receivable process. Again, as with the Accounts Payable system, this workflow process is highly configurable and is largely user-driven. Data selection criteria, particularly at the time of reporting or "as of" file generation, play a major role in the Accounts Receivable workflow.

Deduction Manager

When a customer makes a "short" payment, paying less than the full amount due, a reason code can be entered for the short payment. The short payment can then be reviewed and its disposition determined. The OneWorld Deduction Manager feature is used to review and dispose of such customer payment-related deductions. Using the Deduction Manager, any shortages are typically written off or are

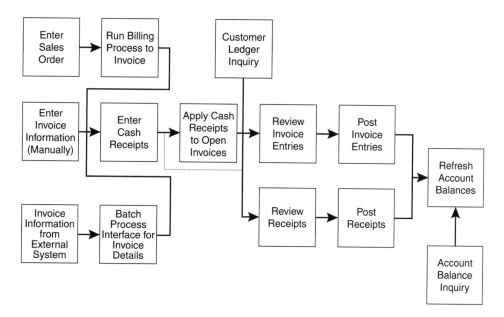

FIGURE 15-3 *The OneWorld Accounts Receivable Process*

disallowed and charged back to the customer, such as when a discount is taken off an invoice but the payment is postdated after the invoice due date.

Stand-Alone or Integrated

OneWorld allows for the creation of invoices and debit memos, called charge-backs, on a manual or direct-entry basis. If your organization is using the OneWorld Sales Order Management system, the creation of invoices can occur on an automatic basis, through the batch process customer billing found in the OneWorld Sales Order Management system.

Bill by Invoice or from an Account Statement

An invoice document can be printed. An invoice document must be requested for invoices that are created on a manual or direct-entry basis. However, when using the OneWorld Sales Order Management system, invoices are typically generated as a part of the customer billing process. For instance, invoice documents are typically printed and mailed to customers as the product is shipped to the customer. Some organizations choose not to print individual invoices. Instead, these organizations typically bill customers by providing a statement of their account activity, much like you might receive for your department store or bank-issued credit card. If your organization has a large customer base, it might be desirable to establish billing cycles. Such cycle codes can then be noted in the OneWorld customer master record. OneWorld can subsequently use these billing cycle codes to produce account statements.

Basic Features

Although the OneWorld Accounts Receivable system has numerous features, its basic features and functionality are provided through these primary interactive forms, batch processes, and reports:

- The Customer Ledger Inquiry form
- The Invoice Entry form
- The Cash Receipts Entry form
- The Credit Refresh batch process
- The Aging report
- The Statement Generation process
- The Statement Print program

Note that the Credit Refresh batch process program should always be run before producing an Aging report. The recommended procedure calls for executing the Credit Refresh batch process on a daily basis. This will ensure that the aging information is current as the credit and collection department of your organization works at collecting delinquent accounts each day.

Advanced Features

Other significant features in OneWorld Accounts Receivable system include the following:

- The ability to produce a "snapshot" or an online statement for a given customer account.
- The ability to receive an electronic bank tape that reflects customer cash payments against their accounts. OneWorld programs can then match cash received against open invoices using invoice number, due date, or amount.

- The ability to generate delinquency and dunning notices. However, it has been my experience that many organizations do not have late-fee policies. Sometimes this failing is due to a legacy system's inability to assess these fees. In other cases, the loss of customer goodwill prevents an existing policy from being implemented. Of course, lending institutions, such as banks, factors, lessors, and credit card companies, regularly assess delinquency fees.

- The ability to generate delinquency and late charges against a customer's unpaid account balances beyond their due dates.

- The ability to record "promises and stories" from customers regarding when a payment can be expected as your credit and collection department works the delinquent accounts list (aging report).

Additional information about the entire OneWorld Accounts Receivable system can be found on the documentation CD-ROM in the Accounts Receivable system reference guide.

World Versus OneWorld Accounts Receivable

Compared to World Accounts Receivable, many new functions have been added to OneWorld Accounts Receivable. These new features have resulted in an incompatibility between World and OneWorld versions of this application—both in terms of functionality and the underlying data models. Therefore, Accounts Receivable is one of the few applications that can't coexist between the two J. D. Edwards software environments.

Fixed Assets

The OneWorld Fixed Assets system administers accounting information and costs related to your organization's fixed assets. The OneWorld Fixed Asset system can be used to amortize or depreciate the costs of an asset based on elapsed time, useful life, or "units of production" basis.

The Fixed Asset system does not need to be maintained monthly. As a matter of fact, the processing fixed asset information can be deferred until an organization is ready to compute period depreciation—whether that is at month end, quarter end, or year end.

The Fixed Asset system includes numerous features, such as automated asset setup and the ability to extract asset-related voucher journal entries for consideration and inclusion as a fixed asset.

Fixed Asset Data Model

The OneWorld Fixed Asset system includes two primary data tables:

- ◆ The Asset Item Master (F1201)
- ◆ The Asset Item Balance (F1202)

In addition to these tables, the General Accounting system transaction, balance, and chart of account-related files play a major role in the Fixed Asset data model.

The Asset Item Master

The asset item master record defines things such as acquisition or depreciation start date, item description, asset class, item or asset number, and serial number.

The Asset Item Balance

The item balance file contains the asset cost and balance information. Asset account balances are maintained by ledger type and fiscal year, much like the General Accounting does for general ledger account balances.

Maintaining Multiple Fixed Asset Books

Multiple books related to depreciation can be maintained. For instance, federal, state, and GAAP books can be maintained. Each book or ledger type must further define the depreciation method and life, which are important in carrying out periodic depreciation calculations.

How It Works: From Acquisition to Disposition

Fixed asset transactions are created by journal entries to the General Accounting account ledger file. Fixed asset accounting in the general ledger is done via subledger accounting, using the asset ID number as the subledger number. All fixed asset transactions are first posted to the general ledger, and then to the Fixed Asset system, except for those generated by the fixed asset subsystem depreciation and transfer functions. Under this scenario, the asset number is established before purchase, and the asset ID number is noted in the subledger field on the purchase order.

Acquisitions

Here are the general processing steps related to fixed asset acquisitions in OneWorld:

1. Approve the acquisition of a new capital asset.
2. Create a purchase order to acquire a new asset.
3. (Optional) Establish the asset in the Fixed Asset system.
4. Receive, against the purchase order, the new asset.
5. Receive and verify the invoice for the new asset. An accounts payable voucher is created for the asset.
6. Review and approve the accounts payable voucher for the asset.
7. Post vouchers to the general ledger. This step posts fixed asset entries to the general ledger, updating account balances.
8. Review and revise the master data information for the newly acquired asset. *Important: Verify the asset's depreciation information (setup) for accuracy.*
9. Review and revise any unposted fixed asset entries.
10. Post the batch that contains the fixed asset entries. This posts transactions from the general ledger account ledger file to the fixed asset item balances file.

If your organization is electing to automatically create new asset item master records from general ledger entries for newly acquired fixed asset acquisitions, Step 3 is not needed. However, if the asset was preestablished, the new asset number could be specified on the purchase order in the subledger field.

Depreciation

OneWorld includes a litany of standard depreciation methods that are acceptable under Generally Accepted Accounting Principles or that are required by the Internal Revenue Service. Table 15-3 lists the standard depreciation methods that are predefined in the OneWorld Fixed Assets system.

Table 15-3 Standard Depreciation Methods in OneWorld

Depreciation Method Code	Description of Depreciation Method
00	No depreciation method used
01	Straight Line Depreciation
02	Sum of the Year's Digits
03	125% Declining Balance to Crossover
04	150% Declining Balance to Crossover
05	Double Declining Balance to Crossover
06	Fixed % on Declining Balance
07	ACRS Standard Depreciation
08	ACRS Optional Depreciation
09	Units of Production Depreciation
10	MACRS Luxury Cars—Domestic
11	Fixed % Luxury Cars—Foreign
12	MACRS Standard Depreciation
13	ACRS Alternative Depreciation
14	ACRS Alternative Real Property
15	Fixed % of Cost
16	Fixed % on Declining Balance to Crossover
17	AMT Luxury Auto
18	ACE Luxury Auto

In addition to the standard depreciation methods listed in Table 15-3, OneWorld also allows for the creation and maintenance of user-defined depreciation methods. During system setup, letters are used to define and segregate user-defined depreciation methods from standard depreciation methods delivered with OneWorld.

OneWorld provides for computing depreciation on a preliminary or final basis. Generally speaking, you should always compute depreciation on a preliminary-run basis. This batch process creates a report simulating the journal entries that will be created when the final depreciation run is made.

After reviewing the results and correcting any depreciation coding errors in the item information, compute depreciation on a final-run basis. This step creates journal entries for accumulated depreciation and depreciation expense. These entries are posted *automatically* to the fixed asset item balances file and to the general ledger account balances file.

Note that it is not necessary to depreciate assets more than once a year. Although it's not a desirable practice, some organizations choose to only compute depreciation on an annual basis.

Asset Transfers

A transfer records the transfer of an asset in the Fixed Asset system. Typically a transfer involves moving or reassigning an asset from one business unit to another (such as moving an asset from one plant to another). The transfer batch process can compute the journal entries related to asset transfers on a preliminary-run basis. The transfer process proof run produces a report simulating the journal entries that will be created when the final asset transfer run is made.

After it is reviewed and accepted, run this process to compute the journal entries related to asset transfers on a final-run basis. This step creates journal entries to transfer an asset between business units. These entries are posted *automatically* to the fixed asset item balances file and to the general ledger account balances file.

Asset Disposals

A disposal transaction is used to record an asset disposal in the Fixed Asset system. Asset dispositions occur for numerous reasons, including physical damage or replacement or sale due to nonuse or obsolescence. The Fixed Asset system creates disposal-related journal entries based on the disposal type specified when the disposal information is entered into the system.

The Fixed Asset system updates the asset master record with the disposal and indicates the method of disposal in the Equipment Status field. The system creates the journal entries related to the disposal, including accounting for any cash from the disposal of the asset.

Here are the four types of asset disposals supported by OneWorld:

- Simple disposal. This invoices no cash proceeds.
- Disposal with cash proceeds. Use this when cash is received for an asset.
- Disposal with a trade-in. Use this when you're trading in an asset in for another asset and no cash proceeds are involved.
- Disposal with cash proceeds and trade-in. Use this when a disposal involves a combination of both cash and a trade-in on a new asset.

Disposal-related journal entries can be computed on a preliminary-run basis. This batch process prints a report simulating the journal entries that are created when the final asset disposal run is made. After they are reviewed and verified for accuracy, compute the journal entries related to asset disposals on a final-run basis. This step creates journal entries for asset disposals. These entries are posted *automatically* to the fixed asset item balances file. Post asset disposal entries to update the general ledger account balances file. Post the general ledger entries to the Fixed Assets system. This final step posts the disposal-related journal entries to the item balances file.

Mass Disposals and Asset Splits

OneWorld includes a Mass Asset Disposals transaction that can be used to dispose of multiple assets instead of a single asset. The mass disposal transaction works only for simple disposals involving no proceeds and for disposals with cash proceeds. Special requirements apply when using the latter method.

An asset split involves splitting an existing asset into one or more new assets. These transactions work similarly to asset transfers. Assets can be split by units, monetary value, or a percentage of their value. Note that the asset does not have to have a quantity greater than one. Here are some typical uses of the Asset Split transaction:

- Removal of a portion of an asset to create two independent assets
- Splitting a component (part) of an asset in order to dispose of it
- Splitting a component of an asset in order to transfer it
- Correcting an asset that was entered as one item but should have been entered as multiple assets

The asset split transaction creates any necessary asset records and updates the appropriate general ledger and asset accounts.

Application Note: Construction in Progress and Project Accounting Using Subledgers

Suppose a new production line is being built. The line is made of many purchased components that typically are not useful on a stand-alone basis. In many cases, each component is recorded as a separate fixed asset. Frequently, these charges are sent to a temporary asset called a construction in progress. However, once the asset is completed and placed in service, depreciation can begin. This requires transferring all component assets from the construction in progress account to the appropriate asset accounts. This can be a laborious process. But there is an alternative approach for construction-in-progress accounting.

A subledger account can be established for the purposes of accumulating, segregating, and reporting of dollars related to a specific project considered construction in progress before it is booked as a fixed asset. In this scenario, purchases flow to the subledger, not to a specific asset at the time of voucher entry. Here are the general steps to follow when using subledger to perform project or construction-in-progress accounting:

1. Create a work order header in the project system. This will be the subledger number.
2. Purchase the asset or components to the construction-in-progress account, with subledger noted. Use subledger type W (work order).
3. Receive the asset or components.
4. Receive and verify invoices against the purchase order receipts, creating payment vouchers.
5. Post journal entries to the general ledger. The subledger account balance is updated for the amount of the asset or components vouchered.

Continue these steps for asset components until the project is considered complete, all expenses have been accumulated and paid, and the asset is effectively ready to be placed into service. Note that a fixed asset does not need to be booked, because subledger accounting can also be used to segregate project-specific expenditures for project analysis and budgeting only.

When using this method for fixed asset construction-in-progress reporting, do not create fixed asset item master entries automatically based on general ledger journal entries to a given account or accounts.

Creating the Asset

A new fixed asset can be accounted for in the aggregate or as an individual component. If it's created as an asset in the aggregate, only one asset is created. If later it becomes necessary to break this aggregated asset into its components, use the asset split feature in the Fixed Asset system to accomplish this requirement. In general, these steps outline the asset creation process:

1. Print a detailed subledger journal for the new construction-in-progress account, where the subledger number equals the project number.

2. Create fixed asset master record(s) as needed.

3. Create a journal entry voucher to debit the asset account for the individual asset(s), with their asset item number as the subledger value. Credit the new construction-in-progress account with the project subledger. The total of the journal should equal the new construction-in-progress account balance for the subledger.

4. Post vouchers to the general ledger that will post fixed asset entries to the general ledger, updating account balances.

5. Review and revise any unposted fixed asset entries.

6. Post the batch that contains the fixed asset entries. This will post transactions from the General Account Balance file to the Fixed Asset Item Balances file.

This is not intended to represent accounting advice, and it might not be appropriate accounting treatment in all instances, because summary instead of detail-level information might be more desirable or even required. This application advice is provided to illustrate the many ways in which OneWorld features can be used to create unique or individualized processes and workflows.

Job Cost

The OneWorld Job Cost system is a formal project cost accounting system that relies on the General Accounting system transaction processing and data model. This system is discussed further in a later chapter.

Integration with Subsystems

The OneWorld General Accounting system is responsible for the basic bookkeeping in most organizations that implement OneWorld. All other OneWorld systems provide information to the General Accounting system about how the subsystem transaction specifically impacts the general ledger central to determining an organization's net worth and any profit or loss it has incurred. Two notably important OneWorld concepts—Automatic Accounting Instructions and General Ledger Posting Category Codes—are central in subsystem accounting and integration with the General Accounting system. This section provides an overview of these two concepts.

Automatic Accounting Instructions

As was previously mentioned, important components in making the integration aspect work in OneWorld are the Automatic Accounting Instructions (AAIs). For example, the accounts payable voucher is created in OneWorld, and a complete or balanced journal entry is not produced. Nor does the program need to tell the system how to account for a given transaction, such as an inventory purchase, every time this type of transaction happens.

Automatic Accounting Instructions can best be thought of as rules governing the accounting for a standard business transaction in OneWorld. OneWorld has logic embedded in its many programs to create general ledger accounting entries for standard business transactions based on generally accepted accounting principles (GAAP). However, your organization controls the account number information that is used to complete these standard journal entries within the general ledger.

These Automatic Accounting Instructions are entered into a system table called the Automatic Accounting Instructions table. It can be referenced as often as is needed by the business transaction processing subsystem. The automatic accounting instruction table first provides the basis for automatic account determination and second provides for automatic journal entry creation.

Generally speaking, the automatic accounting instructions drive the creation of journal entries based on the fundamental principles of a balanced journal entry and complete either one side (the debit or the credit) or both sides (the debit and the credit) of a journal entry. For instance, to increase the value or balance in an asset or expense account, a debit is made to the account. Liability, Capital, and Revenue accounts typically carry a credit balance. Increasing the value or balance in a Liability, Capital, or Revenue account requires a credit to the account.

Most automatic accounting instructions are maintained at the company level. A special company, company 00000, is used as the transaction default when company-specific instructions are missing.

In OneWorld, system integration with the General Accounting system means that any given subsystem must derive credit and debit account information such as the detail account and the contra or control account information from a combination of the following:

◆ Transaction-related values. For instance, an account is specified on a noninventory, nonstock purchase order line.

◆ Automatic Accounting Instructions. For instance, there is no need to note the accounts payable clearing account on a voucher entered. This information will be determined automatically.

◆ Master data information. The G/L category code on the item master record or item branch/plant record serves as a pointer to an automatic accounting instruction that will be used when determining the correct inventory account to use for a given item.

Note that some fundamental accounting principles underpin journal entries made to the general ledger. For instance, asset and expense accounts typically carry a debit balance. Also, when entering an accounts payable voucher, the temporary received-not-vouchered liability is relieved (debited), and the trade payable account (a liability account) is increased by a credit. The implementation of OneWorld requires knowledge of these accounting relationships when you create automatic accounting instructions.

Types of Automatic Accounting Instructions

OneWorld has two major categories of Automatic Accounting Instructions that are maintained separately. The Financial systems (Accounts Payable, Accounts Receivable, Job Cost, General Accounting, and Fixed Assets) have one set of Automatic Accounting Instructions, and the Distribution and Manufacturing systems have another set of Automatic Accounting Instructions. It is important to understand that both the format and content of these two tables containing Automatic Accounting Instructions varies. The finance-related Automatic Accounting Instructions are generally defined by company and instruction or sequence number. The sequence number is the reference to a given business-related event that OneWorld must perform accounting for.

The Distribution and Manufacturing Automatic Accounting Instructions are more granular in definition, including business unit, document type, and category code values. They also include a transaction type or sequence number that references a given business-related event. The thought process and definition behind Automatic Accounting Instructions for the Distribution and Manufacturing systems are considerably more involved than for those found in OneWorld Financial systems.

General Ledger Posting Category Codes

General Ledger Posting Category Codes work closely in conjunction with Automatic Accounting Instructions to help OneWorld determine the appropriate account number to be used when completing a given journal entry post and ultimately complete a balanced journal entry reflecting a subsystem transaction in OneWorld.

General Ledger Posting Category Codes are found throughout OneWorld. For instance, the customer and supplier master records can contain default category codes. The item master and item branch/plant records also contain General Ledger Posting Category Codes to indicate the inventory account to be used on a procurement or inventory management transaction, such as an issue to a work order.

For example, inventory items are grouped for valuation purposes in the general ledger through the G/L posting category code value. When an inventory transaction occurs, such as a material issue or receipt, the OneWorld Inventory Management system looks up the item master record to determine what the G/L posting category is and copies this information into the material transaction for general ledger processing purposes. When the general ledger batch post process is performed, the G/L posting category code is used to determine from the automatic accounting instruction table what G/L account should be used on the transaction for this class of inventory item.

Summary

This chapter introduced the OneWorld Financial systems, including the following:

- ◆ Accounts Receivable
- ◆ Accounts Payable
- ◆ General Accounting
- ◆ Fixed Assets

Financial reporting and financial modeling functionality, including facilities for budgeting and allocations, is an important part of the General Accounting system.

The batch post process employed by OneWorld to integrate all subsystems into the General Accounting system was also reviewed. The importance of and need for periodic integrity reporting were discussed. Automatic Accounting Instructions and the G/L Posting Category Codes and their importance in the integration of OneWorld subsystems into the General Accounting system were also discussed.

Chapter 16

**OneWorld
Distribution
Systems**

This chapter introduces the OneWorld Distribution systems. The OneWorld Distribution systems require substantially greater effort from the standpoint of software configuration and implementation planning than the OneWorld Financial application systems introduced in the previous chapter.

The OneWorld Distribution systems are likely the most important and complex portion of OneWorld that an organization will implement, except for possibly the manufacturing-related systems. It therefore stands to reason that these systems are also the most difficult in terms of configuration and implementation. Many organizations do not implement all of the OneWorld Distribution systems. For instance, it is not uncommon for a nonprofit organization or government entity to implement only the Procurement (Purchasing) system or Procurement and Inventory Management. Table 16-1 outlines the suite of OneWorld Distribution–related systems.

Table 16-1 OneWorld Distribution Systems

System	System Function
Inventory Management	Provides for item master and perpetual inventory capabilities, including base pricing, item costing, and basic stock locator capabilities.
Sales Order Management	Provides for the creation of sales quotations, sales orders, and credit memos.
Procurement (Purchasing)	Provides for the procurement of stock and nonstock materials, services, and consumables. In manufacturing environments, subcontracted or outside operations are also managed.
Transportation Management	Provides for both cost and time efficiency in the selection of freight carriers, the calculation of freight costs, the planning of freight loads, and the continued visibility of customer orders from the point of shipment to customer receipt.
Price Management	Provides for item, item group, customer or supplier, customer or supplier group, and item/customer- or item/supplier-level pricing options.

Table 16-1 OneWorld Distribution Systems (continued)

System	System Function
Warehouse Management	Provides transactions that extend basic stock locator capabilities through rule-driven stock picking and putaway capabilities.

Inventory Management

The OneWorld Inventory Management system has two major functions. The first is to serve as a repository for item-related information. This repository function was discussed in Chapter 14. The second major function of the OneWorld Inventory Management system is to serve as a perpetual inventory system. Within the Distribution suite of OneWorld applications, the Inventory Management system has the simplest data model and the least-complex set of transactions.

Perpetual Versus Periodic Inventory Processes

Generally speaking, it is considered a best business practice to adopt and use a perpetual inventory system. In the case of a perpetual inventory system, a running balance is kept on an item-by-item basis. The accuracy and currency of this running balance are possible only by keeping track of both additions to stock, such as when items are received and stored for later use, and decreases in stock, such as when items are sold, shipped, or consumed. An automated system—such as OneWorld—reduces the effort necessary to maintain a perpetual inventory, especially when a large number of items exist and transaction volume is high. To ensure continuing balance accuracy, most periodic inventory systems are supplemented by a cycle-counting scheme. OneWorld fully supports cycle counting.

A periodic inventory system relies on periodic physical counts of the inventory. Typically, a periodic inventory system does not attempt to maintain continuous, interperiod inventory balance accuracy. Periodic inventory systems are useful for bulk stock, low-value, and noncritical items. Although perpetual inventory methods have largely displaced many periodic inventory systems, if used, this inventory method can be supported by OneWorld using its cycle or tag-counting features. Cycle counting is best if a limited number of items are maintained using the periodic method. Tag counting is the best technique to use if all inventory items are maintained using the periodic method.

Data Model

The data model for the transaction processing portion of the Inventory Management system incorporates portions of the item branch/plant data model. The item branch/plant data model was discussed in Chapter 14. Refer to that chapter for a list of these files.

The item branch/plant-related information provides important order processing-related information, including cost, pricing, reorder points, and stocking levels (for purchased and/or manufactured items), item classifications for valuation and reporting purposes, and the item's on-hand quantity or balance in the primary unit of measure. In addition to the item branch/plant-related information, all inventory transactions are written to the item ledger file (F4111). Also note that the item ledger file is also called the Cardex file.

Stock-Related Transactions

This section introduces the transactions related to the movement of stock into and out of the perpetual inventory in OneWorld.

Receipts

The process of receiving stock into inventory is, technically speaking, a part of the OneWorld Procurement system. As goods are received against an open purchase order, the quantity received is noted in the system through the OneWorld goods receipt transaction. This transaction also relieves the quantity open value for this item on the purchase order, to prevent unnecessary expediting and vendor returns if duplicate shipments are received. For stock items only, the goods receipt transaction updates the stock on-hand balance for this item and also writes a transaction record to the item ledger file.

Other forms of receipt of an item into the OneWorld perpetual inventory include the reporting of a finished good completion through the OneWorld manufacturing system, or a sales order return, which is also treated as a receipt of goods into inventory.

General ledger transactions are also created by a goods receipt. In addition to the quantity update, the general ledger account is also updated to reflect the increase in value of inventory on hand as caused by the receipt of goods. The cost of goods received is determined by multiplying the quantity received times the cost per item received. For instance, the purchase order cost is only one of the "costs" that can be used in this calculation. The cost applied is therefore user-determined by selection of a costing method.

The offset to the general ledger for the increase in inventory by a goods receipt is a temporary liability. The temporary liability is made to a "received not vouchered" account. It has been my experience that most organizations implementing an ERP system for the first time appreciate this OneWorld feature. Most manual receiving processes and legacy systems do not have an equivalent capability. Lack of this feature therefore requires most organizations to manually (if at all) identify any "material" (by dollar amount) transactions at month end and accrue for them. The temporary liability made to a "received not vouchered" account is relieved when the supplier invoice is received and matched to a receipt. This end result is called a three-way match between the purchase order, goods receipt, and invoice quantity and dollar values.

Shipments

Goods are removed from inventory for a number of reasons. Typically, in a non-manufacturing environment, the most obvious reason is to fulfill a customer order. The shipment confirmation process is, technically speaking, part of the OneWorld Sales Order Management system. A special sales order management transaction, the Ship/Confirm transaction, is used for that purpose. This transaction not only relieves the inventory balance for the item by the quantity shipped, but also updates the sales order open quantity to prevent duplicate shipments to the customer.

Issues

A typical manufacturing environment has three classes of inventory: raw materials and purchased components, work in process, and finished goods. Inventory is typically "issued" from the raw materials and purchased component inventory to work in process for either manufacturing or assembly operations. At the conclusion of the manufacturing process, work in process goods flow from work in process inventory to finished goods.

An inventory issue can also occur for other reasons. For instance, inventory can be consumed and expensed against a given general ledger account. In a manufacturing environment, issues for destructive quality testing, research and development, sales samples, manufacturing waste, or scrap are typical. OneWorld supports both manufacturing and consumption-related goods issued from stock.

Adjustments

An inventory adjustment is an increase or decrease in quantity or value of an inventory item. However, typically an adjustment is made in conjunction with the physical count of an item. For instance, an adjustment might be necessary to account for stock shrinkage and shortages, unrecorded issues and receipts, and obsolescence or a substantial impairment in the value of an item caused by spoilage, or possibly water or fire damage.

Transfers

Every stock item managed by the OneWorld Inventory Management system must be maintained, minimally at the branch/plant level. A branch/plant record typically corresponds to a physical facility, such as a warehouse or distribution center. OneWorld allows your organization to create as many branch/plant locations as are necessary to define your organization's physical structure.

In addition, OneWorld also provides for a more finite level of stock control using locations. Locations are typically a subdivision of a physical facility. The typical location is an "aisle/row/bin" designation. In OneWorld, every item must have a primary bin location. In addition, any number of multiple, secondary locations can be defined. In the absence of a secondary location, OneWorld draws stock from or adds stock to the primary bin in order to complete a transaction.

A simple inventory transfer document is used to facilitate the movement of inventory from one storage location or branch/plant defined in OneWorld to another storage location or branch/plant defined in OneWorld. The simple transfer is used most frequently to transfer goods within a single physical facility. For instance, large quantities of goods may be received into a bulk or overstock storage area and then transferred in smaller quantities to another area on an as-needed basis, where order fulfillment is more readily met. Stock quarantine, stock aging, and stock inspection locations also represent another set of transfer transactions that may occur within a single physical facility.

When transfers occur between physical locations, the simple transfer is simply insufficient. The simple stock transfer assumes that inventory moves immediately. However, this is not true when goods move across the country or even across the globe. A better way of including "transportation" time into the transfer process is frequently necessary. The stock transfer transaction in OneWorld fulfills this requirement.

Stock Transfers

The stock transfer is a special type of goods movement within OneWorld. Instead of using a simple inventory transfer document, the stock transfer is a *complex* transfer in that it generates multiple documents, including a purchase order to request transfer of the goods and a sales order that is used to confirm transfer of the goods. In addition to the generation of shipping documents, the inventory-on-hand balance is not immediately updated at the requesting location until the goods are actually "received" in the system, thereby allowing for "in transit" stock.

If your organization frequently moves stock between locations, especially those requiring common carrier deliveries, stock transfers may be the preferred "inter-facility" method for the transfer of stocks. In addition, if your organization employs "branch" accounting and therefore has "interbranch" sales at a transfer price, usually at a cost-plus basis, the stock transfer transaction should be used.

Stock Valuation

Stock valuation is an important concept. There are many approaches to the valuation of inventory. This section introduces the methods of stock valuation available in OneWorld.

Costing

Many ERP systems are designed around a single cost value or definition per inventory or stock item. As stock is removed from or added to inventory, this single cost value is the basis for the transaction. Some ERP systems provide for the definition of multiple costs or methods of valuation at the item level, but not at the branch/plant level. OneWorld provides an extensive amount of control over item costing.

From Where Is Cost Derived?

In OneWorld, a single overall cost can be maintained for an item, or a different item cost can be maintained for each branch/plant. A different cost can also be defined for each location and lot within a branch/plant. OneWorld maintains inventory costs in the Inventory Cost file (F4105). The Inventory Cost Level is a code that indicates whether OneWorld maintains one overall inventory cost for an item, a different cost for each branch/plant, or a different cost for each location and lot within a branch/plant.

Purchase order prices can be established in OneWorld in one of several ways. The simplest method is to specify and control purchase order costing using a cost value from the item master or the item branch/plant record. The second method is to specify price at the supplier and item level, or at the supplier, item, and branch/plant level. The Purchase Price Level code is used to indicate from where a cost is retrieved when creating a purchase order.

Which Cost to Use

Currently, J. D. Edwards predefines 10 of 20 reserved cost methods. An item cost is maintained at the cost method level. OneWorld programs update the cost associated with a specific cost method. Any number of user-defined costs can be added in OneWorld, but user-defined cost methods require manual maintenance. If an item cost is not entered for a cost method that is assigned to any sales, inventory, or purchasing transaction, OneWorld provides a warning message. If this message is bypassed, a cost of 0 is assigned on the transaction.

Costs are established for an item by entering a cost value for each cost method that your organization will use. The cost amount for any cost method can be changed at any time. For example, if the amount associated with the cost method used to calculate costs of goods sold is changed, OneWorld applies the new amount to the item's on-hand quantity. A journal entry is also created to record the difference between the old and the new cost amounts. Table 16-2 lists the predefined costing methods in OneWorld.

Table 16-2 Predefined Costing Methods

Cost Method	Cost Title
01	Last In
02	Weighted-Average
03	Memo
04	Current

Table 16-2 Predefined Costing Methods *(continued)*

Cost Method	Cost Title
05	Future
06	Lot
07	Standard
08	Purchasing (Base)
09	Actual
10	Historical Average

Physical Counts

Most organizations carry out a physical inventory of their stock on hand at least once per fiscal year to ensure the accuracy of their inventory balances. Various procedures can be implemented to satisfy the need for a physical inventory. A physical inventory is conducted at the storage location level. Generally speaking, an organization conducts physical inventories using one or a combination of the following approaches:

◆ Periodic inventory

◆ Continuous inventory

◆ Cycle counting

◆ Inventory sampling

◆ Exception counting

OneWorld provides two facilities to support an organization's physical inventory process. OneWorld has a cycle counting facility and a tag counting facility. Cycle counting is an item-based method of counting stock on hand, and tag counting is a location-based method of counting.

OneWorld Periodic Inventory Support

Using the periodic inventory approach, all stock on hand is physically counted on a given date. Typically, the complete physical inventory is taken at or near a key balance sheet date, such as a month end, quarter end, or fiscal year end. During counting, material movements within the entire warehouse are typically suspended. The OneWorld tag counting feature supports full, periodic physicals.

OneWorld Continuous Inventory Support

If the continuous inventory approach is used, stocks are counted continuously throughout the entire fiscal year. With this approach, every piece of material is physically counted at least once during the fiscal year. Frequently, an organization will create a business day cycle scheme by counting the total stock-keeping locations and then dividing by the number of business days in the year to arrive at the number of items to count each business day. Stocks are then selected on a random or sequential basis for assignment to a business day bucket for counting purposes. Although OneWorld does provide a facility that divides the physical stock into business date buckets, the OneWorld cycle counting feature can be used to support the continuous inventory approach.

OneWorld Cycle Counting Support

Using the cycle counting approach, a physical inventory is conducted at regular intervals throughout the fiscal year. These intervals (or cycles) depend on the cycle counting indicator set for the materials. Use of cycle counting based on an item's ABC classification code allows higher-value items to be counted more frequently than lower-cost items. For instance, some organizations might want to count fast-moving items more frequently than slow-moving items to prevent stock-outs. OneWorld provides support for the former but not the latter method of item selection through its cycle counting facility. A custom turnover analysis program that updates a reporting code within the item/branch plant record would be necessary. This value would in turn be used as the basis for selecting items identified for turns-based counting, made using the OneWorld cycle counting facilities.

OneWorld Sampling-Based Counting Support

If the inventory sampling approach is used, randomly selected stocks must be physically counted as of a given date. This date is usually a key balance sheet date, such as a month end, quarter end, or fiscal year end. If the variances between the result of the count and the book inventory balance are small enough, it is presumed that the book inventory balances for the other stocks are correct and that further counts of stock are unwarranted. OneWorld does not provide support for this method of item selection. A custom sampling program that updates a reporting code within the item/branch plant record would be necessary. This value would in turn be used as the basis for selecting items identified for random counting, made using the OneWorld cycle counting facilities.

OneWorld Exception-Based Counting Support

Exception-based counting assumes that any given item's on-hand balance is accurate unless a physical stock-out occurs. This would happen when OneWorld indicates that a sufficient on-hand balance exists but stock is not physically "found" in the location that matches the information in OneWorld. When any movement request (such as transfer or sales order pick/confirm) can't be completed due to a physical stock-out, the item is physically counted. An item-specific count is made using the OneWorld cycle counting facilities.

How the OneWorld Physical Count Process Works

In general, the first step in conducting a physical inventory is to select the items to be counted. In OneWorld, the selection process builds a record for each inventory item to be counted and notes the current on-hand quantity and the cost of each item from the OneWorld item/balance and location records into a count-related work file. This information is subsequently used when making any adjustments necessary due to a difference between the physical count of the item and the quantity on hand for an item.

Cycle Counting

The following steps are followed in the OneWorld cycle count process:

1. Select items to count.
2. Review the cycle count status.
3. Print the cycle count sheets.
4. Enter the cycle count results.
5. Review any cycle count variances.
6. Recount and revise the cycle count quantity as necessary.
7. Print the variance report.
8. Update the cycle count status and stock on-hand balances, and write adjustments to the general ledger.

As previously stated, item selection is an important prerequisite step in cycle counting. Also, note that a cycle count can be canceled if necessary. In OneWorld, tag counting is a rather formal and extensive counting technique. As a practical consideration, the OneWorld cycle counting process is frequently used in lieu of the tag counting method to carry out a complete physical inventory as well. The results are the same—a physical count is made, differences are noted, and adjustments to both item quantity and ledger balances are made.

Tag Counting

OneWorld tag counting is derived from the concept of count teams, which sweep through the physical facility in two waves. The first team makes an initial count of stock, and the second team verifies the initial count accuracy. Since a complete count in a large physical location can take a considerable period of time, records of receipts and issues from stock must be separately tracked and updated unless all movement operations are suspended during a physical count. In a high-volume distribution operation, such a cessation of operations is not always possible.

The following steps are followed in the OneWorld tag count process:

1. Select items to count.
2. Print inventory tags.
3. Record tag distribution information.
4. Record tag receipt information.
5. Enter the tag count results.
6. Review the tag status.
7. Review any count variances.
8. Perform any recount where necessary.
9. Update the stock on-hand balances and write adjustments to the general ledger.

Note that for a tag count, usually *all* items and locations are involved. As previously noted, tag-based counting requires the distributing and tracking of count tags. OneWorld has built-in facilities for tag tracking.

On a final note, regardless of method—cycle or tag-based counting—OneWorld creates the necessary journal entries to reflect count-based adjustments to the appropriate inventory account to which an item is valued. It should be noted that OneWorld does not "freeze" or "block" stock-related movements when an item has been selected for counting purposes. Cessation of movements during a physical inventory is entirely a business-driven decision.

Stock Valuation

Inventory or stock valuation is an important concern for any organization whose business model includes the distribution or manufacturing of tangible, inventoried products. Although not as controversial as it once was, accounting for inventory has consistently been a widely debated topic in the accounting profession. As a result, there is substantial variation as to what is considered a generally accepted practice for inventory valuation. In addition, most organizations enjoy some latitude in changing their inventory valuation method. For instance, depending on general price levels and economic conditions, a change in method is sometimes desirable, especially for tax considerations, given that the treatment of inventory for financial reporting and tax purposes can differ. It should also be noted that variations exist between inventory accounting practices of the United States and other countries.

With regard to inventory or stock valuation, many standard ERP systems simply do not handle inventory accounting differences easily. By incorporating a Stock Valuation system into its software, J. D. Edwards provides facilities that can help an organization properly identify cost layers in inventory and subsequently adjust the remaining value of cost layers based on the inventory transactions that have occurred.

Reorder Point Planning

For procured or manufactured materials, OneWorld Inventory Management systems provide for simple reorder point planning of items carried in inventory. The item branch/plant record can store information regarding safety stock, minimum and maximum inventory levels, lot sizes, and lead-time information necessary to avoid costly or disruptive stock-out conditions.

The Inventory Management system includes both a Buyers Guide and a Supply/Demand report to help plan inventory replenishment activities. The Purchase Order Workbench program in the Procurement system includes the ability to generate purchase order lines *automatically* based on reorder point information. In World software, this feature was known as the Purchase Order Generator. Note that the Distribution Requirements Planning (DRP) and Materials Requirements Planning (MRP) capabilities found in the OneWorld Manufacturing suite of systems further enhances inventory planning.

Locating and Identifying Stock in OneWorld

OneWorld provides many features to assist your organization in controlling where stock is physically located. In addition, depending on the sophistication of your business requirements, OneWorld also provides features that will assist your organization in identifying specific stock. The stock location and identification features facilitated through OneWorld's Distribution systems are discussed in the following sections.

The highest level that OneWorld defines for both location and valuation purposes is the branch/plant. The branch/plant can represent everything from a storeroom within a warehouse to a rack jobber's truck. It is important to note that *each* branch/plant can be configured differently, depending on your organization's specific requirements.

Location Control

OneWorld provides a stock locator feature through its location control feature. Every item has one and only one primary location in each branch/plant facility and may have any number of secondary stocking locations. A primary location is designated immediately after you assign an item to a given branch/plant. Generally speaking, OneWorld processes an item through its primary storage location. For example, when an item is received, OneWorld assigns the item to its primary location, unless a secondary location is specified.

Each time a specific location is designated in a transaction for an item, OneWorld automatically creates a location record in the item location file (F41021). The sum of the records in the item location table represents the total stock balance for a branch/plant location. Locations can be added merely *by reference* in a transaction. Items can also be *location-controlled*. When an item is location-controlled, it can be assigned only to locations that are preestablished in OneWorld. If you do not configure OneWorld for location control, items can be assigned to any location.

Lot Control

In addition to assigning items to multiple locations within a given branch/plant, it is also possible to assign multiple *lot numbers* within each location. Lot numbers are entered manually when items are received into a specified location. Chapter 14 discussed the item information hierarchy and provides more information on this subject.

Expiration Date

In many industries, including food and life science, lot control is frequently driven by a product's *expiration date*. This is the date on which a lot of items will expire. OneWorld automatically calculates this date when a "shelf life"—in days—is specified for the item in either the Item Master record or the Item Branch/Plant record. OneWorld calculates the expiration date by adding the number of shelf life days to the date an item is received into a location. Note that OneWorld can "commit" inventory based on an item's lot expiration date. Typically, expired lots are quarantined, destroyed, or downgraded—for example, from human to animal use only.

Serialization

In certain situations, the use of a serial number is necessary. In addition to assigning items to multiple locations within a given branch/plant, it is also possible to assign multiple lot numbers to a given location. Consider that a lot number is in effect a serial number. Also note that the use of lot or serial numbers is not mutually exclusive in that either one or the other form of lot control is used, but not both. OneWorld provides special features to force entry of serial numbers when completing certain OneWorld transactions.

Grading and Potency

OneWorld provides for grading or potency control over an item maintained in an item branch/plant location. Note that grade or potency control is applicable to lot-controlled items only. The use of a grading and potency control is on an item-by-item basis. Also note that the use of grading or potency control is not mutually exclusive in that either one or the other form of lot control is used, but not both.

A *grade* enables the classification of items. Lumber is frequently graded. *Potency* is a term associated with many food and life science products. Potency lets you specify the percentage of an active ingredient within a given compound. For example, certain chemicals are mixed in a water slurry mix. The percentage of the active ingredient content in the slurry is a typical potency measure.

When grade or potency control is activated for an item, a standard value and a range of acceptable values are defined for the item. When this item is received or issued, if the event-related reading or lot classification is not within the allowed range, OneWorld provides a warning message. If a grade or potency is not specified, OneWorld uses the standard value from the item branch/plant Additional System Information form.

Also note that items that are "out of range" cannot be shipped under a sales order. It is also possible to specify an acceptable grade or potency range at the customer level using a *preference profile*. For instance, this feature is useful when a client, such as a home builder, accepts only selected grades of lumber from a millwork supplier.

Inventory Reporting

OneWorld includes various management reports related to the valuation, control, and replenishment of stock. This section introduces several important OneWorld inventory reporting concepts.

ABC Analysis

ABC analysis of inventory is based on the principle that a small number of items account for the largest portion of an organization's business or inventory flows. A slightly larger number of items account for a smaller but significant amount of business, and the remaining and larger number of items, taken together, account for only a small amount of business. ABC analysis therefore ranks inventory items with a letter grade of A, B, or C, where A represents the items with the highest total sales, largest gross margin, or largest on-hand value.

In OneWorld, dollar value is used as the basis for measurement in the ABC analysis of inventory. For instance, when items are classified by total sales, they are in fact being classified by a measure of their turnover. Items that turn over faster generate a greater amount of total overall revenues. However, when all items generate roughly the same amount of revenue, a different approach might be needed. Therefore, OneWorld also allows ABC analysis based on an item's gross margin or on-hand (total cost) value.

The ABC analysis ranking determined by OneWorld can be used as the basis for inventory cycle counts, in which A items are counted more often than C items. You can also use different ranking percentages in each category. A, B, and C classification buckets are determined by percentage thresholds. These percentage thresholds are user-defined in OneWorld and typically represent the natural breaks in your overall inventory valuation.

The OneWorld ABC analysis report can be run in two modes—proof mode or final mode. Proof mode prints the ABC rating information without updating the item's branch/plant record. In final mode, the ABC rating is updated in the item's branch/plant record. A processing option determines if the batch process produces a report only or produces a report and performs the update based on the calculation of a new ABC ranking.

The Item Ledger

OneWorld maintains, on a record-by-record basis and by location, both a history and the running or on-hand inventory balance. This net change in inventory is managed through the item ledger or Cardex file. The OneWorld item ledger or Cardex inquiry program is used to view the beginning balance as well as the history of the stock increases and decreases and the current or on-hand balance for any given item.

It is important to note that most movement of stock items has general ledger impact. As a result, inventory corrections should always be handled in the correct manner—through an appropriate inventory-related movement transaction, such as a transfer, adjustment, receipt, issue, or shipment transaction. For organizations that previously relied only on periodic inventory control methods instead of any form of perpetual inventory control, this requires a significant amount of process change and adjustment of business practices—in short, process discipline.

The OneWorld Distribution System Transaction Model

The good news about both OneWorld Procurement and Sales Order Management is that although the two business processes differ substantially—Procure to Pay versus Order to Cash—the basic configuration concepts, data model, and processing model structure driving these two systems are quite similar. OneWorld provides an extensive amount of flexibility in defining custom documents and document workflows.

Both procurement and sales-related documents have basically the same structure. These transactions, or documents as they are called in OneWorld, are made up of a document header and any number of order detail lines. Document headers are stored separately from detail lines in the OneWorld database. Generally speaking, the sales order creation and processing program in OneWorld is more sophisticated than that used for purchase order creation and processing.

When a transaction document is created by a user without copying or referencing an existing document, OneWorld uses its master data records to "build out" the transaction. Therefore, required data entry can be reduced to a minimum. For instance, a sold-to/order-from Address Book value, a requested delivery date and item numbers and quantities are about all that is necessary to complete an order document for an established customer or supplier. Figure 16-1 illustrates on an overall basis how master data influences and populates transaction documents.

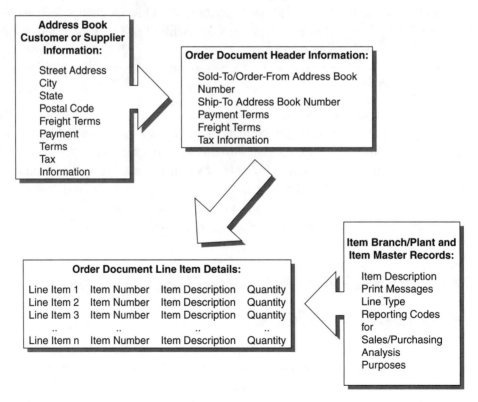

FIGURE 16-1 *Master Data Transfer onto Order Documents*

Document Header Information

General information that is valid for the entire order document is entered in the document header, including the following:

◆ The address number of the sold-to or order-from party

◆ The address number of the ship-to party or location

◆ The requested delivery date

◆ The branch/plant the order is placed against or drawn on

It is important to note that an order header is a "static snapshot" of the master data—the customer master or supplier master—at the given point in time when the order document was first created. Therefore, if any customer master or supplier master changes are made, any pending order documents need to be manually updated to reflect this new information. Your business procedures should include reviewing open orders for a given customer or supplier and then adjusting open orders for these same changes. It might be necessary to review open order information with these external parties to ensure that pending orders should indeed be changed. Typically, it is considered a good practice to not revise any documents that have already been processed.

Information entered into the document header by the user defaults into order line data fields as suggested information. The user may choose to override these defaults. OneWorld program features allow the user to change header-level information and subsequently roll these header-level changes downstream, into the individual order lines that comprise the transaction document.

Order Line Information

While information entered into the document header applies to all the individual order lines of a document, certain item-specific information is entered at the individual order line level in a document:

◆ The item number

◆ Any item-related reporting code values

◆ Quantity ordered

◆ The address number of the ship-to party. Perhaps an alternative ship-to party must be indicated for a given line item on the order.

◆ Pricing and handling-related code values for order lines

Generally speaking, virtually all of the item-specific information related to the individual order line level in a document can be provided by the item master and item/branch plant records and therefore defaults into order line-level data fields as suggested information.

Document Types

The OneWorld Procurement system and the OneWorld Sales Order Management system each provide a predefined set of document types that can be modified to suit your particular business requirements. Note that your organization's business processes dictate to what extent these predefined document types will be used. For instance, not every document type will be needed. In some cases, it might be necessary to create document types that are specific to your organization's business processes. This is a relatively easy process in OneWorld. For instance, I have created a "stock reservation" transaction using a sales order document to place "demand" on inventory for stock planning by purchasing agents. When the order is "filled" using "reserved stock," the planning line is canceled.

For instance, the basic purchase order document type is the OP document, and the Sales Order Management document type is SO. The general rule is that purchase order document types begin with O, and sales order document types begin with S. Although you might think that Purchasing system documents begin with P, that is not the case. P is used to denote Accounts Payable transactions. Table 16-3 lists the major document types defined in OneWorld and the typical use or application for each document type.

Table 16-3 Typical OneWorld Document Types

Document Type	Typical or Intended Use of This Document Type
OB	Blanket purchase order
OD	Direct ship purchase order
OP	Purchase order
OQ	Request for quotation
OR	Purchase order requisition
OS	Subcontracted operations purchase order
OT	Stock transfer order, as received by the "source" facility

Table 16-3 Typical OneWorld Document Types *(continued)*

Document Type	Typical or Intended Use of This Document Type
OV	Purchase order receipt/receipt voucher
SB	Blanket sales order
SD	Direct ship sales order
SO	Sales order
SQ	Sales quotation
ST	Stock transfer order, as requested by the "destination" facility

Inventory Line Types

The OneWorld Inventory system provides for multiple inventory or order line types in OneWorld. These line types apply equally to the OneWorld Purchasing system and the Sales Order Management system. Several important characteristics are related to line type. The first characteristic defines how the inventory will be affected by this line item. For instance, a direct ship or drop ship line type does not affect an item's inventory balance, nor do nonstock items affect an item's inventory balance.

A second characteristic of line type is to determine if a sales or use tax should be assessed on this type of order line. For instance, when passing freight charges, an excise tax, or an installation charge to the client, such charges might be exempt from a sales or use tax calculation. Table 16-4 lists the delivered inventory line types and their uses. Note that an order document line does not need to be associated with an item. Thus, a line type can be created and used for the entry of freight charges, installation, and other nontaxable items as well.

Table 16-4 Typical OneWorld Inventory Line Types

Line Type	Description	Affect on Inventory
S	Stock Item	Impacts inventory and general ledger
N	Nonstock Item	Has no inventory impact. Has general ledger impact, such as expensed when purchased.
D	Direct (Drop) Shipment Item	Has no inventory impact. Has general ledger impact.

Order Processing Rules

One of the hallmarks of OneWorld is its rule-based order processing workflow. The OneWorld order processing workflow can be as simple or as complicated as your organization might care to make it, because it is a configurable process. Workflow steps can be established as required, or they can be considered an optional step, when other allowed steps are defined within an order processing flow.

OneWorld document workflow is determined by a series of sequentially numbered steps called *status codes*. Each order document requires a status code–driven workflow. This requirement must be repeated and changed as necessary for each document and line type combination. For instance, a quotation document that requires sales or product management approval typically has a different document flow from that of a sales order document, which might need a credit approval.

Status codes thus indicate the passing of a document from one status to the next in OneWorld. Therefore, the most important status code value in OneWorld is always the next status that is allowed for the document. An additional or alternative order processing workflow can be established. The alternative workflow step is called the override or other allowed status or workflow step. Tables 16-5 and 16-6 list the representative workflow steps for the sales order and purchase order document types, respectively.

Table 16-5 A Typical Sales Order (SO) Document Processing Status Flow

Last/Next Status Value	Action/Step
520	Sales order line created
540	Print sales acknowledgment
560	Print pick ticket
580	Ready to pick/confirm
600	Ready to invoice
999	Order line closed (shipment completed or order line was canceled)

Table 16-6 A Typical Purchase Order (OP) Document Processing Status Flow

Last/Next Status Value	Action/Step
220	Purchase order line created
240	Print purchase order

Table 16-6 A Typical Purchase Order (OP) Document Processing Status Flow (continued)

Last/Next Status Value	Action/Step
280	Print purchase order receiver
400	Ready to receive
999	Order line closed (received or order line was canceled)

How Status Updates Occur

As mentioned previously, a status code indicates the passing of a document from one status to the next. The obvious question is, what causes the status of a document to be advanced or updated? A status update occurs when a desired action or event related to a document has been completed—usually by another OneWorld program. For instance, the status of a purchase order line is updated from "ready to receive" to "received-complete" status when a receipt is recorded against the purchase order document. Figure 16-2 illustrates a typical OneWorld sales order document path, and Figure 16-3 illustrates a typical OneWorld purchase order document path. Note that optional or "other allowed" paths are shown with dashed lines.

Order Processing Setup

The setup of both the Procurement and the Sales Order Management workflow processes are similar in OneWorld. In general, the steps are as follows:

1. Set up document types. Note the significance of the first letter to particular systems within OneWorld. The second character is generally a user-determined value.

2. Set up order line types. The order line type determines how OneWorld programs will process a detail line contained in an order document.

3. Set up order activity rules. Order activity rules define the sequence of allowable steps that an order document will take from beginning to end. An alternative sequence is said to exist if the next allowed status value is noted for a given activity.

4. Define automatic accounting instructions related to the document type.

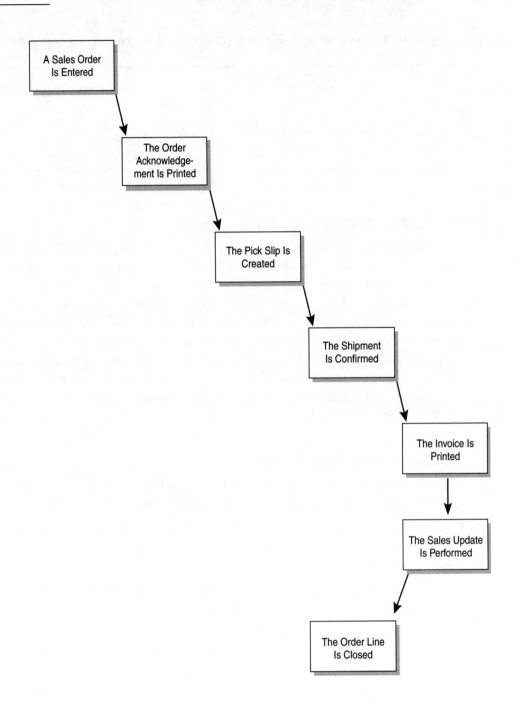

FIGURE 16-2 *A Typical OneWorld Sales Order Processing Cycle*

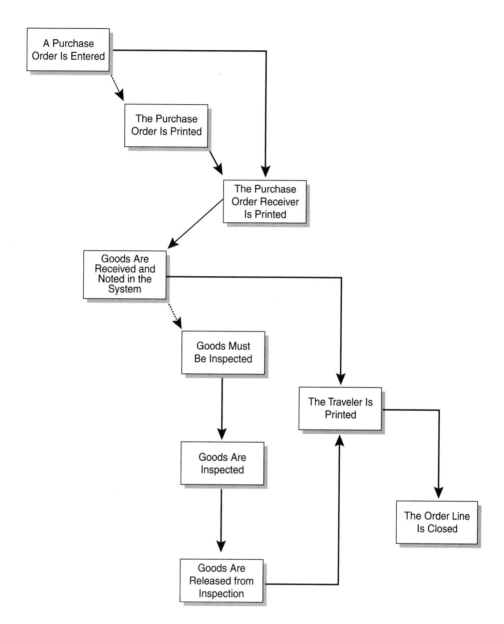

FIGURE 16-3 *A Typical OneWorld Purchase Order Processing Cycle*

5. Create an organization-specific version of the order entry program for each document type created. For instance, a new purchase order document type will require a new version for the purchase order entry program.

6. Review and maintain the processing options related to each organization-specific version of the order entry program for each document type created.

OneWorld provides a tremendous amount of processing power and choice through its user-definable order document process. When comparing OneWorld to SAP R/3, the OneWorld documents and their processing steps are much more fluid. Configuration is also less cumbersome. However, in all fairness to SAP, many more prebuilt document types exist in R/3 than in OneWorld. If your organization requires custom document types, remember that extensive testing should be performed on new document types. Such testing should be done on a full-cycle basis to ensure that all steps—particularly inventory, general ledger, and sales tax processing—work as expected.

Order Processing History

OneWorld also maintains an audit trial or history of the workflow steps if one is required. Generally speaking, it is a good practice to log document creation, change, or disposition events. A log is called a *history* file in OneWorld. For instance, purchase order creation and goods receipt could be captured, but printing a purchase order would not be a logged event.

Note that OneWorld document history does not affect document processing or document information—history creation is the result of document processing. From an information perspective, a transaction history record is both a "subset" and a "snapshot" of the information for a given order line. Again, note that maintaining document history is completely optional. OneWorld stores history records in a separate table that can be viewed through a history file inquiry.

Document Processing Integration

OneWorld Purchasing and Sales Order Management systems rely extensively on the OneWorld foundation systems—the Address Book for customer and supplier information, General Accounting for the chart of accounts, and Automatic Accounting Instructions and Inventory Management for item-related information. The OneWorld order processing configuration—including line types, G/L category codes, and Automatic Accounting Instructions—determines how specific order items interface with both the General Accounting and Inventory Management systems.

Sales Order Processing

The Sales Order Management system provides an overall set of programs that support the "order to cash" processing cycle typically found at most organizations. The OneWorld sales order entry process relies heavily on predefined master data—both customer- and item-related information. Therefore, a minimal amount of information is needed to create a sales order using OneWorld. This improves sales force and customer service productivity by minimizing extensive or redundant data entry while reducing order fulfillment–related errors.

The OneWorld Sales Order Management system has a number of noteworthy features:

◆ The use of customer billing instructions, which are established as part of the customer master record and that serve as rules for processing a customer's order.

◆ Orders can be placed on an administrative hold—for instance, to review pricing or configuration. This is a particularly useful feature for configure or make-to-order product environments. After review, quotations can be released for publication.

◆ Orders can also be placed on a credit hold, based on accounts receivable system activity and the customer master record settings.

◆ Order items can, if appropriate, be placed on backorder.

◆ You can define branch sale markups, which are then applied as transfer costs that apply to interbranch sales or transfer orders.

◆ Commission processing is a challenge in many organizations. Using OneWorld, it is possible to establish a commission structure for a group of salespeople, as well as for a specific salesperson, and use this information when processing a customer order.

◆ Returns from customers and return order credit memoranda can be managed and facilitated through the Sales Order Management system.

◆ Quotations can be created in much the same manner as a sales order is created in OneWorld. A specific quotation document can then be used as the basis for creation of a sales order—without creating a new document from scratch. The final sales order document can be further modified to include customer-requested changes.

♦ Direct ship orders can be created. A direct ship order occurs from the sale of an item that is purchased from a supplier, who then sends the item directly to your customer. The quantity of goods reflected on a direct ship order for a given item does not affect the item's inventory balance. When a direct ship sales order is created, the Sales Order Management system simultaneously creates a purchase order for submission to the supplier. The purchase order requests that the supplier ship the contents of the order directly to the customer noted on the order.

♦ Define and use preferences to customize the way a sales order is processed. Typically, preferences are needed when business requirements aren't consistent for all customers or a group of customers.

The Sales Order Management system includes numerous other features that are beyond the scope of this basic introduction to OneWorld. Many of these features are activated through processing options related to specific OneWorld order management programs. Consult the Sales Order Management system reference guide on the OneWorld documentation CD-ROM for further information.

Procurement

The Procurement system provides an overall set of programs that support the procure to pay processing cycle typically found at most organizations. The OneWorld purchase order entry process relies heavily on predefined master data—both supplier and item-related information. Therefore, a minimal amount of information is needed to create a purchase order using OneWorld. Use of the Procurement system improves the procurement staff's productivity by minimizing extensive or redundant data entry. The Procurement system also improves the buyer's ability to actively manage supplier relationships on a proactive basis. In general, OneWorld provides support for the procurement of the following:

♦ Replenishing end-product inventory used for resale purposes

♦ Replenishing inventory that represents a purchased component or a raw material that will be incorporated into a manufactured end product

♦ Charging purchased goods and services to specific departments, jobs, or projects

♦ Acquiring long-lived assets used in the ordinary course of business

Although what is being procured might vary greatly, as illustrated by this list, the procure-to-pay cycle typically found in most organizations includes these general steps:

- The making of a request or requisition for specific goods or services
- The approval of a requisition for specific goods or services
- If deemed necessary, requesting a quotation regarding the procurement of specific goods or services from one or more qualified suppliers
- Placing an order with the preferred or winning supplier
- Receiving the goods or services from the supplier
- Creating a voucher to schedule pay for the goods or services received

Within OneWorld, there are really two purchasing processes. Depending on the needs of your organization, one or both of these processes will be used for your procurement process. For instance, stock-based procurement is designed to accommodate purchasing for inventory, while all nonstock items and services are procured against specific general ledger account numbers. Several noteworthy features are found in the OneWorld Procurement system:

- The ability to establish supplier performance measures and build statistics from order history for such performance measures.
- Support for evaluated receipt settlement. When evaluated receipt settlement is used, vouchers for purchase order receipts are subsequently created automatically.
- The ability to track purchasing commitments and encumbrances to prevent account deficits. This is an especially useful feature for nonprofit organizations or government entities that use OneWorld.
- The ability to provide order document approval routing.
- The ability to create supplier-related templates. These templates can be used for requisitioning from a standardized or authorized list of purchased items.
- The ability to perform three-way matching of a purchase order to receipt and the invoice to both, or the ability to perform two-way matching of only the purchase order to invoice.
- The ability to immediately recognize the trade payable liability when goods are received. This eliminates much of the month-end guesswork as to what purchases might need to be accounted for as a liability on the balance sheet.

The Procurement system includes numerous other features that are beyond the scope of this basic introduction to OneWorld. Many of these features are activated through processing options related to specific OneWorld order management programs. Consult the Procurement system reference guide on the OneWorld documentation CD-ROM for further information.

Price Management

Although there are a few exceptions in today's highly competitive business environment, such as the "one price for everyone" scheme successfully employed at Saturn in selling its automobile, in the commercial marketplace, few purchasing agents want the term "list price" associated with their names. As a matter of fact, purchasing departments are increasingly responsible for wringing costs out of the supply chain. Therefore, as a general rule, list or base prices are rarely paid, so few customers ever pay the same price for the same item.

As a result, pricing is generally one of the most complex aspects facing most organizations. It is also one area that has to be right from the moment the first sales order is processed through OneWorld. Your customers will expect and demand of your organization such attention to detail. Therefore, when implementing OneWorld, your organization will in all likelihood devote a considerable amount of time to initially planning and setting up pricing schemes and, on an ongoing basis, maintaining pricing information in OneWorld. Price management in OneWorld is facilitated through the Advanced Pricing system. The Advanced Pricing system provides facilities for pricing setup and maintenance.

Once your organization's pricing scheme is established in OneWorld, pricing maintenance is generally straightforward. The amount of maintenance is usually minimal, but the frequency of maintenance is largely a function of the level of "individualized" pricing, general market conditions, and your organization's responses to these conditions through changes in its pricing strategy. Given that with a greater number of products being "commoditized" in today's highly competitive business and economic environment, an organization's market advantage can be significantly enhanced when it can respond quickly to changing market conditions by adjusting or refining its pricing strategy.

There are several dimensions to pricing in OneWorld. The first dimension or level of pricing is called standard price management. Standard price management is an integral part of the Sales Order Management system. It provides the basic pricing architecture in OneWorld. The second dimension of price management is called advanced pricing. The Advanced Pricing system is an additional software system that enhances the basic OneWorld pricing architecture.

Generally speaking, the standard or base price management capabilities should be used unless your organization's pricing procedures require the added features of the Advanced Pricing system. However, in practice, most businesses, regardless of size, employ pricing practices that are complex enough that the standard or base price management capabilities in OneWorld or in any ERP system are generally insufficient for their use. Therefore, most organizations must make use of the OneWorld Advanced Pricing system to some degree.

How OneWorld Pricing Works

The standard pricing capabilities in OneWorld are significant. Both customers and items can be grouped for pricing purposes. This grouping ability allows for straightforward pricing differences between distribution channels and product lines. For instance, the use of customer groups and item groups for pricing purposes largely eliminates the need to establish price adjustment information by item or by customer.

For each item that is sold, a selling price must be defined. This is called the *base* or *list* price. The base pricing structure is defined in the Sales Order Management system. The Sales Order Management system uses this base pricing structure in order to retrieve prices for the items appearing as line items on an order. The base price structure can consist of any combination of items, item groups, customers, or customer groups.

In addition to defining a base price structure, you can define price adjustments. Price adjustments that might be applied to customer orders written by your organization might include the following:

♦ Contract pricing, which typically applies special pricing for an item to a single customer, such as a national or large account

♦ Trade discount pricing, which is a discount percentage on all items for a specific customer group, such as a dealer channel

In general, OneWorld's price adjustment functionality includes the ability to do the following:

♦ Accrue an adjustment amount instead of making the adjustment to the order line itself

♦ Adjust a price by a specified percentage of the base price

◆ Adjust a price by a percentage of the current net price

◆ Adjust a price by a percentage amount of an item's cost

◆ Adjust a price by a specific amount

◆ Adjust a price using an "override" price

In addition, price adjustments are "effective dated" from a given date, through a given date for purposes of providing for a limited-time offer.

On an overall basis, price adjustments can be combined into a pricing structure or price schedule. Within each pricing schedule, any number of price adjustments can be made. For instance, regular discounts and promotional discounts can be combined within the same schedule, thereby allowing multiple adjustments to each sales order line.

Advanced Pricing

Use of the OneWorld Advanced Pricing system enhances standard pricing capabilities by providing additional flexibility for working with pricing groups. Adjustments can be created for single items, single customers, groups of items, or groups of customers. Customers can be further identified by the Sold To, Ship To, or a parent customer number. Using the OneWorld Advanced Pricing system, prices—at the sales order line item level—can be further adjusted.

Price Management and Its Applicability to Procurement

A significant portion of the basic and advanced pricing capabilities available for the OneWorld Sales Order Management system applies equally to the Procurement system and to the management of item/supplier cost relationships. Consult both the Procurement system reference guide and the Advanced Pricing system reference guide on the OneWorld documentation CD-ROM. In addition, a white paper on this subject is available through the Knowledge Garden.

Transportation Management

The Transportation Management system assists your organization in transporting goods and materials from one geographic location to another. The movement of raw materials, components, and finished products, from supplier to manufacturer and from distribution center to customer, represents a significant percentage of the product's final cost.

In addition, knowing the exact location of goods while in transit to a customer is considered an important dimension of world-class customer service. The OneWorld Transportation Management system provides features that help an organization do the following:

◆ Reduce transportation costs

◆ Select the appropriate freight services

◆ Calculate freight charges

◆ Create loads to decrease costs and to meet volume shipping commitments with specific carriers

◆ Create shipping documents

◆ Provide for shipment dispatching and shipment tracking

◆ Improve customer service by making order status and shipment information available on a door-to-door basis

◆ Apply freight charges to sales orders

It is best to view the OneWorld Transportation Management system as an enhancement to the basic Sales Order Management system workflow. Therefore, the use of the Transportation Management system is completely optional.

A *shipment* is the essential transaction in the Transportation Management system. The shipment transaction itself is created through the Sales Order Management system. A shipment is derived from a single sales order document, or it may represent the combination of multiple sales orders for the same customer. The Transportation Management system defines a process flow that any shipment follows from the time an order is picked for shipment until the time that the shipment is delivered to the customer. Figure 16-4 illustrates how the Transportation Management system enhances the basic order-to-delivery cycle.

Landed Costs

The movement of raw materials, components, and end products from supplier to manufacturer to distribution center can represent a significant percentage of an end item's final cost. For instance, it is not uncommon when purchasing items to incur extra fees for delivery, brokerage, and forwarding fees, as well as import duties and taxes. Collectively, these costs are called *landed costs*. OneWorld supports landed costs in one of several ways. Landed costs for an item can be recorded at time of goods receipt or during a follow-on process to the goods receipt process.

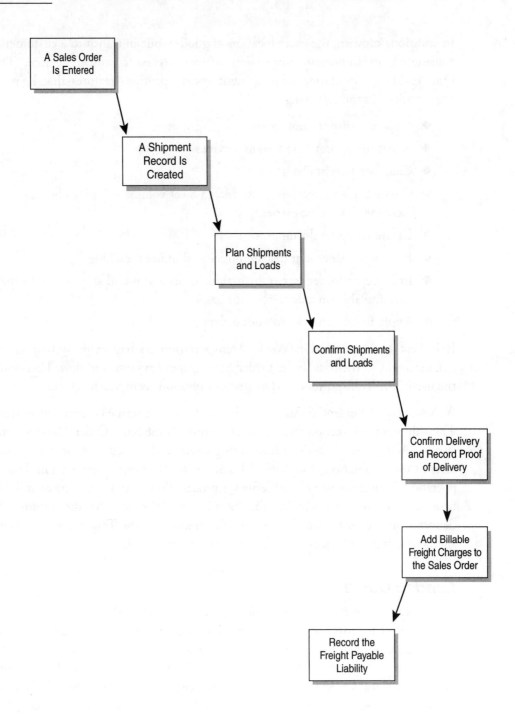

FIGURE 16-4 *The Transportation Management System Workflow*

Although landed costs can be entered during goods receipt, in practice this is not usually when this information is available. Also, you might not want to assign this responsibility to receiving personnel. As a general rule, it is preferable to enter landed cost information as a follow-up process to goods receipt. The stand-alone landed cost processing program is accessed from the Receipts Matching and Posting menu.

OneWorld Warehouse Management

The Warehouse Management system enhances OneWorld's basic inventory management capabilities and is therefore an integral part of OneWorld's distribution and manufacturing systems. Note that use of the warehouse management system is completely optional. In fact, if your organization's requirements can be met through the basic item locator capabilities available in the OneWorld Inventory Management system, it might be best to avoid or at least postpone the implementation of the Warehouse Management system.

The Warehouse Management system significantly enhances control over warehouse operations, from receiving and storing items to their retrieval and shipment. OneWorld Warehouse Management is primarily intended to manage material flows in *a high-volume environment*.

Rule-Driven

The Warehouse Management system is *rule-driven*. These rules establish parameters for how stock is stored, picked, and replenished. Therefore, the Warehouse Management system requires an extensive definition of an organization's stocking locations and the rules that govern the movement of goods to or from these stocking locations, as well as item-specific rules regarding storage conditions. These rules can require a significant amount of forethought, planning, setup, and item maintenance effort.

Transaction-Based

The Warehouse Management system is *transaction-based*. Warehouse Management–related transactions are created based on rules that govern the stocking location from where material is "picked" or to where material is put away within a warehouse. In general, when the Warehouse Management system is used, the material transaction flows in other OneWorld systems are modified so as to generate either picking requests or putaway reservations. These requests or reservations are subsequently confirmed.

In this sense, the Warehouse Management system–related transactions are best thought of as follow-on transactions to selected inventory, manufacturing, purchasing, and sales transactions. These Warehouse Management system–related transactions affect locations and as such do not create any accounting journal entries.

The Warehouse Definition

The definition of the warehouse itself within OneWorld should optimize the use of physical space and employee time and should take into account unique storage requirements related to the goods themselves. The warehouse definition can extend stock control to the lowest levels of detail that will direct distribution personnel to exactly where an item is physically located. Warehouse definition can require a significant amount of forethought, planning, and setup. Also note that changes in your warehouse configuration will require the same, if not more, effort.

Significant Warehouse Management System Features

Some of the more significant features in the Warehouse Management system include provisions for the following:

◆ Monitoring every location in the warehouse, triggering stock movements to replenish picking locations as stock is depleted

◆ Choosing between manual or automatic storage, picking, and replenishment of stock

◆ Moving stock to and from specific locations through manual selection, or automatically, using system-generated suggestions

◆ Confirming stock movements manually or automatically

◆ Preplanning the routes or paths that distribution personnel follow through the warehouse that will maximize their productivity

◆ Defining the use of fixed or randomly selected locations that can be combined to arrive at the most efficient stock distribution, requiring fewer overall movements

◆ Automatic carton selection during the sales order pick/confirm process

Also note that, depending on how the Warehouse Management system is configured, it can adversely impact overall transaction completion times and overall system performance. If the Warehouse Management system is set up wrong, you will in the end find yourself wishing that it had been omitted from the initial scope of your implementation.

Initially, the use of the Warehouse Management system requires *significant* additional setup work. On an ongoing basis, additional transactions are also necessary. These transactions primarily impact the distribution department in a typical organization. As previously mentioned, unless there are compelling business reasons that dictate the use of the Warehouse Management system, your organization might and should choose not to implement this system. In my experience, I have found that if an organization does not already have a complex stock locator system in place, it will not typically be a candidate for warehouse managed stock.

In conclusion, the extent to which an organization uses OneWorld's storage management and item identification features depends on many factors, including the complexity of an organization's distribution model and the "life-critical" nature of the inventoried stock. Your organization must identify its critical stock-related business requirements either prior to or during OneWorld configuration, and especially prior to any master data entry. These features exist at a basic level in the Inventory Management system and are significantly enhanced by the OneWorld Warehouse Management system. Figure 16-5 illustrates a typical OneWorld sales order document path that incorporates warehouse management transactions, and Figure 16-6 illustrates a typical OneWorld purchase order document path that incorporates warehouse management transactions.

Supply Chain Management

Increasingly, discussions in business today revolve around supply chain optimization. Customer-driven supply chain management has emerged as a key element in gaining competitive advantage. As a matter of fact, the greatest threat that most dot-com businesses represent to a traditional brick-and-mortar business is the dot-com's ability to extract activities and players from a product's supply chain where value is not added. This might have more to do with the dot-com's being a pure start-up and therefore having the ability to design its business model from the ground up.

ERP software vendors began recognizing the importance of supply chain management several years ago—not really as a result of the dot-com phenomenon, but, more importantly, through the work of the Supply Chain Council. The Supply

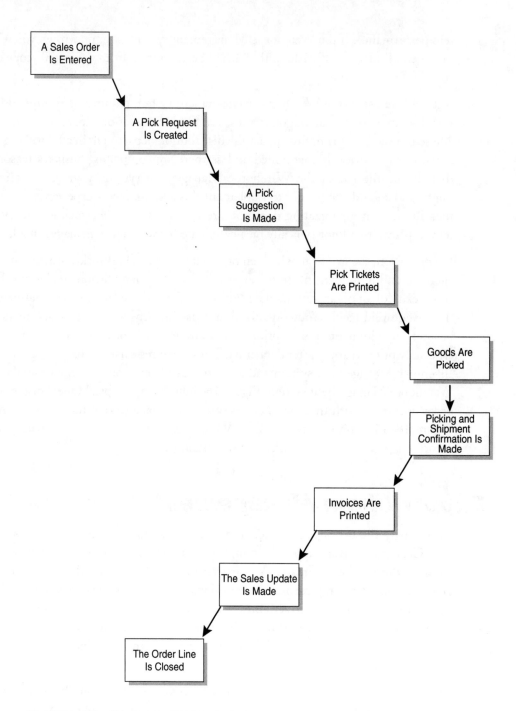

FIGURE 16-5 *A Typical OneWorld Sales Order Processing Cycle Incorporating Warehouse Management*

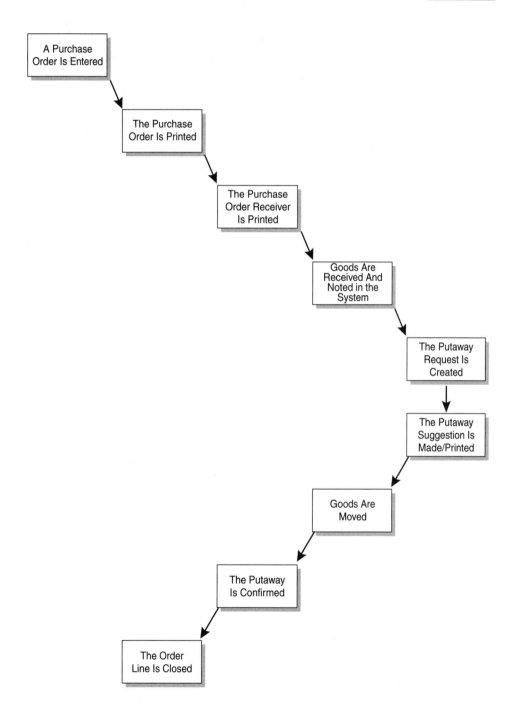

FIGURE 16-6 *A Typical OneWorld Purchase Order Processing Cycle Incorporating Warehouse Management*

Chain Council is a nonprofit trade association founded in 1996 in part by AMR Research, a manufacturing practices think tank. Membership is open to manufacturers, consultants, software companies, and educational institutions that have an interest in applying and advancing supply chain management practices and systems.

The SCOR Model

An important part of the Supply Chain Council's work has been the development and publication of the Supply Chain Operations Reference model, known as SCOR. The SCOR model is a standardized, cross-industry, supply chain management tool. The SCOR process model groups processes into four major categories:

- ◆ Plan
- ◆ Source
- ◆ Make
- ◆ Deliver

As a process reference model, SCOR combines the time-proven concepts of business process reengineering or transformation, best practices benchmarking, and process measurement, typically through using a scorecard or key performance indicators approach.

The Supply Chain Council views the SCOR model as encompassing all the processes from the supplier's supplier to the customer's customer. The SCOR model is intended to span all customer interactions of the Order to Cash process as well as all supplier interactions in the Procure to Pay process. However, the SCOR model does not address product design or post-sale support issues—its focus is squarely on the execution of the customer's current or short-term requirements. A key tenet of the SCOR model is its focus on understanding market interactions through aggregate demand.

As a process reference model, SCOR differs from more classical process models, which tend to decompose a single process configuration. The importance of SCOR as a reference model is to facilitate a common language for communicating between supply chain partners about the supply chain configuration. The SCOR process reference model defines

- ◆ Processes
- ◆ Process categories or configurations
- ◆ Process elements

Using SCOR, an organization's supply chain model is "configured to order" through a core set of processes that are defined by the model. The major processes defined by SCOR include categories for

◆ Stock products

◆ Make-to-order products

◆ Engineer-to-order products

These process configurations are further decomposed into process elements. Process elements define metrics, best practices, and enabling technologies. However, SCOR stops short of specifications regarding implementation. Implementation is carried in a fourth level and is defined by the organization that is using the SCOR model.

SCORx

Since SCOR itself is configurable, it stands to reason that any company heavily involved in implementing a supply chain management initiative based upon SCOR needs enabling technologies—such as enterprise resource planning software that also is configurable. Obviously, this is where ERP software like OneWorld factors in.

Recognizing the importance of this trend, J. D. Edwards has undertaken its own supply chain management initiative. It is known as SCORx, which stands for Supply Chain Optimization and Real-Time Extended eXecution. In many ways, SCORx represents the application of OneWorld, along with ActivEra components, to the configuration and reconfiguration of supply chains in support of SCOR compliance.

The SCORx initiative at J. D. Edwards goes beyond simply a remarketing ActivEra and OneWorld as SCOR-enabling technology. For instance, this initiative includes alliances with other software companies that extend or enhance basic OneWorld manufacturing planning and distribution functionality. For instance, Synquest is an alliance product for Advanced Planning and Scheduling (APS), and Numetrix is a product recently acquired by J. D. Edwards that provides for APS. Both of these products can be integrated with OneWorld.

The purpose of SCOR as described thus far—that it be used as a process reference model and common language for describing and configuring supply chains—is not really its most important goal. The most important goal of SCOR is that it instill a discipline—management and evaluation processes—in the supply chain that will continuously evaluate and improve supply chain performance. Thus, OneWorld's basic and extended capabilities through alliance products are intended to allow a high degree of supply chain configuration, management, and evaluation in conjunction with the SCOR model.

Summary

This chapter provided a fundamental introduction to the OneWorld suite of Distribution-related systems. The OneWorld Distribution systems include the following:

- ◆ Inventory management
- ◆ Warehouse management
- ◆ Procurement
- ◆ Sales order processing
- ◆ Price management
- ◆ Transportation management

The OneWorld Distribution systems are among the most important and complex in OneWorld. Most organizations will likely implement one or more Distribution-related systems. Except for the Manufacturing-related systems, OneWorld Distribution systems are among the most complex programs within the system.

Chapter 17

OneWorld Planning, Control, and Execution Systems

Uncertainty as the Driving Force

It is frequently said that the single most important constant facing every modern organization is change. Given the significance of change, how does the successful organization address it?

The answer is largely through planning. Any successful organization must actively engage in planning—both short-term and long-term. The challenge is to understand market and economic trends—changes—that affect the organization and to respond to these changes quickly, efficiently, and cost-effectively over time. The need for planning challenges every level of management in every organization.

However, planning alone is simply not enough. Plans must be executed, continuously monitored, and frequently updated. It has been previously and eloquently said by others before me that "you must first plan the work and then work the plan." Although often considered manufacturing-driven, enterprise-wide planning, control, and execution are important and fundamental concepts that are common to virtually all organizations and across all industries. This chapter introduces the systems within OneWorld that are related to planning, control, and execution.

The J. D. Edwards ERPx Model

J. D. Edwards refers to the planning, control, and execution systems in OneWorld as its Enterprise Requirements Planning and Execution (ERPx) model. The ERPx model is a collection of systems that facilitate enterprise-wide planning, control, and execution information flows. The systems that comprise the OneWorld ERPx model allow an organization to plan and control its inventory flows and production resources in a planned and deliberate manner, thereby completing products according to an actively and tightly managed schedule.

These OneWorld enterprise-wide planning, control, and execution support systems have features that allow these systems to serve

- ◆ In process manufacturing operations
- ◆ In discrete manufacturing operations, including make-to-stock or make-to-order operations

◆ In high-volume distribution environments

◆ In high-volume service operation environments

In addition, OneWorld planning, control, and execution systems support single- or multiple-location operations.

This chapter provides a brief introduction to the following OneWorld systems:

◆ The Product Data Management system

◆ The Shop Floor Management system

◆ The Product Costing and Manufacturing Accounting system

◆ The Quality Management system

◆ The Forecasting system

◆ The Manufacturing and Distribution Planning system

The first three systems from this list are typically implemented simultaneously and are appropriate for organizations that do not use the full manufacturing resource planning capabilities available in OneWorld. In addition, the Quality Management system can be optionally implemented to supplement these first three systems. The Forecasting and Manufacturing and Distribution Planning systems are typically implemented simultaneously and require either previous or simultaneous implementation of the first three systems in the list.

The Importance of Planning

The importance of planning cannot be understated in light of today's highly competitive, global environment that is increasingly focused on

◆ Reducing the time to market

◆ Driving out costs along the value chain by eliminating waste and any non-value-adding costs

◆ Shortening product life cycles

◆ Increased product differentiation through unique or innovative product features, which requires lean manufacturing techniques and mass customization adeptness

The successful enterprise of the future must be well positioned to balance all of these requirements. If left unchecked, most organizations will find that their operating margins will shrink and their infrastructure costs will soar. The use of a planning, control, and execution support system such as OneWorld is considered a threshold along the way toward achieving sustainable, competitive advantage in an increasingly global, time-driven marketplace.

The success of all organizations in the 21st century will likely hinge upon an increasing use of alliances, partnerships, and linked supply chains that rely heavily on information and collaboration. For instance, the previous chapter discussed the Supply Chain Council's SCOR model, which is intended to form the basis for such collaboration. In short, this balance is achieved by successfully managing the enterprise using a planning, control, and execution support system such as OneWorld. Proactively collecting, analyzing, and sharing information allows an organization to plan and operate more efficiently, regardless of the industry they happen to be in.

Simply put, organizations that actively plan and control their processes are better able to compete. The knowledge-driven organization can also leverage all available information and can adjust rapidly to changing market conditions or customer requirements.

Planning the Work

All planning, control, and execution support systems—including OneWorld—are driven by a concept known as the *planning hierarchy*. The highest level of business planning is called *strategic planning*. The strategic plan corresponds to the organization's mission statement. Strategic planning focuses on establishing the enterprise's "long, wide, and high" vision, and *operational planning* narrows this focus to "short, specific, and real" tasks that support and achieve strategic planning goals.

Although every organization and industry has somewhat unique planning horizons, as a general rule, the horizon of operational planning is typically limited to no more than one year into the future, while strategic plans typically address a span of three to five or more years. The strategic plan establishes overall priorities for the organization, and the operating plan addresses and resolves capacity issues.

After an organization's executive team develops a strategic business plan, the next step is to develop an operating plan. The strategic plan should be the starting point used in developing the operating plan. The operating plan uses long-range sales forecasts included in the strategic plan in conjunction with product-specific resource requirements to project the productive capacity and material requirements. The focus of operational planning therefore emphasizes balancing supply and demand requirements. The typical manufacturing-based operating plan consists of these planning components:

- The capacity requirements plan
- The master production schedule
- The materials requirement plan

The OneWorld Manufacturing and Distribution Planning system includes facilities to address all three of these important areas. After the completion of these components, execution of the overall plan is the next step.

Also note that OneWorld is considered a *closed-loop* MRP system. As a closed-loop system, the OneWorld Manufacturing and Distribution Planning system continuously provides feedback to manufacturing management by alerting management to material and capacity shortages and production bottlenecks.

Manufacturing System Basics

Virtually all products are produced using one of these two manufacturing models:

- The *continuous* model, in which items are produced as a result of a continuous flow process
- The *discrete* model, in which items are produced on a discrete, or one-at-a-time, basis

Regardless of the manufacturing model employed, generally accepted industry practice calls for both of these models to use a Bill of Material, routings, and a Production Order or Manufacturing Work Order as the basis of production planning, control, and execution.

Process Versus Discrete

A process manufacturing operation typically produces end products in batches through a continuous flow process. Material transformations are common in process manufacturing. A process manufacturing operation frequently involves the production of joint or coproducts and byproducts. Also note that discrete processes can result in byproducts or coproducts. For instance, the scrap or waste produced in a discrete manufacturing process, such as punch-press slugs, is considered a byproduct or coproduct if it can be recycled.

A process manufacturing operation is characterized by a series of largely dependent operations that work together continuously. The component items in the process manufacturing operation are typically called ingredients, and the manufacturing process is typically stated in terms of a recipe or formula that is required to complete the end product. Process manufacturing end product units of measure are typically represented and sold in pounds or gallons.

Examples of process manufacturing can be found in the paints and coatings, consumer-packaged goods, pharmaceuticals, chemicals, petroleum, and steel industries. OneWorld has specific capabilities designed to meet the requirements for process manufacturing.

The discrete manufacturing operation typically produces end products one at a time. Material shaping is common in discrete manufacturing. The discrete manufacturing process typically consists of a series of independent operations. A discrete end product is typically comprised of many small, intricately shaped components that must be assembled together. These components are typically called parts. Groups of functionally related parts are said to form subassemblies.

A discrete end product passes through various manufacturing operations in a semicomplete manner until it is ultimately completed. The discrete manufacturing operation uses drawings and parts lists to guide production and assembly of components into an end product. The most common unit of measure for the discrete end product is "each."

Examples of discrete manufacturing can be found in the automotive, electronics, aerospace, and consumer appliances industries. OneWorld has specific capabilities designed to meet the requirements of the discrete manufacturing model.

Make to Stock Versus Make to Order

Discrete manufacturing can be further defined by the degree to which items produced by the manufacturing process itself differ. Products resulting from a discrete manufacturing process are said to be characteristic of either a *make-to-stock* or *make-to-order* environment.

For instance, in the make-to-stock environment, individual products or "families" of related products that are largely homogeneous—possessing nearly identical, if not identical, characteristics—are produced by the manufacturing process. A limited number of options—or manufacturing variations—typically exist in make-to-stock products.

The make-to-stock environment is frequently called the *repetitive* manufacturing model. The repetitive manufacturing model combines a characteristic of process manufacturing—generally producing products in batches and applying this concept to the manufacture of discrete products. Throughput of the make-to-stock or repetitive manufacturing process is typically measured on the basis of a unit capacity per hour or day basis.

The antithesis of the make-to-stock model is the make-to-order model. With a make-to-order product, considerable manufacturing variation is typically found on a product-by-product basis. Any number of names are used to describe a make-to-order manufacturing model, including assemble-to-order, engineer-to-order, and configure-to-order. OneWorld includes features that support either make-to-order or make-to-stock discrete manufacturing models.

Mixed-Mode Manufacturing

Note that many manufacturing operations are really a composite of manufacturing processes, combining both continuous and discrete production operating models within a single production facility or for a single product. This is frequently called *mixed-mode* manufacturing.

OneWorld does not place any limitations on the combination of manufacturing operating models. For example, you can use discrete, process, and repetitive manufacturing in combination or separately for each product manufactured or within each manufacturing facility.

Product Data Management

A central part of the OneWorld ERPx model is the Product Data Management system. The Product Data Management system serves as the repository of manufacturing-related information from which operating plans can be developed and work activities are subsequently defined and controlled.

The Product Data Management system stores "recipes" or "parts lists" on how to assemble or manufacture products. The major Product Data Management system includes these components:

◆ Bills of Material, which list the items or materials and the quantity needed to assemble or manufacture a product

◆ Work Centers, which define the assembly or manufacturing processes

◆ Routings, which define which Work Centers are used, when, and for how long during the assembly or manufacturing process

Items that are to be included in the OneWorld Bill of Material must be defined in the OneWorld Item Master and the Item Branch/Plant tables. Refer to Chapter 14 for additional information on the Item Master and Item Branch/Plant portions of the OneWorld Inventory Management system. The following sections provide a brief overview of the OneWorld Product Data Management system.

Bills of Material

All finished goods and any underlying subassemblies require a Bill of Material. A Bill of Material (BOM) is a formal, structured "parts list" or "recipe" that lists all the component parts or ingredients and the quantities needed of each in order to complete the assembly or manufacture of either a subassembly or semifinished product or the final, assembled, or finished product. The information contained in the Bill of Material plays an essential role in carrying out production planning, control, and execution activities in OneWorld.

Uses of the Bill of Material in OneWorld

The OneWorld Material Requirements Planning (MRP) system is used to "explode" multiple Bills of Material. It then aggregates material requirements and calculates order quantities needed for given future dates that will minimize overall costs—including ordering costs, carrying costs, and stockout costs. When a greater degree of optimization and dynamic adjustment are required by your business than might be offered by OneWorld's core material planning functionality, an advanced planning and scheduling system such as Synquest might be a desirable addition to OneWorld.

The Shop Floor Management system uses the Bill of Material as the basis for generating a parts list and provisioning the materials and resources necessary to carry out the work required to complete a given subassembly or end product.

OneWorld Bill of Material Types

A Bill of Material can be developed and may exist for multiple purposes within OneWorld. Depending on the specific requirements of your organization, the

OneWorld Product Data Management system provides for several types of Bills of Material:

- A planning Bill of Material
- A batch Bill of Material
- A percent Bill of Material
- A manufacturing Bill of Material

The Bill of Material generally represents the list of parts necessary to create at least one item. Or it might represent the parts necessary to create a batch or a quantity greater than one of a given item. This is commonly known as the standard manufacturing lot size or quantity for an item.

Discrete Manufacturing-Related Bills of Material

The planning Bill of Material is used to facilitate master production scheduling (MPS) and material requirements planning (MRP) by categorizing product features or options. This type of Bill of Material is frequently called a modular Bill of Material.

The planning Bill of Material or modular Bill of Material is commonly used to group semifinished products or parts, which are assembled and form a component of a finished product. This is also known as an *assembly* in Bill of Material parlance. Once a subassembly is defined in the form of its own Bill of Material, the subassembly can be combined with other Bills of Material as required. In general, the modular or planning Bill of Material is used to

- Maintain many configurations for an item without creating additional item numbers
- Define quantities of intermediate products in any unit of measure as they progress through a manufacturing process
- Define similar items by copying Bills of Material and routings

The planning Bill of Material is an extremely helpful and versatile tool in the make-to-order manufacturing environment.

Process-Related Bills of Material

The batch Bill of Material is used to accommodate physical constraints, commonly found in process industries, where oven or vat capacity requirements dictate that a given product be produced in batches of fixed quantities.

The percent Bill of Material expresses component quantities as a percent of the parent item or process batch quantity. OneWorld converts the batch quantity to the primary unit of measure for the parent item or process.

How OneWorld Uses a Batch Bill of Material

Note that the OneWorld Material Requirements Planning (MRP) system plans orders to fill net requirements by using one or multiple batch quantities. If the system cannot find a batch quantity for the net requirement, it uses the next larger batch size. If there is not a larger batch size, the closest, smaller batch size is requested until the order amount is supplied.

If only one batch Bill of Material is defined for a given end item, the batch quantity is used both as the multiple if the net requirements are greater than the batch quantity and as the minimum if the net requirements are less than the batch (or full batch) quantity.

OneWorld stores quantities for a percent of Bill of Material's components by calculating a percentage for the component in relation to the batch size and by converting the batch unit of measure to the component unit of measure and storing the quantity of the component.

Note that unit of measure conversions are extremely important if a percent Bill of Material is to work properly. Therefore, it is important to verify that all components or ingredients can convert to the batch-level quantity unit of measure.

Which Bill Matters?

The manufacturing Bill of Material is used to document and track components actually worked. This type of bill is also known as the *as-built, as-configured,* or *frozen* Bill of Material. Regardless of which other Bill of Material types your organization might define and use, only the standard manufacturing bill is actually planned and costed by OneWorld. A planned Bill of Material facilitates master production scheduling, materials requirements planning, and forecasting operations in OneWorld. A *costed* Bill of Material extends the quantity per amount of every component by the cost of the components. In summary, the frozen Bill of Material is used for all short-term planning and scheduling, and a planning Bill of Material is generally used for long-term planning purposes only.

The Single Versus Multilevel Bill of Material

Different forms of Bills of Material are used wherever an end product is assembled from several component parts or materials. Larger, more complex product structures can be broken down into a number of related units. Each unit can be represented by a Bill of Material, called a *single-level* Bill of Material.

In practice, a single-level Bill of Material is often a collection of standardized assemblies. A single-level Bill of Material can be for a complete product or might represent simply an individual part of a much larger, overall product. When additional Bills of Material comprise a single overall Bill of Material, a *multilevel* Bill of Material is said to exist. This is also commonly called an indented Bill of Material.

Relieving Stock Given a Bill of Material Requirement

The OneWorld Shop Floor Management system controls the flow of material from the stockroom to the plant floor. In OneWorld, an Issue Code associated with each component item or part in the Bill of Material is used to control or indicate how OneWorld will relieve stock from inventory and issue stock against a Work Order. Here are some possible "issue from stock" scenarios in OneWorld:

◆ Manually issuing component parts noted on a Bill of Material against a specific Work Order

◆ Issuing component parts against the Bill of Material from floor stock to the Work Order

◆ Backflushing parts by issuing component parts when the final assembly is reported as complete

◆ Preflushing by issuing component parts when the parts list is generated

◆ Superbackflushing by issuing component parts at a pay-point operation

◆ Specifying that a component part is supplied through a subcontracted operation

Although issue codes are established at the branch/plant level in OneWorld, it is possible to override this value by specifying a different issue code within the Bill of Material or Work Order parts list for specific component parts. Understanding these material issue concepts is a critical step in using OneWorld. This is an area where many OneWorld users struggle, especially since more than one of these material issuing techniques is often combined and used on the same Bill of Material.

Phantom Items in OneWorld

OneWorld allows the definition and inclusion of a "phantom" item in a Bill of Material. Phantom items have many aliases and purposes in manufacturing. Generally speaking, a phantom item typically represents an assembly. It is a logical, not a functional, grouping of materials. From a design point of view, materials are often grouped to form an assembly. However, from a production point of view, these materials are not actually assembled to form a physical end item. The Phantom item can exist at any level with a Bill of Material.

Phantom items are never stocked. Any component material requirements for a phantom assembly are against the individual components that make up a phantom assembly, not for the phantom assembly. Planned orders and purchased material requisitions are produced only for the components of the phantom assembly, not for the phantom assembly itself.

The Component Locator Feature

The definition of a subassembly in OneWorld allows for a *component locator* designation. Component locators are used to define a specific assembly sequence. Examples include adding screen-printed key caps or indicator lamp legends to a keyboard, keypad, or front panel of an electronic device in a specific sequence.

Work Centers

A Work Center is typically a physical location within the assembly or production area where a specific assembly- or production-related operation is completed. Work Centers may be machine- or person-centric in that a Work Center may represent a machine, a group of machines, a person, or a group of people.

The definition of a Work Center therefore depends on how your organization's production is designed and whether it is machine- or labor-driven. The Work Center is an essential component in defining your organization's manufacturing process to OneWorld. The OneWorld Work Center record is used to

◆ Define the number of laborers, machines, or machine operators

◆ Define standard costs or rates associated with machine setup, operation, and any associated factory overhead

◆ Define additional information related to the OneWorld capacity planning process

The information contained in the overall Work Center definition plays an essential role in carrying out production planning, control, and execution activities in OneWorld.

The Work Center is comprised of one or more related machines or persons who can perform similar work. Work Centers are typically larger than a machine but smaller than an overall department. Generally speaking, a Work Center demarcation is generally represented by a unique or distinct step or task in an assembly or in a production process. For instance, the Work Center might complete a step or task that transforms raw materials into a semifinished state that will subsequently move to another Work Center for finishing purposes. Generally speaking, Work Center tasks are kept at a generic level and can therefore be assigned or reassigned to any of the machines or persons within the Work Center.

In OneWorld, a Work Center is also defined as a business unit. Business units were first introduced in Chapter 14. A business unit is OneWorld's lowest-level organizational demarcation. In OneWorld, the first step in defining Work Centers is to set up a business unit record for each Work Center that is to be defined. Once the business unit record representing the Work Center is established, the Work Center Revisions form can be used to complete the Work Center definition.

Note that Work Centers are assigned to business units. Several Work Centers can be assigned to a single business unit. For example, a production department might consist of a combination of several Work Centers. However, a Work Center can be assigned to only one business unit at any particular point in time. In addition, Work Centers can be assigned to a business unit for a specified period of time.

Capacity is the ability to perform a task. In OneWorld, capacities define the range of production-related services that labor (persons) or machines can provide within a certain time period. Note that several capacities are associated with a single Work Center. These capacity limitations are distinguished by their categories. For instance, Work Center capacities include laborer or operator and machine capacity by hours per day. The Work Center definition also includes other essential information for Capacity Requirements Planning (CRP) purposes. Note that the Work Center itself is considered the capacity unit for CRP purposes.

The Work Center definition also includes machine, machine setup, machine operator, and overhead rates. Costing activities in OneWorld are performed based on these Work Center values.

Routings

After you define Bills of Material for each of your manufactured products and the manufacturing operations that occur on the factory floor through the use of Work Centers, your next task is to define the course of events necessary to manufacture your organization's products. These instructions are known as *routings* in OneWorld.

A routing is a logically sequenced listing of the operations, or work steps, that represent the processing flow through a given manufacturing process—from beginning to end—to complete the assembly or manufacture of a given item. In many ways, routings are similar to a project plan. The routing also defines the allowances for anticipated yield and scrap from each step in the manufacturing process. Alternative operations can be defined as a part of a routing.

A routing is used to report actual activity against a Work Order, including the time or costs involved in job setup, as well as the labor and machine time required by a work-in-process item at any given point in time. Routings are also used to plan capacity based on Work Center "loading."

Types of Routings

OneWorld provides for multiple types of routings:

◆ Master routings

◆ Batch routings

◆ Alternate routings

The master routing instruction represents a single routing for many parts that use the same manufacturing steps. A master routing eliminates the need for duplicate routing instructions where only nominal changes occur in a manufacturing process, such as a material grade or color change. It should be pointed out that every item must be assigned a master routing. This is the default routing used when a work order is created to make a particular item. Although it is possible that a single master routing can suffice for many items, this is not necessarily always the case.

Batch routing is useful for process manufacturing or where products are manufactured in a fixed quantity, called a batch run. For instance, the process for a smaller batch run might vary from a larger run or between production lines or plants. The batch process feature provides the ability to define a different routing for items based on the quantity or batch size or, alternatively, on the production line or producing plant.

Alternate routing is generally informational in nature. It provides specific directives to your shop floor personnel about optional choices. For instance, if a product is normally produced at work center A, it uses routing A. But if work center A is at capacity, the item might instead be produced at work center B. However, the production rate is different for work center B, so in this case an alternate routing that matches the production rate for work center B is used. Note that OneWorld does not use alternate routing for costing or back-scheduling purposes.

Several other important features of OneWorld routings include the ability to record a tool identification number for each operation and the ability to define an "outside operation" as an alternate path for the routing.

Routings Versus Work Centers

The difference between a routing and a work center is often confusing. Here's a way to understand the difference between these two concepts: A routing represents the rate of capacity consumption, and the work center represents the capacity. A work center is defined in terms of the hours of available use, and a routing is defined in terms of the amount of time required to make each unit.

Engineering Change Management (ECM)

Maintaining all of the engineering, manufacturing, procurement, and sales order management–related information for your organization is no less than a full-time responsibility. This means that in many organizations the basic system information, which is relevant to all OneWorld application processing systems, is often created and maintained by a central department.

Because of the importance of product-related information, many organizations already have informal paper- or e-mail-based Engineering Change Management processes in place. The use of OneWorld's Engineering Change Management is not mandatory. However, for organizations that want a formal Engineering Change Management process, OneWorld's manufacturing suite of applications includes such a facility.

The OneWorld Product Data Management system incorporates an Engineering Change Management subsystem. The Engineering Change Management subsystem is best viewed as a change management and notification process or procedure. The Engineering Change Management system is used to document product-related changes. Changes are generally made to existing products to resolve quality or safety issues or to improve product performance. New products are typically included in the domain of Engineering Change Management at many organizations.

The typical Engineering Change Management process begins when an Engineering Change Request (ECR) is made. The Engineering Change Request process defines and tracks all requested product changes. If the Engineering Change Request is favorably reviewed and approved, it results in the creation of an Engineering Change Order (ECO) or Engineering Change Notification (ECN). The Engineering Change Order is typically used to provide change notification to all affected areas. Most notably, these can include production-related (routing) and product content– or formulation-related (Bill of Material) changes.

In OneWorld, the Engineering Change Management subsystem provides for the creation and management of engineering change request documents and engineering change order documents related to the following:

◆ Drawing changes

◆ Bill of Material changes

◆ Routing changes

◆ New item number assignments

In practice, most smaller and middle-market manufacturing organizations use only the Engineering Change Order process, omitting the Engineering Change Request process from their Product Data Management workflows.

It is important that your organization understand that the OneWorld Engineering Change Management subsystem performs only a limited number of actual changes to your organization's product information within OneWorld. It mainly provides an overall change-related document control and management process. Most of the actual information additions and changes must be done manually. However, the Engineering Change Management system does maintain a revision level in order to help your organization manage modifications to its Bills of Material, Item Master, Item Branch/Plant information, and routings.

Finally, it is also important to note that the use of the Engineering Change Management subsystem does not supplant the need to properly structure OneWorld system security authorizations to specific OneWorld forms to meet your organization's overall requirements. However, the Engineering Change Management subsystem carries out only certain authorization checks that are specific to the Engineering Change Management process.

Many additional OneWorld master data tables should be carefully and, if possible, centrally administered by knowledgeable data administrators. The Item Master, Address Book, Chart of Accounts, Sales and Use Tax Tables, User-Defined Codes, and Payroll Tax Tables are but a few of the master data tables that fall into this category. Other system users should be provided with written or electronic forms to request database changes. At the same time, you could argue for less control in some environments. For instance, in a direct-mail operation, the order-takers generally need Address Book access to add or change customer-related information on-the-fly. As a result, they will in turn require a higher degree of Address Book maintenance–related training than might otherwise be necessary.

 A BEST-PRACTICE TECHNIQUE

Use an Engineering Change Management Process

Whether or not your organization uses the OneWorld Engineering Change Management subsystem, it is considered a best business practice to formally authorize, control, and manage changes to product-related information in a manufacturing environment.

Shop Floor Management

The OneWorld Shop Floor Management system implements the operating plan by managing material flows and work processes on the factory floor. The Shop Floor Management system utilizes data from the shop floor to maintain and communicate status information regarding materials, Work Centers, routings, and remaining operations that are required to complete the manufacturing-related Work Order. The Shop Floor Management system in OneWorld facilitates "working the plan"—in other words, manufacturing execution.

Work Orders

The basis of the OneWorld Shop Floor Management system is the Manufacturing Work Order. When the need to assemble or manufacture a given product arises, a Manufacturing Work Order is created. When something must be done, the Work Order is the initiating or source document. In OneWorld, the Manufacturing Work Order follows a user-defined workflow from its initiation to its cancellation or completion in the system.

In general, there are three basic ways a Manufacturing Work Order can be created in OneWorld:

- ◆ They can be manually created using the Work Order Entry form.
- ◆ Subsequent processing of material requirements planning (MRP) messages can trigger the creation of a Work Order.
- ◆ A sales order document can *directly* trigger the creation of a Work Order.

In OneWorld, after the Manufacturing Work Order document is created, it must be processed through a workflow, or a sequence of predefined steps. Work Order documents and processing steps can be user-defined. Note that typically OneWorld automatically assigns the Work Order number using its "next number" facility. At the time a Manufacturing Work Order is entered, the Manufacturing Work Order Starting Date, or Start Date, is calculated by deducting the Level Leadtime value from the Branch/Plant record of the end product, or subassembly from the Required or Work Completion Date.

There are numerous other uses of the Work Order document in OneWorld. For instance, the Engineering Change Management subsystem is based on the Work Order document. Other uses of the OneWorld Work Order document will be reviewed in the next chapter. Figure 17-1 illustrates a typical Manufacturing Work Order life cycle that can be defined in OneWorld.

Shop Floor Paper Generation

After the creation of a Manufacturing Work Order, Shop Floor Paper can be generated. Creating Shop Floor Paper is a step that is defined in the workflow for a Manufacturing Work Order. In OneWorld, when the Shop Floor Paper batch process is executed, a parts list based on the Bill of Material and a routing is constructed for the Manufacturing Work Order. Therefore, Shop Floor Paper is said to consist of the Manufacturing Work Order along with the parts list, routing, and/or manufacturing instructions.

Work Order Scheduling

When a Manufacturing Work Order is processed, its status changes. In addition, a parts list and routing are attached to the Manufacturing Work Order. Also at

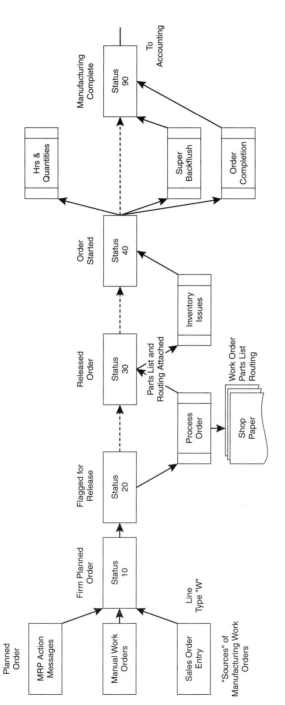

FIGURE 17-1 *The OneWorld Manufacturing Work Order Life Cycle*

this time, each operation is scheduled, with a Start Date and Requested Date for each. This step is in effect a further refinement of the initial Start Date established when the Manufacturing Work Order was created. Each operation is scheduled by calculating the lead time for the operation itself by deducting from the Requested Date the queue setup, run, and move times related to the operation.

Elapsed time values are taken from the routing master. The number of hours per day is taken from the manufacturing constants related to the Branch/Plant. The Branch/Plant Manufacturing Constants are established during system setup. The Prime Load code in the Work Center is used to indicate if scheduling is based on labor time or machine time. Note that Manufacturing Work Order scheduling also affects the determination of capacity requirements. Based on the Prime Load code associated with the Work Center, either the run time or both the setup and run times are used to calculate released capacity load at the Work Center level during the scheduling of this operation.

Lead Time

Determining lead time is an essential factor in a scheduling process. For any product that is purchased or manufactured, a time lag exists between the time when an order is placed or started and when the part is either received or finished. To account for this lag, it is necessary to estimate and account for the extra time—the *lead time*—in the overall manufacturing planning process.

Manufactured Parts

For any manufactured product, OneWorld calculates four types of lead time:

◆ Level lead time

◆ Manufacturing lead time

◆ Cumulative lead time

◆ Per-unit lead time

Level lead time is defined as the number of workdays required to complete a given end product or subassembly after all the component parts are available. Manufacturing lead time is defined as the total number of workdays required to complete a product, from its lowest-level components to the deliverable or end product, assuming that all purchased items are in-house. Cumulative lead time is defined as the number of workdays required to acquire items and complete a product, from its lowest-level components to the final item. Per-unit lead time is defined as the sum of the run times, as defined by the prime load codes for the Work Centers, factored by the routing time basis, and converted to the lead time per unit.

With respect to Work Center operations and their impact on lead time, several additional definitions must be made. The prime load code determines whether a Work Center is labor-intensive or machine-intensive and whether the number of employees or machines is used to determine the daily resource units available in making the lead time and other calculations. The time basis code indicates how many machine or labor hours are needed to produce a given quantity of a specific item. For example, a given item might require 25 machine hours per 1,000 pieces produced. Given these definitions, additional factors also affect lead time in OneWorld.

Machine hours represent the number of machine hours required to produce the amount indicated by the time basis code. *Labor hours* represent the number of labor hours required to produce the amount indicated by the time basis code. *Setup hours* represent the number of hours to prepare a machine to produce a specific item, regardless of the quantity to be produced. *Move hours* represent the number of hours that a Manufacturing Work Order is in transit from the completion of one operation to the beginning of the next operation as defined in the routing. *Queue hours* represent the number of hours that an in-process Manufacturing Work Order waits at a Work Center before any setup or productive work is performed for that Manufacturing Work Order.

Purchased Parts

When a part is purchased from a supplier, a level lead time is specified in calendar days. This is also considered the cumulative lead time for this part. By default, the manufacturing lead time, lead time per unit, total queue and move hours, and setup times for purchased parts are all 0.

Manufacturing Execution

After the creation of the Shop Floor Paper for a given Manufacturing Work Order, the Work Order is scheduled or released to Manufacturing for execution. Note that material shortages might exist, or that subcontracted work might be needed. These two scenarios might delay either the initiation or completion of a Manufacturing Work Order.

Finally, it is entirely possible to use the Shop Floor Management system without using the OneWorld Manufacturing and Distribution Planning system. However, when the Materials Requirements Planning subsystem is not used in conjunction with the OneWorld Shop Floor Management system, both inventory and manufacturing activity *must be manually managed*.

The Dispatch List

In OneWorld, the Dispatch List is used to plan and coordinate productive work within a Work Center. Generally speaking, the production control planner, manager, or supervisor must review active Manufacturing Work Orders—those started or about to start—to determine if capacity exists at each Work Center through which the Manufacturing Work Order will flow or at which it is already being processed. The OneWorld Dispatch List is available as both an online inquiry form and a batch process report.

The Scheduling Workbench

In OneWorld, the Scheduling Workbench is used to monitor and execute changes to the production schedule by making changes to specific Manufacturing Work Orders. For example, the production control planner, manager, or supervisor can monitor the overall progress of the Manufacturing Work Order on the shop floor and determine if any changes have occurred or are needed. The OneWorld Scheduling Workbench is used to effect changes, such as a change in the status, priority, or any other information, including the Requested Date, or actually releasing a Manufacturing Work Order to the shop floor.

When using the OneWorld Scheduling Workbench, Manufacturing Work Orders can be reviewed by item, planner, customer, parent Work Order, status, type, or priority, or by using a combination of these variables.

Reporting Consumption or Completion

Once work begins on a scheduled or released Manufacturing Work Order, component parts or materials can be issued to the Work Order on an as-used basis. Alternatively, component parts or material usage can be backflushed based on production completion. In addition to material usage, scrap can also be recorded against the Manufacturing Work Order. In addition, labor can be reported as it occurs, or it can be backflushed based on standard hours, using a process known as superbackflushing.

Productive work can be recorded or confirmed as complete on a partial basis until the Manufacturing Work Order is considered complete. When a Manufacturing

Work Order is complete, the creation of any material, labor, or overhead variances between the actual and the planned or standard consumption and usage associated with a given transaction is calculated. A final journal entry is then created to reflect manufacturing variances associated with the Manufacturing Work Order.

Note that there are two different methods of planning and reporting production for a Manufacturing Work Order in OneWorld—the Work Order and the rate-based methods. The discussion in this section has focused on the Work Order–based method of planning and reporting production completion. The rate-based method of planning and reporting production is discussed later in this chapter.

Relieving Inventory and Backflushing in OneWorld

As productive work is completed, component parts or items are consumed in the course of production and must be removed from inventory and charged against the Manufacturing Work Order. There are several methods for the relief or issuance of stock from inventory in OneWorld:

- Manually issuing stock
- Preflushing
- Simple backflushing
- Superbackflushing

When making manual inventory issues against a Manufacturing Work Order, it is assumed that an authorized person actually pulls from stock the component parts being requested on the parts list for the Manufacturing Work Order. These manual stock issues are then manually entered or reported in OneWorld, along with the location(s) from which they were picked.

Under the simple backflushing scenario, use of the OneWorld Work Order Completions form automatically triggers the Inventory Issues form. The Inventory Issues form is then prefilled with the quantities based on the standard parts list and the quantity completed. At the time the Inventory Issues form appears, the user may simply accept the prefilled values or may make any known manual adjustments to the quantities and locations before completing the stock issue.

With superbackflushing, a special OneWorld program backflushes both material and labor hours at a standard rate. Superbackflushing can either occur in a blind mode or can trigger the initiation of another form that will provide for modifications before the transaction is actually confirmed. Additionally, the superbackflush can trigger the Work Order Completions form. This allows the location of the completed units to be verified and changed if appropriate.

Outside Operations

Operations performed by a subcontractor are called outside operations in OneWorld. When an operation is defined for purposes of manufacturing, the operation can be flagged as an external operation. The definition of an external operation is at the Work Center level. When a Manufacturing Work Order is created and released for a part and an external Work Center performs one of the operations, a purchase order or requisition is created for this operation. One requisition is created for each operation performed by a subcontractor. The part on the requisition is a purchased part, not an inventory part. If you use a requisition, it is converted into a purchase order in the usual way that has been defined in your OneWorld system setup, using order processing rules and approval routes.

Once the purchase order document is created, it has a life of its own, except for the fact that the purchase-order receiving process automatically triggers the Work Order completion. Note that any outside processed item must have an additional number in both the Item Master file and the Branch/Plant Master file. The item number of this special item must be the same as the original item number but is appended with *OP*nn*, where *nn* is the operation sequence number from the routing. Note that outside operations require the use of a Line Type of X to indicate outside processing and to subsequently trigger the Work Order completion process.

Note that for Outside Operations processing to function correctly, all of the related (required) data and processing options must be properly configured. Carefully review Item Master and Item Branch/Plant information, Shop Floor Management, and Procurement system setups and processing options when troubleshooting problems related to initiating or completing an Outside Operations step.

Rate-Based Manufacturing

In addition to Work Order–based manufacturing, OneWorld also provides repetitive, rate-based functionality. This feature is intended for organizations that manufacture products on a regular or repetitive basis. For example, "every week, on Tuesdays, we produce blue widgets." Instead of entering and processing many small Work Orders, one Rate Schedule is defined. The Rate Schedule defines a specific pattern and expected average rate of production per day over a specified duration of time.

Instead of a Work Order document type and specific Work Order numbers, there will be a two-digit rate schedule code, with multiple date effectivities. Note that no actual Work Order numbers will exist. Unlike many other ERP software packages, OneWorld does not create and track Work Orders on a "behind-the-scenes" basis. There is actually a separate rate-based process, from manufacturing planning through the generation of accounting journal entry transactions.

How Rate-Based Manufacturing Differs from Work Order–Based Manufacturing

Given that a Manufacturing Work Order is not used under a Rate-Based Manufacturing scenario, there are a number of important differences between these two processes. First, there is no attachment of a parts list or routing to rate-based production. As production is reported, the standard Bill of Material and routing are used as the basis of production and inventory reporting. Second, a rate-based schedule does not require processing in order for production and inventory reporting to occur. Labor, machine, and material backflushing can be either visible or completed "behind the scenes" as a "blind" process.

All completed production reporting, along with labor and machine usage and material consumption backflushing, is performed using the OneWorld Scheduling Workbench. Rate-based schedules appear on this form by sequence number, and items scheduled across the production line could be reported easily from this single form every day. The term *sequence* is used to indicate the sequence of running this item relative to the running of other items across the same production line.

Product Costing and Manufacturing Accounting

Accurate product costing and record keeping are vitally necessary in today's manufacturing environment. An organization's product costs have wide-sweeping effects, and they influence everything from gross margins to your future business plans, including product mix decisions, "make versus buy" decisions, and capacity expansion decisions.

For the publicly held company, earnings surprises due to falling inventory values or obsolete inventory are largely unacceptable. The capital structure and operating margins are also adversely affected if an organization has excessive or unwarranted inventory or underutilized plant capacity. In short, active management of the manufacturing process through a formal planning, control, and execution process helps minimize manufacturing costs and manufacturing plant investment in both the short and long term. When all is said and done, in the capitalist system we still measure performance based on profits and margins. Therefore, at the center of any planning, control, and execution system is the need for robust product costing and record keeping. OneWorld includes the Product Costing and Manufacturing Accounting systems as part of its ERPx planning, control, and execution systems model.

System Features

In general, the OneWorld Product Costing and Manufacturing Accounting systems provide a rich set of features that accommodate the needs of most manufacturing environments. Here are some important features provided by the OneWorld Product Costing system and by the OneWorld Manufacturing Accounting system:

◆ User-defined cost add-ons provide for the definition and maintenance of an unlimited number of cost components for tracking specific costs, such as freight, taxes, duty, and electricity.

◆ User-defined cost rollup methods provide for the definition of an unlimited number of cost methods to use in a cost simulation.

◆ User-defined cost factors and rates can be used to allocate cost factors and rates to a specific item. These user-defined cost factors can be used with cost add-ons to calculate additional costs.

◆ You can perform a Bill of Material rollup by calculating total material cost by retrieving the Bill of Material and adding up the total cost of the components appearing in the Bill of Material.

◆ You can perform a cost simulation by running a simulation of costs before any live data is updated as the frozen standard.

◆ You can maintain cost information at the branch/plant level, thereby allowing for cost variances at different locations for identical, manufactured items.

In addition, the OneWorld Manufacturing Accounting system provides a series of inquiries and reports that can be used to evaluate manufacturing performance on the basis of costs incurred and any variances from pre-established or frozen standards.

Product Costing

The OneWorld Product Costing system allows your organization to store and retrieve item-related cost information. Product costing plays a significant role in any manufacturing environment. OneWorld supports a product costing process that relies on the creation of frozen standard cost values related to the underlying component parts and subassemblies and processes that enter into the products that are assembled or manufactured by your organization. In addition, the OneWorld Manufacturing Accounting system relies on these frozen standard costs to calculate manufacturing costs and variances related to the products produced by your organization.

As is the case with most ERP systems, establishing product costs is a multiple-step process in OneWorld. The first step in developing product costs is to define your process-related cost components. The second step is to develop meaningful values for these cost components. The development of meaningful cost components and cost component values is typically done through a careful analysis of your assembly and manufacturing processes. For instance, industrial engineering techniques are frequently employed to determine these major cost components and their typical cost values.

Increasingly, a concept called target costing is being used in manufacturing. Target costing sets an overall total cost threshold before a product is manufactured. It is a common practice among Japanese manufacturers. Target costing sets out to achieve a target cost based on a given product life expectancy or production volume and is based on the cumulative manufacturing experience and efficiencies gained and total program cost outlays. Target costing is typically done in conjunction with the product design and development process.

Once costs are defined by cost component, they are typically calculated in a "simulated" mode. The simulated cost results can be printed for comparative or review purposes. After a review of these simulated costs, changes can be made, and then the costs can be resimulated. After you're satisfied with the results, the costs are then established as *frozen standard costs*.

After frozen standard costs are established in the Product Costing system, the Shop Floor Management and Manufacturing Accounting systems use them for manufacturing process–related and material valuation purposes.

OneWorld Manufacturing Accounting

Transactions created by the OneWorld Shop Floor Management system use the frozen standard costs defined in the OneWorld Product Costing system when performing any manufacturing-related calculations. These shop floor transactions create consumption- and variance-related transactions defined by a series of Automatic Accounting Instructions. These journal entries must be posted to the general ledger account balances in the OneWorld General Accounting system. The OneWorld Manufacturing Accounting system therefore relies on the information contained in the OneWorld General Accounting system.

Based on work in process or production completion reporting in the Shop Floor Management system, OneWorld creates journal entries for Work Order or Rate Schedule transactions based on these work in process movements or end-product completions. These journal entries can be created at either a detail or summary level. Journal entries for manufacturing variances are also created as detail or summary journal entries for both Work Order and Rate Schedule variances. In addition, automatic accounting for any unaccounted units is made during the production reporting process.

Variance Analysis

In OneWorld, a manufacturing cost variance occurs when one user-defined cost value differs from another. These variances can be due to calculated cost differences in material, labor, or overhead or due to changes to the Bill of Material or to a routing. OneWorld provides four different types of variance calculations:

◆ Engineering variances

◆ Planned variances

◆ Actual or consumption-driven variances

◆ Other variances

An engineering variance is based on the difference between the frozen standard costs for a given material, labor, or overhead element when compared to the current cost derived from the Bill of Material, routing, or overhead rate for this same material, labor, or overhead element.

A planned variance is the difference between the current cost derived from the Bill of Material, routing, and overhead rates and the costs based on the Work Order or rate schedule parts list and routing instructions. Planned variances can occur when a Work Order or rate schedule is revised.

An actual variance is the difference between the cost values derived from the Work Order or rate schedule parts list and routing, and the material and labor that were actually reported against that Work Order or rate schedule. Actual variances can occur when material is issued, when hours and quantities are recorded, or when an end-product completion is recorded.

There are two types of actual variances—the labor efficiency variance and the material usage variance. The Labor Efficiency represents the difference between the planned and actual labor costs based on the Work Order or rate schedule routing, and the material usage represents the difference between the planned and actual material costs based on the Work Order or rate schedule parts list.

The "other" variance is derived by comparing the frozen standard costs and the completed Work Order costs, plus scrap. This variance represents the overcompletion or undercompletion costs of the Work Order or rate schedule.

Process Industry Accounting

There are some differences between manufacturing accounting practices in process industries and those found in discrete manufacturing processes. The major difference in manufacturing accounting practice is that in a process-manufacturing environment, production completion is reported against the coproducts and byproducts from the overall process rather than against the overall process itself, while variances are reported at the process level. OneWorld accommodates these differences between process and discrete process manufacturing accounting practices.

Manufacturing Cost Accuracy

Product costs and manufacturing variances are affected by a number of issues. In general, the following guidelines help ensure accurate, complete product costs and minimal disruption in calculating true manufacturing cost variances:

◆ Ensure that all Bills of Material are complete.

◆ Identify and correct any discrepancies in the Bills of Material and routings as they are discovered.

◆ Ensure that all component items have accurate acquisition-related costs, including transportation charges.

◆ Identify all general and administrative overhead elements and their rates.

◆ Ensure that Work Center–related information is accurate and complete.

◆ Establish guidelines for when and how often standards change. For most manufacturers, this is typically an annual process.

◆ Ensure that all standard costs are available before doing the initial cost rollups.

◆ Ensure that correct and consistent units of measure are used.

◆ When items are added to or deleted from the Bill of Material, perform a cost update.

◆ When steps in the routing change, perform a cost update.

Also note that on a day-to-day basis, the shop floor personnel play a vital role in maintaining the accuracy of the cost accounting system. Therefore, it is important to ensure that shop floor personnel input their production completion data on an accurate and timely basis. Also, if they identify any errors in a Bill of Material or routing, it should be elevated to the appropriate parties for immediate attention and correction.

Forecasting

Forecasting is the process of projecting future demand. It is sometimes called *demand planning.* Regardless of the industry or size of an organization, the forecasting of future business activity is an important dimension in the strategic planning process. Ever-astute and prolific business management theorist Peter Drucker once wrote, "If you can't measure it, you can't manage it." In the case of business forecasting, this couldn't be a truer statement.

For most organizations, the development and maintenance of forecasts is a difficult, time-consuming, and frequently inaccurate process. However, the effective management of distribution and manufacturing activities requires anticipating the needs of the market—usually in terms of an organization's sales volume. Implementing a formal forecasting system will allow your organization to anticipate future demand and to quickly assess the impact of changing market trends on your distribution or manufacturing operations. OneWorld provides a formal system for forecasting purposes.

How Forecasts Are Used in Planning and Scheduling

The OneWorld Forecasting system uses sales order history as the basis for projecting future demand. The sales forecast that is generated using OneWorld's sales order historical information can then be used by your organization's executive and operational management team for decision-making purposes. For instance, sales forecasts can help your organization identify important decision points regarding resource acquisition and scheduling, including raw materials and finished-good inventory levels, plant and machinery capacities, warehouse space, workforce requirements, new lines of business, and future product development.

A forecast is the expected consumption of an item that is expressed as a quantity value. It is based on historical sales results and is adjusted for known market activities, including knowledge about new products, market variations, and product life cycle experience.

OneWorld provides a batch process to extract history information from the OneWorld Sales Order Management system. This extracted information is then used as the basis for developing the sales forecast. OneWorld can generate a summary, a product-line-level forecast, a detail, or a product-level forecast. Your organization determines the level of sales forecast that will be generated by OneWorld. Once the forecast table is generated, the forecast information can be manually revised. In addition, planning bill forecasts can be generated. The planning bill forecast is based on groups of items in a Bill of Material format that reflect how items are sold, not how items are built.

The OneWorld Forecasting system generates demand projections that are used as input for the OneWorld Manufacturing and Distribution Planning system. The OneWorld Manufacturing and Distribution Planning system uses forecast input to calculate material requirements at all component levels, including raw materials and subassemblies.

Forecast Consumption

Forecast consumption is the process of decrementing a stored forecast based on the receipt of actual orders. The essence of forecast consumption is that forecast, together with actual demand, represents total demand over the planning horizon. Thus, it is said that actual demand "consumes" the forecast. OneWorld compares and uses the greater of either forecasted or actual sales orders in order to make a forecast consumption adjustment.

Other Forecasting System Features

Significant features of the OneWorld Forecasting system include the following:

◆ The ability to maintain both manually entered forecasts and forecasts generated by the system using sales history

◆ The ability to summarize the sales order history data into weekly or monthly time periods

◆ The ability to enter a "manual" forecast to represent other, independent demands, such as demand related to a product recall campaign

◆ The ability to review and adjust both forecasted and actual sales order figures

◆ The ability to consider and recommend any of 12 forecasting methods as a "best fit" method

◆ The ability to store and display both original and adjusted forecast quantities and amounts

Several of these significant forecasting features are discussed in the next section.

Forecasting Methods

The OneWorld Forecasting system analyzes past sales to calculate forecasts using one of 12 forecasting methods. As previously stated, both detail or single-item and summary or product-line forecasts can be generated. In general, the forecasting method selected should reflect actual product demand patterns. In this regard, the OneWorld Forecasting system will recommend the "best fit" forecasting method.

The "best fit" forecasting method recommendation is made through a trial-and-error approach. On an iterative basis, one or more selected forecasting methods are applied to the sales order history information. The forecast results from each are then compared against the actual sales order history for a specific time period, and a computation is made as to how accurately the forecasting method would have predicted sales for this same time period. When this process is complete, the OneWorld Forecasting system recommends the most accurate forecast as the best fit based on statistical accuracy using the mean absolute deviation (MAD).

The OneWorld Forecasting system incorporates six typical demand patterns or scenarios into its forecasting methods. These include methods to address horizontal, positive or negative trend, seasonal, trend-seasonal, and nonannual demand patterns. The forecasting method is specified when a forecast is produced. Generally speaking, a minimum of 12 to 24 periods of sales history are necessary to calculate most forecasts. Table 17-1 lists the available OneWorld forecasting methods.

Table 17-1 Forecasting Methods

Method	Title/Description of Method
1	Percentage Over or Under Last Year
2	Calculated Percentage Over or Under Last Year
3	Last Year to This Year
4	Moving Average
5	Linear Approximation
6	Least Square Regression
7	Second-Degree Approximation
8	Flexible Method — Percent Over n Prior Months
9	Percent Over n Prior Months
10	Weighted Moving Average
11	Exponential Smoothing
12	Exponential Smoothing with Trend and Seasonality

Forecast Accuracy and Other Considerations

In the forecasting arena, it is generally considered appropriate practice to be "approximately right instead of precisely wrong." Wide margins of error can exist in forecasts. Note that summary-level forecasts are typically more accurate than individual or detail-level forecasts. Therefore, forecasts by product family tend to be more accurate than forecasts for specific products within a product family. Also note that long-term forecasts are generally less accurate than short-term forecasts, because a greater number of fixed forecast assumptions become variables.

Although past information forms the substantive basis of the future forecast for most organizations, it is generally a good practice to *avoid relying exclusively on past data* to forecast future demands. Consider these other influencing factors when reviewing and making forecast adjustments:

◆ The introduction of new products that have no previous sales data

◆ Plans for any future sales promotions, discounts, or rebate programs affecting a product or product line

◆ Changes in the distribution channel for your products

◆ Demographic, economic, and political changes that affect your product, including the impact of interest rates, taxes and tariffs, government regulations, and changing consumption habits or patterns of key markets

◆ Product innovations made by your competitors

In short, your organization's formal forecasting process should include procedures to ensure that appropriate weight is given to the long-term business trends within your particular industry, in the general economy, and, more specifically, to how or why your product is consumed.

Manufacturing and Distribution Planning

The focus of operational planning emphasizes balancing supply and demand requirements. The operating plan uses long-range sales forecasts included in the strategic plan in conjunction with product-specific resource requirements to project what productive capacity and material requirements are necessary to meet anticipated demand.

The OneWorld Manufacturing and Distribution Planning system provides functions that allow your organization to coordinate inventory, purchased materials, labor, and machine resources to deliver products *according to an actively and tightly managed schedule* known as the Master Production Schedule.

As a closed-loop system, the OneWorld Manufacturing and Distribution Planning system provides feedback to manufacturing management on a continuous basis by alerting management to material and capacity shortages and production bottlenecks. This section provides a high-level overview of the OneWorld Manufacturing and Distribution Planning system. A more detailed discussion would require an intimate understanding of generally accepted manufacturing resource planning practices and is therefore beyond the scope of this overview.

Resource and Capacity Planning

The OneWorld Resource and Capacity Planning subsystem allows your organization to prepare a *feasible* Master Production Schedule that reflects both demand forecasts and available productive resources. If sufficient capacity is unavailable, the overall plan must be adjusted, or the capacities themselves must be adjusted. The Resource and Capacity Planning subsystem encompasses the following:

- ◆ Capacity Requirements Planning (CRP)
- ◆ Resource Requirements Planning (RRP)
- ◆ Rough-Cut Capacity Planning (RCCP)

Each planning subsystem validates planning information to a specific level of detail and time horizon. Resource Requirements Planning validates production planning. Rough-Cut Capacity Planning validates Master Production Scheduling. Capacity Requirements Planning validates the Materials Requirements Plan.

The OneWorld Manufacturing Planning Cycle

In OneWorld, the Resource Requirements Plan uses the forecasts of future sales to estimate the time and resources required in meeting your organization's overall business plan objectives. The Resource Requirements Plan is generated after the long-term sales forecast is complete but before the generation of the Master Production Schedule. The Resource Requirements Plan provides an overall estimate of the time and resources that are needed to produce a product.

The next step is to generate the Master Production Schedule. After the Master Production Schedule is created, the Rough-Cut Capacity Plan is used to identify any capacity constraints at critical Work Centers; this in effect determines the shop floor layout. The shop floor layout is typically at a product group level. Therefore, resource validation is also done at this level.

The next planning step is to generate the Materials Requirements Plan. Thereafter, the Capacity Requirements Plan is produced. The Capacity Requirements Plan matches available labor and machine resources to the resource requirements generated by the Material Requirements Plan. The Capacity Requirements Plan indicates whether any revisions to the material requirements plan are needed or if additional resources should be acquired or scheduled.

Integration with Shop Floor Management

After creating the generation or regeneration of the Master Production Schedule, you must create manufacturing Work Orders related to the Master Production Schedule. The OneWorld Order Processing batch process (R31410) is used to complete this step. This step attaches the parts list and routing and generates the corresponding shop floor documents.

Materials Planning

OneWorld Materials Planning provides features to ensure that material requirements are met in order to assemble or manufacture a product. Material Planning analyzes material-related demand from a number of different of sources. Material Planning consists of

- ◆ Distribution Requirements Planning (DRP)
- ◆ Material Requirements Planning (MRP)

A Distribution Requirements Plan provides for the centralized control over distribution center inventories. The Distribution Requirements Plan controls the distribution of finished goods based on demand while also coordinating the replenishment of depleted distribution center inventories. Note that Distribution Requirements Planning is typically run before Master Production Scheduling. The required movement of products from the producing plant to the outlying distribution center locations increases the demand on the producing plant, which must therefore be accounted for in the before Master Production Schedule.

A Material Requirements Plan uses the Master Production Schedule as well as open orders, Bills of Material, and inventory records to calculate time-phased net requirements for every item to create a plan for covering all material requirements.

In OneWorld, the Distribution Requirements Plan or the Material Requirements Plan can be generated for all items or only on a net change basis, which considers only items that have been affected by transactions since the last Distribution Requirements Plan or Material Requirements Plan generation.

Master Production Scheduling

The Master Production Schedule is a "master list" of the items and quantities that an organization *expects* to assemble or produce. A Master Production Schedule is the definitive plan representing what your organization expects to produce based on combining the operating plan with your resource constraints.

Single-level master production scheduling implies that master production scheduling is done only at the end-product or deliverable-item level. Multi-level master production scheduling "explodes" planned orders down to their component level. In general, the OneWorld master production scheduling process consists of the following:

◆ Determining what is needed based on forecasted and actual demand

◆ Subtracting what is available from inventory, purchase orders, and Work Orders

◆ Calculating net requirements and when these items are needed

In OneWorld, the Master Production Schedule can be generated for all items or only on a net change basis, which considers only items that have been affected by transactions since the last Master Production Schedule generation. After you generate the Master Production Schedule, it can be reviewed, and actions can be made to any alerts or scheduling exception messages that were created or logged during the Master Production Schedule generation/regeneration process.

Time Fences and Time Series

A *time fence* is a critical input in the generation or regeneration of the Master Production Schedule in OneWorld. Time fences are points in time when changes to the Master Production Schedule can be made. Your organization's business processes and procedures determine the actual values for these three time fences. OneWorld allows for three time fences: Freeze, Planning, and Message Display.

The *time series* represents the proposed OneWorld Master Production Schedule when its generation or regeneration is requested. The results of the time series or proposed Master Production Schedule are then reviewed, and decisions by your organization's production planners are made as to whether to accept the planning that the system has suggested or to override these suggestions. The alert or action messages generated through the generation/regeneration process are typically reviewed by item number, and appropriate actions are then taken by the production planner. OneWorld provides a time fence inquiry that is used to review and act on these action messages.

Note that the setting of time fences controls the start or requested date of the work order in OneWorld. If these time fences are set incorrectly, late orders can become a significant problem.

Available to Promise and Availability Checking

Item availability calculations are defined for each branch/plant established in OneWorld. The system calculates item availability by defining the factors that subtract from or add to the available quantity of any item. From the standpoint of manufacturing planning, the system calculates an available-to-promise quantity or unreserved quantity based on the totality of known product demand or reservations and expected production.

When activated in Sales Order entry, the system performs availability checking. If desired, when the item's quantity exceeds the stock available, the system issues a warning for this item's quantity. Depending again on the system setup, a back-order is automatically placed for the quantity of the item that is unavailable.

Quality Management

A quality management system helps minimize or eliminate process waste. Process waste takes many forms, including before-sale costs such as rework and scrap, and after-sale costs such as field service trips, product recall campaigns, and the use of inferior purchased component parts that leads to premature end-product failures, fitness of use, or other safety concerns.

The OneWorld Quality Management system provides facilities for recording and managing data related to the material qualities or properties observed in your organization's products. The system allows your organization to record product quality–related testing results in a consistent and controlled manner. The OneWorld Quality Management system can be configured to your organization's specific testing needs through the establishment of user-defined quality tests specific to items or customers.

At any point in the production process, a quality test can be specified. When a test is indicated, samples can be collected, quality tests can be performed, and the results can be recorded in the system. The OneWorld Quality Management system can then be used to review the test results for any given item to verify whether the material produced met your specifications. If the specifications are met, the material can proceed to the next stage in the production process. If the material fails a quality test, the information available from the quality system will help your organization make decisions regarding rework, quarantines, and additional testing, and ultimately take corrective actions at the process level.

Tests

The OneWorld Quality Management system allows for an unlimited number of tests that can be performed within your production process. For each test, minimum, maximum, and target values are defined. Results can be recorded in numeric or alphanumeric format. The number of samples to take for each test and the sample size can be user-defined. Additional text can be entered on tests to indicate tools, testing equipment, and sampling methods related to the test itself. Examples of quality tests that can be processed by OneWorld include dimensional tolerances, color, potency, purity, visual inspection, hardness, and resistance.

Specifications

Specifications enable the grouping of tests that are either related or that should be performed together. Examples of such tests include mechanical, visual, and electronic specifications.

Preference Profiles

After tests and specifications are defined, a preference profile can be created. The preference profile determines which tests to perform and when to perform them. For instance, the preference profile can be specific to an item, item group, customer, or customer group. The preference profile enables maximum control and customization over product tests performed for a customer and the specific items he orders. For example, a preference profile might indicate that one customer requires a lower tolerance of a dimensional specification than another customer might allow.

Test Results Entry

Typically, test results are available or are gathered at various stages in your production process. Test results can be entered directly into the OneWorld Quality Management system as well as from within other OneWorld systems, such as

- When entering receipts for items on purchase orders
- When routing receipts for purchase orders and work orders
- When moving items to stock after completing production
- When entering hours and quantities

◆ When confirming shipments or packages

◆ When entering a sales order

◆ When reviewing lots

After test results are entered, the OneWorld Quality Management system evaluates the results against minimum and maximum values and sets each lot status to pass or fail.

Quality Management Analysis and Reporting

The Quality Management system can print tests and specifications by item and by branch/plant. Test results can be printed by lot number and by sales order number. The test results can be used to print a Certificate of Analysis (COA) if required by your customer. The Certificate of Analysis includes a list of all tests performed and the test results for each lot shipped to the customer. The Quality Management system also provides facilities to review and trace lots through product records and to review nonconforming lots that failed quality tests.

Summary

This chapter provided a brief introduction to the OneWorld planning, control, and execution systems that comprise the OneWorld ERPx model. The ERPx model provides systems that allow an organization to plan and control its inventory flows and production resources in a planned and deliberate manner, thereby completing products according to an actively and tightly managed schedule.

The OneWorld systems introduced in this chapter include:

◆ The Product Data Management system

◆ The Shop Floor Management system

◆ The Product Costing and Manufacturing Accounting system

◆ The Quality Management system

◆ The Forecasting system

◆ The Manufacturing and Distribution Planning system

Virtually all products are produced using one of these two manufacturing models:

◆ The continuous model, in which items are produced as a result of a continuous flow process

◆ The discrete model, in which items are produced on a discrete, or one-at-a-time, basis

Regardless of the manufacturing model employed, the OneWorld planning, control, and execution systems provide support for manufacturing either individually or simultaneously.

It is entirely possible to use the Product Data Management, Shop Floor Management, and Manufacturing Accounting systems without using the Manufacturing and Distribution Planning system. However, when this system is not used, both inventory and manufacturing activity *must be manually managed*. The Manufacturing and Distribution Planning system, when implemented, provides automated scheduling of inventory and manufacturing activity.

As a closed-loop MRP system, use of the OneWorld Manufacturing and Distribution Planning system provides feedback to manufacturing management on a continuous basis by alerting management to material and capacity shortages and production bottlenecks.

The Quality Management system is used to define and record the results of sampling during the production process; use of this system is completely optional.

Chapter 18

OneWorld Human Resource Management, Payroll, and Specialized Business Management Systems

You might be questioning this chapter's long and confusing title. However, when all is said and done, it will become apparent that the subject groupings for this chapter are indeed logical, even though they seem arbitrary at first glance.

As the title of this chapter suggests, the overall content of this chapter is divided into several broad categories. The first topic is an introduction to the OneWorld Human Resource Management and Payroll systems, which are closely related. The second topic introduces a number of specialized Business Management systems, which can be divided into several groups. These groups include Business Management, Project Management, Equipment Management, Service Management, and Customer Management systems. Many of these systems also use information—specifically, time card information—with the OneWorld Human Resource Management and Payroll system and are the basis for work orders created in the Work Order system.

The OneWorld Specialized Business Management Systems introduced in this chapter include systems relevant for the following:

◆ Customer Management

◆ Property Management

◆ Job or Project Management

◆ Equipment Management

◆ Profitability Management

The OneWorld Project Management systems include Job Cost Accounting, Contract Management, Contract Billing, Change Management, and Work Order. The OneWorld Equipment Management systems include Equipment and Plant Management and Equipment Billing. The Customer Management systems include Sales Configurator, Customer Service Management, and Service Billing. The OneWorld Profitability Management systems include Enterprise Profitability Management and Business Intelligence. OneWorld Property Management is a specialized application designed to manage leased space.

Considerable integration exists between all of these systems and other OneWorld systems—specifically, the Address Book, General Accounting, Accounts Receivable, Accounts Payable, Fixed Asset, Inventory Management, Sales Order Management, and Procurement systems. Figure 18-1 illustrates the complex integration that occurs between many of the systems discussed in this chapter.

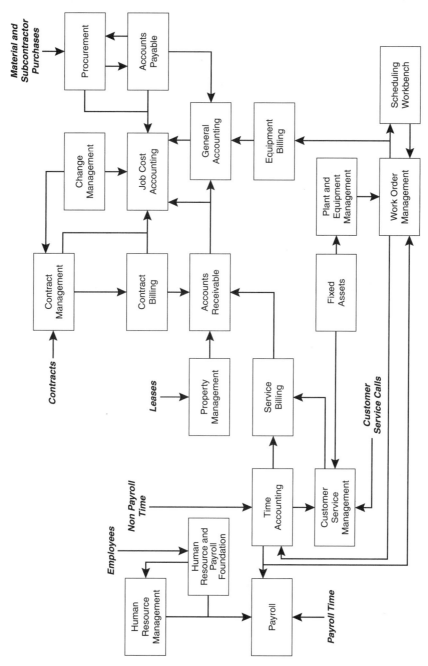

FIGURE 18-1 *Specialized Management System Integration in OneWorld*

Alliance Products

J. D. Edwards has entered into a number of key alliances with other software vendors. These alliances provide for "best of breed" extensions to an organization's OneWorld software investment. The major product alliances discussed in the last part of this chapter are as follows:

◆ The Siebel Sales System for Customer Relationship Management (CRM)

◆ The Vertex Quantum software for state and local tax calculation, rate compliance, and sales and use tax reporting.

Note that J. D. Edwards has other software product alliances. However, the capabilities provided by these representative systems are typically the most sought-after in today's marketplace. A list of additional alliance partners and products can be found in Appendix A.

Human Resource Management and Payroll

In recent years, an increasing number of organizations have chosen to outsource much, if not all, of their human resource–related activities and payroll processing. However, when an organization reaches a certain size, the costs of outsourcing these activities can frequently outweigh the benefits. If your organization currently performs its own human resource–related activities and payroll processing, or it has reached a point where outsourcing these functions has become cost-prohibitive, OneWorld provides both a Human Resource Management system and a Payroll system. These two OneWorld systems are fully integrated through the use of a third system, the Human Resource Management and Payroll foundation system. Together, these systems provide a full range of support for salary, position, and benefit administration; recruitment; workplace reporting; and payroll processing activities.

The Human Resource Management and Payroll Foundation System

The OneWorld Human Resource Management and Payroll foundation system has three basic functions. First, it is used to maintain a central database of information that both the Human Resource Management and Payroll systems share. This foundation system also works in conjunction with the OneWorld Address Book foundation system. The Address Book system is used to maintain employee names, addresses, and tax identification numbers, and the Human Resource Management and Payroll foundation system fulfills the role as the "employee master record" in OneWorld. The information stored in the Human Resource Management and Payroll foundation system includes the following:

- Applicable tax area(s)
- Benefit group(s)
- Departmental assignments
- Education
- Employment status
- Foreign language competencies
- Government-required information
- Job categories
- Job information
- Job skills
- Pay status
- Pay type, deduction, benefit, and accrual (PDBA) information
- Professional licenses
- Time accounting information
- Work experience

The second function of the Human Resource Management and Payroll foundation system is to provide a time card–based system for the accounting and tracking of employee time worked, including the calculation of any overtime hours apart from regular hours.

The third function of the Human Resource Management and Payroll foundation system is to provide for the maintenance of historical or employment event-related information about every employee.

Reporting

Given that the Human Resource Management and Payroll foundation system is used as the basis for maintaining historical or employment event-related information about every employee, this system plays an essential role in all employment-related reporting. Using the information maintained in the Human Resource Management and Payroll foundation system, your organization can respond quickly and efficiently to both government and internal reporting needs by creating reports about employees by department, supervisor, job, or other desired categorizations.

Government Record Keeping and Reporting

Today, a significant body of law covers the employee–employer relationship. Although the most well-known of these laws and regulations are issued by the Equal Employment Opportunity Commission (EEOC), many other laws and regulations are issued by other agencies, including the Department of Transportation (USDOT), the Environmental Protection Agency (EPA), and the Department of Labor. Depending on your line of business, one or all of these agencies of the federal government likely regulate your employee–employer relationships to a certain degree.

Typically, these government agencies require considerable and detailed employment-related record keeping and also require the filing of periodic reports regarding your organization's compliance with these laws and regulations. Such reports are generally based on your employment records. OneWorld specifically supports the following government reporting–related reports:

◆ EE0-1 Annual Report

◆ OSHA 101 Reportable Illness and Injury Report

◆ VETS-100 Veteran's Employment Report

In addition to the federal regulations covering the employee–employer relationship, the state or states in which your organization operates will likely have additional—and different—reporting requirements that must be met. Such additional reporting requirements usually need to rely on OneWorld's Enterprise Report Writer and the employee-related additional and supplemental data fields in the Human Resource Management and Payroll foundation system database.

Additional and Supplemental Data

To meet any data requirements that are unique to your organization, OneWorld includes several features to track such information. In addition to the standard or predefined information contained in an employee record, additional information for the employee can be tracked. OneWorld provides a series of user-defined category codes and user-defined dates that facilitate tracking this information. The use of these codes and dates is generally established when implementing OneWorld. This information can subsequently be used for reporting and analysis purposes.

Turnover

In recent years, most employers have increasingly found substantial truth in the old saying that "Good help is hard to find." Therefore, understanding the cause of employee turnover has become an important activity of the Human Resource department. The Human Resource Management and Payroll foundation system can be used to track employee turnover. Turnover is caused by any employee job change, including promotions, transfers, retirements, terminations, resignations, or any other reason that an employee might leave your employ. Activity reports can be created to monitor history and turnover and determine if a pattern or trend is developing, thereby allowing your organization to initiate steps to resolve any substantive issues that might cause turnover.

Other Uses

Employee information in the Human Resource Management and Payroll foundation system can also be used to track complete job information, including job descriptions and evaluations. This information can then be used for both internal candidate identification and external candidate recruiting. For instance, this information can be used to

- ◆ Analyze jobs to determine appropriate salary ranges
- ◆ Compare jobs and pay ranges
- ◆ Match individuals to appropriate job openings
- ◆ Meet the standards that support equal pay for equal work

In addition to these requirements, your organization might want to track additional information about your employees. Examples of additional information that your organization might need to track include uniform-related information, access and desk key issuance, or the tools and equipment that an employee might have in his possession.

Human Resource Management

The OneWorld Human Resource Management system provides human resource professionals with a set of tools to help them respond to changing workforce needs that are predicated by general economic and labor market conditions, government regulations, and changes by your organization to its employment-related policies and procedures. Features within the OneWorld Human Resource Management system support the following employment life cycle processes:

◆ Position Budget Management

◆ Position Requisitioning

◆ Recruitment and Requisition Tracking

◆ Compensation Management

In addition to these processes, OneWorld also includes facilities for OSHA-related incident management reporting.

Position Budget Management

The OneWorld Human Resource Management system provides features to track and manage headcount authorization, frequently called position budget management. By managing position budgets within the Human Resource Management system, an organization can improve control over the salary administration and budgeting process. The position budget management functions provide for the following:

◆ Automatic updates to the position budget when an employee change occurs

◆ Determination of full-year costs by developing projections based on hours, salary amounts, head count, or full-time equivalents

◆ Online review of the approved head count for a department to ensure that a position is authorized prior to acting on a requisition

◆ Posting of position budgets to salary-related accounts in the general ledger for budgeting purposes

◆ Comparisons of projected salaries through year end using the approved budget for each position

◆ Tracking of position-effective dates and their budgetary impact

◆ Tracking of positions and head count by company and department

A position budget is developed on an annual basis by Position ID, by Business Unit. At the position level, OneWorld uses projected salary expenditures, work hours, full-time equivalents, and budgeted headcount for each position. This information provides the basis for position budget management and reporting, including accounting for part-time and job-sharing arrangements.

When implementing the position budget management functions, it is possible to automatically generate the initial budget using a specific OneWorld batch process. The appropriateness of this step depends on the exact setup of your employee and other position-related information in OneWorld. Keep in mind that automatically generated records in the position can and might need to be manually altered thereafter.

Note that when properly used, position budgets can be used as the basis of the financial budgets related to salaries in the OneWorld General Accounting system. However, in many organizations, the salary budget in the General Accounting system is prepared by the responsible business unit or the accounting department. Therefore, if the position budget management will be used as the basis for salary budgets in the General Accounting system, it is recommended that the Accounting and Human Resource departments collaborate on the implementation and ongoing maintenance of OneWorld's position budgeting features.

Position Requisitioning

OneWorld includes features to create, approve, and manage job requisitions online. Generally speaking, in most organizations the job requisition is created by a department manager who has hiring and firing authority. This usually means that the department also has an authorized or budgeted position that is vacant within the department. Typically, the job requisition includes detailed information about the open position.

Depending on your organization's business policies, after a department manager creates a requisition to fill a position, final management approval is often needed. The approval process can be performed online in OneWorld. Optionally, using OneWorld Workflow Management, e-mail can be used to notify an approver of a requisition awaiting his or her approval. However, the Human Resource Management system can also be used to facilitate online requisition approval exclusive of workflow management. Note that delegating this approval authority to another individual is also possible when a manager will be out of the office for an extended period of time.

OneWorld provides two hard-coded requisition status codes, but additional requisition status codes can be defined. However, OneWorld does have one stipulation:

Any status code related to an approved requisition must begin with the letter A. By monitoring the approval status of job requisitions, the Human Resource department can know what positions have been approved and what they must begin recruiting for.

Recruitment and Requisition Tracking

OneWorld provides a number of features to help the human resource professional identify and qualify candidates for employment opportunities within your organization. The OneWorld Recruitment and Requisition Tracking–related features are described in this section.

Candidate Matching

Using approved, open requisitions, internal job postings can be created and made available for review across your entire organization. As candidates apply, their employment information can be reviewed to determine if a sufficient match exists.

In addition, as resumes are received from external candidates, informational records identifying applicants are also created, and pertinent job-related education, qualifications, skills, and other requirements can be recorded in the system. This information can then be used to identify external applicants who might be qualified to interview for a current job opening.

Employee information stored in the Human Resource Management and Payroll foundation system can also be used to identify internal candidates for open positions, exclusive of a formal job posting system.

Using OneWorld's extensive search capabilities, a list of qualified applicants with appropriate skills can be generated and used as the basis for providing resumes to a department manager for his or her review.

The Applicant Supplemental Database is used to store any information not stored in the applicant's primary record. For instance, previous job experience or scores on job-related tests can be tracked. Using the Supplemental Data's Multi-skill Search function, the Human Resource Department can quickly ascertain which applicants have relevant experience and education that closely match the requirements of the job.

Effective candidate screening requires careful attention to initial design and ongoing maintenance of employee and candidate-related information within the system.

Requisition Tracking

As the Human Resource Department identifies both internal and external candidates through canvas, advertisement, or referral, an applicant or existing employee can be associated with an open requisition.

As applicants are screened, the status of their application can be recorded. For instance, at the conclusion of an interview, an applicant's status can be noted, including steps to indicate offers made or rejected, candidates rejected, and next steps.

OneWorld improves your overall understanding of the recruiting process by tracking requisition-related information. For instance, OneWorld can track recruiting-related costs such as advertising, travel, and any outside agency fees related to fulfilling an open requisition, as well as the length of time the hiring process took for any given position. This information is helpful for planning and budgeting purposes.

Managing the Employee Experience

It's important to get new hires off on the right foot and make them feel good about their choice of employer in today's tight labor markets. To ease the transition from applicant to employee status, OneWorld can optionally be set up to automatically update the person's applicant record to indicate that he or she is now an employee. The system can also be set up to require that someone enter payroll information before the hiring process is complete.

Employee Self-Service

Increasingly, employers want their employees to enroll or maintain their benefit program and address information without Human Resource department intervention. Typically, an organization allows an employee to change his or her benefit plan enrollment status on an annual basis for a limited time. This is generally known as the open enrollment period. This normally places a peak workload on the Human Resource department. Using employee self-service—the moniker for this practice throughout the industry—shifts the burden for managing open enrollment to the employees. However, to make this process appealing to employees, additional value must be provided.

In OneWorld, employees can enroll in or change their benefit plans online. The Open Benefits Enrollment form (P08530) allows an employee to review current benefit program enrollment information, review the new year's benefit plan offerings, calculate total pay period costs for new benefit selections, and repeatedly change open enrollment choices prior to the closing of the open enrollment period.

The Benefits Enrollment form program includes a number of specific processing options that allow the enrollment form to be employment- or life event–driven. Under this scenario, options are limited to changes in employment or changes in the life of an employee. For example, these events may include the employee's initial hiring, or life events such as the birth or adoption of a child or a change in marital status.

A separate version of the Benefits Enrollment form is needed for each such event. The various versions of the Benefits Enrollment form may then be added to a user-defined menu to simplify the online benefits enrollment process for the employee.

Manager Self-Service

OneWorld includes many features intended to streamline and minimize the efforts required of the human resource department to maintain information about employees that can easily be entered at its source, usually by department managers or directly by employees.

In addition to the self-service features available for employees, your department managers have an even greater number of self-service features available. Most of these features are initiated through the Managers Workbench. This OneWorld program serves as a platform for performing a number of employee administration tasks for which a department manager is typically responsible:

- Determining upcoming employee review dates
- Entering employee competency information
- Performing benefit changes for employees
- Requesting an employee status change
- Reviewing employee information, such as name and address, time entry, emergency contacts, paid-time-off balances, and skill competencies
- Reviewing jobs and job competencies for their department
- Setting up new employees, especially at remote locations

These features are in addition to the position requisitioning and compensation management features that are also included in OneWorld. They are typically used by department managers.

Compensation Management

The OneWorld Compensation Management subsystem is intended to streamline the salary review process for both the human resource department and your department managers. The Compensation Management subsystem provides your department managers with a facility for recommending salary adjustments online.

Your organization establishes its promotional and merit increase guidelines as rules within OneWorld. These rules can then be used to guide salary decisions and management approvals. The use of online forms also helps safeguard salary information from both loss and exposure to unauthorized parties.

Benefits Administration

The OneWorld Benefits Administration subsystem is used to manage your organization's benefit plans through online integration with other human resource information and payroll processing. This module is used to enroll employees in the benefit plans that your organization offers and for which an employee qualifies for participation in. The Benefits Administration subsystem addresses the needs of the entire employment life cycle, providing for new hire enrollment, open and ongoing enrollment processing, and post-employment benefit plan changes.

The Benefits Administration subsystem also allows your organization to easily add, change, or terminate benefit plans and the amounts of any payroll deductions associated with these plans. The Benefits Administration subsystem allows for an unlimited number of plans, with varying amount and rate options and eligibility requirements. Other features include the ability to manage separately the employer's and employee's portions of plan costs, generate payroll deductions for employee contributions, administer both pre-tax and post-tax benefits, and track any noncash benefits, such as the use of a company car or a club membership.

Health and Safety Administration

Many regulations govern workplace health and safety. Numerous governmental health and safety regulations impact the typical organization. These programs mandate that an employer track and report any work-related illnesses or injuries. These requirements are frequently called *incident reporting* by health and safety professionals. In addition, "right-to-know" laws require both disclosure and exposure control training regarding any known workplace hazards. OneWorld provides facilities for tracking incident-related information necessary in developing government-required reports. This information can also be used to develop "right-to-know" programs. As discussed previously, OneWorld also provides a series of user-defined and supplemental information facilities within the Human Resource Management and Payroll foundation system that are used to enhance your ability to administer your employee health and safety programs.

Payroll

The OneWorld Payroll system is a complete solution for administering the payroll process. The OneWorld Payroll system automates the compliance with the many federal, state, and local withholding and reporting requirements associated with payroll. Using Quantum software (available from Vertex) as an add-on product for OneWorld, any employee-related withholding amounts can be accurately calculated based on the current tax tables of each taxing authority. Vertex licensees receive periodic rate table updates containing the current payroll-related tax tables of each taxing authority. The updates are then applied electronically. The OneWorld Payroll system includes features that help an organization do the following:

- Calculate and deduct any number of voluntary contributions for benefit programs, such as life insurance premiums
- Calculate and withhold any number of involuntary deductions, such as tax levies, child support, and other garnishments
- Calculate any number of other types of pay, including bonuses, commissions, other incentives, and overtime.
- Provide for user-defined pay cycles and pay periods and corresponding payment dates
- Issue timely and accurate paychecks to its employees
- Keep payroll journal entries in balance when employees work in multiple companies
- Process payments outside the normal payroll cycle
- Process payrolls for multiple companies

- Process payrolls in a union environment
- Provide for both paper-based and electronic (direct deposit) paychecks for its employees
- Simplify tax calculations and allow for any number of taxing entities

The OneWorld Payroll system provides for complete gross-to-net payment calculations and tax calculations. This information is subsequently used to make tax deposits and payments to fund benefit plan contributions. The Payroll system includes a number of standard payroll reports generated from within various stages of the OneWorld payroll processing cycle.

The OneWorld Payroll Processing Cycle

The payroll cycle is a process that you complete in OneWorld each time you need to pay your employees. The OneWorld Payroll processing cycle includes features to do the following:

- Choose the employees to include in a payroll cycle
- Process multiple payroll cycles for different groups of employees
- Review employees' payroll information before creating payments, and make any necessary last-minute adjustments
- Print or create employee payments
- Review and, when necessary, rerun the payroll processing cycle
- Print time entry, pay, summary, and tax reports during the payroll processing cycle
- Create payroll and withholding journal entries automatically during the payroll processing cycle
- Perform the final update—the last step in the payroll cycle. This step updates the payroll history tables and prepares the system for the next payroll cycle.

In addition to the normal payroll cycle, the interim payment feature can be used to process payments outside the payroll cycle. This feature is useful for making special advances to employees, including payroll and vacation advances, or for making termination payments. Note that all payroll-related information can be reviewed online. However, most organizations will want to carefully control access to who within the organization can review this information.

Pre-Payroll Processing

During payroll cycle processing, the system uses time entry records to create payments for employees. Pre-payroll processing involves creating time entry–related work files that the Payroll system requires for generating a payroll. Pre-payroll processing includes the following tasks:

- Recording hours worked on time cards or time sheets
- Entering hours worked, manually, as time cards, into OneWorld
- Generating time cards from these manually entered hours
- Generating time cards automatically for employees whose time cards were not entered manually

Generally speaking, time cards are used for hourly workers. For salaried employees, the system is set up to automatically generate time card records. Time cards are entered into and maintained in OneWorld through the Human Resource Management and Payroll foundation system.

Securing Access to Sensitive Information

No discussion of personnel records in any system is ever complete without a discussion of how this information can be secured. At most organizations, any personnel-related information is generally secured.

OneWorld includes a complete suite of security features that can be used to restrict access to all but the essential information and to provide this information only to those system users who are specifically authorized to use these functions. Typically, an organization designates someone as the OneWorld System Administrator. One of this person's responsibilities is to establish and maintain system security. The System Administrator can set up security for an entire form or even for individual fields on a form.

In addition, OneWorld can be set up to log employee record changes so that each time you add or change employee information, the system automatically creates a historical record of the new information.

Time Accounting

Even if you will not use the Human Resource Management and Payroll system in OneWorld, it is quite possible that your organization will still rely heavily on at least one component from this system—the Time Accounting subsystem.

The Human Resource Management and Payroll foundation system provides for stand-alone time accounting when the OneWorld Payroll system is not used to process time cards. In such cases, the Time Accounting subsystem within the Human Resource Management and Payroll foundation system can be used to generate journal entries into the General Accounting system.

The Time Accounting subsystem has a number of other important uses. It is used to record labor and equipment time by day. The Job Cost system can be used to analyze labor and equipment costs for a job. The Service and Contract Billing systems can subsequently be used to bill customers for the labor and equipment expenses associated with the job. The Human Resource Management and Payroll foundation system is used to record and track work-order labor and equipment charges for job or project work and for equipment maintenance tasks generated in the Equipment and Plant Maintenance system.

Customer Management Systems

This section introduces several additional OneWorld modules that are useful to the customer order management process. The systems provide for installed base management and product configuration.

The Customer Service Management System

Customer service is an important element in today's highly competitive business climate. The "customer experience" before, during, and after the original sale has a significant impact on whether or not a customer becomes a repeat customer. Since the cost of obtaining new customers is many times greater than retaining an existing customer, high levels of customer satisfaction should be an important organizational benchmark. Outstanding pre- and post-sale customer service has brought many accolades to today's most successful companies.

The service organization is an important part of your product or service "value chain." The service organization is typically in contact with your customers more frequently than any other part of your overall organization. It stands to reason that any improvements in the efficiency and effectiveness of your service operations will directly impact the bottom line through increased customer satisfaction and retention levels. Using the OneWorld Customer Service Management system is one way to improve your service-related operations.

The OneWorld Customer Service Management system allows your organization to coordinate all aspects of your customer service operations, including:

- Receiving and responding to calls
- Scheduling depot or on-site equipment repairs
- Generating after-sale revenues, including accessory sales, spare and replacement parts sales, and service contracts
- Tracking customer purchases and service patterns

OneWorld Customer Service Management consists of four subsystems:

- Call Management
- Installed Base Management
- Service Contract Management
- Service Order Management

This section provides a brief overview of each of these subsystems.

Call Management

The Call Management subsystem provides features to record contact between your customers and your service advisers, consultants, and representatives. Increasingly, the customer service center is the central point of contact for most, if not all, post-sale customer interactions at many organizations. This subsystem provides facilities to store and track all customer issues. A customer issue is a question or problem for which your customer wants a solution. A call ticket is typically opened to record the customer issue. Call tickets can be tracked by issue, status of issue, the date and time that an issue is received, the response date and time, or the service team member who "owns" the call. The call ticket can be updated throughout its life based on its analysis and resolution.

Installed Base Management

The Installed Base Management subsystem is used to manage product registrations. The Installed Base Management subsystem provides features to create and track current and historical information for any product or piece of equipment distributed or serviced by your organization. Information such as product model, serial number, purchase date, shipment date, current owner, and warranty information can be maintained in this subsystem.

Service Contract Management

The Service Contract Management subsystem is used to record and manage service contract agreements. A contract is a written agreement between you and your customer regarding services that you will perform for them, such as equipment repairs. Depending on your service capacities and your customer's needs, different service levels might be offered. For instance, equipment service is often performed on-site, at a premium rate, or on a "depot" basis at a lesser rate. The Service Contract Management subsystem allows for the configuration of multiple types of contracts that reflect the service levels and pricing options your organization provides to its customers. The Service Contract Management subsystem can automatically generate contract renewal notices as existing contracts or warranties are set to expire.

Service Order Management

The Service Order Management subsystem is used to create service orders. These are used when a call ticket is inappropriate to the level of service needed. For instance, a service order is entered on the customer's behalf when on-site support or assistance is needed. The Service Order Management subsystem provides a central database for all service and repair information and events. The system also provides facilities to generate and coordinate Returned Material Authorizations (RMAs). The Returned Material Authorization document is an authorization from the supplier for the customer to return a product for credit, replacement, or repair.

Sales Configuration

In today's competitive marketplace, the order of the day is mass customization. Increasingly, customers are requiring manufacturers to build complex product configurations that follow their detailed specifications. Customers are also demanding shorter overall lead times from order placement to product delivery. The emerging model for today's agile manufacturer, especially in discrete industries, is to offer a basic or modular product that can be readily adapted to a customer's unique specifications.

The manufacturer must allow the customer or salesperson to specify unique product configurations from a myriad of options and variations. In order to prepare the pre-sale price quotation and the after-sale manufacturing work order, a precise product configuration must be determined.

Manufacturers are vigorously responding to the pressure and opportunities presented by their customers' configuration and customization needs. However, currently many manufacturers struggle with the manual paperwork and are challenged by slow turnaround times on proposals and quotations and under- or over-bid work due to a lack of accurate or current cost information or product volume versus product complexity constraints. In short, manufacturers need the agility to provide specially configured products at a competitive price in a timely manner.

Three approaches are generally employed to handle complex product configurations. The first is to create unique end part numbers. This approach creates a part number for every combination of features and options and in turn represents an *end* or saleable product. This method can be cumbersome and is not conducive to change because there are simply too many numbers to effectively manage.

The second approach is to create generic end part numbers with extended manual descriptions. Critical information about the features and options that are included in the end product are embedded in the text. All inventory records in the system appear as the same product, because it bears the same part number even though the features and options might be different on each end item. Use of this technique results in a poor audit trail of end products, therefore complicating priority and capacity planning and distorting costs. This is largely due to the fact that the software systems generally do not have a way to retrieve and use embedded text information.

The third preferred approach is to use a product configurator. A product configurator is a specialized software tool specifically engineered to handle complex products. The essence of manufacturing success in the mass customization environment is efficiency. Such efficiencies are demanded throughout the entire product design and build process. In the case of product design, product configuration software provides this efficiency. As for build efficiency, simple, modular designs of manufactured parts are being engineered into scores of products.

The build process is further simplified when a Bill of Material and manufacturing work order can be developed on-the-fly, again based on a product configuration database. Generally speaking, a finite number of rules or combinations of features and options can realistically be provided. In these cases, the product configuration software has a rule-based database that is associated with modular or feature- and option-driven Bills of Material. These modular Bills of Material are subsequently used to develop on-the-fly a parts list for the manufacturing work order.

Configured items are products specified by the customer. They are not make-to-stock items that can be bought off the shelf. Since a customer specifies configured products, features and options are associated with the final product. Although, strictly speaking, there might be infinite combinations of the end item, in reality there usually are practical constraints that limit choices. It might be better said that sometimes the laws of physics simply can't be defied.

J. D. Edwards offers two alternatives to solve the product configuration challenge. For the assemble-to-order model, the OneWorld Sales Configurator is a rules-based product configurator. For the make- or build-to-order model, J. D. Edwards provides a unique and leading-edge parametric-based configurator called CustomWorks that integrates with OneWorld.

Sales Configurator

The OneWorld Sales Configurator system provides functions for establishing and selling configured goods. Although the actual setup for the Sales Configurator is a complex process, the benefits are enormous. The OneWorld Sales Configurator system works like this: As a sales order is entered, if it contains a configured item, a series of questions is displayed. These questions relate to a configured item's features and options.

The configured item's features and options are called *segments* in OneWorld. For the configured item or end product, a segment defines a characteristic or option available for the end product. For example, characteristics of a metal equipment cabinet might indicate a specific paint color or that a door is to be a left- versus right-opening door.

As the configuration-related questions are answered, OneWorld verifies each segment value against a series of user-defined rules and code tables. Segments are associated with the configured item. Cross-segment editing rules are used to prevent invalid combinations of segments. The cross-segment editing rule establishes a relationship between the configured item segments and logic statements.

OneWorld edits segments on the sales order against the applicable cross-segment editing rules. When a cross-segment editing rule is violated, an error results. Also note that assembly inclusion rules control price adjustments, routings, and parts lists for a configured end product. Upon successful validation, the system joins the segments and expresses the configuration as a string of segments separated by a delimiter character, such as a dash.

OneWorld also allows multilevel or nested configurations. Therefore, a configured end product can consist of one or more configured subassemblies. For example, consider the end product known as the "metal equipment cabinet." The metal equipment cabinet consists of two segments—a paint color segment and a door swing segment. If the configuration is valid, the system processes the order.

The setup effort required to make use of the OneWorld Sales Configurator can be substantial. However, the setup process is largely a one-time effort that requires maintenance only as new products are introduced or as features and options change.

The OneWorld Sales Configurator offers your organization the following benefits:

◆ Reduces the number of end item part numbers

◆ Creates parts lists and routings on-the-fly

◆ Improves order accuracy

As an alternative to the Sales Configurator, OneWorld also provides for kit processing. Kit processing allows for the inclusion of features and options in the order-taking process. However, kit processing has limitations that restrict its use when complex specifications are involved that have conditional part requirements, such as when certain features are incompatible with other features.

CustomWorks

CustomWorks is a product that was originally created by the Premisys Corporation. Premisys was a business partner of J. D. Edwards before its acquisition by J. D. Edwards within the past 18 months. CustomWorks is a visual product configurator.

CustomWorks is known as a parametric modeling tool. A parametric modeler can visually create any number of "what-if" product configurations given scaleable component drawings and a set of underlying rules that establish or validate feasible relationships between components.

CustomWorks extends the rules-based nonvisual Sales Configurator to another dimension. CustomWorks actually generates "as-configured" drawings—on-the-fly—that are directly based on product configuration rules. These to-scale drawings represent precise, technical specifications for the make-to-order product that can be used as a medium of communication throughout the selling cycle, from quotation to manufacture. A visual representation helps ensure that the make-to-order product is technically correct and fully understood by both the customer and the manufacturer. These assurances help eliminate confusion and rework.

However, parametric modeling is difficult to implement. This is due in large part to the complexity of rules that are typically required to establish or validate feasible relationships between components. The successful parametric-based product configuration must have "point and click" simplicity. Therefore, building a successful parametric-based product configuration requires tremendous attention to detail. As a general rule, the greater the complexity of the underlying business rules, the greater this challenge.

In order to implement CustomWorks, a number of skills are employed. For instance, AutoCAD-related technical drawing skills are necessary to build the scaleable template drawings. Also, product engineers need to define component compatibility rules and relationships for configuration validation purposes. These rules are established using the CustomWorks Catalog Author. Finally, software engineers must code component compatibility rules and relationships into Visual Basic scripts. Be advised that people who possess these skills and who also can implement CustomWorks are few and far between and are usually in great demand.

Property Management

The OneWorld Property Management system is a record-keeping and billing system related to property leasing. A lease is an agreement between the lessee or tenant and property owner or lessor to use rental property. The lease specifies the duration, the rental payment, and any special calculations or conditions related to the rental.

The Property Management system supports both simple and complex leasing agreements for residential, retail, and commercial properties. The Property Management system provides the ability to collect, store, process, and analyze lease information. Here are some other features of the Property Management system:

♦ Compliance with Financial Accounting Standards Board (FASB) Statement 13, which requires the straight-line method of calculating rental revenues over the life of the lease

♦ Compute interest payable on security deposits

♦ Compute late payment charges

- Provide for expense participation by tenants
- Provide for holdovers after a lease has expired
- Provide for sales coverage leasing agreements for retail tenants
- Provide for periodic escalations in long-term lease agreements
- Set up and generate recurring billings for lease payments
- The ability to require security deposits

For further information regarding the Property Management system, consult the OneWorld reference documentation CD-ROM and view the Property Management system.

Project Management Systems

A major difference between a service-oriented business organization and a distribution or manufacturing business organization is a primary reliance on labor services rather than on material goods or products as a revenue source. The Customer Service Management system is typically used by distributors and manufacturers to provide after-sale product support. However, for the "pure play" service organization, OneWorld provides a series of related systems that are used to administer jobs or projects. Products, if a factor at all to these organizations, are typically needed only to complete a customer's request for service and typically do not represent a major source of revenue to a service organization. The building and construction trades and the consulting industry are examples of industries to which the OneWorld project management–related systems are applicable.

Job Cost

The OneWorld Job Cost Accounting system provides facilities for monitoring both revenues and costs associated with jobs and projects. The Job Cost system is ideally suited to the construction industry. However, the Job Cost system can be used to manage internal capital expenditures or self-constructed assets such as a plant expansion project.

The Job Cost system does not create additional detail-level transactions; instead, it relies on the account balances and the transaction detail in the OneWorld General Accounting system. The Job Cost Accounting system can be used to create and maintain cost code structures for jobs and projects. A cost code structure represents a chart of accounts for the project. Once a cost code structure is developed, a project budget can be established for the job or project. As the actual material purchases are made, or as labor and equipment charges are billed to a customer for a given job or project, they are recorded in the General Accounting system and, in effect, simultaneously in the Job Cost system.

As a matter of fact, the cost code structure for a job is set up much like the General Accounting chart of accounts. Refer to Chapter 14 for additional information about the chart of accounts in OneWorld. Note that the Job Cost system works at the 8 and 9 levels of detail and that the Job Cost system inverts the business unit and object account to form the cost code structure. The OneWorld Job Cost system provides the following important capabilities:

- Maintains time schedules for job tasks
- Generates job-related reports detailing revenues, costs, and other details
- Calculates job progress at any time during the job
- Projects the estimated final values for revenues and costs associated with the job, using any one of several computation methods
- Recognizes and records profit or loss at any point in a job's life
- Creates draw reports on the costs that are eligible to be borrowed against a construction financing agreement
- Sets up unique cost code structures for different jobs

The Job Cost system offers both online job status inquiry forms and reports that allow for monitoring the costs, revenues, and status associated with a job.

Final Projections

The Job Cost system can calculate projected final values for a job at any time during the job's life. Final projections are calculated based on the costs, revenues, and percentage of completion associated with a job at a specified time. Final revenues, costs, profit, and "over or under values" can be projected.

Commitment Tracking

When the Job Cost system is used, the OneWorld Procurement system typically plays a major role in the effective use of this system. The setup of the Procurement system lets job-related purchases be tracked in a purchasing commitments ledger. As an order is placed, the purchasing commitments ledger is updated for the amount of the expenditure now on order. As the purchased materials or services are received and vouchered, the purchasing commitment ledger is "relieved" to avoid double-counting alongside the actual costs now being vouchered.

Profit Recognition

The Job Cost system creates the appropriate profit recognition journal entries for revenues and cost. These entries are based on a job's percentage of completion at any time during job progression. Note that recognized revenue and cost for each job can be manually adjusted if needed.

Budget Revisions

The Job Cost system allows for the entry of budget information for the job. This is called the original budget. The Job Cost system lets you lock in the job's original budget information. After a job budget is locked, a formal budget revision is required in order to change the budget. Revisions are tracked separately. Budget tracking lets you compare the original job budget against the revised job budget.

Draw Processing

The Job Cost system is used to track the progress of your jobs. If your organization has a construction financing arrangement with a lending institution, a draw report can be produced that will identify completed work that is eligible for funding under that arrangement.

Work Order Management

The OneWorld Work Order Management system is designed to administer small, short-term tasks that might be part of a major project. The Work Order system design allows for easy project or task setup, accounting, and basic scheduling of tasks. The Work Order Management system complements the OneWorld Job Cost system. The Job Cost system is used to administer long-term projects in which detailed budget comparisons and final cost projections are typically required. The Work Order Management system provides for simple budget estimates for a Work Order and provides a series of project management reports.

Work Orders are created quickly and easily, without extensive preplanning requirements. Parent Work Orders and Processing Options associated with the Work Order entry form further minimize required information entry. Approval controls, by type of work or dollar amount, can be established over Work Orders, requiring a Work Order to be approved before any work can begin.

Work Order activity rules can be established by Work Order type to define a Work Order life cycle. The activity rules that define the Work Order life cycle govern Work Order processing to ensure that your specific business procedures are followed. In addition, activity rules can be used to indicate whether a Work Order is active or inactive and to control or prevent changes to a Work Order.

The Work Order Life Cycle and the Scheduling Workbench

The life cycle of a Work Order represents the steps or statuses through which a Work Order must pass, indicating the work's progress. For example, a Work Order's life cycle can include steps that represent

- Entry of the request for work to be performed
- Approval for the work to proceed
- That the work needs labor, materials, or equipment resources
- That the work has been started
- That the work has been completed
- That a work order has been revised
- That a work order has been canceled or closed

The OneWorld Scheduling Workbench is used to process Work Orders in OneWorld. Using the Scheduling Workbench, existing Work Orders can be reviewed and updated as the work progresses. For instance, from the Scheduling Workbench, the following tasks can be performed:

- Enter Work Orders
- Approve a Work Order and allow work to begin
- Indicate a change in the status of a Work Order
- Enter the time associated with a Work Order
- Issue material to a Work Order
- Review costs associated with a Work Order, including comparisons of budgeted to actual costs
- Assign personnel to complete a Work Order; the system provides for several different levels of personnel assignments

Work Orders can be assigned priorities. The priority level assigned to a Work Order can be increased or decreased. The Work Order Management system also maintains a number of important dates related to the Work Order. The dates that are maintained for the Work Order include the entry date, the start date, the planned completion date, the assignment date, and the actual completion date. In addition, an unlimited number of narrative remarks can be maintained about each Work Order.

Project Setup and Tracking Using Work Orders

The Work Order Management system can be used to create, plan, organize, and track small projects. The project itself is considered a parent Work Order, and each task within the project is a child Work Order. In fact, the OneWorld Work Order Management system can actually be used to plan and organize your OneWorld implementation project. I've used the Work Order Management system to do exactly this in the past.

Understand that in OneWorld, project management is a status-driven process. The project setup must *manually* outline the task sequence or critical path to be followed. As with any project management system, the accuracy of information in the system relies on the periodic review of all of a project's tasks to determine the date and status changes.

Project Management Reporting

In addition to providing a Work Order document, the Work Order Management system also provides a series of informational reports that can be used to manage projects. These reports include a Cost Summary report, a Cost Detail report, a Work Summary, a Detailed Task Description report, and a Project Status Summary report. In earlier releases of World software, a simple Gantt-style bar chart was available. However, this is not provided in OneWorld.

Service Billing

The OneWorld Service Billing system is designed to provide service-related customer billing and record keeping. Many services involve work that requires varying combinations of time, equipment usage, and materials. The Service Billing system is used to bill for both goods delivered (materials) and services rendered (time and usage). Typically, a service billing process begins through a contractual relationship between a customer and a provider. The customer requests a service. Your organization, as the provider, provides the service and bills the customer for the products and services that were provided. The Service Billing system is used to

◆ Account for the costs of goods and services

◆ Mark up the costs to account for any profit

◆ Bill customers for the goods and services provided

◆ Provide written evidence outlining all customer charges

◆ Create accounting entries related to the goods and services

The OneWorld Service Billing system is ideal for billing services that are provided on a one-time basis, such as a time and materials repair job. The OneWorld Service Billing system also includes a number of industry-specific features.

Retainage

The OneWorld Service Billing system provides for retainage. Retainage is a percentage of the billed amount on an invoice amount that is held back. A retainage is typically paid out after an agreed-upon level or quantity of service has been established and verified as complete by the customer. Typically, retainage is associated with warranty or "punch list" work.

Revenue Recognition

The OneWorld Service Billing system adheres to generally accepted accounting principles regarding the treatment of service or project-related revenue streams, called revenue recognition. Revenue recognition requires that revenue be treated as an inflow of assets, typically a customer prepayment account, until such time that the revenue itself can be considered "earned." At the time revenue is recognized, the prepayment account is relieved, and the revenue account is increased. For instance, it is common in the repair industry to bill on the first service call, even if services aren't fully completed (such as when an additional part must be ordered and installed at a later date). However, any subsequent call to complete a job is made on a no-charge basis. The OneWorld revenue recognition feature creates the required general ledger entries related to revenue recognition without generating new invoices.

The Service Billing system can also be used internally to reallocate internal overhead departments on a pay-per-use basis.

Contract Management, Billing, and Change Management

Together, the OneWorld Contract Management, Billing, and Change Management systems provide a formal contract administration process. Although the Service Billing system is ideal for small-scale projects, for larger projects or contracts a more robust process is usually needed.

Use of a Sales Order Management System is typically inappropriate for contract administration. Generally speaking, in a true build-to-order relationship, called a job or project, nothing is really standardized about the product or service, except perhaps the terms of sale. Because of these complexities, it is typical for a written contractual agreement to exist between the customer and the contractor. The contractual agreement typically outlines the work to be done and the billing terms.

A contract generally establishes guidelines to govern any design or scope changes that affect the job. A change generally means that the work to be done or that is already in process will be altered and that contract billings will also be affected. The OneWorld Change Management system is intended to formalize and administer change orders.

The OneWorld Contract Management, Billing, and Change Management systems include a number of industry-specific features.

Contract Management

When a contract is executed, the information about the contract arrangement must be described to OneWorld. A contract in OneWorld consists of both general information, such as the customer- and contract-related dates, and detailed information, including the goods or services to be billed and how they will be billed. The contract is therefore established in two parts: a contract master record and one or more billing lines.

Contract Billing

The OneWorld Contract Billing system provides a full range of features to perform contract administration and billing. The Contract Billing system relies on a contract master record. After a contract master record is established, the specific details about the contract can be entered into OneWorld. Ultimately, this information is used as the basis for invoicing the customer for payments due under a contract.

Billing Lines and Billing Methods

Billing terms are an important part of contract administration. After a contract master record is defined in OneWorld, billing lines are established. A billing line is used to define a specific, billable event under the terms of the contract. OneWorld uses a billing method or billing type to control invoice calculations. A billing method is always associated with each billing line. The billing method specifies the billing terms for a given invoice line. Billing methods fall into one of two categories in OneWorld. A billing method is either an independent or a dependent billing method.

Independent Billing Lines

An independent billing line includes all the information that OneWorld needs in order to calculate a billing or invoice amount. The following different types of independent billing lines are possible on a contract:

- ◆ Lump sum
- ◆ Milestone billing
- ◆ Progress billing
- ◆ Time and material
- ◆ Unit (quantity) price

In general, billing line amounts can be calculated manually, or the system can calculate the billing amount automatically.

Lump Sum Billing   In OneWorld, a fixed billing amount is considered a "lump sum" billing line. Regardless of the actual expense incurred, the amount billed to the customer is a predetermined, fixed amount. For lump sum billings, the system can also use the lump sum billing line as the basis for calculating revenue recognition. Therefore, a cross-reference to both project-related cost and revenue accounts is necessary.

Milestone Billing   If the milestone billing line is used, the customer is billed only after predetermined and specific milestones are completed over the life of a job or project. Milestones are defined as the completion of a specific phase of work or when a specific date is reached in the life of the project. Each milestone is linked to a billing or event date and a bill rate for the milestone.

Progress Billing   The progress billing line is used to bill the customer only after a specific amount or percentage of total work is completed. The billing event is represented by a cumulative percentage of completion of work on a given date. The last billing represents the residual amount to be billed in order to have "billed out" 100 percent of the contract's value.

Time and Material Billing   The time and material billing term line uses the actual costs of goods and services in order to derive the amount to be billed. Frequently, the customer is billed at cost plus a markup. These arrangements are typically called a cost-plus contract. Note that payroll, equipment, inventory, and accounts payable transactions billed represent the actual costs billed to the project's specific accounts.

Unit (Quantity) Billing   A unit price billing line is based on a quantity and a price per unit. For instance, a contractor might charge a public utility a fixed amount to erect 1,000 towers used for bulk electric power distribution. As each tower is erected, a bill is submitted to the utility. To automatically calculate the billing amount, a cross-reference to the account that represents quantities in place is used in the billing calculation.

Dependent Billing Lines

A dependent contract billing line includes only a portion of the information needed to calculate a billing or invoice amount. OneWorld must then calculate the billing amount using additional information from the OneWorld database. A dependent contract billing line must be associated with an independent billing line. The billing type determines whether or not a contract billing line is dependent. The following billing types are used to define dependent billing lines on a contract:

- Fees
- Prepayments

Fees represent amounts billed to your customer in addition to the value of one or more contract billing lines. The system uses either the invoice amount or the cost amount to calculate the fee amount. The fee billed can represent a percentage of either the costs incurred or the amounts invoiced under a contract.

Prepayments and draws represent advances or deposits that your organization might require from the customer when the contract is executed. These prepayment amounts are then applied against future billings under the contract.

OneWorld supports both direct or fixed-amount draws and prorated draws. The fixed-amount draw reduces the prepayment amount by a fixed amount for each billing over the life of the contract until the prepayment is fully applied. The prorated draw applies the prepayment as a percentage reduction against the billed amount based on the percentage of work completed for the job.

Change Management

The OneWorld Change Management system includes a number of important audit trail and control features that are intended to prevent customer billing errors and misunderstandings related to project scope.

The OneWorld Change Management system is intended to manage the inevitable—change—that will affect a work in process. Changes frequently affect the cost and scope of work to be performed. When a change occurs, a revision is needed to the original contract that will cover the costs associated with the contract change. These amendments to the original contract are frequently called *change orders*. A change order reflects changes to the billing terms for the additional work that have been negotiated with the customer. A change order therefore includes one or more billing lines defining the billing terms that cover the additional work.

OneWorld Change Management is a configurable change management process that suits the needs of just about any organization. For instance, the change request process can be defined as a single step using nothing more than a change request to track any changes to the accounts affected by the job changes. On the other hand, a more comprehensive change process can be created that provides for a multistep approval process for any changes.

Equipment and Plant Maintenance

The OneWorld Equipment and Plant Management system provides features to administer both scheduled and unscheduled maintenance activities associated with your organization's equipment, facilities, fleet, and other machinery assets. The OneWorld Equipment and Plant Management system provides for

- Maintenance work activity planning and scheduling
- Scheduling of maintenance resources

- Purchasing of maintenance parts and materials
- Tracking equipment status and location
- Recording movements or transfers of equipment from one physical location to another
- Tracking the status of all preventive- and corrective-action tasks

The Equipment and Plant Management system works closely with other OneWorld systems. For instance, the Work Order Processing system is used to track and monitor maintenance actions. Note that the Equipment and Plant Management system relies on the OneWorld Fixed Asset system master data model. Therefore, if an equipment asset is already defined in the Fixed Asset system, it does not need to be entered into the database a second time. The Equipment and Plant Management system includes the following maintenance-related features:

- Track the maintenance history of each piece of equipment and target potential problem machines to minimize equipment downtime
- Coordinate maintenance activities based on preventive and corrective maintenance schedules
- Coordinate maintenance activities with materials and labor resources
- Maintain equipment hierarchies called parent/child relationships
- Maintain meter and odometer readings from equipment
- Maintain maintenance rules, and use these rules to project when maintenance actions will be needed
- Maintain detailed cost information about each piece of equipment

In addition, scores of user-defined codes can be associated with any piece of equipment. For instance, licenses and certifications can be recorded and tracked. This information is valuable for the fleet operator.

An important feature of the Equipment and Plant Management system is the online message log. It is used to enter reminder messages and flags about a piece of equipment. For instance, standard message types defined in Equipment and Plant Management system include the following:

- Planned maintenance
- Actual maintenance
- Problem reports

In addition to the online message log, the equipment maintenance schedule stores information about each type of service occurrence for a piece of equipment.

Equipment Billing

Equipment Billing is the billing subsystem of the Equipment and Plant Management system. The Equipment Billing subsystem is used to charge equipment costs or credit equipment revenue to various business units, jobs, and cost codes within your organization. The Equipment Billing subsystem can be used to bill on the basis of usage or on the basis of assignment to a given business unit or job. Note that the Service Billing system is used to charge a customer for equipment-related costs.

Profitability Management Systems

This section of the chapter introduces the OneWorld Profitability Management systems, including the Enterprise Profitability Management system and the Business Intelligence system.

Enterprise-Wide Profitability Management

Activity-Based Costing (ABC) and Activity-Based Costing and Management (ABCM) represent two organizational management practices that have gained widespread attention over the past decade. Activity-Based Costing is based on one simple premise—that an organization's overhead or operating expenses are generated by a number of activities needed to successfully complete its business processes. In Activity-Based Costing, activities consume overhead resources. Processes, products, or projects demand that certain activities be performed. Therefore, the cost of processes, products, or projects is related to the cost of the underlying overhead resources consumed or utilized.

The Activity-Based Costing model is intended to capture information about the origin of costs as accurately as possible. The Activity-Based Costing model works by defining a product or service as a cost object. A cost object is said to consume activities based on activity drivers. An activity driver assigns costs to cost objects. Activities consume resources based on some level of utilization called a *resource driver*. A cost is associated with each resource. A resource driver assigns costs to activities. Costs are subsequently rolled up based on their consumption to the product or service level.

Driver Guidelines

In the Activity-Based Costing model, the selection of drivers is a critical step. An activity driver should reflect the level or quantity of activity that a given cost object requires relative to that of other cost objects. Activity drivers should be root cause-driven. For instance, the poor quality of a given purchased part over another increases or drives inspection costs associated with that purchased part over other inspected parts that have a higher delivery quality. The frequency and intensity of inspection therefore influences the cost of the product using that component. Quantifying the activity driver must be both possible and practical. Therefore, always weigh the relative cost of collecting the data versus its relative precision.

As a general rule, it is best to consult the persons actually engaged in the day-to-day work when developing background information and in making decisions about activity drivers. Here are some general guidelines to follow when developing or selecting drivers:

♦ The driver should fit well with the type of activity

♦ The driver should closely correlate to the consumption of the activity

♦ The driver selected is at a level that minimizes the overall number of drivers needed

♦ The driver selected will be useful in promoting performance or process improvements

♦ The driver selected does not require any new measurements

Table 18-1 provides representative examples of activities, and Table 18-2 provides representative examples of drivers used in an activity-based cost model.

Table 18-1 Representative Activity-Based Costing Activities

Activity Category	Typical Activities
Customer Management	Contact customers, prepare quotes, invoice and collect money
Engineering	Perform product engineering work
Production	Plan production, purchase materials, receive and handle raw materials, manage production on the shop floor
Distribution	Store and ship final product
Human Resource Management	Hire and train employees

Table 18-2 Representative Activity-Based Costing Drivers

Type of Driver	Consumption Unit of Measure	Description of Driver
Activity	Unit	Drilling a hole
Activity	Batch	Setting up a machine
Activity	Product (service)	Designing a new product or service
Cost	Raw material quality	Inspecting goods
Cost	Complexity of assembly	Assembling components
Cost	Hiring actions	Human resources
Cost	Samples analyzed	Quality control
Cost	Engineering changes requested	Engineering
Resource	Percentage of time	Department or person
Resource	Percentage of machine time	Equipment or machinery depreciation

By design, Activity-Based Costing is intended to provide accurate, activity-driven cost information. It is said that Activity-Based Costing corrects the distortions of an organization's product and service costs. For example, Activity-Based Costing can demonstrate that, given a certain sales volume, profit margins can vary dramatically when other factors are taken into account, such as product mix, shipment size, special packaging, or a customer's special handling requirements.

Activity-Based Costing or Activity-Based Cost Management is often used to direct organizational and business process improvement efforts. For instance, Activity-Based Costing or Activity-Based Cost Management has been used in conjunction with other process improvement tools, such as just-in-time (JIT), and total quality management (TQM), and business process reengineering (BPR) initiatives. The removal of non-value-adding costs is a major objective of most improvement initiatives. Most frequently, Activity-Based Costing or Activity-Based Cost Management is used as a measurement tool to affirm the value of these other improvement initiatives. Activity-Based Costing or Activity-Based Cost Management helps identify activities that aren't value-adding.

The OneWorld Enterprise Profitability system provides a foundation within OneWorld for utilizing the Activity-Based Costing model by allowing for the identification and capture of direct or indirect costs related to specific products, services, or customers using root cause relationships. The OneWorld Enterprise

Profitability system provides the ability to collect, track, and assign activities to specific cost objects. The Enterprise Profitability system includes the following features:

◆ The ability to track transactions using cost objects

◆ The ability to capture quantity information

◆ The ability to reassign costs based on cost drivers

Detailed product costs are captured for analysis by the OneWorld Enterprise Profitability system based on transactions that occur in other OneWorld systems. The relevant transactions are selected based on user-defined cost-gathering criteria. A cost-gathering criterion is defined as either a cost object rule or a flex accounting instruction. Which cost-gathering criterion applies depends on the underlying OneWorld system. As automatic journal entries are produced by other OneWorld systems, the desired product costs are captured based on the pre-established cost-gathering criteria. The establishment of the cost-gathering criteria is therefore an important setup task when implementing the Enterprise Profitability system.

The OneWorld Enterprise Profitability system supports Activity-Based Cost Management by producing unique views of an organization's financial information. At the core of the OneWorld Enterprise Profitability system is the Cost Analyzer Table. It provides for collecting and arranging managerial accounting information *without affecting* the organization's underlying financial accounting information. Once the Cost Analyzer Table is established, it is used as the basis for management review and information analysis purposes.

Business Intelligence

Generally speaking, a Business Intelligence system focuses on establishing criteria that represent key performance indicators or measures and preparing on a regular basis some style of balanced scorecard reporting.

The "balanced scorecard" strategy translates an organization's strategy into tangible objectives and measures. These tangible objectives and measures typically include a mix of outcome measures (revenue, profit, growth rate) and performance drivers (cycle times, defect rates) that are organized into four categories:

◆ Customer Knowledge

◆ Financial Performance

◆ Internal Business Processes

◆ Learning and Growth

J. D. Edwards is currently working on a Business Intelligence system enhancement to OneWorld.

Data Extraction and Data Warehousing

A Business Intelligence system typically relies on a data warehouse. It is used to store representative data that your organization chooses to extract from OneWorld detail-level transaction files, header-level files, and balance files. The OneWorld Business Intelligence system provides a data warehouse facility and data extraction features to use in conjunction with other OneWorld database tables, such as the Sales Order Detail Transaction table or the Account Balance table.

Data Analysis and Reporting

The OneWorld Business Intelligence system provides facilities for defining key performance indicators or measures. The Business Intelligence system is then used to analyze and summarize transaction information into these key performance indicators or measures. These types of metrics are becoming increasingly important to an organization's top decision-makers. In addition, in order to gain a complete view of the organization's business model, the decision-maker must have the ability to drill down into transaction-level details when necessary.

Alliance Products

The last section of this chapter and of this book is devoted to a discussion of the products represented by a few key alliances between J. D. Edwards and other software vendors. These alliance relationships provide for "best of breed" extensions to OneWorld. The major product alliances discussed in this section include:

◆ Siebel Systems for Customer Relationship Management (CRM)

◆ Vertex Quantum Software form for federal, state, and local tax compliance purposes

J. D. Edwards has other software product alliances. A list of additional alliance partners and products can be found in Appendix A.

Siebel Systems

Over the last few years, a new class of business application software products has emerged—Customer Relationship Management (CRM) systems. The Customer Relationship Management system meets an increasing desire to provide sales force automation and contact management to the field sales force. Customer Relationship Management also relies on widespread acceptance of the client/server model and the ability to "store and forward," or synchronize information with an enterprise system.

Rather than expand its own product line into this arena, J. D. Edwards has chosen to partner with Siebel Systems. Siebel Systems is considered the leading Customer Relationship Management software vendor and has won wide acclaim for its Siebel Sales software. Siebel Sales software helps the sales and business development force manage accounts and new business opportunities. Some of the basic features of Siebel Sales software are discussed in the following sections.

Account Management

Siebel software can help focus selling efforts toward your existing accounts. Account management features provide facilities for creating accounts and entering account information, including identifying any parents or subaccounts. Account information can be viewed, including accounts with any associated contacts, activities, and opportunities.

Opportunity Management

An opportunity is defined as a potential revenue-generating event. Opportunities typically include a projected close date, revenue amount, and win probability. Siebel software provides facilities to enter information about new opportunities, view opportunity details, record notes about opportunities, and track the status of an opportunity throughout the sales cycle from creation to closure.

Contact Management

Siebel software provides capabilities to efficiently manage your business and personal contacts. Using Contact Management, business contact information can be recorded. Contact Management also allows for the creating and tracking of activities for a contact and creating and sending e-mail or written correspondence to a contact.

Activity Tracking

Siebel software allows for defining and tracking various sales cycle activities. An activity is a task or event that is generally but not always performed for a contact, account, or opportunity.

Appointment Scheduling

Siebel software allows for scheduling appointments and time management. The software provides for daily, weekly, and monthly views of appointments.

Sales Quotations

Your organization's product catalog and price list can be entered into Siebel Sales software. Using this information, a salesperson can generate quotations for customers and prospects. Siebel Sales also can verify the configuration through its Product Configurator option.

Forecasts

Siebel Sales software allows salespeople to generate sales forecasts in a variety of time slices, such as weeks, months, quarters, or years, and in a variety of formats. The salesperson can select which opportunities to include within his or her forecast.

Marketing Information Library

Siebel Sales software provides a facility for cataloging marketing-related materials into its database. The salesperson then can view this information or add it to correspondence sent to a customer or prospect.

Competitive Comparisons

Siebel Sales software provides a facility for cataloging competitive information, such as product cross-references and feature comparisons. This information is entered and maintained in the Siebel Sales software database. It is used when salespeople need comparative information to help sell their products against those from competitors or to help customers make product substitutions.

Integration with OneWorld

OneWorld and Siebel Sales integrate in a number of key areas. Table 18-3 summarizes the inbound and outbound interfaces between OneWorld and Siebel Sales software.

Table 18-3 Interfaces Between OneWorld and Siebel Sales

Inbound to OneWorld

Quotations—Sales order header and detail records

Outbound from OneWorld

Sales orders—Sales order header and detail records

Address Book and customer master information

Item master and item branch/plant records

Item base price records

Vertex

The J. D. Edwards approach to calculating sales and use tax information is quite simplistic. For instance, J. D. Edwards provides defaults that can suffice for a number of order-processing scenarios. For smaller and mid-sized companies that do not vigorously pursue tax relief, or that operate in fewer markets or in markets where tax rules are straightforward, the standard OneWorld sales and use tax functionality is generally sufficient.

For organizations that have more sophisticated tax-processing requirements than might be accommodated through OneWorld's standard functionality, J. D. Edwards has a product alliance with Vertex. Vertex offers a product called Quantum. Quantum replaces OneWorld's tax calculator with a more robust calculation function and provides periodic updates to its internal tax tables that can be applied electronically.

OneWorld's Standard Sales and Use Tax Processing

Before discussing Vertex, a basic understanding of the standard tax calculations in OneWorld is prerequisite knowledge. In general, the OneWorld approach applies a tax rate based on the ship-from or ship-to address value or on the branch/plant applicable to the order. Using this logic, it is possible to have a special, lower rate at the customer level, or it is possible to exempt the customer from tax treatment altogether. The order header–level tax default rate or exemption is then used at the order line level during tax calculation.

At the item level, an indicator on the item master (or, in its absence, an indicator in the branch/plant item master) indicates tax treatment. If both of these values are missing, the line type can be used to provide a default value for the tax treatment. At the line level, taxation is simply a matter of fact; the item is either taxable or not taxable. If the item is taxable, the default tax rate and tax status value from the order header are used, unless the user entered a specific override tax rate and tax status value during order entry.

When Basic Sales and Use Tax Calculations Aren't Enough

Sometimes OneWorld's basic sales and use tax calculations are insufficient to handle all the convoluted types of sales taxes and exemptions that state and local governments levy. In addition, keeping up with changes to the thousands of tax rates levied by an equal number of tax jurisdictions is an onerous process—and it grows as the number of states in which your organization does business grows. In addition, your organization might be faced with an ever-growing list of other tax challenges, including the following:

- Customer exceptions
- Enterprise zone exemptions
- Item/customer exceptions
- Ship-to-location exceptions
- Special exemptions or private letter rulings

Many of these exceptions are not easily accommodated—if they're accommodated at all in OneWorld. However, note that J. D. Edwards is not alone in its ignorance about sales and use tax exceptions. For instance, I am familiar with SAP and Ross Systems ERP systems, both of which have similar weaknesses. Several companies provide bolt-on solutions that serve as tax calculators. Increasingly, organizations are turning to Vertex to provide sophisticated and up-to-date sales and use tax processing capabilities to extend the basic tax calculations in an ERP system.

Vertex can resolve many tax calculation exceptions. For instance, a user-determined override rate can be specified for a given item shipped to a specific customer. Certainly, the key is converting percentages of applicable tax to a reduced user exception rate in the Vertex model. However, note that these exception tables are not automatic. They must be administered, and that can be the source of a great deal of initial work on the part of your tax department and your OneWorld and Vertex implementation specialists. However, these definitions can provide the highly customized tax calculations that your organization might need to ensure accurate customer invoices.

How Vertex Quantum Works

Vertex interfaces with OneWorld as a remote function call to an external program that in effect replaces the basic tax calculator in OneWorld. Vertex Quantum interfaces to OneWorld in the following areas:

- ◆ Accounts Payable
- ◆ Accounts Receivable
- ◆ Procurement
- ◆ Sales Order Processing

Once the Vertex tax calculation is complete, the calculated tax value is passed back to the OneWorld transaction and replaces the OneWorld calculated tax. Thereafter, the exact rate that was applied is available only from within the Vertex database.

Tax Decision-Maker Engine

When a OneWorld program calls upon the Vertex Quantum Tax Decision-Maker Engine to perform a tax calculation, the Engine determines the following:

- ◆ Whether the transaction is interstate or intrastate
- ◆ The transaction's taxing jurisdiction
- ◆ The appropriate tax rate
- ◆ The maximum tax base
- ◆ Any excess amounts, if applicable
- ◆ Any tax exceptions, if applicable

The Vertex Quantum Tax Decision-Maker Engine then

- ◆ Retrieves the appropriate tax rate
- ◆ Calculates the tax amount
- ◆ Returns the calculated tax amount to the calling OneWorld program

The Vertex Quantum software can also store tax history independent of OneWorld. This information can be used as an audit trail, for management reports, and to prepare tax returns. Because the Data Module isolates the state, county, city, and district rates, Quantum can calculate to these four levels individually.

Considerations

Before setting up the J. D. Edwards/Quantum Sales Tax Interface to reflect your organization's operating environment, carefully consider the specific conditions and requirements of any organizational, product, customer, supplier, and international tax obligations you might have.

First, it is necessary to understand any special accommodations, dispensations, or private letter rulings your organization has arranged with any state or local jurisdictions regarding the applicability or collection of sales and use taxes. Second, it is necessary to understand how products sold, consumed, or used by the organization fit into various tax categories. For example, new machinery might be treated differently from used machinery or even spare parts. Finally, your organization must identify the tax category to which its customers and suppliers belong. For example, an exempt customer might be a reseller or a charitable organization.

What Vertex Quantum Offers

Besides the handling of any sales tax calculation exceptions, there are several other sound reasons to consider using Vertex Quantum:

◆ Periodic updates, provided by Vertex, keep your sales and use tax rates current. Vertex replaces the standard tax rate area in J. D. Edwards with a geo-code. There are literally thousands of geo-codes, which are based on the various tax rates that apply at the local and state jurisdiction levels. Geo-code-based rates are regularly updated by Vertex.

◆ Detailed audit trail of tax calculations.

◆ Automates tax return preparation through an optional module.

◆ Even if your tax processing needs are simple today, future exceptions can be handled more easily using Vertex Quantum.

Finally, it is quite possible that your organization's tax accounting department is already using hard copy versions of Vertex sales tax guides. They are well-known throughout corporate America as a premier provider of state and local tax information.

Alliance Product Integration

The integration of alliance products with OneWorld is typically not a "load and go" process. Understand that each of these alliance products has its own installation, setup, and processing idiosyncrasies that your organization must accommodate. In addition, these products require ongoing maintenance. From an operational point of view, although these systems operate in conjunction with OneWorld, they really operate independently of OneWorld and rely on interfaces with OneWorld. It is necessary to constantly monitor these interfaces to ensure that they are operating correctly.

Summary

This chapter introduced a number of special-purpose OneWorld systems:

- ◆ Human Resource Management system
- ◆ Payroll system
- ◆ Human Resource Management and Payroll foundation system
- ◆ Time Accounting subsystem
- ◆ Customer Service Management system
- ◆ Sales Configurator system
- ◆ CustomWorks Visual Product Configurator
- ◆ Job Cost Accounting system
- ◆ Work Order Management system
- ◆ Service Billing system
- ◆ Contract Management and Billing system
- ◆ Change Management system
- ◆ Equipment and Plant Management system
- ◆ Equipment Billing system
- ◆ Enterprise Profitability Management system
- ◆ Business Intelligence system

As was noted in this chapter, considerable integration exists between all of these systems and other OneWorld systems—specifically, the Address Book, General Accounting, Accounts Receivable, Accounts Payable, Fixed Asset, Inventory Management, Sales Order Management, and Procurement systems.

Finally, this chapter concluded by introducing several alliance products that are available from third-party affiliates of J. D. Edwards. These alliance products represent "best of breed" extensions to OneWorld. The major product alliances include the Siebel Sales System for Customer Relationship Management and the Vertex Quantum software, which provides for state and local tax calculations, rate compliance, and reporting.

Appendix A

**OneWorld Product
Alliance Directory**

This appendix provides a summary listing of the add-on products available for OneWorld from third-party vendors who have entered into formal alliances with J. D. Edwards. Note that J. D. Edwards has a certification program to ensure third-party software compatibility with OneWorld. Please check with the software vendor or with J. D. Edwards to determine if a specific product of interest is certified.

J. D. Edwards' OneWorld Product Alliances

Product Name	Product Focus	Vendor Name	Vendor Internet Address
Agile Anywhere	Internet-based procurement	Agile Software Corporation	www.agilesoft.com
Metify ABM product suite	Value-based decision-making using activity-based modeling and cost analysis	Armstrong-Laing Group	www.armstronglaing.com
PATROL	Application management	BMC Software	www.bmc.com
WinFrame and MetaFrame	Windows Terminal Server extensions	Citrix Systems	www.citrix.com
ScreenPhone and Computer Telephony Integration System (CTIS)	Connects phone switches to the OneWorld telephony plug-in, providing enhanced call management	ComTek International	www.comtek-intl.com
Create!form	Electronic form solution that utilizes OneWorld PDF output	Create!form International	www.createform.com
Transformation Server	Bidirectional data replication allows sharing and synchronization of data across all OneWorld-supported databases	DataMirror Corp.	www.datamirror.com

J. D. Edwards' OneWorld Product Alliances *(continued)*

Product Name	Product Focus	Vendor Name	Vendor Internet Address
dcLink	Automated data collection of transaction data	Data Systems International	www.dsionline.com
ExpressBridge	Ship and track common carrier-based shipments from within OneWorld	Federal Express (FedEx)	www.fedex.com
Panagon Document Warehouse for OneWorld	Integrated document management (IDM) software	FileNET Corporation	www.filenet.com
FormScape	Output management middleware for manipulation, migration, and distribution of print data for viewing, printing, distributing, and archiving purposes	FormScape	www.formscape.com
AutoRelease and VendorRelease	Electronic Data Interchange (EDI), release accounting, shipping control, and bar code application software for automotive suppliers	Future Three Software	www.future3.com
Enterprise, Pillar, and Spiderman	Application software for reporting, analysis, modeling, and planning, including a single global view of financial information across multiple locations and diverse general ledgers	Hyperion Solutions Corporation	www.hyperion.com
ERP Connect	Automated data collection of transaction data	IBM Corporation	www.ibm.com
W-6 Service Scheduler	An advanced enterprise service scheduling solution that takes into account variables such as skill level, availability, location, and service-level agreements	Intelligent Electronics	iet-w6.com

J. D. Edwards' OneWorld Product Alliances *(continued)*

Product Name	Product Focus	Vendor Name	Vendor Internet Address
Image Management	High-volume production document management imaging systems	Image Integration Systems	www.iissys.com
JetForm Design and JetForm	High-quality professional forms with output comparable to preprinted forms using documents from OneWorld applications and virtually any laser printer	JetForm Corporation	www.jetform.com
LLM-WINPDE/ NT for ERP/MRP	High-end bar code printing solutions for shop floor, manufacturing, and warehouse environments	Loftware, Inc.	www.llmwin.com
SpyView and SpyImage	Computer Output to Laser Disk (COLD) archiving and document imaging	Magellan Software	www.magsoft.com
Matrix and Matrix OneWorld Integration	Automates the format and delivery of product information by seamlessly sharing Bill of Material and item master data between Matrix and OneWorld	MatrixOne Inc.	www.matrix-one.com
OptioDCS, OptioFAX, OptioCheckBook, Optio e.comPresent, and Optio DesignStudio	Output management	Optio Software	www.optiosoftware.com
TrustedLink EDI/ 400 and TrustedLink Enterprise	Electronic Data Interchange (EDI) software, catalog content, and enterprise data management	Peregrine Connectivity, Inc.	www.peregrine.com

J. D. Edwards' OneWorld Product Alliances *(continued)*

Product Name	Product Focus	Vendor Name	Vendor Internet Address
Personic WorkFlow	Applicant tracking and recruitment automation system	Personic Software, Inc.	www.personic.com
FastFax	Provides for sending, receiving, and managing purchase orders, invoices, quotes, and order acknowledgments produced by OneWorld via fax and e-mail	Quadrant Software	www.quadrantsoftware.com
Seagate Crystal Reports, Seagate Info, and Seagate Holos	Provides enterprise reporting, advanced data analysis, and ad hoc query capabilities for OneWorld	Seagate Software	www.seagatesoftware.com
Siebel Sales	Customer Relationship Management (CRM) solutions	Siebel Systems	www.siebel.com
MDLINK	Automated data collection of transaction data	Sirius Computer Solutions	www.siriuscom.com
CZAR DLL Rating Engine	Transportation price management provides less-than-truckload (LTL) transportation pricing	SMC Systems	www.smcsystems.com
GENTRAN	Provides electronic commerce (EC) software and value-added services, including high-volume, commercial-grade message management and translation	Sterling Commerce	www.sterlingcommerce.com
SynQuest Supply Chain Performance Series	Integrated, real-time supply chain planning and execution software	SynQuest	www.synquest.com

J. D. Edwards' OneWorld Product Alliances *(continued)*

Product Name	Product Focus	Vendor Name	Vendor Internet Address
Quantum for Sales and Use Tax	Sales and use tax calculation, exception management, and return preparation	Vertex, Inc.	www.vertexinc.com
Business Forms	A full-service business forms publisher providing OneWorld-compatible preprinted forms	Western Business Systems	www.wbsforms.com

Appendix B

**OneWorld
Vocabulary**

This brief guide defines many of the terms related to OneWorld, project management, and ERP software in general that you will encounter in conversations with colleagues, peers, and consultants during your OneWorld implementation project.

application program   A computer program used to accomplish a given business task. For instance, OneWorld has interactive application programs and batch application programs.

Application Programming Interface (API)   A call or request from one computer program to another for purposes of invoking the functionality provided by another program.

application server   A server within a local area network (LAN) that is dedicated to application processing.

application system   A group of related computer programs that are used to administer a specific business process. Some examples of business applications include Accounts Payable, Inventory Management, and Sales Order Processing.

assemble-to-order   A manufacturing process or technique in which a large number of finished products are assembled using a group of common or core components. Generally speaking, the common or core components used to complete the finished product are planned and stocked in anticipation of a customer order, and the actual receipt of a customer order initiates assembly of the finished product.

audit trail   A detailed and verifiable history of a processed transaction.

Automatic Accounting Instruction (AAI)   A code associated with a transaction type that is used to reference an account number in the Chart of Accounts by the General Ledger posting program that will automatically generate journal entries. Each system that interfaces with the OneWorld General Accounting system has Automatic Accounting Instructions, which must be set up after the Chart of Accounts has been designed.

base functionality   See *standard functionality*.

batch application program   The processing of a group of transactions that is treated as a single unit during processing. OneWorld performs batch application processing with little or no user interaction. For example, a report is considered a batch application. In OneWorld, a batch application program number is readily identifiable, because it begins with R.

batch control   A feature that verifies the number of transactions and the total amount in each batch to be entered into OneWorld.

batch input processing   The processing of a group of transactions loaded from an external source through a special program called a batch input processor. The batch input processor treats these transactions as if they were entered manually and performs all required validations. Batch input processors are used for conversion to and integration with OneWorld.

bucketed system   A time-phased manufacturing or distribution resource planning (MRP/DRP) system in which all time-phased data is accumulated into predefined time periods called *buckets*.

bucketless system   A time-phased manufacturing or distribution resource planning (MRP/DRP) system in which all time-phased data is processed, stored, and displayed using dated records rather than predefined time periods.

business function   Represents a set of related business rules and logic that can be called from any OneWorld application program. Business functions are combined with other business functions, forms, event rules, and other components to make up a typical OneWorld application.

business view   The method used by OneWorld to access specific columns from one or more data tables used in OneWorld application programs, such as transaction forms or reports. A business view does not contain any data and can't be used for data access except from within the OneWorld environment.

Capacity Requirements Planning (CRP)   A manual or systemic process for determining how much labor and how many machine resources are required by the production workload within a given time span. Both actual and planned orders are considered inputs to Capacity Requirements Planning, which uses these orders as the basis for calculating demands against available labor and machine capacity.

category code   A user-defined code field for which both the meaning and the list of acceptable values are fully user-defined. Also called a reporting code.

change management A process to control change. Generally speaking, a change control process is an administrative process that is exercised over both configuration changes and object customization in the OneWorld system.

Chart of Accounts Defines your organization's financial reporting structure. It includes definitions of both the organizational structure (companies and business units) and the account structure (object accounts and subsidiary accounts) used to prepare basic financial statements (the balance sheet and income statement).

check in/check out A procedural process for moving program-related objects from client workstations to a central server. Objects that are created locally, such as a report version, must be checked into a central or deployment server from a client workstation. From the deployment server, the checked-in object can be replicated to other client workstations and servers. When a program-related object must be modified, it must be checked out to a local client workstation.

client/server computing In a client/server environment, business application processing workloads are divided among several computers. The server computer provides on-demand services to a network of client computers.

client workstation The personal computer workstation on which a user operates OneWorld software applications.

closed-loop MRP A manufacturing system built around resource planning that includes forecasting, production planning, master production scheduling, and capacity requirements planning. In a closed-loop system, manufacturing execution functions provide feedback so that the plans can be revised and kept continuously up-to-date.

coexistence An arrangement whereby an existing AS/400-based J. D. Edwards' World software user can install OneWorld software and then share data between OneWorld and World software. However, not all OneWorld applications have a database structure that is compatible with World applications. In such cases, those applications cannot coexist.

communications middleware See *middleware*.

conference room pilot The process of modeling or prototyping a business process using OneWorld software functionality after it has been configured to your business requirements. Piloting of business processes is typically iterative until proof of concept is reached. Pilots are often conducted for specific OneWorld software systems (called *unit testing*) and are then piloted as an integrated process (called *integration testing*). For instance, integrated piloting would test the entire order-to-cash or procure-to-pay cycle in total versus piloting only the Procurement system.

conference room pilot environment   A testing environment used for simulating production transactions to confirm that the software system has been configured in such a way as to satisfy business processes and maintain data integrity. Generally speaking, all configuration settings are applied to this environment, and a subset of master data is loaded into this environment that will support the range or scope of simulated transactions.

Configurable Network Computing (CNC)   The OneWorld application architecture. Configurable Network Computing allows for connecting multiple computers and databases across a common a TCP/IP-based network to execute a common set of interactive and batch application programs, using data contained in one or more relational databases using structured query language (SQL) as the access method.

configuration   The process of adapting, configuring, or tailoring the unmodified standard or base software functionality. In OneWorld, this capability is provided through a series of switch settings, such as processing options, order processing rules, system constants, and line types, or through tables such as tax rate/areas and payment terms and other user-defined codes that represent an organization's standard business rules. These settings subsequently influence OneWorld applications to function in a way that represents your specific business process, transaction, or event.

constants   Parameters or codes that are set in the system and are used to standardize the processing of information by associated programs.

continuous manufacturing   A type of manufacturing process that produces physical items in bulk or in batches and lots, usually based on chemical reactions.

conversion   The conversion of master or transaction data from existing or legacy systems into OneWorld. Table conversion, Electronic Data Interchange (EDI), and batch input processors count as the technical methods used to migrate data from other systems into OneWorld.

core functionality   See *standard functionality*.

core system   The central or foundation system in an ERP system. For instance, the Address Book, General Accounting, and Inventory Management systems can be considered foundation systems.

Customer Relationship Management (CRM)   A system used to manage ongoing customer and prospect relationships. A Customer Relationship Management system can be used to manage business opportunities, make quotations, and reply to other presale or postsale requests.

customization   When the unmodified, standard, or base functionality provided by a software package is not robust enough to support a business process, the package might need to be customized. In such cases, an underlying application program that provides such functionality must be either modified or supplemented through new application processes that fulfill the business process or functionality gap.

database middleware   See _middleware._

Data Dictionary   A centralized database table used by OneWorld to manage the definitions and guidelines for database columns and certain text information.

database server   A server within a local area network (LAN) that is dedicated to database (file) processing and storage operations.

deliverable   The tangible result of a project task. Examples of specific deliverables in an implementation project include the project plan, a status report, conference room pilot test results, a configured application system, and a converted master data table.

deployment server   The computer used to install, maintain, and distribute OneWorld software to other servers and client workstations across a network.

design-to-build   An encapsulation of the new product development process and engineering steps required to bring a product idea from concept to production.

detail   The specific information that makes up a record or transaction.

detail area   The OneWorld form that displays detailed information associated with the records or data rows displayed on a grid.

development environment   The OneWorld environment used to test any modified development objects before they are promoted to other OneWorld environments.

development workstation   Used to modify OneWorld objects. The object must be checked out from the central server to a development workstation and then checked back in after modification.

discrete manufacturing   A type of manufacturing process that produces distinct physical items such as automobiles, appliances, or computers.

Distribution Requirements Planning (DRP)   A variation of materials requirements planning that focuses on staging end or final products at various warehouse locations for efficiency in customer order fulfillment.

Electronic Data Interchange (EDI)   The paperless, computer-to-computer exchange of business transactions, such as purchase orders and invoices, in a standardized format.

end-user   Someone who uses OneWorld software on a daily basis as a part of his or her job. For instance, a purchasing agent is an end-user who uses the OneWorld Procurement system on a daily basis to create, print, and manage purchases.

engineer-to-order   A manufacturing process that relies on customer specifications to design, engineer, or customize an end or final product for customer use. Each customer order results in a unique set of item numbers, Bills of Material, and routings on the shop floor.

Enterprise Report Writer   A development tool in the OneWorld software environment used to create custom reports when a standard OneWorld report will not suffice. The Enterprise Report Writer combines the separate capabilities of the FASTR, STAR, and World Writer products found in the World software environment into a visual development report-writing environment.

Enterprise Resource Management (ERM)   See *Enterprise Resource Planning*.

Enterprise Resource Planning (ERP)   The planning, tracking, and managing of all resources utilized by the business in fulfilling its business activities (such as making a product or performing a service).

Enterprise Server   Combines the functions of a database server and an application processing or logic server.

event-driven programming   Event-driven programming is best understood by reviewing the operation of the OneWorld interactive form. Traditionally, computer programs were procedurally driven, and end-users had relatively little control. The advent of graphical user interfaces allows end-users to exercise relatively full control or discretion over a computer program's operation. It makes possible the graphical user interface environment, in which the user can move anywhere within the form window, point to a form control, and click to activate the control, which in turn represents an event that redirects program execution.

event rule   Business logic that directs an application program to behave in a certain manner. Examples of events include performing a mathematical calculation, passing data from a field on a form to a field on another form, or performing a record retrieval operation. In OneWorld, event rules define complex business logic without using a traditional computer programming language. An event rule can be defined as a reusable business function, or it can be embedded in a specific event or operation in a OneWorld interactive form or batch application, such as a report.

environment   A key element in the OneWorld Configurable Network Computing architecture. The path code is used in conjunction with Object Configuration Mapping (OCM) to specify the location of data or a specific set of objects within the context of the network.

executable object   A computer program that can be executed or run from a computer's operating system. This term is synonymous with *application* and *executable program*.

executive sponsor   See *project sponsor*.

functionality gap   Occurs when the unmodified standard or base functionality provided by a software package is not robust enough to support a business process without modifications to the program(s) or source code related to that business process.

gap   See *functionality gap*.

Graphical User Interface (GUI)   A computer interface that is graphics-based as opposed to character-based. Graphics-based interfaces present information to the system user through a series of "windowpanes" of information. They use a pointing device connected to the computer in conjunction with graphic symbols called icons and buttons to let the user navigate the software by pointing and clicking on these symbols. A character-based user interface presents all information as alphanumeric characters and requires navigation by keystroke. Graphical User Interfaces rely on event-driven programming and objects.

grid   The portion of the window that displays detailed information on a form. The grid is arranged in rows and columns, which represent data records and data fields, respectively.

header   Common information such as identity or control information for a related group of records. For instance, purchase order header information indicates from whom materials were purchased, and purchase order detail information indicates exactly what was ordered. Many OneWorld data models and forms use header information.

install   The process of loading OneWorld software onto a computer.

installation plan   The standard means of installing, upgrading, or updating the OneWorld configuration. Plans contain information about data sources, environments, and packages.

integration   The process of extracting information from one system and introducing it into another system. The desirable state of affairs is the *seamless and unattended* integration of data from one system to another. OneWorld systems are integrated, but a non-OneWorld system is not necessarily integrated with OneWorld. Interfaces are custom computer programs created to interface or integrate another system with OneWorld.

integrity test   A process used to supplement internal balancing procedures by locating and reporting out-of-balance conditions, typically caused by data inconsistencies, between the General Accounting system or general ledger balance and a subsidiary ledger in another system, such as Accounts Payable or Accounts Receivable.

interactive application program   An entry or inquiry form that is used to interact with the computer under the immediate control of the end-user. In OneWorld, an interactive application program is readily identifiable, because it begins with P.

interactive processing   Interactive forms are an integral part of every OneWorld application. Forms allow the user to access business data in one or more tables based on a business view. The form is then used to add, modify, or view data in the underlying data tables. Forms are designed by defining controls, such as data grids, edit fields, pushbuttons, and radio buttons, and by defining event rules. Events are activities that occur in an application. For instance, whenever data is entered into a form field or a pushbutton is clicked, an event occurs, and an event rule is activated.

interface   See *integration*.

issue   A major problem that impedes the progress of the OneWorld implementation project and cannot be readily resolved by the project manager or the project team without outside assistance.

JDEBASE   See *middleware.*

JDENET   See *middleware.*

job   A batch application program. Jobs are typically initiated by selecting a menu option or submitting a version from a Versions List. Or they are automatically submitted based on day and date information through the OneWorld Scheduler.

job queue   A logical or software-driven segmentation of the computer's processing resources by the operating system. The job queue represents a location where a series of batch application programs can wait to be processed.

job queue processing   Batch jobs are typically processed on a first in/first out basis or by priority ranking. In some cases, batch jobs must be processed in a certain sequence, such as where order processing rules might be updated, or on a single-threaded or one-at-a-time basis, such as in the case of the General Accounting batch post.

just-in-time installation (JITI)   A method used by OneWorld to dynamically replicate objects upon first use from the central server where objects are stored to a client workstation.

just-in-time replication (JITR)   A method used by OneWorld to replicate new (added) records in tables to an individual client workstation.

legacy system   An existing system that is being replaced or supplemented by OneWorld.

make-to-stock   Manufacturing processes that rely on finished products that are shipped from inventory, or "off the shelf." Manufacturing takes place *before* a customer order arrives. The master scheduling and final assembly scheduling are conducted at the finished goods level.

manage the enterprise   A generic reference to business processes that do not directly impact product flows from suppliers or to customers. These processes include business performance measurement and resource administration and maintenance activities such as plant maintenance, fixed asset accounting, general accounting, and human resources.

Manufacturing Resource Planning (MRP)   A method of planning and staging the utilization of labor, machinery, and material resources in a manufacturing process. Ideally, it addresses operational planning in units and financial planning in dollars and has a simulation capability to answer "what if" questions. It is made up of a variety of linked functions, and it uses business or strategic plans, including sales forecasts, to develop operating or production plans. Production plans are then carried out, or executed, in an organized and controlled manner. The planning, control, and execution systems are integrated with the procurement, sales order management, and financial systems. Frequently called "big MRP."

master business function   Provides a central location for storing standard business rules about entering documents, such as invoices, vouchers, and journal entries. The master business function includes processing options that are shared by certain programs.

master data table   A database table used to store data and information that is considered permanent and necessary to the system's operation. Master data tables include information such as all possible tax rates to assess orders or all customer, employee, and supplier names and address information.

Material Requirements Planning (MRP)   A planning, control, and execution method that focuses on managing and planning material resources—usually raw materials and subassemblies—in a manufacturing operation. Frequently called "little MRP."

message queue   As jobs are submitted and processed, or when a report is ready to print but requires a specific form to be loaded, a message can be sent to the end-user regarding the job's status, including the need for the form. An informational message, such as a job completion message, requires no action when a job completes normally. An action message, such as a form load or printer attention message, requires specific action by the end-user.

middleware   A general term that covers all the distributed software needed to support interactions between clients and servers. The software provides application software independence by resolving incompatibilities in a network of disparate client workstations, server computers, databases, and operating systems. JDEBASE is J. D. Edwards' proprietary database middleware package for OneWorld, and JDENET is J. D. Edwards' proprietary communications middleware package for OneWorld.

migration   See *conversion*.

milestone   The completion of a given task, group of tasks, or an entire project phase in the OneWorld implementation project. See also *deliverable* and *project plan*.

mixed-mode manufacturing A manufacturing process that combines elements of several manufacturing models. For instance, a plastic bag manufacturer might produce coils, or rolls of plastic tubing, using process or batch manufacturing techniques. As customer orders are received, the bag manufacturer assembles the bags by cutting and sealing the tubing on one edge to form the bags to the dimensions indicated on the customer order.

modification See *customization*.

network computer A network computer, or thin client workstation, does not have the full features of a personal computer workstation, typically called a "fat client" or "thick client." For instance, the network computer typically lacks a local hard disk drive and therefore must rely strictly on network resources for data access or program execution. The network computer uses either a Web browser or Windows Explorer to locate network resources. One or more terminal servers are used to provide the "missing pieces" to a thin client workstation in terms of "local" program execution. In reality, programs are executed on the terminal server. Screen and cursor data is sent to the local network computer, and keystrokes and mouse movements are sent to the terminal server.

network operating system See *operating system*.

next numbers A OneWorld feature used to control the automatic numbering of data, such as new transaction documents and master data records in OneWorld. For master data (items and Address Book records), it is recommended that OneWorld's check digit control feature be used. For transaction documents, the sequential or next number alone is usually sufficient.

object In object-based design and programming, objects are the "building blocks" used to assemble or build an application. Typically, an object represents both data and an encapsulation of the methods used to manipulate the data. Each object has its own specification, which is stored at both the server and the client workstation.

Object Configuration Manager (OCM) The nerve center or traffic manager over the OneWorld runtime environment. It keeps track of the locations of objects—both executable programs and transaction data. When an object is referenced by a client workstation request, the Object Configuration Manager builds an "access path" to a specified object for a given environment. The environment selected during the end-user's initial sign-on influences the access path.

Object-Oriented Programming A software development approach aimed at generating reusable programs. It ultimately simplifies the development of applications by reducing what must be developed anew for each additional software application or business process that is automated. See also *event-driven programming*.

Open Database Connectivity (ODBC) A standards-based interface or method used to provide access to data among different applications from different data sources. The ODBC interface is made up of a set of connectivity methods and rules that are unique to an application or data source on the back end but that allow transparent access on the front end using standard connectivity methods and rules.

operating system (OS) The software that directs the operation of the computer hardware and any attached computers or other devices, such as printers and disk drives. UNIX, OS/400, and Windows NT are examples of operating systems.

order-to-cash process See *quote-to-cash process*.

output queue See *print queue*.

package OneWorld objects are installed to workstations in packages from the deployment server. A package can be compared to a Bill of Material or a kit that specifies the necessary objects that a workstation or server configuration will need and where on the deployment server the installation program can find the objects.

package build Before objects are deployed, a package build must be performed. A package build precedes actual deployments of objects to servers and workstations. The package build is a point-in-time "snapshot" of the central objects on the deployment server.

partitioning A technique or approach used to reduce network traffic and enhance performance in the OneWorld Configurable Network Computing environment. The OneWorld design allows partitioning of its business function components. OneWorld transaction-oriented applications can perform transaction edits locally, at the client workstation, while database transactions are executed on an application server, thereby minimizing network traffic and improving overall application performance.

path code A pointer to a specific set of objects.

personalization See *configuration*.

plan to produce   The combination of planning, controlling, and work execution business processes leading from a sales forecast, or firm order, to raw materials procurement, and then transformation through various manufacturing operations until a finished product is produced.

platform independence   Application programs or systems are said to be platform-independent or portable when the application program or system executes regardless of the underlying combination of database, machine, or operating system employed.

primary key   A column or combination of columns that uniquely identifies each row in a table.

print queue   A location on the print server where a list of reports that were spooled during a batch process are now available to be written to an output device, such as a printer or a disk-based report management and storage system.

print server   A server within a local area network (LAN) that is dedicated to receiving output from various applications and directing output to the desired network resources (such as printers) as they become available.

pristine environment   If your organization will modify OneWorld objects, this environment is required and is used to compare or test unaltered objects against altered objects.

processing option   The OneWorld feature that alters or directs the operation of an application program or establishes default values or other parameters used by the program.

procure to pay   The basic business process of placing an order with a supplier and receiving the goods or services associated with that purchase order. Includes the procuring of materials, receipt of the material to fulfill the order, logging of a supplier's request for payment, supplier payment, and application of payment against the supplier's account.

product code   A code that identifies the specific OneWorld application system. For example, product code 01 represents the Address Book. For World software users, applications that cannot coexist typically include a B in the product code. For instance, Accounts Receivable is product code 03B in OneWorld.

production environment   The OneWorld environment where end-users conduct their "real" daily business activities.

project   A temporary work structure or organization formed to complete a specific defined deliverable or set of deliverables, such as the implementation of OneWorld in your organization. A project has a specific begin date and end date, specific objectives, and specific resources assigned to perform the work. A project manager has overall responsibility and authority over a project. When the objectives are met, the project is considered complete.

project manager   The person with authority to manage a project. This includes directing the planning and development of all project deliverables. The project manager is responsible for managing the budget, the project work plan, and all project management procedures, such as scope or change management, issue or gap management, and risk management.

project phase   A major, logical grouping of work on a project. A phase also represents the completion of a major deliverable or set of related deliverables.

project plan   A time-sequenced, logical grouping of work on a project. Each project task is assigned a specific start and completion date, resulting in a measure of task duration in workdays. Certain tasks depend on the completion of one or more preceding tasks. Therefore, the actual completion of a preceding task affects the start of one or more subsequent tasks. The project's critical path is determined by adding together the duration of all tasks on each possible path or the combination of tasks in a project. The critical path is the path represented by the highest overall duration.

project risk   A circumstance, event, or task that is usually external to the project itself that, if not completed, would prevent or stop further work on a project. If an event or task is within the control of the project team, such as having conference room piloting complete by a certain date, it is not a risk. If an event has a 100 percent chance of occurring, it does not represent a risk to the project. See also *stoplight report*.

project scope   The boundaries of a project. Scope defines what the project will deliver and what it will *not* deliver.

project sponsor   The person(s) from the organization's executive team with ultimate authority over the project. The sponsor(s) are responsible for providing project funding, resolving issues and scope changes, approving major deliverables, and setting overall, high-level direction for the project.

project steering committee A group of high-level stakeholders who are responsible for providing guidance and overall strategic direction for a project. The steering committee does not take the place of the project sponsor(s); rather, it provides strategic input and communicates anticipated organizational changes required by the project throughout the organization. The steering committee is usually made up of organizational peers and is a combination of direct customers and indirect stakeholders of the project.

proof of concept The result of modeling or prototyping a business process using OneWorld software functionality after it has been configured to your business requirements.

protocol A set of formalized rules specifying how server and workstation hardware and operating system and middleware software interact when transmitting and receiving information over a network.

prototyping See *conference room pilot*.

pull replication A method of replicating data to individual client workstations from a central server in OneWorld. A client workstation must be established as a subscriber. A subscriber is then notified of changes, updates, and deletions as specific information is requested by the client workstation from the central server.

purge The process of removing data records from the OneWorld database table. Special programs are used to remove data records. Data records can then be stored on magnetic or optical media in a format accessible through Structured Query Language for historical uses.

push replication A method of data replication between multiple servers. For any given object, one server is typically called the publisher, and the remaining servers are treated as subscribers. The publisher must notify subscribers of any changes to an object. If the subscriber is not running when a change notification is sent, the subscriber receives the change notification upon startup.

Query by Example (QBE) A table inquiry method or technique. In OneWorld, virtually every data grid on a form includes a Query by Example entry row where a table inquiry can be structured. Each successive entry in a column forms an "and" relationship with the prior inquiry.

quote-to-cash process The basic business process of taking an order from a customer and fulfilling that customer order. Includes making a quotation or proposal to the customer, converting a quotation into a firm order, making or procuring materials, delivering the materials to fulfill the order, billing the customer for the order, receiving and applying payments from the customer, and applying the amount received against the customer's account.

record   A collection of related, consecutive data columns or fields, which the system treats as a single unit of information.

relational database   In OneWorld, business data is stored in tables in a relational database. A data file or table consists of columns, representing data fields. A collection of related data fields is called a data record. All physical data in a database is stored in tables. One or more fields that are common between individual tables can relate separate tables of business data to one another.

release   A software version that contains major new functionality. Also called the base release.

release level   The specific level of OneWorld software. A release level is achieved by installing a base release of the software and then applying one or more release updates to the software.

release update   An accumulation of software fixes and performance enhancements that generally contains no new functionality. A release update is applied against a base release level of the software.

repetitive manufacturing   A manufacturing process where various items are made across the same manufacturing operations, in separate batches or continuously.

replicated object   A copy of a central object. An object must be replicated to and reside on each client workstation or server that runs OneWorld. The path code is used to locate central objects in the OneWorld Configurable Network Computing environment.

replication   The process of copying objects from one computer to another across a network. In a replicated environment, multiple copies of the same object are maintained on multiple computers across the network. However, a single computer, or source, must ultimately own and publish the objects to any other computers in the network, thereby ensuring that the latest copies of the objects reside in a primary place and are then replicated as appropriate to subscribers.

server   A computer that is specifically intended for managing or providing computing resources to other computers attached through a common network. A single server can perform all computing tasks. However, for performance reasons, servers are frequently dedicated to providing specific tasks. For instance, servers can provide a common storage area for executable programs, also called a deployment server in OneWorld. A server can provide a common storage area for business data when used as a file or database server, or the server can manage communications with network computers when used as a terminal server. A batch server can provide batch application processing resources, and a print server can manage printer operations for multiple computers.

Software Action Request (SAR)   The J. D. Edwards terminology for requesting a fix in or modification of OneWorld software. Software Action Requests initiated by J. D. Edwards reside in the Knowledge Garden and can be searched by release or by object. Software Action Requests are also used to initiate and control local changes to OneWorld objects through the Object Management Workbench.

standard functionality   The unmodified standard or base functionality provided by a software package. The core functionality in a software package can frequently be tailored (configured) or personalized without requiring modifications to the software programs or the software package's source code.

steering committee   See *project steering committee.*

stoplight report   A report produced by the project manager. It is used to summarize project progress and status and to highlight project issues and risks. The stoplight color represents the risk assessment or impact of a given project issue.

store-and-forward   A transaction method that allows a client application to perform work locally and to complete the work later by connecting to a server application, usually to upload data originating on the client to a central server.

Structured Query Language (SQL)   An industry-standard data manipulation language used for relational database access. Structured Query Language is used to create databases and to retrieve, add, modify, or delete data from databases.

subscriber   The computer that is responsible for a replicated copy of a published data table.

Supply Chain Management (SCM)   The process of managing the supply chain. The supply chain is the network of facilities, options, and resources to perform procurement of materials from suppliers, transformation of these materials into intermediate and finished products, and distribution of finished products to customers. Supply chains exist in both service and manufacturing organizations, and they vary in complexity from industry to industry and firm to firm. In general, the emphasis of supply chain management is to reduce non-value-adding activities and total inventory investment throughout the supply chain.

system administrator The individual(s) responsible for performing system-level tasks in the OneWorld Configurable Network Computing environment. These tasks include maintaining end-user sign-on security and object-level security, maintaining replication tables, building and deploying packages, installing new workstations or printers, applying software updates, and installing new releases.

system code See *product code.*

table See *relational database.*

table conversion Specific OneWorld programs designed to convert the business data from one table into another table, usually with a different format or arrangement of the data. Table conversions are typically part of a software upgrade and are performed automatically as a step in the upgrade plan. Table conversion is also used to convert, migrate, or integrate data from legacy systems into the OneWorld database.

tailoring See *personalization.*

terminal server A server within a local area network (LAN) that is dedicated to servicing and administering network computers or thin client workstations.

test environment The OneWorld environment used to test OneWorld software after any modifications are made, prior to promoting or deploying software changes throughout the network for general use. After a developer uses the test environment to test modifications, end-user representatives typically test the modifications through the conference room pilot environment, which contains a broad sample of an organization's business data and an image of its system configuration.

Universal Batch Engine (UBE) In OneWorld, batch processing application programs are submitted to the Universal Batch Engine for scheduling and processing by the computer. A server can be designated as the Universal Batch Engine on which OneWorld batch processing requests are processed. A user or the OneWorld Scheduler submits, to a job queue on the server, a batch-processing request. The operating system processes the batch-processing request by job priority or arrival sequence and then directs any output to an output or print queue. See also *job queue* and *job queue processing.*

upgrade The process of refreshing software from the current release level to a new, higher release level.

User-Defined Code (UDC) A code that can be defined to represent your organization's business data or its policies and procedures. Virtually every data field or column on any OneWorld master data or transaction entry form is defined by an underlying user-defined table. User-defined tables codify business data, reduce errors, promote consistency, and ease inquiry for analysis purposes.

user profile The formal definition of an end-user in OneWorld. The definition of a user typically provides for access to specific environments and specification of a local or preferred print queue. The definition of an end-user also includes object-level security, allowing or denying a specific user access to certain business data or application program functions within OneWorld.

vocabulary overrides The OneWorld feature that is used to override the J. D. Edwards–supplied description for a field, row, or column on forms and reports.

workflow A predefined, procedural process whereby documents, information, or other work in process is passed from one individual to another for further review or processing action until the process is considered complete. Examples of OneWorld workflow processing include document approval routes and document order processing rules.

workgroup server A remote database server usually containing subsets of data replicated from a master database server. The workgroup server does not perform any application or batch processing.

Epilogue

Despite reports to the contrary, Enterprise Resource Planning (ERP) systems are having a profound impact on the way many organizations perform basic business record keeping, conduct their basic business processes, and manage the organization itself. Organizations both large and small in all types of industries have already adopted or will adopt an ERP system to increase their back-office productivity. To this end, J. D. Edwards is poised to be a significant, long-term player in the ERP software marketplace. For example, in October of 2000, OneWorld achieved its 1,000th installation.

During the weeks leading up to the completion of this book, J. D. Edwards also announced the OneWorld Xe product. This announcement represented a rebranding of sorts for OneWorld. With every new release of a software package as complex as OneWorld, we old-timers in the ERP business get to relearn what we thought we already knew. But more importantly, during my early test drive of OneWorld Xe, I was increasingly impressed with OneWorld's performance, completeness, and production readiness.

It was not possible to cover every aspect of OneWorld in this book. However, that was never my intent. What I did intend was to provide a broad overview of this increasingly important ERP software package, as well as offer some sage advice and general information on OneWorld implementation. To that end, I feel my work is done here.

The completion of this book was a watershed event. It represents the culmination of an effort that has consumed much of my free time for the past year. It was also a humbling experience. Much like teaching, writing requires comprehension and mastery of the subject material. Although I have made every effort to ensure the accuracy of the material contained in this book, in the end what you have read is still largely the informed opinion of the author.

Robert W. Starinsky

Index